American Literary Scholarship

1978

American Literary Scholarship

An Annual / 1978

Edited by J. Albert Robbins

Essays by Wendell Glick, J. Donald Crowley, Donald B. Stauffer, Hershel Parker, Willis J. Buckingham, Louis J. Budd, Robert L. Gale, George Bornstein and Stuart Y. McDougal, Panthea Reid Broughton, Jackson R. Bryer, William J. Scheick, Thomas Wortham, David Stouck, Jack Salzman, James H. Justus, Richard Crowder, James E. Breslin, Winifred Frazer, Darwin T. Turner, Michael J. Hoffman, Maurice Couturier, Hans Galinsky, Rolando Anzilotti, Keiko Beppu, Rolf Lundén

Duke University Press, Durham, North Carolina, 1980

© 1980. Duke University Press. Library of Congress Catalogue Card number 65–19450. I.S.B.N. 0–8223–0443–0. Printed in the United States of America by Heritage Printers, Inc.

Foreword

In keeping with our recent practice of alternating the editing of these volumes, Professor James Woodress of the University of California, Davis, will supervise and edit *American Literary Scholarship 1979*, to be published in 1981.

One innovation this year is an abbreviated citing of publishers. For those familiar with the standard publishers of scholarly books, this, I feel sure, will cause no particular problems. For example, instead of "(Cambridge, Mass.: Harvard Univ. Press)" we now cite only "(Harvard)"; and in place of "(New York: Charles Scribner's Sons)" we will specify only "(Scribner's)." We have provided a list of publishers' abbreviations in the front matter. Citing publishers by this short form has two merits: a saving of space and less interruption to the flow of sentences in which citations appear. In the case of more exotic and seldom-cited publishers, we have retained full citation in the text.

For a variety of reasons we have an unusually large number of author changes to announce for *ALS 1979*. The Hawthorne chapter, previously written by J. Donald Crowley, will be done by David B. Kesterson, North Texas State University; the Poe chapter, done by Donald B. Stauffer, will for one year be written by the present editor; the Fitzgerald and Hemingway chapter, contributed for eight years by Jackson R. Bryer, will be handled by Scott Donaldson, College of William and Mary, Williamsburg, Va.; the essay on 19th Century Literature, provided by Thomas Wortham, will be covered by Kermit Vanderbilt, San Diego State University; Fiction: The 1950s to the Present, done by James H. Justus, will be written by Jerome Klinkowitz, University of Northern Iowa; Black Literature, contributed this year by Darwin T. Turner, will be handled by John M. Reilly, State University of New York, Albany; and the general chapter, "Themes, Topics, Criticism," written by Michael J. Hoffman, will be provided by Jonathan Morse, University of Hawaii.

We appreciate the services and fine work of these retiring contributors, who leave us for a variety of personal and professional reasons. Professor Stauffer will serve for a year in China and will be unable there to keep up with current scholarship on Poe. Some have served long tenures with us and wish to free themselves from this annual drain upon their time and energies. Professor Justus, who, with his essay in this volume, completes a full decade, has contributed close to a total of 400 pages—the equivalent of a substantial book. The quantity of words he has perused in hundreds of books and articles is vast and the skill in reducing all this to some 400 pages of thoughtful and readable evaluative prose is indeed impressive.

Michael J. Hoffman, who has been responsible for the very difficult assignment, "Themes, Topics, Criticism," has these thoughts upon retirement.

I have done this chapter for six years now, and it is time to turn the task over to someone else. As I wrote last year, this job has been perhaps the most educational experience I have had as a scholar. The past six years have witnessed a subtle transition in American criticism. The influences of continental scholarship and the "new criticism" have been increasingly obvious in the practice of American and British critics. It is hard to know where this transition will take us, but it is hard to believe that American criticism will ever be quite the same again. As to that, however, my successor will keep ALS readers informed.

Professor Woodress and I thank the seven retiring contributors for work well and faithfully done. Their service in these volumes will continue to be a resource for scholars.

It might be in order, once again, to inform readers of ALS that we do not profess to cite and comment upon every published article and book. More and more, as scholarship and criticism multiply, the need increases to become more selective—however much our aim remains to touch upon all scholarship of merit. The scholar seeking full coverage should consult the MLA International Bibliography and appropriate specialized bibliographies.

Occasionally in ALS one encounters citations whose publication antedates the ALS volume by one or even two years (that is, in ALS 1978, items dated 1977 or 1976). In a few instances we have overlooked these pieces and feel them worthy of tardy mention, but more likely than not the article or book did not appear in the year of its copyright or serial date. In other words, the date on the journal or the date of copyright in a book is not always as reliable as the date of publication. A journal bearing the date "Fall 1977" can in reality be as late as December 1978 in appearing.

We are grateful to Eileen M. Mackesy, managing editor of the *MLA International Bibliography*, for arranging to provide us with advance proof sheets of the American section of the bibliography. And thanks also to James L. Harner (Bowling Green State University), section head for Festschriften, for providing us with appropriate entries from his files in advance of publication. This early information is essential to our tasks.

J. Albert Robbins

Indiana University

Table of Contents

Key to Abbreviations

Festschriften, Essay Collections, and Books Discussed in More Than One Chapter

American Contributions / Victor Terras, ed., *American Contributions to the Eighth International Congress of Slavists, Zagreb and Ljubljana, September 3–9, 1978* (Columbus, Ohio: Slavica Publishers)

Les Américanistes / Ira D. and Christiane Johnson, eds., *Les Américanistes: New French Criticism on Modern American Fiction* (Port Washington, N.Y.: Kennikat Press)

American Visionary Fiction / Richard Finholt, *American Visionary Fiction: Mad Metaphysics as Salvation Psychology* (Port Washington, N.Y.: Kennikat Press)

California Writers / Charles L. Crow, ed., *Essays on California Writers* (Itinerary 7) (Bowling Green, O.: Bowling Green Univ. Press)

Comic Relief / Sarah Blacher Cohen, ed., *Comic Relief: Humor in Contemporary American Literature* (Urbana: Univ. of Illinois Press)

Cosmic Satire / John W. Tilton, *Cosmic Satire in the Contemporary Novel* (Lewisburg, Pa.: Bucknell Univ. Press, 1977)

Democracy and the Novel / Henry Nash Smith, *Democracy and the Novel: Popular Resistance to Classic American Writers* (New York: Oxford Univ. Press)

Earthly Delights / Wright Morris, *Earthly Delights, Unearthly Adornments: American Writers as Image-Makers* (New York: Harper & Row)

The Evidence of the Imagination /

Donald H. Reiman et al., eds., *The Evidence of the Imagination: Studies of Interactions between Life and Art in English Romantic Literature* (New York: New York Univ. Press)

Feminist Criticism / Cheryl L. Brown and Karen Olson, eds., *Feminist Criticism: Essays on Theory, Poetry and Prose* (Metuchen, N.J.: Scarecrow Press)

Gyascutus / James L. W. West, III, ed., *Gyascutus: Studies in Antebellum Southern Humorous and Sporting Writing* (Atlantic Highlands, N.J.: Humanities Press)

The Hole in the Fabric / Strother Purdy, *The Hole in the Fabric: Science, Contemporary Literature, and Henry James* (Pittsburgh: Univ. of Pittsburgh Press, 1977)

Literature and the Occult / Luanne Frank, ed., *Literature and the Occult: Essays in Comparative Literature* (Arlington: Univ. of Texas at Arlington, 1977)

The Modern American Novel / Gerald Peary and Roger Shatzkin, eds., *The Modern American Novel and the Movies* (New York: Ungar, 1977)

Neither White Nor Black / Judith R. Berzon, *Neither White Nor Black: The Mulatto Character in American Fiction* (New York: New York Univ. Press)

New Perspectives / Faith Pullin, ed., *New Perspectives on Melville* (Edinburgh: Univ. of Edinburgh Press)

Poetry in America / Bernard Duffey, *Poetry in America: Expression and Its Values in the Times of Bryant, Whitman, and Pound* (Durham, N.C.: Duke Univ. Press)

Remembering Poets / Donald Hall, *Remembering Poets: Reminiscences and Opinions—Dylan Thomas, Robert Frost, T. S. Eliot, and Ezra Pound* (New York: Harper & Row)

Studies in Biography / Daniel Aaron, ed., *Studies in Biography* (Cambridge, Mass.: Harvard Univ. Press)

Vulnerable People / Josephine Hendin, *Vulnerable People: A View* of American Fiction since 1945 (New York: Oxford Univ. Press)

What Manner of Woman / Marlene Springer, ed., *What Manner of Woman: Essays on English and American Life and Literature* (New York: New York Univ. Press, 1977)

Where the West Begins / Arthur R. Huseboe and William Geyer, eds., *Where the West Begins: Essays on Middle Border and Siouxland Writing, in Honor of Herbert Krause* (Sioux Falls, S.D.: Center for Western Studies, Augustana College)

Periodicals, Annuals, Series

AEB / *Analytical & Enumerative Bibliography*
AF / *Anglistische Forschungen*
AfricaI / *Africa: International Business, Economic & Political Monthly*
Agenda
AI / *American Imago*
AIQ / *American Indian Quarterly*
Akzente: Zeitschrift für Literatur
AL / *American Literature*
AlaR / *Alabama Review*
ALR / *American Literary Realism*
ALS / *American Literary Scholarship*
AmerS / *American Studies*
AmerSI / *American Studies International* (supplement of *AQ*)
AmerSS / *American Studies in Scandinavia*
Amst / *Amerikastudien/American Studies*
AN&Q / *American Notes and Queries*
APR / *American Poetry Review*
AQ / *American Quarterly*
AR / *Antioch Review*
ArielE / *Ariel: A Review of International English Literature*
ArmD / *Armchair Detective*
ArQ / *Arizona Quarterly*
ASch / *American Scholar*
AtM / *Atlantic Monthly*

ATQ / *American Transcendental Quarterly*
BALF / *Black American Literature Forum*
BB / *Bulletin of Bibliography*
BBr / *Books at Brown*
BCM / *Book Collector's Market*
BI / *Books at Iowa*
BIS / *Browning Institute Studies*
BlackS / *Black Scholar*
Boundary / *Boundary 2: A Journal of Postmodern Literature*
BRH / *Bulletin of Research in the Humanities* (formerly *Bull. of the N.Y. Public Library*)
BuR / *Bucknell Review*
Calamus: Walt Whitman Quarterly, International (Tokyo)
Caliban (Toulouse, France)
Calibano (Pisa)
CE / *College English*
CEA / *C.E.A. Critic*
CEAA / *Center for Editions of American Authors*
CentR / *The Centennial Review*
CeS / *Cultura e Scuola* (Rome)
ChiR / *Chicago Review*
CimR / *Cimarron Review*
Cithara
CLAJ / *CLA Journal* (College Language Assn.)

CLQ / *Colby Library Quarterly*
CLS / *Comparative Literature Studies*
CollG / *Colloquia Germanica*
CollL / *College Literature* (West
    Chester [Penn.] State College)
ComM / *Communication Monographs*
Commonweal
ConL / *Contemporary Literature*
ConP / *Contemporary Poetry*
CP / *Concerning Poetry*
CRAA / Centre de Recherches sur
    l'Amerique Anglophone
CRCL / *Canadian Review of Com-
    parative Literature*
CRevAS / *Canadian Review of
    American Studies*
Crit / *Critique: Studies in Modern
    Fiction*
CritI / *Critical Inquiry*
Criticism
CritQ / *Critical Quarterly*
CSE / Center for Scholarly Editions
DAI / *Dissertation Abstracts
    International*
*Degrés: Revue de Synthèse à Orienta-
    tion Sémiologique*
Delta (Montpellier)
*Descant: The Texas Christian Univ.
    Library Journal*
DN / *Dreiser Newsletter*
DnS / *Dickinson Studies* (formerly
    EDB)
DQR / *Dutch Quarterly Review of
    American Letters*
DVLG / *Deutsche Vierteljahrsschrift
    für Literaturwissenschaft und
    Geistesgeschichte*
EA / *Etudes Anglaises*
EAL / *Early American Literature*
EAS / *Essays in Arts and Sciences*
    Univ. of New Haven [Conn.]
    Lib.)
EDB / *Emily Dickinson Bulletin*
*Edda: Nordisk Tidsskrift for
    Litteraturforskning*
EdL / *Etudes de Letters*
EGN / *Ellen Glasgow Newsletter*
EigoS / *Eigo Seinen* [*The Rising
    Generation*] (Tokyo)
EIHC / *Essex Institute Historical
    Collections*
EIP / *Essays in Poetics*

Éire / *Éire-Ireland: A Journal of Irish
    Studies* (St. Paul, Minn.)
ELH / *English Literary History*
ELN / *English Language Notes*
ELT / *English Literature in Tran-
    sition* (1880–1920)
ELWIU / *Essays in Literature*
    (Western Ill. Univ.)
Encounter
EngR / *English Record*
ES / *English Studies*
ESA / *English Studies in South Africa*
    (Johannesburg)
ESC / *English Studies in Canada*
*ESQ: Journal of the American
    Renaissance*
ETJ / *Educational Theatre Journal*
EurH / Europaisch Hochschuls-
    chriften/Publications Univer-
    sitaire Européenes/European
    University Studies
EuWN / *Eudora Welty Newsletter*
Expl / *Explicator*
Extrapolation
FDP / *Four Decades of Poetry*
    (Toronto)
FemS / *Feminist Studies*
FHA / *Fitzgerald-Hemingway An-
    nual, 1978*
FOB / *Flannery O'Connor Bulletin*
*Foundation: Review of Science
    Fiction*
GaR / *Georgia Review*
Genre
GeoR / *Geographical Review*
Glyph: Johns Hopkins Textual Studies
GrLR / *Great Lakes Review: A
    Journal of Midwest Culture*
Gulliver
HC / *Hollins Critic*
HJ / *Higginson Journal* (formerly
    Higginson Journal of Poetry)
HK / *Heritage of Kansas* (Emporia)
HLB / *Harvard Library Bulletin*
HSL / Hartford Studies in Literature
HudR / *Hudson Review*
IEY / *Iowa English Bulletin:
    Yearbook*
IFR / *International Fiction Review*
IJAS / *Indian Journal of American
    Studies*

IJWS / *International Journal of Women's Studies*
IllQ / *Illinois Quarterly*
Innisfree (Southeastern La. Univ.)
InR / *Intercollegiate Review: A Journal of Scholarship and Opinion* (Bryn Mawr, Pa.)
IowaR / *Iowa Review*
JAAI / *Journal of Afro-American Issues*
JAmS / *Journal of American Studies*
JBlackS / *Journal of Black Studies*
JEngL / *Journal of English Linguistics*
JGE / *Journal of General Education*
JHI / *Journal of the History of Ideas*
JLN / *Jack London Newsletter*
JNT / *Journal of Narrative Technique*
JPC / *Journal of Popular Culture*
JQ / *Journalism Quarterly*
KAL / *Kyushu American Literature*
Kalki: Studies in James Branch Cabell
KanQ / *Kansas Quarterly*
KASL / *Kasseler Arbeiten zur Sprache und Literatur*
KN / *Kwartalnik Neofiloloqiczny* (Warsaw)
L&P / *Literature and Psychology*
L&U / *The Lion and the Unicorn: A Critical Journal of Children's Literature* (Brooklyn [N.Y.] College)
Lang&S / *Language and Style*
LC / *Library Chronicle* (Univ. of Penn.)
LFQ / *Literature/Film Quarterly*
LGJ / *Lost Generation Journal*
LitR / *Literary Review*
Lituanus: Baltic States Quarterly of Arts & Sciences
LJGG / *Literaturwissenschaftliches Jahrbuch der Görres-Gesellschaft*
LMonog / *Literary Monographs*
LNL / *Linguistics in Literature*
LRN / *Literary Research Newsletter*
LWU / *Literatur in Wissenschraft und Unterricht* (Kiel)
Manuscripta
MarkhamR / *Markham Review*
McNR / *McNeese Review*
MD / *Modern Drama*
Meanjin / *Meanjin Quarterly* (Univ. of Melbourne)

MELUS: Multi-Ethnic Literature of the United States
MFLL / *Memoirs of the Faculty of Law and Literature: Literature* (Shimane Univ., Japan)
MichA / *Michigan Academician* (replaces *PMASAL*)
MidAmerica (East Lansing, Mich.)
MinnR / *Minnesota Review*
MissQ / *Mississippi Quarterly*
MLA / Modern Language Association
MLQ / *Modern Language Quarterly*
MLR / *Modern Language Review*
MoR / *Missouri Review*
Mosaic / *Mosaic: A Journal for the Comparative Study of Literature and Ideas*
MP / *Modern Philology*
MPS / *Modern Poetry Studies*
MQ / *Midwest Quarterly*
MQR / *Michigan Quarterly Review*
MR / *Massachusetts Review*
MSE / *Massachusetts Studies in English*
MSEx / *Melville Society Extracts* (formerly *Extracts*)
MSpr / *Moderna Språk* (Stockholm)
MSzA / *Mainzer Studien zur Amerikanistik*
MTJ / *Mark Twain Journal*
Names: Journal of the American Name Society
NCF / *Nineteenth-Century Fiction*
NCHR / *North Carolina Historical Review*
NConL / *Notes on Contemporary Literature*
NDEJ / *Notre Dame English Journal*
NDQ / *North Dakota Quarterly*
NEQ / *New England Quarterly*
NER / *New England Review* (Hanover, N.H.)
NewRep / *New Republic*
NM / *Neuphilologische Mittelungen*
NMAL: Notes on Modern American Literature
NMW / *Notes on Mississippi Writers*
NOR / *New Orleans Review*
Novel: A Forum on Fiction
NR / *Nassau Review*

NsM / Neusprachliche Mitteilungen aus Wissenschaft und Praxis
NYRB / New York Review of Books
Obsidian: Black Literature in Review
Odyssey: A Journal of the Humanities (Rochester, Mich.)
ON / Old Northwest (Miami [Ohio] Univ.)
OntarioR / Ontario Review
Overland (Melbourne)
Paideuma: A Journal Devoted to Ezra Pound Scholarship
Paragone (Florence)
Parnassus: Poetry in Review
PBSA / Papers of the Bibliographical Society of America
PCLS / Proceedings of the Comparative Literature Symposium
Peeble, A Magazine of Poetry (Crete, Neb.)
Phylon: The Atlanta University Review of Race and Culture
PLL / Papers on Language and Literature
PMHB / Pennsylvania Magazine of History and Biography
PMLA: Publications of the Modern Language Assn.
PMPA / Publications of the Missouri Philological Assn.
PoeS / Poe Studies
Poetica: Zeitschrift für Sprach- und Literaturwissenschaft (Amsterdam)
Poetics: International Review for the Theory of Literature
Ponte / Il Ponte: Revista Mensile di Politica e Letteratura
PR / Partisan Review
Prospects: An Annual of American Cultural Studies
PQ / Philological Quarterly
Proof: Yearbook of American Bibliographical and Textual Studies
PrS / Prairie Schooner
PsychocultR / Psychocultural Review
PsyR / Psychoanalytic Review
PULC / Princeton University Library Chronicle
QH / Quaker History
QJS / Quarterly Journal of Speech

RAAA / Regensburger Arbeiten zur Anglistik und Amerikanistik
RadT / Radical Teacher: A Newsjournal of Socialist Theory and Practice
RAIC / Review of Afro-American Issues and Culture
RALS / Resources for American Literary Study
ReAL / RE/Artes Liberales (Nacogdoches, Tex.)
Renascence
Rendezvous: Idaho State University Journal of Arts and Letters
RevI / Revista/Review Interamericana
RFEA / Revue Française d'Études Américaines
RFI / Regionalism and the Female Imagination (formerly the *Kate Chopin Newsletter*)
RFN / Robert Frost Newsletter (College Station, Tex.)
RLV / Revue des Langues Vivantes
RS / Research Studies (Wash. State Univ.)
RSQ / Rhetoric Society Quarterly
RUS / Rice University Studies
SA / Studi Americani (Rome)
SAB / South Atlantic Bulletin
SAF / Studies in American Fiction
SAJL / Studies in American Jewish Literature
SALit / Studies in American Literature (Kyoto)
Salmagundi
SAQ / South Atlantic Quarterly
SAR / Studies in the American Renaissance (Twayne)
SatR / Saturday Review
SAVL / Studien zur Allgemeinen und Vergleichenden Literaturwissenschaft
S&W / South & West: An International Literary Magazine
SB / Studies in Bibliography
SCN / Seventeenth-Century News
SCR / South Carolina Review
SDR / South Dakota Review
SEEJ / Slavic and Eastern European Journal
SELit / Studies in English Literature (Tokyo)

Semiotica
SFQ / *Southern Folklore Quarterly*
SFS / *Science-Fiction Studies*
Shenandoah
SHR / *Southern Humanities Review*
Sigma (Turin)
Signs: Journal of Women in Culture and Society
SIR / *Studies in Romanticism*
SJS / *San Jose Studies*
SLJ / *Southern Literary Journal*
SN / *Studia Neophilologica*
SNNTS / *Studies in the Novel* (North Tex. State Univ.)
SoQ / *Southern Quarterly*
SoR / *Southern Review*
SoSt / *Southern Studies: An Interdisciplinary Journal of the South* (formerly *LaS*)
Soundings: A Journal of Interdisciplinary Studies
SovL / *Soviet Literature*
SpM / *Spicilegio moderno* (Pisa)
Sprachkunst: Beiträge zur Literaturwissenschaft
SR / *Sewanee Review*
SSE / Stockholm Studies in English
SSF / *Studies in Short Fiction*
STA / Studien und Texte zur Amerikanistik (Frankfurt am Main), Peter Lang)
StHum / *Studies in the Humanities*
STTH / *Science-Technology & the Humanities* (Melbourne, Fla.)
StQ / *Steinbeck Quarterly*
STZ / *Sprache im technischen Zeitalter*
Sub-Stance: A Review of Theory and Literary Criticism
SUF / Schriften der Universitätsbibliothek Freiburg
SwAL / *Southwestern American Literature*
SWR / *Southwest Review*
TAH / *The American Hispanist*
TCL / *Twentieth-Century Literature*
TDR / *Drama Review*
Thought
ThQ / *Theatre Quarterly* (London)
ThS / *Theatre Survey*
TriQ / *TriQuarterly*
TSB / *Thoreau Society Bulletin*
TSE / *Tulane Studies in English*

TSL / *Tennessee Studies in Literature*
TSLL / *Tennessee Studies in Literature*
TUSAS / Twayne United States Authors Series
TWN / *Thomas Wolfe Newsletter* (Univ. of Akron [Ohio])
UDQ / *Denver Quarterly*
UES / *Urisa English Studies: Journal of the Department of English*
UMSE / *University of Mississippi Studies in English*
USP / *Under the Sign of Pisces: Anaïs Nin and her Circle*
UTQ / *University of Toronto Quarterly*
UWR / *University of Windsor Review* (Windsor, Ontario)
VMHB / *Virginia Magazine of History and Biography*
VQR / *Virginia Quarterly Review*
WAL / *Western American Literature*
WascanaR / *Wascana Review*
WCR / *West Coast Review*
WCWN / *William Carlos Williams Newsletter* (Penn. State Univ., Middletown)
WIRS / *Western Illinois Regional Studies*
WLWE / *World Literature Written in English*
WMQ / *William and Mary Quarterly*
WQ / *Wilson Quarterly: A National Review of Ideas and Information* (Washington, D.C.)
WS / *Women's Studies, An Interdisciplinary Journal*
WStJ / *Wallace Stevens Journal*
WVUPP / *West Virginia University Philological Papers*
WWR / *Walt Whitman Review*
WWS / *Western Writers Series* (Boise, Idaho: Boise State Univ.)
YER / *Yeats Eliot Review* (formerly, *T. S. Eliot Review*)
YES / *Yearbook of English Studies*
Yiddish
YR / *Yale Review*
YULG / *Yale University Library Gazette*
ZAA / *Zeitschrift für Anglistik und Amerikanistik* (East Berlin)
ZK / *Zeitschrift für Kulturaustauch*

Publishers

ALA / Chicago: American Library Association

AMS / New York: AMS Press

Anchor / Garden City, N.Y.: Anchor Press, Doubleday

Archon / Hamden, Conn.: Archon Books

Arno / New York: Arno Press

Basic / New York: Basic Books

Beacon / Boston: Beacon Press

Black Sparrow / Santa Barbara, Calif.: Black Sparrow Press

Bowker / New York: R. R. Bowker Co.

Brigham Young / Salt Lake City, Utah: Brigham Young Univ. Press

Bucknell / Lewisburg, Pa.: Bucknell Univ. Press

Calif. / Berkeley: Univ. of California Press

Cambridge / Cambridge, Eng.: Cambridge Univ. Press

Chicago / Chicago: Univ. of Chicago Press

Col. & Univ. / New Haven, Conn.: College and University Press

Columbia / New York: Columbia Univ. Press

Cornell / Ithaca, N.Y.: Cornell Univ. Press

Crowell / New York: Thomas Y. Crowell

Delacorte / New York: Delacorte Press

Dial / New York: Dial Press

Doubleday / New York: Doubleday & Co.

Dover / New York: Dover Publications

Duke / Durham, N.C.: Duke Univ. Press

Dutton / New York: E. P. Dutton

Edinburgh / Edinburgh: Univ. of Edinburgh Press

Exposition / Hicksville, N.Y.: Exposition Press

Fairleigh Dickinson / Madison, N.J.: Fairleigh Dickinson Univ. Press

Farrar / New York: Farrar, Straus & Giroux

Florida / Gainesville: Univ. Press of Florida

Fordham / Bronx, N.Y.: Fordham Univ. Press

Gale / Detroit: Gale Research Co.

Garland / New York: Garland Publishing Co.

Georgia / Athens: Univ. of Georgia Press

Greenwood / Westport, Conn.: Greenwood Press

Grossett / New York: Grossett & Dunlap

Grove / New York: Grove Press

Hall / Boston: G. K. Hall and Co.

Harcourt / New York: Harcourt Brace Jovanovich

Harper / New York: Harper & Row

Harvard / Cambridge, Mass.: Harvard Univ. Press

Harvard-Belknap / Cambridge Mass.: Belknap Press of Harvard Univ. Press

Hendricks / New York: Hendricks House

Hill & Wang, New York

Holt / New York: Holt, Rinehart and Winston

Hopkins / Baltimore: Johns Hopkins Univ. Press

Houghton Mifflin / Boston: Houghton Mifflin

Howard / Washington, D.C.: Howard Univ. Press

Humanities Press / Atlantic Highlands, N. J.: Humanities Press

Illinois / Urbana: Univ. of Illinois Press

Indiana / Bloomington: Indiana Univ. Press

Iowa State / Ames: Iowa State Univ. Press

Kansas / Lawrence: Regents Press of Kansas

Kennikat / Port Washington, N. Y.: Kennikat Press

Kentucky / Lexington: Univ. Press of Kentucky

Knopf / New York: Alfred A. Knopf

Lib. of Congress / Washington, D.C.: Library of Congress

Lippincott / Philadelphia: J. B. Lippincott

Little, Brown / Boston: Little, Brown

LSU / Baton Rouge: Louisiana State Univ. Press

Macmillan / New York: Macmillan Publishing Co.

Macmillan-L / London: Macmillan Press

Mass. / Amherst: Univ. of Massachusetts Press

Methuen / London: Methuen

Minn. / Minneapolis: Univ. of Minnesota Press

Miss. / Jackson: Univ. Press of Mississippi

Missouri / Columbia: Univ. of Missouri Press

Nebraska / Lincoln: Univ. of Nebraska Press

New Directions / New York: New Directions Publishing Corp.

New Mex. / Albuquerque: Univ. of New Mexico Press

N. Car. / Chapel Hill: Univ. of North Carolina Press

No. Ill. / DeKalb: Northern Illinois Univ. Press

Northwestern / Evanston, Ill.: Northwestern Univ. Press

Norton / New York: W. W. Norton & Co.

Notre Dame / Notre Dame, Ind.: Univ. of Notre Dame Press

NYU / New York: New York Univ. Press

Ohio / Athens: Ohio Univ. Press

Oklahoma / Norman: Univ. of Oklahoma Press

Oxford / New York: Oxford Univ. Press

Penn. State / University Park: Pennsylvania State Univ. Press

Pittsburgh / Pittsburgh: Univ. of Pittsburgh Press

Prentice-Hall / Englewood Cliffs, N.J.: Prentice-Hall

Princeton / Princeton, N.J.: Princeton Univ. Press

Purdue / West Lafayette, Ind.: Purdue Univ. Press

Putnam's / New York: G. P. Putnam's Sons

Random / New York: Random House

Rodopi / Amsterdam: Rodopi

Rowman / Totowa, N.J.: Rowman and Littlefield

St. Martin's / New York: St. Martin's

Scarecrow / Methuchen, N.J., Scarecrow Press

Schocken / New York: Schocken Books

Scribner's / New York: Charles Scribner's Sons

Shoe String / Hamden, Conn.: Shoe String Press

Simon & Schuster / New York: Simon and Schuster

SMU / Dallas, Tex.: Southern Methodist Univ. Press

So. Ill. / Carbondale: Southern Illinois Univ. Press

SUNY / Albany: State Univ. of New York Press

Swallow / Chicago: Swallow Press

Tenn. / Knoxville: Univ. of Tennessee Press

Texas / Austin: Univ. of Texas Press

Texas A&M / College Station: Texas A & M Univ. Press

Thoreau Soc. / Geneseo, N.Y.: Thoreau Society

Twayne / Boston: Twayne Publishers

Ungar / New York: Frederick Ungar Publishing Co.

Univ. Microfilms / Ann Arbor, Mich.: University Microfilms International

Viking / New York: Viking Press

Virginia / Charlottesville: Univ. Press of Virginia

Wash. / Seattle: Univ. of Washington Press

Wayne / Detroit: Wayne State Univ. Press

Wesleyan / Middletown, Conn.: Wesleyan Univ. Press

Wis. / Madison: Univ. of Wisconsin Press

Yale / New Haven, Conn.: Yale Univ. Press

Part I

1. Emerson, Thoreau, and Transcendentalism

Wendell Glick

The locus of this year's interest in Transcendentalism and the Transcendentalists is with Emerson: five critical studies were published, ranging from pedestrian and idiosyncratic to new and scholarly. Volume 14 of *The Journals and Miscellaneous Notebooks* issued from the Harvard-Belknap Press, as that edition makes steady progress. Two new volumes deal with Fuller; none were published on Thoreau. The publication of the first two volumes of Joel Myerson's *Studies in the American Renaissance* is an important event: they bring into print a quantity of hitherto unpublished primary material, as well as a number of distinguished critical essays.

i. General Studies, Textual Studies, Bibliography

The volume that comes closest this year to a reinterpretation of Transcendentalism is Robert D. Richardson, Jr.'s *Myth and Literature of the American Renaissance* (Indiana), a study that settles fairly comfortably into the scholarly genre of the history of ideas. Richardson's thesis is that writers of the American Renaissance can be divided into two groups on the basis of their *conscious* attitudes toward myth: those first of all who saw myth as "deeply and importantly true" and those secondly who viewed myth as "dangerous, delusive, false." The American Transcendentalists, Alcott, Emerson, and Thoreau, constitute the first group. Particularly penetrating is the chapter on Thoreau, which treats Thoreau's unorthodox use of myth as a *process* by which he universalized individual experience. From this point of view, *A Week*, *Walden*, *The Maine Woods*, and "Walk-

Again this year I acknowledge the substantial aid of Professor Roger Lips in covering the year's Emerson scholarship.—W.G.

ing" yield new meanings. Richardson's "Greek Myth: Prometheus
on Ktaadn" (pp. 105–17) can profitably be read in conjunction with
Frederick Garber's analysis of Thoreau and Ktaadn in *Thoreau's
Redemptive Imagination* (*ALS 1977*, p. 9). Emerson's more conventional response to myth, when compared with Thoreau's, illuminates
the significant differences between the aesthetic sensibilities of the
two men. Richardson's substantial study deserves a wide audience.
Also dealing broadly with Transcendentalist thought is Peter C.
Carafiol's "James Marsh to John Dewey: The Fate of Transcendental Philosophy in American Education" (*ESQ* 24:1–11). Despite its
scope of 70 years, this essay is a keen summary of the educational
principles of James Marsh, developed at the University of Vermont
in reaction to Lockean thought, and their impact on John Dewey
in the latter part of the century. "Dewey's educational ideas rever-
berate with Marsh's principles," is Carafiol's claim, "both [men]
celebrating individual differences between students that Lockean
education overlooked." The "fate of Transcendental philosophy" is
the capitulation of Marsh's faith in "transcendent truths" to Dewey's
relativism.

Under this rubric it is perhaps fitting to call attention to Joel
Myerson's *Studies in the American Renaissance* (Twayne). Myerson's attractive, new, illustrated annual appeared in June. Five of
the fourteen articles and monographs in Volume 1, and seven in
Volume 2 deal with Transcendentalism and its exponents, for the
most part the minor Transcendentalists, whose contributions have
never been systematically assessed. The opening essay, Richard
Francis's "The Ideology of Brook Farm" (pp. 1–48) raises again the
question addressed by H. C. Goddard in 1908 (in *Studies in New
England Transcendentalism*) of the disjunction between the overt
Fourieristic reform impulses of the Brook Farm group and the more
passive mode assumed in the 1840s by Emerson and Thoreau. Francis's principal contribution in this essay is not so much to advance
us beyond Goddard as to clarify William Henry Channing's relationship with the ideology of the Brook Farm phalanx. The point
contended for is that "Brook Farm was both a manifestation of the
Transcendental impulse and an attempt to create a better world"
and that "there is no need to see a conflict between these two descriptions." Perhaps not, but there is clearly a wide divergence in
reform methodology between Emerson and Thoreau on the one

hand, and George Ripley on the other. Robert N. Hudspeth's "A Calendar of the Letters of Margaret Fuller" (pp. 49–143) locates all known Fuller letters preparatory to a thorough, scholarly edition. David Robinson in "Christopher Pearse Cranch, Robert Browning, and the Problem of 'Transcendental' Friendship" (pp. 145–53) details the disintegration of the friendship of the two men in Florence as Browning's accelerating fame in the 1850s lifted him into aristocratic society. Thomas Blanding's "Daniel Ricketson's Sketch Book" (pp. 327–38) prints Ricketson's pencilled impressions of Thoreau, Ellery Channing, Alcott, and others from the cache of drawings in the manuscript collections of the New Bedford Whaling Museum. And Madeleine B. Stern, who has contributed much to a new understanding of Louisa Alcott, traces in "Louisa M. Alcott in Periodicals" (pp. 369–86) the dramatic story of Alcott's rise to fame as a contributor of some 210 poems, sketches, stories, and serials to periodicals between 1852 and 1888, impelled by her father Bronson's inability to support his family.

Volume 2 of Myerson's annual, which also appeared in 1978, is a mine of primary materials, with half the volume given over to the Transcendentalists. The lead essay by Robert A. Gross, " 'The Most Estimable Place in All the World': A Debate on Progress in Nineteenth-Century Concord" (pp. 1–5), I find the least valuable of the group. It forces its point by arbitrarily juxtaposing Thoreau's alleged view of the Concord economy against that of a conservative contemporary, Edward Jarvis. Gross concludes that "within the bounds of a single town, Jarvis and Thoreau had identified almost all of the central issues that later historians and social scientists would contest when they came to assess the consequences of the industrial revolution." But the parallels are strained; and to use Thoreau to the ends of social and economic commentary is to miss widely the core of his thought. Joel Myerson's "Bronson Alcott's 'Journal for 1836'" (pp. 17–104) makes available in print for the first time in its entirety Alcott's journal for a year crucial to New England Transcendentalism, and 11 pages of annotative notes lend perspective to the text. Annette M. Woodlief's "Emerson's Prose: An Annotated Checklist of Literary Criticism Through 1976" (pp. 105–60), though selective, will be useful to scholars for its careful and descriptive annotations in particular. John W. Clarkson, Jr.'s fine biographical essay on Sanborn in "Mentions of Emerson and Thoreau in the Letters

of Franklin Benjamin Sanborn" (pp. 387–420) reminds us again of
our need for a full-length biography of this thoroughly disliked ex-
ploiter of his acquaintanceship with the great of Concord. Clarkson
has performed a service to students of Emerson and Thoreau by
sifting out of the copious correspondence the 183 letters that contain references to the two men, since publication of Sanborn's complete correspondence is unlikely and probably unwarranted. Suzanne
S. Lewis in "Thoreau's Use of Sources in *Cape Cod*" (pp. 421–28)
claims that Thoreau in writing *Cape Cod* used a succession of guide-
books in combination with his own experience to portray "the steps
necessary for sincere perception of reality and the nature of the
heroic frame of mind," a novel reading of the book to say the least.
Alleging that "it is time . . . to examine closely the nature and extent
of Louisa Alcott's feminism," Madeleine B. Stern in "Louisa Alcott's
Feminist Letters" (pp. 429–52) prints 12 original Alcott letters to
demonstrate that "'Louisa Alcott's feminism was the feminism of a
human being impatient with indifference, apathy, and intolerance."
Her feminism was thus "dynamic without being militant." David
Robinson's "The Career and Reputation of Christopher Pearse
Cranch: An Essay in Biography and Bibliography" (pp. 453–72) is
a corrective to Perry Miller's estimate that Cranch "ultimately
proved one of the most futile and wasted talents" among the Transcendentalists. Robinson believes that much that Cranch wrote,
though not all, will repay "extremely close attention." All in all,
Studies in the American Renaissance has earned our support, if only
for its printing of primary holograph materials.

"James Burrill Curtis and Brook Farm," edited by Myerson,
prints 17 letters to his father filled with details of Brook Farm life
(*NEQ* 51:396–423). And in "Convers Francis and Emerson" (*AL*
50:17–36), with just enough commentary of his own to put Francis
in perspective, Myerson prints the passages from Francis's unpublished journal in the Houghton Library that have to do with the
responses of this ecclesiastical conservative to Emerson and to his
lectures. Of Emerson's introductory lecture to his "Human Culture"
series delivered in Boston on 6 December 1837, Francis commented:
"He was perpetually opening such rich, lofty, far reaching veins of
thought, that we sat breathless, as it were, and the mind ached with
pleasure in following him." Myerson's sifting of the unpublished
papers at the Houghton for primary material is a genuine service.

In "Channing's Unfinished Autobiographical Novel" (*ESQ* 24:42–55) Francis B. Dedmond publishes a 50-page holograph fragment of a novel by Channing (found at the Folger) that reflects the early onset of self-searching and loneliness that was to be Channing's lot throughout his life. One looks forward to Dedmond's studies of Channing's two unpublished autobiographical novels written ten years later: "Leviticus" and "Major Leviticus: His three days in Town." David Robinson and Lawrence Buell in "The Poems of Joseph Stevens Buckminster" (*RALS* 7:41–52) publish five poems (three for the first time) from this influential Boston minister, noted for his introduction of German scholarship into America. And Jesse Ishikawa in "Convers Francis to Theodore Parker: Boston in 1844" (*ESQ* 24:20–29) publishes from manuscript a lengthy, droll letter from Francis to Parker in Berlin, filling him in on gossip in the transcendental world of 1844.

I count it a matter of first importance when our stock of definitively edited texts is augmented. It is gratifying, therefore, that steady progress is being made in the publication of *The Journals and Miscellaneous Notebooks of Ralph Waldo Emerson* (Harvard-Belknap). Volume 14 appeared this year, edited by Susan Sutton Smith and Harrison Hayford, and bearing the seal of the Center for Editions of American Authors. The chronicle is thus continued of an aging but great mind, brooding the issues of black slavery and the coming war, though it is a mind beginning to question its own vitality. Despite Emerson's arduous lecture schedule during this period (1854–61), he published *English Traits* and *The Conduct of Life*. References to Thoreau, Alcott, and Ellery Channing are numerous. Reading them leads one to question whether Emerson was not too close to Thoreau's eccentricities to perceive the subtlety of Thoreau's thought. But one senses also that Emerson saw much more in Alcott and Channing than we in the 20th century have recognized, and he may well have been right.

Several useful checklists appeared during the year. Richard H. Dillman's "Resources for the Study of Transcendental Rhetoric: Emerson and Thoreau" (*RSQ* 8:165–75) attempts the perhaps impossible task of separating from the mass of scholarship on Transcendentalism and the Transcendentalists that portion dealing with rhetoric. Walter Harding's issuance of "A Catalog of the Thoreau Society Archives in the Concord Free Public Library" (Thoreau

Soc.) calls attention to that large accumulation of useful primary source material on Thoreau. The running bibliographies appearing in each issue of the *Thoreau Society Bulletin* constitute, as always, the most current listing of scholarship on Thoreau. Matthew J. Bruccoli and colleagues are continuing their ambitious *First Printings of American Authors* (Gale, 1977–78). Volume 1 includes Margaret Fuller; volume 2, Emerson; volume 3, Jones Very, George Ripley, Elizabeth Palmer Peabody, Frederic Hedge, and the Unitarian ministers Samuel Longfellow and Samuel Johnson. Joel Myerson carefully researched the textual history of *Margaret and Her Friends* (*PBSA* 72:187–200), the most complete record we have of Margaret Fuller's "Conversations." And finally, in the area of textual research, two articles appeared dealing with my editing of Thoreau's "Resistance to Civil Government" ("Civil Disobedience") in *Reform Papers* (Princeton [1973]). Thomas Woodson's "The Title and Text of Thoreau's 'Civil Disobedience'" (*BRH* 1:103–12) argues from the doctrine of "usual practice" that Thoreau made the substantive alterations in the 1849 text of "Resistance to Civil Government" that appeared in the 1866 posthumous printing of "Civil Disobedience." My essay, "Scholarly Editing and Dealing with Uncertainties: Thoreau's 'Resistance to Civil Government'" *AEB* 2:103–15) demonstrates the editorial untrustworthiness of Ellery Channing, who edited the posthumous 1866 edition, and argues that the burden of proof that Channing was being guided by instructions left by Thoreau, now lost, is clearly on those who desire to emend the 1849 copy-text, if modern textual principles formulated by Greg are to be honored. That Thoreau's usual practice was to revise his texts is incontrovertible. Also incontrovertible, unfortunately, is Ellery Channing's promiscuous altering of every Thoreau text that he handled.

ii. Emerson

a. **Life and Thought.** For those who must choose among the several books on Emerson appearing during the year, I recommend as a first choice David Porter's *Emerson and Literary Change* (Harvard). The power and influence of Emerson upon later writers have often been remarked (by Waggoner, Pearce, and others). Porter provides an explanation for that influence by examining Emerson's

poems as aesthetic constructs, not as philosophical or cultural products. He is "single-mindedly concerned," he tells us in his Introduction (p. 5), "with the basic structure of his poetic theory and the
nature of his formal innovation," and he sees in "the passage Emerson made from closed poetic vision to a broad reconciliation of art
and reality" a foreshadowing of Eliot, Pound, Williams, Stevens,
Robert Lowell, and others. "Emerson's prose is his power," Porter
argues, but the power of his prose results from his reattachment "of
language to process rather than to conclusion." To Porter "Emerson
was an aesthetic adventurer of an independence we have not sufficiently appreciated before," "the American artist who altered the
frontier": strip the idealism from Emerson's conscious aesthetics,
Porter suggests, and we are left with the key to understanding the
20th century. I find Porter's case to be strong and strongly reasoned;
his book holds its power to illuminate to the very end. My only reservation is that if the strength of the book is its undeviating deduc-
tion of Emerson's aesthetic principles from the poetry (where paradoxically they do not live and grow), the book's weakness may well
be that detaching Emerson from his Puritan past (after all, the Puritans applied language to experience also) has led Porter to make
claims for Emerson's innovativeness that are extreme. But I predict
that the argument of this book will alter our view of Emerson.

Not so Kenneth Marc Harris's *Carlyle and Emerson: Their Long
Debate* (Harvard), a portion of which (pp. 87–96) is reprinted in
Studies in Biography, pp. 103–12, under the title "Transcendental
Biography: Carlyle and Emerson." Where Porter develops his new
thesis in authoritative prose, Harris rehashes an old one with mushy
generalizations that lead often into frustrating cul de sacs. The essential formlessness of this book and its tendency toward the broad
statement may be the result of attempting too much: one cannot develop the philosophy of Emerson and that of Carlyle and draw
parallels between them in 170 pages. One comes away from this
book doubting that it was needed at all, unclear as to what the point-
by-point comparisons between the two men are supposed to reveal.

R. A. Yoder in *Emerson and the Orphic Poet in America* (Calif.)
undertakes much the same task that Porter undertook but with less
success. From the outset Porter's book deduces the principles of
Emerson's aesthetics from his poetry, by careful sequiturs leading
the reader through evidence cited from Emerson to its conclusions

on Emerson the aesthetician who sought structures for "a new veracity and reconciliation with experience." Yoder, on the other hand,
imposes his critical scaffolding on Emerson from the outside. Beginning with the assumption that "Emerson's conception of poetry
and the poet belongs to a special Romantic tradition, one larger
than American literature and encompassing much of it," Yoder over-
plays Emerson's absorption with the Orphic tradition, citing too
little evidence from Emerson to convince the reader that Orpheus
so dominated his thought. That Emerson's last word on Orpheus
"came significantly early, in 1849" according to Yoder (p. 173), and
that "this is indeed the culmination of his Orphic inquiry" suggests
to me that Orpheus was less absorbing to Emerson than he is to
Yoder. Porter links Emerson's aesthetics to Emerson's prose, which
is his "poetry," as Hyatt Waggoner has convincingly shown. Yoder's
mention of the prose is fleeting and casual. Porter's study of Emerson's aesthetics envelops the whole man. Yoder is selective and con-
strictive, and (for me) murders to dissect. The best of Yoder's
criticism is his essay on Emerson's prose comprising chapter 7,
"Toward the Titmouse Dimension," but this essay was previously
published (*PMLA* 87:255–70).

William J. Scheick in *The Slender Human Word: Emerson's
Artistry in Prose* (Tenn.) argues for an "aesthetic device" which
allegedly gives unity to Emerson's individual essays, Emerson's em-
ployment of what Scheick calls "a central hieroglyph or picture" that
provides in each case "a unique internal structural principle." During 1837 and 1838, Scheick believes, "Emerson perfected his use of
a hieroglyph as an aesthetic device, as the ordering visual center
of an essay" (p. 30). Since it is fairly obvious that Emerson often
makes one image dominant in a particular essay, Scheick may be
expanding upon and giving a new name to an old fact. We have,
of course, been seeking unifying principles in Emerson's essays for
a long time, and one reads Scheick with the feeling that he might
profitably have leavened his book with recent insights of other
scholars who have addressed the same concern. Ralph La Rosa's
monograph, "Necessary Truths: The Poetics of Emerson's Proverbs"
(*ALS 1966*, p. 5) comes to mind, for example, with its suggestion
that Emerson's essay structures are sometimes extensions of proverbs
that he loved. A good portion of Scheick's book is given over to
explications of individual essays, the essays being those most amen-

able to interpretation with Scheick's "hieroglyph" key. To name just a few of the "hieroglyphs": "The American Scholar" (One Man), "Experience" (The Planet Earth), "Success" (The Traveling Geographer), and "The Poet" (Pan).

Though Emerson's thought received its most noteworthy attention during the year in books, there was no dearth of shorter studies. Joel Porte's "Emerson in 1838: Essaying to Be" (*Studies in Biography*, pp. 183–99) calls attention to the very early emergence of Emerson's self-doubt and despondency, as reflected in "Literary Ethics," and "the delicate balance Emerson strikes between his hopes and fears." Here is an essay that achieves much in short space, that restores Emerson to us with zest. Wesley Mott's "Emerson and Antinomianism" with its attentiveness to Emerson's early sermons (*AL* 50:369–97) should be read as a corrective to those scholars who detach Emerson wholly from the Puritan tradition and view him as a scion of European Romanticism. Mott's position is perhaps extreme: in spite of Emerson's "occasional indulgence in Transcendental hyperbole," Mott concludes, "he remembered the basic truths about human nature he had learned as a minister." James B. Reece, with "Emerson's 'The Sphinx' and the Perception of Identity" (*ESQ* 24:12–19), enters the lists with the dozen or more critics who have tried to interpret this "bafflingly paradoxical poem," and emerges, in my opinion, still firmly astride his horse. Reese's close reading of the poem leads him to conclude that "the key to understanding the secrets of nature [the Sphinx] is the 'perception of identity' in all physical things." Porter's insights in his chapter 1 (see above) which reveal how Emerson's poetry distances the reader from immediate experience complement and illuminate Reece.

b. **Emerson and Other Writers.** In addition to Kenneth Marc Harris's *Carlyle and Emerson*, six or so shorter studies appeared, linking Emerson to other writers. Most are influence studies, some set on quicksand. One wonders why historian Merrill D. Peterson's "The American Scholar: Emerson and Jefferson" in *Thomas Jefferson and the World of Books* (Lib. of Congress, pp. 23–33) was written. When Peterson's clichés are not simply innocuous, they are, with respect to Emerson, wrong. "How could [Emerson and Jefferson] possibly have understood each other?" Peterson asks. "Jefferson's intellectual world was that of the eighteenth-century philosophes,

whose heroes were Bacon, Newton, and Locke." For his answer
Peterson might examine Walter Harding's *Emerson's Library*, or
even better, Emerson's lists of readings in his *Journal*. Hardly a single 18th-century thinker of consequence would he find missing.
Philip D. Beidler in "Billy Budd: Melville's Valedictory to Emerson" (*ESQ* 24:215–28) argues ingeniously that it is this novel's
"failure of form that provides Melville's ultimate testimony to the
deficiency of a Transcendentalist aesthetic." If Beidler is correct,
and I for one doubt his premises, Melville is distinctly in the minority now when critic after critic (e.g., Porter) attribute the vitality
of our literature in this century to the very Emersonian aesthetic
that Melville allegedly found deficient. This won't (and shouldn't
be) the final reading of *Billy Budd*. In "Emily Dickinson, Emerson,
and the Poet as Namer" (*NEQ* 51:467–88) John S. Mann undertakes
the "complicated and perilous task" of exploring "the possibility of
Emerson's presence in Emily Dickinson's life and poems, focusing
particularly on the shared interest of the two writers in "the role
of the poet as namer." By holding Dickinson's poetry firmly against
Emerson's thought Mann releases fine insights into Dickinson, leaving unresolved, however, the question of his influence on her. Unlike the Beidler essay, where the conclusions drawn clearly outrun
the evidence, Mann's restraint gives his thesis authority. David Robinson, using the same device that Mann found useful of holding
another author against Emerson, develops a new reading of Strether
from *The Ambassadors* "as a protagonist growing toward self-reliance" ("James and Emerson: The Ethical Context of *The Ambassadors*" [*SNNTS* 10:431–46]).

iii. Thoreau

a. **Life and Thought.** The floodtide of books on Thoreau in 1977
was followed by an ebb in 1978, and the periodical literature,
too, was scant. Two addresses delivered at annual meetings of the
Thoreau Society in Concord found their way into print, and unlike
many addresses, make substantive contributions. Joel Porte's " 'God
Himself Culminates in the Present Moment': Thoughts on Thoreau's
Faith" (*TSB* 144:1–4) argues that Thoreau, like Wallace Stevens,
finds God "not somewhere off in space and time, separated from
his being in the world, but rather embedded in 'the reality that sur-

rounds us.'" And Paul O. Williams in "The Influence of Thoreau on the American Nature Essay" (*TSB* 145:1–5) traces Thoreau's influence through John Burroughs, Edwin Teale, Loren Eiseley, Joseph Wood Krutch, and other nature writers. A thoroughly researched analysis of Thoreau's attitude toward the Irish by George E. Ryan corrects what I had always disturbingly felt to be an uncharacteristic dislike in Thoreau of the Irish as a national group: "Shanties and Shiftlessness: The Immigrant Irish of Henry Thoreau" (*Éire* 13:54–78) finds little inclination in Thoreau (as distinguished from Emerson) to denigrate the Irish en masse, but instead a very genuine sensitivity toward the exploited New England Shanty Irish that grew as the years passed. Steven G. Kellman's "A Conspiracy Theory of Literature: Thoreau and You" (*GaR* 32:808–19) begins with a long prologue that argues the predisposition of Americans to "conspire" against establishment norms, and ends with the thesis that *Walden* is Thoreau's invitation to his reader to be an active collaborator with him in the "conspiratorial goal" of self-reliance. That the audience of *Walden* is an active participant with the author in the mutual search for the "self" is a more tenable position, perhaps, than that they are fellow conspirators, a description that seems extreme. Michael West's "Versifying Thoreau: Frost's 'The Quest of the Purple Fringed' and 'Fire and Ice'" (*ELN* 16:40–47) argues that "Thoreau's *Journal* is the unrecognized source" for both poems. If West's reading of sexual implications for both Frost and Thoreau into their comments on the fringed purple orchis seems somewhat far-fetched, his careful matching of the Frost poems with their Thoreau counterparts gives him a strong case for influence. Though space limits preclude mention of each short article in the little journals devoted exclusively to Thoreau, I call particular attention to *The Thoreau Society Bulletin*, which prints pieces of scholarly interest in most issues, and to *The Concord Saunterer*, which has become a respected vehicle for scholarly essays and newly discovered primary material.

b. **Studies of *Walden*.** Charles Child Walcutt's "*Walden* as a Response to 'The American Scholar'" (*ArQ* 34:5–30) ingeniously finds the structure of *Walden* to be dictated by its point-by-point refutation of Emerson's arguments in "The American Scholar." Walcutt's claim is that "Thoreau's book is organized as a refutation of Emer-

son's essay and . . . the discipline and intellectual effort involved
in bringing off this task helped make *Walden* the wonderful and
extraordinary book that it became." The claim is too broad, though
Walcutt's careful demonstration that the successive chapters of
Walden can be read as counterarguments to Emerson's main con-
tentions in "The American Scholar" dramatize the differences in
thinking between the two men. The interval between the two works,
however, is 17 years. Neill R. Joy's "Two possible Analogues for 'The
Ponds' in *Walden*: Jonathan Carver and Wordsworth" (*ESQ* 24:
197–205) moves onto the slippery terrain of influence studies. Joy
tries to make his point by discovering parallels in feeling, tone, image,
structure, diction, and subject matter. But he mentions in summarizing that "if Thoreau did preoccupy himself with Wordsworth's
passages, he transformed them so that only faint echoes of the original sounds are retained." His case is weak. Jim Springer Borck and
Herbert B. Rothschild, Jr., in "Meditative Discoveries in Thoreau's
'The Pond in Winter'" (*TSLL* 20:93–105) do a running explication
of chapter 16 of *Walden*, seeing it as a kind of microcosm of the book
as a whole, a statement of many of *Walden*'s accepted themes, and
a self-contained unity. The claims of the essay seem extravagant.
No year passes without its study of the language of *Walden*: this
year's contribution is Judy Schaaf Anborn's "Thoreau in the Bean-
Field: The Curious Language of *Walden*" (*ESQ* 24:179–96). The
word "Curious" is troublesome from the outset, and the article fails
to clarify it. This essay develops no momentum: it is long, yet it lacks
direction and a single informing principle.

iv. Minor Transcendentalists

Interest in Margaret Fuller during the year easily outdistanced interest in all other members of this group. Two books, both by Joel
Myerson, typify this interest: *Margaret Fuller: A Descriptive Bibliography* (Pittsburgh) and *Margaret Fuller: Essays on American Life
and Letters* (Col. & Univ.). *A Descriptive Bibliography* "provides
an analytical description of all book-length publications by Fuller
and lists all her known contributions to magazines, newspapers, and
collections" (p. xiii). Entries are accessible and completely described; and the volume is unusually attractive, with its facsimile
illustrations of title pages, boards, and wrappers of Fuller books.

In this volume and Myerson's *Annotated Secondary Bibliography* (*ALS 1977*, p. 5) scholars have available two authoritative and useful tools. *Essays on American Life and Letters* is a selection from Fuller's works, including all of *Woman in the Nineteenth Century*; reviews of works of Hawthorne, Lowell, Emerson, Poe, Longfellow, Melville, and Charles Brockden Brown; and commentaries on current events. The reader is thus given a sense of the complete range of Fuller's interests. The selections are prefaced by a lucid biographical introduction and a useful bibliographical note. Bell Gale Chevigny followed her biography, *The Woman and the Myth* (*ALS 1977*, p. 13), with an absorbing essay, "Growing out of New England: The Emergence of Margaret Fuller's Radicalism" (*WS* 5:65–100). Having a deep knowledge of Fuller, Chevigny is able to dramatize Fuller's struggle for self-actualization in an environment hostile to its fulfillment. This is an intelligent essay, written with feeling, showing how by a succession of steps Fuller worked her way through the influence of New England, of her parents and Emerson, to an understandable political and social radicalism that reached its fruition in Rome.

Two studies of Jones Very and one of Louisa Alcott deserve mention. James A. Levernier's essay, "Calvinism and Transcendentalism in the Poetry of Jones Very" (*ESQ* 24:30–41), argues that Very's poetry should be read as his personal exploration on "whether or not it was possible for an orthodox Christian to be a Romanticist." "In coordinating a Transcendental view of nature with a Calvinistic perception of reality, Very concludes that only a Calvinist can be a successful Transcendentalist." Levernier's claim that this alleged conclusion of Very's explains his "apparent inconsistencies" is debatable. More convincing is David Robinson's "The Exemplary Self and the Transcendent Self in the Poetry of Jones Very" (*ESQ* 24: 206–14). Robinson claims less and accomplishes more; he accords Very "a careful strategy of composition," calling attention to Very's "conscious manipulation of voice" in his poems, "his use of what can be called the exemplary self and the transcendent self." Much of his essay Robinson devotes to explication of poems illustrating Very's use of the two personae. Eugenia Kaledin's "Louisa May Alcott: Success and the Sorrow of Self-Denial" (*WS* 5:251–63) invites comparison with Madeleine Stern's comments on Alcott's feminism in "Louisa Alcott's Feminist Letters" (see above). Whereas Stern sees

Alcott's feminism as "dynamic without being militant," to Kaledin "what becomes apparent as we study Louisa Alcott's life and her work is that her acceptance of the creed of womanly self-denial as much as her willingness to buy success by catering to middle class ideals aborted the promise of her art and led her to betray her most deeply felt values." Like Chevigny's article on Fuller (also noted above) Kaledin's is a sensitive rendering of the plight of a talented 19th-century woman whose personal and artistic growth was blocked by crippling social norms. Upon reading studies like these one wonders how many of Hawthorne's "damned mob of scribbling women" who fed the midcentury appetite for sentimental fiction were driven to artistic debauchery by the same forces of bias and proscription.

University of Minnesota, Duluth

2. Hawthorne

J. Donald Crowley

Hawthorne criticism in 1978 is rather thin compared to the work done in recent years. Although major studies of Hawthorne's life and of the English years as well as further volumes of the Centenary Edition are in press, none of these appeared in 1978. Nor did the *Nathaniel Hawthorne Journal* for 1977, now two years behind. Thin, then, and unfortunately of the usual uneven quality, with Chillingworth popping up as "Robert" and Goodman Brown as minister among similar strange growths here and there. Still there are worthwhile, even valuable additions to Hawthorne studies. In the criticism itself the most persistent interest focuses on Hawthorne's ambivalences about and intricacies of storytelling, as suggested by the number of essays which see *The Blithedale Romance*, "Rappaccini's Daughter," and a few other similar works as self-reflexive metafictions.

The only book-length critical study is Taylor Stoehr's *Hawthorne's Mad Scientists: Pseudoscience and Social Science in Nineteenth-Century Life and Letters* (Archon), a loose-limbed account of the popular pseudoscientific cultural phenomena and movements that flourished in Hawthorne's America. The sometimes bizarre practices and the wide public faith in mesmerism, phrenology, homeopathy, and associationism, spiritualism, feminism, and prison reform—each of which had multifoliate subspecialties—define Stoehr's social history. Insofar as the study shows Hawthorne making such contemporary theories and practices the stuff of his fiction, Stoehr's work is a welcome corrective to the view of Hawthorne as a moonshiney romancer disengaged from his actual world, and a corrective as well to recent structuralist deconstructions of Hawthorne's meanings. But its contributions are to social history rather than to literary criticism. Stoehr is true enough to his Preface to be distracting to most readers: "I admit to being just as interested in the trivia that

went into *The Blithedale Romance* as I am in the book itself, marvel
that it is." The book takes its shape from this preference, and *The
Blithedale Romance*, being at the center of Stoehr's interest, becomes the centerpiece of Hawthorne's art. The other half of Stoehr's
affection is devoted to this or that "ism" or "ology" with only the
slightest thread of conjecture to relate it securely to the fiction.
Thus, Margaret Fuller's "miraculous" cure of her spinal curvature
"by 'Odic irradiation and absorption'—that is, by vampiristic drain-
ing of her husband's sexuality"—is an anecdote "relevant to *Blithedale* and must be treated in full." Every aspect of the question except
its relevance is indeed treated in full. Stoehr's single literary historical intention is to analyze this romance as a transitional innovation by which Hawthorne transforms the conventions of Gothic
into emergent utopian fiction.

i. Manuscripts, Texts, Life, Bibliography

The chief event of 1978 in this category is the publication of *Hawthorne's Lost Notebook, 1835–1841* (Penn State), which reproduces
on facing pages a facsimile of the manuscript and a transcription
determined by Barbara S. Mouffe, the possessor of the notebook,
and Hyatt H. Waggoner. A "Reader's Edition," the text is as free
as possible of editorial emendations. Mouffe's Preface traces the
route by which the manuscript came into her family's hands, and
Waggoner's brief introduction describes the dominant qualities and
preoccupations of Hawthorne's entries and comments on the motives and manner of Sophia Hawthorne's revisions when, in 1866,
she prepared *Passages from the American Note-Books*. The present
edition restores for the first time Sophia's deletions, material amount-
ing to approximately one-fourth of the manuscript. Carefully and
handsomely done, it provides Hawthorne scholars with the last direct evidence they will ever have of the so-called solitary years before his marriage.

Two other texts, these of Hawthorne's consular papers, also appeared: John R. Byers, Jr., compiled "Selections from the Official
Consular Despatches of Nathaniel Hawthorne" (*EIHC* 113:239–
322), and Mark F. Sweeney edited the documents of the first half
of Hawthorne's tenure in "An Annotated Edition of Nathaniel Hawthorne's Official Dispatches to the State Department 1853–1857"

(*SAR 1978*, pp. 331–85). Byers's selections include all of the most important communications together with a large number of lengthy and interesting technical enclosures ranging over shipping and trade subjects as well as depositions involving questions of misconduct at sea. Sweeney's text prints all the dispatches, many of which are lacking in biographical or literary historical interest, but only refers in annotations to these enclosures no doubt assembled by the consul's knowledgeable and efficient clerks. Sweeney's introductory comments restate the earlier assessment of Randall Stewart regarding the effects of Hawthorne's consular duties on his later attempts to write fiction and suggest besides that, as Hawthorne's confidence grew, he was willing to color his reports with vigorous advocacy, especially on moral issues. A spot check of the two transcriptions reveals a number of discrepant readings, which point to the difficulty of Hawthorne's hand even in these years. Readers will want to use both texts together.

A biographical study that should add a new dimension to our understanding and teaching of *The Scarlet Letter*—and other works —is Stephen Nissenbaum's "The Firing of Nathaniel Hawthorne" (*EIHC* 114:57–86), an analysis that reconstructs Hawthorne's vacillations and poses of quiet detachment during his last unsettling months at the Custom-House in 1849. Charles W. Upham, the local Whig leader who plays the villain in Hawthorne's version of his dismissal, sounds most convincing in the records cited by Nissenbaum when he protests that the inevitabilities of party politics, not personal animosity, were responsible for the decapitation. Nissenbaum demonstrates too that there was real if regrettable substance to some of the charges leveled against Hawthorne, that it was the writer's misfortune to be caught in a common, unavoidable political squeeze-play much as he had, several years earlier, been willing to cooperate in, in order to gain the surveyorship. Nissenbaum traces deftly the desperate protective strategies that Hawthorne employed in his attempts to keep his position. His astute analysis of the political circumstances intimates cogently the ways in which "*The Scarlet Letter* itself, rather than 'The Custom-House,' is Hawthorne's autobiographical testament." It was in that work that Hawthorne transformed his vengeful drop of venom into rich symbolism and thus exorcized it. Any future critic will be obliged to take this essay into account.

A work of value primarily to collectors but of more general use as well is C. E. Frazer Clark, Jr.'s *A Descriptive Bibliography of the Writings of Nathaniel Hawthorne* (Pittsburgh). Clark has sections listing chronologically all separate publications, all collected works through 1900 published under the imprints of Ticknor and Fields and their successors, all first-appearance contributions to books and pamphlets, all first-appearance contributions to American and English magazines and newspapers together with selected reprints through 1850, special material and selected ephemera, selected bibliographical material, prose attributions, and verse by Hawthorne and verse attributed to him. The book abounds with handsome illustrations, the index appears comprehensive, and the study clearly supersedes all others of its kind.

Hawthorne and Melville students alike will welcome Walker Cowen's "Melville's Marginalia: Hawthorne" (*SAR 1978*, pp. 279–302), which includes exacting descriptions and locations of Melville's notations and identifies page-line references in both the personal copies of Melville and the appropriate volumes of the Centenary Edition. The rarity of actual comments will be a disappointment, however. Melville's habits of quick reading led him generally to merely underline or check rather than elaborate his thoughts; furthermore, Cowen speculates, numerous annotations were destroyed in one way or another after his death.

ii. General Studies

"Why was Hawthorne melancholy, and what made Poe drink liquor and why did Henry James like England better than America?" asks Marion Montgomery, quoting Flannery O'Connor, at the beginning of "Hawthorne's Imagination and the Sacredness of the Common" (*CLS* 15:43–52). The essay concludes with the lamenting insinuation that Hawthorne's being and art suffered because he could not "bring himself to the shelter of that Church's [St. Peter's] great world." Whether taken as an attempt to counter the secular/skeptical bent of much recent criticism or as something else, the piece seems, unfortunately, pretentious and simplistic. More modest but equally innocent of purposeful focus is Madison Jones's "Variations on a Hawthorne Theme" (*SSF* 15:277–83), which chooses "Young Goodman Brown," "Rappaccini's Daughter," and "The Birthmark" as illustrations of Hawthorne's credal commitment to the Calvinist notion that, in spite of their total depravity, individuals still contain within themselves the divine image: hence the erroneous ways of Brown, Giovanni, Aylmer. But why stop here? one asks first. And then, why go on? since the donnée presented as discovery Jones tends to assume rather than demonstrate. Critics of all persuasions have always accepted Hawthorne's characters as endowed with the virtue of value.

Roberta F. Weldon's "From 'The Old Manse' to 'The Custom-House': The Growth of the Artist's Mind (*TSLL* 20:36–47) proposes that Hawthorne consciously intended his audience to consider the two sketches as parts of a single one in which he traces the different effects the two places had on him and his art. The Concord home, having allowed Hawthorne at least the illusion of solitude and society equally sweet, encouraged imaginative writing as well as a kindly paternalistic appreciation of his reader. The custom-house experience, on the other hand, alienates from society, self, and art even in permitting the development of "a Romantic concept" of the author-reader relationship. And here Hawthorne writes a sketch, "not to invest the experience with a certain immortality, but to kill its power and bury its memory." In offering up "The Custom-House" as purge, Weldon's conclusion is in opposition to Nissenbaum's. Weldon's analysis tends, I think, to accept as literal truth Hawthorne's fictional version of himself there and seems to lose sight of the implications of the fact that Hawthorne had already written *The Scarlet Letter*, his achievement in having done so interposing itself between the two sketches. That Hawthorne's earliest narrative practices are subtler and more sophisticated than Weldon would imply is one of the points made by C. S. B. Swann in "The Practice and Theory of Storytelling: Nathaniel Hawthorne and Walter Benjamin" (*JAmS* 12:185–202). Swann's discussion of "Mr. Higginbotham's Catastrophe," "Wakefield," and the conclusion of "The Story Teller" takes place against a background of only loosely related theoretical concerns that would show Hawthorne anticipating metafiction and antifiction. Swann's argument is that Dominicus Pike and his tale enjoy a comic triumph over the persistent intrusion of abundant "news" that constantly threatens to strip common experience of all value. Intriguing but more tenuous are his speculations about "Wakefield," a "story," Swann says, told "three times"

and making us aware all the while that it stands in lieu of the "novel"
Hawthorne might have written. The last section of the essay and
the claims the author makes for Oberon's home return I find not
dull but incoherent—rather like tracking a Twain meditation on the
possible compounds of *Schlag* and *Zug*. In "Rappaccini's Garden of
Allegory" (*AL* 50:167–86) Don Parry Norford charts his way—and
his readers'—through another labyrinth of critical considerations to
conclude that Hawthorne's ideal of allegory could never find "its
appropriate embodiment" because of his perception of "an unbreach-
able gap between the ideal and the actual, spirit and matter, art and
life, which may be healed only in the next life." In such works as
The Scarlet Letter, "The Birthmark," "The Prophetic Pictures," and
"Rappaccini's Daughter" allegory is "daemonic" and the artist an
anti-Pygmalion who cannot avoid transforming characters into artifacts. Parry's view has it that Hawthorne himself—and not just his
artists and narrators—labored under the "Puritan feeling that [he]
blasphemously usurps the power of God" and that whatever redemptive moments allowed art are limited for Hawthorne to its self-
reflexive dramatization of these irreversible difficulties.

iii. Long Romances

The single substantial essay on *The Scarlet Letter* itself is John
Franzosa's " 'The Custom-House,' *The Scarlet Letter*, and Hawthorne's Separation from Salem" (*ESQ* 24:57–71). An intricate
analysis that should be read with Nissenbaum's reconstruction of
Hawthorne's firing, Fransoza's is a largely Freudian study which,
like Nissenbaum's, finds the romance addressing more fully than
does Hawthorne's introductory sketch the central, angry "themes
of dependence—nourishment, loss, and rejection—" that were the
upshot of his removal from office and the painful death shortly
thereafter of his mother. Hawthorne works off an oedipal rage in
his creation of Hester as a composite parent figure, "a type of phallic
mother" who, representing "a denial of loss," leads him imaginatively to his "profound discovery." So "hell-fired" in this sense was the
romance for Hawthorne that his chief aim in the sketch was to dispel
" 'its stern and somber aspect' " by inviting a conception of the no-
toriety of his fictional self. Still, for Franzosa, Hawthorne's resolution was short-lived, since he shared with Dimmesdale the haunting

conviction that "to live is to exist inauthentically." Though psychological jargon intrudes here and there, Franzosa's insights are many and make their claims on both text and reader.

In "Art vs. Utopia: The Case of Nathaniel Hawthorne and Brook Farm" (*AR* 36:89–102) Taylor Stoehr examines the writer's "daring" attempt to stare down "the antithetical claims of social conscience and literary consciousness" and to confront "the almost metaphysical anxiety that the practice of art seemed to arouse in him." Not all of what Stoehr says is new, but his comments on Thoreau's and Emerson's differing responses to this problem are instructive. What's to be doubted is Stoehr's assertion that Hawthorne had reopened in this romance "the old issues that two dozen stories and as many years had served to smooth over and neutralize in habitual formulations." Such a judgment plainly distorts the early short fiction, tale and sketch alike. A much stranger set of premises and conclusions is announced in Edward Stone's "The Spirit World of *The Blithedale Romance*" (*CLQ* 14:172–76). Stone has the romance being "more than all else" a history of utopian aspirations "finally smothered"; yet Coverdale's imagination, he says, combining (somehow) "Alpha and Omega," redeems and gives new life to the "group pursuit of the American dream." Still larger, more sweeping claims for Hawthorne's and Coverdale's mutual success and profundity are made by Irvin Stock in "Hawthorne's Portrait of the Artist: A Defense of *The Blithedale Romance*" (*Novel* 11:144–56). Most of these claims seem to rest on a name and a comparison: like *Moby-Dick*, *The Magic Mountain*, *The Counterfeiters*, Hawthorne's romance "belongs to a class of what may be called wisdom-novels, novels whose texture and themes rise, not out of one idea of what is so or another, but out of the conflict between all ideas—indeed, between the truth-seeking human mind—and the complexities of human experience." Rather than construct conflicts amenable to "problem-solving theory," Hawthorne's steady purpose was to write "a novel to expose what the art of fiction usually conceals" and to cast doubt on "its own pretensions to truth." Stock's own assessment smacks of an attenuated, overly subtle critical problem-solving itself, and it leaves readers wondering why some wisdom-novels are wiser and more interesting than others.

In "Progress and Providence in *The House of the Seven Gables*" (*AL* 50:37–48) John Gatta examines the problem of Hawthorne's "prosperous conclusion" with perception and precision. Hawthorne, he attempts to demonstrate, charts the question of progress under three different ontological aspects: the moral and spiritual development of the individual, the amelioration of public life and social history, and the "teleological drama of redemption" whose terms are knowable only to Providence. Agreeing with other recent critics that Hawthorne is most of all skeptical about social progress systematic or otherwise, Gatta presents forcefully the controversial argument that the principle of "causality linking all three notions of progress" in the romance is nothing less than providential design —mysterious, paradoxical, announcing individual spiritual growth with "circumstances of outward failure." Phoebe is in this scheme intended as "the Incarnation of a transcendent religious principle of redemptive love," and Hawthorne's failure to make her role and the happy ending "real" is a failure of his sentimental and at times pious language. Gatta suggests, finally, that we may share Hawthorne's failure "in our inability *as* moderns to understand or appreciate that brighter side of Hawthorne's divided sensibility which he declared more characteristic of his nature." The question remains why Hawthorne, at least in his finest fiction, seems no less unable than we to believe in that side of himself.

iv. Short Works

In "House Symbolism in Hawthorne's 'My Kinsman, Major Molineux' " (*ATQ* 38:167–75) J. C. Nitzsche finds a Robin who, initially deluded by the blandishments of earthly, material homes (the barbership, inn, harlot's house), comes to the truth of Ecclesiastes in perceiving the figurative, spiritual homes presented him (the church, grave, stately mansion) and in realizing that worldly fortune is heavy baggage "for the good man who wishes to rise—in the Other World." Even readers of religious bent will be unable to bear witness to so didactic a reading. Likewise oversimplified is Denis M. Murphy's reading of the tale in "Poor Robin and Shrewd Ben: Hawthorne's Kinsman" (*SSF* 15:185–90), which for the most part says what others have implied or understood—that, insofar as Franklin's *Autobiography* is alluded to, Robin's journey is "a derisive mockery of the Franklin ideal" of the easy way to wealth and wisdom. And this is to say nothing of the objections Franklin scholars might have. If both essays are notable for what they are willing, or wish, to leave out, they nonetheless pale beside Edwin Haviland Miller's "'My Kinsman, Major Molineux': The Playful Art of Nathaniel Hawthorne" (*ESQ* 24:145–51), which bristles with objections to virtually every interpretation that has elaborated the tale's resonant symbolic —even historical—suggestiveness. Robin is not a latter-day version of "Odysseus, Dante, the Red Cross Knight, Everyman, Christian, or Ben Franklin," and his kinsman is no scapegoat figure. "America does not come of age in this tale," and nowhere "is Robin concerned with ethical problems." Stripped of criticism's veneer of "intellectual-historical-mythical profundities," Robin's tale is a portrayal, affectionate and "comi-tragic," of "a boy-man at the difficult, anxiety-ridden age of eighteen." Its center is a psychological and erotic realism, done up in the playful manner of one who enjoys a throaty authorial laugh. Phallic imagery is admitted into the funhouse, as is oedipal conflict. So is the scarlet petticoat who, except for her "sly freedom," could be "Phoebe!" Hawthorne's first long, deliberately dry-as-dust paragraph of historical setting or antisetting is as good as nonexistent. And though Miller pauses over the name "Robin," he ignores altogether the historical import of the surname of this boy-man, only one of whose names is Robin and who, after all, paid a double fare just to get into town.

In "The Hieroglyphic Rock in Hawthorne's 'Roger Malvin's Burial'" (*ESQ* 24:72–76) William J. Scheick writes astutely about the completeness with which the rock as hieroglyphic mystery permeates nature, the human heart, language, even the tale itself. Reuben's burden is shared by both Hawthorne and the reader: "the tale mimetically conveys an impression of the irresolvable dilemma of human existence in a world which appears to invite knowing even while it remains unknowable." Though brief, the essay is fresh and stimulating.

Along with defenses of Coverdale, the year brings charges against other Hawthorne narrators. Mark M. Hennelly, Jr., in "'Alice Doane's Appeal': Hawthorne's Case Against the Artist" (*SAF* 6: 125–40), takes one of the critical paths more traveled by in arguing that, far from being chaotic and contrived, this is a "uniquely masterful tale" the key to whose understanding is, we're told, the tired formula that Hawthorne is not to be confused with his "prying and perverted Artist-Narrator." The frame is itself the story, the "tales" within—the "history of the Doanes and the final nightmare vision of Cotton Mather"—simply "allegorical insets" which illustrate the frame's situation. All this done up in a cohesive five-act drama in which Hawthorne's purpose is to level irony at "the probing Intellect he always feared he might become." Frame does displace tale traditionally understood here, but Hennelly's logic leaves dangling the reasons why, if Hawthorne so decisively separated himself from his dehumanized storyteller, he still felt compelled to refuse to acknowledge the piece in his last collections. As other essays this year argue, it was Hawthorne's habit to share the dark powers of his narrators rather than to morally separate himself from them.

There is clearly no evidence of an emerging consensus yet regarding the meaning of "Rappaccini's Daughter" and the exact reasons why Giovanni goes wrong. The view Richard L. Predmore advances in "The Hero's Test in 'Rappaccini's Daughter'" (*ELN* 15:284–91) is that Giovanni, confronted with the responsibility of the traditional hero of myth and fairy tale to redeem the captive princess by solving the riddle she is, fails, not so much because of his empirical attitudes as because of the "wild vagaries which his imagination ran riot continually in producing." Since his "tormenting confusion" is his Inferno, our judgment of his shortcomings is softened. What Predmore fails to clarify is why, how Giovanni is only "partly" responsible: Beatrice *is* enigmatic, after all, Giovanni's empiricism and riotous fancy notwithstanding. The literary historian is likely to feel reduced, or elevated, to Giovanni's perplexities when he reads Lloyd Spenser Thomas's "'Rappaccini's Daughter': Hawthorne's Distillation of His Sources" (*ATQ* 38:177–91), which reaches conclusions only slightly different by way of a radically different trail. Hawthorne craftily "mingles borrowings from Dante, Ovid, Indian literature, and Renaissance iconology, as well as arcane oenological and toxological lore to symbolically gauge Giovanni's aberration" and "heighten his own narrative irony." The essay is delightfully formidable in its erudition and threatening in the web of pedantry that, at so many points, hides well the whole to examine the part. One works his way through "sigh" motifs and other Dante allusions through a number of sculptural images (of which that of Vertumnus "is only one") and various pertinent etymologies to find himself at statements such as: "The only real poison in the story is that of misconception." The essay lacks coherence, but there is about it a steady honesty and an episodic brilliance. The year's most thoughtful and balanced essay on this tale is Kent Bales's "Sexual Exploitation and the Fall from Natural Virtue in Rappaccini's Garden" (*ESQ* 24:133–44). Bales threads his way among readings religious and Freudian, arguing that both Beatrice and the garden appear steadily in two forms: Beatrice as "an un-self-conscious natural creature, proper inhabitant of Eden, and as a self-denying saint who ascends from her human martyrdom to an Eden beyond this fallen world"; the garden as at once "a mysterious survival of Eden" and as "a microcosmic world." Beatrice's fate is to be victimized by civilization and its sexual discontents that politicize all human relationships. Bales manages to be his own best critic in questioning whether his evaluation of the tale is altogether consistent with Hawthorne's dissatisfaction with both Enlightenment rationalism and Romantic naturalism.

v. Hawthorne and Others

In an essay overlooked last year, "The Impact of American Literature on French Writers" (*CLS* 14[1977]:119–34) Roger Asselineau surveys, among others', Hawthorne's popularity in France to find it problematic. Given the still worse fates of other American writers, Hawthorne might have taken joy in his discovery in 1860 at a Marseilles train station that he was known there most of all for a translation (bad) of *A Wonder-Book*. Asselineau's analysis of the reasons for the French reception of American writers is illuminating. Suggestive, too, for different reasons is Rainier Sell's "Hawthorne and Wilder: From 'Main-Street' to *Our Town*" (*LWU* 11:149–60), which tries to show half a dozen "affinities" between the two works, from Hawthorne's "showman" and Wilder's "Stage Manager" to a reliance on allegory. Sell's comparisons seem forced the more they press their generalizations into specific illustrations. But the argument is sufficiently sound that the reader is left wondering whether there isn't a subtler, more significant tissue of connection between the two works than Sell claims. Instead of an authentic comparison, there is only an artificial occasion to make do with in Anna Balákían's ". . . 'and the pursuit of happiness': *The Scarlet Letter* and *A Spy in the House of Love*" (*Mosaic* 11,ii:163–70). Why the writer chooses Anaïs Nin's novel rather than one or more of dozens of others whose "subject is adultery" is never made clear. Try as Balákían might to disguise or conceal her predisposition for the contemporary-feminist version of the cult of self-discovery, her rhetoric leaves no doubt that Hawthorne's vision and Hester's plight will not measure up to the stressful complexities of Nin's and her heroine Sabina's. Thus, the A's fire in Hester's breast is "nonetheless a localized fire" and her guilt "imposed from the exterior" whereas Sabina's "ingrained" scars result from that "forbidden knowledge" required of her in her strenuous efforts, through many "sexual encounters," to "reinvent love." The essay seems only to prove that, when "human sexuality" is so deep in the saddle as to be the latest fashionable idolatry, Hawthorne's story of Hester Prynne will finish a distant second. In "The House and the Railroad: *Dombey and Son* and *The House of the Seven Gables*" (*NEQ* 51:3–22) Jonathan Arac, on the other hand, clarifies a matrix of common metaphor and a similar literary historical rationale that justify the pertinence of his useful comparison. Arac demonstrates convincingly the similarities and differences in the ways the two writers develop their materials in terms of the established patterns of the Gothic tale (the house) and those of the essayistic sketch of contemporary life (the railroad). His distinctions here are measured, acute, as they are in regard to the divergent views Dickens and Hawthorne had of the burdens and the beneficial possibilities of writing social fable: Dickens's instinctive faith that "the representation of social reality carries a moral power that moves people to action" distinguishes him from Hawthorne, who could not recognize "the existence of society without needing to reduce it to its psychological substrata."

University of Missouri, Columbia

3. Poe

Donald B. Stauffer

The big event of the year was the publication of the second and third volumes of Mabbott's edition. Also noteworthy was a handsome, well-edited symposium on *Pym*, a work that continues to fascinate Poe scholars. Some interesting studies of Poe's cultural milieu appeared; aside from these bright spots the scholarship and criticism were routine. If we are to judge by the number of popular books published on Poe, he is still interesting to the reading public. Three commercial books appeared: Wolf Mankowitz's *The Extraordinary Mr. Poe* (Simon & Schuster), Peter Haining's *Edgar Allan Poe Scrapbook* (Schocken), and Julian Symons's biography. The first two are loaded with interesting pictures and misinformation, while the biography makes some claims on our attention. Many of the dissertations this year were comparative, so in the next year or two we shall probably see articles comparing Poe to Lovecraft, Baudelaire, Thomas Cole, Gogol, James, Hawthorne, and Valéry.

i. Texts

It has become customary over the past 25 years to refer to the "long-awaited" edition of Poe's *Collected Works* which the late Thomas O. Mabbott was preparing for the press. That wait is now nearing its end with the appearance of volumes 2 and 3: *Tales and Sketches 1831–1842* and *Tales and Sketches 1843–1849*, ably edited by Mabbott's widow, Maureen Cobb Mabbott, and her associate Eleanor D. Kewer, and handsomely printed by the Belknap Press of Harvard University Press. The editors prepared the final copy from the manuscript left by Mabbott at his death in 1968, and they have rechecked every note, silently correcting and adding information where necessary.

Unlike recent editions of most other American authors, this one does not follow the guidelines of the Center for Scholarly Editions (formerly the CEAA), but that does not mean it is lacking in textual and bibliographical apparatus. It is the first edition that collates the various versions of Poe's texts since the venerable 1902 "Virginia Edition" of the *Complete Works* by James A. Harrison, and it reflects the discoveries of Poe scholarship over the past three quarters of a century, many of them made by Mabbott himself. Mabbott saw and collated the revisions in over 50 more manuscripts and printed versions of the tales than Harrison had access to.

He decided to call these volumes "Tales and Sketches" in order to be able to include some pieces that might be called essays by some; his principle of selection was to include any piece that involves narration. Accordingly, he prints nine definitely new pieces which did not appear in Harrison: "The Lighthouse" (including a photograph of the MS.), "A Dream," "Instinct vs. Reason," "Cabs," "Morning Chapters," "Desultory Notes on Cats," "The Swiss Bell-Ringer," "Theatrical Rats," and "A Reviewer Reviewed." None of these, with the possible exception of "The Lighthouse," is going to add much to our knowledge or estimate of Poe's work, and they will be of interest mainly to Poe specialists. But the edition as a whole is of great interest and value, containing as it does the fruits of Mabbott's years of research. In addition to the extensive notes, glosses, and lists of sources, such items as his conjectures on the identities of the narrators of the Folio Club tales, his views on the use of vampirism in "Usher," his opinion on the reasons for the different versions of "The Spectacles," his printing of Mrs. Whitman's MS. copy of "Morella," to mention just a few at random, make these volumes a must for every student of Poe. Unfortunately, the principles of selection of copy-text do not follow modern editorial procedures and therefore limit its usefulness as a text. Some of the objections to Mabbott's choices of copy-texts are presented by Joseph J. Moldenhauer in his review in *PoeS* 11:41–46.

An example of Mabbott's arbitrariness in textual matters is the case of "The Spectacles." Mabbott chose not to reprint a manuscript version now in the possession of the University of Texas at Austin, giving the unimportance of the tale as his reason for choosing the late Griswold text over Poe's own manuscript revision. He therefore printed "the form long known to the world" and collated it with the manuscript. This is the manuscript that was sent to the English poet Richard Hengist Horne shortly after the earlier version had been reprinted in the Philadelphia *Dollar Newspaper*. Moldenhauer has provided a superb edition of the text of the later version with textual commentary and notes that make it more easily accessible than do the collations in Mabbott ("Poe's 'The Spectacles': A New Text from Manuscript," *SAR* 1977:179–234).

Roland Nelson's "Apparatus for a Definitive Edition of Poe's *Eureka*" (*SAR* 1978:161–205) is a reworking of the material that appeared in his dissertation (see *ALS 1975*, p. 58). Burton Pollin explores the variants in Poe's spelling of Hans Pfaall and those mistakenly used by critics and scholars, including the false variant, "Pfaal," which resulted from a copying error in A. H. Quinn's 1941 biography. He points out that Poe himself changed the spelling from "Phaall" to "Pfaall" for his proposed "second edition" of the *Tales of the Grotesque and Arabesque*. He denies that Poe had any intention of sexual innuendo in this or such other tales as "Lionizing," in which some critics have found suggestive passages: "Poe apparently wished to guard against any 'phallic' references by changing the spelling" ("Hans Pfaall: A False Variant and the Phallic Fallacy," *MissQ* 31:519–27).

ii. Biography and Miscellaneous

The continuing popularity of Poe is the most obvious explanation for still another book about him written for a general audience. Julian Symons, the English novelist and mystery writer, has written *The Tell-Tale Heart: The Life and Works of Edgar Allan Poe* (Harper) as a serious chronicle of the facts of the life and a study of the works. Symons does not perpetuate or capitalize upon the legend, but gives a straightforward life based on reliable sources. He is largely sympathetic to Poe and his work, although he concludes that he was a "literary psychopath of genius." In his comments on the work he pooh-poohs most criticism of the past 20 years, but holds Marie Bonaparte in high regard.

There were four articles on Poe's influence. One is an interesting study of the relationship between literature and art, Renée Riese Hubert's "The Other Worldly Landscapes of E. A. Poe and René Magritte" (*Sub-Stance* 21:68–77). Hubert pays particular attention to Poe's aesthetic theories in "The Domain of Arnheim" and their

relation to Magritte's two paintings with that name. In "American
Gothic: Poe and *An American Tragedy*" (*AL* 49:515–32), Thomas P.
Riggio maintains, with many illustrative examples, that the principal influences on chapters 42–47 of the novel, depicting Clyde's
murder of Roberta, were Poe's tales and poems.

In "*Pym* and *Moby-Dick*: Essential Connections" (*ATQ* 37:73–
86) Grace Farrell Lee shows convincingly how the two novels may
be connected by the mythic forms their journeys take: the myth of
the eternal return and its variations in the pattern of descent and
return, and its analogue, death and rebirth. Lee supports her belief that Melville must have recognized these motif patterns in *Pym*
and wove them into his own narrative. Her examples are many, and
though most citations from both books are familiar, she succeeds in
matching them in striking ways that provide fresh insights into both
books and help build the case that Melville had read and was influenced by *Pym*. And Adeline R. Tintner shows how Henry James
adapted the theme and structure of *Pym* in *The Golden Bowl*, in
"James Corrects Poe: The Appropriation of *Pym* in *The Golden
Bowl*" (*ATQ* 37:87–91).

Benjamin Franklin Fisher's collection, *Poe at Work: Seven Textual Studies* (Baltimore: Edgar Allan Poe Society) is a republication
in hardcover of the essays Fisher edited for *LC* 41 (see *ALS 1976*,
pp. 36–42 passim). The book includes one additional item, Robert W.
Burns, "Poe and His Revisions: A Checklist of Materials," pp. 100–
110. Recent German criticism of Poe beginning with Link and
Schuhmann and going up through the early seventies is surveyed by
Roger Forclaz in "Poe in Europe" (*PoeS* 11:49–55).

There were only three poetry items, one of which was published
in 1977. Deborah K. Nagy, in " 'Annabel Lee': Poe's Ballad," *ReAL*
3,ii[1977]:29–34, analyzes the poem's structure, rhyme, rhythm and
repetition to show how Poe draws his effects from the ballad tradition. Nagy defends the poem against critics who find it weak and
obscure. Lou Ann Kriegisch, in " 'Ulalume'—A Platonic Profanation
of Beauty and Love" (*PoeS* 11:29–31), develops a close reading of
the poem as a Platonic struggle between earthly and spiritual love,
based on parallels with the *Phaedrus*. James Voss, in "Poetry and
Mythic Thought: a Structural Approach to the Love Sonnet and to
Poe's 'Sonnet—To Science' " (*Edda* 5:271–92), is interested in developing a structural approach to the love sonnet by analyzing its

underlying mythic structure. By examining "Sonnet—To Science" in the light of the Western love sonnet tradition Voss discovers a mythic structure which leads him to some interesting new readings of the poem.

iii. General Studies

If there is any trend this year it is toward a greater interest in the historical context of Poe's writing and in the philosophical backgrounds, particularly of the 18th century. The Baudelairean image of Poe as a man without a country is dying, as more attention is paid to his response to contemporary political and social issues. This trend cannot help but deepen our understanding of all his work, not merely the satires. The best of these studies is Brian M. Barbour's "Poe and Tradition" (*SLJ* 10:46–74), which explores some of the ways Poe's work is related to American traditions. Barbour's historical and philosophical approach uses the tales as examples of Poe's efforts to criticize American thought and morality in the 1830s and 1840s. Poe's well-known hostility to science and the scientific method is directly stated in his own voice in the poems; but in the tales Poe speaks indirectly through his narrators, to show his readers their own shortcomings. The rationalistic outlook which prevents speculation or seeing things whole is clearly attacked in "The Purloined Letter," where the unifying power of the imagination is set against narrow rationalism in the solution of the problem. The narrator of "The Fall of the House of Usher" embodies another essentially American attitude: the superiority of common sense over more complicated forms of thinking and feeling. Poe makes this common-sense narrator become more and more obtuse and inadequate in the face of events he does not understand. And the American emphasis on the primacy of the individual will is shown to be grotesque when it becomes the will to dominate, as in "The Cask of Amontillado" or "Ligeia." The essay is a welcome one in its use of American historical and philosophical contexts and its efforts to place Poe in them.

In "Poe and American Society" (*CRevAS* 9:16–33) Stuart Levine covers more familiar ground, pulling together many reasons why we should consider Poe a writer of his time and place. Levine provides a variety of topics, including Poe's reactions to modernization, the similarity of his ideas to those of Emerson and other contemporaries, his fascination with technology, his interest in the possibilities of magazine publishing, and his response to popular culture. He uses these familiar points to attack some writers of 30 and 40 years ago who failed to see what most of us today are more clearly aware of, but he has already made his point more thoroughly in the notes to his and Susan Levine's anthology of the tales (see *ALS 1976*, p. 35).

Another article showing Poe to be a writer of his time is Ronald T. Curran's "The Fashionable Thirties: Poe's Satire in 'The Man That Was Used Up'" (*MarkhamR* 8:14–20). Curran points out the variety of 19th-century social values that Poe was attacking in his tale. Poe first takes his narrator through a variety of encounters with typical gospel preachers, playgoers, cardplayers, duellers, and ballroom dancers. His description of General A. B. C. Smith is a satirical attack on 19th-century scientific ingenuity, in which the general is seen as a ridiculous machine, an infernal automaton. Poe is therefore attacking the materialistic tendencies of the age rather than a specific person, according to Curran.

Some interesting speculations about the relation of Poe's ideas to 19th-century American ideas about sexuality are made by Jules Zanger in "Poe and the Theme of Forbidden Knowledge" (*AL* 49: 533–43). Drawing upon some of the common imagery and themes in "Morella," "Ligeia," "MS. Found in a Bottle," and "A Descent into the Maelstrom," Zanger sees two types of forbidden knowledge associated with these tales. In the first two the narrator acquires his knowledge under the guidance of another, while in the last two he is under the control of forces outside of himself. In all of them, however, knowledge is associated with the Fall. The whirlpool and woman are therefore linked, although to arrive at a strictly Freudian interpretation would be not as useful as seeing that Poe is using a sexual metaphor. Asking what the explicit metaphors of forbidden knowledge and whirlpools suggest about the significance to Poe of the implicit sexual metaphor, Zanger concludes that it is associated in Poe's mind with the entire carnal condition of man, from birth through aging to death, and is associated with pain, rather than the autonomous, never-changing, purely intellectual condition of an Israfel.

Kenneth Dauber, in "The Problem of Poe" (*GaR* 32:645–57), bravely takes on the task of reassessing Poe, after finding that most recent criticism has not succeeded in placing him. Dauber thinks we have been looking for Poe in the wrong places; that there is no discoverable meaning in his stories; rather his fiction is nothing more than fiction, and he reduces the world to the status of a fiction, an abstraction. Poe's work is not meaningless, however; it is "a deferral of meaning. It absorbs and thereby empties the world, rewriting it at the level of a language which now becomes all." What Dauber is saying, in the fashionable language of phenomenological criticism, is that Poe's fiction is self-reflexive and self-enclosed: a solipsistic art which becomes its own end. He says it well, however, and along the way offers some interesting observations on Poe's need to feel that he is being plagiarized and on his need to use phony erudition.

Victor J. Vitanza, in " 'The Question of Poe's Narrators': Perverseness Considered Once Again" (*ATQ* 38:137–49), challenges James Gargano's concept of the unreliable narrator of Poe's tales by looking at the major tales collectively rather than individually. Vitanza argues that the narrators are indeed "reliable" if the pattern in each tale is seen as a reflection of the principle of perverseness: the basic pattern, which varies from tale to tale, is *impulse: reason: self-destruction*. He demonstrates admirably how this concept of perverseness carries on through the major Gothic tales, the tales of ratiocination, and finally to *Eureka*. The term "reliable," however, becomes very slippery as he moves from the question of the reliability of narrators in individual tales to reliability in the larger sense of reflecting Poe's notions of perverseness. One could agree that Poe's narrators reliably reflect his views and still accept Gargano's thesis that each deranged narrator is unreliable when he attempts to tell his story. Vitanza does not really invalidate Gargano's thesis, but he does have interesting things to say about the theme of perverseness in the tales.

Alcohol and Poe are linked in a somewhat different way than usual by Benjamin Franklin Fisher IV, in his Edgar Allan Poe Society lecture, *The Very Spirit of Cordiality: The Literary Uses of Alcohol and Alcoholism in the Tales of Edgar Allan Poe* (Baltimore: Enoch Pratt Free Lib.). Fisher surveys the tales, particularly those in the Folio Club group, which use references to alcohol or drinking, or use wordplay suggesting them. He collects many of the already well-known references to drinking in the comic tales, such as "Bon-

Bon" and "The Duc de l'Omelette," but he also points out that "The Assignation" and "MS. Found in a Bottle" become humorous when they are understood to be told by drunken members of the Folio Club. In fact, he believes that much of the intended humor of the tales was to be derived from their Folio Club context.

David Karnath peevishly scolds Poe for not being wholly consistent in adhering to his critical principles of unity of effect, in "Poe's Baroque Space and the Unity of Effect" (*SSF* 15:263–68).

iv. The Tales

As a more detailed illustration of his thesis that the Folio Club tales were originally intended to be comic and that revisions were made when they were published individually, Benjamin Franklin Fisher IV examines the revisions of "MS. Found in a Bottle" in detail. He finds that Poe drops phrases that suggest humor and exaggeration and revises to create a greater sense of horror. The brief discussion and a reprinting of the rare 1833 *Baltimore Saturday Visiter* version are appended to Fisher's Poe Society lecture (pp. 19–32).

Joseph P. Roppolo, in "Undercurrents in Poe's 'The Fall of the House of Usher'" (*TSE* 23:1–16), ignores the work of practically every recent critic and claims that no one has looked for allegorical meaning in the tale. Roppolo's own allegorical reading makes Roderick the Artist, the House of Art. Roderick loses the rational control (Intellect) necessary to create a work of art. Madeleine is the externalized symbol of Roderick's reason who rejoins him too late to prevent the house's collapse.

Poe's quarrel with Lockean associationist theory, explored in detail by Barton L. St. Armand's study of "Usher" (see *ALS 1977*, p. 42), is further documented by Kent Ljungquist in "Burke's *Enquiry* and the Aesthetics of 'The Pit and the Pendulum'" (*PoeS* 11: 26–29). Burke's sensationist aesthetics are contained in his *Enquiry into the Origins of Our Ideas of the Sublime and the Beautiful*, in which Burke argues that blackness evokes sublimity and that the sublime could be used to portray subjects that defy the restrictions of ordinary language. Poe, in Ljungquist's view, used qualities of the sublime he found in Burke as a literary device to impart terror to the narration of "The Pit and the Pendulum."

In "The Geometric Structure of Poe's 'The Oval Portrait'" (*PoeS*

11:6–8), William J. Scheick looks at the "fictive space" of the tale and discovers a series of "more or less circular layers," descending from the turret to narrative frame and finally to the eyes of the portrait itself. The inward-outward movement suggested by these concentric circles resembles the pulsations of *Eureka*; they also suggest to Scheick a mandala, or yantra, which induces a dreamlike state in the reader.

J. Gerald Kennedy's "Poe and Magazine Writing on Premature Burial" (*SAR* 1977:165–78) places Poe's tale in the context of contemporary treatments of the theme. Kennedy demonstrates that the theme was treated in various ways in Poe's time: realistically, satirically, and romantically; and that by the time Poe used all three approaches in his tale it had already become a cliché which he used to display his own virtuosity as a writer.

Burton Pollin's "Poe's 'Murders in the Rue Morgue': The Ingenious Web Unravelled" (*SAR* 1977:235–59) contains the fruits of the author's research into Parisian street names, house architecture, and other matters which convince Pollin that many of the inaccuracies and inconsistencies in the tale are deliberate: they are "pleasant caprices of the author's imagination," "mere *plaisanteries*," "delightfully whimsical inventions," etc.

Ottavio M. Casale looks at Poe's allegorical technique in "William Wilson," which he considers, rightly, his most overtly symbolic tale. Casale notes that Wilson's double becomes progressively less material, more internalized, and therefore more symbolic in value, to the point where, at the end, he has become dematerialized. Poe, he says, carefully created a "cumulative allegory," or symbolic construct, in which aspects of the mind are incorporated as characters that begin firmly in physical reality and end up in the mind. This is a shrewd observation, although I wish he had been less reluctant to deal with precisely what the tale allegorizes ("The Dematerialization of William Wilson: Poe's Use of Cumulative Allegory," *SCR* 11:70–79).

v. The Narrative of Arthur Gordon Pym

A special symposium issue of *ATQ* edited by Richard P. Benton was devoted to *Pym*, called "Journey Into the Center—Studies in Poe's *Pym.*" In addition to the essays discussed here, the issue contained a translation by Gerald Bello of Roger Forclaz's 1964 article, "A Voyage to the Frontiers of the Unknown," a bibliography by Burton Pollin of editions and translations of *Pym*, and some plates from Charles Wilkes's *Narrative of the United States Exploring Expedition, During the Years, 1838, 1839, 1840, 1841, 1842*. Although these essays are interesting, they do not as a group measure up to the quality of other works on *Pym* that have appeared in the last three years.

The widely accepted view of J. V. Ridgely and Iola S. Haverstick that Poe changed his mind several times about the direction of Pym's story line and that he worked on it at several periods between 1836 and 1838 has been challenged by Alexander Hammond after a close look at the original copyright entry and the circumstances surrounding it. Hammond's interpretation of the evidence is that *Pym* was essentially complete when its title was recorded on 10 June 1837, and that its composition was rushed during that spring in order to exploit public interest in Wilkes's Antarctic expedition, which did not actually depart until 1838. Hammond thus calls into question the contention that some parts of the book were written in 1838, and he thinks that the publisher held the completed manuscript until its publication would coincide with the expedition's departure. He also points out some elements of hoax that may have been part of the novel's appeal to the publishers ("The Composition of *The Narrative of Arthur Gordon Pym*: Notes Toward a Re-examination," *ATQ* 37: 1–20).

David Ketterer also takes issue with Ridgely and Haverstick—in this case arguing against their claim that the work lacks unity. His argument is based on the thematic unity of deception which occurs throughout, and on a unity of structure first discerned by Edward Davidson and Charles O'Donnell. Ketterer refines their notions of structural unity by noting that the prologue is followed by two halves paralleling each other and "implying" an epilogue which parallels the prologue. His catalogue of examples of deception follows the work of other scholars, and the article as a whole would serve as a good introduction to the novel but adds little to what has already been said elsewhere ("Devious Voyage: The Singular *Narrative of A. Gordon Pym*," *ATQ* 37:21–33).

In "The Dragon and the Uroboros: Themes of Metamorphosis in *Arthur Gordon Pym*," *ATQ* 37:57–71, Barton Levi St. Armand uses alchemical lore and Jungian psychology to provide new perspectives on the changing and deceptive qualities of the tale. Adopting two alchemical symbols, the Dragon and the Uroboros, St. Armand explores image clusters that appear to define two opposite poles of archetypal metamorphosis in the novel. At one pole is the complete reconciliation of opposites, symbolized by the Uroboros, an age-old symbol for eternity; at the other is incomplete transformation, symbolized by the Dragon, with its grotesque appendages. The narrative is itself a monstrous tale, full of grotesque excrescences, monsters, and monstrous events. But in addition to these Dragon-like aspects, St. Armand finds imagery and events suggesting the prenatal state, which Jung's disciple Erich Neumann links to the Uroboros symbol. St. Armand therefore sees the novel in a way similar to that of Edward Davidson, as, in Davidson's words, "a moving backward through the natural order as it presently exists and into the world's original condition, as primal first cause."

Leonard W. Engel enumerates in a mechanical way some images of enclosure already noted by other critics and arrives at the not-very-new conclusion that Pym's emergence from these various confinements suggests death to an old self and rebirth of a new one ("Edgar Allan Poe's Use of the Enclosure Device," *ATQ* 37:34–44).

As he does for "The Pit and the Pendulum," Kent Ljungquist sees *Pym* as another example of Poe's using the aesthetic of the sublime, in "Descent of the Titans: The Sublime Riddle of *Arthur Gordon Pym*" (*SLJ* 10:75–92). Pym's responses to various events correspond to the sensations described by Edmund Burke on the sublime. But Ljungquist also finds elements of Romantic Titanism, which Poe was aware of in Shelley and Keats, but possibly found also in Jacob Bryant's *A New System; or, An Analysis of Ancient Mythology* (1807). Other parallels between *Pym* and Bryant suggest that Poe used his source to make the white Titanic figure at the novel's close a sublime evocation of the history of man's degeneration from original harmony into savagery.

vi. Eureka

Two studies of *Eureka* take opposing viewpoints as to Poe's tone and attitude, one taking his rhetorical flights seriously, the other suspecting them to be partly a hoax. Alan C. Golding, in an excellent analysis of *Eureka*'s semantic strategies, discovers a parallel between the language he uses and the level of sublimity he achieves. The pattern is similar to that in Poe's tales, where the narrator moves from an everyday, rational level to the fantastic or irrational or sublime. Golding ("Reductive and Expansive Language: Semantic Strategies in *Eureka*," *PoeS* 11:1–5) shows how Poe first points out to his reader the limits of simple (reductive) language for explaining ideas lying beyond its capacities and then goes on to use a figurative, "expansive" language which points toward the sublime. Golding builds on John Hussey's study (see *ALS 1975*, pp. 56–57), showing the relationship between *Eureka* and Hugh Blair's discussions of sublimity in his lectures on rhetoric. Although he derives the term "expansive" from Dawson Gaillard's discussion of Poe's use of language (see *ALS 1975*, p. 58), he goes beyond Gaillard to show that Poe's concern with language tends toward finding precise definitions as well as toward resisting them. Poe's intention is to use reductive statements which "clear the reader of mistaken assumptions that he knows what words mean so that the mystery of the universe can be revealed" through language which is extravagant, metaphorical, and nonreferential, that is, expansive, and thereby suggests the sublime. This is a well-written, closely reasoned essay which builds on recent rhetorical studies of *Eureka* and is consistent with the general view that Poe as an artist moves away from the realistic and the precise toward the poetic and the vague.

Then there is Peter C. Page, who, in "Poe, Empedocles, and Intuition in *Eureka*" (*PoeS* 11:21–26), finds that the influence of Empedocles on Poe's cosmological work is significant in several ways. Page finds the proof for Poe's having been influenced by the ancient Greek cosmologer in the fact that both use the terms "attraction" and "repulsion," and in *Eureka* Poe follows Empedocles' cycle of periods of primal unity alternating with periods of diffusion. But, like Poe, Empedocles was a duplicitous figure, a trickster who did not always mean what he said. Page sees numerous possibilities for irony and double-entendre in *Eureka* and suggests that Poe is covertly ridiculing his cosmologer-persona through multilingual puns and other devices. Page suspects that Poe does not mean his speaker to be taken seriously and that his "stance toward his intuited cosmology is as derisive as his attitude toward Emerson's Transcendentalism, to which it bears a resemblance." Page is among a growing number of critics who feel that Poe was ridiculing the idea of being able to know intuitively the ultimate nature of things while seemingly taking pains to explain it.

State University of New York at Albany

4. Melville

Hershel Parker

I suspect that more was published on Melville this year than in any earlier year, most of it predictably weak, some of it unpredictably good. The unevenness is obvious in an ambitious collection of 11 new essays edited by Faith Pullin, *New Perspectives on Melville* (Edinburgh). Six of the contributors are British, six American; the collaborative essay on *Pierre*, as Pullin says, "is a truly Anglo-American enterprise." The collection deals with most of Melville's works, casually or penetratingly, but omits the intimidating *Clarel* altogether. I don't think the collection coheres, or that it succeeds in not being "just another contribution to the Melville industry," but it contains some essays of permanent value. From across the Atlantic also came other precious cargo—sometimes too precious—in the form of two issues of *Delta* on "Bartleby." Bowing to the need for terseness in *ALS*, I am ignoring some three dozen routine, superficial, derivative notes and articles (mainly on *Moby-Dick*, "Benito Cereno," and *Billy Budd, Sailor*), along with some weak pages in books and a couple of the pieces in *New Perspectives*. I start this policy with trepidation that I might omit something important because I did not see it, but amends can be made for such oversights. As the ultimate proof of my dedication to brevity, I am restraining the urge to exhort. Everything I have said in the opening paragraphs of *ALS 1972, 1973, 1975,* and *1977* still applies, anyhow.

i. Biography, Bibliography, Reputation, and Miscellaneous

The best ongoing biographical work is by the team of Joyce Deveau Kennedy and Frederick James Kennedy. Their two-part "Elizabeth and Herman" (*MSEx* 33:4–12; 34:3–8) is a significant supplement to the *Log*, one that will take some time to absorb. The Kennedys' greatest coup so far is the recovery of a wonderful Melville letter and some other interesting new documents: see "Herman Melville and Samuel Hay Savage, 1847–1851" (*MSEx* 35:1–10); the letter is reproduced full size on pages 3–5. As Jay Leyda says, documents are still out there, but they are dwindling every day as offices get moved, houses get torn down, people die, and libraries discard bulky, crumbling newspapers without microfilming them. Right now the Kennedys, bless them, are about the only gleaners after Leyda, except for another team, Donald and Kathleen Malone Yannella, whose "Evert A. Duyckinck's 'Diary: May 29–November 8, 1847'" (*SAR* 2:207–58), a fascinating preview of their full edition of the diaries, puts the well-known Melville entries into context. Stanton Garner's "Melville in the Customhouse, 1881–1882" (*MSEx* 35:12–14) offers some sordid background on Melville's working conditions. If a contemporary allegation is true, "all" of the inspectors (including Melville) were strongarmed into contributing some 2 percent of their annual salary to the Republican State Committee in 1881.

Merton M. Sealts, Jr., answers "yes" to his question "Did Melville Write 'The Fiddler'?" (*HLB* 26:77–81), reminding us that the attribution rests on Mrs. Melville's file of Melville's magazine pieces and her notations on them. George Monteiro's "*Clarel* in the *International Review*" (*MSEx* 34:9) reprints in facsimile a newly discovered January 1877 review, and Nelson C. Smith reprints some hitherto unknown "Melville Reviews in the London *Sun*" (*MSEx* 36:8–12). I pried an essay from Walker Cowen for *Recognition* (1967), but the first real sampling of Cowen's 1965 dissertation, long a cult object on the interlibrary loan circuit, is his "Melville's Marginalia: Hawthorne" (*SAR* 2:279–302), in which the descriptions of Melville's annotations and markings are helpfully keyed to the Centenary Edition as well as to the actual editions which Melville marked up. More, Cowen, more!

The long-promised *A Concordance to Melville's "Moby-Dick"* (Univ. Microfilms), edited by Hennig Cohen and James Cahalan, appeared in three hefty volumes. Yet this is a makeshift operation since the choice of the Feidelson text was fortuitous, the result of the discovery that a machine-readable tape of it had been made by the Princeton University Computer Center. As I pointed out in 1973 (*Proof* 3, p. 375), this text derives, not without error, from the Mansfield-Vincent edition. The Norton text (1967) is not "definitive," but I think its list of variants between the American and English editions

is complete, and any standard concordance to *Moby-Dick* will incorporate those English readings which must be Melville's own corrections and those which are almost surely his own revisions. Such
a concordance would also find a way to incorporate certain conjectural emendations, even if it retains, e.g., the 1851 reading "argued"
cross-referenced to the conjectured "augured" (Norton Critical Edition, p. 340, l. 3). The editors propose to offer a supplementary key
to the pagination of the Northwestern-Newberry Edition, when it
appears, but even so cumbersome an apparatus would not solve the
problem of which words are included. Pending the NN publication,
a usable concordance could have been made from the first American
edition supplemented with the Norton substantive variant list and
certain of the Norton emendations. Consult Watson Branch's review-
essay on the Cohen-Cahalan concordance in *Computers and the
Humanities* (1979) before you rush to lay out your $126.75. Another
wasted opportunity is Eugene F. Irey's *"Moby-Dick" Index Concordance* (Hendricks), which lists (1) "those references, with the exception of the names of characters and ships in the narrative, which
Melville for whatever reason chose to emphasize by capitalization";
(2) some of the same words which appear without capitalization;
and (3) "references to the characters and ships in the narrative."
(The ascription of all first-edition capitalization to Melville is, to
say the least, naïve.) These pages are marvelous to skim down but
impossible to use seriously. Go to "Presbyterian" and you won't find
that Ishmael was "born and bred in the bosom of the infallible Presbyterian Church": that's under "Church, Presbyterian." "Dutch" has
a cross reference to "Low Dutch" but "German" has no cross reference to "High German." Under "Coffin, Charley" is listed "only a
Perseus . . . a Coffin," while "A Coffin my Innkeeper" is listed separately. Sexism triumphs when Hosea Hussey gets into the main index
along with his brindled cow while poor Mrs. Hussey, being merely
a character in *Moby-Dick*, is relegated to the third section. My favorite historical personage in the main section is Harry ("the adul-
terer that broke jail in old Gomorrah"). Irey, who names the names
of people who helped him create this mess, threatens us with "a
forthcoming complete concordance to *Moby-Dick*." I hope it manages to get more of Melville's words than Cohen-Cahalan did, and
that it manages to avoid some of the awkwardness of format which
Branch details. Now that universities have decided that the old

staples of dronework (editions and reception studies) are too de-
meaning, they are granting Ph.D.'s for computer concordances to
literary works. If that boggles your mind, good. But the dissertation
directors, or computer concordance directors, now at least owe it to
us to think out how the available technology can best serve the purposes of real live users of the concordance. There is, as Melville said,
an aesthetics in all things.

In "*BAL* Addenda: Melville" (*PBSA* 72:243–45) G. Thomas
Tanselle indicates "some of the principal items (or categories of
items) that the *BAL* fails to include." An intimidating compilation
is Masao Tsunematsu and Sanford E. Marovitz's "A Bibliography of
Herman Melville Studies in Japan," in *MFLL* 1:13–68. The Mar-
ovitz-Tsunematsu "Melville Studies in Japan" (*MSEx* 36:1–6), a
discursive survey, will suffice most of us.

Robert Milder's "'Knowing' Melville" (*ESQ* 24:96–117), a review essay of the books by Gerard M. Sweeney (1975), Richard H.
Brodhead (1976), and T. Walter Herbert, Jr. (1977), gives the most
thoughtful reviews those books have had and also a fascinating discussion of the 1962 book by Warner Berthoff. Like Milder's 1976 and
1977 essays in *ESQ*, this is one of the year's best pieces.

ii. General

Last year I missed Ann Douglas's "Herman Melville and the Revolt
Against the Reader" in her *The Feminization of American Culture*
(Knopf [1977], pp. 289–326) and now will join Willard Thorp (*AL*
50:523–24) in a minority view of its value. William Charvat, to whom
Douglas gives less than adequate thanks, wrote much better on the
same subject, mainly because his knowledge was so much more
sweeping and his spirit so much more generous. I am dismayed by
the careless citing of editions (the wrong ones); by pointless speculations (if Melville had known Margaret Fuller, "he would have
respected her and her work"); and by her contempt for accuracy
(Melville was older than Whitman).

An item in Italian, "Herman Melville e Daniel Defoe: Un'Ac-
coppiata 'Storica' Rivisitata" (*Ponte* 33:931–39), by Michele Puglisi,
looks to me like a pointless culling of some comparisons to Defoe
in contemporary reviews of Melville; the quotations come from such
nonexhaustive sources as Hetherington's *Melville's Reviewers* and

Branch's *Melville: The Critical Heritage.* But "Defoe and Melville" is one of those old topics on which a splendid article could yet be written, maybe by a student of the development of aesthetic terminology in the 19th century. Paul McCarthy takes on an unhackneyed topic in "Melville's Rascals on Land, Sea, and in the Air" (*SoQ* 16:311–36), although his land-sea-air division may not be a useful strategy; certainly one misses examples from the poetry and much of the prose, notably the short stories. Edwin M. Eigner in *The Metaphysical Novel in England and America: Dickens, Bulwer, Melville, and Hawthorne* (Calif.) will probably satisfy few readers with his definition of metaphysical, but the book has a sprinkling of aperçus on Melville that could set critics thinking—e.g., the first paragraph on page 26 or the remarkably provocative one on pages 95–96.

H. Bruce Franklin's chapter on Melville in *The Victim as Criminal and Artist* (Oxford, pp. 31–70), is a redone, expanded version of his chapter in *Weapons of Criticism* (1976). Franklin sees Melville as "an artist whose creative imagination was forged in the furnace of his labor and oppression, an artist who saw the world of nineteenth-century American society and its commercial empire through the eyes of its victims." Confessing that in *The Wake of the Gods* he cut *Moby-Dick* from its roots in Melville's whaling experience and thereby drained the life from it, Franklin again drains the life from Melville's works, this time by ignoring Melville's self-education in world literature, the complicated play of his pondering mind, and the sizable admixture of the conservative and aristocratic in his character. A glance at the Northwestern-Newberry *Typee* could have saved Franklin from his repeated assertions that certain "radical" passages from the English *Typee* were not printed in the United States until 1893. The first American printing was only very slightly censored, and in fact the first American reviewers had read the very words Franklin says they never saw. Here is your basic comicbook-Marxist Melville, if you want him.

iii. Early Books—*Typee, Omoo, Mardi*

Faith Pullin wrote the first essay, "Melville's *Typee*: The Failure of Eden," for her collection (*New Perspectives*, pp. 1–28). This is a straightforward introduction to *Typee*, hardly new but refreshing in this day of lopsided, partial readings. Gerard M. Sweeney in "Melville's Smoky Humor: Fire-Lighting in *Typee*" (*ArQ* 34:371–76) responds bug-eyed to "an amazingly graphic description of masturbation" that some of us hoped would never be written about. Sexual innuendo just stops being funny if you call it "doubly purposeful, pointing toward both the themes of the book and the character of the narrator." At least Sweeney does not strive toward the high solemnity of my favorite academic title, "The Serious Functions of Melville's Phallic Jokes." More subtle is David Ketterer's simultaneously published note on the same passage, "Censorship and Symbolism in *Typee*" (*MSEx* 34:8). I would have ignored Michael Clark's "Melville *Typee*: Fact, Fiction, and Esthetics" (*ArQ* 34:351–70) had Clark not included this sentence which epitomizes the lingering academic contempt for scholarship: "Although any report of a South Seas adventure might have had an inherent interest to the receptive, curious audience of mid-nineteenth-century America, Melville manages to transcend the bland reportage that, we might imagine, characterized the average travel book of the period, the majority of which have long since been forgotten." A scholar from the generation of Charles Roberts Anderson would have *found out* what those average travel books were like; one or two of those books may survive in libraries even unto the 1980s, awaiting the Kennedys.

Joyce Sparer Adler in "Melville's *Typee* and *Omoo*: Of 'Civilized' War on 'Savage' Peace" (*MinnR* 10:95–102) gives an obvious survey of Melville's social criticism in his first two books. This slight article does not rank with Adler's earlier series of long, complexly argued, controversial articles. In "*Omoo*: Germinal Melville" (*SNNTS* 10:420–30) Steven E. Kemper makes the over-obvious point that the narrator has a "strong but rudimentary conservatism" as well as a "seemingly libertine and antiauthoritarian vigor." "Melville, Marriage, and *Mardi*" (*SNNTS* 9[1977]:247–60) by Charles Haberstroh Jr. (actually published in 1978), sounds as if it were written about Thoreau's "fear of sexual surrender," his "puritanical confusion over the whole idea of physical involvement with women," and his sense that "sexual activity demeans the one who allows himself to succumb to it." But Haberstroh is talking about Melville. The grain of truth drifting somewhere near here is that by 1849, anyhow, Melville had begun to feel that being a responsible family man was incompatible with being a great writer. "Melville's *Mardi*: One

Book or Three?" by J. Michael Sears (*SNNTS* 10:411–19) reasonably stresses neoplatonic elements, but the article is a testimony to the impulse to perceive unity in anything that is, by definition, a work of art. Sears fails to ask theoretical questions, such as what kinds of or degrees of unity can be provided by recurrent imagery.

In "*Mardi*: Creating the Creative" (*New Perspectives*, pp. 29–53), Richard H. Brodhead is also notably slippery with scholarship, most obviously in pages that assert similarities between the narrative mode of "*Mardi*'s opening phase" and that of Poe's *Narrative of Arthur Gordon Pym*, only to conclude that what "is important about this is not so much that it reveals particular debts on Melville's part as that it demonstrates what kind of a book Melville is writing in *Mardi*'s first fifty chapters." Then Brodhead seems to assert an actual debt when he says "Melville closes his Poe and opens his Rabelais." The evasiveness, Milder makes clear in his review of Brodhead's book (see section *i*), comes from a New Critical bias so strong that it overpowers a recurrent impulse to acknowledge, if not engage in, scholarship. Here Brodhead's real essay (pp. 41–52) deals with the emergence of "the Melville who compulsively engages in ontological heroics." These pages are fine—obvious, but well expressed, and employing details never mustered in previous arguments. (For Robert D. Richardson, Jr.'s discussion of *Mardi*, see section *iv*.)

iv. *Moby-Dick*

Classic essays on *Moby-Dick* are nearly as scarce as big white whales, but another has been published—Harrison Hayford's "Unnecessary Duplicates: A Key to the Writing of *Moby-Dick*" (*New Perspectives*, pp. 128–61). Buttressing his argument not only by a close reading of *Moby-Dick* (can a reading be closer?) but also by the knowledge of Melville's compositional methods gained in working with Sealts on the manuscript of *Billy Budd, Sailor*, Hayford offers the hypothesis that at a "crucial stage of the book's development" four central characters, Bulkington, Queequeg, Ahab, and Peleg, were involved "in a multiple reassignment of roles, which also redefined a fifth, the narrator." In this remarkable essay Hayford exposes himself as, after all, a more awesome deconstructionist than any of the French or their faddish East Coast imitators. What he argues cannot be proved, although the analysis of anomalies in Peleg's and Bildad's departure from the *Pequod*, to single out one passage, approaches irrefutability. For what it's worth, examples of the same compositional practices can be adduced from other writers as well as Melville himself in *Billy Budd, Sailor*; when I read this essay I had been working with the manuscript of *Pudd'nhead Wilson*, and kept seeing places where precisely what Hayford conjectures about Melville is demonstrable in Twain. As Wilson Heflin said in his review of *New Perspectives* (*MSEx* 37[1979]:9), "Hayford advances his theories, modestly, tentatively, and perhaps compulsively ('All of us must go on with our fumbling—with any combination of keys we can find . . .'). To summarize . . . here would be to do disservice to a brilliant essay, one which should be required reading for all true Melvilleans."

If it were not such a clumsily written Jungian primer I would call another study a classic, Edward F. Edinger's *Melville's "Moby-Dick": A Jungian Commentary—An American Nekyia* (New York: New Directions). Edinger is worse than useless on anything having to do with the aesthetic experience of reading *Moby-Dick*, and humor is always suspect ("Why did you laugh, Ishmael?"). Yet despite all weaknesses, he is almost alone among recent critics in understanding the psychology of Melville as a writer, as in the brilliant passage on pages 70–71 about Melville's pitting "the powers of his own creative imagination against the ultimate mystery of human existence," with personal trauma and tragedy but at the gain of "a new symbolic image to be added to the collective cultural consciousness." Edinger belongs with the great responders to Melville—a club which includes Frank Jewett Mather, J. W. N. Sullivan, Lewis Mumford, E. L. Grant Watson, Henry A. Murray, Jay Leyda, and Harrison Hayford. Dismiss any prejudices you have against Jungian jargon and buy this book so you can mark it up, for it's one of those rare studies which pays tribute to the majesty of Melville. It is also, almost incidentally, one of the best treatments of the Americanness of Ahab.

After those very different, very powerful pieces, everything else was anticlimactic. Robert D. Richardson, Jr., devotes a blandly written but sensible chapter to Melville in *Myth and Literature in the American Renaissance* (Indiana), pp. 195–233. His discussion of *Mardi* as "Melville's book of myths" I found unsatisfying because it leaves out about 85 percent of the memorable parts, but his discussion of *Moby-Dick* deals with a crucial topic. As he says in contrasting *Moby-Dick* to *Mardi*, "Instead of our being given an abstract and mythical allegory, we are shown, by means of the thoroughly real figures of Ahab and the white whale, not only how myths arise but how they come to be believed by ordinary people like us." In presenting both Ahab and Moby Dick, "Melville not only provides a reasonable explanation of how this change happens, but he compels us ourselves to believe in these grand creations of the mythic imagination." Richardson's grasp of the shifting attitudes toward myth in the 19th century nicely supplements Edinger's concerns, for Edinger warns that he is "not a scholar but a depth psychotherapist" and that his own book "is an effort not so much to understand Melville as to understand the psyche, especially the collective psyche, through the genius of Melville's imagination."

A. Robert Lee's "*Moby-Dick*: The Tale and the Telling" (*New Perspectives*, pp. 86–127), is a determined effort to understand how "Melville first proposes to tell, then actually tells, his tale." The essay is slow-starting and overlong but charming in its hyperbolic evocation of Melville's own gamesomeness. Larzer Ziff's "*Moby-Dick* and the Problem of a Democratic Literature" (*YES* 8:67–76) mentions none of the recent scholarship and criticism on the topic, and offers nothing new. Henry Nash Smith's chapter on "The Madness of Ahab" in *Democracy and the Novel* (Oxford) tries to "determine what Ahab's madness means: that is, in what ways Melville elaborates or qualifies the basic proposition that the controlling power in the universe is evil, by declaring Ahab, who holds a view something like this, to be insane." In the process Smith looks at legal definitions of the new term "monomania," including one by Judge Lemuel Shaw in 1844, and tries explicating some problematical passages in *Moby-Dick*. Smith's deep-seated dissatisfaction with aspects of *Moby-Dick* (his feeling that Ahab's madness is "overdetermined" and that we are never "given enough fictional substance concerning Ahab's prior experience to account for his state of mind when he first meets the White Whale") is more provocative than the usual assumption that perfect unity in the printed text only awaits demonstration by the latest explicator. Smith quotes from what seems to

be an important essay which I will try to find before next year—
Armin Staats's "Melville—*Moby-Dick*" in *Der amerikanische Roman
von den Anfängen bis zur Gegenwart*, edited by Hans-Joachim Lang
(Düsseldorf, 1972). Awhile back we passed the stage where we
could safely assume that anything in a foreign language would be
superficial and derivative; what Smith translates and quotes sounds
impressive. Rodolphe Gasché's "The Scene of Writing: A Deferred
Outset" (*Glyph* 1[1977]:150–71) is a coterie-piece of deconstructionist criticism, awkwardly written because it tries, unsuccessfully,
to be mannered rather than clear. Gasché focuses upon the words, if
not the meanings, of chapter 32, "Cetology," and the games a critic
can play with those words. The idea that "Cetology" is a new beginning required by the "coercion of narration" (a typically clumsy
phrase) is potentially a very fruitful one, as is the idea of "deferred
outset" (see Hayford's article for what can be done with *that* notion); and Melville's talk of his books' being botched should have
struck more fire from a deconstructionist connoisseur of disorder.

v. Pierre

In "Radical Disunities: Models of Mind and Madness in *Pierre* and
The Idiot" (*SNNTS* 10:234–50) Joan Magretta sensibly examines
these "models" as "part of the peculiar framework of attitudes and
ideas which shaped the perception and experience of unreason in
the nineteenth century." This essay should be read along with
Henry Nash Smith's chapter on *Moby-Dick*. Hershel Parker's chatty
"Conjectural Emendations: An Illustration from the Topography of
Pierre's Mind" (*LRN* 3:62–66) focuses on the mental processes, such
as they are, involved in detecting one kind of textual error.

Much more ambitious is the piece by Brian Higgins and Hershel
Parker, "The Flawed Grandeur of Melville's *Pierre*" (*New Perspectives*, pp. 162–96), an attempt first to lay out ways in which Melville
had control of his material, especially his analysis of Pierre's psychology and of human psychology in general, then to chart the ways
in which the last half violates the expectations so carefully built up.
An essential difference between the stance taken here and that of
most critics—including Leon Howard in the Northwestern-Newberry
"Historical Note"—is that Higgins and Parker see the first half of

the book as the great part, despite the high interest and intermittent power of the second half. Rather than dismissing the opening "books" as melodramatic and mawkish, Higgins and Parker argue that Melville achieves there "an extraordinary conversion of gothic sensationalism into profound psychological exploration." The essay may have one or two feet in the Hayfordesque camp of homegrown deconstructionist criticism, since it also recognizes both the order and the disorder that appears on the printed page. Anyhow, Heflin links it to Hayford's very different one as two "essays in which very close textual analysis and genetic considerations reveal new insights about the composition of *Moby-Dick* and *Pierre* respectively" (*MSEx* 37[1979]:9).

vi. "Bartleby"

Delta, the new journal published at Paul Valéry University, Montpellier, normally concerns itself with southern writers, but this year it devoted both issues to "Bartleby" and accompanied the first with a paperback supplement containing on facing pages the 1856 text, in English, and the Pierre Leyris French translation, thoroughly revised from its 1951 publication. The editor of both issues and the introducer of the translation was Philippe Jaworski. The *Delta* contributors almost never questioned the adequacy of the translation, perhaps because several of those who wrote in French quoted the English text (as, of course, did those who wrote in English). There are some awkwardnesses (did Leyris understand "He ran a day and night line"?) and a serious problem in the use of the idiomatic "Lettres au Rebut," which cannot convey the English connotations of "Dead Letter Office." The *Delta* issues will be of little interest to Melvilleans. Most of the essays in English are routine, even Joseph J. Moldenhauer's lengthy " 'Bartleby' and 'The Custom-House' " (7: 21–62), an attempt to show that "Bartleby" is informed by "Melville's responsiveness to Hawthorne and 'The Custom-House.' " Ordinarily Moldenhauer persuades me, but not this time. Thomas P. Joswick's "The 'Incurable Disorder' in 'Bartleby the Scrivener' " (6: 79–93) is excellent on the ironic humor of the story. Joswick pays repeated lip-service to deconstructionist bleakness (as in mention of "the empty masquerade of western metaphysics that would assure us of origin, purpose, and end for our history"), but he seems to be mouthing the catchphrases the way critics used to (or still do) talk about irony, texture, and ambiguity. This is just the kind of essay Henry Sussman has in mind when he talks about the academic establishment's assimilating deconstructionism (see section *viii*). Melville critics will not need to read the other articles in English, and they will need to read the articles in French only if they are curious to see what happens to "Bartleby" in the hands of French followers of such critics as Roland Barthes, Jacques Derrida, and Gérard Genette. I recommend Patrick F. Quinn's review, "The *Delta* 'Bartleby' Symposium" (*MSEx* 39[1979]:11–12); and see Professor Courturier's comments in chapter 21, below.

To finish up with the foreigners, I will mention Arno Heller's "Herman Melvilles 'Bartleby the Scrivener': Eine kritische Rezeptionsanalyse" (*Sprachkunst* 9:316–27). Heller briefly places much of the recent writing on the story in the perspective of changing trends in criticism. In "Monroe Edwards and Melville's Bartleby" (*ELN* 15:291–94) Douglas Robillard adds to the pool of information about the swindler whose trial in 1842 was a great sensation, helpfully citing books and pamphlets on Edwards in the Beinecke. (I was surprised that Edwards is not in the *Log*; what Melvillean first looked him up?) Morris Beja's "Bartleby and Schizophrenia" (*MR* 19:555–68) is temperate and sophisticated, alert to the perils of psychological criticism, but it quickly becomes reductive in the attempt to pigeonhole Bartleby as a victim of "'schizophrenia, catatonic type, withdrawn'" and to identify him as a victim of what R. D. Laing calls "'ontological insecurity.'" Robert E. Abrams's "'Bartleby' and the Fragile Pageantry of the Ego" (*ELH* 45:488–500), a too brief treatment of a major topic, unstrenuously moves from one numbered section to the next, citing Freud on the uncanny, Bergson on the comic, and a couple of times symptomatically allowing quotations from diverse sources to carry what argument a paragraph has. Most intriguing is the observation about the narrator's attempt to elicit some angry spark from Bartleby: "This same tarbaby routine between earnest gesticulator and autistic incommunicado, lost in an unruffled and undisturbed dream, can be comic on the vaudevillian stage."

The hands-down winner of the prize for the most cliché-ridden piece of the year is "The Gothic Formula of 'Bartleby,'" by Steven T. Ryan (*ArQ* 34:311–16), which begins with adjectival and adverbial pyrotechnics and builds to this triumph: "The narrator may see the American dream blossoming, but Bartleby sees the destructive power of dream transformed to nightmare." My sanguine friend Donald Pizer may hope that public complaints such as his (*SNNTS* 10:130) will have some effect on the editor of *Arizona Quarterly*, if not on the trustees of the University of Arizona–Tucson.

vii. Other Stories

There were three articles on "The Encantadas," the most substantial being Robert Sattelmeyer's and James Barbour's "The Sources and Genesis of Melville's 'Norfolk Isle and the Chola Widow'" (*AL* 50: 398–417), an overlong and somewhat disjointed essay (several pages are not about the Eighth Sketch at all, despite the title). Richard Ogden and Leon Howard had suggested that newspaper accounts of an Indian woman who was rescued from an island off Santa Barbara in 1853 might have influenced Melville; now Sattelmeyer and Barbour have located reports in two of the newspapers likely to have met Melville's eye, the Albany *Evening Tribune* and the Springfield *Daily Republican*. For all the interest of this possible analogue, or loose source, it strikes me as too tenuous to bear the weight the authors put on it as a link between the Agatha letters and the Eighth Sketch. They exaggerate, surely, in claiming that "'Norfolk Isle and the Chola Widow' is perhaps the only tale in the Melville canon which can be traced from its beginnings as a story 'instinct with significance' to its eventual enactment as completed tale." Other accounts of the Galapagos need to be explored, such as the interesting passage the authors have found in Benjamin Morrell's *Narrative*. All in all, an interesting but overblown article. Monique Pruvot's "L'espace imaginaire de Melville dans les *Encantadas* et les significations de trois symboles thériomorphes" (*RLV* 44:15–27) is a meditation on bird, fish, and tortoise.

Caroline Moseley in "'Old Virginny' in Melville's 'The Paradise of Bachelors'" (*MSEx* 33:13–15) points out that the allusion is not to the still familiar song ("No place on earth do I love more sincerely / Than old Virginny, the state where I was born"), which

was not published until 1878, but to Edwin P. Christy's 1847 song
of the same title, for which she prints the text and part of the music.
Good work.

viii. The Confidence-Man

There were two deconstructionist essays of widely different merits.
In "Figuring the Beginning: Melville's *The Confidence-Man*" (*Genre*
11:389–409), Thomas P. Joswick tries to reestablish what Melville
scholars have for years been laboriously removing: the indeterm-
inacy of meaning. Joswick begins interestingly but does not work
through enough of the text to justify his claims; he asserts the
novel's indeterminate meaning rather than demonstrating it. The
mechanicalness of the essay is signaled by the casually strewn deconstructionist catchphrases: "figurative play," "rhetorical subversion," "ground and shadow," "conceptual problematic," "deferred
presence," lack of "self-presence and center." By contrast, one of
the most comprehensive readings of the book in recent years is
Henry Sussman's "The Deconstructor as Politician: Melville's *Confidence-Man*" (*Glyph* 4:32–56); furthermore, in his bountiful self-
presence Sussman (a co-editor of *Glyph*) concludes with a wry,
self-challenging analysis of the way the academic community has
assimilated—has tamed—just such writers as himself. Joswick's essay—like his essay on "Bartleby" (section *vi*)—is a plainer example
of assimilated deconstructionism, I would say; Sussman is still out
there thinking at the edge of disorder. Ironically, Sussman justifies
the second half of the book in a way that would delight a New
Critic, and like run-of-the-mill academics, he ignores some important criticism and sometimes reads too hastily, as in taking the P. I. O.
Man for a slave-trader. The faults of deconstructionists should be
cosmic, not petty.

I find it hard to discuss Q. D. Leavis's "Melville: The 1853–6
Phase" (*New Perspectives*, pp. 197–228) because it so wildly mixes
grossly erroneous information into a sensible popularization of Elizabeth S. Foster, Jay Leyda, and others; but the erratic pages on
The Confidence-Man (210–28) do contain some on-target readings.
Another unoriginal article in the Pullin book, Larzer Ziff's "Shakespeare and Melville's America" (*New Perspectives*, pp. 54–67) comes
to life stylistically toward the end in the claim that "aboard the

Fidèle the Shakespearean canon is handled the way the Bible is: a commonly accepted account of the human condition that furnishes a treasury of illustrations with which to lubricate the cogs of conversation between strangers; a collection of ethical maxims that are agreed to by all in the abstract but that yield contradictory meanings when pursued in the particular."

ix. Battle-Pieces

Matthew O'Brien's " 'The Maddest Folly of the Campaign': A Diarist and a Poet Confront Kennesaw Mountain" (*Civil War Hist.* 23 [1977]:241–50) pleasantly but factitiously links an account "by a youthful eyewitness-participant" and a nine-line poem in *Battle-Pieces*. In "Parallels in Melville and Whitman" (*WWR* 24:95–108) Jerry A. Herndon uncompellingly suggests that Whitman's "Year of Meteors (1859–60)" influenced Melville's "The Portent." In the argument "if" builds upon "if," but the account of newsworthy meteors of 1859–60 is interesting.

x. Billy Budd, Sailor

Watson Branch's "Melville's 'Incompetent' World in *Billy Budd, Sailor*" (*MSEx* 34:1–2) advocates "incompetent" as the variously deciphered word in what Hayford and Sealts call the "coda." The suggestion seemed implausible to me, but Branch shows that for Melville this innocuous word had special connotations relevant to the context. It would have helped to reproduce the parallel use of "fully competent" which Branch tellingly cites from a draft title for *The Confidence-Man*; a reproduction of the "coda" does accompany the article.

In "Exigencies of Composition and Publication: *Billy Budd, Sailor* and *Pudd'nhead Wilson*" (*NCF* 33:131–43) Hershel Parker and Henry Binder summarize at length what Hayford and Sealts say about the ending before going on to generalize about some implications of Melville's having seen the story "as complete with different endings." (The article was written for a special issue on "Narrative Endings," reprinted by the Univ. of Calif. Press as a paperback under that title.) In "An Organic Hesitancy: Theme and Style in *Billy Budd*" (*New Perspectives*, pp. 275–300), C. N. Manlove after a slow start gets down to some interesting reading but he fails to look at the Genetic Text in order to see how some of the complicated passages reached the form he is explicating. Stanton Garner's "Fraud as Fact in Herman Melville's *Billy Budd*" (*SJS* 4: 82–105) is another of those grand revelations which Melville occasionally inspires. Garner believes that every error of historical fact in *Billy Budd* was deliberately, diabolically put there by sneaky, perverse, graybearded old Herman. The editorial bearing of the argument is explicit: no textual emendation should be made to this book "in the sole interest of factual accuracy." What Garner does not face is the question of whether all factual errors in all of Melville's earlier works were deliberate signals to the sleuthing reader that the narrative was not on the up-and-up.

University of Delaware

5. Whitman and Dickinson

Willis J. Buckingham

It is unlikely that 1978 will come to be recognized as a landmark year for scholarship on either writer. Nevertheless there is satisfaction to be taken in William White's careful edition of Whitman's *Daybooks and Notebooks* and in perceptive critical approaches to Whitman taken by David Cavitch and Joseph Cady. On Dickinson's side, the first-rate work of substance this year is also critical and is largely constituted in essays by Sharon Cameron, Evan Carton, and John S. Mann. The year may also mark a turn in our understanding of the poet's relationship with her sister-in-law. From her accustomed niche as the dark lady of Dickinson biography, Susan Dickinson takes at least a few steps into the light of common day.

i. Whitman

a. **Bibliography, Editing.** The latest addition to the New York University Press's CEAA edition of "The Collected Writings of Walt Whitman" are two volumes which reproduce the poet's jottings and ledger entries from 1876 to 1891 and a third which consists mainly of Whitman's record of an 1880 trip to Canada and his notebook reflections on language: *Daybooks and Notebooks*, edited by William White in three volumes (New York: New York Univ. Press). Aside from the Canadian diary and a portion of the notebooks published as Whitman's *An American Primer*, most of this material has been available only in manuscript. Since the daybooks merely served the poet as a place to record business expenses and various other minutiae and memoranda of his daily life, it is not surprising that they seem sketchy and lifeless. Nevertheless, these entries constitute

Preparation of this chapter was greatly facilitated by the research assistance of Norman J. Gehrlein, Jr.–W.J.B.

a kind of Whitman log during his years of decline, and taken together with the apt and extensive annotation White gives them, the
Daybooks will be steadily useful for verifying information about the
poet's outward life. Though only a little less fragmentary, the heretofore unpublished material in the third volume is of considerable
literary interest, for it offers the fullest evidence we have of Whitman's early and intense interest in language. The notebooks and
miscellaneous shorter pieces, many of them composed before 1855,
also provide new workbench perspectives on Whitman's artistry, for
they contain the apparent first drafts of lines and phrases he would
later incorporate into *Leaves of Grass*. The only other addition to the
primary record this year is William White's facsimile reproduction
of a recently discovered note of thanks Whitman wrote in 1888 ("A
New Post Card to Samuel Hollyer," *WWR* 24:133–34).

Whitman at Auction, 1899–1972 (Gale), compiled by Gloria A.
Francis and Artem Lozynsky, photographically reproduces pages
from 43 auction catalogues containing substantial Whitman material. The book might have been much longer, for the compilers
made their selection from nearly 500 catalogues available to them.
Nevertheless this sampling can reward the diligent searcher in a
number of ways. Some titles are accompanied by a salesroom full-
ness of description that far exceeds standardized citations in scholarly bibliographies. Moreover, these listings provide otherwise inaccessible information about particular copies of a given work, noting
for example, Whitman's flyleaf inscriptions, thereby adding to our
knowledge of what other writers owned Whitman and were known
by him. Catalogue descriptions also occasionally furnish the texts,
sometimes in facsimile, of letters and other manuscripts which have
since been lost. In addition to an index of names and titles, and a
brief history of Whitman auction sales in their foreword, the compilers include two essays by Charles E. Feinberg: one a reprinted
essay on early Whitman collections, the other a personal and win-
some description of his own experiences as a collector.

Of minor interest are some 15 items about Whitman drawn from
the crumbling files of *The Long Islander*, a community newspaper
which Whitman launched in 1838. They are reprinted by William
White in the "Walt Whitman Supplement" he edits annually for the
paper in "Whitman in *The Long Islander*, 1849–1919" (*Long Islander* [Huntington, N.Y.], 8 June, pp. 24–25). The most notable

clipping records an 1881 visit of Whitman, accompanied by Richard
Maurice Bucke, to his birthplace at West Hills. These fugitive pieces
show that the paper's attitude toward its founder underwent considerable change. An 1858 editorial denounced *Leaves of Grass* as
"repulsive and nasty" but 30 years later its author was "a grand old
man with a good big heart."

b. **Biography.** The image of the "good grey poet," so visible in
The Long Islander's revised estimate of its founder, was, as we know,
the joint creation of Whitman himself and his earliest biographer-
disciples, Burroughs, O'Connor, and Bucke. Leandro Wolfson shows
that this superficial and glorified conception of the poet continues
to dominate Latin American biographical and critical studies ("The
Other Whitman in Spanish America," *WWR* 24:62–71). In a brief
overview of the nature of biography, Justin Kaplin asks whether
the bard can ever be fully demythologized since Whitman played
such a large part in shaping his biography to tally with the self-
image his followers were promulgating. In "The 'Real Life' " (*Studies
in Biography*, pp. 1–8), Kaplin regards Whitman as the prime ex-
emplar of the artist who hides behind apparent self-disclosure.
"Whitman's overflowing records," he says, "so accessible and careless, were ultimately guarded and recalcitrant, like their owner."

Artem Lozynsky and John R. Reed furnish new evidence that
"guarded" is perhaps the best word for Tennyson's opinion of Whitman in their pamphlet publication, *A Whitman Disciple Visits Tennyson: An Interview Describing Dr. Richard Maurice Bucke's Visit
of 9 August 1891 at Aldworth* (Lincoln, Eng.: Tennyson Research
Centre [1977]). The man who aspired to be Whitman's Boswell,
Horace Traubel, questioned Bucke about the visit shortly after the
latter's return from England and it is the heretofore unpublished text
of this interview that Lozynsky and Reed have edited. Tennyson
and Bucke, as it turns out, spoke mostly about spiritual matters; the
former's comments on Whitman as a writer are polite but noncom-
mittal. A less cordial exchange that occurred in 1884 issues of *The
Critic* raises the possibility that Whitman once sent Longfellow
proof-sheets of *Leaves of Grass* and asked for permission to dedicate
his book to the Cambridge poet, a request Longfellow later rid-
iculed. In "Longfellow, Whitman, and 'A Fabulous "Episode" ' "
(*Odyssey* 2:22–23), William White cautions, however, that Whit-

man denied the story as soon as he learned of it, and that no evidence exists to corroborate *The Critic's* hearsay account.

***c.* Criticism: General.** Most of the articles here considered take a thematic rather than stylistic approach to their subjects, all enduring ones in Whitman studies: the poet's relation to self, place, history, and God. The first of these issues elicited the most penetrating contributions, even, and especially, John Updike's nonspecialist assessment, "Walt Whitman: Ego and Art (*NYRB* 25[9 Feb.]:33–36). This essay has the freshness and force of Randall Jarrell's well-known tribute, "Some Lines from Whitman," first published 25 years ago. Like Jarrell's, Updike's admission of certain embarrassments serves only to italicize his larger affection and respect. If Whitman manifests a faintly absurd solipsism (Updike's phrase is "Panoramic egotheism"), his work is redeemed by "almost mischievous" realism, "ardor" for others, good humor, and artistic courage. A more conventionally documented account of Whitman's self-awareness is Donald Stauffer's "Walt Whitman and Old Age" (*WWR* 24:142–48). Stauffer argues that although Whitman idealized age in a rather facile way in his early poetry, numerous short verses about the subject written during his last years ring true to the poet's life experience and deserve greater recognition as having intrinsic poetic merit. It is a pleasure to rediscover in Stauffer's brief essay these late-in-life poems. It is satisfying too to report on David Cavitch's study of the poet's inner life, "Whitman's Mystery" (*SIR* 17:105–28). "More than we have yet recognized," Cavitch believes, "Whitman's poetry is about *knowing*—that is, conceptualizing—a new insight to human nature through closer, freer attention to subjective experience." He finds that the key passages in "Song of Myself" are those in which the speaker struggles to fuse both poles of his personality—his essential self or soul and his immediate consciousness. The discovery of self-love evoked in these passages leads the poet, in opposition to the rationalistic scruples of his own time, to anticipate 20th-century interest in unconscious and irrational levels of experience. In repeatedly giving himself over to unharnessed and perplexing intuition, the poet makes transfiguring discoveries of inner power and coherence. In this reading Whitman's "egoism" is not the quaint reflection of 19th-century expansionism that Updike intimates; it is the embrace of a profound self-apprehension.

Though the book as a whole is treated in another chapter of this volume, Bernard Duffey's *Poetry in America* (see pp. 64–75) deserves notice here as the year's major attempt to situate Whitman among other American poets of his period and to define Whitman's response to the dissolution of a harmonious public belief system that occurred in America during the latter half of the 19th century. Whitman's poetry therefore imagines, Duffey says, a world of natural processes in which the individual can only "assert reality" rather than "reflect transcendence." Change itself became the primary fact of American life and of Whitman's verse. A similar approach to Whitman, though much less elaborately worked out, is adopted by James E. Mulqueen in "Toward a Morphology of American Poetry" (*ArQ* 33[1977]:293–310). Taking his cue from Oswald Spengler, who argued that the Renaissance was a time when the European culture-soul awakened into full "Faustian" self-consciousness and power, Mulqueen says that the comparable period in America was the 19th century and that Whitman was its celebrant. Thus, in concord with the soul of his country, Whitman's poetry "is eternally restless, constantly striving upward, and possessed of a sense of spiritual infinity."

There is, of course, considerable evidence that Whitman would have agreed with Spengler's notion that by the 19th century European culture was in decline. As Michael Dressman shows in " 'Names are Magic': Walt Whitman's Laws of Geographic Nomenclature" (*Names* 26:68–79), the poet believed that "all aboriginal names sound good" and that cities named after saints, royalty, or from the classics should be changed. Whitman thought, moreover, that there should be a direct relationship of name to place, as in far-Western newspapers like the *Tombstone Epitaph* and in nicknames given to inhabitants of certain Western states (Hoosiers, Buckeyes, Wolverines). That the American West, and particularly its prairies, was a geographic metaphor of special value for Whitman is noted by P. S. Lehmberg in " 'That Vast Something': A Note on Whitman and the American West" (*StHum* 6:50–53). Whitman imaginatively associated the plains with democracy and the divine average and he believed that it would be in the Western states that American individualism and brotherhood would find their fullest development. Nevertheless, it is just when we begin to suppose that Whitman was doctrinally oblivious to America's immediate historical

antecedents, to saints, to royalty, and to Europe, that we need most
to be reminded of his lifelong interest in the past. In " 'To Span Vast
Realms of Space and Time': Whitman's Vision of History" (*WWR*
24:45–62) Jeffrey Steinbrink provides a balanced and informed view
of ambivalences in the poet's thought. He concludes that Whitman's
"confidence in the continuity of history forbade his asserting the
absolute autonomy of the present, while his sense of America's historical uniqueness and the premium he placed on originality encouraged him to resist the imposition of tradition."

Whitman's simultaneous use of and resistance to tradition is
evident as well in his theology, as David Kuebrich shows in two
companion articles, "Whitman's New Theism" (*ESQ* 24:229–41)
and "Whitman's Politics: Poetry and Democracy" (*BuR* 23[1977]:
116–30). Both are on the poet's spirituality as it applies to science
and politics in 19th-century America. The first essay also makes connections between Whitman's religious convictions and his literary
method of "indirection," while the second explicates the religious
character of Whitman's ideal body politic. Though in defining mystic elements in Whitman's thought Kuebrich repeats much that has
already been said, he does show—and with salutary incisiveness and
precision—how ideas current in his own time, such as evolution,
shaped Whitman's revaluation of God. In "Whitman's 'Mystic De-
liria' " (*WWR* 24:77–84) Beth Lynne Lueck remarks on a cluster
of six words that Whitman uses to characterize heightened experience. The most satisfying assessment of Whitman as a religious poet
this year is the chapter Robert D. Richardson, Jr., devotes to him in
Myth and Literature in the American Renaissance (Indiana, pp.
138–64). Richardson shows that though Whitman valued old religions, and the impulses behind them, he sought to displace myth
with "symbols, images of man himself, a new religion of humanity,
and prophecy." Particularly useful is Richardson's discussion of
Whitman's interest in Egyptian lore and in the religion of patriotism
espoused by the French historian Jules Michelet.

Treated last year by Myrth Jimmie Killingsworth (*ALS 1977*,
p. 73), Whitman's interest in electricity is taken up again by Harold
Aspiz in " 'The Body Electric': Science, Sex, and Metaphor" (*WWR*
24:137–42). His is the first substantial account of this subject since
Edmund Reiss's "Whitman's Debt to Animal Magnetism" (*PMLA*
78[1963]:80–88. Aspiz's essay, however, is virtually disarmed as a

source for further study because it has received publication in its unrevised lecture form—tantalizing allusions to "a manuscript jotting" and "a book the poet read," for example, are left unidentified. Richard Freed indirectly provides evidence for the importance of magnetism in "An Approach for Teaching Whitman to College Freshmen" (*EngR* 29:9–12). He finds that surging and pulsing movements are an "animating principle" in all the poet's work.

d. **Criticism: Individual Works.** Complementing Richardson's inquiry into Whitman's use of Egyptian religion (noted above) is Stephen J. Tapscott's "Leaves of Myself: Whitman's Egypt in 'Song of Myself'" (*AL* 50:49–73). He argues that the role of the speaker in that poem in "translating" the signs of the natural world parallels Whitman's interest in the discovery and deciphering of the Rosetta stone, about 1831. He also points out that in those places where the poem seems indebted to Hebrew verse, the influence of Egyptian literature is also clear (e.g., equality before the throne of God and resurrection of the body). Another critic sensitive to Biblical echoes in the poem is John Berryman, whose "'Song of Myself': Intention and Substance" was written in 1957 but first published only in a posthumous collection of his prose, *The Freedom of the Poet* (Farrar [1976], pp. 227–41). Although Berryman begins by confessing "I like or love Whitman unreservedly" and though his study is punctuated by expressions of enthusiasm ("exquisite," "ravishing," "great"), he proceeds in rather orderly fashion to address two central questions in the poem: who is the speaker? what is his message? He stresses that Whitman thought of the poem as a "work of *life*" as opposed to literature and that he intended the poet's presence to be felt as a "voice for others" exploring the content of religious experience. He observes the poem to have the somewhat inchoate form of an exultation even though it can be said to fall into four musically derived movements. David Charles Leonard connects the concept of evolution in "Song of Myself" with the four laws of Larmarck's theory of progress in "Lamarckian Evolution in Whitman's 'Song of Myself'" (*WWR* 24:21–28).

Among studies of portions of "Song of Myself" this year is William J. Sabo's "The Ship and Its Related Imagery in 'Inscriptions' and 'Song of Myself'" (*WWR* 24:118–23). Sabo notices that the ship image helps to unite the two poems and strengthens several motifs in "Song of Myself," especially that of the perpetual journey. The most startling contribution to studies of the poem this year is Dennis K. Renner's remarkable interpretation of the "twenty-eight young men" passage (section 11) as a figurative treatment of the admission of Texas as the 29th state into the Union ("The Conscious Whitman: Allegorical Manifest Destiny in 'Song of Myself'" *WWR* 24:149–55). Assembling evidence from Whitman's reading and writing about this event, Renner proposes that the men are the 28 brother states, alluring to the 28-year-old "richly dressed" woman as they would be to a territory that in the poet's eyes had been controlled for that number of years by a "degenerate Mexican aristocracy." Section 25 of the poem receives close scrutiny by Lawrence I. Berkove in "Biblical Influence on Whitman's Concept of Creatorhood" (*Calamus* 16:18–26), an essay that was originally published in *ESQ* for 1967 (47:34–37) but not previously noted in these pages. One can find a Biblical passage of arguable interest for almost every other line of Whitman, but there is need for caution in imposing Biblical contexts on the poet's meaning simply because the same word or phrase is used in Scripture, a danger not entirely avoided here.

Noteworthy among discussions of shorter works is Joseph Cady's "Not Happy in the Capitol: Homosexuality and the *Calamus* Poems" (*AmerS* 19:5–22). Cady argues that since the poet's difficult task in this group of poems was to invent a way of speaking affirmatively about homosexual love to a presumably homophobic popular audience, the poems reveal an ambivalence between proclaiming new sexual standards and conforming to old ones. In exploring the poet's "divided consciousness" in these poems, he offers provocative and searching interpretations of "Scented Herbage," "Whoever You Are," and "When I Heard at the Close of Day." In a more traditional exegesis of "Scented Herbage," Roberts W. French understands Whitman to turn away from his art in the gradual realization that only love and death endure whereas poetry is but a transitory "emblem" of life ("Whitman in Crisis: A Reading of 'Scented Herbage of My Breast,'" *WWR* 24:29–32). That Whitman elsewhere celebrated the timeless flow of natural processes is French's argument in "Symbolic Values in 'The Dalliance of the Eagles'" (*WWR* 24:124–28).

Edwin H. Miller's Jungian analysis of "Out of the Cradle" in

Walt Whitman's Poetry (*ALS 1968*, pp. 52–53) is extended by Susan G. Feinberg, who cites archetypal components used in the poem to express the psychic "regression and progression of the child-hero" ("Whitman's 'Out of the Cradle Endlessly Rocking,'" *Expl* 37,i:35–36). Jungian categories are also employed by Steve Carter to suggest that one of the *Drum Taps* poems provides a model for the way the soul accommodates experience in Whitman's poetry as a whole ("The Metaphor of Assimilation and 'Rise O Days From Your Fathomless Deeps,'" *WWR* 24:155–61). Useful as such psychoanalytic study may be for much of Whitman's work, it will always fail to elucidate "Passage to India," according to Roger Asselineau ("'Passage to India,'" *Calamus* 16:11–14). The serene spirituality of that poem, he says, is missed by psychological critics. Two other studies view "Passage to India" as the culminating statement of the poet's considerable interest in India: Egbert S. Oliver, "Whitman's Use of India as Fact and Symbol" (in *Challenges of Societies in Transition*, edited by Manotama Barnabas et al., Delhi: Macmillan Co. of India, pp. 359–65) and C. N. Sastry, "Glimpses of India in *Leaves of Grass*" (*Calamus* 16:2–10). Spiritual connotations for a single phrase in another well-known work are exhaustively explored by Susan Strom in "'Face to Face': Whitman's Biblical Reference in "Crossing Brooklyn Ferry'" (*WWR* 25:7–16). Strom believes that all six appearances of the words "face to face" in the Bible serve to explain the poem's meaning. Finally, Louise M. Rosenblatt studies the relevance of Whitman's democratic ideals to separatist ethnic tendencies currently developing in American Life ("Whitman's *Democratic Vistas* and the New 'Ethnicity,'" *YR* 67:187–204). Whitman's vision of a pluralistic yet fraternal nation, Rosenblatt says, is essential to our survival.

e. Affinities and Influences. Aside from studies of Egyptian lore and Lamarckian evolutionary thought in "Song of Myself" noted above, most influence studies this year focus on how Whitman affected others. Though Whitman never met the other great New York writer of his day, it is tempting to imagine that he and Melville were at least aware of each other's work. Making the most of meager evidence, Jerry A. Herndon in "Parallels in Melville and Whitman" (*WWR* 24:95–108) argues that some of Whitman's lines may derive from his reading of *Moby-Dick* and that Melville's "The Portent" may have made poetic use of Whitman's "Year of Meteors (1859–60)." Lewis Leary's conviction that echoes of "Out of the Cradle" can be heard in Kate Chopin's novel, *The Awakening* (*ALS 1970*, pp. 67–68) is confirmed with new evidence by Gregory L. Candela in "Walt Whitman and Kate Chopin: A Further Connection" (*WWR* 24:163–65). The response of another American woman writer is recorded by Myra Stark, who finds that a number of themes and techniques in "Song of Myself" are similar to those in Anne Sexton's "In Celebration of My Uterus" ("Walt Whitman and Anne Sexton: A Note on the Uses of Tradition," *NConL* 8:7–8). If Whitman's presence in America has been gauged too exclusively in his effect on writers and thinkers, that preoccupation has been somewhat counterbalanced by essays in *The Artistic Legacy of Walt Whitman* (*ALS 1970*, pp. 69–70) and by Peter J. Abernethy's study of Whitman and Frank Lloyd Wright (*ALS 1977*, p. 75). In another excellent article, Kent Blaser traces continuities principally between Whitman and Thomas Eakins, George Bellows, Robert Henri, John Sloan, and Alfred Steiglitz ("Walt Whitman and American Art," *WWR* 24:108–18).

Of Whitman's legacy abroad, Rosemarie Arbur adds to our knowledge of Whitman's influence on D. H. Lawrence (" 'Lilacs' and 'Sorrow': Whitman's Effect on the Early Poems of D. H. Lawrence," *WWR* 24:17–21). Lawrence, Arbur says, "really depended on Whitman when he struggled to articulate poetically his feelings about his mother's death." Though Gerard Manley Hopkins, like Lawrence, was deeply ambivalent about Whitman, Jerry A. Herndon sees marked resemblances between the latter's "On the Beach at Night" and Hopkins's "Spring and Fall: To a Young Child" ("Hopkins and Whitman," *WWR* 24:161–62). A portion of Betsy Erkkila's dissertation on Whitman's reception in France (*ALS 1977*, p. 75) is published this year as "Walt Whitman and Jules Laforgue" (*WWR* 24:71–77). Though Laforgue did not imitate Whitman, the American writer "freed Laforgue to be himself," an effect particularly noticeable in poems composed during the few years before Laforgue's premature death.

Finally, two essays notice parallels with Whitman but make no claims for influence. Wendy Greenberg analyzes the style of a paragraph from Victor Hugo's preface to an 1840 volume of his poems (*Les Rayons et les ombres*) and compares it to a paragraph from

Whitman's 1855 preface to *Leaves of Grass* to show that both writers had similar ideas about the visionary nature of poetry ("Hugo and Whitman: Poets of Totality," *WWR* 24:32–36). L. Edwin Folsom remarks that both W. S. Merwin and Whitman are obsessed with the meaning of America but he goes on to show that where Whitman is enthusiastic, Merwin is doubtful ("Approaches and Removals: W. S. Merwin's Encounter with Whitman's America," *Shenandoah* 29:57–73). Merwin's *The Lice*, for example, is "an anti-song of the self" about a "ruined American Adam."

ii. Dickinson

a. **Bibliography, Editing.** Following the meticulous and informed procedures of his earlier editorial work on Dickinson's manuscripts (ALS 1967, p. 53), R. W. Franklin discusses three recently discovered holographs which, in varying degrees, modify texts of five poems published in the Johnson variorum ("Three Additional Dickinson Manuscripts," *AL* 50:109–16). In the case of "One Sister have I in the house," a poem Dickinson wrote in tribute to her sister-in-law, Susan Gilbert, shortly after Sue's marriage to Austin Dickinson, Franklin shows that after the poet's death family feeling against Sue was so strong as to cause Austin or Lavinia, or both, and with the probable assistance of Mrs. Todd herself, to mutilate the poet's autograph copy of the poem. Franklin also disentangles the textual history of an important Dickinson poem in "The Manuscripts and Transcripts of 'Further in Summer than the Birds' " (*PBSA* 72:552–60). He presents the various versions of the poem chronologically, adding to them an 1883 holograph, the poet's latest fair copy, which has never been published. This final version, however, does not differ substantially from the 1866 text given major representation in the variorum.

The growth of Dickinson's reception in India is partially documented by Willis J. Buckingham, who describes critical volumes on the poet appearing there in "Three Studies of Emily Dickinson Published in India" (*PBSA* 72:97–100). (A more recent Indian volume on Dickinson is noted in section *c*, below.) Buckingham also provides a second gathering of items overlooked in his 1970 volume ("Second Addendum to the Buckingham Bibliography," *EDB* 33: 61–75). The following issue of the same journal (its name having

been changed to *Dickinson Studies*) contains Buckingham's checklist of recent scholarship and ana, "Emily Dickinson: Annual Bibliography for 1976" (34:42–55).

b. **Biography.** No one in Dickinson's immediate family was more
important to her growth and maturity as a poet than her sister-in-
law, Susan Gilbert Dickinson. Though most of the evidence bearing
on their relationship suggests that it was a mutually sustained and
lifelong friendship, there are scattered documents that point to interruptions in their mutual regard. Recent biographers have tended
to weight these contrary indications heavily in the balance—too
heavily, one thinks after reading Jean McClure Mudge's "Emily
Dickinson and 'Sister Sue'" (*PrS* 52:90–108). Having sifted through
the poems, notes, and unpublished family correspondence as thoroughly as anyone, Mudge speaks persuasively for the constancy of
their affection. Moments of strain, she says, normal in any long relationship, should not obscure the overwhelming evidence that Sue
"claimed and returned" Dickinson's extraordinary love and remained
the poet's critic of choice before and long after Dickinson had given
up on Bowles and Higginson. Susan Dickinson addresses us directly, and with marked geniality, on manners and customs in mid-
19th-century Amherst in the first publication of her essay, written
about 1900, "Two Generations of Amherst Society" (in *Essays on
Amherst's History* [Amherst, Mass.: The Vista Trust], pp. 168–88).
Though she includes only a passing reference to Emily Dickinson,
Susan's own poise and command of language is impressive here and
her amused reflections on the social and religious gravity of her
elders in the community match well with the delightfully astringent
notes of social subversion heard frequently in her friend's poems and
letters. In this essay it is possible to experience firsthand some of the
qualities Emily Dickinson found so appealing in her "other" sister.
    Having surveyed last year some of Dickinson's letters as evidence
of her emotional attachment to women (*ALS 1977*, p. 77), Lillian
Faderman turns to examine those love poems which seem or clearly
are addressed to women ("Emily Dickinson's Homoerotic Poetry,"
HJ 18:19–27). "Read as a whole," Faderman concludes, "these poems
present a picture of a woman whose love for another woman is characterized often by a quality akin to worship . . ." and "it was unhappy
love because the beloved was cruel or because the dictates of custom

and necessity guaranteed its impermanence." These are the same themes, of course, that one finds in the love poems (and "Master" letters) presumably addressed to men. The first to give serious attention to Dickinson's interest in women was Rebecca Patterson, who in 1951 advanced Kate Scott Anthon as the poet's beloved. In "E[mily] D[ickinson]'s Elusive Lover" (*HJ* 18:28–34) Frederick L. Morey sketches the reception of Patterson's biography from the outrage and silence that attended its publication to the guarded but somewhat more positive recent assessments that reflect changing ideas about sexuality. In regard to another of Dickinson's presumed lovers, the Rev. Charles Wadsworth, so much is made of the poet's supposed distress on his removal to San Francisco that it is good to be reminded that he returned to Philadelphia only seven years later and remained for her an important friend. Vivian R. Pollack tells us that the famous preacher suffered diminution in his powers of speech in his latter years and lost, as a consequence, much of his congregation ("After Calvary: The Last Years of E[mily] D[ickinson]'s 'Dearest Earthly Friend,'" *DnS* 34:13–18). That Dickinson must have known of his affliction throws light on her image of Wadsworth as a fellow-sufferer and on the tact of her letters about him after his death.

c. Criticism: General. Phenomenalist study of Dickinson this year is measurably advanced in two essays by Sharon Cameron and a third by Evan Carton. All three examine structures of consciousness enacted in the poems; they attempt to define various and delicate psychic equilibriums erected in the face of intense, unfathomable interior experience as it is occasioned particularly by pain and loss. In "Naming as History: Dickinson's Poems of Definition" (*CritI* 5: 223–51) Cameron finds that Dickinson's speakers are repeatedly confounded by contradictory forces that resist identification because the persona cannot achieve even momentary distance from them. Despair and death resist explicit naming, she says, because "They flood conception, overwhelm it, so that it gives way to tenuous, incomplete, and multiple representation." Thus the poems honor the opacity of inner experience by deliberately fumbling at coherence. In offering only "disengaged" meanings, they articulate stunned experience. In contrast to these passive maneuvers against temporality, Cameron locates speakers in other poems who adopt an eruptive,

angry voice as a stronghold against those forces that bind her to
time and require sacrifice and choice ("'A Loaded Gun': Dickinson
and the Dialectic of Rage," *PMLA* 93:423–37). (These two essays
will appear as chapters in the author's forthcoming book-length
study of Dickinson.) Concerned also with ambivalence in crucial
Dickinsonian situations is Evan Carton's "Dickinson and the Divine:
The Terror of Integration, the Terror of Detachment" (*ESQ* 24:242–
52). In those poems which reflect a quest for union with the divine,
Carton observes that the speaker characteristically hovers between
fear of failure and fear of success. On the one hand, to give up the
possibility of the sublime is to fall back into finitude and death,
but so overwhelming is the presence of the divine that union with
it equally means certain annihilation. Nevertheless, knowing well
that her hope of ecstatic union is illusory, Dickinson does not re-
nounce her search "for she understands also that the willingness to
be deceived is a requisite for true faith." These thoughtful and just
reflections are sometimes called into question, however, by needless-
ly inflationary claims, as in Carton's portrayal of the poet's dichot-
omous vision as idiosyncratic and the poetry based on it somewhat
peculiar, even "a sado-masochistic exercise in temptation and denial." Description of the divine presence as at once annihilating
(*mysterium tremendum*) and elevating (*mysterium fascinosum*) is
a theological commonplace.

Relevant to Sharon Cameron's study of Dickinson's poems of
definition is John S. Mann's "Emily Dickinson, Emerson, and the
Poet as Namer" (*NEQ* 51:467–88). Their different approaches, in
this case, yield converging results. Though his essay begins as a
source study, locating in Emerson's essay, "The Poet," some of Dickinson's beliefs about the vitality of language, particularly its Adamic
power to possess the external world, Mann goes on to suggest that
Dickinson was innovative in adopting definition as a poetic strategy
for clarifying a turbulent and tangled inner life. Yet her efforts at
identification do not result in simplifying or "explaining" that complexity; instead, she reflects the always problematic experience of
selfhood by resisting any singleness of interpretation that Emersonian naming might convey. Her poems imply "a vision of the essential doubleness of things." That ambivalence is described as a
"resolute dualism" in Steve Carter's more broadly based, if less original, effort to delineate Dickinson's mental universe by reference to

some of the leading philosophical sources for her thought ("Emily Dickinson and Mysticism," *ESQ* 24:83–95). Her vision is neither wholly orthodox nor wholly secular, he maintains, because she constitutes some elements of her spirituality from the Christian drama of salvation (e.g., the "way of suffering and self-denial") and others from Transcendentalism (e.g., the almost gravitational growth of the soul). Her individual fusion of mystical ideas from these sources, he concludes, "points toward the subjective and arbitrary systems of the Symbolists of a later generation."

Perhaps too broadly concerned with these subjects to yield fresh insight is E. M. Tilma-Dekkers's "Immortality in the Poetry of Emily Dickinson" (*DQR* 8:162–82). The author claims that since Dickinson experienced the limits of human spiritual aspiration, "she devised an 'emotional strategy' by arguing that it might, after all, not be desirable to have complete knowledge." She cared little about an afterlife, preferring to cultivate moments of heightened awareness in this life whereby the soul becomes conscious of its immortal essence. Reaching similar conclusions, James M. Hughes notes that because they know full well the brevity of their tenure in time, Dickinson's speakers rebelliously postpone ultimate salvation knowledge available only at death in order to relish this world and make experiments relative to their future in the next ("Dickinson as 'Time's Sublimest Target,'" *DnS* 34:27–37). Dickinson's poetic paradigm for this pulling back from complete spiritual knowledge, according to Anthony Hecht, is her frequent use of the riddle form ("The Riddles of Emily Dickinson," *NER* 1:1–24). She chose that device out of a "profound sense that neither life itself nor the holy text by which we interpret it is altogether intelligible, and both require a riddling mind or interpretive skill." On another subject, Hecht quite correctly observes that there is more variety in Dickinson's poetic styles and forms than is usually recognized. His discussion of her range, from a poet's knowledge, is, though brief, uncommonly illuminating and persuasive.

That Dickinson entertained religious ideas about immortality much less profound than those just sketched was the conviction last year of Barton L. St. Armand (*ALS 1977*, p. 83) and his argument is taken up again by George Monteiro in " 'Love & Fame' or 'What's A Heaven For?': Emily Dickinson's Teleology" (*NEQ* 51:105–13). Monteiro believes that in some of her poems on marriage and fame

Dickinson fashions a "personal, corporeal Paradise" where she was certain to receive "deferred rewards as lover and poet." Especially helpful is his identification of "Checks" in "1 never saw a Moor" as commercial drafts on immortality cashed in at death. The portrait of Dickinson as artist consciously working for her literary, if not heavenly, reputation among subsequent generations emerges in Ruth Miller's "Poetry as a Transitional Object" (in *Between Reality and Fantasy*, ed. Simon A. Grolnick and Leonard Barkin [New York: Jason Aronson], pp. 449–68). Offended that no one would take her seriously as a poet, she thought to "link herself to posterity" by binding up her verses in fasicles. The evidence? Poems such as "Tie the Strings to my Life, My Lord."

Poems fit the argument more readily in another study of Dickinson's perception of herself as an artist, Joanne Feit Diehl's " 'Come Slowly—Eden': An Exploration of Women Poets and Their Muse" (*Signs* 3:572–87). Diehl attempts to answer the question, taking Dickinson as her principal case, How do women poets perceive their relation to a male-dominated tradition? She finds in Dickinson persistent ambivalence toward a combined male figure (precursor, lover, God), fearful that if she casts him off she will relinquish her muse as well. Fear of the other's powers and uncertainty of her own informs those poems in which the speaker withdraws equally from self-abandonment and self-possession. In separate critiques of this essay, Lillian Faderman and Louise Bernikow claim that a residuum of patriarchal bias blinds Diehl to Dickinson's manifest interest in women, both as symbolic figures of power and as writer-precursors ("Comment on Joanne Feit Diehl's " 'Come Slowly—Eden': An Exploration of Women Poets and Their Muse,'" *Signs* 4:188–95). Diehl's vigorous rejoinder takes back nothing ("Reply to Faderman and Bernikow," *Signs* 4:195–96). Dickinson's perception of herself as a 19th-century woman, economically and physically dependent on others, is the subject of Barbara J. Williams's "A Room of Her Own: Emily Dickinson as Woman Artist" (in *Feminist Criticism*, pp. 69–91). The essay begins well by noting imagery of diminution and disenfranchisement in the poems but ends with conclusions that seem a little amorphous and preachy.

In his overview of American poetry (Whitman, section *c*, above), Bernard Duffey considered Whitman as exhibiting a spirit of incoherence. That spirit turning inward and becoming self-communing, he says, is the case with Dickinson (pp. 129–37). Her poems are "fictions of incoherence" because in them the self reaches for momentary rather than universal truths and in the process is frequently immured in a "labyrinth of its own making." Though it has been little studied, one of the moments of awareness Dickinson deftly articulates is that of dream and its relinquishment into waking consciousness. John S. Mann furnishes modest but exemplary comment on a cluster of these poems in "Dream in Emily Dickinson's Poetry" (*DnS* 34:19–26). He concludes that "Dreams help to record the processes of mind working in response to a turbulent, an erupting inner life." Published in India is a full-length critical volume on Dickinson by Abha Agrawal, *Emily Dickinson: Search for Self* (New Delhi: Young Asia Publications, 1977). It discusses motifs and stratagems of self-exploration in the poetry though not in such a way as to afford new understanding. Nevertheless, it deserves notice as the most reliable study of Dickinson in India to date and its appearance is further evidence of the poet's growing reputation in that country.

d. **Criticism: Individual Works.** The most arresting single suggestion of the year is John Cody's visceral reading of "Tankards scooped in Pearl" in "Dickinson's 'I taste a liquor never brewed'" (*Expl* 36, iii: 7–8). Those drinking vessels, Cody says, are not fashioned *of* pearl, they are scooping into it, as one would dip into ice cream. They must therefore be the speaker's lungs, filling and refilling themselves in the dewy and pearllike intoxicating atmosphere of summer. Less exceptional is Cody's line-by-line paraphrase in "Dickinson's 'I can wade Grief'" (*Expl* 37,i:15–16). Cody regards the poem's message, that adversity strengthens whereas prosperity weakens, as a well-known psychological truth. Attempting again (cf. *ALS 1975*, p. 101) to decipher the "fading ratio" in "Dickinson's 'As by the dead we love to sit'" (*Expl* 36,iii:32–33), Laurence Perrine understands it as a temporarily inflated estimate of the recently lost friend over against the "collective emotional value" of the speaker's remaining friends. In "Dickinson's 'A House upon the Hight'" (*Expl* 36,iii:14–15) Perrine argues that the empty mansion of the poem is a metaphor for heaven, expressive of the poet's doubts about immortality. Radhe Shyam Sharma, though, wonders whether another poem, often taken to reveal the same disillusionment, does in fact make any

prediction about the unrelieved finality of death ("Emily Dickinson's 'I heard a Fly buzz—when I died'—A Reconsideration," *IJAS*
8:50–54). Sharma feels that the fly stands not for putrefaction but
for intimations, however stumbling, of another world outside the
confining windows of mortality. According to Clarence Gohdes, the
fly might well be staggering from having been harnessed to over-
weighty critical speculation ("Emily Dickinson's Blue Fly," *NEQ*
51:423–31). "Is there really a hidden meaning," Gohdes asks, "in
this simple imaginary death scene beyond the implicit oblique irony
that Nature can be 'caught without her diadem' even at the solemn
moment of death?"

The first full-scale explication, adopting R. W. Franklin's reediting of the poem, is David Robinson's "Text and Meaning in
E[mily] D[ickinson]'s 'A Pit—but Heaven over it' (J1712)" (*EDB*
33:45–52). Robinson contends that the "Pit" is a condition of insanity the speaker feels herself on the brink of. If Franklin's added
stanzas properly conclude the poem, they reflect, Robinson thinks,
the speaker's decision to protect those around her by maintaining,
at least outwardly, her mental poise. Kenneth L. Privratsky similarly
finds a desperate equilibrium but little cheerfulness in Dickinson's
best-known poem ("Irony in Emily Dickinson's 'Because I could
not stop for Death,'" *CP* 11:25–30). The speaker is less than happy
to have been tricked into thinking that her last ride to death was
just another country excursion. Despite the mountain of existing
comment on this poem, Privratsky manages to make two or three
unfamiliar suggestions. For example, "The Dews drew quivering
and chill" he reads as describing the speaker's dying and chilled
body attracting drops of condensation to itself. Among briefer contributions, Cynthia Griffin Wolff comments insightfully on the relation of structure to theme in "Dickinson's 'Much Madness is divin-
est Sense'" (*Expl* 36,iv:3–4) and George Monteiro mentions erotic
implications in "Dickinson's 'For every Bird a Nest'" (*Expl* 37,i:
28–29).

Several studies consider sources for individual poems. Chester
P. Sadowy identifies the bewildered Persian worshipper as a Manichaean in "Dickinson's 'He touched me, so I live to know'" (*Expl*
37,i:4–5). Dickinson could have read about the pluralistic beliefs
of that faith in one of her textbooks at Mt. Holyoke. Walter H. Eitner
explores the applicability of the myth of Daphne, the virgin who

was turned into a laurel tree, to "I started Early—Took my Dog" ("E[mily] D[ickinson]: Another Daphne?" *EDB* 33:35–39). Epic parallels interest Wolfgang E. H. Rudat in "Dickinson and Immortality: Virgilian and Miltonic Allusions in 'Of Death I try to think like this'" (*AN&Q* 16:85–87). Similarities with Eve's situation in *Paradise Lost* seem to mean that Dickinson's speaker has no certain knowledge of an afterlife, despite indications to the contrary in Virgilian contexts for the poem observed by Nancy McClaran (*ALS 1976*, p. 75). Dickinson's treatment of the love situation in Shakespeare's sonnet number 43 is sensibly discussed by Jane F. Crosthwaite in "Dickinson's 'What I see not, I better see" (*Expl* 36,iii:10–12). In the Amherst poet's redaction Crosthwaite finds an added note of stubborn complaint against God. Because *Othello* was a favorite of Dickinson's, Robert F. Fleissner wonders whether she was seeing a black man as well as peaty wastes in "I never saw a Moor" ("Dickinson's 'Moor,'" *DnS* 34:7–12). If she had *the* Moor in mind, Fleissner would paraphrase the opening line "I never yet saw death."

e. **Affinities and Influences.** Lois A. Cuddy has already proposed that Dickinson modeled her metrics on the forms for Latin verse she studied as a schoolgirl (*ALS 1976*, p. 76). In "The Latin Imprint on Emily Dickinson's Poetry: Theory and Practice" (*AL* 50:74–84) Cuddy goes on to urge that the poet's syntactical displacements also follow rules in her Latin textbook. The linguistic parallels, worth noting, are exhaustively set forth here, but one must take exception to Cuddy's conclusion that "it was not license which dictated Dickinson's innovations, for she never violated the rules." It may be wondered whether Dickinson's distinctive grammar caused her the sort of moral self-accusation only Latin constructions could ease. As for the influence of Emersonian and Transcendental ideas on Dickinson, both John S. Mann and Steve Carter offered notes of qualification (section *c*, above). Lawrence Buell valuably supplies another in "Calvinism Romanticized: Harriet Beecher Stowe, Samuel Hopkins, and *The Minister's Wooing*" (*ESQ* 24:119–32). Though principally occupied with Stowe, Buell suggests that both she and Dickinson epitomized a "late Edwardsean sensibility" in which Calvinist doctrinal rigor and supernaturalism combine somewhat uneasily with a religion of the heart. In literary works where these two motifs are mutually honored, he says, we can expect "an equation between self-fulfillment and self-denial rather than self-assertion or self-reliance in the Emersonian sense." Buell is certainly right in calling for assessments of the poet's 19th-century religious milieu which do more than extract simplified versions of Emerson and Calvin.

George Monteiro continues his investigation of Dickinson's influence on Robert Frost (see ALS 1977, p. 84) with a description of books by and about her in Frost's library ("Robert Frost's Dickinson Books," EDB 33:3–7). In one, Frost had marked 48 poems, the first lines of which Monteiro provides. Robert F. Fleissner is convinced that Dickinson's "Apparently with no surprise" was the source for Frost's "Fire and Ice" in " 'Frost . . . at . . . Play': A Frost-Dickinson Affinity Affirmed" (RS 46:28–39). Fleissner's argument, though carefully researched, is tenuous and overdrawn. The critic whose 1924 edition of her poems initiated Dickinson's 20th-century rehabilitation gives notable other evidence of his regard for her work in the Selected Letters of Conrad Aiken, edited by Joseph Killorin (Yale, passim). Dickinson is also mentioned with respect in Tillie Olsen's reflections on women as writers, though her only comment of substance is a long footnote having to do with external resemblances between the lives of Dickinson and Gerard Manley Hopkins (Silences [New York: Delacorte], p. 128). Similarities in imagery are only external, according to John Ditsky, in two poems on hope by Emily Dickinson and Emily Brontë, which Ditsky says reveal profound differences in tone and feeling ("The Two Emilies and a Feathered Hope: Shared Imagery in Dickinson and Brontë," KAL 19:28–31).

Arizona State University

6. Mark Twain

Louis J. Budd

In "They Keep Mixin' Fact and Fiction in Hannibal, Mo." (*Smithsonian* 9,vii:155–60) William Zinsser guesses at the motives of those who, often as families, keep flocking to Mark Twain's boyhood home. He decides, "We were pilgrims to an American childhood that no longer exists. Tom Sawyer is the child we wish we had been and that some of us would still like to be." Such appeal means that the general magazines regularly carry articles not vital to *ALS*. Still these articles help to answer the charge that scholars in the humanities are educating only each other; today a popular "story" on Mark Twain is far more accurate and insightful than one done in 1940 or even 1960. His fame also keeps encouraging essays that claim a tenuous link for some other writer; furthermore, hardly any long essay, much less book, on the American character can resist discussing him. While *Adventures of Huckleberry Finn* will always command the most respect, there is growing interest in his other books. In a more fundamental trend scholars now often set any specific work within a knowledge of his biography and *oeuvre* and an awareness of textual problems. My four sections should be regarded therefore not as categories but simply as indications of the most helpful side of the book or essay discussed.

i. Bibliography

Without a breather after the monumental *Mark Twain: A Reference Guide* (*ALS 1977*, pp. 87–88) Thomas A. Tenney has already published his "Second Annual Supplement" (*ALR* 11:157–218), which reaches back all the way to 1868 to pick up more reviews and articles whose titles had not given an earlier lead. He continues to annotate each entry with judgmental detail. Those "data banks" that New Wave librarians are projecting will be valuable only to the extent

that specialists like Tenney gather and evaluate what is punched
into the tapes. Likewise, Edgar M. Branch's review (*ALR* 11:311–
16) of the *Reference Guide* has more substance than the ordinary
high-flying essay. Branch produces both a reassuring though cau-
tionary verdict on its quality and a fine introduction to using it most
effectively.

Unlike Paul Fatout's *Mark Twain Speaking* (*ALS 1976*, p. 80),
his *Mark Twain Speaks for Himself* (Purdue) is not an enduring
book. Its potpourri of 76 items is already known to Twainians, taken
collectively. Still Fatout supplies many expert touches as well as
seasoned wisdom on the S. L. Clemens–Mark Twain dichotomy,
which strikes him as "vague and shifting" because the "outward
image and private image merge and exchange places" frequently.
Mark Twain Speaks for Himself can be enjoyed and trusted if the
reader recognizes that it does not exhaust any of the kinds of material included, such as letters to the editor or statements to the
press. Because of his own special knowledge, Carl L. Anderson, in
"Mark Twain in Sweden: An Interview and Commentary" (*ALR* 11:
80–91), can translate an out-of-the-way and interesting item; while
filling in the background for the Clemenses' single visit to Scandinavia, Anderson establishes that Dr. Kellegren had higher medical
standing than many now realize.

Only an apprentice needs reminding that the *Twainian* appears
every other month. For 1978 it mostly printed family letters, some
already available in whole or in part, and a further set of marginalia
by Clemens, who seldom read a book passively. Another very personal if fitful enterprise, the *Mark Twain Journal*, has benefited from
the competition to get published, and its quality keeps rising, though
it still has a weakness for articles that offer any kind of case for Mark
Twain as a figure of world literature. Evidently it does not submit
proof to its contributors, who will not enjoy my saying that its Summer issue has so many typos (e.g., "People" for "Pope") that it suggests a Mark Twain parody. The new *Bulletin* of the Mark Twain
Society of Elmira, New York, will be produced carefully and even
handsomely, judging by its first two numbers. Based upon the sound
guess that Elmira is the best site left for prospectors, it hopes to
record anecdotes, letters, and memorabilia. Not scholarly yet de-
pendable is Ralph Tyler's list in "Classic Corner / The Works of
Great Writers Available Today" (*Bookviews* 1,viii:17–19) of all

printings, hardcover or paperback, currently on the market. Not complete yet useful is "The Age of Mark Twain," pp. 69–83, in James C. Austin, *American Humor in France* (Iowa State), which surveys the changing but always mixed reception of our humorists by French critics, who often reveal more about their own culture than ours.

ii. Biography

Though the highpoint of the year, the writing about Clemens's actions and character ranged so widely in approach that the order of precedence here must be subjective. Wilson H. Faude, *The Renaissance of Mark Twain's House: Handbook for Restoration* (Larchmont, N.Y.: Queens House), might even seem too tangential since it explains the ingenious craft of reestablishing the "original text" (as Norman Holmes Pearson put it) of the Hartford residence. Faude's claim about its present "jewel-like condition" is justified by the glittering reality which overshadows any account of the expensive setting (such as the ombra or the stenciled ceilings and marble window in the billiard room) of Clemens's family life. While in the neighborhood we should recognize Ellen Moers for "A Note on Mark Twain and Harriet Beecher Stowe," pp. 39–47, in *Harriet Beecher Stowe and American Literature* (Hartford, Conn.: Stowe-Day Foundation). Moers reminds us that Mrs. Stowe asserted a clear-minded presence during most of the Clemens years in Nook Farm. Another famous personage with whom Clemens associated leads to "Grant and Twain in Chicago: The 1879 Reunion of the Army of the Tennessee" (*Chicago History* 7:151–60) by Charles H. Gold, who draws on local sources to confirm that Mark Twain scored a triumph with his speech capping the major banquet.

On a totally new trail Ulysses S. Smith, in *Up a Tree with Mark Twain* (Quincy, Ill.: Shondo-Shando Press), which depends basically on cryptograms, claims to reconstruct two incognito escapades in Hannibal during the 1880s which brought on blackmail after a husband caught Clemens in bed with his wife, who went on to bear an illegitimate daughter—the mother of Smith. This grandson plunges on to reveal that Clemens is the true author of *The Strange Case of Dr. Jekyll and Mr. Hyde*, salted with further anagrams confessing to his misdeeds. If all of this is a hoax, Smith carries it on in a letter to me about improving his case, already elaborated in 531 pages that are clear and sober except for a cheerful anticipation of being hooted. Undoubtedly Smith "takes the belt" (as his "Sir Grandpap" liked to say) for shock value in 1978 though Thomas P. Riggio, in "Mark Twain and Theodore Dreiser: Two Boys Lost in a Cave" (*MTJ* 19,ii:20–25), would be runner-up if he could prove the Dreiser story, which he resurrects, that in a New York City saloon in 1907 or so Clemens professed ambivalence toward his dead wife and complained about the restraints of his marriage.

Mark Twain in England (Humanities Press) by Dennis Welland is mistitled. Less broadly framed than Howard G. Baetzhold's *Mark Twain & John Bull* (1970), it depends mainly on the archives of Chatto and Windus and becomes authoritative for the English printings, arguing convincingly, for instance, that *Following the Equator* is an "abridged variant" of the English *More Tramps Abroad*. But Welland grows debatable when he expands into contending that during the 1880s Clemens had a crisis of confidence in himself as a writer and a human being. From the start Welland holds that he felt and thought consistent approval of Victorian England, a view that gets untenable when it gives no ground in *A Connecticut Yankee in King Arthur's Court*. Another denial of reality might seem to be the conclusion that Clemens remained cordial toward Andrew Chatto for 35 years, but Welland proves that he never blamed his own blunders on Chatto or charged that still another publisher was cheating him. According to M. E. Grenander, in "California's Albion: Mark Twain, Ambrose Bierce, Tom Hood, John Camden Hotten, and Andrew Chatto" (*PBSA* 72:455–75), he was in truth too hard on Hotten, whose alleged piracies may deserve a kinder name within the copyright legalities at that time. The most intriguing pattern in Grenander's weave of old and new sources is the relationship between Clemens and Bierce, who passed up chances to become good friends yet never sought or took occasion to clash.

Particularly relevant to *Following the Equator*, detail on the world tour of 1895–96 is getting quite rich. While *Mark Twain in India* (Bombay: Noble Publishing House) uses the major collections in the United States, Keshav Mutalik is best qualified to correct Clemens's errors about India and offer a native's reactions to his judgments, especially those about the British raj. Perhaps the most solid chapter deals with the "At Home" performances, but Americans will value Mutalik's analysis of the impact of India, which fascinated Clemens and "changed his attitude to life." Though that claims too much, India may have lured him closer to the conviction that existence is "only a vision, an unfulfilled dream"; likewise, he would have been happier if the misery he saw and smelled had indeed reconciled him to suffering as an integral part of experience. At least, surely his "careful study of Indian customs and practices intensified his tolerant attitude to aliens." His meeting with a most princely alien, who enjoyed his resulting portrait in *Following the Equator*, is recounted by Mohamed Elias, in "Mark Twain and the Aga Khan: Mutual Impressions" (*IJAS* 8,i:46–49). Though E. Daniel Potts and Annette Potts, in "The Mark Twain Family in Australia" (*Overland* 70:46–50), are also working their home turf, their freshest element comes through heavy use of letters from Olivia Clemens to her sister Susan Langdon Crane. Coleman O. Parsons, in "Mark Twain: Paid Performer in South Africa" (*MTJ* 19,ii:2–11), amends his earlier verdict of an "almost uniformly triumphal" tour. Parsons's sleuthing, backed by visits to the halls where Mark Twain performed, deepens our gut sense of a weary professional adjusting to the acoustics, balky audiences, and other variables.

During their stay in a sumptuous Australian home, Olivia wrote fondly of her husband: "He was born for this kind of luxury." Yet that baffling man had enjoyed barnstorming in India. In the drivingly reasoned and stated "Mark Twain: The Writer as Pilot" (*PMLA* 93:878–92) Edgar J. Burde, speculating on his "identity problems," proposes that Clemens never wrote about his experience as a pilot (rather than cub) because he could not order his feelings toward them. More generally, in the face of other obvious dynamisms Burde argues with finesse that Clemens's mind or psyche fused the "figurative master pilot" with his creative self and his conception of the artist. (Burde's readers should note the apology in *PMLA* 94[1979]: 7 for transposing 11 lines of type in his article.) Just as speculative though meticulous in procedure and summed up in graphs is "Content Analysis of Mark Twain's Novels and Letters as a Biographical Method" (*Poetics* 7:155–75) by Robert R. Sears, Deborah Lapidus, and Christine Cozzens, who extend Sears's earlier probe (*ALS 1976*, p. 82) of Clemens's "separation anxiety" by classifying 599 "episodes" from nine novels into categories involving "attachment and loss." Humanists willing to go interdisciplinary had better look for themselves at what two reputable social scientists, assisted by a graduate student in literature, present as a methodology applicable to other writers too.

iii. General Essays

Three books that will get rounded treatment elsewhere demand mention. Since the authors are Walter Blair and Hamlin Hill, it was a sure bet that the chapters on Mark Twain would mark a high point of their *America's Humor from Poor Richard to Doonesbury* (Oxford). Their analysis is orthodox yet packed with original insights, fully appreciative of Twain's writings before 1890 yet alert to his later modernity of attitude and method that in some ways anticipated the nihilistic humorists of our times. Incidentally, Blair and Hill successfully run the risk of inserting sly touches of their own. Henry Nash Smith, with his usual conciseness, makes one chapter do for Mark Twain in *Democracy and the Novel*. This time Smith most notably raises our consciousness concerning Huck's much-admired decision to go to hell rather than turn in Jim; we have been too charmed by the moral politics to recognize that Huck falls into rhetorical grandiosity added to overacting. Smith's chapter is masterful in itself though it does not fit Mark Twain perfectly into the overall problem posed. Since three other authors get the most attention in Martha Banta's sweepingly interpretive *Failure & Success in America: A Literary Debate* (Princeton), I will merely report that self-effacing Huck emerges as the "lowest mark to which the American might come and yet survive, survive *significantly*." To support this view, Banta challenges those explicators who wish that the saints on the river could forever stay clear of the town society.

After these three books it is hard to avoid the phrase "mere essays." In one of these—Paul F. Boller, Jr., "Mark Twain's Credo: A Humorist's Fatalistic View" (*SWR* 63:150–63)—the author reviews thoroughly the tension between the desire to believe and revulsion at pointless suffering, between free will and determinism. These problems are posed with much greater resonance in John Irwin Fischer, "Mark Twain, Mount Tabor, and the Triumph of Art" (*SoR* 14:692–705), where Clemens's drive to judge according to his inner light is contrasted with the "georgic" tradition, which teaches man to find in nature the "source of his own identity and a final home for his thoughts." More specifically Fischer dissects one of the *Quaker City* letters to find out whether artistic instinct overrode Mark Twain's rationalism. Fischer proceeds with such sophistication that, once again, *ALS* readers must decide for themselves whether the mixed, practical-minded tactics of the *Quaker City* letters undercut their value as a philosophical crux. Ostensibly less ambitious, St. George Tucker Arnold, Jr., in "The Twain Bestiary: Mark Twain's Critters and the Tradition of Animal Portraiture in Humor of the Old Southwest" (*SFQ* 41[1977]:195–211), nevertheless comes close to giving us a major article, flawed only because some texts bend his patterns. His main argument runs that while one group of humorists made comparisons with animals to ridicule their provincial characters, a few saw the closeness of frontier man and animal as an "appealing bond"; for Mark Twain this bond passed into a "total identification," a "kinship Twain the pagan felt for the truer life beneath the human level." Arnold ends with the appealing notion that his "totem" ought to be the bird and more particularly the brash, irreverent Bombay crow of *Following the Equator*.

Among four more limited but first-rate essays, Alan Gribben, in "Mark Twain Reads Longstreet's *Georgia Scenes*" (*Gyascutus*, pp. 103–11), continues his expert studies based on the books Clemens owned. Here Gribben confronts the still murky problem of just how closely he knew the masters of the Old Southwest. Ironically the problem may stay unsettled because most of the relevant books he enjoyed during the 1880s were torn apart to furnish printer's copy for *Mark Twain's Library of Humor*. On a different kind of reading Gribben, in " 'A Splendor of Stars & Suns': Twain as a Reader of Browning's Poems" (*BIS* 6:87–103), deals with his penchant for oral interpretation; this subject leads into crosscurrents of taste within his household and his other preferences in texts for semipublic performance. As for the results of knowing Browning well, Gribben declines to claim any benefits for Clemens beyond "aesthetic gratification and intellectual challenge"—a good return after all. In " 'The Babes in the Wood': Artemus Ward's 'Double Health' to Mark Twain" (*PMLA* 93:955–72) Edgar M. Branch also handles a literary influence with as much authority as delicacy. After reconstructing one of Ward's zaniest lectures, Branch proves that it did have a structure of subtle devices from which Mark Twain learned

much at a period when he knew enough to be able to do so but
had matured too far to let Ward skew his development toward a
still greater mastery. "Mark Twain and the American Indian: Earthly Realism and Heavenly Idealism" (*AIQ* 4:223–42) by James C.
McNutt gathers passages over a span of half a century to show that
Clemens's Nevada years made him believe he knew the redman at
firsthand and that for the rest of his life he would burlesque the
Romantic stereotypes while slowly acquiring a cultural relativism
which sensitized him to the results of white injustice. Clear and judicious, McNutt does especially well at eliciting the social-political
attitudes latent in often slapdash humor.

iv. On Individual Pieces

Whatever the immediate trends, *Huckleberry Finn* will never be
ignored if only because some of those who "teach" it conclude eventually that they have found a further perspective. But the relative
neglect of *A Connecticut Yankee*, given its reach and passion, is
being remedied, and the racial tangle in *Pudd'nhead Wilson* makes
it the liveliest area of discussion at present. Also current is a notion
that the final Mark Twain writings are the most profound.

Except for those who will apply Fischer to *The Innocents Abroad*,
the first article in order is "Feminist Fools: Women in the Political
Novels of the 1870's" (*JGE* 30:154–64) by Martha S. Grise, who
gives Mark Twain sole responsibility for *The Gilded Age*, which
she takes as warning beauties like Laura Hawkins not to let pride
betray them into pursuit of "power and independence" and conscious
rebels like Ruth Bolton not to forget that "weakness and dependency
are the nature of the true woman." Surprisingly *The Adventures of
Tom Sawyer* elicited only "Darkness at Morning: The Bitterness in
Mark Twain's Early Novel *Tom Sawyer*" (*MTJ* 19,iii:4–5) by Joseph
J. Feeney, S.J., who must have submitted his note before seeing recent essays in the same vein such as that by Tom H. Towers (*ALS
1976*, p. 86). Despite Clemens's sporadic faith in the Liberal or
Whig version of history, in "*The Prince and the Pauper*: Mark
Twain's Once and Future King" (*SAF* 6:193–202) Towers somewhat
similarly interprets the second "boy" book as controlled by nostalgia
that can accept a purely rural England as the one imaginable setting for a just, contented society. This essay has the innovative vir-

tue of treating the Prince-King as the more important of the two boys and therefore the more instructive character.

In "Love and Power in *Huckleberry Finn*" (*TSE* 23:17–37) Towers finds the creative impetus focused not by bitterness or nostalgia but by the complexities that any form of human involvement brings. Though ending up less revisionist than his opening sally, he attacks the recent consensus as Romantic in essence, as imperceptive of the fact that all of Mark Twain's heroes desire acclaim, wealth, and even some kind of power rather than escape. On a modest scale Huck yearns for social standing and tries at times to affect his world; his resolve to light out for the Territory springs from the frustration of having embroiled himself in society. As a formalist way of finding more depth in him Watson Branch, in "Hard-Hearted Huck: 'No Time to be Sentimentering'" (*SAF* 6:212–18), draws a fruitful distinction between Huck as narrator and as participant in the action; his supposedly low level of emotion displays simply his intentness on telling what happened instead of how he felt at the time. The only other notable essay moves the searchlight directly upon the author and then on his reader. In "Literary Masters and Masturbators: Sexuality, Fantasy, and Reality in *Huckleberry Finn*" (*L&P* 18:85–92) Charles E. May charges both that Clemens semiconsciously linked literary creation (or fantasy) to sexual fantasy and that critics prefer Huck over Tom because they have their own fears of trifling too far with actuality. To the dismay of anti-Freudians May earns the right to expect a reasoned judgment on the dialectic between playfulness and work that he develops for *Huckleberry Finn* as well as its author. At least May must be right in suggesting that Tom's boyhood is closer in spirit to the one most of us had than Huck's.

Discussions of *A Connecticut Yankee* will now have to take account of Alan Gribben, "'The Master Hand of Old Malory': Mark Twain's Acquaintance with *Le Morte D'Arthur*" (*ELN* 16:32–40), which corrects the current data about when Clemens first dipped into Malory and, more important, reveals his lasting fascination with two passages. In effect Evelyn Schroth also warns sourcehunters to invoke Malory with discretion; "Mark Twain's Literary Dialect in *A Connecticut Yankee*" (*MTJ* 19,ii:26–29) gives systematic detail to the fact that only an "illusion" of archaic speech was skillfully created. Abandoning pre-1889 sources, Sam B. Girgus, in "Conscience in Connecticut: *Civilization and Its Discontents* in Twain's Camelot" (*NEQ* 51:547–60), borrows Freudian concepts to reinforce those critics who see Hank Morgan ultimately rejecting technology; without extrapolating backward from the ending, Girgus contends that to install a factory system Hank tried to make the Arthurians internalize a work-oriented conscience against which the aggressive or death instinct inevitably rebelled. I wish that Girgus could review for us "The Meaning of *A Connecticut Yankee*" (*AL* 50:418–40) by Everett Carter, who judges between the "hard" (antisentimental) and "soft" (anti-industrial) impact of the book, measured by what the author thought he was getting said. Building on explicit statements of intent, Carter decides that Mark Twain admired Hank's progressivist goals up through the ending, which was planned as an indictment of the Church, and that the delirious Hank's regrets flow from "private" sadness about his lost wife and child. It will be interesting to see whether Carter's learned and lucid polemic discourages what has become almost a shibboleth among Twainians.

Another lion in the path may prove to be "Exigencies of Composition and Publication: *Billy Budd, Sailor* and *Pudd'nhead Wilson*" (*NCF* 33:131–43) by Hershel Parker and Henry Binder, who warn that late improvisation can twist an original design badly. To illustrate their thesis that emerging problems can often have an "often crucial" bearing on why a manuscript ends as it does, Parker and Binder argue that the discovery of the murderer rounded off "very little of what had been written before it" because Mark Twain was salvaging his plot through a spectacular scene around his titular hero. Those who respect *Pudd'nhead Wilson* as a mordant fable cannot ignore this formalist-textual verdict of a cobbled together "farce-melodrama." They will also have to reject Robert E. Morsberger, "*Pudd'nhead Wilson* and the Iron Mask" (*MarkhamR* 7:25–27), which draws parallels with popular novels of the period while deciding that it is "more theatrical than significant . . . ranks higher as entertainment than as social commentary." Indeed Earl F. Briden, in "Idiots First, Then Juries: Legal Metaphors in Mark Twain's *Pudd'nhead Wilson*" (*TSLL* 20:169–80), has already demurred by contending that the novel built up toward that murder trial through an "analogical matrix"—that is, an underlying pattern of figures based on legal idiom (which includes "swear" in any context or any stage of ossified metaphor). Not concerned with esthetic quality, Judith R. Berzon (*Neither White Nor Black*, pp. 36–48) clarifies the heredity vs. training debate before concluding that Mark Twain was stressing the "institutions and social conditioning" that perpetuated slavery; yet she does complain of some shallow melodrama centered on the false Tom. As defenders of the novel regroup they may benefit from two basically factual enterprises. In "Pudd'nhead Wilson's Calendar" (*MTJ* 19,ii:15–19) Thomas W. Ford, after classing the maxims by whether they relate to the chapters they head, reports that the free-standing group is by far the larger and also the more pessimistic. Sidney Berger's precise work with the text is extended in "Determining Printer's Copy: The English Edition of Mark Twain's *Pudd'nhead Wilson*" (*PBSA* 72:250–56), which through dogged rather than showy logic demonstrates that the *Century Magazine* printing of the last five chapters has better authority than any other version.

Among a handful of articles on Mark Twain's final phase one stands out. Distilling half of a dissertation based on thorough research, Hunt Hawkins, in "Mark Twain's Involvement with the Congo Reform Movement: 'A Fury of Generous Indignation'" (*NEQ* 51:147–75), presents cogently the background, genesis, and reception of *King Leopold's Soliloquy*, which, though not designed for immortality, has some political bite left. In "Mark Twain's Joan of Arc: An 'Asbestos' Character Rising from the Ashes" (*MTJ* 19,iii: 13–19) Yvonne A. Amar, who at least does the service of insisting that the *Personal Recollections* is not a curious mutant, rates Joan herself as vibrant and rounded through action when the vaporings of the narrator are brushed away. With "In Quest of Redemptive Vision: Mark Twain's *Joan of Arc*" (*TSLL* 20:181–98) James D. Wilson still more forcefully acclaims the book as vintage Mark Twain—on his lesser-known hopeful side. Taking it as a religious-historical allegory, Wilson joins the few who accept Joan as an engaging "proof that spiritual and cultural regeneration is possible." Raymond Varisco, in "A Militant Voice: Mark Twain's 'The Man That Corrupted Hadleyburg'" (*RevI* 8:129–37), opts likewise for a supportive effect, if obviously more subdued, from what is potentially a mechanistic story. Essentially satisfied with the explication by Clinton S. Burhans, Jr., (*AL* 34[1962]:375–84), Varisco adds little more than examining how the story's narrator is tightly restrained so that characters and their dialogue can project the moral issue. After assiduously reviewing the criticism, Vincent Carretta, in "The Roots of Mark Twain's Pessimism in *What Is Man?*" (*Cithara* 18:46–60), also detects bright rays within the late despair. Again mostly within the bounds of past commentary, Richard Tuerk, in "Appearance and Reality in Mark Twain's 'Which Was the Dream?' 'The Great Dark' and 'Which Was It?'" (*IllQ* 40,iii:23–34), helpfully places the confusing of reality and illusion not in the aged Clemens's mind but in the perception he grants to baffled humanity.

My chapter is spared from a diminishing end by Sholom J. Kahn, *Mark Twain's Mysterious Stranger: A Study of the Manuscript Texts* (Missouri). Buoyed up by admiration for Mark Twain's intellectual reach, Kahn steadily broadens his probing of two key questions: "how good" are these writings and "what is the nature and degree" of their unity? While reasoning toward his highest accolade for "No.44, The Mysterious Stranger" he also claims solid intrinsic value for "Schoolhouse Hill" and much more for "The Chronicle of Young Satan." He feels no need to denigrate the earlier texts before concluding that "No.44" is not only virtually complete but also unique beneath the obvious similarities with them. Crucial to comprehending "No.44" are the makeup of the truly eerie stranger and his relation to August along with the various aspects of the Duplicate, whose "ambiguous, shifting status" anticipates Freudian insights. Conceding some blurs of meaning does not impugn the "aesthetically satisfying" craft with which Mark Twain fleshed out his climactic "dream of life." Though many will continue to prefer "The Chronicle of Young Satan," anybody who has followed Kahn's paragraph-by-paragraph discussion of the manuscript will feel compelled to give "No.44" a sympathetic reading.

Along with the Fischer, Arnold, Carter, and Parker-Binder essays and the Blair-Hill chapters, Kahn poses enough mental challenge to keep us invigorated. We may as well stay fit because it already seems certain that in 1979 the Mark Twain fraternity will buck the trend of the economy and have an unusually productive year.

Duke University

7. Henry James

Robert L. Gale

Criticism of Henry James showed no sign of abating in 1978. There were 7 new books on him, at least 3 new editions of some of his work, 70 or so articles devoted exclusively or partly to him, and 16 dissertations. Much is naturally short, tangential, or somewhat trivial; but the year also saw a good deal of solid and some brilliant work. It is hard to single out specific critics for special praise; but I regard as unusually commendable books by Stephen Donadio, Sergio Perosa, Mary Doyle Springer, and Edward Wagenknecht, and essays by Paul B. Armstrong, Jean Frantz Blackall, Sara DeSaussure Davis, Jane Nardin, Elsa Nettels, Adeline R. Tintner, and J. W. Tuttleton. Voluminous work was accomplished in the field of sources, influences, and parallels. James's *Bostonians, What Maisie Knew,* "Turn of the Screw," and *Golden Bowl* received concentrated attention.

i. Life, Texts

David W. Pancost, in "Henry James and Julian Hawthorne" (*AL* 50:461–65), surveys the social and intellectual relations between James and Nathaniel Hawthorne's thin-skinned son Julian, whom James interviewed in February 1879 on the occasion of his writing *Hawthorne,* and whom James later saw, in London in the 1880s, in California in 1905. Julian deplored "James's enthusiasm for literary realism," while James was more legitimately put off by "Julian's anglophobia, superficiality, and lack of culture."

Leon Edel's biography of James is happily available in an inexpensive five-volume paperback reprint (New York: Avon).

As for new texts, it is good to be able to note that Maqbool Aziz's meticulous but overpriced edition of the short stories is continuing: the second volume of *The Tales of Henry James* (Oxford), covering the years 1870–74, has appeared. In addition, a facsimile of the manuscript of *The Europeans* was issued (New York: Fertig). The best new edition this year of a James work is the Norton Critical Edition of *The Wings of the Dove*, edited by J. Donald Crowley and Richard A. Hocks. The format is the same: text (with the 1909 New York Preface and photographic illustrations, and maps of contemporary London and Venice), textual appendix, selections from James pertinent to his novel (from his *Notebooks*, letters, *Italian Hours*, *Notes of a Son and Brother*, and "Is There a Life After Death?"), selected critical pieces, and bibliography. The work is a model of careful scholarship. Why no Norton Critical Edition of James's dozen best short stories?

ii. Sources, Influences, Parallels

In "Henry James' *Winter's Tale*: 'The Bench of Desolation'" (*SAF* 6:141–56), Joseph Milicia notes the "curious resemblance" of James's "most unjustly neglected tale" to Shakespeare's late play. Each work features a man who is unjust to a woman, separated from her, then reunited after many years; each concerns terrible harm followed by "debilitating remorse," but then forgiveness and rekindled love; and each combines pathos with comedy and miracle. Well and good, but Milicia seems far too kind to Kate Cookham.

It is well known that Claire Clairmont, friend of Shelley and Byron, provided James a partial model for Juliana Bordereau in "The Aspern Papers." Less is known about Claire's real-life niece, Pauline "Plin" Clairmont (1825–91), who attended her old aunt in Florence, Italy, much the way Miss Tina Bordereau attends her aunt in Venice, in James's story. Shedding light on Pauline is "Miss Tina and Miss Plin: The Papers Behind *The Aspern Papers*," pp. 372–84, in *The Evidence of the Imagination: Studies of Interactions Between Life and Art in English Romantic Literature*, edited by Donald H. Reiman et al. (NYU), by Marion Kingston Stocking. Plin was refreshingly peppy and modern, visited her aunt in Florence occasionally, then was a paying guest, and finally did unremunerated housekeeping for her until old Claire died in 1879. Stocking fascinatingly tells us about Plin and also how her Shelley-expert whilom lover Edward Augustus Silsbee, some little while after Claire's death, bid on her Shelley letters but lacked cash to outbid a better-financed competitor, whose money Plin finally preferred to anything else.

George Sebouhian, in "Adam Verver: Emerson's Poet" (*MarkhamR* 7:39–40), develops the thesis that "James meant Adam Verver [of *The Golden Bowl*] as a straight portrait of the new American, an American whose spiritual ancestor was born in the pages of Ralph Waldo Emerson"; Verver is a poet projecting his vision of life through collecting for his museum and thus depicts "the American imagination fulfilling its . . . promise to provide . . . artistic experience for . . . the people"—even as James saw himself functioning. Yes, but Verver is uncreative. In her "James Corrects Poe: The Appropriation of *Pym* in *The Golden Bowl*" (*ATQ* 37:87–91), the indefatigable Adeline R. Tintner demonstrates how James, characteristically rethinking another author's creative work, "used 'the imaginative effect' of the 'blind white fog' which contributes the climax of Poe's *Narrative [of Arthur Gordon Pym]* (rather than 'wasted' it) by incorporating it analogically and metaphorically within the consciousness of the Prince [Amerigo]." Further, Tintner, in "A Source for Prince Amerigo in *The Golden Bowl*" (*NMAL* 2:Item 23), shows that the Prince's lineage parallels that of the Marchese Simone de Peruzzi de Medici, husband of Edith Story, whose sculptor father is the subject of James's *William Wetmore Story and His Friends*. (In her essay on "Lady Barberina," Tintner incidentally discusses parallels involving it, *Gulliver's Travels*, and Oscar Wilde. See below, where the careful reader will notice the variant spelling, "Barbarina.")

In "'An Honorable Emulation of the Author of *The Newcomes*': James and Thackeray" (*NCF* 32:399–419), R. D. McMaster offers a convincing demonstration of James's general admiration for William Makepeace Thackeray and also his specific debt to *The Newcomes*, not only when it came to writing *Roderick Hudson* but, though to a lesser extent, *The American* as well. Both *The Newcomes* and *Roderick Hudson* develop "the combined theme of unsuccessful artist and marriage market"; Christine relates to Ethel, Roderick to Clive, and Singleton to Ridley. Further, "the moral contrast of Roderick and Singleton" parallels that of Clive and Ridley. In addition, "James and Thackeray share a Victorian interest in the basic ambiguity of facts and in the power of the shaping mind to interpret and arrange facts so as to flesh out its own idiosyncratic view of the world, morally or aesthetically." As for *The American*, in which the marriage-market theme is again central, old Madame de Bellegarde derives partly from Thackeray's Lady Kew.

David Gervais's *Flaubert and Henry James: A Study in Contrasts* (Macmillan-L) is a slow, sophisticated defense of Gustave Flaubert against James's adverse criticism of him. Gervais tries to show that James partly misread the Frenchman. But James disappears from Gervais's defensive book too much. The two novelists' theories of tragedy were radically different (see *ALS 1977*, p. 116). Preferring Flaubert's, Gervais, when he gets to James's *Portrait of a Lady*, subjects it to one of the most savage treatments on record: James's intention in his story of Isabel Archer is at variance with its meaning, James is fooled by his too-remote heroine, she is shallower than she (or he) thinks, she admires passive Ralph Touchett too much (as does James), she hides her moral timidity by silly pseudo-wit, she is not numbed enough by sorrow, and she wrongly links sex and death. Gervais seems guilty of the critical sin for which he rebukes James: just as James wanted Flaubert to write more like James, so Gervais wants James to write more like Flaubert. (See Jeannette King, *Tragedy in the Victorian Novel: Theory and Practice in the novels of George Eliot, Thomas Hardy and Henry James* [Cambridge], for more temperate critical comparisons.)

A. R. Tintner's essay "James's 'The Beldonald Holbein' and Rollins' 'A Burne-Jones Head': A Surprising Parallel" (*CLQ* 14:183–90) shows that James's 1901 story is indebted to the 1894 story entitled "A Burne-Jones Head" by Clara Sherwood Rollins. "The basic situations" are identical: "the function of the heroine in James's story is exactly that of the 'Burne-Jones Head.' She is imported to embellish her patron's social career, but banished when she outshines her." There are even verbal echoes.

Next, Tintner, in "James Writes a Boy's Story: 'The Pupil' and R. L. Stevenson's Adventure Books" (*ELWIU* 5:61–73), argues that James's "Pupil" (1891) is replete with "similes and metaphors . . . built out of terms involving mutiny, shipwreck, and sea weather" reminiscent of Stevenson's *Treasure Island* (1883) and *Kidnapped* (1886); and, further, that the plot of "The Pupil" is partly modeled on that of *Kidnapped*. Tintner details parallels between James's "boy's book" and *Kidnapped*, between Pemberton and Jim Hawkins of *Treasure Island*, between aspects of the Moreen family and "that smooth and formidable 'adventurer' " John Silver of *Treasure Island*. More boldly, Tintner then compares the Moreens with Stevenson in boyhood and maturity, and concludes with a comparison of Stevenson and Ray Limbert, hero of James's short story "The Next Time."

The influence of James on Conrad concerns Ian Watt, who in "Marlow, Henry James, and 'The Heart of Darkness' " (*NCF* 33: 159–74) shows how Conrad tried to adapt James's technique of the "sensitive central intelligence" point of view, specifically Fleda Vetch's in *The Spoils of Poynton*, which Conrad was ecstatic about, in creating Marlow, especially in "Heart of Darkness." However, Marlow "represented . . . a much more extreme and overt break with the distance, impersonality, and omniscience of [Flaubertian] third-person narration" than pleased James, who accordingly disapproved of Marlow's extreme " 'mixing himself up with the narrative' " and further registered his "distaste for the infinite pluralism of Marlow's narrative functions."

Devoted to other critical concerns, William J. Scheick, in "The Fourth Dimension in Wells's Novels of the 1920's" (*Criticism* 20: 167–90), contrasts in passing H. G. Wells's *Meanwhile: The Picture of a Lady* (1927) with James's *Portrait of a Lady*.

In their odd "Hemingway and Brooks: The Mystery of 'Henry's Bicycle' " (*SAF* 6:106–09), Fred D. Crawford and Bruce Morton trace Ernest Hemingway's derisive, parodic reaction to the anti-expatriation theories of Van Wyck Brooks, as expressed in his *Pilgrimage of Henry James*. It seems that Hemingway has Bill Gorton in *The Sun Also Rises* postulate that "Henry's bicycle," not expatriation, caused a creativity-blocking impotence. Much ado, but fun.

Lillian Faderman's "Female Same-Sex Relationships in Novels by Longfellow, Holmes, and James" (*NEQ* 51:309–32) asserts that "the female-female relationship in *The Bostonians* has obvious parallels to those in [Henry Wadsworth Longfellow's] *Kavanaugh* and [Oliver Wendell Holmes's] *A Mortal Antipathy*." Faderman urges us to read all three novels through 19th-century, pre-Freudian eyes; they will then dramatize healthy, romantic, serious female-female friendships which post-Freudian critics are all too ready to castigate as "unhealthy," even "lesbian." Curiously, Faderman praises James for characterizing so complexly that he discourages reductive criticism, and voices annoyance with many recent critics for nonetheless downgrading Olive Chancellor and exalting Basil Ransom; but she then simplistically hints that Verena Tarrant would have matured better with Olive than with Basil. (Sara Davis and Susan Wolstenholme are more careful; see below.)

The most impressive book of 1978 on James is Stephen Donadio's *Nietzsche, Henry James, and the Artistic Will* (Oxford). Aware that philosophy and fiction "sustain . . . and offer . . . criticisms of one another," Donadio juxtaposes aspects of the writings and lives of Nietzsche and James. One was feverish, almost clownish at times; the other, detached, restrained. But they agreed that art keeps the ugliness of truth from killing us, that art muffles actuality's ache; further, the two identically respected the Emersonian concepts of self-reliance and the need to transcend historical cultures to attain inner culture. Donadio begins by showing that James and Nietzsche, not knowing each other but still breathing the same "intellectual air . . . during the closing decades of the nineteenth century," were connected to each other indirectly by Thomas Sergeant Perry, Paul Bourget, Violet Paget, Oscar Wilde, and especially William James. Both Nietzsche and Henry James believed that art's being superior to the limitations of any epoch frees the artist to convert himself into a work of art, to play God. Next, we are shown that James's freeing himself of national limitations parallels Nietzsche's call for *der gute Europäer*: both writers hoped to shop thereby at "a kind of cultural Common Market, a Pan-European confederation whose citizens would be by definition cosmopolitan." Further, the ramifications of James's theory and practice of the restricted point of view relate to Nietzsche's "perspectivism." The chapter called "The Artist of the Real" contains Donadio's most spectacular writing; the critic here relates his two figures' attitudes toward artistic unity, nature, the ability of the writer to redeem life by imaginatively re-presenting it, the agony and joy of creative loneliness, and finally Napoleon. Then Donadio stresses the Emersonian monism fusing diversities—necessity and freedom, victims and victors, the ferocious and the lassoed, Caesar and Christ, strong man and saint, nightmare and counter-attack, real island marooning each of us and our common continent of wit and hope, two-sided coin. Donadio commands an austere style, syntactically complex like James's. This book has an original concept and is stunningly executed.

Evelyn A. Hovanec's *Henry James and Germany* (Rodopi) is a

thorough treatment of the slight subject of James's views on "Germany, Germans, and things German." Hovanec discusses James's time spent in Germany, his nonfictional comments on aspects of the German people and their accomplishments, and his frequent use of Germans and things German in his fiction; then she offers reasons for his pervasive "feelings of discomfort and antipathy with reference to Germany." This final section is the most valuable. James found Germany too much like America; he recalled his student days in Germany and Switzerland with distaste; he preferred French, Russian, English, and American literature, and Italian and Dutch painting, to German literature and art—and perhaps Henry's immemorial rival William James respected the Germans too much.

Leon Edel's "Portrait of the Artist as an Old Man" (*ASch* 47:52–68) is on aging. It compares Leo Tolstoy, Henry James, and William Butler Yeats; and discusses James with respect to family, sexuality, life and art, personal crises leading to "private successes and public failures," facing the truth, supposed freedom, "living . . . by imagination," loneliness, nostalgia, sensitive stoicism, and abiding faith in art.

John Snyder, in "James's Girl Huck: What Maisie Knew" (*ALR* 11:109–23) begins by laying out this tidy blueprint: "Where Twain and James come together . . . is in their romantic commitment to the vision of their young protagonists' triumph over circumstance, Maisie's and Huck's freedom to expand beyond the confines of convention, to create on their own new values which are as humane and lovely as the older generation's are selfish and crude." Snyder stresses Maisie, with only occasional asides to Huck Finn and his " 'open-air' ethics."

William R. Goetz, in "The Allegory of Representation in *The Tragic Muse*" (*JNT* 8:151–64), briefly discusses Stéphane Mallarmé's "Crayonne au théâtre" (1887) as "a parallel to James's description of Miriam [Rooth, of *The Tragic Muse*]." (For fuller discussion of Goetz's article, see below.)

In "The Esthetics of Perversion: Gothic Artifice in Henry James and Witold Gombrowicz" (*PMLA* 93:992–1002), Patricia Merivale sees James's "Turn of the Screw" and *Sacred Fount* and Gombrowicz's *Pornografia* (1960) and *Cosmos* (1965) as similar through being not only "Gothic artist parables" but also fictions in which their central characters immorally manipulate others. Merivale adduces no evidence of influence by James "the uneasy realist" on Gombrowicz "the zestful artificer," and even finds James's two samples "double-plotted" whereas *Pornografia* is "hyperplotted" and *Cosmos* "underplotted." But *The Sacred Fount* and *Cosmos* are both "intriguing, thorny, valuable works in which the novelists explore by way of epistomological uncertainty and moral unease the perils, folly, and perverseness of their craft," whereas the other two works concern evil and eroticism, and are technically more satisfying.

iii. Criticism: General

With successful single-mindedness Daniel J. Schneider, in *The Crystal Cage: Adventures of the Imagination in the Fiction of Henry James* (Lawrence: Regents Press of Kansas), offers the thesis that James is overwhelmingly concerned with dramatizing the struggle of various types of free spirits to avoid or to escape captivity. James sees life as a trap. Further, he sees the purpose of the free spirit to be the attempt to avoid that trap. Schneider is original, captivating, and sound in his review of James's main works of fiction. He relates biographical and autobiographical material to his central discussion; in addition, he integrates his thesis with much of James's literary criticism of other authors.

Henry Nash Smith's *Democracy and the Novel* deserves brief mention here for its bearing on James. At the outset Smith confesses that he was "long . . . fascinated by the solidity, the durability, the imperviousness of the secular faith or ideology lying at the base of American popular culture. . . ." His *Democracy and the Novel* then evolved from his "gradual realization that each of the major novelists examined here [including James] came into collision with it." Smith analyzes James's ironic response to "lowbrow" fiction, his criticism of personalities formed by a taste for "middlebrow" literature, and his difficulties in locating and reaching an audience which would pay.

Paul B. Armstrong's "Knowing in James: A Phenomenological View" (*Novel* 12:5-20) would appear to be a trial balloon, the published beginning of a future book on James and phenomenology. It is known that William James was "a pioneering precursor of phenomenology"; Armstrong is asking "whether similar ties might join Henry's achievement to the world of [Edmund] Husserl and his followers—or whether, in particular, this novelist's notion of the 'impression' and phenomenological theories of consciousness might prove mutually illuminating." For James, the novel is an impression of life. The impression is miraculously revealing, has a "teleological impulse," and leads to "a leap of faith." The impression-seeking consciousness is best when aggressive. People's impressions differ because of differing temperaments and sometimes should not be "trust[ed] uncritically." Armstrong relies heavily on James's "Art of Fiction."

"Henry James and the Idea of Race" (*ES* 59:35–47) by Elsa Nettels is complex and valuable. It discusses James's acceptance and use of racial (i.e., nationalistic) stereotyping; both his admiration of Hyppolyte Taine and his sporadic use of some of Taine's ideas on "distinctive heredity [i.e., racial] traits"; and James's simultaneous hope for the interracial "collaboration of gifted spirits" and fear of "the chaotic mingling" of races (as in New York City) with the effect of "the obliteration of traditional [national] distinction." Nettels treats the following Jamesian characters well: Lady Barbarina ("Lady Barbarina"), Count Valerio ("The Last of the Valerii"), Hyacinth Robinson (*The Princess Casamassima*), and Prince Amerigo (*The Golden Bowl*), as well as several Americans generously "seek[ing] to form themselves through new [international] associations."

A. R. Tintner's essay "The Books in the Book: What Henry James' Characters Read and Why" (*AB Bookman's Weekly*, 15 May:3468, 3470,3472,3474,3476–94) proves that James was bookish, that his fictional characters read books—often those which James read or wrote, but sometimes books he invented—and that he described his characters as resembling other fictional characters. Tintner's "Henry James and Fine Books" (ibid., 3 April:2406,2408–10) discusses James's knowledge of bookbinders and fine bindings, and how the novelist related both to Hyacinth Robinson (*The Princess Casamassima*) and Nanda Brookenham (*The Awkward Age*).

"Henry James and the Art of Biography" by Elsa Nettels (*SAB* 43:107–24) concerns James's theory and practice of the art of biography. Many of his more than 150 reviews present biographical sketches rather than mere reviews; thus, they often also explain facts, historical ambiance, and authorial method. His *Hawthorne* and *William Wetmore Story* demonstrate his Sainte-Beuve impartiality, pro-Taine tenets, and high critical seriousness. Hawthorne transmuted and transcended his heritage, whereas Story was too scattered to be worthy of his adopted Italy and of his friends. James opted for truth in biography, but truth with discriminating generosity, never with cruelty.

The best work of the year on the theory behind James's fictional practice is Sergio Perosa's *Henry James and the Experimental Novel* (Virginia). Perosa is better at telling how James is "a father of modernism" than at explicating specific examples of his modernism, although Perosa does both well. He starts slowly (with the three massive novels of the later 1880s, plus *The Reverberator*) but soon gains momentum, especially after he gets both James's *Sacred Fount* and his curious part in *The Whole Family* out of the way. Perosa is at his best once he arrives at the novels providing him his supreme challenge: *The Sense of the Past* and *The Ivory Tower*. He combines previous scholarship with insights of his own. His book is in two parts. In part 1 Perosa deals with experimental themes, experimental techniques, and then *The Sacred Fount* (suggesting that in it James with "mastery and assurance . . . put forward the highest and most consistent plea for fiction as 'rival creation,' for the novel as providing an autonomous world of its own that is almost opposed to the actual world"). Part 2 begins almost hopelessly with *The Whole Family* but concludes with a pair of sustained critical crescendoes, first on *The Sense of the Past* and then on *The Ivory Tower*. We have in the former a vast binary system involving England and America, Ralph Pendrel and Aurora Coyne, past and present—all in a tension only increased by the international-ghost theme. As for the latter novel, Perosa writes that "Here we see how his [James's] abstract fictional worlds and ways were consciously conceived and nourished, tested and projected, realized and . . . canceled in the process. There is no better place to study his stretching of the possibilities of the novel to their breaking point, while always stopping short of the actual break. Going from the Notes to the completed books (and vice versa) is a perfect exercise in fictional hermeneutics. The Notes are there to support and at the same time to *deny* the novel. They provide the scaffolding, the characters and the plot, the time and space relationships, the moral bearing and the thematic links, the development and the purport of the subject." It is both tragic and apt that James died before completing *The Ivory Tower*. Had he lived, the novel would have been technically and thematically awesome.

But James in dying passed the baton to such modernist continuators as Joyce, Mondrian, Beckett, Gass, Proust, Mann, and Woolf. Perosa's book is grandly designed and executed.

In *Eve and Henry James: Portraits of Women and Girls in His Fiction* (Oklahoma), Edward Wagenknecht analyzes Daisy Miller (of "Daisy Miller"), Euphemia de Mauves ("Madame de Mauves"), Isabel Archer (*The Portrait of a Lady*), Christina Light (*Roderick Hudson* and *The Princess Casamassima*), Miriam Rooth (*The Tragic Muse*), Fleda Vetch (*The Spoils of Poynton*), Maisie Farange (*What Maisie Knew*), Nanda Brookenham (*The Awkward Age*), Milly Theale and Kate Croy (*The Wings of the Dove*), Maggie Verver and Charlotte Stant (*The Golden Bowl*), George Stransom's friend ("The Altar of the Dead"), May Bartram ("The Beast in the Jungle"), and Alice Staverton ("The Jolly Corner"). Wagenknecht threads his way through previous pertinent criticism, agreeable to him and otherwise, to pick up support for his insights. He seems more temperate than usual in this sparkling study of selected Jamesian females, since he commends other scholars quite gracefully, although, as usual, he can be counted upon to lambaste the offbeat and the irresponsible. Part of his technique is to favor the reader with his usual serpentine informational footnotes. In a typical chapter Wagenknecht considers James's sources (both personal and literary), his mode of composition, popular and critical responses to the work, and then Wagenknecht's own interpretations; occasionally, the critic also compares the given heroine and other women, both in James and elsewhere. Wagenknecht says little new about Daisy or Euphemia, not very much about Isabel, Nanda, Milly, Charlotte, or May, but plenty about the others. His successive chapters on Christina, Miriam, Fleda, and Maisie are steadily illuminating. He relates Christina to the seven major figures around her, praises Miriam for her admirable but often hidden traits, explains Fleda's relationship to Mrs. Gereth, and is tender in treating Maisie. He suggests that James's women are individualistic, self-sacrificial, scheming, and sometimes naive. His choices among James's gallery of females is arbitrary, and one wonders why certain others were omitted. Wagenknecht's best attributes are his comprehensive recall of pertinent nuances from the fiction, his unflickering sagacity, and his urbane lucidity.

Compared to Wagenknecht, Mary Doyle Springer in *A Rhetoric of Literary Character: Some Women of Henry James* (Chicago) writes more on fewer characters, and adverts to fewer other critics. Wagenknecht's book and Springer's overlap on two characters—Euphemia de Mauves and Alice Staverton—but not interestingly. Springer writes the sort of criticism that James would have approved of: it is gracious, discriminating, subtle, and verbose. Her book is too long, but every sentence is written with clarity and devotion. She theorizes on a variety of female characters in James and how he designs them to function in their aesthetic wholes. Springer finds Kate Cookham ("The Bench of Desolation") to be an example of a suppressed character, one about whom James's narrator shows us Herbert Dodd, "hero" of the story, to be mistaken; and yet Dodd is not weak or clownish. Kate is suppressed because we initially misread her, and we do so because of James's deliberate presentation of sad Dodd's misperceptions of her. Aunt Penniman (*Washington Square*) and Flora ("The Turn of the Screw") are singled out as " 'extra' characters," who through James's handling become essential to their fictions; the woman becomes the fourth side of a triangle converted into a square, while the "baby girl" is passive, reacts normally, is there to tell off the governess, and escapes but not to cause more evil later. Alice Staverton is a frame character, appearing in "The Jolly Corner" only early and late, does not oppose Spencer Brydon openly, but lets him learn for himself that the ghost or apparition is a here-and-now, submerged element from within himself. The weakest chapter of Springer's generally magnificent study deals with the technique of characters in apologue, "which [we read] aims at the fullest realization of character and dramatization short of obscuring the dominant emphasis of the work." Springer's women here include the Countess and Scholastica, from James's "Benvolio." Springer tries hard to rescue the chapter by nicely discussing the barbaric titular heroine of "Lady Barbarina" as apologically subordinated to the message that international marriages pitting aristocracy of wealth against that of blood were not consummations whose happy time had come in James's epoch. "Discovering the Main Character" would be a more fascinating chapter but for the pedestrian choices of illustrative characters. Springer does better when she discusses James's strategies in slowly unrolling evidence of characters so that the reader can see it "accumulate," whether those characters change during this emergent process or are fixed; here she also discusses characters in antithesis and in apposition.

Her final chapter relates the rhetoric of character to real life; she defends James's preference for art over "the real thing," discusses the preponderance of feeding and sleeping in real life, and their proper downplay in fiction, and praises James for his coherent fictive wholes. Springer is to be praised for her unfailing enthusiasm, suavity of tone, sweetness of temper, and professional generosity.

Christine M. Roman, in "Henry James and the Surrogate Mother" (*ATQ* 38:193–205), begins with the valid assumption that contact with the biological mother is so important that, if denied it, a young woman will habitually seek a substitute mother. Such surrogates, though rare "in the mainstream of literature," appear often in James's early fiction, but with this twist: Jamesian surrogates see the consequences of motherlessness in the lives of characters like Daisy Miller ("Daisy Miller"), Fleda Vetch (*The Spoils of Poynton*), Catherine Sloper (*Washington Square*), and Tina Bordereau ("The Aspern Papers"), and take on "the self-appointed role of guide." More dramatically, several characters in *The Portrait of a Lady* offer themselves as substitute mothers for Isabel Archer, who seems independent but accepts guidance from others. She learns from them and thus fits herself to be a maternal guide to Pansy Osmond.

Brian Lee's *Novels of Henry James: A Study of Culture and Consciousness* (St. Martin's) is an exasperating little book, which is both too short and tedious. Its thesis is this: James's pertinent long fiction dramatizes the truism that from 1865 to 1910 or so the American moral consciousness, both at home and abroad, changed from Adamic to acquisitive and pessimistic. Lee finds his evidence in 16 of James's novels. He discusses *The Europeans, The Portrait of a Lady, The Spoils of Poynton,* and *The Ivory Tower* best; the others, less effectively. In spite of his title, Lee sandwiches a discussion of *The Tragic Muse* between parts of a chapter on four short stories which he says "show James singlemindedly struggling with the problems of art and moral action at a time when most of his contemporaries were taking aestheticism to its logical extremes." As final annoyances, this book is weirdly punctuated, capriciously documented, and badly proofread.

Marianna Torgovnick, in "James's Sense of an Ending: The Role Played in Its Development by the Popular Conventional Epilogue" (*SNNTS* 10:183–98), separates traditional novelistic epilogues into the philosophic, the parodic, and the popularly conventional; then

she "examine[s] the role James's *notions* of the epilogue play in the
development of his own fictional endings." James resented the popular conventional epilogue and therefore evolved as its replacement
"the scenic ending, bare of authorial commentary, focused intently
on the final conversation of two protagonists, and rich in formal connections to the body of the novel." Yet, interestingly, this evolution
"work[ed] through the popular conventional epilogue which he despised." Torgovnick presents much evidence to support her ideas.

In "Henry James and the Art of Illustration" (*CentR* 27:77–94),
Ralph F. Bogardus explains James's ambiguous attitudes toward the
art of illustration. James long delighted in illustrations of the works
of Charles Dickens, among others, and he admired examples of the
art, particularly when satirical, as practiced by George Du Maurier
and Honoré Daumier; but he also felt that fiction should stand on
its own feet, without pictorial support. Bogardus draws his evidence
mainly from James's *Picture and Text* and "Real Thing."

iv. Criticism: Individual Novels

A bandwagon misreading of *Roderick Hudson* is that of Robert K.
Martin, who in "The 'High Fidelity' of Comradeship: A New Reading of *Roderick Hudson*" (*ALR* 11:100–108) sees the novel as the
narrative of Rowland Mallet's unrequited homosexual passion for
Roderick. (It is revealing that Martin finds literary analogues in "the
inner, secret love story of Nick and Gatsby" in *The Great Gatsby*,
and in Miles Coverdale's "unconvincing" terminal revelation of his
love for Priscilla in *The Blithedale Romance*.)

J. W. Tuttleton's "Propriety and Fine Perceptions: James's 'The
Europeans'" (*MLR* 73:481–95) is as fine an essay as has ever been
published on James's fictional follow-up of the controversy caused
by his *American*, "Daisy Miller," and "International Episode." Hurt
by what he called the "imperfect reciprocity" shown by Europeans
to Americans abroad, James still was alarmed by criticism of his provocative fiction, since he wanted both European and American sales.
So in *The Europeans* he distances a safer contrast between cultural
thinness and richness, inhibitions and spontaneity, the view of life
as duty and the view of life as opportunity, by contrasting European-
ized Americans Eugenia Münster and Felix Young in Boston and
nearby. The two are nonnational and hence seem "romantic," and

differ in ambition, sincerity of manners, and generosity of spirit. Jane Missner Barstow begins her "Originality and Conventionality in *The Princess Casamassima*" (*Genre* 11:445–58) in discontent with previous critics, who "explain away the strangeness [of Hyacinth as victim, and of relationships between characters] as part of a central conflict between politics and culture." So she theorizes that the novel "continually deconstructs the dichotomies and polarities it presents." Barstow then explicates the statement in the novel that Hyacinth "had been provided with the best opportunities for choosing between the beauty of the original and the beauty of the conventional." Conventional Millicent Henning is at odds with the beautiful Princess, and most characters clash "with the conventions of the[ir] social classes." Much that is either conventional or original in the characters not only can be interpreted two ways but also can become objects of "competition over mimicry." By processes of acting, which "is the place where originality and conventionality come together," the central characters tie the two modes of life together but also ravel both and each of them. This essay is too original for me to follow, perhaps because its jargony terminology is, alas, too conventional now.

We have two fine essays on *The Bostonians*. Susan Wolstenholme's "Possession and Personality: Spiritualism in *The Bostonians*" (*AL* 49:580–91) argues forthrightly that Verena Tarrant first is spiritually, psychically, and materially possessed by her father Selah, then is psychologically possessed by Olive Chancellor, and finally is to be personally and sexually possessed by unprincely Basil Ransom. Each of these three possessors lacks a voice and therefore converts Verena into his or her voice: ". . . she herself has no will and can decide nothing without the inspiration of one of her guiding spirits." It is her past which evokes "her three successive possessing spirits": her father was a domineering radical; Olive replaces him but only encourages the girl to give vent to more radicalism; then Basil acts as a new aggressive paternal figure to Verena, fated to become as muffled and submissive in marriage as her own "lost soul" of a mother has been. Sara DeSaussure Davis also dislikes Basil. In her essay "*The Bostonians* Reconsidered" (*TSE* 23:39–60), she offers a persuasive argument, first, in derogation of him as a pseudo-chivalric, hypocritical, tyrannical, and brutal man; and, second, in partial defense of Olive, who—when compared to Basil, anyway—

is relatively considerate, honest with herself, and just. Running through or near these critical corrections Davis has a less fully argued line to the effect that "the story of Verena seems almost an allegory of post-war feminism." William R. Goetz tries in "The Allegory of Representation in *The Tragic Muse*" (*JNT* 8:151–64) to rescue *The Tragic Muse* from its current disrepute by "recognizing that the novel is *about* representation, that representation is not so much its own (missing) mode as its primary subject-matter." Goetz documents the skill with which James expands on the word "representation" in its political, pictorial, and dramatic senses, and how he uses such words and phrases as "stands for," "reproduction," "present" (verb), "show," "exhibition," "figuration," and their variants. Goetz notes that *The Tragic Muse* is aptly a transitional work between James's earlier "pictorial phase" and his later " 'dramatic' nineties."

Two splendid critical essays concern *What Maisie Knew*. Paul B. Armstrong's "How Maisie Knows: The Phenomenology of James's Moral Vision" (*TSLL* 20:517–37) urges that Maisie's story combines epistemology and moral drama, probes "freedom, limitation, and our relations with others" more than it does any "issue of ethical norms," asks *how* not *what* the girl can know, and then asks how her initiation into the process of knowing relates to liberty and interpersonalism. Often citing the text, Armstrong concludes that "Maisie's triumph is both epistemological and existential in an inextricable unity." Jean Frantz Blackall's "Moral Geography in *What Maisie Knew*" (*UTQ* 48:130–48) plumps for the majority critical view, that Maisie "escape[s] untainted" from experiences which a few critics see as ruinously corrupting. Blackall regards the girl as achieving "a fusion of moral and aesthetic impulses." As for the tone of the novel, Blackall here "affirms a middle view [between seeing the work as evoking Dickensian laughter and as filled with Jacobean horror]. Because Maisie's perspective matures, the nature of the reader's response shifts gradually from a qualified laughter, dependent on her naivety, towards compassion and respect, consequent upon her growing spiritual autonomy."

Joanna A. Higgins, in "The Ambassadorial Motif in *The Ambassadors*" (*JNT* 8:165–75), sees Lambert Strether's renunciation of Maria Gostrey as "thematically and formally necessary," given the context of "an ambassadorial motif in the novel." This motif is stressed by incidents in which characters use ambassador-like go-betweens, and also by the hero's gradually learning as ambassadors do to mistrust "all appearances, including the illusion of freedom." A more complex and successful reading is "James and Emerson: The Ethical Context of *The Ambassadors*" (*SNNTS* 10:431–46), by David Robinson. This painstaking essay shows the relationship between Emerson's theory concerning the interconnection of the artistic life and the moral life, on the one hand, and—on the other—Strether's changing friendships with Mrs. Newsome, Madame de Vionnet, and Maria Gostrey, and his concomitant growth through Emersonian "self-culture" and self-reliance to loneliness.

v. Criticism: Individual Tales

Roger Seamon, in "Henry James's 'Four Meetings': A Study in Irritability and Condescension" (*SSF* 15:155–63), examines the bases for reading the story as neither moral fable nor melodrama but as realistic fiction. In the opening paragraph of the story, the narrator is thus seen as mixing "condescension and indignation." Why? The word left blank may mean that he does not really know; but we learn that the narrator resists Caroline Spencer's sequence of implicit demands both by judging the woman unworthy and by anger not only at her but also at himself. At the last meeting he permits "politeness, alienation and safety [to] win out over candor, intimacy and risk" —all allegedly in the name of good breeding.

"Lady into Horse: James's 'Lady Barberina' and *Gulliver's Travels*, Part IV" (*JNT* 8:79–96) by A. R. Tintner is a four-part essay on a neglected story. In the first part Tintner argues that James here uses "the metaphor of horse trading . . . to analogize the Anglo-American marriage market." She provides an amusing plot summary and theme analysis, highlighting James's equine puns, showing how the heroine is less human than splendid animal, and concluding that the society in which aristocratic daughters are dickered for suffers "consequent dehumanization." The second and fourth parts of Tintner's essay suggest that "James was using [Jonathan] Swift's tale [of the Houyhnhnms] as a model or parallel," then that James's 1884 tale influenced Oscar Wilde's "Canterville Ghost" (1887). The third part of the essay reinforces the first by providing a biographical basis for James's wanting to satirize England's horsy set.

"In Fairness to the Master's Wife: A Re-Interpretation of 'The Lesson of the Master'" (*SSF* 15:385–89) is a rigorous reading by Peter Barry, who sees Paul Overt as misunderstanding the lesson of the master Henry St. George. Overt thinks that it is a warning against marriage, but in reality it is more likely to be simply a warning against indolence. Later, young Overt, after accepting the master's praise of the deceased Mrs. St. George as sincere, freely decides to remain single in spite of recognizing that the master has thus retracted his "warning against marriage." Thus both writers are self-reliant; further, "we are given no guarantee that the [again] married and vigorous St. George will not produce good work, or that the celibate Overt will."

David Eggenschwiler's essay "James's 'The Pupil': A Moral Tale without a Moral" (*SSF* 15:435–44) is an almost precious reading, which suggests that James asks us to shift back and forth from sympathy to detachment as we morally assess Pemberton. Like ourselves, Pemberton alternately is charmed by and clinically evaluates Morgan Moreen. Later Pemberton, unlike the wiser reader, worries about difficulties which he has partly created. When poverty and sickness intrude, Pemberton becomes condescending, starts a contest with Morgan's mother for the boy's affection, and thus hastens the castastrophe. We would condemn Pemberton more except that "often he has responded as we have" in the face of moral, tragic-ironic drama.

Pauline Lester, in "James's Use of Comedy in 'The Real Thing'" (*SSF* 15:33–38), sees the story as partly a comic one, which makes the reader laugh at times but which also deals with serious issues and has a sober ending. The narrator is comically impecunious and hence deferential to the Monarchs, whom he amusingly resembles somewhat. They become his upper-handed employees. He feels inferior, even filial, before the bigger Monarch. So he "tries to exorcise them [both] with childish malice," although he remains reluctant "to grow up by sacking [them]." Further, Oronte is a Roman-comic figure.

Next, "The Turn of the Screw," which never stops generating critical essays, produced a few more in 1978. Barbara Bengels's "The Term of the 'Screw': Key to Imagery in Henry James's *The Turn of the Screw*" (*SSF* 15:323–27) relentlessly pursues the thesis that "in the word *screw* James virtually reveals [*sic*] every twist of the novella." The word relates to the pressure the governess puts on Mrs. Grose, Flora, and Miles in turn; jailer figures (the governess and also Peter Quint); a propellor of figurative boats in the story; teacher implications; a person "with a screw loose"; sexual activity; and finally the governess's squeezing of Miles at the climax. Susan Clark's iffy essay "A Note on *The Turn of the Screw*: Death from Natural Causes" (*SSF* 15:110–12) suggests that Miles may have had a heart murmur and was therefore sent home from school; further, that his uncle was discreetly informed but neglected (perhaps deliberately, through boredom and practicality) to tell the governess. If so, perhaps Miles later confesses to saying nasty things at school because he feels he has to admit something "bad" to the governess, who then embraces him into "precocious cardiac arrest." Jane Nardin's splendid essay "*The Turn of the Screw*: The Victorian Background" (*Mosaic* 12:131–42) "argue[s] that *The Turn of the Screw* can be read as a tale which exposes the cruel and destructive pressures of Victorian society, with its restrictive code of sexual morality and its strong sense of class consciousness, upon a group of basically sane and decent individuals." Thus, "society . . . [becomes] the demon of the piece." Nardin asks that we make certain assumptions concerning Douglas, the governess's earlier life, Miles's conduct at school, and so on; then she shows how rigidities of the Victorian social hierarchy hurt incipient love relationships between Douglas and the governess, Peter Quint and Miss Jessel, and the governess and her employer; and how everything is spoiled because of "conventional ideas about 'proper' marriages." Mrs. Grose judges Quint and Miss Jessel meanly, and issues "dark hints" about them. They might have been the subject of innocent comments by Miles at school. But he and Flora might have become "emotional substitutes for the legitimate family they [Quint and Miss Jessel] would never have." So the morally rigid governess, who is not unbalanced, sees ghosts anyway because they "are the logical offspring of . . . [her] attempts to understand a complex human situation in terms of a cultural tradition incapable of yielding real insight." And in "The Unfixable Text: Bewilderment of Vision in *The Turn of the Screw*" (*TSLL* 20:538–51), Kevin Murphy, following a trend now, sees James employing "strategies . . . to *prevent* a consistent reading of the text." Murphy examines doubling techniques and effects, which through "duplicitous replication" create an "ultimate opacity."

Finally, Michael P. Peinovich and Richard F. Pattison, in "The Cognitive Beast in the Syntactic Jungle: A Study of James's Language" (Lang&S 11:82–93), build on the work of Ian Watt, Seymour Chatman, and Michael Schreiber, to treat James's cognitive apparatus most illuminatingly. The upshot is that James in "The Beast in the Jungle" merits praise for making syntax reinforce theme. What seems important, grammatically and thematically, isn't; what ought to be active and singular, as well, isn't either; grammatical elements get shunted and buried, as do John Marcher (and his ideas) and May Bartram. James "passivize[s]" not only forms of the verb "is" but also therefore the subjects thereof. He frequently uses "recipient" rather than "performant" precognitive and cognitive verbs in his tale, to underscore Marcher's passivity; and he seldom uses "know" plus propositional clause, which infrequency stresses his hero's inconclusiveness.

University of Pittsburgh

8. Pound and Eliot

George Bornstein and Stuart Y. McDougal

i. Pound

The period when Pound studies fit Pound's own view of Browning's *Sordello* as "a rag-bag to stuff all its thoughts in" appears to have ended. New work recognizably continues the main trends noted last year. First, the relation between the life and work continues strong, this year focusing particularly on the period from World War II onwards. Secondly, comparative studies again attract much of the major effort, this time with Provence and de Gourmont in the fore. And finally, *The Cantos* rightly continues preeminent in studies of individual works. A writer as encyclopaedic as Pound will always generate diverse studies, but centers of common concern seem to have emerged.

a. **Texts and Biography.** Textual and biographical contributions relate so closely this year that they warrant being considered together. The two chief items concern both the Fascist years and their aftermath. The more important is Leonard W. Doob's edition of *"Ezra Pound Speaking": Radio Speeches of World War II* (Greenwood), which supersedes the few scattered texts printed elsewhere. It includes all 105 available manuscripts for the broadcasts recorded by the FCC during the period 1941–43, along with 5 others available only from the FCC's own transcripts and 10 earlier scripts selected by Mary de Rachewiltz. Appendices offer a quantitative tabulation of recurrent themes, statistics on aspects of the broadcasts cited by Pound critics, and rudimentary remarks on style and technique; a glossary and index of names concludes the volume. For those of us who know and love Pound at his best, this record of him

George Bornstein has contributed the section on Pound and Stuart Y. McDougal the section on Eliot.—*J.A.R.*

at his worst will shock and dismay, yet must be faced. By turns coy and vicious, learned and gullible, coherent and chaotic, these broadcasts make clear Pound's antisemitism, support of Fascist regimes, and hopes for America to leave or to lose the war. Among other things, he thought both the war itself and Russian communism to be Jewish conspiracies, admired Hitler and Mussolini, fomented racism, urged American soldiers to return home, and hoped that Roosevelt ("Rosenfeld") could be legally hanged. Readers unable to make their way through the entire volume will gather the gist of Pound's performance by scanning the 16th broadcast (15 March 1942). The venom betrays on every page the principles of clear thought and accurate perception fundamental to Pound's best art and debases thinkers such as Confucius, whom Pound elsewhere put to better use. Rather than continuing to overreact to postwar controversies like the Bollingen by excusing, understating, or distorting Pound's descent into Fascist hatreds, Pound scholars must honestly confront the roots of his decline even in his great early period and the results of his passage through hell during his later recovery. William Chace's *The Political Identities of Ezra Pound and T. S. Eliot* offered us a start in that direction a few years ago.

Pound's own later remorse comes across clearly in the long "Fragments of Ezra Pound" section of Donald Hall's *Remembering Poets*. Largely an account of Hall's 1960 meetings with Pound in Rome for the celebrated *Paris Review* interview, *Remembering Poets* movingly portrays the aged Pound wavering between energy and exhaustion, resolve and remorse. "You have driven—all the way—from England—to find a man—who is only fragments," Pound told his startled interviewer. For the next few days Pound's conversation alternated between his wartime activities and his desire to continue work on *The Cantos*, seeking absolution for one and confidence for the other from the surprised young poet who had come to interview him. Hall indicates that the published version of his influential interview "contains no words that Pound did not speak (or write) and no ideas or implications that he did not, I'm sure, intend; neither does it correctly represent, for any stretch longer than two inches of text, the dialogue that took place on the Via Angelo Poliziano." Records of briefer glimpses of Pound by Virgil Geddes in 1924 and John P. Sullivan in 1960 appear in *Paideuma* 7:281–86; David Gordon's "Zuk and Ez at St. Liz" is the most pertinent piece in the special Zukofsky memorial number of that journal (7:581–84). Snippets from two unpublished letters praising the section on Greek metric in Albert Lavignac's *Encyclopédie de la musique* accompany Mary Bernard's "A Communication on Greek Metric, Ezra Pound, and Sappho" (*Agenda* 16:62–68).

Two other items demand mention. The "Catalogue of the Pound Exhibition" at Sheffield University includes useful textual notes and establishes a definitive chronology for the Pounds' trip to France in 1919. It is conveniently reprinted at the end of *Ezra Pound: The London Years, 1908–1920*, edited by Philip Grover (AMS); the six essays in that volume (five of them originally read at the Pound Conference at Sheffield in 1976) will be discussed where relevant below. Peter Schneeman's "Pound's 'Englischer Brief': A Look Toward Germany" (*Paideuma* 7:309–16) introduces a previously unknown little article by Pound giving his views on worthwhile recent English literature for the short-lived German journal *Europa Almanach* in 1925; the text is the only known instance of Pound's composing in German for publication. Although Schneeman states at the outset that the German text "is reprinted here, with a translation," his article inexplicably includes only the translation. Further, the letter appears to be identical with the "Lettre Anglaise" published by Pound in André Breton's *Littérature* in 1920, reproduced as appendix 6 in Andrew Clearfield's article in the same number of *Paideuma*, discussed below. The relation of these two texts clearly needs further study.

b. General Studies. The few general studies this year emphasize the early Pound. Three appear conveniently together in Grover's *Ezra Pound: The London Years.* In "Modernists and Edwardians" (pp. 1–14) Eric Homberger argues against the pervasive view of Edwardian culture as hostile to modernism and instead notes "signs of evolution and continuity," especially in regard to widespread French influence. He concludes his survey by observing that "it was the discovery of modernity *within* Edwardian culture itself which seems such a remarkable phenomenon: Pound and Eliot were distinctly part of that culture, they were themselves Edwardians." William Pratt's "Ezra Pound and the Image" (pp. 15–30) adds to his earlier Imagist studies the important suggestion that Imagism represents a displacement of religious patterns or symbols onto secular literature. Although Pratt does not say so, that transference accords with a pervasive characteristic of post-Romantic literature as postulated by M. H. Abrams in *Natural Supernaturalism* (1971). Pratt is less successful in trying to establish Imagist principles as a credo of modernism in general, however; few readers will agree that "*Ulysses, Mrs. Dalloway, The Sound and the Fury* . . . are in essence extended Imagist poems" (p. 27). Donald Monk's uneven "How to Misread: Pound's Use of Translation" (pp. 61–88) includes the interesting claim that Pound's division of poetry into melopoeia, phanopoeia, and logopoeia corresponds to the order of his successive involvements as translator of Provençal, Chinese, and Latin verse. Monk offers worthwhile incidental remarks on the Bertrans de Born poems, *Cathay* and *Propertius*.

Donald Davie's "Ezra Pound and the English" (*Paideuma* 7: 297–307) nicely complements Homberger's essay. Davie contrasts Pound's literary professionalism with the English taste for cultivated amateurism, which he sees as an insular debasement of the Renaissance ideal of the cultivated courtier. He marshalls remarks by Phyllis Bottome, Max Beerbohm, W. H. Auden, and others, and instructively compares Pound's intransigence to Eliot's more subdued infiltration of the London milieu. Adopting a more American perspective, Bernard Duffey in the few pages on Pound in his *Poetry in America* competently places him within the developing context of modern American verse, with emphasis on Imagism, *Mauberley*, and *The Cantos*. Although Buckminster Fuller's "Pound, Synergy, and the Great Design" (*Agenda* 16:130–64) expounds its author's own ideas with only incidental reference to Pound, the congruences first noted by Hugh Kenner remain of interest.

c. **Relation to Other Writers.** Two books and several articles dwelled upon Pound's relation to other writers. The best of them, Richard Sieburth's fine *Instigations: Ezra Pound and Remy de Gourmont* (Harvard), aims "to elicit affinities rather than stress debts, for Gourmont did not influence Pound in the usual sense of the term: he provided, both by his personal example and his works, something far more important—a range of instigations, a series of incitements to experiment and discovery." Rather than falling into the traps of license inherent in such an approach, Sieburth has instead limned the impact of Gourmont's principal works on the broad contexts of Pound's interests. In Gourmont's overtly symbolist verse *Litanies,* Pound responded particularly to elements of rhythm and naming which he could exploit for very different Imagist purposes. From *The Latin Mystique* he took particularly the notion of Goddeschalk's formula "amas ut pulchram facias." In *The Problem of Style* Pound saw an active sense of tradition similar to his own internationalism, while he termed other essays "the best portrait available . . . of the civilized mind from 1885–1915." Gourmont affected Pound's crucial sense of Flaubert and contributed the tool of "dissociation" as a method of distinguishing confused or conflated thoughts. Finally, Pound found Gourmont's *The Natural Philosophy of Love,* which he translated, a validation of his own insights into the struggle between the forces of procreation and those of repression. Occasionally Sieburth collapses the critical distance between himself and Pound too much, and at others he raises issues—e.g., "evaluating Pound's antisemitism"—whose significance he evades; but in general he has made a graceful, concise, and illuminating contribution to Pound studies.

Like Gaul, Peter Makin's *Provence & Pound* (Calif.) is divided into three parts: the first emphasizes Bertrans de Born; the second traces the cultural tradition which Pound detected from William IX of Acquitaine to Dante by way of Queen Eleanor, Bernart de Ventadorn, Arnaut Daniel, and Sordello; the third defends Pound's linkage of Provençal heresy to the cult of Eleusis rather than to Manichaean or Cathar doctrines. For all its learning, the book suffers organizationally from attempts to attract too many audiences. In striving "to present the Provençal culture to those who know Pound, and Pound to those who know Provençal culture; and both, if possible, to those who know neither" Makin oscillates between the recondite and the elementary. Pound scholars may learn rather more than they seek about disputes in current Provençal studies, even while being grateful for some of the information. They will learn rather less about Pound himself, for whom Makin goes over a great deal of well-trod ground before getting to some of his best contributions, such as the discussion of Canto VI (pp. 73–96). Surprisingly in a book with over 100 pages of notes, Makin makes little but querulous use of previous Pound scholarship on Provence (except for that of Hugh Kenner) and instead "takes advantage of the very full discussions of the way Pound used Provençal material in his early

verse and in the metamorphosis-Cantos by ignoring these matters
as far as possible." His related article in *The London Years*, "Pound's
Provence and the Medieval Paideuma: an Essay in Aesthetics" (pp.
31–60), explores Pound's occasional use and ultimate rejection of
much Latin medieval poetry. The remarks on the impact of de
Gourmont's *Latin Mystique* should be read along with Sieburth's
book.

Touched on in passing by both Sieburth and Makin, Pound's
esoteric interests serve as main subject of the featured essays in
Paideuma this year. Most give primary attention to *"The Little
Review* Calendar" constructed by Pound in 1922, which declared
that "The Christian Era came definitely to an END at midnight of
the 29–30 October (1921) old style," proposed a new era "p.s.U."
(post script *Ulysses*), and assigned pagan names to the cycle of
months. Forrest Read finds the calendar and the Seal of the United
States to be twin loci of esoteric Pythagoreanism underlying the
works, especially *The Cantos*, in "The Mathematical Symbolism of
Ezra Pound's Revolutionary Mind" (7:7–72). The thesis of the article (Read mentions two books of elaboration currently seeking
publishers) is provocative but unconvincing, party because, as Read
concedes, Pound "never explicitly disclosed its application"; a long
concluding section usefully calls attention to the illustrated capitals
of the deluxe *XVI Cantos* and the deluxe *Cantos 17–27*. Akiko
Miyake argues more circumspectly from the same document in "The
Greek-Egyptian Mysteries in Pound's 'The Little Review Calendar'
and in Cantos 1–7' (7:73–111). Yet in basing much of her search
for source on Thomas Taylor's *Eleusinian and Bacchic Mysteries*
(first published in 1790), Miyake runs into a problem analogous to
Read's: Pound never mentions Taylor's name. That fact also fails to
deter Carroll F. Terrell in "Mang-Tsze, Thomas Taylor, and Madam
YΛH" (7:141–54), which begins with the reference to Madam YΛH
in Canto XXX. Only Andrew Clearfield's "Pound, Paris, and Dada"
(7:113–40) emphasizes the comic aspect of *"The Little Review*
Calendar," which it describes as a "Dada gesture." Whether mining
the calendar for esoteric exegeses will reveal mysteries or only itself
become a Dada gesture remains to be revealed.

Two studies of Pound's relation to later writers emphasize habits
and theories of language. In his misleadingly titled "Pound's Wordsworth; or Growth of a Poet's Mind" (*ELH* 45:660–86) David Simp-

son helpfully discriminates between Pound's Imagist faith in a "natural language" of poetry adequate to objectivity and Wordsworth's persistent doubts about the capacity of language to embody "things." Simpson's remarks about Pound's language and his relation to the romantics should be supplemented with Herbert N. Schneidau's "Pound and Wordsworth on Poetry and Prose" and George Bornstein's *The Postromantic Consciousness of Ezra Pound,* both discussed in these pages last year. Loy D. Martin's "Pound and Fenollosa: the problem of influence" (*CritQ* 20:48–60) uses syntactic analysis to suggest that Fenollosa's essay influenced Pound little but did provide him with ready ammunition for the literary wars. Martin makes the interesting proposal that Fenollosa's essay has less value as an interpretation of Chinese art than as "a partial analysis of Victorian literary norms."

d. **Studies of Specific Works.** Attention continues to center on *The Cantos,* but studies of a few shorter works may be mentioned at the outset. In "Mauberley's Barrier of Style" (*The London Years,* pp. 89–115) Ian F. A. Bell locates in contemporaneous discussions of science the "extraordinary system of polysyllabic vocabulary" by which Mauberley distances himself from experience. Concentrating on poems II and III of the second sequence, Bell shows how Mauberley never moves beyond the stage of descriptive measurement to that of making conclusions about the measurements. Elsewhere Franz Link offers a Biblical source for the word "passing" in "Gentildonna" and a parallel between Jesus and Dionysus for the honeycomb in "Ballad of the Goodly Fere" in his "Two Notes on the Early Poetry" (*Paideuma* 7:185–86), while Richard Ingber discusses "Ezra Pound's 'Women of Trachis': A Song for the Muses' Garden" (*AmS* 23:131–46). Charles O. Hartman's "Some Notes on Poetic Value" (*ConP* 2[1977]:24–50) compares translations of "The River-Merchant's Wife" by Pound and by Witter Bynner.

The two fine chapters on Pound in M. L. Rosenthal's *Sailing into the Unknown: Yeats, Pound, and Eliot* (Oxford) derive from his pair of articles praised in these pages last year. The second—"Dimensions of Pound: the Structuring of the Cantos"—adds important remarks on the earlier poetry and explores *The Cantos* in additional detail. Rosenthal's entire book deserves reading not only for its individual insights but also for its provocative thesis that balances

of feeling and awareness generate the very structure of modern
poetry.

Equally striking on theme rather than structure, John Lauber's
"Pound's 'Cantos': a Fascist Epic" (*JAmS* 12:3–21) coincides with
publication of the wartime broadcasts. In contrast to attempts to
minimize or to compartmentalize the role of Pound's Fascist beliefs
in the poem, Lauber sees them as fundamental to its ideology. He
delves far beneath the poem's recurrent praise of Mussolini to expose its congruence to the historian Richard Hofstadter's notion of
"the paranoid style in American politics," with emphasis on a vast
conspiracy as the motive force in historical events. Although he
sometimes too easily conflates various sections of the poem and
occasionally proposes parallels not unique to Fascism, Lauber convincingly establishes a Fascist orientation for the middle sections
of the poem and implies its roots in Pound's earlier ideas. The next
question for Pound studies should be a sophisticated inquiry into
what role such concerns play in an aesthetic evaluation of the poem.
No such advances attend Robin Graham's rambling "Will and Sensibility in The Cantos" (*ESA* 21:89–97), which too often exagger-
ates criticism into caricature.

Four articles attend to groups of cantos. The most provocative,
Herbert Schneidau's "Pound's Book of Cross-Cuts" (*Genre* 11:505–
21), first explores "the parallel of [Pound's] thinking to the advances
of the diacritical age" before sketchily surveying the unpublished
drafts of the UrCantos at Yale. In "Ezra Pound and the Words off
the Page: Historical Allusion in Some American Long Poems" (*YES*
8:95–108) Stephen Fender contrasts Whitman's and Crane's use of
accessible public documents to Pound's and Williams's penchant
for more obscure sources; along the way Fender clears up a few
obscurities in the Jefferson Cantos. Fred Moramorco's "The Mal-
atesta Cantos" (*Mosaic* 12:107–18) is a competent introductory
survey with little new for the specialist, while his "Thirty Years with
the Pisan Cantos" (*MPS* 9:1–17) consists mostly of simplified summaries of each canto.

In the most interesting of the articles on individual cantos, "The
Structure of Canto IV" (*The London Years*, pp. 117–37), Walter
Baumann moves through syllabic scansion, vocabulary, syntax, ty-
pography, and theme to arrive at overall structural unity. His re-

marks on accent, syntactic fragments, and the "Actaeon: Vidal" subject rhyme are particularly apt. Scholars have yet to evaluate properly the curious absence of verbs in much of Pound's best verse. *Paideuma* continues its documentary work with long articles by John J. Nolde on "The Sources for Canto LV" (7:189–247) in the Jesuit de Mailla's *Histoire Générale de la Chine*; and by Ben Kimpel and T. C. Duncan Eaves on "The Sources of the Leopoldine Cantos [XLII–XLIV]" (7:249–77) in documents of *Il Monte dei Paschi*. Eva Hesse more briefly identifies So-Shu in Canto II and (more tentatively) the Tree of Visages from Canto IV in "New Light on Old Problems" (7:179–83). Finally, John Driscoll also utilizes de Mailla in "Canto LX and Ezra Pound's Use of 'Histoire Générale de la Chine'" (*SN* 50:215–32). In showing Pound's heavy reliance and occasional oversimplification of his source, Driscoll sometimes speaks more critically about the adaptation than do the contributors to *Paideuma*.

ii. Eliot

Studies of Eliot's work this year center almost exclusively on *The Waste Land* and *Four Quartets*, with nothing of importance on the drama and relatively little on the criticism and minor poetry. Interest in the process of composition remains high, and will no doubt receive further stimulus by the publication of Dame Helen Gardner's fine study of *Four Quartets*. Biographical essays continue to appear, contributing to an increase in Eliot's "visibility."

a. Texts. Dame Helen Gardner's meticulous study of *The Composition of "Four Quartets"* (Oxford) provides the reader with an opportunity to examine the drafts and sources of these poems. Eliot's "intolerable wrestle / With words and meanings" ("East Coker, II") during the years when he was struggling with these poems becomes considerably clarified by Dame Helen's study. Although Eliot's revisions lack the excitement of those of *The Waste Land*, they contribute substantially to our understanding of *Four Quartets*, and in particular "Little Gidding," where the drafts are most extensive. Dame Helen also identifies difficulties with the existing texts and suggests possible emendations.

b. **Biography.** The most interesting biographical essay is Donald Hall's "Notes on T. S. Eliot" in his *Remembering Poets*. Hall writes with humor and sensitivity about his encounters with Eliot, which began while Hall was still an undergraduate at Harvard in 1949 and continued for nearly 15 years. Hall contrasts Eliot at 62, aged, stooped, and imperious, with the remarried Eliot of 70, "debonair, sophisticated, lean, and handsome." In view of this transformation, Hall proceeds with a very tactful speculation on Eliot's early life and first marriage, with which he illuminates Eliot's development as a poet. "When we read his poems," Hall counsels, "we must be conscious that they are 'personal,' as well as historical or doctrinal, or we do not read them."

Eliot's friendship with Stravinsky is the subject of Robert Craft's informative essay, "Stravinsky and Eliot: 'Renard' and 'Old Possum'" (*Encounter* 50:46–51). Although Eliot first publicly noted his admiration for Stravinsky in 1921, he did not meet him until 1956. A friendship between the two men, whose mutual interests ranged from music to detective novels, was quickly formed. They often discussed the possibility of a collaboration, but it was never realized, although Stravinsky based his anthem, *The Dove Descending* (1962), on "Little Gidding." Eliot's much longer friendship with Conrad Aiken, dating from the time they were both undergraduates at Harvard, is examined by Ted R. Spivey in "Aiken's Eliot: Toward a Revision" (*SoQ* 17:29–41). Spivey draws upon his conversations with Aiken from 1965 to 1969, but he fails to add any new material of genuine interest to this subject. Another biographical essay which covers familiar ground is Doris L. Eder's summary of Eliot's life ("The Exile of T. S. Eliot" [*UDQ* 11,iv:95–111]) published last year (1977). H. Bibesco describes his successful efforts to end the pugilistic career of "The Possum" in his amusing "Lunch with T. S. Eliot" (*AtM* Feb:46–49), a companion piece to his "Lunch with Uncle Ez," reviewed last year.

c. **General Studies.** Some of the best discussions of Eliot's poetry this year occur in M. L. Rosenthal's *Sailing into the Unknown: Yeats, Pound, and Eliot* (Oxford). Rosenthal assesses Eliot's poetic achievement by analyzing "Little Gidding," a poem Eliot "inhabits with his mind entire." Rosenthal praises the virtuosity of the first two sections but does not hesitate to criticize "the heavy dose of sheer prosiness [which] constitutes a real barrier in the rest of the poem." In his second, more general chapter on Eliot ("Essences and Open Forms"), Rosenthal shows how Eliot developed the "extended lyric structure in sequence form" by combining fragments written and published at different times. In this way Eliot was able to stretch his "powers of distilled intensity" to longer works. Rosenthal's observations about "the undeveloped potentialities suggested by excised portions of the earlier draft" of *The Waste Land* are particularly provocative. This is a book from which all students of modern poetry can profit.

Two other book-length studies survey Eliot's work from more specialized vantage points. In *Landscape as Symbol in the Poetry of T. S. Eliot* (Miss.), Nancy Duvall Hargrove provides a thorough interpretation of Eliot's poetry on the basis of its symbolic use of setting. Her detailed explications serve largely to confirm what we have already known about Eliot's poetry, and her observations about his use of landscape could have been presented in a briefer format. Hargrove also tends to overvalue works (e.g., "Landscapes") which develop physical settings extensively. The book is illustrated with attractive photographs of the major sites of Eliot's verse which demonstrate the accuracy of his perceptions even if they do not add substantially to our understanding of his poetry.

Ann P. Brady's *Lyricism in the Poetry of T. S. Eliot* (Kennikat) has more modest aims than Hargrove's study, but suffers from some of the same faults. Brady's enthusiasm for lyric poetry causes her to slight Eliot's nonlyric poetry. Lyricism becomes an evaluative criterian, and hence "Marina" receives the highest praise of Eliot's short poems, while *Poems, 1920* is dismissed as "particularly unlyrical." In her examination of the long poems there is virtually no discussion of the poetic relationship between the lyric and nonlyric passages.

Two general essays cover familiar territory without contributing anything significantly new to their subjects. In " 'Intimate and Unidentifiable': The Voices of Fragmented Reality in the Poetry of T. S. Eliot" (*CentR* 22:1–27), Thomas J. Morrisey traces Eliot's "conception of reality" to F. H. Bradley, whose views he summarizes, and then contends that Eliot "never fully abandoned his early beliefs in the fragmentary nature of human experience or in the deficiencies of language as a means of expressing experience." Alan

Weinblatt considers Eliot's "anguished struggle . . . to hold at bay the overwhelming tide of the past" in "T. S. Eliot and the Historical Sense" (*SAQ* 77:282–95). Weinblatt postulates Eliot's creation of a "poetics of feeling" in his later critical writings. "But," he notes, "even while practicing it, Eliot was convinced that a poetics of feeling was certain proof of a twilight age in poetry, an age doomed to impotence and insignificance, and to counter this flood of gloom he evolved not simply a poetics of neoclassicism, but a poetics of compensation, in which the classics as models played a major role in staving off utter paralysis and silence."

A considerably more astute analysis of the implications of Eliot's critical theory is Eugene Goodheart's provocative chapter on Eliot in *The Failure of Criticism* (Harvard). In his study Goodheart explores the relationship between the ebbing of criticism's moral authority and the rise of modernism, concluding that "the triumph of modernism is the defeat of criticism." In "The Reality of Disillusion in T. S. Eliot" Goodheart associates Eliot "with the anti-critical tendency of modernism" an association which, as he notes at the outset of his chapter, is "paradoxical, if not perverse." He observes that Eliot's criticism lacks the "dynamic principle of change counter to the mechanical principle that prevails in the world" which animated the beliefs of Carlyle, Ruskin, and Arnold. Goodheart convincingly demonstrates that Eliot's feeling for "the impotence of the modern" coupled with a commitment "to a religious ideal which has already been realized both institutionally and doctrinally in a dead past is to be continually tempted by despair." He concludes by asserting that "The anomaly of Eliot's originality is his discovery of the aesthetics of modern ineffectuality. Paradoxically, this discovery is the most effectual principle of his art. And it is a paradox that his immense prestige as a critic has contributed to the undoing of his criticism."

d. **Relation to Other Writers.** In his lucid and well-written study, "The Adventures of Tiresias: France, Gourmont, Eliot" (*MLR* 73:29–37), Michael Hancher uncovers remarks about Tiresias by Anatole France and Remy de Gourmont which Eliot is known to have read prior to writing *The Waste Land*. France is responsible not only for a line M. L. Rosenthal (p. viii, *Sailing into the Unknown*) misattributes to Victor Hugo ("The good critic is he who relates the adventures of his own soul among masterpieces") but for the following lines, taken from the same essay: "We cannot, like Tiresias, be a man and have recollections of having been a woman. We are shut up in our own personality as in a prison." Hancher sensibly concludes that Eliot's "Tiresian reference is the common and classical one. . . . But in writing his epic of frustrated spirituality and perplexed sexuality Eliot did write in a contemporary tradition. The sexual experience of Tiresias and the spiritual entrapment of the self were two related topics prepared for Eliot's attention by French writers at the start of the modern century." Alice Levine's essay, "T. S. Eliot and Byron" (*ELH* 45:522–41) considers the "unconscious, sub-surface relationship between the poets" rather than the question of "direct influence." After a summary of Eliot's comments on Byron's verse, Levine examines *Childe Harold's Pilgrimage* and *The Waste Land* as a pair of poems revealing "differences of degree rather than kind, of transformation rather than opposition." Levine successfully clarifies "the relationship between the nineteenth- and twentieth-century sensibilities as represented by Byron and Eliot." In "George MacDonald's *Lilith* and the Later Poetry of T. S. Eliot" (*ELN* 16:47–51), Kathryn Walls attempts to uncover parallels between "Burnt Norton" and *Lilith*, but they are simply not close enough to be convincing. Nor does Walls show the significance of such parallels. Two more persuasive source studies are Gordon N. Ross's "*The Waste Land* and *The Deserted Village*" (*NMAL* 3:7) and Hans Borchers's "The Patient Etherised Upon a Table: A New Source" (*YER* 5:9–13). Ross glosses a line from the episode of the "typist home at teatime" ("On the divan are piled [at night her bed]") with a couplet from Goldsmith: "The chest contrived a double debt to pay, / A bed by night, a chest of drawers by day." Given the verbal similarities and the close proximity of another allusion to Goldsmith, the parallel is a convincing one. Borchers argues that the famous opening simile in "The Love Song of J. Alfred Prufrock" could have as a source two stanzas from W. E. Henley's "In Hospital" where a patient upon a table awaits being chloroformed. William Harmon briefly compares Eliot's encounter with the "familiar compound ghost" in "Little Gidding" to Pound's encounter with the "spirit or hypostasis" in Canto LXXXI in "Visions of Perfection: Some Recurrent Figures in the Poems of Eliot and Pound" (*YER* 5:18–20). Harmon shows that the visions are culminations of quests begun early in the careers of both poets.

e. Studies of Specific Works. Keith Alldritt's *Eliot's Four Quartets: Poetry as Chamber Music* (London: Woburn Press) consists of three long essays, each considering different aspects of the "principle of musicality as it informs *Four Quartets*." Alldritt traces Eliot's interest to the symbolist's preoccupation with music, and he argues that *Four Quartets* must be considered a symbolist poem. After an historical survey of the form of the sonata, Alldritt demonstrates how Eliot employed this form to manipulate the voices of different speakers. One need not agree with Alldritt's classification of these speakers (lecturer, prophet, conversationalist, and conjuror) to accept his analysis of the way Eliot can "interweave and combine" these voices. Alldritt views *Four Quartets* primarily as "a thing of words" with one of its subjects being the "layers of verbal consciousness," and he considers Eliot's achievement here to be a "pre-eminently verbal" one.

Two articles this year consider different aspects of "spiritual renewal" in *The Waste Land*. Jeffrey L. Spear examines the concluding lines of Part I in "'The Burial of the Dead': Eliot's Corpse in the Garden in a Christian Context" (*AL* 50:282–85). After noting the Christian hope for life after death as expressed by St. Paul's response to the question of how the dead are raised (I Cor. 15:35–54), Spear points out that Eliot's lines present just the reversal of this, a "fear that the symbol of our mortality will be exposed to view." Spear concludes that "the passage thus perfectly caps the failure of spiritual renewal suggested at the beginning of the poem by the cruelty of April . . . but also suggests additional promise in the rain that comes at last at the end of the poem." Paul Lewis interprets the fate of Phlebas in "Life by Water: Characterization and Salvation in *The Waste Land*" (*Mosaic* 11:81–90). He argues that "Phlebas is the first of Eliot's characters who achieves spiritual renewal through an extinction of personality and an escape from time," but one principal difficulty here is in considering Phlebas a fully developed character. As a result, it is hard to accept Lewis's contention that Phlebas represents the "highest level of consciousness in the poem."

Bruce Bailey provides a chronological survey of humorous responses to Eliot and his poem by such varied writers as James Joyce, Richard Aldington, W. Hodgson Burnet, Christopher Morley, Amy Lowell, and Thomas Wolfe in "T. S. Eliot's *The Waste Land* in Parody, Travesty, and Satire" (*YER* 5:3–8). For Bailey, the value of these works ("aside from their worth as entertainment") "lies mainly in their casual parallels to the general course of more serious criticism and in their own sometimes illuminating attacks on *The Waste Land* itself." I would add that they often reveal more about their respective authors than about the work they are purporting to describe.

Only two articles were devoted to Eliot's short poems. In a detailed analysis of "Gerontion," Nancy K. Gish proposes that we consider the poem as looking forward to the "poetry of thought" more fully developed in *Four Quartets*, rather than seeing it as an extension of the techniques of "The Love Song of J. Alfred Prufrock" ("Thought, Feeling and Form: The Dual Meaning of 'Gerontion,'" [*ES* 59:237–47]). Gish distinguishes the "intellectual," "moral," and "emotional" cores of the poem and shows how they interact. She convincingly demonstrates that Gerontion's thoughts are arranged in a "logical pattern" which "moves from his self absorption and compulsive self analysis towards a crystallization of meaning—a statement of his personal and historic plight in clear rational terms —and dissolves again into terror." George Whiteside provides "A Freudian Dream Analysis of 'Sweeney Among the Nightingales'" (*YER* 5:14–17), in which he views the poem as Sweeney's nightmare of "male desire and fear of alluring females' retaliation for it."

University of Michigan

9. Faulkner

Panthea Reid Broughton

In 1978 Faulkner criticism can hardly be said to have overcome its two basic problems of scholarly irresponsibility and theoretical sameness. Mistakes in spellings, dates, and facts as well as neglect of previous relevant scholarship continue to be all too prevalent in Faulkner studies. Also too prevalent are overviews and summaries which simply generalize. Such work is not so much wrong as beside the point and redundant; also it cheapens as it softens the critical enterprise.

But if scholarly irresponsibility and theoretical sameness were not vanquished in 1978, each suffered major setbacks. Though errors persist, they are less plentiful this year. Also, the year's attention to Faulkner's early work and to the function of allusions establishes a model of scholarly responsibility which will, I hope, serve as an example for the future. And finally, though little meaningful psychobiographical or structuralist or phenomenological criticism was directed towards Faulkner, 1978 saw the best of such new approaches melded with more traditional rhetorical methods. I am particularly pleased with the results such hybrid approaches yield when applied to Faulkner's technique (the topic most severely neglected in the past). In this review I have changed category *b* under "Special Topics" (section *iv*) from "Language and Style" to "Style and Structure." My intention is that language and style be subsumed under the topic "Style" and that the rubric include "Structure" to cover the significant topic of technical form in Faulkner.

i. Bibliography, Editions, and Manuscripts

In 1978 the special Faulkner number of the *Mississippi Quarterly* included two previously unpublished works by William Faulkner. The first is "Eunice" (*MissQ* 31:449–52), a ballad written between

1920 and 1922. The poem is interesting less in its own right than for
its anticipation of things to come: associations between a house and
a woman, the connection between sexual fulfillment and sudden
death, and the fascination that the subject of loss held for the early
Faulkner. This text (owned by Louis Daniel Brodsky) is printed
with a helpful collation comparing it with the version housed at the
Alderman. It is worth noting that Faulkner seems to have written a
remarkable number of ribbon copies of this rather unremarkable
poem. The second piece, untitled in typescript but titled here by
James B. Meriwether "Frankie and Johnny," was apparently written
early in 1925. One of the story's four sections was published with
minor changes in *The Double Dealer* in 1925; the rest of the story
was not published until 1978. The story suggests that in 1925
Jamesian niceties about point of view escaped Faulkner; the omniscient narrative voice records Frankie's father's thoughts as he
drowns: " 'Poor kid, she'll have it tough now,' he thought among
green bubbles." Nor had Faulkner developed an ear for consistency
of style and tone: just after Frankie says, " 'Beat it, bum; or I'll slam
you for a row,' " Faulkner writes, "Johnny retained his sangfroid
admirably." Other startling shifts in diction show Faulkner consciously experimenting with radically different writing styles. But if
Faulkner lacked a sense of style and tone, he did not lack a sense
of structure: the story is broken into architectural units and the last
ends, one generation later, where the first begins.

    In 1978 George F. Hayhoe provided a valuable bibliographical
tool. His "Faulkner in Hollywood: A Checklist of His Film Scripts
at the University of Virginia" (*MissQ* 31:407–19) lists all the scripts
(or parts of scripts) now housed at the Alderman Library. By an
improved format this list includes much more thorough information
than Bruce Kawin's Filmography in *Faulkner and Film* (*ALS 1977*,
p. 142). It provides precise physical descriptions of the treatments,
accurate information about pagination, and much fuller production
information. Also it seems to have corrected a number of errors in
Kawin's listing. Hayhoe's checklist registers 25 treatments (some
with more than one version) now housed at the Alderman. It would
have been useful to know the source of each script (some were
Faulkner's, some were recently given by M-G-M and Twentieth
Ceutury-Fox), but otherwise this list tells us everything such a list
can about available resources.

Also of interest is Jack L. Capp's note on "The Faulkner Concordance" (*LRN* 3:72–73) which summarizes proceedings at the meeting of the Faulkner Concordance Advisory Board at the 1977 MLA. Discussion included suggestions about possible future broadening of the transcriptions so that they will facilitate analysis of stylistics.

ii. Biography

No significant biographical materials on Faulkner appeared in 1978, though a handsome book of photographs did offer us a few special glimpses into his life. Jack Cofield's *William Faulkner: The Cofield Collection* (Oxford, Miss.: Yoknapatawpha Press) is a book of photographs either taken by or collected by Jack's father (and Faulkner's contemporary), J. R. Cofield. As Carvel Collins's introduction makes clear, Cofield has always been generous with his collection of Faulkner materials. That generosity means that most of the pictures of William Faulkner have been seen before; but the collection does make available some less familiar and some new shots of Faulkner, his family, and his natural habitat. (Incidentally, Cofield's generosity was an appropriate compensation for his habit of collecting prints by silently making his own copies when, say, William Faulkner brought a roll of film to him to develop.) Though intended as much for the coffee table as for the scholar's library, *William Faulkner: The Cofield Collection* manages to be informative and certainly offers pleasant viewing and reading.

Dorothy Commins's *What Is an Editor: Saxe Commins at Work* (Chicago) devotes two chapters to Commins's relationship with Faulkner. These chapters include portions of 13 letters from Faulkner to Commins, only 5 of which were printed in *The Selected Letters of William Faulkner* (see *ALS 1976*, pp. 120–22). Although Dorothy Commins's anecdotes suggest the closeness of Faulkner's relationship with his friend and editor, her narrative is too disjointed and incomplete to be especially informative or convincing.

Though luridly titled and rather sentimentally written for the popular press, one of the articles Sally Davis has written about Meta Carpenter—"The Secret Hollywood Romance of William Faulkner" (*Los Angeles Mag.* 23:131–34,206–07)—does include a few new photographs, one of Faulkner's cartoon depictions of a typical day

with Meta, and excerpts from Faulkner's letters which differ slightly
from those printed in *A Loving Gentleman* (see ALS *1976*, 122–23).
And, finally, Richard F. Peterson's "An Early Judgement of Anderson
and Joyce in Faulkner's 'Artist at Home' " (see section *ix*) makes
some interesting suggestions about Faulkner's relationship with
Sherwood and Elizabeth Anderson.

iii. Criticism: General

a. **Books.** I am reviewing Arthur F. Kinney's *Faulkner's Narrative
Poetics* under the topic "Style and Structure" (section *iv*, *b*); but
four books remain under the broader rubric of "General" criticism.
By far the most significant of these is Cleanth Brooks's *William
Faulkner: Toward Yoknapatawpha and Beyond* (Yale). Apparently, Brooks's intention here was to turn over every stone left unturned
in *The Yoknapatawpha Country* (see ALS *1963*, pp. 75, 78–79).
Thus, though the book's title suggests that it will deal with Faulkner's early works and with his non-Yoknapatawpha novels, two of
its appendices deal with *Absalom, Absalom!*. Such a portmanteau
format makes for a certain awkward disproportion; appendices and
notes make up over a third of the book's entire length. Brooks's notes
cover everything from an eight-and-a-half page list of allusions to
a detailed review of actual cases of mutiny during World War I.
They examine Miss Rosa Coldfield's "poetry" (i.e., her poetic rhetoric) and analyze the logic (or lack of it) in the Old Marshall's
military and political ideology. This section of notes may sound as
if it is a formless compendium of odds and ends, but I think it is
one of the book's major strengths. It is full of hard information and
relevant observations in pithy form. Brooks, no doubt, could have
embroidered each of these notes into a speech or an essay. I, for
one, am glad he did not.

Toward Yoknapatawpha and Beyond is especially commendable
for the serious attention paid to little-known and seldom-discussed
works by Faulkner. Certainly one of its best chapters is the discussion of *A Fable*; there Brooks thoroughly examines the book's
strengths and analyzes the causes of its logical and artistic failures.
Brooks's careful tracing of Faulkner's sources is another of this
study's major accomplishments. Further, Brooks makes very revealing comparisons between certain themes and motifs in the early

prose and poetry and in the later fiction. He also makes at least satisfactory explanations of the qualitative disparities between Faulkner's mediocre and his best work.

There are a number of questions Brooks does not answer. Some of them he asks himself, concluding that they are unanswerable. And there are some questions, such as why Faulkner sees in antitheses, which remain only implicit in his treatment of Faulkner. The only real omission in this book is its lack of a conclusion. To be sure, *Toward Yoknapatawpha and Beyond* covers multifarious materials and it is hardly a thesis book, so a tidy summing-up would have been impossible. Nevertheless, certain insights become almost motifs throughout the book; among them are Faulkner's romanticism, his fascination with the unattainable, his desire to "have it both ways," his tendency to see in opposed pairs, his sense of man's divided nature, and his conviction that art is inferior to life. I would have preferred that Brooks address himself in a conclusion to a statement about the significance of such continuing concerns. Nevertheless, the sound scholarship, the critical insight, and the human wisdom make it a very significant study.

There are three other books of general criticism to be reviewed here. Each of these books is a collection of essays from the annual Faulkner conference at the University of Mississippi. The explanation for this backlog of supposedly annual volumes is that the organizers of the first "Faulkner and Yoknapatawpha" conference in 1974 did not then plan to print the speeches; apparently, it was only after the 1975 conference that they determined to print the proceedings of prior and subsequent conferences; thus the 1974 and 1975 volumes have appeared very late. Though they are not listed in MLA bibliographies, they are available now for reviewing along with the proceedings of the 1977 conference (see *ALS 1977*, pp. 140–42, for comments on the 1976 volume). Each of these collections raises the question of the appropriateness of printing speeches. Certainly that problem is most obvious with the first volume (*UMSE*, vol. 14 [1976]). This volume, titled "Faulkner and Yoknapatawpha, 1974, Selections," includes a capsule "History of Northern Mississippi" by David Sansing (pp. 5–21), which, though useful, offers no information not available elsewhere. Elizabeth Kerr's "The Evolution of Yoknapatawpha" (pp. 23–62) reviews the Yoknapatawpha fiction, tracing its interrelationships and pointing out when continuity breaks; this discussion is interesting, but hardly groundbreaking. Joseph Blotner's speeches were not available for publication in this volume; instead, the editors have printed a transcript of a relatively informative and revealing seminar discussion. Malcolm Cowley's two talks—"Dilsey and the Compsons" (pp. 79–88) and "Ike McCaslin and the Wilderness" (pp. 89–97)—are engaging summary treatments of the novels under consideration. Clearly, all these materials worked well as oral presentations, but they work less well as written documents. The volume also includes materials intended, apparently, to fill out its pages. There is an essay by a student at the conference (on female characters) but it only begins the task it undertakes. The volume also includes three panel discussions of such general topics as "The Riches of Yoknapatawpha" (pp. 141–61). Nothing in this volume convinces me of the appropriateness of the editors' belated decision to publish it.

The other collection—(*UMSE*, vol. 15 [1978])—is definitely a superior collection, though it too suffers because requirements for speeches and essays differ markedly. There are two speeches by Cleanth Brooks. In "The Sense of Community in Yoknapatawpha Fiction" (pp. 3–18) Brooks effectively defines and explains how a community functions in Faulkner. In "Gavin Stevens and the Chivalric Tradition" (pp. 19–32) he provides an entertaining character study. These essays are clarifications and expansions of work Brooks has done elsewhere, but they are not significant additions to it. Blyden Jackson's "Faulkner's Depiction of the Negro" (pp. 33–47) sees progression throughout Faulkner's career in his resistance to stereotypes and willingness to see blacks as individuals; this is another persuasive and engaging paper which reemphasizes but does not discover. Jackson's "Two Mississippi Writers: Wright and Faulkner" (pp. 49–59) is really about Wright, not Faulkner. Elizabeth M. Kerr's "*Absalom, Absalom!*: Faust in Mississippi, or The Fall of the House of Sutpen" (pp. 61–82) is an impressive tally of gothic elements in that novel. Her "The Women of Yoknapatawpha" (pp. 83–100) summarizes social mores regarding women in the Mississippi environment and reviews Faulkner's treatments of major Yoknapatawpha women. William Boozer's "Collecting Faulkner" (pp. 125–37) is a practical and unpretentious talk which offers useful, even valuable, advice on the rudiments of collecting Faulkner. Such a nonliterary topic is a welcome addition to the volume, as are the fascinating anecdotes about Faulkner told in the panel discussions by those who knew him.

By far the most successful essays in this second volume are those by Carvel Collins and Richard Godden. Collins's "Faulkner: The Man and the Artist" (pp. 217–31) seems to be printed just as he delivered it (even references to the cash bar afterward are included). Collins's lively style insures that the speech remains entertaining as an essay. Further, Collins readily acknowledges when he is reworking old ideas, but he adds new insights to established lines of argument so that the essay is a fresh and effective attack upon certain mistaken assumptions about Faulkner's artistry and his use of autobiographical materials. Collins's other essay "Faulkner and Mississippi" (pp. 139–59) is, despite its title, a survey of mythic elements in Faulkner. Collins refutes the sociological approach to Faulkner by offering in more detail than in earlier works a number of mythical parallels in *The Sound and the Fury* and *As I Lay Dying*. While other essays in these volumes read like speeches, not articles, Richard Godden's "William Faulkner, Addie Bundren, and Language" (pp. 101–23) reads like an article, not a speech. (It appeared, by the way, twice in 1978: once in this volume, and once, in slightly expanded form, under the title "William Faulkner, and Addie Bundren's Words with God" [*EIP* 3:25–46].) Godden too covers a great deal of ground; in fact the only problem with his densely packed essay is Godden's attempt to treat Addie, Faulkner, language, and even (by implication) God in just over 20 pages. Godden relates Addie's words to events in the Garden of Eden and to the linguistic assumptions of modernism by arguing from the text; this essay is specific and revelatory in its illustrations of how silence and virginity, language and fertility are related for Addie and for Faulkner. One of the essay's virtues is that, while it shows how Faulkner and Addie do think alike, it insists that Addie's distinction between words and deeds is "patently a falsification."

The third of these collections from the Faulkner conference— *The Maker and the Myth: Faulkner and Yoknapatawpha, 1977*, edited by Evans Harrington and Ann J. Abadie (Miss.)—prints eight essays. Apparently, Harrington and Abadie rethought the question of appropriateness for print; this year they did not publish transcripts of discussions and they must have asked that the essays be written or revised with publication in mind.

The collection is flanked by two essays by Calvin S. Brown. In the first, "Faulkner's Localism," Brown follows a now-familiar pattern of pointing out local prototypes for characters, scenes, and events in the fiction. His distinction between tone in Faulkner and in local-color writing is familiar but useful, as is his categorizing of different levels of dialect. In "Faulkner's Universality," the last essay in the collection, Brown takes another hackneyed topic. Though his facetious spoof of myth-mongering criticism is beside the point, he does make a cogent attack upon those who assume that "other nations are entitled to their myths, but the South is not." That issue is, however, more complicated than Brown acknowledges. Brown's knowledge of specifics and his willingness to classify barely save these essays from the vapidity which often characterizes treatments of such general topics.

Ilse Dusoir Lind took another hackneyed topic, and she did succeed in saying something new. Her major point in "Faulkner's Women" is that "*Faulkner is the only major American fiction writer of the twenties and thirties who incorporates into his depiction of women the functioning of the organs of reproduction.*" Unfortunately, though, not everything she says is new. She explains that, other than experience and observation, Faulkner's sources for treatments of female sexuality are Louis Berman and Havelock Ellis; but that point was made several years ago in an article by Mick Gidley to which Lind does not refer (see *ALS 1971*, p. 109). Lind's failure to do her scholarly homework, nevertheless, does not detract from the importance of her conclusion: "What a probing of two of his medical sources here shows is that he was far more modern than we have allowed, far more audacious than we have perceived, far more reverential of human life as it manifests itself in woman than we have credited."

Unfortunately, Margaret Walker Alexander's treatment of "Faulkner and Race" is not successful. In her essay on this large and important topic Alexander announces that Faulkner "made a great beginning" in creating understanding between the races. But some of her comments about the fiction seem to contradict her own conclusion. Her essay is filled with unfounded generalizations, non-sequiturs, and blurred distinctions. Most seriously, her statements about "Pantaloon in Black" and *Huckleberry Finn* suggest that she does not acknowledge that, though a fictional character may make a racist slur in a given work, its author's intent may be not to condone but to expose the narrow insensitivity of such racism. Alexander's muddled presentation does no credit to her important topic.

The collection includes two essays by Lewis P. Simpson which continue and expand the focus of Simpson's earlier "Faulkner and the Legend of the Artist" (see *ALS 1976*, p. 125). Here and elsewhere Simpson writes intellectual and cultural history. We turn to him for understanding of central issues in Western civilization, not for readings of particular texts. His approach contains certain liabilities: one is distance from the text (suggested here by a couple of careless errors—bringing Reverend Shegog from Chicago; making Mink, Flem's brother); another is terminology used in a self-reflexive, sometimes idiosyncratic manner. The sheer complexity of his subject makes for dense but rewarding reading.

In the first of these essays, "Sex and History: The Origins of Faulkner's Apocrypha," Simpson argues that modern Western civilization has deprived humanity of mystery and the hope of transcendence offered by earlier mythological civilizations. Feeling his "world historical alienation" especially severely, the artist seeks to reclaim in art the ecstasy and oneness lost through modern historicism. Simpson characterizes that longing as sexual; thus he considers the frustrated sexuality in Faulkner's early work an expression of the artist's frustrated desire to return to a mythological or cosmological mode of existence. Simpson never explains whether he is suggesting an analogy between mythological consciousness, artistic creation, and sexuality; or whether he means that art is really sexual. These matters need clarification, as do terms such as the "isolation of the individual in history," the "isolation of history in the individual," and the "closure of history in the self." On the other hand, Simpson astutely relates the individual and the transcultural; he sees in Faulkner an epitome of the "tension between the cosmological and historical modes of existence."

In his second essay, "Yoknapatawpha and Faulkner's Fable of Civilization," Simpson argues that Faulkner's intent in *A Fable* was to "transfer the Christian myth into the realm of a mystical humanism, which in his writings had developed as an uncertain foil to the ruthless historicism of modernity." This mystical humanism was apparently more an idea than an actuality; thus Simpson exposes in Faulkner's ambivalence toward the general the novel's central flaw;

for the old general is, like Faulkner, "world historical poet"; and the
novel finally endorses the general's value system, not, as intended,
the corporal's. Simpson also offers a convincing, but brief, explanation for the failure of southern literature in the 19th century and
for the failure which characterizes Faulkner's late work.

Two essays by Albert J. Guerard complete this collection. In
"The Faulknerian Voice" Guerard effectively distinguishes voice
from style and proceeds to classify the elements of Faulkner's voice.
Also he makes a useful distinction between the "two major variants
of the fully liberated or fully realized Faulknerian voice": the first
he terms "Jamesian," the second "Miltonic." Guerard too sees the
connection between sexuality and art in Faulkner; he illustrates how
significantly in the early work "Faulkner did not repress his sexual
fantasy or suppress his verbal audacity." In "Faulkner the Innovator" Guerard focuses upon Faulkner's "striking innovation"—the exploration of different levels of consciousness within a single work
or a single passage. Guerard adds to the critical debate about Quentin Compson's conversation with Henry Sutpen and points out how
Faulkner's literary imagination thrived when presenting imagined
scenes. This work, of course, is an expansion of what Guerard has
already said in *The Triumph of the Novel* (see *ALS 1976*, pp. 127–
28), but Guerard does not simply re-dress old arguments in new
clothes; when he repeats himself, he does so in quotation marks.
When he expands on a point he has already made, he does so with
fresh illustrations. Thus Guerard manages in these two essays to
say something new and useful about a topic on which he had seemed
to have already had the last word.

b. Articles.   Like the speakers at the Faulkner conferences, authors
of articles on the topic "Faulkner" face the problem of writing at
once a broad overview and an original and significant contribution
to scholarship. Few succeed. One who did succeed is Philip M.
Weinstein in his "Precarious Sanctuaries: Protection and Exposure
in Faulkner's Fiction" (*SAF* 6:173–91). As Weinstein notes, his
thesis is similar to my own (see *ALS 1974*, pp. 127–28), but his emphasis upon the positive value of creating mental sanctuaries differs
from mine. Also Weinstein insightfully chooses fresh paradigmatic
instances which further reveal the significance in Faulkner of encounters with "*the maelstrom of unbearable reality.*" In "Cavaliers,

Calvinists, and the Wheel of Fortune: The Gambling Instinct in Faulkner's Fiction" (*NMW* 11:3–14) Richard A. Milum provides a reminder of how central to both theme and plot in Faulkner's fiction is the gambling instinct.

Mary Jane Dickerson's "Faulkner's Golden Steed" (*MissQ* 31: 369–80) reviews Faulkner's major treatments of horses in order to establish the mythical dimension they carry in his work. Though interpretive subtleties must be sacrificed in such an overview, the essay offers an interesting explanation of how "Faulkner's unique relationship with horses informed his fiction with the revelation of myth." In "Faulkner's Images of the Past: from *Sartoris* to *The Unvanquished*" (*YES* 8:109–24) Arnold Goldman focuses upon the "image of the Southern gentleman shot dead in his tracks in chivalric pursuit" as the epitome of the legend of the southern past. Goldman's use of that motif is an effective device for tightening and unifying his essay, but it cannot entirely compensate for a clumsy style and an absent conclusion. And in "Homer Was Blind: John Steinbeck on the Character of William Faulkner" (*StQ* 11:15–20) Richard F. Peterson considers Steinbeck's attack upon Faulkner for supposedly plagiarizing one of his essays. Peterson's objective coverage establishes Faulkner's blamelessness and suggests that there were some issues at certain times about which Steinbeck was slightly paranoid. Also, the chapter "Faulkner: The Etiology of His Art" in Malcolm Cowley's *—And I Worked at the Writer's Trade* (see chapter 20) is largely a reprint of Cowley's perceptive review in the *Southern Review* of John T. Irwin's *Doubling and Incest—Repetition and Revenge*, but it also offers fresh insight into Faulkner's writing process.

Harley D. Oberhelman's "William Faulkner's Reception in Spanish America" (*TAH* 3:13–17) is an informative, factual view of translations, reviews, criticism, and events which have furthered Faulkner's reputation in Spanish-speaking America. But other articles of general criticism were less successful. The treatment of Faulknerian materials in Fred Langman's "Landscape and Identity in the American Novel" (*AmerSI* 16:34–47) is simply too brief for its own good. Essays such as Harley D. Oberhelman's "Faulknerian Techniques in Gabriel García Márquez's Portrait of a Dictator" (*PCLS* 10:171–81) and Nikolai Anastasyev's "The Necessity of Faulkner" (*SovL* 8[1977]:180–83) and Pyotr Paliyevsky's "Faulkner's America" (*SovL* 8[1977]:177–80) testify to Faulkner's influence elsewhere but are too generalized to be of value. The failure of Christopher Muller's "On William Faulkner's Manner of Narration" (*KN* 25:201–12) is more difficult to explain. Unlike most essayists writing on general topics, Muller defends his propositions with specific supporting evidence; in fact, his essay is filled with tallies of everything from word frequencies to techniques. But these tallies are a spotty and unreliable attempt to "present the typical characteristics which can be found in all of Faulkner's works."

It is not appropriate here to review another review similar to this chapter, but Faulkner scholars should be aware of a new annual evaluation of scholarship: "Faulkner 1977: A Survey of Research and Criticism" (*MissQ* 31:429–47). The salient facts are these: it is based chiefly upon the Southern Literature Bibliography in the Spring *MissQ*; it is the work of a committee, headed by Thomas L. McHaney; it follows the topical organization of McHaney's bibliography (see *ALS 1976*, p. 120); and it appears about a half year before the Faulkner chapter in *ALS*. Those are the facts, to which I would like to add one statement of judgment: I must disagree that the works noticed are the significant ones for 1977, for I find several trivial works present and several worthy essays absent. Articles by Kerry McSweeney, David Middleton, Carl E. Rollyson, Jr., and John L. Cleman, for instance—all cited in the Faulkner chapter of *ALS 1977*—are omitted from the McHaney survey. The committee's inclusion/exclusion policy may not be entirely objective.

iv. Criticism: Special Studies

a. **Ideas, Influences, Intellectual Background.** The varied essays for 1978 which covered these topics remind us again how valuable is specificity. Michael Millgate's "Faulkner's Masters" (*TSE* 23:143–55) pursues a distinction Faulkner made between those contemporary writers who influenced Faulkner in specific or limited ways —who taught him "the tricks of the trade"—and those masters such as Conrad and Melville who influenced him in the "broadest and deepest sense." The essay offers a fine overview, but it does not have the length to treat the topic in sufficient detail. Millgate remarks that "Faulkner's awareness of French literature deserves far closer study than it has yet received." Millgate does not deal with that topic, but the essay following his in the same collection does. In "The French Face of William Faulkner" (*TSE* 23:157–73) Roger Asselineau offers a valuable brief summary of Faulkner's early reception in the states and in France. (Asselineau frames his essay with references to Arthur Hobson Quinn's attack on Faulkner—a disturbing though amusing reminder now of how misunderstood Faulkner was by those who should have known better.) Asselineau offers factual and theoretical explanations for Faulkner's fame in France and traces the influence of a substantial list of French writers on Faulkner. His essay is flawed only by a blindspot about Faulkner's craftsmanship: Asselineau feels that, though Faulkner "admired Flaubert's meticulous craftsmanship, he felt closer to Balzac's slap-dash manner." Nevertheless, Asselineau has written a valuable overview of Faulkner's debt to the French. The year's two major full-length studies of Faulkner—Cleanth Brooks's *Toward Yoknapatawpha and Beyond* (see section *iii*) and Arthur Kinney's *Faulkner's Narrative Poetics* (see section *iv, b*)—also offer insight into the question of influence.

The year saw the publication of two other influence studies which were more limited in scope but which also added to our knowledge of Faulkner's sources. "William Faulkner and Willard Huntington Wright's *The Creative Will*" (*CRevAS* 9:169–77) is another in the series of investigations of Faulkner's extraliterary reading which Mick Gidley has been writing over the last eight years or so. This essay is a detailed and well-documented analysis of several specific ways in which Wright's aesthetic ideas may have influenced Faulkner's work. James H. Krefft's "A Possible Source for Faulkner's Indians: Oliver La Farge's *Laughing Boy*" (*TSE* 23:187–92) is a responsibly researched and convincing essay whose topic is announced by its title. As serendipity, Krefft also offers further evidence of Faulkner's debt for the "living is motion" theory.

One 1977 item published in an unlikely spot for Faulkner criticism is Charles S. Aiken's "Faulkner's Yoknapatawpha County: Geographical Fact into Fiction" (*GeoR* 67:1–21). The essay is of interest to the Faulknerian for its terminology, statistics, maps, and its nonliterary sources.

Two generalized surveys that contribute nothing to our understanding should be mentioned here chiefly as warning. They are Thadious Davis's "Southern Literature: From Faulkner to Others"

(*CEA* 40:14–18) and Luther Stearns Mansfield's "The Nature of Faulkner's Christianity" (*Descant* 22:40–48).

b. **Style and Structure.** Though Arthur F. Kinney's *Faulkner's Narrative Poetics: Style as Vision* (Mass.) shows the influence of structuralist and phenomenological schools of criticism, it cannot be so neatly labeled; for Kinney writes out of conviction, not about literary methodology, but about Faulkner's accomplishment and the response it compels from readers. Kinney's basic understanding is that "ripples of *narrative consciousness* . . . spread out through the various scenes of Faulkner's novels to embrace our sense of the work *as a whole,* our *structural consciousness*" and that we gain "a sense of the significance of the accumulation of incidents and images as we put them together [with] what we may term our *constitutive consciousness.*" This approach establishes narrative point of view, vision, and form as interrelated phenomena calculated to affect the reader in specified ways. As Kinney writes, "There may be thirteen ways of looking at blackbirds, but Faulkner felt reasonably assured of the reader's own, fourteenth view. . . ."

As introduction to the powers and potentialities of his approach, Kinney offers a detailed analysis of the scene in *Light in August* when we first meet Byron Bunch, who recalls the first time he saw Joe Christmas. This is a masterful treatment of the elements of Byron Bunch's perception, of Faulkner's arrangement of the scene in terms of perception and conception, and of the cognitive acts involved in reading this passage.

Believing that we can get at Faulkner's nonlinear novels best if we consider the arrangement and relationship of their parts, Kinney shows us how the novels are structured by analogy, synecdoche, image chains, correlatives, juxtaposition, counterpointing, conciliation, parallelism, replication, synonymity, circularity, and clustering. Applied to Faulkner, such terms are not entirely new. What is new though is that Kinney does not just make off-handed generalizations about counterpointing or clustering; he shows how such devices work and how they convey a particular vision. He also examines Faulkner's debt to other experimenters in the novel form and he provides a workable justification for the distinction between Faulkner's best and his least effective fiction. Kinney's prose is not always crisp, his coverage is spotty, and he allowed a careless error about the dating of *Sanctuary* to go undetected. Nevertheless, he has written a benchmark study, for *Faulkner's Narrative Poetics* is one of those rare books which change our way of approaching a body of literature.

With its catchy title and its framing reference to Mickey Mouse, Richard Pearce's "Reeling Through Faulkner: Pictures of Motion, Pictures in Motion" (*MFS* 24:483–95) promises to be about Faulkner and film. Instead, it is about the peculiar tension in Faulkner between motion (as subject) and motion (as narrative technique). Pearce makes effective use of film terminology to describe Faulkner's style, but the essay's major achievement is attention to passages in which the subject is static but (as Pearce illustrates) the medium itself is in motion. In "Faulkner: Short Story Structures and Reflexive Forms" (*Mosaic* 11:127–37) James G. Watson also distinguishes between motion as subject and as technique. Insisting that "each narrative perspective is a reflexive form—if not a precise reflection —of each other one," Watson deals with a major device of construction in Faulkner's novels. His essay, however, covers a great deal of ground at a very rapid pace. Other essays which are concerned with the style or structure of Faulkner's writings are those by Guerard (see section *iii*), Godden (see section *iii*), and DeSpain and Jacobs (see section *vi*).

c. **Race.** The only essays explicitly devoted to this topic were those by Blyden Jackson and Margaret Walker Alexander (see section *iii*). However, James Stuart's "The Ironic Voices of Faulkner's *Go Down, Moses*" (section *vii*) offers real insight into Faulkner's exposure of the limitations and consequences of stereotypical attitudes about race.

v. Individual Works to 1929

In *Toward Yoknapatawpha and Beyond* Cleanth Brooks offers a valuable, extended treatment of Faulkner's early work. Also several short studies add substantially to our understanding of this heretofore largely neglected material. One—Margaret Yonce's " 'Shot Down Last Spring': The Wounded Aviators of Faulkner's Wasteland" (*MissQ* 31:359–68)—is an imaginatively but misleadingly titled piece. The essay deals principally with the poem "The Lilacs" and offers a valuable key (in the concept of the split personality) to reading that poem. Gail Moore Morrison's " 'Time, Tide, and Twilight': *Mayday* and Faulkner's Quest Toward *The Sound and the Fury*" (*MissQ* 31:337–57) is an excellent treatment of these two works' shared motifs and possible sources. This meticulous study of allusions, especially to Arthurian materials, is a valuable resource for readers of the early work and of *The Sound and the Fury* as well. Robert W. Hamblin's "*The Marble Faun*: Chapter One of Faulkner's Continuing Dialectic on Life and Art" (*PMPA* 3:80–90) is marred by a failure to explain the relation between characters' opinions and Faulkner's. Nevertheless, the essay deals with a significant topic, shows the continuity in Faulkner's work, and includes some useful observations about the function of personification in *The Marble Faun*. John Ditsky's "William Faulkner's *The Wishing Tree*: Maturity's First Draft," (*L&U* 2:56–64) promises much but provides little more than a plot summary. In "Women and Myth in Faulkner's First Novel" (*TSE* 23:175–86) Philip Castille explores Faulkner's mythical method in *Soldier's Pay*. Arguing that Faulkner employs and inverts the myth of Diana and Hippolytus, Castille convinces us that Faulkner's first novel is deepened by these associations. Also, though he sometimes seems unkind to Margaret Powers, Castille offers a sensible analysis of her sexuality and of that of Emmy and of Cecily Saunders.

Fred Chappell's "The Comic Structure of *The Sound and the Fury*" (*MissQ* 31:381–86) is an impressionistic and somewhat puckish reminder that the basic events in *The Sound and the Fury* (excluding Quentin's suicide) are comic. Chappell does not consider the irony that, abstracted from context, tragic events and characters often do form the stuff of comedy; whether inflexibility, for instance, is comic or tragic is chiefly a matter of tone and outcome. Nevertheless, Chappell does well to remind us how many elements of farce are present in *The Sound and the Fury*. Richard C. Sterne's "Why Jason Compson IV Hates Babe Ruth" (*AN&Q* 16:105–08) succeeds in answering the question its title poses because Sterne has uncovered not only facts but rumors current in 1928.

Karl F. Zender's note on *The Sound and the Fury*, "Jason Compson and Death by Water" (*MissQ* 31:421–22), effectively explains the parallel structure which frames Jason's references to the ways Compson men die. Zender's point of departure for the note was

Calvin Brown's query about Jason's projected death for himself by nosespray. Though Zender shows us how Jason thinks by analogy, Brown's question—why a nosespray?—still calls for an answer. Three 1977 items not available to me in time for last year's chapter should be mentioned here. In "The 'Sojer Face' Defiance of Jason Compson" (*Thought* 52[1977]:188–203) David Aiken finds in the Reverend Shegog's sermon the book's ethical norm by which Jason's self-assertive defiance is condemned. Though not couched as a refutation of those critics who dismiss the sermon's importance, this essay nevertheless serves as a counter to them. Yasuko Idei in "Time as a Means of Conveying Nihilism in Faulkner's *The Sound and the Fury*" (*KAL* 18[1977]:24–32) writes another of those overviews which are sound enough but which do not add anything new to our understanding. M. D. Faber's "Faulkner's *The Sound and the Fury*: Object Relations and Narrative Structure" (*AI* 34[1977]:327–50) offers some observations about structure in the Quentin section, but mostly explores the terms of the maternal and paternal voids in the Compson household. Several predictable liabilities typify such psychological studies: misspellings, jargon, a disregard for literary criticism, and a predilection for the Compson family. To Faber's credit, his essay (though it includes its share of misspellings) is less jargon-ridden and more thorough and insightful than most such studies.

vi. Individual Works, 1930–39

This was a big but uneven year for *As I Lay Dying*; critics explored, with mixed results, several questions not heretofore addressed to this novel. In one of the best essays, "Fate and Madness: The Determinist Vision of Darl Bundren" (*AL* 49:619–33), Charles Palliser confronts the issue of Darl's apparent insanity and its connection with his alleged clairvoyance. Both are explained, Palliser argues, by Darl's absolutely deterministic vision. Though he is more convincing on the subject of clairvoyance than on madness, Palliser's careful explanation of relationships between symptoms and causes offers a welcome corrective to studies which too readily assume that Darl is somehow possessed of magical powers and that he must be mad. In "Natural Rhythms and Rebellion: Anse's Role in *As I Lay Dying*" (*MFS* 24:556–64) Leon F. Seltzer and Jan Viscomi argue that because he lives in harmony with natural rhythms, Anse not only prevails but also establishes the novel's value system. Thus "judging the morality of Anse's actions is problematic because they seem to originate less from vindictiveness than from instinct." I have an instinctive resistance to this argument, and I do find strained reasoning here; the authors argue from Anse's "iron shoes" to his being rooted "firmly in nature's ground" and from his new false teeth to a renewal of fertility. Nevertheless, this is the most carefully defended and compelling presentation of this point of view that I have seen. Richard Godden's essay on Addie and language (see section *iii*) was also an important study of this novel.

As I Lay Dying cries for an analysis of its spatial form, and that is why Betty Alldredge's "Spatial Form in Faulkner's *As I Lay Dying*" (*SLJ* 11,i:3–19) is such a disappointing essay. Alldredge seems to define spatial form as the use of disparate viewpoints; therefore, her essay summarizes different viewpoints. Presumably, the idea here is that each perspective is modified by the others and that the reader must see them at once, as in space, before understanding the novel. But Alldredge herself does not allow a character's viewpoint to be modified; she accepts Addie's viewpoint and writes, for instance, that Addie "practices no deceit in her affair with Whitfield." Therefore, it is difficult to see how Alldredge thinks spatial form functions here. One item from 1977 just now available is LeRene DeSpain's and Roderick A. Jacobs's "Syntax and Characterization in Faulkner's *As I Lay Dying*" (*JEngL* 11[1977]:1–8). The authors begin with a fascinating comparison of syntax in one passage from Molly Bloom's monologue and one from Jewel Bundren's. This analysis puts into question traditional assumptions about the interior monologue as a representation of "pre-speech levels of consciousness." It also makes a rather startling but undeveloped suggestion about Darl's voice and Faulkner's discovery of his own voice. The authors expect us to take on faith the representativeness of their examples and thus the validity of their hypotheses. Instead, their selectivity and brevity detracts from the potential significance of their essay. Yasuko Idei's "A Quest for Identity and the Meaning of the *Be-Verb* in Faulkner's *As I Lay Dying*" (*KAL* 19:32–44) fails to focus on its announced topic, nor does it offer a substitute topic. And finally, in "The Complex Pastoralism of *As I Lay Dying*" (*PMPA* 2[1977]:46–52) Albert J. Devlin opens an interesting topic for discussion but fails to develop it; his engaging style almost obscures the fuzziness of his argument.

Thomas J. Morrissey's "Food Imagery in Faulkner's *Light in August*" (*NR* 3:41–49) is marred by two gross errors: Morrissey refers to the dietician's punishment of Joe and to Joanna Burden's pregnancy. Also he makes no use of previous criticism. Nevertheless, Morrissey does use specifics well to establish just how thematically and structurally central to *Light in August* is food imagery.

Pylon received minimal attention in the essay on *The Tarnished Angels* by Michael Stern in *The Modern American Novel*.

The past several years have seen a number of excellent essays on narrative structure in *Absalom, Absalom!* This year added excellent work by Brooks (see section *iii*), Kinney (section *iv, b*), Rimmon-Kenan, Brodsky, and Muhlenfeld. A minor contribution of Shlomith Rimmon-Kenan's "From Reproduction to Production: The Status of Narration in Faulkner's *Absalom, Absalom!*" (*Degrés* 16: 1–19) is that it illustrates how appropriate to an analysis of *Absalom, Absalom!* are structuralist terms like "intradiegetic" and "extradiegetic." Classifying the ways in which Faulkner undermines the reliability of different narrative perspectives in the novel, the essay explains how narration proceeds despite the unreliability of evidence. The model used here for that process is not religious, artistic, or historical, but rather psychoanalytical.

Another essay which deals with that process is Claudia Brodsky's "The Working of Narrative in *Absalom, Absalom!*: A Textual Analysis" (*AmSt* 23:240–59). This essay reminds me of Richard Forrer's (*ALS 1976*, p. 136). Both authors consider the function of an external narrative voice; both see *Absalom, Absalom!* as a celebration of the powers of the imagination; but whereas Forrer spoke of a mode of transcendence, Brodsky speaks of an "overpass to love." Another refreshing contribution to the study of this novel was Elisabeth Muhlenfeld's " 'We have waited long enough': Judith Sutpen and Charles Bon" (*SoR* 14:66–80). Muhlenfeld's careful distinction between fact and speculation and her sensitive readings of the few facts available shed considerable light upon the characters of Charles and Judith and upon their relationship. Muhlenfeld makes a sound analysis of the ways in which Mr. Compson and Quentin and Shreve as well misunderstand the two lovers, and she

also provides more evidence of the unreliability of the narrative
voice. Especially effective is her reading of Bon's letter. Through
such careful readings she persuades us that "the possibility of Judith
and Bon's love brightens and strengthens *Absalom*."

Arthur F. Kinney's "Form and Function in *Absalom, Absalom!*"
(*SoR* 14:677–91) considers sources and models for *Absalom*. Here
Kinney writes somewhat impressionistically so that this essay seems
more a meditation than an argument. But Kinney does show how
the romantic desire to make life cohere constitutes subject matter
and decrees form in a number of sources including (and this is his
most interesting point) Col. W. C. Falkner's *The White Rose of
Memphis*. In a brief note on "Matthew Arnold, the North, and *Absalom, Absalom!*" (*AN&Q* 16:105) Richard L. Newby suggests the
significance of the Arnoldian allusions in Faulkner's "best of thought"
and the "best of ratiocination." In "A Possible Source for the title
Absalom, Absalom!" (*MissQ* 31:423–24) Lynn Dickerson makes a
strained and unconvincing attempt to find in Grace Lumpkin's *To
Make My Bread* a "source" for this novel's title. In his *The Critical
Act: Criticism and Community* (Yale) Evan Watkins devotes a
chapter to *Absalom, Absalom!* Watkins's treatment is a persuasive
refutation of Georg Lukács's attack upon Faulkner for "the lack of a
consistent view of human nature," but Watkins offers no new discoveries about the novel. Nor does Patricia Tobin in her chapter on
Absalom, Absalom! in *Time and the Novel: The Genealogical Imperative* (Princeton).

M. E. Bradford's "*The Unvanquished*: The High Cost of Survival" (*SoR* 14:428–37) is typified by political rhetoric and extraliterary
judgments: the northern invasion of the South was "a dramatic illustration of American millenarianism, gnostic secular Puritanism
at its worst"; *The Unvanquished* makes people uneasy "because it
renders with such telling force a teaching on community which is
offensive both to the statist totalitarian and to the atomistic liber-
tarian who occupy the conventional antipodes of contemporary
cultural history"; and "Each act of reading Faulkner as I believe he
expected to be read is for Southerners also an act of piety." Bradford's real thesis is that the protagonist in *The Unvanquished* is no
single hero but "*res publica*, the Commonwealth," but his thesis gets
lost in his chauvinism. Also lost on Bradford is the irony in his considering Ringo a member of the Sartoris family. In "Faulkner's

'Riposte in Tertio' " (*AN&Q* 16:88) G. Jennifer Wilson provides a helpful note on the appropriateness of using duelling terminology here and in the rest of *The Unvanquished.* In "Faulkner, Scott, and Another Source for Drusilla" (*MissQ* 31:425–28) Richard A. Milum provides a thorough, well-researched, and convincing note on the significance of associations between *The Unvanquished* and *Rob Roy.*

No work on *The Wild Palms* appeared in 1978, but Marion W. Cumpiano wrote an interesting treatment of "Old Man" which has, I believe, implications for the novel as a whole. In "The Motif of Return: Currents and Counter Currents in 'Old Man' by William Faulkner" (*SHR* 12:185–93) Cumpiano uses a rather contrived analogy to the different levels of the flood to characterize the different levels at which we may read the convict's desire to return to prison. Despite that contrivance and despite the essay's independence of previous criticism, Cumpiano presents insight into the ways images are clustered and return is associated with escape in this half-novel.

vii. Individual Works, 1940–49

The Hamlet did not fare especially well in 1978. Robert A. Fink in "Comedy Preceding Horror: *The Hamlet's* Not So Funny Horses" (*CEA* 40,iv:27–30) makes a useful comparison between the Stamper/Snopes and the Snopes/Armstid trades, but his attribution of innocence to the one, horror to the other is too simple. Beth Burch's "A Miltonic Echo in Faulkner's *The Hamlet*" (*NConL* 8,iv:3–4) comes closer to convincing us that "Elegia Quinta" echoes through Faulkner's early work than that it is a specific source for the Ike Snopes/Houston's cow scene.

In 1978 *Go Down, Moses* fared very well indeed. James Stuart's "The Ironic Voices of Faulkner's *Go Down, Moses*" (*SDR* 16:80–101) reminds us that "the larger truth of *Go Down, Moses* is an old one: Power is a function of authority, and things don't change much." But the special contribution of this essay is Stuart's insistence that "irony is [*Go Down, Moses's*] chief mode." Thus Stuart illustrates how the context of the whole novel undermines and corrects characters' limited perspectives on such topics as race and sex. Also the essay serves as another reminder of the distance Faulkner keeps between himself and his characters and of the complex manner in which he structures his novels. Stuart only touches on "Pantaloon in Black," but Warren Akin IV's " 'The Normal Human Feelings': An Interpretation of Faulkner's 'Pantaloon in Black' " (*SSF* 15:397–404) further exemplifies Stuart's point; that is, Stuart establishes that it is insensitivity to other human beings that echoes despairingly throughout *Go Down, Moses*. Akin's careful discussion of the terms of Rider's sensitivity heightens our sense of the story's irony and of its centrality in *Go Down, Moses*.

In "Faulkner as Historian: The Commissary Books in *Go Down, Moses*" (*MarkhamR* 7:31–36) Carl E. Rollyson considers the process exemplified in Isaac's reading of the ledgers. Rollyson finds this process significant because "the commissary books in *Go Down, Moses* constitute Faulkner's one extended attempt to deal with the type of evidence that is the stuff out of which historians fashion their version of the past." Rollyson's essay exemplifies the process it describes, since it extrapolates from Buck's and Buddy's entries in the ledgers to make valuable readings of their characters and their times. Walter A. Davis's *The Act of Interpretation: A Critique of Literary Reason* (Chicago) uses "The Bear" as the principal text to illustrate how a systematic criticism can work. His attention to function, structure, and purpose, "the primary categories of interpretation," in "The Bear" considers the intent behind the form, provides a useful reading, and reveals how effective affective criticism can be.

Regina K. Fadiman's *Faulkner's 'Intruder in the Dust': Novel into Film* (Tenn.) deals with interrelationships between fiction and film in general, but Fadiman works by analysis and documentation over what she terms a "particularized case history" of one novel and the film made from it. Her study includes a discussion of the differences between the two media, analyses of both novel and film, detailed explanations of changes made and of their motivation and effects, one copy of the screenplay of *Intruder in the Dust* by Ben Maddow, a number of illustrations, and a useful set of appendices. Fadiman makes a number of astute observations on such central topics in Faulkner as initiation and the homogeneous community. Especially interesting is her examination of alterations in the final filmscript for *Intruder in the Dust* which were probably (and here we need more documentation) done by Faulkner himself; if indeed Faulkner did make these changes, they indicate that he was especially determined that Stevens not appear as a spokesman either for himself or for the South. Fadiman's initial theory that "looking at an adaptation can sharpen our eyes to see more of the original" may seem somewhat dubious; but she writes an intriguing study of the film. By contrast, in "Rites of Passage: Novel into Film," an essay on *Intruder in the Dust* in *The Modern American Novel*, E. Pauline Degenfelder summarizes the film and tells us nothing valid about the novel.

Edmond L. Volpe's "Faulkner's 'Knight's Gambit': Sentimentality and the Creative Imagination" (*MFS* 24:232–39) is an interesting discussion of the appeal that the image of Mrs. Harriss as an untouched young girl held for Gavin Stevens. Though Faulkner treated such image-making ironically in the fiction, Volpe suggests that it was a seductive habit of mind for Faulkner himself. Unfortunately, Volpe's essay is too brief for a full discussion of this topic. (Also, he misspells "Harriss" as "Harris" throughout the essay.)

viii. Individual Works, 1950–62

In "The Narrative Structure of Faulkner's *Requiem for a Nun* (*MissQ* 31:387–406) Hugh Michael Ruppersburg offers a "critical key" for proper understanding of this novel. That key is the awareness that the dramatic sections of *Requiem* too are narrative. As an exploration of narrative modes, *Requiem* is, Ruppersburg argues, a unified novel. His essay serves both to make this novel more accessible and to enhance our estimate of its stature. Ruppersburg's article was the only one printed in 1978 on work from this period, though Cleanth Brooks devotes a chapter in his *Toward Yoknapatawpha and Beyond* to *A Fable* and Lewis Simpson also considers *A Fable* in his "Yoknapatawpha and Faulkner's Fable of Civilization" (section *iii*).

ix. The Stories

It was a good year for Faulkner's short fiction because more essays, more widely distributed among the stories, were published. Thomas Bonner, Jr.'s " 'Once Aboard the Lugger'—An Uncollected Faulkner Story" (*NMAL* 3:item 8) is a descriptive account which offers a number of suggestions about theme and technique in this early, little-known story. Though these suggestions could have been further developed and the story's history further expanded, Bonner has performed a useful service in reclaiming this tale. Richard A. Milum's "Faulkner's 'Carcassonne': The Dream and the Reality" (SSF 15: 133–38) is a reading which resolves most of the story's enigmas by paraphrasing and by associating it with the dream/reality conflict in Faulkner's major work. Milum seems to lack an appreciation of the irony with which such idealism is treated elsewhere and to rely upon the label "stream of consciousness" to explain away the story's technical difficulties; nevertheless, he provides a welcome treatment of a neglected story. In "Faulkner's 'Uncle Willy': A Childhood Fable" (Mosaic 12,i:177–81) Edmond L. Volpe reads "Uncle Willy" as a fable opposing the innocent, joyful childhood world with the self-righteous, repressive, and dull adult world. These are appropriate observations; Volpe only goes wrong when he makes comparisons between "Uncle Willy" and Huckleberry Finn, or between Uncle Willy and the tall convict in The Wild Palms: for if irony is missing in "Uncle Willy," it certainly is not missing in those works. Paul Debreczeny's "The Device of Conspicuous Silence in Tolstoj, Čexov, and Faulkner" in American Contributions focuses upon "Dry September." Comparing the effects of omitting crucial scenes in one work by each author, Debreczeny writes a competent, interesting essay.

And finally another neglected story received attention in Richard F. Peterson's "An Early Judgement of Anderson and Joyce in Faulkner's 'Artist at Home'" (KAL 18[1977]:19–23). The essay's title suggests its failures. Peterson shows how a borrowing from Joyce's "The Dead" works in "Artist at Home," but that allusion is not a "judgment" of Joyce, and it certainly is a different class of allusion from Faulkner's use of details from Sherwood Anderson's life. Peterson's title then suggests his failure to focus and to make distinctions. Also he makes Faulkner's portrayal of Anderson harsher than it is: Howe (the Anderson figure) gets the dying poet (a Faulkner figure) a good nurse and later pays both hospital and funeral costs, but Peterson writes that "The Howes never see Blair after the incident, but they do find out that he died shortly after leaving town." Another flaw is that Peterson begins by suggesting that Faulkner might have written "Artist at Home" in 1926, but by the end of the essay he has moved from supposition to assumption as he refers to "the phase marked by Mosquitoes and 'Artist at Home.'" But the real failure of this essay, and the reason I am paying it so much attention, is that the biographical suggestions Peterson makes are quite significant. Peterson should have couched his essay as an argument about the dating of "Artist at Home."

Again, "That Evening Sun" was the subject of more studies than any other Faulkner story. John B. Rosenman's "The Heaven and Hell Archetype in Faulkner's 'That Evening Sun' and Bradbury's *Dandelion Wine*" (*SAB* 43:12–16) sees in each narrative a recurrence of an archetypal pattern; certainly, the very unrelatedness of the two works suggests that the archetypes are at work here. Rosenman's suggestions about the eschatological associations in "That Evening Sun" are appropriate, but a more fully developed treatment would have been welcome. In "Faulkner's 'The Village' and 'That Evening Sun': The Tale in Context" (*SLJ* 11,i:20–31) Philip Momberger provides a sensitive reading of the story and suggests that "The Village" grouping in the *Collected Stories* was not just topical but thematic. While this is not a discovery piece, it is a well-written, well-researched, and well-argued basic study of certain crucial themes here and elsewhere in Faulkner.

Louisiana State University

10. Fitzgerald and Hemingway

Jackson R. Bryer

This has hardly been a "quiet year" in Fitzgerald and Hemingway studies. It was marked by the appearance of two full-length critical studies of Fitzgerald (the first in six years), an excellent biography of Maxwell Perkins which includes much valuable material on both Fitzgerald and Hemingway, Matthew J. Bruccoli's edition of Fitzgerald's complete *Notebooks*, Bruccoli's definitive study of the Fitzgerald-Hemingway relationship, a book-length collection of contemporary reviews of Fitzgerald's books, the first publications of a full Fitzgerald screenplay and of the plays Fitzgerald wrote as a teenager, and a number of provocative and original essays which advance study of these writers' works a good deal.

i. Bibliographical Work and Texts

As has often been the case in recent years, some of the most important and most original work done on Fitzgerald and Hemingway in 1978 falls into this category. The best of the textual pieces is Scott Donaldson's "Preparing for the End: Hemingway's Revisions of 'A Canary for One' " (*SAF* 6:203–11). In a clear and conclusive wedding of textual evidence and critical analysis, Donaldson examines the three drafts of the story in order to show how Hemingway made subtle changes which established the groundwork for his revelation of the impending separation of the American couple. His conclusion, that Hemingway "has done everything possible to lay a sound foundation for his 'surprise ending' " and that his textual revisions "contribute brilliantly to that foundation," is indisputable in view of the evidence he presents. In "The Manuscripts of *To Have and Have Not*: Ernest Hemingway's Social Turning Point" (*RFEA* 2[1976]: 139–47), Geneviève Hily-Mane similarly uses textual evidence to make an effective critical observation. Hily-Mane observes that the

This essay could not have been completed without the research assistance of Ruth M. Alvarez.—*J.R.B.*

first draft of *To Have and Have Not* was centered on the "problem of the writer faced with his art and with social pressure" and its "real hero" was the painter Thomas Bradley, "a true artist" and "a man of action." Only major last-minute changes made by Hemingway transformed Harry Morgan into the major character and focused the novel thematically on social issues. Although not as clearly presented as Donaldson's, Hily-Mane's thesis is equally provocative. Less ambitious than either but nonetheless valuable is Peter M. Griffin's note on "A Substantive Error in the Text of Ernest Hemingway's 'Summer People'" (*AL* 50:471–73), in which Griffin points out that in the 1972 Scribner's edition of *The Nick Adams Stories* and in the Bantam paperback edition, ten lines of the original manuscript of the story (the only complete new work published in the collection) are omitted. Griffin reprints the missing lines, concluding quite sensibly that the piece is "deeply flawed" without them.

The other bibliographical studies are more narrowly focused on textual matters exclusively and hence do not make the critical claims advanced by Donaldson and Hily-Mane. Matthew J. Bruccoli, in "'An Instance of Apparent Plagiarism': F. Scott Fitzgerald, Willa Cather, and the First *Gatsby* Manuscript" (*PULC* 39:171–78), reprints a letter from Fitzgerald to Cather enclosing two pages from a working manuscript of *Gatsby*. These are all of the surviving pages of the working draft which preceded the complete manuscript now at Princeton and reprinted in facsimile form in 1973 (see *ALS 1973*, p. 151). As such, Bruccoli observes, they provide evidence that Fitzgerald "was working on the final plot of *Gatsby* earlier than has been thought. . . . These manuscript pages attest to the existence of at least a partial working draft in 1923, which Fitzgerald then completely rewrote—not revised—in 1924." Geneviève Hily-Mane's "On Some Technical Aspects of the Manuscripts of Ernest Hemingway" (*RFEA* 3[1977]:95–110) marshals a great deal of material to show that Hemingway made lists of titles for his novels and stories both during and after their composition and that he also often used names of real persons and real situations in the manuscripts of his works and then made changes in successive drafts which gradually "transformed their identities as well as their personalities." Hily-Mane provides lists of these name and title changes as appendices to her article, which is a workmanlike piece of research.

James L. W. West III, in "The Bantam 'Gatsby'" (*BCM* 3,vi:

15–18), studies the covers and jackets of the 1945, 1946, 1949, and 1951 paperback impressions of *Gatsby* as reflecting the changing reputation and image of its author. Jackson R. Bryer's "Notes Toward a Corrected Edition of *Dear Scott/Dear Max*" (*FHA*:177–80) lists corrections in the first American edition of the Fitzgerald-Perkins correspondence which Bryer and his coeditor John Kuehl sent to Scribner's for insertion in the English and paperback reprintings, corrections which Scribner's only partially incorporated in the paperback and did not incorporate at all in the English edition.

Virtually all of what might be termed the "reference work pieces" on Fitzgerald and Hemingway this year are updatings or supplementings of previously published standard volumes. The only exceptions are Robert B. Harmon's *Understanding Ernest Hemingway: A Study and Research Guide* (Scarecrow, 1977), inadvertently overlooked in last year's survey, and two items in the 1978 *Fitzgerald/Hemingway Annual*, James D. Brasch's and Joseph T. Sigman's "The Library at Finca Vigia: A Preliminary Report, 1977" (pp. 185–203) and John J. Fenstermaker's "Marketing Ernest Hemingway: Scribners' Advertising in *Publishers Weekly* and the *New York Times Book Review*, 1929–1941" (pp. 283–95). The redundancy and uselessness of Harmon's book is best suggested by noting that Harmon includes only 25 periodical articles about Hemingway in his listing (by contrast, he lists 77 dissertations), fails to annotate the very selective review entries he presents, and makes several outrageous errors (he calls Hadley Richardson "a childhood acquaintance" of Hemingway's and makes no mention of Maria in summarizing the plot of *For Whom the Bell Tolls*). Brasch and Sigman, on the other hand, present a very useful survey and description of Hemingway's library which they feel "demonstrates the extraordinary range of [his] reading and his somewhat scholarly cast of mind, especially in the later years," thus supporting "the contemporary trend in Hemingway criticism . . . which sees the novels less as autobiographical accounts of Hemingway's experience than as intellectually shaped works that owe a great deal to Hemingway's reading and his sense of literary content and style." Although it is written blandly and is limited in scope to two advertising outlets, Fenstermaker's piece breaks new ground in surveying the techniques Scribner's used to publicize the seven Hemingway volumes it published between *A Farewell to Arms* and *For Whom the Bell Tolls*. Fenstermaker ex-

presses understandable surprise that the publisher "made no real
attempt to capitalize on the interests, travels, and other activities of
[the] celebrity-author, even though well-known biographical material could have been used effectively to sell most of Hemingway's
work in the Thirties."

The additions to and corrections of existing reference works divide into those which add or correct material by Fitzgerald or Hemingway and those which do so for material about them. The annual
checklists in the *Fitzgerald/Hemingway Annual* (Fitzgerald by Carol
Johnston, pp. 437–47; and Hemingway by William White, pp. 449–
63) include both sorts of items; but, otherwise, we have notes by
William White correcting errors in and announcing additions to the
Hemingway bibliography (*PBSA* 72:247–49 and 360–61); George
Monteiro adds to known early reviews and notices (*PBSA* 72:245–
46), as does Ray Lewis White (*LC* 43:81–98; *FHA* 273–82). The
latter also calls attention to an unrecorded review of Fitzgerald's
one published play, *The Vegetable* (*FHA*:97–98).

Although *The Vegetable* was the only one of Fitzgerald's ven-
tures into dramatic writing to appear in print in his lifetime, he did
write other plays—for the stage and for the screen—and 1978 saw
the first publication of five of these. In *F. Scott Fitzgerald's St. Paul
Plays, 1911–1914* (Princeton, N.J.: Princeton Univ. Lib.), Alan
Margolies has presented a meticulously prepared edition of the four
dramas Fitzgerald wrote for the Elizabethan Dramatic Club in his
hometown. Inasmuch as the plays were written when their author
was in his middle and late teens, they show a remarkable grasp of
dramatic structure, character differentiation, and control of essentially melodramatic situations. There is considerable improvement
from the first one, "The Girl from Lazy J," which is little more than
a sketch, to the last, "Assorted Spirits," in which a complex plot line
is handled quite effectively. All suffer, however, from unfortunately
truncated second acts and from an overabundance of terrible puns
("No doubt you catch my drift, or shall I snow again?"). Margolies's
Introduction is excellent, as are his briefer prefaces to the individual
plays; and his Textual Apparatus section is a model of scholarly
thoroughness.

The 1938 MGM production of *Three Comrades* remains the only
movie-writing assignment of the many Fitzgerald undertook during
his three visits to Hollywood for which he received actual screen

credit; and in *F. Scott Fitzgerald's Screenplay for "Three Comrades"* *by Erich Maria Remarque*, edited by Matthew J. Bruccoli (So. Ill.), we have the full text between covers. It is a good screenplay, possibly because Remarque's novel, like so much of Fitzgerald's own fiction, centers on the relationship between a poor young man and a girl also pursued by a man of wealth. Bruccoli provides a fascinating Afterword which tells in detail how producer Joseph Mankiewicz butchered Fitzgerald's script by demanding extensive revisions (many of the revisions are printed as an Appendix); and the full volume is a testimony to how a screen-writing talent like Fitzgerald's was abused and ignored rather than nurtured and improved.

Just how much Fitzgerald's understanding of the screen-writing process developed is graphically illustrated by comparing the *Three Comrades* script with the "treatment" of *Lipstick*, which he prepared in 1928 for United Artists and star Constance Talmadge. A 45-page typescript of this "screenplay" survives and Bruccoli has printed it in the *Fitzgerald/Hemingway Annual* (pp. 3–35). It is little more than a short story, with occasional attention paid to the visual details necessary for a movie; it contains none of the sophisticated references to camera angles and descriptions of settings which are in the later script; and, in fact, it is not even rendered in dialogue form but instead is a narrative. The *Annual* also includes (pp. 61–62) a reprinting from the 10 September 1934 New York *Sun* of Fitzgerald's listing of his ten "outstanding impressions in the theater," ranging from "Charles Chaplin in 'The Pilgrim'" through "My own performance in a magicians' show at the age of nine" to "Ernest Truax's face when he was carrying through bravely in a flop of my own [*The Vegetable*] that opened cold in Atlantic City"; and Fitzgerald's 1923 choice of an English drinking tale as his "favorite story," printed in the New York *Herald*, and here reprinted by Richard Winslow (p. 67).

The most important new Fitzgerald or Hemingway text to appear in 1978 is Matthew J. Bruccoli's edition of *The Notebooks of F. Scott Fitzgerald* (Harcourt). About 60 percent of this material appeared in Edmund Wilson's 1945 edition of *The Crack-Up*; but here we not only have the full notebooks exactly as Fitzgerald gathered them—divided into sections entitled, to choose just a few, "Descriptions of Girls," "Moments (What people do)," "Rough Stuff," "Jingles and Songs," and "Feelings & Emotions (without girls)"—

but also Bruccoli's customary helpful editorial apparatus. In this instance Bruccoli includes "Editorial and Explanatory Notes" for many of the entries, identifying persons and places as well as, most helpfully where applicable, indicating where Fitzgerald used the entry in his fiction.

ii. Letters and Biography

The only significant new Fitzgerald letters to appear are a group of seven written in 1920–21 to Carl Hovey, the editor of *Metropolitan Magazine*, or to his screenwriter wife, Sonya Levien Hovey. Edited by Katherine B. Trower, "The Fitzgeralds' Letters to the Hoveys" (*FHA*:55–60) include one Zelda Fitzgerald letter and are primarily concerned with the serialization of *The Beautiful and Damned* in Hovey's magazine. Of much less significance is Gerald F. Peterson's unearthing of "An Unpublished Letter from F. Scott Fitzgerald" (*FHA*:82–83), a brief 1924 note to John Myers O'Hara, a translator of Greek poetry who had apparently sent Fitzgerald a copy of his version of Sappho's poetry.

Despite Hemingway's own strictures, his letters seem to find their way into print one way or another. Just how this has happened and how often are two of E. R. Hagemann's major concerns in his valuable and fascinating "A Preliminary Report on the State of Ernest Hemingway's Correspondence" (*LRN* 3:163–72). As of 1978, Hagemann finds that a total of 594 letters in full, in part, and in paraphrase are in public print. These include 46 reproduced in full (facsimile), 44 in part (facsimile), 50 printed in full (no facsimile), 423 letters excerpted, and 219 letters paraphrased. Hagemann's piece, which also includes a selected list of letter-groups to 28 addresses and a break-down by years, is enormously useful.

A great deal of biographical material on both Fitzgerald and Hemingway appeared in 1978. Much of it dealt with the literary friendships they both cultivated. The most relevant of these of course was the relationship they had with each other. In *Scott and Ernest: The Authority of Failure and the Authority of Success* (Random) Matthew J. Bruccoli skillfully gathers all the documentary evidence —letters, reminiscences, interviews with mutual friends, published autobiographical accounts, and previously published research—to present the fullest and most accurate account we will ever have of the very complex relationship which existed between these two artists. Each appreciated the other's skill as only another practitioner could while at the same time envying in the other skills which they felt they themselves did not possess. One of the central figures in Bruccoli's study is Maxwell Perkins, who, because he served as editor and confidante to both writers, provides a major source of linkage between them. A. Scott Berg's brilliant biography, *Max Perkins: Editor of Genius* (Dutton), is thus filled with material about both Fitzgerald and Hemingway, most particularly detailed accounts of the publications of each of their works which Perkins saw into print during the 1920s and 1930s. One of the book's other great values for students of Fitzgerald and Hemingway is that Berg has presented excerpts from all of Perkins's correspondence so that we not only get Hemingway's and Fitzgerald's own words about one another (much of this is also in Bruccoli's book), we get views as well of both of them from such other Perkins authors as Thomas Wolfe, Edmund Wilson, Marjorie Kinnan Rawlings, and Morley Callaghan. Bruccoli provides a footnote to Berg's volume in "The Perkins/Wilson Correspondence About Publication of *The Last Tycoon*" (*FHA*: 63–66), which summarizes the contents of the 30 letters which passed between Perkins and Wilson in 1941, when the latter was preparing an edition of Fitzgerald's last novel. His conclusion is that the "preparation of *The Last Tycoon* for publication was Edmund Wilson's sole responsibility. There is no evidence that Maxwell Perkins or anyone else collaborated in editing Fitzgerald's drafts."

Fitzgerald's relationships with Ring Lardner and Erskine Caldwell and Hemingway's with Wolfe and Sherwood Anderson are also the subjects of recent pieces. In "Harmony in Great Neck: The Friendship of Ring Lardner and F. Scott Fitzgerald" (*SatR* 9 July 1977:23–25,36), an article adapted from his Lardner biography, *Ring* (Random, 1977), Jonathan Yardley focuses on the period 1922–24 when both writers lived in Great Neck. Despite "profound differences," the two shared love of drink, "delight in foolery and talk," generosity, their mutual "taste for gossip of show biz and the literary world," and, above all, a sense of themselves as "outsiders" in Great Neck because they were writers and "serious men." James E. Devlin's note, "Fitzgerald's Discovery of Erskine Caldwell" (*FHA*:

101–03), traces Fitzgerald's role in bringing Caldwell's work to Perkins's attention in 1930, a story which A. Scott Berg tells in much greater detail in his Perkins biography.

Lex Gaither's "Hemingway and Wolfe" (*TWN* 2,ii:29–30) also duplicates Berg's research in reviewing the attacks Hemingway made on Wolfe's work and the occasions on which they met. Hemingway's fractured friendship with Sherwood Anderson, a break caused by the publication of *The Torrents of Spring*, is the subject of Anthony F. R. Palmieri's "A Note on the Hemingway-Anderson Rupture" (*FHA*:349), in which Palmieri quotes Mrs. Anderson as having written him that Anderson told her just before he died that Hemingway had apologized.

Two coffee-table-type biographical volumes on Hemingway appeared in 1978. Anthony Burgess's *Hemingway and His World* (Scribner's) is a highly personalized account, filled with self-indulgent writing ("The amorous field was not exactly wide open for Hemingway, but he was a sort of guardian of the gate."), much redundant biographical information, occasional critical insights, and a good deal of irrelevant material, especially on the film versions of Hemingway's novels and stories. The book is filled with photographs, but many of them are of Hemingway's friends. Such is not the case with Peter Buckley's *Ernest* (Dial), which opens with a stunning and revealing 100-page chronological portfolio of Hemingway portraits from 1899 to 1961. These pictures portray better than any text possibly could the astonishing physical decline Hemingway experienced in the last decade of his life. Buckley's biographical account is much less satisfactory, shifting disconcertingly from a straightforward year-by-year narrative to personal reminiscences to questionable assertions of how Hemingway felt about a wide variety of subjects; and it is weighed down with Buckley's determination to blame everything bad in Hemingway's life on the influence of his mother. Both Burgess's and Buckley's books would have been better had there been less prose and more pictures.

Personal reminiscences of Fitzgerald and Hemingway continue to appear as articles as well. In "The Fitzgeralds Were My Friends" (*FHA*:37–54) C. Lawton Campbell chronicles his long association with Scott and Zelda, beginning in October 1913 at "horsing" week at Princeton down to fleeting glimpses of Scott in Hollywood in the 1930s. Henry S. Villard knew Hemingway only for a brief time, in

1918 when they were both in the American Red Cross Hospital in Milan; but he writes effectively of this experience in "In a World War I Hospital With Hemingway" (*Horizon* 21[Aug.]:85–93). Villard provides vivid glimpses of Agnes von Kurowsky, Elie Macdonald, and Captain Enrico Serena and speculates plausibly on Hemingway's use of them as models for characters in *A Farewell to Arms*; he also tells of a 1975 meeting with Agnes in which she discussed Hemingway, agreeing with Villard that the manner in which they all idolized him at the hospital might well have served as "the foundation for the self-centeredness that would transform his fresh, boyish character in the years to come." Forrest (Duke) MacMullen was Hemingway's friend and hunting companion during the last 15 years of the writer's life; and John Unrue, in "Duke Remembers Papa" (*FHA*:205–14), records MacMullen's memories of that friendship, correcting some of A. E. Hotchner's 1966 account, and, along with Lloyd Arnold's recently reissued book (see *ALS 1977*, p. 167), giving us vivid material on Hemingway in Idaho in the 1940s and 1950s.

Finally, in "Justice Holmes on Hemingway" (*MarkhamR* 8:7–8), George Monteiro records Holmes's responses—in letters (1928–30) to Sir Frederick Pollack, Harold J. Laski, and Lewis Einstein—to Hemingway's fiction, finding the older man's reactions "evidence of a classic encounter between the generations" (Holmes three times called attention to the role fornication played in Hemingway's novels and stories). Sterling S. Sanford's chart of "Hemingway Genealogy" (*FHA*:343–44) traces the family back to Ralph Hemingway, born in England and "known to have been living in Roxbury, Massachusetts, as early as 1633."

iii. Criticism

a. **Collections.** Jackson R. Bryer's *F. Scott Fitzgerald: The Critical Reception* (New York: Burt Franklin) is virtually identical in format to Robert O. Stephens's Hemingway volume (see *ALS 1977*, p. 168) in presenting a sizable selection of the contemporary reviews of Fitzgerald's novels, short story collections, and one published play. Many of the notices are reprinted from local newspapers and thus this book makes available much material which would otherwise be nearly impossible to locate. Bryer provides an Introduction which surveys reviewers' responses to Fitzgerald's work through the

1941 posthumous publication of *The Last Tycoon* (unlike Stephens, Bryer does not include reviews of the numerous gatherings of material which have appeared in the years since the author's death); and he also reprints from Fitzgerald's scrapbooks at Princeton several reviews which could not be located.

b. **Full-Length Studies.** For the first time in six years, 1978 saw the appearance of a full-length critical book on Fitzgerald; in fact, there were two. The title of Joan M. Allen's study, *Candles and Carnival Lights: The Catholic Sensibility of F. Scott Fitzgerald* (NYU), suggests her thesis—that Fitzgerald's nature was divided, personally and as a writer, between "the lights of the carnival . . . the apparently glamorous life" and "his profound moralism, the realization of sin and destructiveness which underlie and permeate the temporal world." Allen's concern is with the second of these and with how Fitzgerald's "Roman Catholic early education and family experiences, the complexities of a Catholic upbringing in an atmosphere of inadequate paternity and oppressive maternity and ambivalence about money, formed his moral consciousness." The book is strongest when Allen documents the facts of Fitzgerald's Catholic training. Her readings of the fiction are uneven, primarily because she too often overreaches in her efforts to find evidence of Catholic elements. Even so, there is much here of worth.

Rose Adrienne Gallo's *F. Scott Fitzgerald* (Ungar) is a short general survey in Ungar's Modern Literature Monographs series. It contains a brief, choppily written biographical chapter and individual chapters on each of the novels, on the short stories, and, for no apparent reason, on film adaptations of Fitzgerald's works. As is usual in books of this sort, there is a lot of plot summary and the level of critical insight only occasionally rises above that suitable for students not well acquainted with Fitzgerald; but there are a few surprises. These include an interesting suggestion of parallels between *Tender Is the Night* and Ovid's *Metamorphoses* and between "the elemental human situation" of the novel and the ancient myth of Diana of the Wood; a full and useful discussion of "Babylon Revisited"; and intriguing ideas regarding similarities between *The Last Tycoon* and the myths of the love of Apollo for the muse Thalia and of the Hindu god Siva. Throughout, Gallo's interpretations are sound (although she seriously undervalues *This Side of Paradise*), making her book a useful introductory volume.

The one book on Hemingway, Ben Stoltzfus's *Gide and Hemingway: Rebels Against God* (Kennikat), is, in reality, simply two independent essays; and, because the one on Hemingway deals entirely with *The Old Man and the Sea*, it will be discussed below.

c. General Essays. Continuing the recent trend, there are quite a few general essays this year. Four of these deal with Fitzgerald and Hemingway. The best is James W. Tuttleton's "'Combat in the Erogenous Zone': Women in the American Novel Between the Two World Wars," in *What Manner of Woman*, pp. 271–96. Tuttleton's subject is Fitzgerald's, Hemingway's, and Faulkner's responses to the emergence of the New Woman in America, responses the author labels "fundamentally ambivalent," adding that "at times they were clearly hostile to what they felt as a threat . . . to an older ideal of women. . . ." Thus, Fitzgerald powerfully expressed his ambivalent feelings so that "we are as attracted to his heroines as he was, but in the end are equally disillusioned with the self-indulgent uses to which the American girl of the twenties, as he saw her, had put her freedom." Tuttleton sees Hemingway as having "a deep fear—if not of women, at least of man's 'weakness' in 'succumbing' to his own emotional need for woman." His "'undefeated'" men are "redeemed by an inwardness of stoic strength in which, finally, women have no part—except as poignant memories of love the hero once momentarily had but lost." Heroines like Catherine and Maria celebrate "an ideal of womanhood" which Hemingway felt had "largely vanished after World War I, except perhaps in Europe." This is an excellent essay, with a wealth of insight. It is far more penetrating than Hans Schmid's "The Switzerland of Fitzgerald and Hemingway" (*FHA*:261–71), which gives details of each writer's visits to Switzerland and how each utilized those experiences in his fiction, concluding only that their use of the common setting "appealed to Fitzgerald's and Hemingway's sense of seeing the antinomies in life."

The burgeoning "film and literature" industry has spawned three essays this year on television and cinema adaptations of Fitzgerald's and Hemingway's works. In "*Gatsby, Tycoon, Islands*, and the Film Critics" (*FHA*:297–306), Michael Adams surveys the response to the three most recent movie adaptations, noting not surprisingly that each "failed with most of the critics and the public because of bad script-writing, directing, casting, and acting." Gregory Sojka, in "The American Short Story Into Film" (*SSF* 15:203–04), has more positive things to say about the "painstaking efforts" involved in adapting "Bernice Bobs Her Hair" and "Soldier's Home" for television. And in the most useful of the pieces, DeWitt Bodeen's "F. Scott Fitzgerald and Films" (*Films in Review* 28:285–94), the author surveys all the movie and television adaptations, praising the earliest, silent, versions, and, for the most part, harshly criticizing the more widely known and more recent film versions of the fiction.

Of the three general essays on Fitzgerald, the best of a not very distinguished lot is Gary Scharnhorst's "Scribbling Upward: Fitzgerald's Debt of Honor to Horatio Alger, Jr." (*FHA*:161–69). Through brief analyses of *This Side of Paradise, The Vegetable, The Great Gatsby,* and "Forging Ahead," Scharnhorst shows convincingly how Fitzgerald "revived faded memories of the Alger books, not to celebrate them or the Myth of Success which they promoted, but in all instances to satirize them, for the mature Fitzgerald transformed the incredible success won in the Alger stories popular in his childhood into a symbol of the crass materialism rampant in his maturity, a symptom of the acute spiritual malaise which afflicted his achievement-oriented generation." In a much more disjointed essay, "Madness and Sexual Mythology in Scott Fitzgerald" (*IJWS* 1:263–71), Madonna C. Kolbenschlag ranges uncertainly back and forth between discussions of Fitzgerald's fictional women and of his relationship with Zelda, relating both fiction and reality to Freud's and Laing's theories of madness and sex role behavior. Her conclusions are not strikingly original. The same can also be said of Stephen L. Tanner's "Fitzgerald: 'What to Make of a Diminished Thing'" (*ArQ* 34:153–61), which seems highly redundant in viewing Fitzgerald's fiction as "composed of two parts"—"Romantic Promise . . . the complex of hope, dream, yearning, aspiration, expectation, idealism, mystery, confidence, and future possibility," and "the Diminished Thing . . . the unavoidable aftermath of Romantic Promise: hopes and dreams thwarted, the mystery and excitement become commonplace, the future devoid of expectation and possibility."

Of the seven general essays on Hemingway, three are excellent, two are of uneven quality, and two are unoriginal. In the first category are Larzer Ziff's "The Social Basis of Hemingway's Style" (*Poetics* 7:417–23), William Adair's "Ernest Hemingway and the Poetics of Loss" (*CollL* 5:12–23), and Nicholas Joost's and Alan Brown's "T. S. Eliot and Ernest Hemingway: A Literary Relationship" (*PLL* 14:425–49). All are characterized by a combination of clear presentation and highly original ideas. Ziff's contention is that the famous Hemingway style "stems not only from a distrust of a debased public language of feeling but from a disapproval of the sensibility that would want to express feeling directly in whatever language" and that this style "works effectively only in conjunction with material that supports the view that public ideals are false and truth resides solely in unverbalized private experience." Thus, the later Hemingway works became self-parodies as a result of changes in his world view. Adair's thesis is that "Hemingway's work is more concerned with loss, the fear of loss (almost always more important than the fear of violence and death), and the aftermath of loss— longing, confusion, remorse, 'hunger,' nostalgia—than it is with violence, the threat of violence, and death." He ranges intelligently over Hemingway's life and works, citing numerous examples of this pattern. Joost and Brown are similarly precise in pointing out that, despite Hemingway's "generally negative" opinion of Eliot and of *The Waste Land*, his "compulsion to rework after the model of Eliot's writing his own language, themes, and structure (not solely the architecture or design but the reiterative patterns of his work) ensured the precocious achievement of his fiction and indeed the style displayed in all his writing." Their knowledge of both writers and the evidence they amass is simply too great to be denied.

Both Jacqueline Tavernier-Courbin's "Striving for Power: Hemingway's Neuroses" (*JGE* 30:137–53) and Donald Monk's "Hemingway's Territorial Imperative" (*YES* 8:125–40) are difficult to follow, probably because they exist at too great a distance from Hemingway's texts. Both authors try to read the fiction within the context of external sociological or psychological theories; in doing so, they offer some intriguing readings but they also often smother or obscure the very material they are trying to explicate. Tavernier-Courbin uses the writings of Karen Horney and Snell and Gail Putney to explain Hemingway's suicide as well as his need to prove himself— to the world and to himself—as it was expressed in his fiction. Monk applies Lorenz's and Ardrey's work on the "territorial imperative"

to an examination of Hemingway's heroes, asserting that "Caught
in his true vulnerability . . . [the Hemingway hero] holds just enough
space to live, his right to that space being that he has measured what
factors will make it defensible."

Gary D. Elliott's "The Hemingway Hero's Quest for Faith"
(*McNR* 24[1977–78]:18–27) and Sunita Jain's "Of Women and
Bitches: A Defense of Two Hemingway Heroines" (*JSL* 3,ii[1975–
76]:32–35) do little more than rehearse well-worn ideas.

d. **Essays on Specific Works: Fitzgerald.** The disproportionate attention paid to *Gatsby* continues, with 12 of 26 essays on that novel;
but there are also encouraging signs. Several of the *Gatsby* essays
break new ground; the year's four essays on *Tender Is the Night*
are all of high quality; and most important of all, we have six essays
on the short stories.

The three best *Gatsby* essays all view the novel by imposing a
pattern or framework upon it. In *"The Great Gatsby* as Pastoral
Elegy" (*FHA*:141–54) John H. Kuhnle uses studies of the elegy
form by W. W. Greg, Richard P. Adams, and William Empson in
focusing on four major elements which are present in Fitzgerald's
novel: form, pastoralism, biography, and resolution. Kuhnle carefully and convincingly explores each of these areas, concluding that
Gatsby is "in form, convention, and theme . . . a pastoral elegy emphasizing Nick's interpretation of the life and death of Gatsby and
their effect on the survivors." Peter L. Hays, in "*Gatsby*, Myth, Fairy
Tale, and Legend" (*SFQ* 41[1977]:213–23), also argues plausibly
that the novel combines characteristics of the fairy tale with those
of the legend, contending that Fitzgerald has used this combination
"to mock the American dream, to show that it is no more than a
legend to those who believe in it, and a fairy tale, in the most pejo-
rative sense, for most of us." Hays is particularly mindful of the need
to define his terms. H. Keith Monroe is on slightly more tenuous
ground in "Gatsby and the Gods" (*Renascence* 31,i:51–63) when
he claims that "what has, at first glance, seemed a desultory ironic
linking of Gatsby with Christ seems, on closer examination, to be an
expression of a philosophical dualism that recognizes the chasm between the material vegetative world and the imaginative ideal
world." But Monroe does not insist nor does his essay become shrill,
so its effect is convincing.

Three of the *Gatsby* essays focus on specific characters, two on Daisy and one on Tom. All three present radically new ideas and overstate their cases; but each includes some valuable new material. Judith Fetterley's *"The Great Gatsby*: Fitzgerald's *droit de seigneur"* in her *The Resisting Reader* (Indiana), pp. 72–100, is a very strident view, filled with extraliterary assertions such as "When men invest women with the significance of ultimate possessions, they make them the prime counters in their power games with each other." Nonetheless, Fetterley does discern useful patterns of "investment/divestment" and "advantage/disadvantage" in the novel and her reading is often as challenging as it is lively. Leland S. Person, Jr., in " 'Herstory' and Daisy Buchanan" (*AL* 50:250–57), adopts a similarly critical view of the men in *Gatsby*, especially Nick, who "abstracts women into objects of selfish wish fulfillment." Person sees Daisy as misinterpreted by both Nick and Gatsby; neither can "realize (and communicate) the essense of [her] meaning." She is thus "victimized by a male tendency to project a self-satisfying, yet ultimately dehumanizing, image on woman." For Person, Daisy is Gatsby's "double" and the novel describes "the death of a romantic vision of America and embodies that theme in the accelerated dissociation —the mutual alienation—of men and women before the materialistic values of modern society." In "Tom Buchanan: Patrician in Motley" (*ArQ* 34:101–11), Robert Roulston, like Person, is somewhat insensitive to the complexities of the Buchanans; but he challenges us with his interpretation of Tom as "one of the great comic characters in literature." Comparing Tom with Falstaff and Twain's Pap Finn and Duke and King, Roulston sees him sharing with them "shrewdness," "self-evident fatuousness," "exuberant amorality," a "lack of self-knowledge," and an "earthy, even a coarse nature." Roulston is most persuasive when he points out that, like Falstaff and Pap, Tom is a force of nature; and Fitzgerald, like Shakespeare and Twain, knew that he must exorcise him with laughter, for to rail against him would have been futile.

The year's two comparative pieces on *Gatsby* are only moderately absorbing. Christine M. Bird's and Thomas L. McHaney's *"The Great Gatsby* and *The Golden Bough"* (*ArQ* 34:125–31) is not nearly as thorough nor as convincing as Robert J. Emmitt's 1976 essay (see *ALS 1976*, pp. 152–53) in its discovery of "striking parallels" between Frazer and Fitzgerald (Bird and McHaney are apparently unaware of Emmitt's work). Kiyohiko Tsuboi's "Steinbeck's *Cup of Gold* and Fitzgerald's *The Great Gatsby*" in *John Steinbeck: East and West*, edited by Tetsumaro Hayashi and others (Muncie, Ind.: Steinbeck Soc. of America), pp. 40–47, does little more than restate the obvious assertion that both authors were products of the same era and thus subject to similar mythic and sociological influences.

Of the four notes on *Gatsby*, two do make useful identifications, but the other two are worthlessly redundant. In the former category are James Ellis's "The Shadow-Figure Behind *The Great Gatsby*: James, Duke of Monmouth" (*FHA*:171–75) and William P. Keen's "*The Great Gatsby* and 'The Golden Windows'" (*NMAL* 3:item 5). Ellis points out that Nick's early reference to "the Dukes of Buccleuch" and Gatsby's later mention of "the Earl of Doncaster" both are titles created for James, Duke of Monmouth, and, as such, strengthen the relationship of Nick and Gatsby as "doubles." Keen suggests that the phrase "French windows, glowing now with reflected gold" implies a connection between *Gatsby* and Laura Richards's popular children's story "The Golden Windows" (1903). The link seems at best a very shaky one. Hiromi Kawachino's "*The Great Gatsby* as a Story of America" (*KAL* 19:73–76) is a totally unoriginal piece, as is V. N. Arora's "*The Great Gatsby*: The Predicament of the Dual Vision" (*IJAS* 8,i:1–9).

In the best of four good essays this year on *Tender Is the Night*, "Fitzgerald's 'Figured Curtain': Personality and History in *Tender Is the Night*" (*FHA*:105–36), Bruce L. Grenberg calls Fitzgerald "a 'critical,' a 'philosophical,' and, if you will, a 'moral' historical novelist, intent on comprehending and explaining in rational terms the motives and implications of human events, viewed simultaneously as personal experience and public phenomena." Nicole's schizophrenia thus becomes "metaphorical as well as clinical," typifying rather than merely illustrating "the experience and suffering of an immature America in the opening decades of the twentieth century." In a similar way, Devereux Warren's rape of his daughter is "an apt metaphor for the intra-familial self-destructive conflict of World War I, a war in which two opposing nations were led by grandchildren of Queen Victoria." Dick represents 19th-century American idealism and his failure illustrates "the tragic failure of American idealism in the twentieth century." In Grenberg's view, then, the novel as a whole "depicts an America whose ideals, noble in themselves, are becoming untenable, whose idealists, by the very virtue of their ideals, are being corrupted, or crushed and cast out by a new culture progressively giving itself over to material, amoral pleasure." This is a seminal essay, one of the best in print on *Tender Is the Night*.

Robert Roulston has two solid articles on *Tender*, both dealing with the role of place in the novel. In "Slumbering with the Just: A Maryland Lens for *Tender Is the Night*" (*SoQ* 16:125–37), Roulston contends that Fitzgerald's view of Maryland as combining northern "industriousness" with southern "genteel repose" embodied for him "the scheme of values which pervades *Tender Is the Night*." Roulston also comments sensibly about England, the Mediterranean, and Virginia as settings in the novel, seeing Virginia as "in certain respects a surrogate for Maryland." In "Dick Diver's Plunge Into the Roman Void: The Setting of *Tender Is the Night*" (*SAQ* 77:85–97), Roulston focuses more narrowly on the five chapters set in Rome, a locale which he labels "a symbolic embodiment of larger cultural and political forces and simultaneously . . . a spiritual landscape that reflects the state of mind of the central character." Accordingly, besides being "a perfect microcosm of all that has been great and all that has become debased in Western civilization," Rome provides "an x-ray of Dick's psyche—a kind of waking nightmare in which . . . wish fulfillment and punishment combine in a kind of *pas de deux* . . . between the id and the ego." Both of Roulston's essays—and Grenberg's as well—are close and careful readings; and all three suggest dimensions and resonances in *Tender Is the Night* which are surely there and which, hopefully, will serve to place it more securely alongside *Gatsby* as a scrupulously crafted work of fiction. The fourth essay on the novel, Suzanne West's "Nicole's Gardens" (*FHA*:85–95), also reveals this craftsmanship, albeit on a more limited scale, by noting Nicole's association with three different gardens.

The year's one essay on *The Beautiful and Damned*, Robert Roulston's "*The Beautiful and Damned*: The Alcoholic's Revenge" (*L&P* 27[1977]:156–63), is intriguing, although overly biographical in emphasis. Roulston contends that, while he was writing his second novel, Fitzgerald "was experiencing a psychological crisis of a sort likely to confound the most disciplined intellect"—he had "marital and professional tribulations which were exacerbated by his growing dependence upon alcohol"—and that the novel he wrote records "the progress of Fitzgerald's malady." To this ailment is attributed the novel's and its author's "across the board, all-out assault upon his boyhood years . . . and obliquely upon values embodied by his own parents—in fact, upon those forces which had shaped his character and aroused expectations which recent events had shattered." Roulston's perspective here is severely limited; but he does provide a plausible interpretation of this strangely sprawling and bitter novel which has been, for the most part, ignored by critics.

Neither of the year's two pieces on *The Last Tycoon* is very substantial. John Callahan's "The Unfinished Business of *The Last Tycoon* "(*LFQ* 6:204–13) deals primarily with the recent film version; his observations about the novel do not go very far beyond those in Callahan's 1972 book on Fitzgerald (see *ALS 1972*, p. 138). Neill R. Joy, in "Fitzgerald's Retort to Hemingway's 'Poor Scott Fitzgerald'" (*NMAL* 2:item 13), strains to make what, if convincing, would be a quite minor point. In "*This Side of Paradise*: A Study of Pathological Narcissism" (*L&P* 28:178–85), Madelyn Hoffman argues that Amory Blaine's "ultimate equation of beauty with evil represents an awareness on some level that the narcissistic personality's weakness for charisma in others represents a quest for reunion with the original narcissistic charismatic parent." Hoffman's insights, which draw upon the theories of Heinz Kohut and Otto Kernberg, are fascinating but she does not really explore their applications to Fitzgerald's novel as a work of art.

The fact that there are six essays on Fitzgerald's shorter fiction this year is of greater significance than the actual pieces themselves. The best, Janet Lewis's "'The Cruise of the Rolling Junk': The Fictionalized Joys of Motoring" (*FHA*: 69–81), deals with what, strictly speaking, is not a short story at all, but is rather Fitzgerald's account of a 1924 motor trip he and Zelda took from Connecticut to Alabama. Lewis skillfully shows how the piece combines "fact and fancy in describing the actions and the participants" and how it also anticipates its author's future fiction in its perceptions that "Southern nostalgia" is "contrived" and that "one cannot, in fact, repeat the past." Her essay totally supports her conclusion that this is a work that Fitzgerald "worked on with care and real interest, a genuine attempt to bridge autobiography and storytelling." Charlotte LeGates's "Dual-Perspective Irony and the Fitzgerald Short Story"

(*IEY* 26,vii[1977]:18–20) applies to the short stories a view that has often been applied to Fitzgerald's novels: "Because he is able to convey, simultaneously, two diametrically opposed views, he creates dual-perspective irony. . . ." LeGates's study, while suggestive, remains quite superficial. Robert K. Martin's "Sexual and Group Relationships in 'May Day': Fear and Longing" (*SSF* 15:99–101) is more original but also certainly more debatable in its suggestion that, in Gordon Sterrett, Fitzgerald is "treating, albeit covertly and perhaps unconsciously, the problems faced by the repressed homosexual when he is forced to leave a place of relative happiness and security, such as the military or a men's college, and take up a place in a heterosexual world which he fears." In "Fitzgerald's 'Crazy Sunday': Cinderella in Hollywood" (*LFQ* 6:214–21), Kenneth Johnston locates the key to the story in Joel Coles's trustworthiness as a narrator. His inability "to distinguish between appearance and reality" provides the "major source of dramatic irony" which pervades the story. This failure, in turn, "is primarily the result of having lived and worked too long in a world of make-believe"; and "when he comes face to face with genuine, shattering grief, he fails to recognize or respond to it." Thus, it is Joel's "blunted and uncertain perception which is responsible for the inconsistent portrayal of character, the blurred relationships and motivations, and the 'structural disharmony'" which critics have found in the story. Although Johnston never develops his idea that the story is a "variation of the Cinderella tale," his essay is coherent and helpful. So too is James B. Twitchell's "'Babylon Revisited': Chronology and Characters" (*FHA*:155–60), which reexamines the chronology of the story in order to "exonerate Charlie from the charge of being a conscious or unconscious coconspirator in his ultimate disappointment." In "Fitzgerald and Pulp Fiction: From Diamond Dick to Gatsby" (*FHA*: 137–39), Daryl E. Jones finds in Fitzgerald's 1924 story, "Diamond Dick and the First Law of Women," in "provisional form, significant elements later incorporated in" *Gatsby*. These include "frequent allusions to a series of pulp Westerns issued at the turn of the century, and . . . its assignment of values espoused in these Westerns to a female prototype of Gatsby." Jones makes a good case for taking this minor story more seriously thematically, but he admits that, artistically, it is "perhaps the least effective of the potboilers" which Fitzgerald wrote in the winter of 1923.

e. **Essays on Specific Works: Hemingway.** The trend of recent years (Hemingway criticism more evenly distributed over the full range of his fiction than Fitzgerald criticism) was broken in 1978. Nine of the year's 20 essays on specific novels deal with *The Sun Also Rises.* Unfortunately in this case, quantity does not guarantee quality; none of the pieces is distinguished. Given this fact, liveliness and originality become the major criteria for choosing among them. On this basis, Leon F. Seltzer's "The Opportunity in Impotence: Count Mippipopolous in *The Sun Also Rises*" (*Renascence* 31,i:3–14) comes off quite well. Seltzer's controversial "key supposition" is that the Count, like Jake, is impotent. As evidence, he offers "verbal repetitions and dramatic details" from the text, adding that the Count can live comfortably with his impotence because he "has rejected the conventional estimation of physical passion and come to value love on a higher, more 'aesthetic' level—one that ignores the narrowly sexual and celebrates not the platonic but the universally sensuous" and because he has the financial resources "to exchange money for happiness." This is a very suggestive essay, especially in its conclusion that "impotence in *The Sun Also Rises*—at least as it is embodied in the Count—describes, paradoxically, not man's deficiency but his amazing potentiality." Margaret Calvert's analyses, in "Style and Structure in *The Sun Also Rises* (*LNL* 3,ii:1–91), are equally challenging. Calvert applies the techniques of detailed linguistic analysis to four selected passages from the novel to arrive at several interesting insights regarding Hemingway's style, most particularly how variations in that style signal important thematic or symbolic effects. Her work with image sets in the novel seems most rewarding. But the whole essay repays careful reading.

Three of the year's essays focus on Jake primarily, although one of them, Sam S. Baskett's "'An Image to Dance Around': Brett and Her Lovers in *The Sun Also Rises*" (*CentR* 22:45–69), is more worthwhile for what it has to say about Brett. Baskett notes that she "is principally a contained figure to whom her suitors react, rather than a human being whose motives are susceptible to psychological analysis." Thus, the value each suitor "affixes to Brett is a function of his value of himself and the life he is able to live." In "The Morality of Asceticism in *The Sun Also Rises*" (*FHA*:321–30), Kathleen L. Nichols writes well but not very originally of Jake's "progress from romantic to realist." Her article is specific and very clearly articulated; but, in calling Jake's solution to his problems "a secularized morality based on the Catholic ideal of asceticism," Nichols appears merely to be giving a new label to a previously critically overworked idea. Bates Hoffer does not go very far beyond earlier studies either, in "Jacob: As the Sun Rises" (*LNL* 3,ii:93–108), where he discusses parallels between Hemingway's novel and various sections of the Bible. Hoffer's citing of similarities in Revelations and *Sun* are shaky and, ultimately, not very valuable. Jeffrey Hart's "*The Sun Also Rises*: A Revaluation" (*SR* 86:557–62) virtually defies summary; it employs an unfocused scattershot approach and never develops what appears to be its central thesis, that *Sun* is Hemingway's "real novel about the thirties."

Of three notes on *Sun*, the most substantial is Scott Donaldson's " 'Irony and Pity': Anatole France Got It Up" (*FHA*:331–34), which plausibly offers biographical evidence that Bill Gorton's use of the catch-phrase "irony and pity" derives from Donald Ogden Stewart's (one of the real-life models for Gorton) having found the phrase in Anatole France's *Le Jardin d'Epicure*. In "Hemingway and Brooks: The Mystery of 'Henry's Bicycle' " (*SAF* 6:106–09), Fred D. Crawford and Bruce Morton attribute Hemingway's mocking parody of criticism of expatriate art to his outrage at Van Wyck Brooks's *The Pilgrimage of Henry James*, in which Brooks had contended that all great writers stay at home. James Ellis's suggestion, in "Hemingway's *The Sun Also Rises*" (*Expl* 36,iii:24), that Jake's "playing with the idea" that his wound is "funny may very well be a reference to a World War I joke that the British medal for gallantry, the Distinguished Service Order, stood for 'dick shot off' " seems tenuous at best.

Three of the year's four essays on *A Farewell to Arms* focus on the character of Catherine Barkley; and two of these come to very different conclusions about her. In "Beyond the Feminist Perspective: Love in *A Farewell to Arms*" (*FHA*:307–12), William K. Spofford argues a reasonable position very timidly and simplistically. Spofford feels that to see Catherine as "a mindless creature who makes no demands upon her man and who exists only to satisfy his needs" is "to do an injustice to her and to the special relationship that exists between her and Frederic Henry." But the arguments he offers in support of this view are weak, depending as they do on assertions of the two characters' "mutual self-denial" and on his own

statements rather than material from the text. By contrast, Judith
Fetterley, in "A Farewell to Arms: Hemingway's 'Resentful Cryp-
togram'" in her The Resisting Reader (Indiana), pp. 46–71, 193–95,
presents a far more controversial and debatable viewpoint but does
so in an extremely lively and provocative fashion. As in her essay on
Gatsby, Fetterley's stance is blatantly and stridently feminist; but
one need not totally accept remarks such as "While the novel's surface investment is in idealization, behind that idealization is a hostility whose full measure can be taken from the fact that Catherine
dies and dies because she is a woman" in order to derive thoughtful
insights from her piece. It is filled with food for further critical consideration: Catherine's death is the fulfillment of Frederic's "unconscious wish, his need to kill her lest she kill him" and "the logical
consequence of the cumulative hostilities Frederic feels toward her,
and the final expression of the connection between the themes of
love and war"; "In an ironic reversal of expectations, the real danger
to Frederic Henry turns out to be not the world of war, the outer
world that is so obviously threatening, but the world of love, the inner world that seems overtly so secure"; Catherine is "the scapegoat
whose ritual death allows the hero to survive." Placed alongside
these remarks, J. F. Kobler's inconclusive answers to the question
"Why Does Catherine Barkley Die?" (FHA:313–19) appear very
tepid. Colin S. Cass's " 'Nothing Happened . . .': The Tip of a Hemingway Iceberg" (FHA:247–59) is the year's best essay on a Hemingway novel in its detailed exploration of the irony and implications
to be found in Frederic's remark, after Miss Van Campen finds the
empty liquor bottles in his hospital room, that "Nothing happened
except that I lost my leave." Cass's piece brilliantly demonstrates
how this seemingly innocuous explanation conceals a multitude of
important thematic materials—the Van Campen episode clearly does
have a good deal more significance than Frederic's dismissal of it
indicates. Throughout Cass is sensitive both to the overall design
of the novel and to the details of the specific scene he is analyzing.

   Of the three pieces on For Whom the Bell Tolls, only one is a
substantial full-length essay. Carole Moses' "Language as Theme
in For Whom the Bell Tolls" (FHA:215–23) argues persuasively
that the "limitations of language" in the novel constitute "a major
sub-theme": "As a political tool, as a means of communication, and
as an art form, language again and again fails to describe reality

adequately, even though many characters express idealistic views about the potential of language." Moses ranges widely but carefully through the text and brings authority to her interpretation of the meaning of this sub-theme—"all men are outsiders because of their failures to communicate, failures based on the inherent limitations of language." R. H. Miller, in "Ernest Hemingway, Textual Critic" (*FHA*:345–47), collates Hemingway's epigram with its 17th-century spelling text original, noting that, in correcting the galleys, Hemingway made 13 corrections, and concluding that "he wanted Donne's prose in its seventeenth-century purity, and he did a good job getting it." In "Garbo as Guerilla: *Queen Christina* and *For Whom the Bell Tolls*" (*FHA*:335–38), H. Keith Monroe overreaches in suggesting that parallels between Maria and the character Garbo played in the film *Queen Christina*, along with references to Garbo in the novel, may constitute "Hemingway's acknowledgment of a debt to *Queen Christina* which provided him with at least part of the structure of the novel's love story."

The year's two articles on *Across the River and Into the Trees* present two different, and in many respects opposing, views of Richard Cantwell. A. Sidney Knowles, Jr., in "Hemingway's *Across the River and Into the Trees*: Adversity and Art" (*ELWIU* 5:195–208), takes a biographical approach, viewing the novel as "fundamentally self-serving," "a bitter requiem for himself," "a settler of scores, old and new," and a memorial to "certain aspects of his relationship with Adriana Ivancich." In this view, of course, Cantwell becomes Hemingway and "the bitterness of Cantwell's recollection of World War II is not a product of some generalized hatred of war, but of Hemingway's disdain for a war that was managed badly and for generals and politicians who corrupt the military art." Knowles is thorough and convincing; his portrait is of a Cantwell full of self-pity and bitterness drawn by an author who was using his fiction "to strike back bitterly at a long siege of misfortune." James L. McDonald, in "The Incredible Richard Cantwell" (*NMAL* 2:item 3), also regards Cantwell as a "mouthpiece for Hemingway"; but McDonald sees him embodying Hemingway's "prowess" and validating his "sense of his own masculinity."

In "Hemingway's Battle with God" in his *Gide and Hemingway: Rebels Against God* (Kennikat), pp. 39–84, Ben Stoltzfus offers the theory that *The Old Man and the Sea* is not religious in a traditional

sense but rather "should probably be classified as a pagan poem to
existential man." Santiago "is not a Christ figure because of his faith
in man's ability to conquer, man's supremacy, power, intelligence,
and need to assert his manliness." Stoltzfus sees the philosophy underlying the novel as close to the existentialists' belief that death
is essential to living—the killing of the fish suggests that death gives
life meaning—and he views the novel's "messages" as "that 'living
death' is at the heart of things" and that "human dignity is based on
a full appreciation of life and what a man can do." Although some
of Stoltzfus's allusions appear far-fetched, his reading is a useful
counterbalance to those which consider *Old Man* as a religious allegory. By contrast, William Adair's "Eighty-Five as a Lucky Number: A Note on *The Old Man and the Sea*" (*NConL* 8,i:9) is utterly
spurious.

As usual, Hemingway's short stories continue to attract far more
criticism than do Fitzgerald's. This year we have 13 essays on 11
different individual stories, as well as 3 which deal with several
stories as a group. In a well-executed and carefully articulated article, "Opposites Meet: Melville, Hemingway, and Heroes" (*KanQ*
7,iv[1975]:40–54), Paul McCarthy points out similarities in themes,
techniques, and structure between *Redburn* and the Nick Adams
stories. McCarthy amasses so much evidence and urges his thesis
so gently that his piece is useful and convincing. Sharon Robinson's
claim of Emerson's influence on the characterization of Nick Adams
is not nearly as persuasive in "Hemingway, Emerson, and Nick
Adams" (*StHum* 7,i:5–9). J. R. Pici's "Hemingway: Openings of the
Master Strategist" (*LGJ* 5,i[1977]:9, 23), although brief, is remarkably suggestive in its examination of the opening passages of five
Hemingway stories and its observations regarding style and length
of these openings with respect to the rest of the story. This is a topic
deserving of further, more extended, study.

There are two essays this year on "The Short Happy Life of
Francis Macomber." In "The Macomber Case" (*RLV* 43[1977]:
341–47), Charles R. Lefcourt views the Margot-Francis relationship
against the background of other frustrated American couples in
Hemingway's fiction, noting that in each case it is "indifference on
the part of the American boy-man that alienates the female." In this
interpretation Margot "is not 'bitchy' through an ingrained drive for
dominance, but because of the sheer and continual frustration of

her desire to be an individual" and the shooting at the end is tragic because she "strikes down a man who only now shows signs of being able to satisfy her needs by taking his rightful role as dominant partner in their marriage." This is a radical view of the story and Lefcourt's disjointed style does not help him in presenting it.

Of two notes on "The Battler," Glen W. Singer's "Huck, Ad, Jim, and Bugs, A Reconsideration: *Huckleberry Finn* and Hemingway's 'The Battler'" (*NMAL* 3:item 9) is an insightful piece. Singer elaborates on and amends Philip Young's comparisons of the two works, seeing Hemingway's story as "the debasement of an American myth" in which "the white man and the man of color still sit side by side before a campfire, engaged in inarticulate communion, but the wilderness is gone, having been replaced by the hobo jungle, and the ultimate escape of the river has been cut off by the railroad." Kenji Nakajima's "Nick as 'The Battler'" (*KAL* 19:45–48) merely restates the obvious.

Most of the other pieces on the short stories this year are notes which make minor observations. There are, however, two more substantive essays, Wayne Kvam's "Hemingway's 'Under the Ridge'" (*FHA*:225–40) and Gertrude M. White's "We're All 'Cats in the Rain'" (*FHA*:241–46). Kvam does a brilliant job of explicating an infrequently studied story, showing how Hemingway transformed his experiences in the Spanish Civil War into fiction, producing on one level "a miniature dramatization of the entire Loyalist Civil War defeat" and on another level a "parable of the fiction writer who goes to study war at any time." Working with a story which has received much more critical attention, White nonetheless provides much new insight into its resonances. She is particularly effective in assigning symbolic meanings and in describing the tone of the story. Concerning the latter, she calls it "detached and neutral, the viewpoint . . . of aloof observation."

Looking briefly at the new notes on individual stories, one of the most worthwhile is Kenneth Johnston's "In the Beginning: Hemingway's 'Indian Camp'" (*SSF* 15:102–04), which points to two differences between the published story and the deleted opening of it (later published as "Three Shots" in the 1972 edition of *The Nick Adams Stories*). In "Hemingway's Nun's Tale" (*RS* 46:50–53), George Monteiro helpfully traces the biographical background of "The Gambler, the Nun, and the Radio," concluding that the story "tells us 'how it was' during a fixed period during which nothing was going well with the author or his fictional surrogate [Frazer]." In another note, "Hemingway's Unnatural History of the Dying" (*FHA*:339–42), Monteiro argues that Hemingway erred when, in reprinting this section of *Death in the Afternoon* separately as a story, he included in it his treatise mocking naturalists, travelers, and humanists. Paul Witherington, in "Word and Flesh in Hemingway's 'On the Quai at Smyrna'" (*NMAL* 2:item 18), offers a detailed close reading which finds the key to the story in "Hemingway's gradual merger of the inner narrator, the one to whom the war experiences happened, with the outer or frame narrator who is listening to the account, presumably years later, and turning it into this two-page sketch." Jack F. Stewart's subject in "Christian Allusions in 'Big Two-Hearted River'" (*SSF* 15:194–96) is suggested by his title, as is Matthew O'Brien's in "Baseball in 'The Three-Day Blow'" (*AN&Q* 16[1977]:24–26). O'Brien does a better job of showing how his insights help us understand the story than does Stewart. William V. Davis's "'The Fell of Dark': The Loss of Time in Hemingway's 'The Killers'" (*SSF* 15:319–20) seems neither very clear nor original; while Andrew Crosland's "Hemingway, Heller, and an Old Joke" (*AN&Q* 16:73) is truly the ultimate in scholarly absurdity in its assertion of *lack* of influence between Heller in *Catch-22* and Hemingway in "The Friend of Spain: A Spanish Letter."

f. Dissertations. Deborah A. Forczek's "Fitzgerald and Hemingway in the Academy: A Survey of Dissertations" (*FHA*:351–85) is an extremely useful and exhaustive analysis and listing of the 138 dissertations done on the two writers between 1949 and 1976. Only five new dissertations were abstracted in 1978, two on Fitzgerald and one on Hemingway, one a comparison of Hemingway's *In Our Time* and Anderson's *Winesburg, Ohio*, and one with the intriguing title "Howard Hawks: An American *Auteur* in the Hemingway Tradition."

University of Maryland

Part II

11. Literature to 1800

William J. Scheick

This year studies of colonial American literature and culture convey an impressive vigor. Perhaps interest in trivia, demonstration of the obvious, and (as in other areas of literary study) duplication of what has already been established surface a mite too often, but significant advancement occurred in 1978. And it appeared in unexpected places. Whereas the major Puritan poets and Benjamin Franklin attracted minimal attention, the millennium, jeremiads, drama, travel narratives in general and nature reporters in particular, the influence of the Scottish Enlightenment, and interaction between Puritans and Native Americans emerged as vital subjects rich in potentiality for ongoing literary studies in the period.

i. Puritan Poetry

Robert Daly's well-written and appealing *God's Altar: The World and the Flesh in Puritan Poetry* (Calif.) discusses the verse of several New England poets in relation to each other. The strengths of the book include its range, its codification of a tradition to which Edward Taylor belongs rather than from which he appears to depart, its distinction between "naturalist" and "Gnostic" tendencies in the poetry, its clarification of Puritan attitudes toward imagery, its analysis of Anne Bradstreet's elegies and "The Vanity of Worldly Things," and its insight into the function of metaphor in Taylor's elegies. Daly's thesis, that Puritans were not hostile to poetry, to the sensible world, to sensuous imagery or to symbolism, is not original; nor is his general assessment or coverage of previous commentary on the poetry quite accurate or complete. Among other weaknesses are a questionable conflation of periods of time and a problematical use of the term "Puritanism," neither of which are clarified by the simple assertion that Puritan attitudes toward the sensible world "were far more pervasive and uniform than a doctrinaire pluralist would expect." Troublesome as well is the undefended attribution of "I Walk'd and Did a Little Mole-Hill View" to Michael Wigglesworth, which poem figures importantly in Daly's study but which has not commonly been accepted as part of Wigglesworth's canon, not even now by Richard Crowder, who first made the attribution. Daly's book would have benefited, as indeed would discussions of Taylor generally, from an awareness of E. Brooks Holifield's *The Covenant Sealed* (1974). Finally, Daly fails to reveal any value in the poetry itself, never suggests why anyone should read it, reduces all of it—even Taylor's work, which is denied any greater degree of artistic achievement—to thematic content. Nevertheless, revisionist studies often evince such difficulties, and these defects notwithstanding, Daly's book accomplishes its purpose and contributes intelligently to our understanding of Puritan verse.

Another limitation in Daly's approach is pinpointed in " 'The Crucified Phrase': Sign and Desire in Puritan Seminology" (*EAL* 13:278–93), in which Michael Clark cogently emphasizes the Puritans' uncertainty over visible signs of election, their awareness of a gap between the legibility of the world and fallen humanity, their rejection of the material world as a basis for an epistemology, and their certainty of a permanent dialectic between sign and spirit.

Less rigorous and original, though competent, are the introductory remarks in *Early American Poetry* (Wis.), an anthology in which Jane Donahue Eberwein offers in-depth selections from the work of Bradstreet, Taylor, Timothy Dwight, Philip Freneau, and William Cullen Bryant, as well as representative poems by Wigglesworth, Ebenezer Cooke, and Joel Barlow. Spot-checking suggests careful editing, and the selections are judicious, though those by Bradstreet and Taylor only somewhat augment examples presented in Harrison T. Meserole's anthology. The annotations, disappointing in my opinion, might have been more extensive.

Essays on individual poets were scarce this year, though Edward Taylor fared moderately well. In "Edward Taylor to Samuel Sewell[,] Nov. 17, 1704" (*EAL* 13:107–9) Thomas M. Davis edits a letter by Taylor concerning public worship; and Karl Keller documents a Taylorian relationship in "Edward Taylor and the Mathers" (*MSpr* 72:119–35). The way in which Taylor's typological concepts determine the logical connections between stanzas of a meditation is the subject of Peter White's "An Analysis of Edward Taylor's *Preparatory Meditation 2.1*" (*CP* 11,ii:19–23). In "Taylor's 'Meditation Thirty-Eight' (Second Series)" (*Expl* 37,i:3) Caroline Zalboorg mentions some basic features of legal imagery in one of Taylor's poems. Focusing on two poems in "Edward Taylor's 'Problematic' Imagery" (*EAL* 13:92–101) Michael Shuldiner reminds us of the importance of influence on both the meaning and the pattern of Taylor's verse. Although limited in range and despite its tendency to stumble over the question of Taylor's alleged inconsistencies, this essay inclines in the right direction. On the other hand, an ill-advised foray into the bog of number symbolism is attempted by Karen Grube, in "The 'Secret Sweet Mysterie' of Numbers in Edward Taylor's 'Meditation 80,' Second Series" (*EAL* 13:231–37).

Anne King's polemical "Anne Hutchinson and Anne Bradstreet: Literature and Experience, Faith and Works in Massachusetts Bay Colony" (*IJWS* 1:445–67) concludes insipidly that the iconoclast and the creative person represent two types of heroic American women. In "Two Sermons and a Poem by Benjamin Colman" (*SCN* 26:91–93) Howard C. Adams locates two heretofore missing Colman publications and reprints a poem. The poetic ambition of Colman's daughter is remarked in Pattie Cowell's "Jane Colman Turell: 'Inclinations to Poetry'" (*SCN* 26:93–94). And new biographical details are unearthed by Peter White in "William and Benjamin Tompson: The Light and the Dark" (*SCN* 26:96–99).

ii. Puritan Prose

Although perhaps blemished by a reductive treatment of previous commentary, Walter P. Wenska's "Bradford's Two Histories: Pattern and Paradigm in *Of Plymouth Plantation*" (*EAL* 13:151–64) raises several interesting questions about the composition of, the impulses behind, and the purposes informing the first and second books of Bradford's account. An unpretentious review of current opinions about Bradford's work is provided by Perry D. Westbrook's *William Bradford* (TUSAS 317). The Latin of a contemporary of Bradford's is briefly annotated in Leo M. Kaiser's "Some Remarks on the Text of *The Simple Cobler of Aggawam*" (*EAL* 13:302–4). And another first-generation divine, who arrived in New England within a year after Nathaniel Ward, is the subject of Baird Tipson's "The Routinized Piety of Thomas Shepard's Diary" (*EAL* 13:64–80). This essay commences with a thoroughly routine account of the polarities of presumption and despair in Puritan psychology and then provides some insight into this pattern by tracing its origin to the suspended assurance characteristic of Reformation and Pietistic notions. An attempt to limn certain features of Shepard's mind appears in Andrew Debanco's "Thomas Shepard's America: The Biography of an Idea" (*Studies in Biography*, pp. 159–82).

Of the third generation divines Cotton Mather has emerged over the last few years as an increasingly attractive subject for critical investigation. The trend continues this year. Charles J. Nolan, Jr., reviews scholarly interest in Mather in "Cotton Mather: An Essay in Bibliography" (*RALS* 8:3–23). Several of Mather's classical allusions are identified in Leo M. Kaiser's "Six Notes" (*EAL* 13:294–98); and Ronald A. Bosco, in "The Dates of Composition and Initial Audience of 'Paterna,' Cotton Mather's Unpublished Autobiography" (*RALS* 7 [1977]:27–40) argues that "Paterna" divides into two sections, the first written during the period 1699–1702 and addressed to Mather's son Increase and the second composed in 1717 or later and addressed to his son Samuel. Larger concerns characterize David Levin's *Cotton Mather: The Young Life of the Lord's Remembrancer, 1663–1703* (Harvard). This life-and-times biography fails in my judgment to provide a major illuminating reassessment, but I hasten to say that it is a competent and readable attempt, beyond previous efforts, to establish a context for Mather's actions as well as to humanize the man. Oddly Levin eschews interpretative implications and tends to reduce Mather's personality; at times he seems deliberately to evade the darker corners of Mather's mind. Levin's book also falters, for me at least, in coming to terms satisfactorily with previous scholarship on Mather, in its confusing commentary on Increase Mather's adoption of the Half-way Covenant (cf. pp. 4, 9, 194), and its silence about similarities and differences between Mather and other colonial ministers (not to mention Benjamin Franklin) in the matter of identifying one's life with the historical prospects of America. Despite such deficiencies, Levin's book is a generally useful contribution to the Mather revival.

The jeremiad character of various sermons, including several by Mather, is reviewed in "Lectures at the Pillory: The Early American Execution Sermon" (*AQ* 30:156–76) by Ronald A. Bosco, who also compiled "Early American Gallows Literature: An Annotated Checklist" (*RALS* 8:81–107). A major statement on the jeremiad appears in Sacvan Bercovitch's *The American Jeremiad* (Wis.), a lucid and thoughtful extension of ideas explored in his *The Puritan Origins of the American Self* (1975) and his study in *LMonog* 3 (1970). Arguing that the jeremiad has served as a vehicle of cultural expression, particularly of middle-class ideology, from colonial to modern times, Bercovitch analyzes the European origins of the genre and discloses how the American version inverts the theme of divine retribution in order to produce a comforting celebration of communal success and, as well, how the American version, in a ritual of progress through consensus, fuses secular and sacred history. Striking is the inadvertent correspondence between Bercovitch's portrait of American self-consciousness and Bruno Bettelheim's notion of the development of a child's psyche, in particular the idea that as a child achieves a self over which he can be unambivalent, he slowly accepts the possibility that the self may also evince a more dubious nature. Bercovitch's study exhibits an impressive mastery of primary materials and a somewhat less satisfactory recognition of previous scholarship in related areas (e.g., John Kouwenhoven's pertinent concept of the patterns of process in American culture, earlier identifications of a "collective self" in Puritan writings, and recent investigations of Edwardsean millennialism). Although not convincing at every point, the book offers a supurb overview which future approaches to the subject will clarify rather than repudiate.

Whereas Bercovitch tends to evade the question of how the New England jeremiad came to represent the views of middle and southern, as well as northern, colonists, John F. Berens faces this historical problem directly, suggesting that the Great Awakening partially destroyed regional boundaries, that itinerant and transplanted New Englanders served as agents in various geographic areas, and that the French and Indian Wars served catalytically in the emergence of a belief in the providential foundation of American patriotism. In *Providence and Patriotism in Early America, 1640–1815* (Virginia) Berens covers the same ground as does Bercovitch, with a mutual emphasis upon the rhetoric and the biblical imagery of the jeremiad. But whereas Bercovitch details differences between the European and American versions of the jeremiad, Berens focuses on how northerner and southerner, loyalist and patriot, Federalist and Anti-Federalist, elite and popular spokesmen shared the providential language and imagery of the jeremiad. This emphasis permits Berens to surpass Bercovitch's observations about national consensus and to demonstrate how the rhetoric of the jeremiad led to partisan conflict within the providential framework. Berens is perhaps sometimes too quick to infer that an author personally endorses everything he says in a public document—e.g., identifying Thomas Paine's actual belief with remarks about national sins in the *American Crisis* papers. In summary, to read one of these two books is to read much of the other; but Bercovitch's deft portrait of the American psyche and Berens's expert framing of that portrait with referential details of American and European history remarkably complement each other.

iii. The South

In the field of southern colonial studies the publication of Richard Beale Davis's three-volume *Intellectual Life in the Colonial South, 1585–1763* (Tenn.) is a major event. The work overwhelms; the reader comes away from it with great respect for its impressive scope, consistency, and readability. Old-fashioned in the best sense, Davis's study presents encyclopedic literary history at once rich in synthesis and revisionism (e.g., it refutes various observations made by Perry Miller, Roy Harvey Pearce, and Alan Heimert). Different readers may object to one or another specific matter, they may express skepticism over the environmental determinism implicit at certain points in Davis's discussion, and they may wince at the use of such words as "primitive," "savage," and "natives" in reference to Native Americans, often specifically in contrast to "the civilized southern colonial." Nevertheless, only the myopic will fail to appreciate the degree to which Davis's exceptional work is simultaneously a defense and a challenge, a wonderful landmark celebrating Davis's entire career and guiding others to this too often neglected area of literary inquiry.

Impressive as well is Marion Tinling's two-volume edition of *The Correspondence of the Three William Byrds of Westover, Virginia, 1684–1776* (Virginia, 1977). The letters are edited with care, the annotations are full, and the volumes are attractively designed, illustrated, and printed—in every respect a laudatory performance. In response to the edition Carl Dolmetsch has written a review-essay entitled "Three Byrds of Virginia" (*MissQ* 31:615–22). The Byrds's neighbor in Maryland is the subject of Donald V. Coers's "New Light on the Composition of Ebenezer Cook's *Sot-weed Factor*" (*AL* 49:604–06), which cites evidence to support arguments for 1708 as a realistic date for the composition of Cooke's satiric poem. In "Ebenezer Cooke's *The Sot-weed Factor: A Satire on Pride*" (*SoSt* 17: 363–73) David Robinson stresses pride as the cause of sin and as the moral (in contrast to the usually asserted social) center of the poem. Finally, Gregory A. Stiverson and Patrick H. Butler have edited "Virginia in 1732: The Travel Journal of William Hugh Grove" (*VMHB* 85[1977]:18–44).

iv. Edwards and the Great Awakening

Appropriately Jonathan Edwards, especially his millennial thought, received significant attention this year. In "The Impolitic Mr. Edwards: The Personal Dimension of the Robert Breck Affair" (*NEQ* 51:64–79) Charles Edwin Jones connects Edwards's role in the offensive against the ordination of Breck and Breck's later role in the dismissal of Edwards from his Northampton parish. "The Calvinist Psychology of the Heart and the 'Sense' of Jonathan Edwards" (*EAL* 13:181–92), by Terrence Erdt, ratifies with useful detail the arguments of others (particularly Conrad Cherry) that Edwards's concept of the "sense of the heart" was not innovative but rather an application of an idea available from several sources, including Calvinism. Edwards's notion of self-love is contrasted with that of a contemporary in Charles W. Akers's "Religion and the American Revolution: Samuel Cooper and the Brattle Street Church" (*WMQ* 35:477–98). And Edwards's views on singing in church by note, as well as the observation that the Great Awakening did little to resolve the controversy about such singing, are noted in Joyce Irwin's "The Theology of 'Regular Singing'" (*NEQ* 51:176–92).

An important, heretofore undisclosed feature of Edwards's thought is revealed in *Apocalyptic Writings* (Yale, 1977), the fifth volume of The Works of Jonathan Edwards. Expertly edited and annotated by Stephen J. Stein, who has also written a full and useful introduction, this valuable contribution revises certain specific claims made by Alan Heimert, among others, and implicitly agitates for a reassessment of Edwards's originality generally. In "Providence and the Apocalypse in the Early Writings of Jonathan Edwards" (*EAL* 13:250–67) Stein demonstrates how Edwards's view of the apocalypse varied, even in the early notebooks, and exhibits a greater reconciliation of the theologian's concern with earthly realities and otherworldly considerations than has been previously detected.

Concepts of the millennium, including Edwards's views, figure significantly in the books by Bercovitch and Berens, discussed above, and are the central concern of John West Davidson's *The Logic of Millennial Thought: Eighteenth-Century New England* (Yale, 1977) and Nathan O. Hatch's *The Sacred Cause of Liberty: Republican Thought and the Millennium in Revolutionary New England* (Yale, 1977). Surveying the writings of several ministers, Davidson refutes the conventional application of pre- and post-millennial classifications, demonstrating that 18th-century millennialism cannot be categorized according to any prediction of events, in terms of a contrast between pessimistic catastrophism and optimistic progressivism, or in relation to its effect on Revolutionary ideology. At the foundation of 18th-century eschatology is a model of progress reinforced by the Puritan morphology of conversion. Not everything Davidson says convinces—e.g., his claim that Revolutionary ideology assumed human nature would remain depraved—but his book is indeed valuable for future literary and historical studies of 18th-century New England writings.

In contrast, Hatch's book avoids a penetrating probe into the eschatological notions so crucial to his thesis: that traditional Puritan apocalyptic rhetoric and 18th-century political discourse formed a "civil millennialism" in accord with which the advancement of freedom is God's cause. Its many limitations notwithstanding, Hatch's book raises several worthy questions, makes good use of Timothy Dwight's writings, and supports Davidson's belief that neither the Great Awakening nor New Light factionalism can be designated as the primary agency in the development of the idea of redemptive history in New England. Ideally Hatch's study should be read in conjunction with the books by Davidson, Bercovitch, and Berens. Such intensive exposure may transform the unwary reader into a stargazer, but those less vulnerable will learn enormously about millennial ideas generally and Edwards specifically. Clearly, and rightly, there has been a renaissance of interest in both.

While Edwards was a neophyte minister for a Presbyterian congregation in New York, John Leverett labored at Harvard, where he delivered several orations, one of which now appears in Leo M. Kaiser's "A Latin *Oratiuncula* of President John Leverett of Harvard, October 23, 1822" (*Manuscripta* 22:109–22). The way "turning within" should move one to outward and forward action is discussed in William A. Christian's "Inwardness and Outward Concerns: A Study of John Woolman's Thought" (*QH* 67:88–104). And Yale University Press has made available *The Papers of Ezra Stiles*, 22 reels of microfilm including all the manuscripts and printed works (in the Yale collection) by the man who believed that Edwards's writings would "pass into . . . transient Notice perhaps scarce above Oblivion."

The influence of Edwardsean tradition in America is documented in Ann Douglas's *The Feminization of American Culture* (Knopf, 1977), Laurence Buell's "Calvinism Romanticized: Harriet Beecher Stowe, Samuel Hopkins, and *The Minister's Wooing*" (*ESQ* 24:119–32), and an essay by Conrad Cherry to be remarked shortly. Edwardsean tradition, its transmission and influence, deserves much more attention than it has received to date.

v. Franklin and the Revolutionary Period

Scholarship on Benjamin Franklin did not advance appreciably this year. Stephen J. Whitfield observes the obvious in "Three Masters of Impression Management: Benjamin Franklin, Booker T. Washington, and Malcom X as Autobiographers" (*SAQ* 77:399–417), whereas in "Metamorphoses of Spiritual Autobiography" (*ELH* 44 [1977]: 108–26) Robert Bell remarks Franklin's investment of fragments of experience with meaning, so that some whole or pattern is suggested, as a departure from the models of spiritual autobiography provided by Augustine and Bunyan. In "Benjamin Franklin, Universal Genius," which appears in *The Renaissance Man in the Eighteenth Century* (Los Angeles: William Andrews Clark Memorial Lib., Univ. of Calif., pp. 1–44), J. A. Leo Lemay details Franklin's performance in public affairs, science, and literary endeavors, noting in particular several levels of the American dream theme in the *Autobiography*. A catalogue of certain interests, attitudes, intentions, methods, and tonal qualities identifying similarities between the *Autobiography* and Addison's and Steele's influential writings is presented in Janette

Seaton Lewis's " 'A Turn of Thinking': The Long Shadow of the *Spectator* on Franklin's *Autobiography*" (*EAL* 13:268–77).

Franklin's ideas, rather than his artistry, are scrutinized in three essays. In "Benjamin Franklin's Vision of a Republican Political Economy for America" (*WMQ* 35:605–28), Drew R. McCoy instructively points to the conceptual significance of virtue in Franklin's repudiation (evincing typical republican inconsistencies) of British political economy, especially its emphasis on production for export. A theory of habit accenting nurture over nature is the topic of Norman S. Fiering's "Benjamin Franklin and the Way to Virtue" (*AQ* 30:199–23), which refers to Edwards in passing while devaluing the influence of Puritanism on Franklin. Franklin's resistance to peace short of formal independence is noted in Cannon Garland's "Sir William Jones and Anglo-American Relations During the American Revolution" (*MP* 76:29–45).

"Franklin's and Crèvecoeur's 'Literary' Americans" (*EAL* 13:50–63), by Philip D. Beidler, contributes somewhat to the generally held view that the *Autobiography* and *Letters from an American Farmer* exhibit a correspondence between an evolving individuality and representative cultural identity. For Mary E. Rucker, in "Crèvecoeur's Letters and Enlightenment Doctrine" (*EAL* 13:193–212), the *Letters* reveals a tension emanating from a narrator who is emotionally idealistic and an author who is rationally pessimistic about humanity, nature, and America. The essay fudges on the question of "whether or not Crèvecoeur here deliberately engages in a dialectic, which legitimatizes intentional inconsistencies and contradictions," an essential matter for anyone wishing to believe that the *Letters* are elaborately ambiguous rather than merely ambivalent.

John Adams and Thomas Paine figure in "Revolutionary Rhetoric and Puritanism" (*EAL* 13:45–49), Larzar Ziff's brief reminder that Puritan history was cited in the cause of liberty. The book of a political colleague, whom Adams in 1793 accused of being as deceptively ambitious as was Oliver Cromwell, is the subject of Dorothy Medlin's "Thomas Jefferson, André Morellet, and the French Version of *Notes on the State of Virginia*" (*WMQ* 35:85–99). Medlin documents Jefferson's disagreement with Morellet's view that a translation might surpass the original version of a work, an approach which led the Frenchman to rearrange the *Notes* into four categories. Clayton W. Lewis makes a modest effort, without regard to precedent attempts, to discuss a worthy topic in "Style in Jefferson's *Notes on the State of Virginia*" (*SoR* 14:668–76). James M. Cox, in "Jefferson's *Autobiography*: Recovering Literature's Lost Ground" (*SoR* 14:633–52), offers a relaxed ramble through the logical and unornamented style of the *Autobiography*; Cox cogently says at one point: "The assurance and the detachment of Jefferson's narrative breathe a confidence which is at the heart of the stillness and purity of his life of himself."

Inventing America: Jefferson's Declaration of Independence (Doubleday), by Garry Wills, refutes the frequently expressed assumption that Lockean thought underlies Jefferson's political and social ideals. Attending closely to the language of the Declaration Wills elucidates the correspondence between the thought and expression of Jefferson and that of leading thinkers of the Scottish Enlightenment, especially Francis Hutcheson. Aside from a somewhat rash prologue, an annoying failure to take into comprehensive account what others have observed about the language of the *Declaration*, and too heavy a reliance upon what is well-known among Jefferson scholars, Wills's book is convincing in its thesis and frequently illuminating on specific matters. Especially noteworthy is Wills's analysis of Jefferson's language and manner in the Natural Bridge passage in the *Notes*. Rarely has Jefferson's thought been discussed as well as in *Inventing America*, a work providing an opportunity for entertaining reading and good thinking.

In "Eulogy or Symbolic Biography: The Iconography of Revolutionary Leadership, 1776–1826" (*Studies in Biography*, pp. 131–57) Michael T. Gilmore demonstrates that the Christian and Classical traditions, especially underlying the metaphor of paternity, utilized by patriot eulogists in 1776 to justify separation from Great Britain, were used again by them at the turn of the century to legitimatize America. The importance of the image of the yeoman farmer as a moral symbol of the Revolutionary age is explored by William D. Liddle in " 'Virtue and Liberty': An Inquiry into the Role of the Agrarian Myth in the Rhetoric of the American Revolutionary Era" (*SAQ* 77:15–38).

The development of freedom of the press in the colonies is traced in Clark Rivera's "Ideals, Interests and Civil Liberty: The Colonial Press and Freedom, 1735–76" (*JQ* 55:47–53, 124). By making important documents public and by presenting a consistent ideological

view of the emergent struggle, according to Allan R. Raymond's
heavily documented "To Reach Men's Minds: Almanacs and the
American Revolution, 1760–1777" (*NEQ* 51:370–95), almanacs con-
tributed importantly to American attitudes toward the break from
Great Britain. Another significant vehicle for ideas during this time
and later is the subject of *American Essay Serials from Franklin to
Irving* (Tenn.) by Bruce Granger and of *Newsletters to Newspapers:
Eighteenth Century Journalism*, edited by Donovan H. Bond and
E. W. Reynolds McLeod (Morgantown: West Va. Univ. School of
Journalism, 1977). The latter presents ten essays on printing and
the press, including two on Franklin: "Non-Indigenous Influences
on Benjamin Franklin's Journalism" by Robert W. Hudson (pp. 119–
28) and "Benjamin Franklin's 'Silence Dogood' as an Eighteenth-
Century 'Censor Morum'" by Mark Lipper (pp. 73–83). Although
more descriptive than evaluative, Granger's *Essay Serials* supports
certain established distinctions between northern and southern
serials, provides useful comparisons, and generally succeeds in reminding us of the merits of 18th-century essays written by Franklin,
Francis Hopkinson, Joseph Dennie, Judith Sargent Murray, and especially Philip Freneau and John Trumbull.

vi. The Early National Period

An acquaintance of Trumbull, Timothy Dwight, as well as two of
Dwight's students, figure in Conrad Cherry's "Nature and the Republic: The New Haven Theology" (*NEQ* 51:507–26). Cherry convincingly detects a paradox at the core of Yale Divinity thought: that
in conjunction with their rejection of an Edwardsean view denying
the free agency of man, they applied a Newtonian world view which
nonetheless imprisoned the individual within an inflexible scheme
of cosmic government. Another Hartford Wit is discussed in "The
Enlightenment View of Myth and Joel Barlow's *Vision of Columbus*"
(*EAL* 13:34–44), in which Robert D. Richardson, Jr., conducts an
informative survey of 18th-century notions of myth in order to suggest that although Barlow evinced a typical skepticism towards myth,
his epic on America reflects the more affirmative current of his day.
The views of a contemporary, who made more of a career in law than
did Dwight or Barlow, are investigated in Michael T. Gilmore's
"Eighteenth-Century Oppositional Ideology and Hugh Henry Brack-

enridge's *Modern Chivalry*" (*EAL* 13:181–92), which argues that Brackenridge shared the English neoclassicists' attachment to country, commonwealth, and old Whig ideology.

One of Brackenridge's friends is approached as a systematic and serious poet in Richard C. Vitzthum's *Land and Sea: The Lyric Poetry of Philip Freneau* (Minn.). Vitzthum argues that as a young man Freneau believed in the superiority of fancy over reason and, so, romanticized nature in his poetry, whereas by the mid-1780s he became skeptical, dismissed fancy and pastoralism as deceptive, and adopted a rationalistic stoicism. During this time he developed personal and consistent symbolic patterns, most notably reflected in masculine sea and feminine land imagery. After 1790, he again returned to nature in his poetry, not in terms of fancy or skepticism, but in the light of deism, which permitted him to perceive stability in nature and harmony between nature and humanity; at this time he abandoned his private symbolism for public expression. Not everyone will agree at every point with Vitzthum's interpretations, or with all of his attempts to regularize apparent exceptions to his thesis, or with every claim for Freneau's talents (e.g., "syntactic ambiguity is a device Freneau uses . . . in a number of his best poems to mask disturbing meanings from unwary readers"). But Vitzthum makes excellent use of Freneau's revisions and offers interesting, if sometimes very contestable, readings of Freneau's marginalia. Vitzthum successfully elevates Freneau's status as a poet and in the process invites others to take a more serious look at the poetry.

American drama of the period has become increasingly attractive as a topic for critical inquiry. With an interesting thesis worth debating, Jay Martin's "The Province of Speech: American Drama in the Eighteenth Century" (*EAL* 13:24–33) suggests that early American theatre served as a medium for indigenous imagery reflecting American social existence and that this vision underwent three distinct evolutionary phases. A pre-Revolutionary War play, in which history serves as a metaphor expressing the audience's fear of tyranny and irrationality as well as permitting that audience to advance the claim for independence from Great Britain, is illuminatingly approached in Frank Shuffelton's "The Voice of History: Thomas Godfrey's *Prince of Parthia* and Revolutionary America" (*EAL* 13:12–23). For Donald T. Siebert, Jr., the juxtaposition of laughter and sentiment and the use of bawdiness and of audience involvement as well exemplify original features of *The Contrast* ("Royall Tyler's 'Bold Example': *The Contrast* and the English Comedy of Manners" [*EAL* 13:3–11]). Tyler also wrote fiction, and sketches from one of his unpublished works have been edited by Martha R. Wright, in *The Bay Boy, or the Autobiography of a Youth of Massachusetts Bay* (Exposition). A minor, student-authored work reflecting an altercation among Windsor citizens surfaces in "Drama as Social Corrective: A Performance at Windsor, Vermont, in 1791" (*NEQ* 51:99–105).

Approached with certain expectations, Walter J. Meserve's *An Emerging Entertainment: The Drama of the American People to 1828* (Indiana, 1977) may disappoint. Its aims are to survey chronologically the plays written and published in early America; to describe them in general terms and synopsize the plots of the most important of them; to relate some details of the biography of their authors; and to suggest broad connections between them and the cultural and historical matrix they reflect. Aside from such strange lapses as changing Michael Wigglesworth's name to William (pp. 4, 337) and attributing to Charles Brockden Brown a work entitled *Armond* (p. 94), Meserve's book generally succeeds as an act of critical description and enumeration.

Concern with travel narratives of the period, particularly by nature reporters, is typified by Bruce Silver's "William Bartram's *Travels* and Other Eighteenth-Century Accounts of Nature" (*JHI* 39:597–614), which cites regional characteristics and the lack of an argument for the existence and goodness of God as chief differences between the *Travels* and similar contemporary works. Also of interest are Neill R. Joy's "Two Possible Analogues for 'The Ponds' in *Walden:* Jonathan Carver and Wordsworth" (*ESQ* 24:197–205) and Percy Adams's "Travel Literature of the Seventeenth and Eighteenth Centuries: A Review of Recent Approaches" (*TSLL* 20:488–515).

The study of American colonial naturalists received a major boost with the appearance of David Scofield Wilson's *In the Presence of Nature* (Mass.). Wilson explores how, in the work of Jonathan Carver, John Bartram, and Mark Catesby, nature reportage intermingles with protonational ideas, often initiating the reader by means of the reporter's subjective mediation between his own personality (self, art) and nature (other, science). Although it would have benefited from an application of several insights from recent studies by such anthropologists as Mary Douglas and Victor Turner, the book

succeeds marvelously in recapturing the original excitement informing the naturalists' texts, in indicating aesthetic dimensions in these
works (especially in Catesby's paintings), and in setting an enviable
model for how felicitously an academic book can be written. Beautiful intrinsically and extrinsically, Wilson's book is in a sense a pioneer
study, one which invites others to follow its pace-setting example.

vii. Brown and Contemporaries

Travel literature figures centrally in William C. Spengemann's *The
Adventurous Muse: The Poetics of American Fiction, 1789–1900*
(Yale, 1977), a suggestive and elegantly written book as important
for what it says about narratives by William Wood, William Bradford, Sarah Kemble Knight, Timothy Dwight, and William Bartram
as for its revelation of how the heritage of such narratives is mirrored
in American fiction. When contrasting this heritage with the equally
influential poetics of domesticity, Spengemann occasionally errs:
e.g., concerning Augustine's concept of motion, Irving's narrative
variation in *A Tour on the Prairies*, and Cooper's notion of gifts; and
there are misjudgments or, perhaps, eccentric moments in the work.
But these are minor matters compared to his formidable overall
achievement and specifically to his commentary on Freneau's "The
American Village," Brackenridge's *Modern Chivalry*, Susannah Row-
son's *Charlotte Temple*, Royall Tyler's *The Algerine Captive*, and
Charles Brockden Brown's *Arthur Mervyn*.

Mark Seltzer has written an intelligent essay on Brown's currently most popular work. "Saying Makes It So: Language and
Event in Brown's *Wieland*" (*EAL* 13:81–91) convincingly demonstrates that Clara's language compensates for her perception of
broken causal sequences, that her speech emerges as the central
action of the romance. The cogency of this approach becomes even
more apparent, I think, if one applies to it observations by Michel
Foucault and Jacques Derrida on the problem of origination. Detective work of a different sort characterizes "*Ormond*: How Rapidly
and How Well 'Composed, Arranged and Delivered'" (*EAL* 13:238–
49), in which Sydney J. Krause argues that *Ormond* was written
with somewhat less haste and with somewhat more care than generally thought. An interesting fragment by Brown appears in Hans
Borcher's edition of *Memoirs of Stephen Calvert* (Bern: Peter Lang).

In "Samuel Miller's Nation 'Late Become Literary': The *Brief Retrospect* in Brockden Brown's *Monthly Magazine*" (*EAL* 13:213–16) Walter H. Eitner identifies passages in *Brief Retrospect* as revisions of an article by Miller in Brown's publication. Sources also concern Edward W. Pitcher, who in "A Note on the Source of 'The Child of Snow' and 'The Son of Snow'" (*EAL* 13:217–18) points to a 13th-century French tale. And in "Signatures and Sources for Fiction in [Noah] Webster's *American Magazine* (Dec. 1787–Nov. 1788)" (*EAL* 13:102–06) Pitcher suggests that 17 of 19 works of prose in one publication were not written by American authors, a fact alerting critics to be wary of relying on signatures as evidence; see also Pitcher's "Sources for Fiction in *The Royal American Magazine* (Boston, 1774–5)" (*AN&Q* 17:6–8). Finally, in "A Letter of William Hill Brown's" (*AL* 49:606–11) John R. Byers, Jr., seeks clues to Brown's physical appearance.

viii. Miscellaneous Studies

Puritan relations with Native Americans received more attention than usual. In *Puritans, Indians, and Manifest Destiny* (Putnam's, 1977) Charles M. Segal and David C. Stineback have compiled 55 documents by Native Americans and by New England colonists or visitors in order to demonstrate that the history of the interaction between the two was characterized by a cultural conflict with philosophical and theological bases—specifically each culture's spiritual perception of itself—and that this conflict reveals the essential difference between them during the westward movement in America. The paperback edition of this instructive collection should make useful supplementary reading in the classroom.

In *The White Man's Indian: Images of the American Indian from Columbus to the Present* (Knopf) Robert F. Berkhofer gives a good synthesis of current studies of the idea of the Native American. Occasionally Berkhofer's method may trouble historians and his tendency to generalize may raise eyebrows. Too often he reduces texts so that they illustrate a thesis rather than emerge as complex wholes; and he is particularly inaccurate in his comments on Cooper. His book, however, is sensitive and serves as an excellent resource for anyone interested in literary images of Native Americans. Also of value in this regard is David C. Stineback's "The Status of Puritan-

Indian Scholarship" (*NEQ* 51:80–90) and James Axtell's "The Ethnohistory of Early America: A Review Essay" (*WMQ* 35:110–44).

Ann Stanford's "Images of Women in Early American Literature," included in *What Manner of Woman*, edited by Marlene Springer (NYU, 1977, pp. 184–210), suggests that whereas women in 17th-century literature appear as heroic figures (e.g., Anne Bradstreet, Anne Hutchinson, and Mary Rowlandson), women in 18th-century literature suffer a decline in status (e.g., Charles Brockden Brown's women, who are victims of circumstance rather than self-willed individuals). In " 'To Render Home a Paradise': Women in the New World Landscapes," in *Women's Language and Style*, edited by Douglas Butturff and Edmund L. Epstein (Akron, Ohio: Dept. of English, Univ. of Akron, pp. 36–46), Annette Kolodny demonstrates that in the late 18th century northern and southern colonial women expressed frustration over entrapment within landscapes beyond their control, in contrast to men who felt a legal and experimental power to alter landscapes.

Not to be overlooked is Ronald J. Vander Malen's "Providence as Mystery, Providence as Revelation: Puritan and Anglican Modification of John Calvin's Doctrine of Providence" (*CH* 47:27–47), which is pertinent to students of American as well as English Puritanism. On the other hand, Stephen L. Fluckiger's "The Idea of Puritanism in the Plays of Eugene O'Neill" (*Renascence* 30:152–62) can be skipped.

In summary, 1978 was a rather full year for colonial studies, with several outstanding contributions, no major embarrassments, and in general a respectable progress in an evolving sophistication of critical method and a consequent enrichment of analytic texture.

University of Texas, Austin

12. 19th-Century Literature

Thomas Wortham

Feminist criticism was less strident, explications less ingenuous, and scholarship founded on recovered fact, not imagination: such are the predominant characteristics of the year's work in 19th-century literature. The first volume of a new edition of Irving's letters, Nina Baym's superb study of women writers active at midcentury and Ben Vorpahl's considered analysis of Remington's artistic vision are works that will endure. The other books and many articles, if not all of the first importance, are nevertheless a happy indication that the continuing discovery of our literary past is real and ultimately important.

i. General Studies

In his attempt to locate the meaning or meanings of the American Revolution in the American imagination during the past two centuries, Michael Kammen, in a bold, intriguing, but disappointing book, *A Season of Youth: The American Revolution and the Historical Imagination* (Knopf), examines, among other evidences, the role the Revolution has played in American popular culture, including iconography, poetry, drama, and historical novels. Kammen significantly notes that the novels whose actions center on the Revolution—whether Cooper's, Simms's, Kennedy's, early, or Churchill's, Jewett's, S. Weir Mitchell's later in the 19th century—"normally enjoyed an enormous but ephemeral popularity, and then mostly lapsed into obscurity." So with the poetry and drama; and so with, the book seems to imply, the meaning of the Revolution. But this implication Kammen denies at the end, where he declares that "the Revolution has remained the foremost provenance of nationality and of tradition in the United States." The wealth of knowledge Kammen brings to the book is immense and almost always interesting, but like much wealth in the world it is not always used to the best effect.

This is not true of an essay too briefly noted last year (see *ALS 1977*, p. 193): Sacvan Bercovitch's "How the Puritans Won the American Revolution" (*MR* 17[1976]:597–630). A complex and densely informed consideration of the various responses of 19th-century writers to the significance of the Revolution, Bercovitch's discussion centers on George Bancroft's *History of the United States*; in particular, how "it transmutes the colonial past into myth, and in epic form sets forth God's unfolding design for America, the revolution of revolutions that was born aboard the *Mayflower* and *Arbella* and matured in the struggles of 1776." Vital to this myth is the view of revolution as a national rite of passage (Kammen devotes a chapter to this idea): "This," writes Bercovitch, "works to increase the tension of transition. One need only think of the peculiarly adolescent concerns of our classic writers, their emphasis on freedom from prescribed roles, on confrontations with the absolute, on the disparity between social and 'ultimate' values, even while they return insistently to the meaning of America." What is distinctive about 19th-century American literature, as opposed to European, is that American writers tend to uphold middle-class ideals "even when they most bitterly assail the middle class." What "might have been a search for social alternatives" is turned "into a call for symbolic revitalization." Thus the culture is perpetuated. Both in style and economy the essay is to be recommended.

Other essays of a general nature are Bernard Rosenthal's "The Urban Garden: Nineteenth-Century American Views of the City" (*TSLL* 20:119–38), which proposes that "contrary to the modern myth of early nineteenth-century America cherishing an agrarian dream, the great vision of the age was preeminently urban"; and Daniel L. Guillory's "The Mystique of Childhood in American Literature" (*TSE* 23:229–47), a competent essay that would have been much better had Mark Twain not so expectedly stolen center stage.

ii. Irving, Cooper, and Their Contemporaries

Two important titles are added to the growing shelf of "The Complete Works of Washington Irving" (Twayne): *The Sketch Book of Geoffrey Crayon, Gent.*, edited by Haskell Springer, and the first volume of Irving's *Letters*, ably edited by Ralph M. Aderman, Herbert L. Kleinfield, and Jenifer S. Banks. *The Sketch Book*, Irving's best-known and worthiest work, demands the care and intelligence Springer brings to its enormously complicated text. While the editorial apparatus is nearly two-thirds as long as Irving's text, it is not space wasted; it fulfills two important purposes: Irving's methods of composition and the vagaries of early 19th-century publishing are finely illuminated, and the justification for the present text is admirably and convincingly argued. On the evidence of this work, the misgivings some felt toward the earlier volumes in the Irving series no longer appear warranted.

Important for all those interested in the literary milieu of the early republic is the appearance of the first of four projected volumes of Irving's *Letters*. Though as many as one half of the extant letters have over the years found their way into print in some form or another, the lack of a comprehensive collection of all Irving's known and available letters has been a serious hindrance to Irving scholars. A large book of nearly 800 pages and containing 382 letters written by Irving between 1802 and 1823, the edition is a model of sensible editorial policy and scholarly decorum. Annotations are detailed, but are throughout held in check and never become distracting; the introductory materials are likewise well tailored to the demands of the occasion, modest and gracefully expressed.

Until publication of this new edition the most valuable source of Irving's letters was his nephew's *The Life and Letters of Washington Irving*—written over a century ago (1862–64). Pierre M. Irving, his uncle's companion and literary aide for nearly 30 years, came to know better than any other his uncle in the full range of his activities, and, as Wayne R. Kime points out in *Pierre M. Irving and Washington Irving: A Collaboration in Life and Letters* (Waterloo, Ontario, Canada: Wilfrid Laurier Univ. Press, 1977), "exerted a great influence in shaping his posthumous fame." Kime's approach to Irving's biography through the biography of his younger confidant is an original and, it seems in this case, a worthwhile venture. The danger is in overemphasizing those aspects of Irving's later life his nephew most fully shared, but Kime generally avoids this. As long as Pierre's *Life and Letters* remain a primary source of information about Irving's career, Kime's careful study will remain an important means of interpreting and measuring that work.

Recent interest in Irving's attitudes toward the American West
in his later writings remains current in two worthy essays by William J. Scheick and William Bedford Clark. Taking as their starting
point Wayne Kime's superb analysis of Irving's A Tour on the Prairies (ALS 1973, p. 209), both authors agree in essentials with Kime
that in Irving's undeservedly neglected book the values of the wild
West effectively challenge, if not defeat, those of the civilized East.
Clark's "How the West Won: Irving's Comic Inversion of the
Westering Myth in A Tour on the Prairies" (AL 50:335–47) characterizes A Tour as "a kind of mock-heroic quest that quietly sub-
verts the perennial American myth of westering, a myth that pre-
supposes that civilization must inevitably conquer the wilderness.
. . . Civilized man's assault upon the virgin West, a theme rich with
heroic possibilities, is portrayed as an exercise in comic futility, a
lesson in human limitations." In "Frontier Robin Hood: Wilderness,
Civilization and the Half-Breed in Irving's A Tour on the Prairies"
(SwAL 4:14–21) Scheick focuses on Pierre Beatte, the half-breed
whose role in A Tour "represents a hybrid race epitomizing the radical tension between civilization and the wilderness which permeates
the narrative." Whereas Irving managed "to suspend his ambivalence" in A Tour toward these conflicting values as they are pre-
cariously integrated in Beatte, in his subsequent books about the
West his sympathies turned increasingly to the civilized state.

By examining Irving's use of his Spanish sources and various
responses of later historians to his History of the Life and Voyages
of Christopher Columbus (1826–27), John Harmon McElroy methodically defends "The Integrity of Irving's Columbus" (AL 50:
1–16), laying effectively to rest Stanley T. Williams's unworthy
charge "that anyone who praises the scholarship of Irving's Columbus can have made 'no genuine investigation' into the matter." More
fashionable in its critical approach is a short section (pp. 1–11) of
Judith Fetterley's polemic, The Resisting Reader: A Feminist Approach to American Fiction (Indiana), which takes as the book's
premier text "Rip Van Winkle." "How," she asks, "is [a woman]
to read our 'first and most famous' story in which the American
imagination is born if the defining act of that imagination is to
identify the real American Revolution with the avoidance of adult-
hood, which means the avoidance of women, which means the
avoidance of one's wife? What is the impact of this American dream

on her?" The answer: disastrous. Undervaluing, it seems to me, Irving's irony and sometimes subtle humor, Fetterley casts Irving headlong into Outer Darkness, the dwelling place of antifeminists, thereby getting her book—worth reading—off to a roaring start.

Though more properly reviewed elsewhere in this volume, Bruce Granger's *American Essay Serials from Franklin to Irving* (Tenn.) concludes, as the title suggests, with an intelligent and sensitive discussion of Irving's *Salmagundi* papers and the *Letters of Jonathan Oldstyle, Gent.*, the latter edited by Granger for the Irving edition (see *ALS 1977*, p. 209). When I wrote in my essay last year that Granger claimed in his introduction to the Oldstyle letters that "these early pieces foreshadow the more mature work of Irving" (*ALS 1977*, p. 210), I misspoke myself, at least in emphasis. What Granger said and repeats in the present work is more qualified: "Only occasionally do these early works point clearly to the later"; connections there are, but tenuous and hardly noticeable except in retrospect. Finally, it is pleasant to note that another facsimile edition, this time of *Bracebridge Hall*, has been issued under the imprint of the Sleepy Hollow Restorations of Tarrytown, New York, and introduced, with appropriate charm, by Andrew B. Myers.

Book-length studies of Cooper's life and art happily appear to have become annual occurrences, a far cry from a few years back when only Robert Spiller seemed to value Cooper as novelist and man of letters worth reading. I suppose most of us still do not read that much of him, though the promised appearance of the first volume of the new Cooper edition (State Univ. Press of N.Y.), to be followed quickly by many more, will provide diligent readers an excellent opportunity for (re)reading the novels and important works of nonfiction. In the meantime, one can peruse Warren S. Walker's compilation, *Plots and Characters in the Fiction of James Fenimore Cooper* (Archon) to find out all he or she has missed or forgotten. Though no substitute for the works themselves, such guides—when as well done as Walker's work—are useful reference tools.

It is unfortunate that Stephen Railton's *Fenimore Cooper: A Study of His Life and Imagination* (Princeton) should follow so closely on Blake Nevius's illuminating study of the novelist's picturesque vision, *Cooper's Landscapes* (see *ALS 1976*, p. 199; see also Dennis Berthold's review article: "Literary Pictorialism," *ESQ* 24:163–76), and Daniel Peck's *A World by Itself* (*ALS 1977*, p. 211), a bold interpretation nicely complementing and extending in interesting areas Nevius's work. Comparison is inevitable, and it is Railton's book that is found wanting. His concern is with "the way Cooper's novels responded to the complicated and conflicting demands of his unconscious"; Railton's tools, the well-worn theories of psychoanalysis. Central to his understanding of Cooper is the dominance in his life and writings of his father, William Cooper; the insights this biographical approach cast on several of Cooper's works —most notably *The Pioneers* and *Home as Found*—are instructive (especially the inconsistent and contradictory behavior and patterns previous critics have noted) but in the end they seem remarkably old-fashioned.

Much more important is Terence Martin's relatively short piece, "Beginnings and Endings in the Leatherstocking Tales" (*NCF* 33: 69–87), one of nine distinguished essays in a special issue of *Nineteenth-Century Fiction* devoted to "narrative endings." Addressing himself to the five Leatherstocking tales, Martin sees in all endings necessary beginnings, and in the ending of *The Deerslayer* the beginnings of the earlier novels; or in Martin's concluding words: "For the ending of the series is a celebratory beginning that prefigures the death of a hero who longs for beginnings."

Advancing still further our understanding of Cooper's artistry and especially his command of an effective style, Carl Nelson demonstrates in "Cooper's Verbal Faction: The Hierarchy of Rhetoric, Voice and Silence in *The Prairie*" (*WVUPP* 24[1977]:37–47) that "each character's voice possesses more or less human worth, establishing a qualitative interplay between levels of rhetoric and the points of view they represent." Those points of view, however, are mostly negative, as Nelson points out, since at the end of the novel "wisdom [represented by the trapper, Natty Bumpo] remains undisturbed, having no voice and no role among the living."

Minor in their purpose, but entirely competent, are J. Gary Williams's "The Plot-Shift in Cooper's *The Oak Openings*" (*ELN* 16: 25–32), which examines Cooper's changing focus between the time he initially sketched the novel and its ultimate publication; and Isaac Sequeira's "The Frontier Attack on Cooper, 1850–1900" (*IJAS* 8,i: 25–35), a narrative catalogue of complaints by professional frontiersmen and men of letters to Cooper's representation of the frontier, particularly its Indian inhabitants, in his novels. Much less satisfactory is a free-wheeling, cliché-ridden essay by Martin Green on "Cooper, Nationalism and Imperialism" (*JAmS* 12:161–68), a prime example of the sort of "cultural criticism" that has made American Studies suspect for many. Finally there is Barton Levi St. Armand's carefully argued article, "Harvey Birch as the Wandering Jew: Literary Calvinism in James Fenimore Cooper's *The Spy*" (*AL* 50:348–68), which dwells "on the character of Harvey Birch as the domestication of an international Romantic archetype," but still upholds "the genuine Americanness of Cooper's treatment of this symbol."

Perhaps it is in the nature of things that to one not "bred or bawn in a brier-patch!" the continued and energetic critical interest in William Gilmore Simms's writings, especially his Revolutionary romances, appears sometimes a rather vapid form of parochialism. The principal theme in most of the recent writing on the southerner is intelligently rehearsed by Stephen Meats in an essay, first presented as a paper at a Bicentennial Symposium, "Artist or Historian: William Gilmore Simms and the Revolutionary South" (*Eighteenth-Century Florida and the Revolutionary South*, edited by Samuel Proctor [Florida], pp. 94–109); one may, however, find himself somewhat dissatisfied with Meats's answer to the question implied in the title of his essay: "Simms was not artist *or* historian; he was artist *and* historian."

Lieutenant Porgy, a character central to the series of Revolutionary romances and described by Simms as a "laughing philosopher," but whom others have seen in a decidedly Falstaffian light, is the focus of two fine articles this year. L. Lynn Hogue in "The Presentation of Post-Revolutionary Law in *Woodcraft*: Another Perspective on the 'Truth' of Simms's Fiction" (*MissQ* 31:201–10) sees that it is the law—"one source of order and decorum in Simms's fiction"—that supplies "thematic and structural cohesion" for this work, Simms's masterpiece; its role is both to help "develop character, and provide opportunity for comic scenes." In Mary Ann Wimsatt's opinion, Porgy functions throughout the series "to link two halves of a setting commonly associated with romance"—in Simms's works these are the world of the plantation and the world of the forest—"and to speak for the plight of the Southern militia in defeat at Camden and limited success at Eutaw Springs." As should be obvious, Wimsatt relies for her formulation in "Simms's Porgy, the Romance, and the Southern Revolutionary Militia" (*SHR* 13:1–12) on Frye's enduring *Anatomy of Criticism*, and throughout, to good purpose.

Adding to Simms's authenticity in his representation of the Revolutionary period in South Carolina was, according to James E. Kibler, Jr., in "Simms as Naturalist: Lowcountry Landscape in His Revolutionary Novels" (*MissQ* 31:499–518), his intimate knowledge of the black-water swamp which he was able effectively to draw upon, and his strong sense of the land's importance to the humans it supports.

"Simms's Benedict Arnold: The Hero as Traitor" (*SoSt* 17:273–89), by Miriam J. Shillingsburg, argues that the importance of Simms's little known composition, *Benedict Arnold: The Traitor. A Drama in an Essay* (1863), rests on two grounds: the light it casts on our understanding of Simms as a literary critic, especially in his observations on the relationship between history and art, and as another demonstration of "the nineteenth-century obsession with the Arnold-André intrigue." Another essay concerned with Simms's mediating position between historian and romancer is Charles S. Watson's "De Soto's Expedition: Contrasting Treatments in Pickett's *History of Alabama* and Simms's *Vasconselos*" (*AlaR* 31:199–208), the first, a formal work of history published in 1851, which Simms "criticized as being only a chronicle instead of what [he] deemed a true history." Accordingly, Simms rendered his version of de Soto's expedition, the subject of the first chapter of Pickett's book, in his historical novel, *Vasconselos: A Romance of the New World* (1853): "whereas Pickett gave a straightforward, factual account of de Soto's expedition," Watson explains, "Simms graphically presented unflattering characteristics of the Spanish explorer and the moral lessons to be learned from his deeds." Simms did not always go to such lengths, however, to "improve" the work of conventional historians. Frederick Wagner shows in "Simms's Editing of *The Life of Nathanael Greene*" (*SLJ* 11:40–43) that the 1849 biography of Greene described on the title page as "edited" by Simms was just that and not an original work as some of his biographers have supposed. His source was William P. Johnson's *Sketches of the Life and Correspondence of Nathanael Greene* (1822); Simms, Wagner demonstrates, merely "abridged and paraphrased the two-volume work by

Johnson," whose name was only in passing mentioned in the book's preface.

It is Simms, the historian-novelist, it would appear, who obviously interests his modern southern literary descendants. This is as William R. Trent predicted long ago; writing in 1892, Trent expressed the hope that even after 50 years Simms's Revolutionary and Colonial romances would be read: "When the Southern people get a true history of themselves, they will find that they have many things to learn and to unlearn; and one of the things they will vainly wish to forget will be their utter indifference to the unseconded and uncheered efforts of men like Simms, to rescue the history of their State and section from the dust of oblivion." Even to an unfeeling Yankee, this makes eloquent sense.

Two reasons Donald A. Sears, author of *John Neal* (TUSAS 307), cites as contributing to Neal's meager reputation today are "the unavailability of his works and . . . a scarcity of studies of them." The first of these is in part remedied by a short anthology of his writings, *The Genius of John Neal*, STA 1 (Texte), intelligently edited and introduced by Benjamin Lease and Hans-Joachim Lang; tales, extracts from novels, essays and critical writings are all represented. Sears, acknowledging his debt to Lease and Lang, addresses himself in his study to the second need in Neal studies. Though he wishes to present Neal in the completeness of his brilliant career, and does so to a largely satisfactory degree, Sears's discussion of Neal as a writer of fiction is the book's strongest contribution. Certainly the case he makes for a modern edition of Neal's short stories about New England is convincing; "Neal's lack of sentimentality, his fine control of actual speech, and his achievement of an effective tone," Sears concludes in the book's best chapter, "mark his stories as significant contributions to a native literature." Neal's achievement in terms of the fiction produced contemporaneously in his native state, while touched upon in Sears's book, is treated more fully in his "Maine Fiction before 1840: A Microcosm" (*CLQ* 14:109–24).

Though Bryant is a pivotal figure in Bernard Duffey's challenging survey of *Poetry in America* and his poetic merits are well represented in those poems of his Jane Donahue Eberwein has selected for her anthology of *Early American Poetry* (Wis.), critical interest in Bryant's work is, as in the recent past, slight. Calling our attention

to "The Disappearing Image in William Cullen Bryant's 'To a Water-
fowl' " (*CP* 11,ii:13–16), E. Miller Burdick finds the poem a far
more complex work than previous critics have realized; it "is a 'lesson' not only about how the poet is like the bird, but about how the
'Power' which creates nature's symbolism in the first place compels
the poet to go beyond symbols to the unsymbolizable, transcendent
idea which is the 'Power' itself." David J. Baxter argues in "Timothy
Flint and Bryant's 'The Prairies' " (*AN&Q* 16[1977]:52–54) that
Flint, the western writer and editor, was a more direct influence on
Bryant's poem than was Bryant's 1822 journey to Illinois.

Mary Kelley's discussion, "A Woman Alone: Catharine Maria
Sedgwick's Spinsterhood in Nineteenth-Century America" (*NEQ*
51:209–25), of Sedgwick's ambivalent attitudes toward the role of
the unmarried woman in a social order in which only the married
woman, dedicated to husband and child, could achieve real fulfillment is a solid piece of work, especially for its rich use of the
unpublished Sedgwick papers in the Massachusetts Historical Society. Also admirable in its scholarship is Raymond H. Schmandt's
account of "A Forgotten Philadelphia Writer: William Joseph Walter (1789–1846)" (*PMHB* 102:27–39), whose career coincided with
Philadelphia's brief moment of literary distinction.

iii. Popular Writers of Midcentury

In view of the plethora of "research guides" of dubious value that
we have experienced in recent years, Nina Baym's *Woman's Fiction:
A Guide to Novels by and about Women in America, 1820–1870*
(Cornell) seems most unfortunately titled. But the title is honest,
and the book a major contribution to our understanding of 19th-
century fiction, both by women and men. No one that I know of
has had both the courage to read the best-selling novels of that
generation of women writers Hawthorne so ungentlemanly damned,
and the critical and historical sophistication to make so much, and
sometimes so little, out of them. Women writing for women, about
what women then and perhaps now in America dream: beset by all
sorts of adversity, but strengthened by independence, the popular
heroine does in the end succeed. Baym's detailed analysis is based
upon her reading of some 130 novels written between 1822 and 1869
by authors now largely forgotten: Sedgwick, Maria Jane McIntosh,

Caroline Lee Hentz, Elizabeth Stuart Phelps, E. D. E. N. South-
worth, Caroline Cheseboro', the Hale sisters, and many others. Their
tales are basically the same, but the variations, and of course the
similarities, importantly illuminate the culture these many novelists
felt so often imprisoned by. Related is an earlier piece by Baym,
"Portrayal of Women in American Literature, 1790–1870" (*What
Manner of Woman*, pp. 211–34), broader and more general than her
perspective allowed in the book, but equally informed and informative.

If after Baym's study one should wish to know still more about
the Warner sisters, especially Susan, the elder, a profligate senti-
mentalist responsible for such works as *The Wide, Wide World*
(1850) and *Queechy* (1852), he will find Edward Halsey Foster's
Susan and Anna Warner (TUSAS 312) useful, but also irritating for
its excessive repetitiveness. In addition Foster too often appears
unnecessarily embarrassed to be found writing about two women
of such slender talents, and as a result tends to resort to sales figures
to prove that what he is doing is worthwhile. It is, and so is the book.

According to Baym, Harriet Beecher Stowe's interests "set her
apart from the other American women writing fiction in her day,"
and, except as a point of contrast, she is not figured in Baym's book.
But more than a half-dozen other pieces well make up for that omission. The best of these is Lawrence Buell's "Calvinism Romanticized:
Harriet Beecher Stowe, Samuel Hopkins, and *The Minister's Wooing*" (*ESQ* 24:119–32), which examines "the literary implications
of Stowe's particular branch of New England thought, the late Edwardsean sensibility," and thereby furthers our understanding of
the role New England orthodoxy played in the working of the mid-
19th-century New England imagination. *The Minister's Wooing*,
Stowe's third novel (1859) and, as Buell says, "the one serious novel
of the period which deals most directly with the Edwardsean tradition" is reissued in handsome facsimile by the Stowe-Day Foundation of Hartford, Conn., Sandra R. Duguid writing an introduction
which emphasizes Stowe's choice in the novel of the "aesthetic pattern" of comedy to reflect her optimistic hope for mankind.

Also to be praised is Howard Kerr's "'The Blessed Dead': The
Transformation of Occult Experience in Harriet Beecher Stowe's
Oldtown Folks" (*Literature and the Occult*, pp. 174–87). Kerr,
whose book, *Mediums, and Spirit-Rappers, and Roaring Radicals*

(see *ALS 1972*, p. 195), remains the best study of spiritualism and
19th-century American literature, argues here that Stowe's own participation in seances in 1868 "animated major occult episodes of her
most important New England novel, *Oldtown Folks* (1869)."

Ellen Moers's attempt in her short pamphlet, *Harriet Beecher
Stowe and American Literature* (Hartford, Conn.: Stowe-Day Foundation), "to put *Uncle Tom's Cabin* back in American literature
where it belongs," not simply as a document in the history of slavery
in America, but as an early example of literary realism, is a welcome
change from most studies of Stowe's great novel. "We have forgotten," Moers tells us, "that *Uncle Tom's Cabin* won its vast public
. . . not only for its slavery matter, but also for its dedication to the
American Real, its priceless evocation of the national character and
daily ways. We have forgotten that the first time the phrase 'The
Great American Novel' was used, *Uncle Tom's Cabin* appeared to
its inventor, John William DeForest, to have been the only pre-
tender to the title, because of its 'national breadth.'" Appended to
Moers's essay is a brief "Note on Mark Twain and Harriet Beecher
Stowe." Other essayists writing on *Uncle Tom's Cabin*, however, are
less interested in the novel as literature: Jane Gardner covers familiar ground in "The Assault upon Uncle Tom: Attempts of Pro-
Slavery Novelists to Answer *Uncle Tom's Cabin*, 1852–1860" (*SHR*
12:313–24); and Harold Beaver in "Time on the Cross: White Fiction and Black Messiahs" (*YES* 8:40–53) insists on reading the novel
"as a kind of Methodist allegory." Opposite this razzle-dazzle is the
sober scholarship of Susan Geary's "Harriet Beecher Stowe, John P.
Jewett, and Author-Publisher Relations in 1853" (*SAR 1977*, pp.
345–67).

With the exception of Madeleine B. Stern's bibliographical essay, "Louisa M. Alcott in Periodicals" (*SAR 1977*, pp. 369–86), interest in Alcott this year focuses on what Ann Douglas in a review
of Martha Saxton's *Louisa May: A Modern Biography of Louisa
May Alcott* (see *ALS 1977*, p. 216) describes as "the discrepancy
between the literary persona and the reality of Louisa May Alcott"
("Mysteries of Louisa May Alcott," *NYRB*, 28 Sept., pp. 60–63).
What becomes apparent to Eugenia Kaledin in "Louisa May Alcott:
Success and the Sorrow of Self-Denial" (*WS* 5:251–63) is that Alcott's "acceptance of the creed of womanly self-denial as much as her
willingness to buy success by catering to middle class ideals aborted

the promise of her art and led her to betray her most deeply felt values." The reticence such a stance necessarily involved was in part responsible for the suppression of Alcott's *Diana and Persis* (Arno, 1977), a story written in 1879, but only now published in an able edition by Sarah Elbert. This, too, is a principal theme in Nina Auerbach's superb reading of *Little Women* in her *Communities of Women: An Idea in Fiction* (Harvard), pp. 55–73.

The lot of women in the 19th century was indeed a sorry one, overcome only by an expenditure of emotional and intellectual energy greatly disproportionate to the meager rewards to be won. But there were winners, among them the largely anonymous female writers whose rebellious verse Gail Dickerson gathers in "Notes on Nineteenth-Century Feminist Verse" (*FemS* 4:115–26). Julia Ward Howe's enormous popularity and her life-long devotion to the cause of women's rights are reflected quite naturally in this verse, the familiar cadence of "The Battle Hymn of the Republic" unmistakable in one "poem":

> In the past they've made us playthings,
>   toys to charm an idle hour;
> That is over, and, my sisters, they must
>   now concede our power. . . .
> Mothers, sisters, wives and sweethearts,
>   gird your armor for the fight,
> Traced across our floating standard be
>   our watchword, *Equal Rights.*

The "Fireside Poets" fade deeper into oblivion, a result, it seems, not only of current fashion, but also of ignorance. Janet Harris quite rightly makes no literary claims for Longfellow's *Poems on Slavery* [1842]" (*CLQ* 14:84–92), but her discussion of Longfellow's contribution to the antislavery cause is interesting for its historical perspective. Robert A. Ferguson also considers Longfellow's political attitudes and the way they are reflected in several of his poems in an attractive essay, "Longfellow's Political Fears: Civic Authority and the Role of the Artist in *Hiawatha* and *Miles Standish*" (*AL* 50:187–215). Ferguson's Longfellow is no escapist, but rather one "emotionally and intellectually engaged in the collapse of the Union" during the 1850's. Daniel F. Littlefield's belief that he has discovered the key to the enormous popularity of "Long-

fellow's 'A Psalm of Life': A Relation of Method to Popularity"
(*MarkhamR* 7:49–51) in Longfellow's "aphorizing in the tradition
of such works as *The Proverbs, The New England Primer*, and *Poor
Richard's Almanac*" will seem to most a commonplace. And an auto-
graphed inscription is made to pass as "An Unpublished Longfellow Poem" (*PBSA* 72:349–50), communily described by Philip
C. Kolin, David Goff, and Linda Goff.

Longfellow's *Kavanaugh* (1849), Oliver Wendell Holmes's *A
Mortal Antipathy* (1885), and Henry James's *The Bostonians* (1885)
are the texts of Lillian Faderman's "Female Same-Sex Relationships
in Novels by Longfellow, Holmes, and James" (*NEQ* 51:309–32),
a stunning display of literary sensitivity and good common sense.
Attempts by modern critics, Faderman argues, to explain away these
relationships are manifestations of our prejudices, not of the historical and authorial realities reflected in the novels. Faderman's
"analysis of the nineteenth-century author's milieu indicates that in
such cases he probably said exactly what he meant, that he was
indeed describing love relationships between women, and that . . .
while such relationships were not merely platonic but sensual or
amatory as well, they were not regarded as 'abnormal' or 'perverted.'" Another of Holmes's novels is the subject of Lewis Fried's
"*Elsie Venner*: Holmes and the Naturalistic Tradition" (*ZAA* 26:
305–13), an interesting and reasonable attempt to place Holmes
within the perimeters of philosophical naturalism.

Three Southern poets, *Sidney Lanier, Henry Timrod and Paul
Hamilton Hayne*, share a "Reference Guide" (Hall), compiled by
Jack De Bellis. Whether their literary merit warrants such expense
of time and press is a question one must answer for himself.

iv. Local Color and Literary Regionalism

Three readings of Sarah Orne Jewett's little masterpiece, "A White
Heron" (1886), are a happy indication that her artistry, admired so
greatly by Howells, James, and Cather, is now not so neglected as
in years past. It was Cather's belief that Jewett's stories lost readers'
interest during the 1930s because of the advent of Freudianism in
literary criticism. Ironically it now appears that it is the hidden or
submerged psychological dynamics of Jewett's fiction that attract
the most critical interest. Utilizing the formulations of Norman O.

Brown's *Life Against Death* (1959), Theodore R. Hovet proposes in "America's 'Lonely Country Child': The Theme of Separation in Sarah Orne Jewett's 'A White Heron'" (*CLQ* 14:166–71) that Sylvia, the young girl of the story, remains attached to nature, the world of childhood, and thus must reject the "'unsatisfactory activity'... of the cities," the world of the young adult male who briefly enters her realm. In another essay on the story, "'Once Upon a Time': Sarah Orne Jewett's 'A White Heron' as a Fairy Tale" (*SSF* 15:63–68), Hovet applies Vladimir Propp's notion of "the morphology of the fairy tale" in order to reveal "how Jewett turned to the fairy tale in order to explore the mythic roots of the conflicts generated by the encounter of modern social forces with provincial America." And according to Richard Brenzo in "Free Heron or Dead Sparrow: Sylvia's Choice in Sarah Orne Jewett's 'A White Heron'" (*CLQ* 14: 36–41), Jewett's symbolic treatment of the story's elements "universalizes and enriches the meaning of the girl's inner experiences"; her rejection of the male is her means of preserving "her integrity and independence." James and Gwen L. Nagel's *Sarah Orne Jewett: A Reference Guide* (Hall, 1977) will hopefully find significant use in the future as our appreciation of this important writer increases.

Further advances toward a definition of a midwestern imagination and its art are made by Walter Havighurst in an address he delivered to the Ohio-Indiana American Studies Association, "Lighting Out for the Territory" (*ON* 4:311–18), and by Bud T. Cochran's examination of "The Indianas of Edward Eggleston's *The Hoosier-School-Master*" (*ON* 4:385–90). Among the midwestern writers of the 19th century, none, according to Madonna C. Kolbenschlag in "Edward Eggleston and the Evangelical Consciousness" (*Mid-America* 5:19–29), was more preoccupied with the evangelical consciousness than Eggleston. The field of midwestern literature is still so largely unexplored that one might be justified in withholding assent to the extremity of Kolbenschlag's statement, but her analysis of several of Eggleston's novels in terms of Max Weber's theory of the "Protestant Ethic" is certainly worthwhile. Much less successful is John E. Hallwas's "The Varieties of Humor in John Hay's Pike County Ballads" published in the same journal (pp. 7–18), but if Hallwas fails, Robert L. Gale more than succeeds in his sensible and highly literate study of *John Hay* (*TUSAS* 296), an attractive addition to the Twayne series.

R. Bruce Bickley, Jr., also demonstrates that the Twayne format, which has defeated many in the past, can be made to work intelligently. His *Joel Chandler Harris* (TUSAS 308) is based on the assumption that Harris's work is worthy of serious critical attention, and by the end of his book readers should be convinced that "the texture of Harris's writing [is] much more sophisticated and complex than its often humorous or facile surface suggests." Bickley's *Joel Chandler Harris: A Reference Guide* (Hall), done in collaboration with Karen L. Bickley and Thomas H. English, and his several bibliographical checklists in *ALR* supplement the bibliographical apparatus of the book. A fellow Georgian is the subject of Bert Hitchcock's *Richard Malcolm Johnston* (TUSAS 314), but, unlike Bickley, Hitchcock sees his author's importance as strictly historical, not literary, a competent but unremarkable "local colorist."

Thomas Nelson Page, the best of the "plantation romancers," enjoyed enormous popularity 50 years ago, and his formula for success seems still to work if one is to judge by the historical "novels" supermarkets and drugstores deal in. Lucinda H. MacKethan analyzes Page's fictive vision in a fine article, "Thomas Nelson Page: The Plantation as Arcady" (*VQR* 54:314–32), and finds its cornerstone to "be his dual focus of pride and loss; the strength of his fictional recreations of the Old South as Arcady . . . rests primarily in his ability to balance his belief in his idealizations with his awareness of threat and inevitable doom facing them." Another popular southern writer at the end of the last century, admired and read throughout the country, was Mary Noailles Murfree, but we are warned by Allison Ensor not to trust "The Geography of Mary Noailles Murfree's *In the Tennessee Mountains*" (*MissQ* 31:191–99); it's of the mind, not of the land.

In a continuing series of articles on southern magazines, Edward L. Tucker tells the sprightly history of a literary monthly that existed briefly in the 1840s, the editors being two young Englishmen, William Carey Richards and Thomas Addison Richards, or in the phrase of Tucker's title, "Two Young Brothers and Their *Orion*" (*SLJ* 11:64–80). Titles are important, and it will be a pity if that of Richard Walser's essay, "Biblio-biography of Skitt Taliaferro" (*NCHR* 55:375–95), scares away readers who can only benefit from Walser's detailed account of this minor humorist of the Old Southwest.

Paul T. Bryant's opinion that "Western Literature: A Window

on America" (*CEA* 40,iii:6–13) can provide students with "a clear understanding . . . of their own culture, their own vision of America, and their own relationship to the landscape" is reinforced by Ralph Mann's excellent study of the literature written about California in the 1840s and 1850s, "The Americanization of Arcadia: Images of Hispanic and Gold Rush California" (*AmerS* 19:5–19). According to Mann these early writings "did not espouse an escape from Eastern institutions and mores but, on the contrary, championed their expansion." Just as Bishop Berkeley had predicted.

v. Henry Adams and Late 19th-Century Nonfiction

A grievous flaw in the established curriculum of American literature is the negligible role prose nonfiction plays in it. Not so with British literature, especially of the 19th century, as David J. DeLaura's *Victorian Prose: A Guide to Research* (1973) more than amply attests. After the period of Transcendentalism in America, only Henry Adams and a few naturalists and essayists, John Burroughs, John Muir, and Clarence King, receive any significant attention, and even Adams's literary reputation is fairly recent, as a glance through Earl N. Harbert's *Henry Adams: A Reference Guide* (Hall) clearly illustrates. Partly that was the fault of Adams and the posthumous publication of *The Education*. Harbert considers in "Henry Adams and the Critics of His Time" (*TSE* 23:71–84) the interesting question of what Adams's place would be in American letters had he never written his acknowledged masterpiece; expectedly the answer is "not much." An earlier essay by Harbert, "Henry Adams's *Education* and Autobiographical Tradition" (*TSE* 22[1977]:133–41), rightly insists that "the *Education* must be seen to offer us something much larger than the usual understanding of 'autobiography' allows. . . . The genius of Adams's experiment in modernity lies in his dramatic conversion of the narrative and didactic convention he had inherited—the stuff of traditional autobiography—to his own unique purpose," the creation of a work of art, of course. It cannot be long before the applied insights of Jacques Derrida, Paul DeMan, and their confrères rid even more effectively the taint of autobiography from Adams's curious work. Less informing is Thomas J. Schlereth's "Fiction and Facts: Henry Adams's *Democracy* and Gore Vidal's *1876*" (*SoQ* 16:209–22), a comparison of the two novels, which, in spite of the century that separated their publication, are as "striking" in their similarities as in their differences.

Though they were closely associated during the early years of the *Nation,* Adams and E. L. Godkin never managed to create a close friendship; in fact, Adams soon came to distrust the more self-serving Godkin. In this he was probably justified, if one is to trust William M. Armstrong's *E. L. Godkin: A Biography* (SUNY). Armstrong, whose edition of *The Gilded Age Letters of E. L. Godkin* (SUNY, 1974) contains many important letters to prominent literary figures, portrays his subject as having been "neither a deep nor an original thinker. . . . It is as a man of his age that his stature must be weighed." One must add, however, that it was a stature enormously influential for over half a century.

That John Muir's early Calvinistic training was never annulled by the Romantic sensibility visible in his outlook in later life is the argument of Harold P. Simonson in "The Tempered Romanticism of John Muir" (*WAL* 13:227–41); it was this conflict that accounts for Muir's darker side—"a recurring sense of mortality, discordance, and judgment—that intermingled with his Romanticism, deepened and enriched it, and enhanced his searching literary consciousness." In another thoughtful article, Richard F. Fleck charts "John Muir's Evolving Attitudes Toward Native American Cultures" (*AIQ* 4:19–31), the direction being from initial misconception and prejudice to later acceptance and compassion.

vi. Realism and the Age of Howells

To the very end Howells thought himself a "Buckeye," the rest had just been addresses, and as Edwin H. Cady once pointed out, the realistic vision in American fiction of the last century was a result in part of seeing "the world in midwestern eyes" (see *ALS 1963,* p. 112). Unfortunately Robert Cosgrove's "Realism: The Midwest's Contributions" (*ON* 4:391–401) possesses neither some controlling sense of what realism was nor an adequate awareness of the historical, social, and intellectual causes for midwestern writers' dominance of American fiction between 1870 and 1930. As a result we get many names, a few titles, but no direction.

This is not true of Martha Banta's long article on women in postbellum fiction, titled (!) "They Shall Have Faces, Minds, and (One

Day) Flesh: Women in Late Nineteenth-Century and Early Twentieth-Century American Literature" (*What Manner of Woman*, pp.
235–70). Banta knows right where she stands, and what her standing there means. As a result, her reflections on "the images of women
emerging from the period immediately after the Civil War, and the
literary forms used to convey them" should satisfy all readers, feminists and fogies. More limited is Martha S. Grise's "Feminist Fools:
Women in the Political Novels of the 1870s" (*JGE* 30:154–64), an
examination of "the antifeminist sentiment of varying types and degrees" in three novels of political satire, Clemens's and Warner's
The Gilded Age, DeForest's *Playing the Mischief*, and Adams's *Democracy*; regardless of their differences their common "message . . .
was unambiguous: women must not attempt to change the age-old
pattern of their lives." Success, happiness, and sometimes life itself
came in staying at home. By examining nearly a dozen novels in
order to determine what the attitudes were toward "Miscegenation
in the Late Nineteenth-Century American Novel" (*SHR* 13:13–24),
William L. Andrews finds that the opinions reflected in and by the
novels were as complex and varied as those in the political and social
worlds they purported to represent.

The Minister's Charge; or, The Apprenticeship of Lemuel Barker,
introduction and notes to the text by Howard N. Mumford, text established by David J. Nordloh and David Kleinman, is the only
volume of "A Selected Edition of W. D. Howells" (Indiana) to appear this year, but several titles are announced for publication in
1979, including the first volume of a new edition of Howells's letters.
In the meanwhile a handsome piece of work by Brenda Murphy and
George Monteiro, "The John Hay–William Dean Howells Relationship as Reflected in Their Letters" (*BBr* 26:1–22) provides valuable
insights into the epistolary character and maneuverings of both men,
and critical interest in Howells's writings remains active and varied.

Jacqueline Tavernier-Courbin's "Towards the City: Howells'
Characterization in *A Modern Instance*" (*MFS* 24:111–27), though
well-written, is finally disappointing in its rehearsal of lecture-room
commonplaces: in Howells's Boston one sees "the chaos of modern
values"; Bartley Hubbard epitomizes an "amoral involvement in the
current of life, [and] becomes the paradigm of commercial Boston,
and by extension, of the modern world"; Atherton and the Hallecks
are "dramatic characterizations of the moral confusion and physical

inactivity associated with Proper Boston"; and so on. Howells's attitude toward the city, or rather the urban ideal, is far more complex than Tavernier-Courbin represents. "It was not the city itself he rejected," Gregory L. Crider writes in "William Dean Howells and the Antiurban Tradition: A Reconsideration" (*AmerS* 19:55–64); "he was able, even in his most anticapitalistic novels, to envision an urban utopia founded upon socialistic principles," having "recognized the intrinsic—and for him indispensable—advantages of urban life." While on the subject of Howells and cities, it is appropriate to mention Elizabeth Waterson's "Howells and the City of Quebec" (*CRevAS* 9:155–67), which considers Howells's use of this "great city of civilization and sophistication and tradition" in several of his early writings.

The literary friendship of Howells and James and its consequences have not much interested commentators on the art of either novelist in recent years; perhaps the absence of a complete record of their correspondence is responsible, or, more likely, the different directions their critical reputations have taken. Regardless, their contemporaries thought them a pair, a fact that later annoyed both. William L. Stull chronicles in "The Battle of the *Century*: W. D. Howells, 'Henry James, Jr.,' and the English" (*ALR* 11:249–64) a part of the "beautiful war" between Realists and Romanticists that followed upon Howells's 1882 article on James and, at least in its early years, seemed to stand the two Americans up against the whole of the British literary establishment. But they were aware of their differences, Howells, according to Barbara C. Ewell, perhaps more consciously in his art than James. By noting some "Parodic Echoes of *The Portrait of a Lady* in Howells's *Indian Summer*" (*TSE* 22: 117–31), Ewell makes a valuable observation about the two men's artistic vision: "Their shared commitment to realism did not prevent the two . . . from viewing reality from very different windows of the house of fiction. James saw life in its essence of tragic consciousness; Howells, at least in *Indian Summer*, saw in that vision the comic parody that is also the consequence of being human." Less convincing is the connection George Knox finds between "Mark Twain's and W. D. Howells' Green Moldy Dwarfs" (*MTJ* 19,iii:8–12), the "shriveled, shabby dwarf" that appears to the narrator of "The Facts Concerning the Recent Carnival of Crime in Connecticut" (1876) and the opium-induced dwarfish apparition that is seen by Lorenzo Hawbeck in Howells's *The Son of Royal Langbrith* (1904).

The Son of Royal Langbrith is the focal text of Elsa Nettels's valuable "Howells and Ibsen" (*TSLL* 20:153–68), a carefully considered study of Howells's profound response to the Norwegian dramatist's works. Nettels has examined the relevant documents and texts, including some unpublished materials, and, more important, sees through to their meaning: "Howells responded as he did to Ibsen's plays because he saw in them the expression of his own aim, first realized in *A Modern Instance*, to unite social criticism and psychological analysis in studies of characters whose actions and mental states reflect the disorders of a whole society."

Two fine studies of individual novels are Gary P. Storhoff's "Ironic Technique in *The Landlord at Lion's Head* (*NDQ* 46,ii:55–64) and Allen F. Stein's "A New Look at Howells's *A Fearful Responsibility*" (*MLQ* 39:121–31). Storhoff believes that if we examine the characters, especially Westover, in *The Landlord* who are most critical of the novel's protagonist, Jeff Durgin, we will find their moral visions wanting and even prejudiced. Critics, not adequately recognizing this, have failed to understand the novel "as an ironically contrived masterpiece in which Howells first exposes the pomposity of Westover's nineteenth-century moralistic vision, then accepts—with reservations—Jeff's immersion in the ambiguity of experience." Stein's "new look" at *A Fearful Responsibility* (1881) shows it to be "not only Howells's first predominantly bleak work but also the first revelation of his profound doubts about the essentially pragmatic orientation of his whole literary program."

In "From History to Realism: Howells Composes *The Leatherwood God*" (*ON* 4:195–218), Eugene H. Pattison studies in greater detail than opportunity afforded him in the introduction to his recent edition of *The Leatherwood God* (see *ALS 1976*, p. 215) Howells's use of his primary source, Richard H. Tanneyhill's historical account of the 1828 incident. And lest a year goes by without some mention of "Howells' *The Rise of Silas Lapham*" (*Expl* 36,iii:37–40), R. B. Jenkins examines the functions of a subplot in the novel involving the beautiful, young clerk-typist, Zerilla Dewey.

The multifaceted achievement (in this instance no cliché) of Thomas Wentworth Higginson, already the subject of five book-length biographies, is most fortunate in its most recent chronicler and critic. James W. Tuttleton's *Thomas Wentworth Higginson* (TUSAS 313) reveals the man in his full, paradoxical magnitude: radical activist and man of letters; quintessentially of New England, but defender of the Union; the "preceptor" of Emily Dickinson and the writer of very ordinary verse; and the author of *Army Life in a Black Regiment* (1870), the discussion of which merits the reader's heartiest praise.

That there exist (in the Denver Public Library) "The *Sub Rosa* Writings of Eugene Field" (*PBSA* 72:541–52) does not surprise, and the clarification and corrections offered by Harry J. Mooney, Jr., about them is appreciated. But Richard H. Crowder's discovery of "Sexuality in the Sonnets of James Whitcomb Riley" (*ON* 4:143–50)—*credite, posteri!*

vii. Fin de Siècle America: Stephen Crane and the 1890s

It is Crane's "boldness" that assures Thomas A. Gullason of "The Permanence of Stephen Crane" (*SNNTS* 10:86–95); in Gullason's words, Crane "has left us indelible portraits of the chaos, the mystery and wonder of the spirit of Man and his environment, of life and death, with a vision and a style that are still highly individual and unduplicated even today." Gullason is by no means alone in his appreciation of Crane; 40 other articles and notes speak to the facts of Crane's life and art this year, and by sheer number suggest the major importance of Stephen Crane. Or do they? First it is necessary to see if and how they alter or augment our understanding of this American Chatterton.

Much will be made of Henry Binder's "*The Red Badge of Courage* Nobody Knows" (*SNNTS* 10:9–47), the lead article of a special number of *Studies in the Novel* edited by Hershel Parker with James T. Cox. What Binder sets out to do is to reconstruct the text of Crane's acknowledged masterpiece as Crane intended the novel to be read. Between the time he submitted the manuscript (mostly extant) of the story to Ripley Hitchcock, his editor at D. Appleton & Co., and its eventual publication, two series of deletions in the novel were made, "apparently in response to editorial suggestions," but to which Crane assented. These cuts, according to Binder, "confused the original irony; reduced the psychological complexity of Henry Fleming, the main character; also obscured the function of

Wilson and the tattered man; and left the text incoherent at several places, in particular the final chapter." This is obviously important, and Binder's careful reconstruction of the text, now available in the new *Norton Anthology of American Literature*, edited by Ronald Gottesman and others, will demand the careful attention of every Crane specialist, just as the Hayford and Sealts text of *Billy Budd* did some years back. But Melville had no part in the publication of his novella; Crane did, and that's the great difference. There is no doubt that Binder's reconstructed text is superior to the Appleton text of 1895. The critical confusion and disagreement that has surrounded the novel for the last thirty years, and which Steven Mailloux intelligently discusses in "The Red Badge of Courage and Interpretive Conventions: Critical Response to a Maimed Text" (*SNNTS* 10:48–63), is now resolved, and the coherence of Crane's ironic vision is solidly established. But the manuscript does not represent Crane's "final" intention, any more than does the Appleton text. *The Red Badge of Courage* nobody knows is *The Red Badge of Courage* nobody will ever read because it was never completed in full accordance to Crane's artistic vision. Further complications are explained by Binder in his "Unwinding the Riddle of Four Pages Missing from *The Red Badge of Courage Manuscript*" (*PBSA* 72: 100–06), and an essay by Binder's former teacher, Hershel Parker, "Aesthetic Implications of Authorial Excisions: Examples from Nathaniel Hawthorne, Mark Twain, and Stephen Crane" (*Editing Nineteenth-Century Fiction*, edited by Jane Millgate [Garland], pp. 99–119), further helps illuminate the problems Binder so masterfully confronts.

The text of the 1896 Appleton edition of Crane's *Maggie*, as everyone must by now know, is also "maimed," but here a solution readily offers itself as Hershel Parker and Brian Higgins point out in "Maggie's 'Last Night': Authorial Design and Editorial Patching" (*SNNTS* 10:64–75). If one wants "to read Stephen Crane, not what his Appleton editor left of him," then one must read the 1893 edition of *Maggie*, privately printed at Crane's own expense. Unfortunately Fredson Bowers failed to heed this warning, already made by Joseph Katz and Edwin H. Cady when Bowers edited Crane's little book for the "Virginia Edition" of Crane's *Works* (see *ALS 1969*, p. 176). Bowers's "definitive" edition of the *Works* has since been completed in ten volumes, sloppily performed, "inaccurate and unreliable," a sorry monument to wasted opportunity. David J. Nordloh's meticulous and judicious indictment, "On Crane Now Edited: The University of Virginia Edition of *The Works of Stephen Crane*" (*SNNTS* 10:103–19), will touch with despair the heart of even the staunchest deconstructionist.

Except for James Nagel's competent but fairly commonplace consideration of "Stephen Crane and the Narrative Methods of Impressionism" (*SNNTS* 10:76–85), the remaining essays and notes in the Crane number of *Studies in the Novel* are biographical or bibliographical, most of them of such specialized interest not to warrant special mention here. Donald Pizer's "Stephen Crane: A Review of Scholarship and Criticism since 1969" (pp. 120–45) is of general interest, however, in that it brings up to date the chapter on Crane he contributed a decade ago to *Fifteen American Authors Before 1900* (1971); and Robert Morace's edition of "Stephen Crane's 'The Merry-Go-Round': An Earlier Version of 'The Pace of Youth'" (pp. 146–53), accompanied by an amusing commentary, lays to rest the "ghost" of a novel that never was.

In a short but thoughtful consideration of "Women in the Writings of Stephen Crane: Madonnas of the Decadence" (*SHR* 12:141–48), Donald Vanouse finds that "Crane was one of those who struggled to deviate from intellectual timidity and sexist arrogance in discussing women." Thomas A. Gullason turns his attention to "The Prophetic City in Stephen Crane's 1893 *Maggie*" (*MFS* 24:129–37), a work he describes as "the experimental novel of its day, an anti-novel, where Crane ignores traditional plot, character, theme, style, and cause-and-effect relationships, to expose a City of Unreality and an American tragedy."

Robert Shulman's "Community, Perception, and the Development of Stephen Crane: From *The Red Badge* to 'The Open Boat'" (*AL* 50:441–60) is a valuable and admirably written essay which takes up an important aspect of Crane's vision: his "developing sense of the value of human community." The ideas of Tolstoy, sanctioned by Howells's approval, must certainly have helped Crane discover his own sense of the "solidarity" of mankind, but further debt to the great Russian remains an area of speculation, sometimes helpful as in the case of James B. Colvert's "Stephen Crane's Literary Origins and Tolstoy's *Sebastopol*" (*CL* 15:66–82), but more often likely to recall in one's mind Joseph Conrad's remark, "I could not see the relevancy." This is likely to be the response of most to Clarence O. Johnson's "Stephen Crane and Zola's *Germinal*" (*AN&Q* 16:40–43).

Conrad's preface to Beer's 1923 biography of Crane remains a noble testimony to a happy literary friendship, but Peter L. Hays adds importantly to our understanding of the dimensions of that relationship in his "Joseph Conrad and Stephen Crane" (*EA* 31: 26–37) where he argues that "Crane did influence Conrad's early work," and that one sees "that influence not only in Conrad's style but also in his choice and treatment of subject matter." Hays's position is by no means novel; as Donald W. Rude shows in "Joseph Conrad, Stephen Crane and W. L. Courtney's Review of *The Nigger of the 'Narcissus'*" (*ELT* 21:188–97), it was current during Crane's lifetime, but Hays's argument is commendably supported and documented.

In dealing with Crane's relations with editors and publishers our natural response is to side with Crane; but Walter H. Page's rejection of *The Third Violet* (see George Monteiro, "Stephen Crane and the *Atlantic Monthly*: Two New Letters," *AN&Q* 16:70–72) seems better founded than William L. Andrews's defense of the book in "Art and Success: Another Look at Stephen Crane's *The Third Violet*" (*WascanaR* 13:71–82). While admitting the novel's weaknesses, Andrews still finds it "a significant and suggestive work . . . one drawn from the fires of an authentic and fundamentally serious creative forge."

Jamie Robertson's "Stephen Crane, Eastern Outsider in the West and Mexico" (*WAL* 13:243–57) hopefully will correct several serious misreadings of Crane's stories of the West, especially Raymund A. Paredes' charge of Crane with racism (see *ALS 1971*, p. 186); "Crane's use of the myth of the West is effective," Robertson writes, "not because he seriously believes in it, but because he uses it as a medium to delineate the heroic action of men who, above all things, come to realize their own insignificance."

"'The Ideal and the Real' and 'Brer Washington's Consolation': Two Little-Known Stories by Stephen Crane?" (*ALR* 11:1–33) prints in facsimile and in transcribed text two stories in the Crane collection of the Clifton Waller Barrett Library at the University of Virginia; a short introduction by Lyle D. Linder is both rather silly and annoyingly sketchy. And as usual this year, there is a good handful of explications of individual Crane stories and biographical notes. The most interesting of these is Ellen A. Brown's and Patricia Hernlund's "The Source for the Title of Stephen Crane's *Whilomville Stories*" (*AL* 50:116–18), showing as it does the word "whilom" rich in family associations and childhood memories.

Don Graham's *The Fiction of Frank Norris: The Aesthetic Context* (Missouri) is "an attempt to define and set forth the best of Frank Norris, and to try to understand what is valuable about his fictional world and what is artistically successful in his presentation of that world." The perspective Graham adopts for this worthy endeavor is one provided by what he calls "aesthetic documentation . . . the extensive references to all manner of art in Norris's fiction." This creates a "rhetoric of aesthetic detail" in the novels, which in turn serves as a guide to important themes and previously unappreciated dimensions of the works. Of related interest is Graham's "Frank Norris and Les Jeunes: Architectural Criticism and Aesthetic Values" (*ALR* 11:235–42), "Les Jeunes" being five young aesthetes with whom Norris associated in San Francisco during the mid-'nineties.

In "Frank Norris: A Biographical Essay" (*ALR* 11:219–34), Joseph R. McElrath, Jr., examines the various biographical resources that exist for Norris and finds emerging "the picture of a divided personality: the suave, elegant, boyish-looking man of ease; and a more idiosyncratic and excitable creature who ran on nervous energy in private"; in large part this was "the result of his transition from adolescence to sober maturity," arrested, of course, by an early death. In the same journal, McElrath suggests Richard Harding Davis's *The West through a Car-Window* (1892) as "A Source for Norris's 'A Deal in Wheat'" (11:141). In another "source-study" Stephen Tatum argues "Norris's Debt in 'Lauth' to Lemattre's 'On the Transfusion of Blood'" (*ALR* 11:243–48). Again, what such findings mostly prove, it too often seems, is that Norris, like most writers, read books other than his own. Much more worthwhile is George M. Spangler's analysis of "The Structure of *McTeague*" (*ES* 59:48–56); "from start to finish," Spangler concludes, "the character McTeague is presented as continuously oscillating between repose and disturbance—the repose dependent on sexual dormancy and the disturbance on fear of the destructive female, though the fear is at first disguised as a rational consideration of sexual instinct in general and then as a grim parable of greed." Also to be praised is the wisdom of publishers to make available in soft-cover and almost affordable price texts of less than first-rank novels, in this instance, Norris's *Vandover and the Brute* (Nebraska), introduced by Warren French.

Certain of the "Chicago School of Fiction," to use Howells's convenient phrase, receive abundant attention this year, and the quality of the criticism is good. It was an interesting group of writers, striving to work their art in the "Columbian" city. One contemporary observer was Harriet Monroe's younger sister, and, as James Stronks points out, "Lucy Monroe's 'Chicago Letter' to *The Critic*, 1893–1896" (*MidAmerica* 5:30–38), 135 of them, in fact, "freshens our interest and adds a wealth of detail existing nowhere else to what we have known previously of the city's cultural life during its yeasty mid-1890's."

It's "the Chicago Years" that Charles Fanning focuses on in his study of *Finley Peter Dunne & Mr. Dooley* (Kentucky). Later the newspaperman and humorist would move on to New York and national fame, but in the mid-'nineties Dunne's audience was mostly local, or rather the audience of his happy creation, Martin Dooley, the Irish saloon keeper of Archey Road whose many dialogues in Irish dialect helped an ethnic community define its place in a strange, new world. Though Fanning's praise of "Mr. Dooley" and his writings will appear to some rather extravagant, his study is nonetheless valuable.

Joseph B. McCullough makes no extraordinary claim for the artistry of *Hamlin Garland* (TUSAS 299), but does point out that "whenever he was able to maintain a tension between his radical individualism and the oppressive social and economic forces threatening individual freedom, his work retains a compelling vitality." "Desertion and Rescue on the Dakota Plains: Hamlin Garland in the Land of the Straddle-Bug" (*SDR* 16:30–45) is an examination by Robert F. Gish of Garland's two Dakota novels, *A Little Norsk: Ol' Pap's Flaxen* (1892) and *Moccasin Ranch: A Story of Dakota* (1909); "in and behind both novels," Gish's careful reading shows, "various ideas of desertion and rescue function as controlling motifs." Gish's psychological speculations in regard to these patterns, specifically Garland's "need to restore his mother-wife to her former, civilized life and make right his father's wrong," are entirely in accord with Garland's biography. In "Hamlin Garland's Indians and the Quality of Civilized Life" (*Where the West Begins*, pp. 51–62), Jack L. Davis calls our attention to Garland's Indian fiction, *The Captain of the Gray-Horse Troop* (1902) and *The Book of the American Indian* (1923), designating them "truly landmark treatments of Indians": Garland "opened himself to the seductive possibility that native life possessed a quality missing from, but perhaps necessary to, American civilization . . . a spiritual sense of identity with the material/spiritual world." Finally, Randall L. Popken compares two early works by Garland and Willa Cather in "From Innocence to Experience in *My Ántonia* and *Boy Life on the Prairie*" (*NDQ* 46,ii: 73–81), claiming that Garland's autobiographical volume measures up well against Cather's better-known novel.

Kenneth Scambray's "The Romance in Decline: Realism in Henry Blake Fuller's *The Cliff-Dwellers*" (*NDQ* 46,ii:19–28) is a perceptive reading of Fuller's first realistic novel in terms of the "realism-romance debate" that centered on Howells in the 1880s and 1890s. According to Scambray, Fuller consciously set out in his novel "to redirect the American novel away from the European tradition in fiction as he had experienced it in the sentimentality of Charles Dickens and in the historical romances of Sir Walter Scott." The fact that the novel deals with the business world is less important.

Adhering to a recent decision to devote its pages primarily to bibliographical scholarship, *American Literary Realism* serves Frederic scholars with a reprint of a minor short story, difficult to obtain in its original publication, but now edited by Thomas F. O'Donnell, "Harold Frederic's 'Cordelia and the Moon': Text, with Comment" (11:34–51), and Robert A. Morace's annotated edition of "Arthur Warren's and Robert Sherard's Interviews with Harold Frederic" (11:52–70), two items originally published in 1895 and 1897. In the same issue L. Moody Simms, Jr., briefly discusses "The Georgia Background of Will N. Harben's Fiction" (11:71–79) and reprints Harben's own essay on his native "Georgia," commissioned by *The Bookman* in 1913.

Ben Merchant Vorpahl's *Frederic Remington and the West: With the Eye of the Mind* (Texas) is an important book. Arguing that "any formulaic linkage between Remington and the West is misleading rather than enlightening," Vorpahl believes we should "not consider Remington a 'western' artist, except in the unique sense generated by his own work—the sense less of a region than of a direction." Remington's achievement "was not only to include all the sordidness of the event in his recorded vision but also to expand that vision until both sordidness and transience were absorbed in a universal interrogative and the West lost its substance to emerge as perception only—the same variety of transformation Melville worked on the whaling industry in *Moby-Dick.*"

James H. Justus's conviction that Kate Chopin's *The Awakening* will prove a "permanent 'rediscovery'" in American fiction is undoubtedly correct, and his fine essay, "The Unawakening of Edna Pontellier" (*SLJ* 10,ii:107–22), is a noteworthy testimony to the novel's substantial aesthetic achievement. What appeals most to Justus "is the way in which Chopin's coolly assured psychological insight and technical skill of portraiture merge in the study of one woman." "Edna's process of awakening is," he explains, "a kind of enlightenment, but it can hardly be called growth. What she discovers does not set her free but binds her even more tightly to a destined end." Gregory L. Candela's further recognition of echoes of Whitman's "Out of the Cradle Endlessly Rocking," in Chopin's novel, "Walt Whitman and Kate Chopin: A Further Connection" (*WWR* 24:163–65), nicely complements Justus's reading.

"Kate Chopin and the Fiction of Limits: 'Desiree's Baby'" (*SLJ* 10,ii:123–33), a careful analysis of Chopin's popular story by Cynthia Griffin Wolff, finds the vision in this story, as in all of Chopin's best fiction, to be "consummately interior"; "it draws for strength upon [Chopin's] willingness to conduct the bleak fact of life's tenuous stabilities." Read independently, the story is a "superb piece of short fiction," but when "seen in the more ample context of Chopin's complete work, the story accrues added significance as the most vivid and direct statement of her major concern—the fiction of limits." Also bleak is the treatment of "Childbirth and Motherhood in Kate Chopin's Fiction" (*RFI* 4,ii:8–12); though ideally "Chopin saw the tremendous positive potential of childbirth and motherhood," Patricia Hopkins Lattin finds that in actuality, "motherhood in Chopin generally proves disastrous, causing insanity, death, and . . . a woman's loss of self"(!).

Though it is too often neglected, even in our literary histories, the economics of authorship is an important and even fascinating subject, especially when approached with the intelligence and impressive knowledge of someone like Nelson Lichtenstein. His "Au-

thorial Professionalism and the Literary Marketplace, 1885–1900"
(*AmerS* 19:35–53) examines the emergence of literary syndicates,
authors' societies, and the literary agent during this period when
"professional authorship in America achieved its modern dimensions."

University of California, Los Angeles

13. Fiction: 1900 to the 1930s

David Stouck

In 1978 there were fewer books and articles on the major writers from this period, probably because centenary studies for most of these authors are now in the past. If there was a trend in the scholarship it was to examine some of the minor works by these authors and to rediscover the writings of their lesser known contemporaries.

In the search for opportunities for original research critics have also turned increasingly to examining aspects of the popular imagination, particularly as regards the Western and the treatment of literature in film. Typical is Gary Topping's "Zane Grey: A Literary Reassessment" (*WAL* 13:51–64) in which Topping argues that Grey was unfairly reviewed by his critics because they looked for realism and naturalism when Grey was writing romances. Grey, says Topping, should be appreciated for the exoticism of some of his characters, the grand scale of scenery and action, and for his "nostalgia for an earlier, simpler, and morally more vital time." In another essay, "The Pastoral Ideal in Popular American Literature: Zane Grey and Edgar Rice Burroughs" (*Rendezvous* 12,ii[1977]:11–15), Topping shows how the works of Grey and Burroughs reflect the turn-of-the-century "wilderness cult" when America, no longer a frontier society, was trying "to preserve as many of the frontier-nourished institutions and values as possible." Both writers, says Topping, saw man as a mixture of the civilized and primitive and felt he could not realize his potential happiness "unless both elements in his nature were given room for expression." But where Burroughs leaves Tarzan caught unhappily between the two forces in his nature, says Topping, Grey in some of his novels is able to envision for his characters a pastoral society which possesses elements of both the primitive and civilized.

The Classic American Novel and the Movies, edited by Gerald

Peary and Roger Shatzkin (Ungar, 1977), is a collection of essays
discussing film treatments of several works of fiction from this period.
The essays reveal how novels like *Sister Carrie* and *An American
Tragedy*, considered politically subversive, were drastically altered
so that Dreiser's amorality and his socialist ideas were deleted, and
how in the film version the happy ending replaced the compromise
and defeat that conclude such novels as *Main Street* and *Alice Adams*.
An essay on *The Sea Wolf* on the other hand shows how the film
improved on some of the novel's salient weaknesses, particularly the
love affair between Humphrey and Maud Brewster. These essays
are concerned largely with film, but descriptions of the process by
which novels became films often reveal some significant aspects of
the fictions.

Most of the writers from this period were influenced or affected
by the reviews and critical writings of H. L. Mencken. There are
two recent book-length studies which give an overview of Mencken's
career and analyze his ideas and assumptions as a literary critic.
W. H. A. Williams's *H. L. Mencken* (TUSAS 297[1977]) is a short
book committed to surveying briefly all the facets of Mencken's
work, whereas Charles A. Fecher's *Mencken: A Study of His Thought*
(Knopf) is a much longer, more leisurely study with considerable
biographical material included. While the scope of the two books
differs (Fecher naturally gives us more detail), they make a similar
impression, for the two authors are agreed on the essential points
concerning Mencken: the influence of Nietzsche on his early thinking, the iconoclastic rather than systematic nature of his literary
criticism, and his failure to ground his social criticism in a genuine
theoretical concept of politics and society. Both writers make clear
that Mencken was not an original or profound thinker but they show
how important he was in freeing American culture from the pro-
hibitive and imitative standards of the Genteel Tradition.

i. Willa Cather

Mencken thought highly of Willa Cather and critics today continue
to explore the substance of this writer's deceptively simple craft.
What is interesting is that Cather not only received the lion's share
of attention in 1978 but that critics examined most of the works in
her canon. The best essays focused on *The Professor's House* and

Death Comes for the Archbishop. In " 'The Thing Not Named' in *The Professor's House*" (*WAL* 12:263–74) Barbara Wild argues that the novel's deep theme is that of a great friendship between two unusual men, Tom Outland and Godfrey St. Peter, and suggests that the Biblical friendship of Christ and Peter might have been in Cather's mind when she wrote the novel. As in the New Testament story, says Wild, there is a strong feeling of loss and betrayal surrounding the professor's friendship and in Christian terms he undergoes a symbolic death and rebirth. In "The Art of Willa Cather's Craft" (*PLL* 14:61–73) Cynthia Chaliff states that "at the heart of Cather's fiction there is a wish to return to the happiness of childhood." Chaliff suggests that Cather's technique of yoking together two apparently unrelated stories in *The Professor's House* represents a flight from present reality.

In a fine essay entitled "Willa Cather's Archbishop: A Western and Classical Perspective" (*WAL* 13:141–50) John J. Murphy shows how Cather gives Father Latour the characteristics of both the American hero and the heroes of classical literature, "particularly Aeneas, whose destiny was to shape a new culture in Italy by transplanting the home gods of Troy." Latour, writes Murphy, "reflects Cather's cyclical view of history, in which the American experience repeats the European, and our West the larger West." In a note, "The Genesis of the Prologue of *Death Comes for the Archbishop*" (*AL* 50:473–78) James Woodress describes a painting, "The Missionary's Story," by the popular 19th-century artist Jehan George Vibert, which in an interview Cather referred to as an inspiration for the first scene of her novel. What would have intrigued Cather in this rather insignificant piece, says Woodress, is the "sharp visual contrast between the sophisticated Old World cardinals surrounded by the amenities of life and the austere missionary priest just back from the wilderness." Woodress's note rightly draws attention to the highly visual aspect of the prologue, particularly the author's use of color. In a longer piece, "Willa Cather and History" (*ArQ* 34:239–54), James Woodress writes that Cather gradually abandoned her youthful belief in progress and came to view history "as a series of disconnected epochs, each to be dealt with separately." Her two historical novels, *Death Comes for the Archbishop* and *Shadows on the Rock*, says Woodress, dramatize the romantic Emersonian idea of history embodied in representative men; and in these novels, he adds, she is like Hawthorne, more concerned with capturing the feeling about another period than with faithfully recording historic fact. In a similar vein Patricia Lee Yongue suggests in "Willa Cather on Heroes and Hero-Worship" (*NM* 79:59–66) that one of the allusive contexts in which *Death Comes for the Archbishop* might be read is Carlyle's *On Heroes, Hero-Worship, and the Heroic in History*, for, as Yongue argues, Cather shared Carlyle's idea that significant human history consists of the accomplishments of great men and, like Carlyle, believed in the necessary bond between the artist Hero and the heroic Ordinary Man who gives the Hero's vision concrete substance.

Increasingly critics are concerned with Cather's presentation of women characters and with her handling of sexuality. In "Finding Marian Forrester: A Restorative Reading of Cather's *A Lost Lady*" (*CLQ* 14:221–25) Anneliese H. Smith, with the authority of Cather's statement that nothing mattered in the story but the portrait of the heroine, examines Marian Forrester carefully and finds her repeatedly betrayed by masculine ignorance and self-interest, including that of the novel's narrator, Niel Herbert. And in a probing article entitled "Narrative Technique in Cather's *My Mortal Enemy* (*JNT* 8:141–49) S. J. Rosowski shows how the narrator of the novel gradually exchanges the romantic myth of young Myra Driscoll for the reality of the older, disillusioned woman who has lost her world of romantic love but has gained human wisdom. In "The Unity of Willa Cather's 'Two-Part Pastoral'; Passion in *O Pioneers!*" (*SAF* 6:157–70) Sharon O'Brien argues that the two stories combined in *O Pioneers!* are both parables about passion. Alexandra Bergson's taming of the soil, says O'Brien, "chronicles the heroic results of passion regulated and channeled," whereas the story of Emil and Marie "records the destructive outcome of sexual passion indulged and unleashed." This novel, continues O'Brien, "reflects one of Willa Cather's most persistent fictional preoccupations: the insufficiency, even the danger, of sexual passion and the opposing grandeur of passion deflected from the personal to the impersonal object."

In *"One of Ours:* Willa Cather's Losing Battle" (*WAL* 13:259–66) Marilyn Arnold argues reasonably that Cather's war novel fails because she has put a weak character at its centre and provided no clear values for him to believe in. Claude Wheeler, says Arnold, glorifies war because it frees him from the bonds of a materialistic society; but at the same time, Arnold points out, Cather makes clear to the reader that war is a false ideal, so that her protagonist at best emerges simply a pathetic victim. Less clearly argued is Richard Giannone's "Willa Cather and the Unfinished Drama of Deliverance" (*PrS* 52:25–46), which asserts that Cather's fiction, taken as a whole, recounts a pilgrimage of the human soul in search of freedom and wholeness. Giannone considers specifically *Sapphira and the Slave Girl*, which he sees as a paradigm of the movement from enslavement to liberty; but his reading of the novel is overwrought and implies a cunning and design which I doubt was either Cather's method or purpose. Robert Alan McGill's "Heartbreak: Western Enchantment and Western Fact in Willa Cather's *The Professor's House*" (*SDR* 16,iii:56–79) is an even more muddled article which makes one wonder about editorial policies. McGill, however, does identify two important ideas in *The Professor's House*—letting go with the heart and feeling the ground under one's feet—as having their source in Robert Frost's poem, "Wild Grapes."

Finally there were two short articles concerned with literary conventions in *My Ántonia*. In "The Iconography of Vice in Willa Cather's *My Ántonia*" (*CLQ* 14:93–102) Evelyn H. Haller argues that "the minor characters in this novel are described not so much in terms of personality as in terms of morality," although the schema of vices they portray is one of Cather's own making. Haller relates many of the minor figures such as Mrs. Shimerda and Wick Cutter to the list of sins given by Chaucer's Parson. In "Renaissance Pastoral Conventions and the Ending of *My Ántonia*" (*MarkhamR* 8:8–11) Richard C. Harris draws attention to the triple enclosure of fence and hedges surrounding Ántonia's orchard, which imitates, he says, the special geography of Renaissance pastorals and implies that Jim Burden finds peace, not loss, there.

ii. Gertrude Stein

A special issue of *Twentieth Century Literature* (*TCL* 24,i) resulted in some interesting new articles on Stein, emphasizing her importance as a technical innovator. Leon Katz, who is editing Stein's "Notebooks," has discovered that she was influenced in the development of her ideas about personality by a dubious book of psychology, *Sex and Character* by Otto Weininger. In "Weininger and *The Making of Americans*" (pp. 8–26) Katz discusses how Stein appropriated

Weininger's system for describing character, particularly the notion of the whole or completed individual, and developed her own ideas about a character's "bottom nature" and the possibility of success and failure as dependent on the relationship between different levels of one's being. Two articles show how ongoing process and changing relationships are the fundamental elements of composition for Stein. In "Spreading the Difference: One Way to Read Gertrude Stein's *Tender Buttons*" (pp. 57–75) Pamela Hadas argues that the "objects" in the book are described by means of associative word play which transforms the objects, and that the process reveals how one lives with perceptions of changes and differences of all sorts, from the unreliable meanings of language to those psychological differences between men and women, past and future, brothers and sisters. In "Gertrude Stein's 'Composition as Explanation'" (pp. 76–80) Bruce Bassoff gives a brief but lucid account of Stein's essay relating it to the fundamental principles of French structuralism. Stein's emphasis, says Bassoff, like that of Lévi-Strauss, is not on the individual elements of a composition but on the relations between those elements. She believed, he continues, that a composition forms out of things happening in the world without the artist knowing until later how those things happened. Bassoff relates the latter idea to the critical principles of Walter Benjamin and Jacques Derrida, who argue that the meaning of a text is continually deferred.

There was a range of interest reflected in the articles in the special Stein number of *TCL*. Cynthia Secor's "*Ida*, A Great American Novel" (pp. 96–107) is a feminist reading of the late Stein book. The heroine, Secor argues, is engaged in a quest for self-actualization which cannot be resolved in a permanent marriage until she comes to term with the question of her own entity. Ida's "restlessness and rootlessness, her lack of enduring connection with place or family," says Secor, is what makes her the modern American heroine. Kate Davey's article, "Richard Foreman's Ontological-Hysteric Theatre: The Influence of Gertrude Stein" (pp. 108–26) discusses the influence of Stein's "continuous present" on the experimental theatre of Richard Foreman. Elsewhere (*IFR* 5:91–95) Ethel F. Cornwell traces another influence in "Gertrude Stein: The Forerunner of Nathalie Sarraute."

One of the best articles in the special number is Lynn Z. Bloom's

"Gertrude Is Alice Is Everybody: Innovation and Point of View in Gertrude Stein's Autobiographies" (pp. 81–93). Bloom describes the form of Stein's *The Autobiography of Alice B. Toklas* as autobiography-by-Doppelgänger in which the writer has created a ventriloquist persona (Alice) "to distract the reader from the egotism inherent in conventional autobiography." This narrative technique, says Bloom, avoids the confessional mode and allows the real speaker (Stein) to give what appear to be objective and honorific interpretations of Stein's life and work. There were three other articles in 1978 which focused on Stein's experiments with autobiography. In a perceptive article entitled "The Autobiography as Generic 'Continuous Present': *Paris France* and *Wars I Have Seen*" (*ESC* 4:224–37) Shirley Swartz shows how Stein constructed biography out of a series of anecdotes and observations that "recreate things being." Stein, says Swartz, wanted to recreate not the self remembering but the self knowing and experiencing, and so made her autobiographies an activity of the "human mind" without beginning or ending. In a densely written but challenging essay entitled "Portrait, Patriarchy, Mythos: The Revenge of Gertrude Stein" (*Salmagundi* 40:69–91) Neil Schmitz examines Stein's posture and purposes in writing autobiography. Most significant in the ruse of Alice as narrator, says Schmitz, is Stein's fundamental belief that a true portrait or definition of a person is not possible, that the imposed ordering of memory is bogus. This shattering of her own portrait, concludes Schmitz, allies Stein with Whitman and Twain's Huck Finn, who insist on new beginnings and the primordial function of language as naming. Unlike the above articles Lawrence Raab's "Remarks as Literature" (*MQR* 17:480–93) adds nothing to one's understanding of Stein's purposes or techniques in writing autobiography.

Linda Simon's *The Biography of Alice B. Toklas* (Doubleday, 1977) provides another picture of Stein's life because, like the famous *Autobiography*, it inevitably deals with Stein as much as with Toklas. Simon's book confirms the view that Toklas's life was wholly dedicated to serving Gertrude Stein both while the author lived and during the more than 20 years that Toklas survived after her death. There were two more items touching on Stein's life. In "Two Revolutionaries: Gertrude Stein and Emma Goldman" (*STTH* 1,i:70–78) Winifred L. Frazer parallels the careers and personalities of these two innovative thinkers, while in "Baby Woojums in Iowa" (*BI* 26[1977]:3–18) Bruce Kellner gives an overview of the literary friendship between Stein and Carl Van Vechten.

iii. Theodore Dreiser

Although Dreiser is known chiefly for his novels, there were some interesting articles recently on his short fiction. In "The Making of Dreiser's Early Short Stories: The Philosopher and the Artist" (*SAF* 6:47–62) Yoshinobu Hakutani shows that Dreiser's stories frequently had their source in personal experiences so that inconsistencies arose between his philosophical determinism and his artistic creation of a character or incident. "Dreiserian characters," says Hakutani, "are often sometimes larger than the author's occasional philosophy . . . and his understanding of humanity often goes beyond the philosophy he learned from Spencer." In "Psychological Veracity in 'The Lost Phoebe': Dreiser's Revision" (*SAF* 6:100–105) Don Graham compares the magazine version of "The Lost Phoebe" with that collected in *Free and Other Stories* and finds that in the later version Dreiser has added detail which makes the original ghost story a study in perceptual derangement as well. And in "Dreiser's Later Short Stories" (*DN* 9,i:5–10) Joseph P. Griffin examines six late stories which remain uncollected and demonstrates that Dreiser was becoming less preoccupied with a destructive view of life and that he was moving towards more documentary kinds of fiction, blurring the distinction between short story and personal sketch.

An American Tragedy, however, continues to receive the greatest amount of critical attention. In Michael Spindler's "Youth, Class, and Consumerism in Dreiser's *An American Tragedy*" (*JAmS* 12,i:63–79) there is a good reading of the novel in the light of postwar social and economic forces, showing how Clyde Griffiths is caught between the new consumer capitalism, which emphasized spending and gratification, and the ascetic ideology of the old Protestant work ethic. In an awkwardly written but provocative essay entitled "Looking Around to See Who I Am: Dreiser's Territory of the Self" (*ELH* 44[1977]:728–48) Philip Fisher argues that Clyde Griffiths has no identity of his own but experiences himself as an extension of the world around him. Dreiser's city, says Fisher, exists as a projection of human desires, and Clyde is drawn and repelled by this centre of being which exists outside his body. In *"An American Tragedy*: Constitutional Violations" (*DN* 9,i:11–19) Mona G. Rosenman argues that it was Dreiser's purpose to show that "Clyde Griffiths had neither adequate counsel nor a fair trial" and to illustrate the ways in which the specific American principles of liberty and justice were violated during the trial. And in "An American Tragedy: Novel, Scenario, and Films" (*LFQ* 5[1977]:259–67) Bernice Kliman examines the three film versions of Dreiser's novel and finds that not only does the medium of film necessitate changes from the novel, but that the director's point of view is also crucial to the novel's translation into film. Eisenstein's scenario, says Kliman, is close to Dreiser's novel because it puts the blame for the murder not on Clyde but on society; whereas Von Sternberg, only interested in the personal relationships, presents Clyde as a callous brute in his film; and George Stevens, studying the ways a man can get ahead, presents him in *A Place in the Sun* as a victim of chance circumstances.

One of the best Dreiser articles was Fred G. See's "The Text as Mirror: *Sister Carrie* and the Lost Language of the Heart" (*Criticism* 20:144–66), which demonstrates that Dreiser's language allows no metaphysical "elsewhere," that it is a language of material surfaces. Throughout the novel, says See, the appearance of metaphor recalls a religious and romantic order that is gone, that no longer has the power to give meaning to or fulfill desire in the heroine's life. Finally, there were a couple of miscellaneous items dealing with Dreiser's career rather than specifically with his fiction. In "Theodore Dreiser and the Nobel Prize" (*AL* 50:216–29) Rolf Lundén asks why Sinclair Lewis and not Dreiser won the Nobel Prize in 1930 and explains that Lewis had the advantage over Dreiser because he was a bestseller in Scandinavia and his criticism of American society was more explicit. It is hard to avoid thinking, says Lundén, that the prize went to Lewis because his satirical caricatures allowed Europeans to laugh at America. And in *ALR* 11:284–94 Thomas P. Riggio has published an interview "transcribed from an unmarked recording in the Dreiser collection at the University of Pennsylvania." The interview appears to have been given in San Francisco in 1939 and is of interest because it contains a rare instance of Dreiser's discussing publicly his reading and his aesthetics.

iv. John Dos Passos

The purpose of Iain Colley's *Dos Passos and The Fiction of Despair* (Rowman) is to trace and diagnose the special variety of pessimism that evolves in Dos Passos's writing. Colley describes the pessimism of the author's first novel, *Streets of Night*, as simply "an adolescent feeling that the world is hopelessly wrong." The sense of urban loneliness, says Colley, is the book's most significant and lasting impression. The two war novels that followed describe the more genuine experience of the young American sharing the pain and bewilderment of the common soldier. *One Man's Initiation— 1917* intimately records the shock and outrage felt as the innocent American collides with the brute, terrifying realities of the war, while *Three Soldiers* describes the failure of a soldier "to discover a means of personal self-realization that will redeem the impersonal and inhuman mechanism of army existence." The implications of that failure are set forth, continues Colley, in one of Dos Passos's best novels, *Manhattan Transfer*, where characters are simply part of a giant metropolis and life is viewed as motion without purpose or meaning. The alienation felt by modern man is the subject of *USA* and though Dos Passos was not a Marxist, he argues, he did employ the rhetoric and imagery of class warfare to dramatize the hardships of a chaotic social system and the permanent human condition of loneliness. Dos Passos's achievement was to show "the sick futility of life" in the accumulated detail of daily defeats, and though the picture is an ignoble one, says Colley, there is truth and courage in its portrayal. This is a good discussion of Dos Passos's fiction with a number of useful parallels drawn between Dos Passos and other writers of the "lost generation."

In contrast Sharon Fusselman Mizener's *Manhattan Transients* (Exposition, 1977) is a naive and badly written extended essay purporting to examine character, technique, and social ideology in *Manhattan Tranfer*. Mizener's discussion of the characters focuses largely on the sexual irregularities of their lives and her chapter on ideology simply restates the common view that *Manhattan Transfer* is "a massive indictment of modern industrial society," but not a Marxist or anarchist novel. The best chapter is the detailed discussion of imagery which focuses on the idea that the images "create an impressionistic landscape appropriate for the habitation of souls in purgatory," but a purgatory which does not hold hope of another world to come.

From the Dos Passos collection at the University of Virginia Townsend Ludington in "The Hotel Childhood of John Dos Passos" (*VQR* 54:297–313) has summarized the contents of two unpublished essays Dos Passos wrote about his childhood. The essays, according to Ludington's account, reveal the author intimidated by the decorum of his upper-middle-class surroundings and by the loneliness of his illegitimate condition. Ludington suggests that his best fiction is a form of rebellion against Victorian gentility and the false strictures of a hypocritical society.

v. Jack London

There were only a few articles on London and most of those were concerned with his short fiction. In " 'To Build A Fire': Physical Fiction and Metaphysical Critics" (*SSF* 15:19–24) Charles E. May takes exception to the symbolic readings of London's best-known story and argues that it is a naturalistic story with physical significance only. The death of the protagonist, says May, does not represent man's cosmic loneliness but rather "the simple physical discovery that the self is body only." In "Jack London's Portrayal of the Natives in His First Four Collections of Arctic Tales" (*JLN* 10:127–37) Jacqueline T. Courbin writes that London creates both sentimental and complex portraits of natives, but that throughout his Arctic stories the superiority of the Anglo-Saxon is taken for granted. Don Graham's article, "Jack London's Tale Told by a High-Grade Feeb" (*SSF* 15:429–34) is a brief appreciation of both the serious and comic ironies in London's story, "Told in the Drooling Ward." Graham points out the uniqueness of the story in London's canon, and places it in the context of other fictions such as the Benjy section of *The Sound and the Fury* and Kesey's *One Flew Over the Cuckoo's Nest*, which employ feeble-minded personae.

There were two other articles of some interest on London. In "Jack London's *The Iron Heel*: Art as Manifesto" (*SAF* 6:77–92) Paul Stein examines *The Iron Heel* as a "literary version of the *Communist Manifesto*," which insists on the revolutionary overthrow and destruction of capitalism; while in a more conventional literary manner John S. Mann in "The Theme of the Double in *The Call of the Wild*" (*MarkhamR* 8:1–5) describes the patterns of division that permeate the novel, particularly as they inform the central theme of savagery versus civilization.

vi. Sherwood Anderson

Most of the Anderson articles, like those on London, deal with the author's minor works. In "Sherwood Anderson's *Kit Brandon*: A Study in Oral Form" (*GrLR* 5:42–48) Philip A. Greasley shows how Anderson's last novel embodies the values implicit in the oral style, particularly the dignity and importance of the common man. And in "Black Mystics, French Cynics, Sherwood Anderson" (*BALF* 11[1977]:49–53) Michael Fanning analyzes *Dark Laughter* and Anderson's preoccupation with the life of the senses. Two models for the instinctive life, says Fanning, existed for Anderson: the European and the black. But, continues Fanning, Anderson felt that European sensuality had been degraded to promiscuity by the war, while black American sensuality remained an inaccessible mystery to the white, so that neither form was available to the white American. These are interesting articles, but neither alters the status of these minor novels. The most ignored of Anderson's minor works is the novel *Many Marriages*. Fifty years out of print, the book has been resissued in a new critical edition, edited by Douglas G. Rogers (Metuchen, N.J.: Scarecrow Press). In the introduction Rogers discusses the novel's place in the Anderson canon, the reasons for its long obscurity and neglect, and gives an account of Anderson's attitudes and experiences during the writing of the book. Finally, there is even a textual study of an unpublished Anderson novel. See William S. Pfeiffer's "*Mary Cochran*: Sherwood Anderson's Ten-Year Novel" (*SB* 31:248–57).

vii. Edith Wharton

There are only three recent articles on Wharton worthy of mention here. In the best of these, "The Ordered Disorder of *Ethan Frome*" (*SNNTS* 9[1977]:237–45), David Eggenschwiler carefully scrutinizes Wharton's novel to assess whether the protagonist should be classified as a tragic hero or a pathetic victim of circumstances. Eggenschwiler argues persuasively that Ethan Frome, viewed with both irony and sympathy by the narrator, moves in a middle ground, a man deficient in courage but suffering more than his due. In "Edith Wharton's Debt to Meredith in 'The Mortal Lease'" (*YULG* 53:100–108) Arline Golden identifies Meredith's sonnet sequence *Modern Love* as the source of Wharton's title for "The Mortal Lease" and as a thematic paradigm for her poem's conflict between mortality and the inability to accept it. In "Edith Wharton's Final Alterations of *The Age of Innocence*" (*SAF* 6:21–31) Joseph Candido shows how Wharton's deletion of adjectives and phrases in the galley proofs makes her statements less explicit and heighten the subtlety of characterization in her novel. This is a valuable consideration of Wharton's sensitivity to style, but I wonder why Candido or his editors would let stand a statement that Wharton at the time of writing *The Age of Innocence* was "embroiled in an arduous love affair with Walter Berry," when R. W. B. Lewis's biography has more or less proved such an assumption to be false.

viii. Lewis, Hergesheimer, and Wescott

These three writers were once considered to be among the most important literary figures of their generation. Today, however, they are more often read for the light they cast on social history and receive only occasional attention from literary critics. Sinclair Lewis is the most important of these writers and Dick Wagenaar's substantial essay, "The Knight and the Pioneer: Europe and America in the Fiction of Sinclair Lewis" (*AL* 50:230–49), attests to a residue of lasting interest in his work. Wagenaar argues that the romantic need to embellish quotidian reality is one of the fundamental postures in Lewis's life and art. Initially, says Wagenaar, Lewis located his vision of an ideal life in Europe which by contrast emphasized, in books like *Main Street* and *Babbitt,* the gritty reality of materialistic America. But Lewis's travellers to Europe such as Sam Dodsworth still yearn for the purposeful, self-reliant life of the frontier, writes Wagenaar, and Europe, mellow with tradition, becomes a place where weary Americans die. In his last novel, *World So Wide,* says Wagenaar, Lewis posits the inner world of the mind and self as the new frontier, but unfortunately he did not have the turn of mind or fictional technique to demonstrate the central character's growing self-knowledge. Joseph Hergesheimer was one of the most promising young writers of the 1920s. Today he is almost completely forgotten, but for the benefit of the few who are still fascinated by his novels Edward L. Tucker has published in its original and complete form a letter which contains important autobiographical information. See "Joseph Hergesheimer to Mr. Gordon: A Letter" (*SAF* 6:218–27). In a good article entitled "The Midwest and the Expatriate in the Fiction of Glenway Wescott" (*ON* 4:25–34) Paul J. Ferlazzo finds interesting the fact that Wescott, more than any of his contemporaries, examined his life as an expatriate with continual reference to the midwestern heritage that nurtured him. In *The Grandmothers*, says Ferlazzo, Wescott views pioneering and expatriation as part of a similar questing pattern, while in *Good-bye Wisconsin* he indicts the Midwest "as a region incapable of satisfying the longings of the self."

ix. Ring Lardner

In "Southwestern Humorists and Ring Lardner: Sport in American Literature" (*IllQ* 39[1977]:5–21) Christian Messenger asserts that "Lardner saw the sports world as emblematic of a disorder in society, and his popular heroes were presented as lost and unhappy." Messenger also illustrates the similarity between the conventions in Lardner's stories (the physical peculiarities of the characters, the criticism of social customs, the narrator as outsider) and those devices used by such Southwest humorists as Longstreet and Harris as early as the 1830s. Lardner as a sports writer is a special interest in Jonathan Yardley's *Ring: A Biography of Ring Lardner* (Random, 1977). Yardley's own interest in sports and his experience as a journalist make him eminently qualified to write about the life of this author. But *Ring* is an account of Lardner's life which also charts his development as a writer. Yardley singles out Lardner's mother's interest in literature, religion, and music as having a significant influence on the writer and he considers in some detail Lardner's earliest pieces of journalism, tracing the development of his quick laugh and off-handed style. There is much about Lardner the man, his reticence to reveal his emotions, his fastidiousness on sexual matters, his eventual alcoholism; but Yardley does not presume to psychoanalyze his subject. There are good discussions of Lardner's fiction, particularly the creation of Jack Keefe. To emphasize the fact that Lardner wrote in a vernacular "that has had a lasting effect on the way American writers describe American talk," he quotes Virginia Woolf's assessment that Lardner was, like the game he wrote about, a remarkable instance of native American culture. Yardley also documents Lardner's influence on such writers as Sherwood Anderson, James T. Farrell, and Hemingway. This well-balanced account of Lardner's life and work will admirably serve the needs of biography for some time to come.

x. Glasgow, Cabell

There was very little new scholarly material of interest about these two writers from Virginia. The only Glasgow article was C. Hugh Holman's "*Barren Ground* and the Shape of History" (SAQ 77:137–45), which examines the way in which the characters of Glasgow's most personal and psychological novel are still representatives of social classes intermingled in the complex patterns of Virginia's history. Issue 9 of *EGN* includes a special supplement, "Ellen Glasgow: An Annotated Checklist, 1973 to the Present," by Jan Zlotnick Schmidt, which updates Edgar E. MacDonald's "An Essay in Bibliography" (*RALS* 2:131–56; 3:249–553). Of special interest to teachers is the fact that *The Sheltered Life* is in print again at last, published by Hill and Wang.

    Kalki 7:115–28 reprints an early Cabell story entitled "An Amateur Ghost" and in the same number Paul Spencer in "Jurgen and the Ghost" (pp. 129–33) discusses the changes Cabell made when he incorporated the story into the novel *Jurgen*. Chief among the changes, says Spencer, are the shift from first to third person narration, the identity of the young man as Jurgen, the change of turn-of-the-century England to medieval Glathion, and the change of the school-boy humor to the more sardonic, bawdy humor of Cabell's middle age.

xi. Proletarian Writers

The quest for fresh subjects to research also resulted in a number of studies of muckraker journalists and fiction writers. Louis Filler's purpose in *Voice of the Democracy: A Critical Biography of David*

Graham Phillips (Penn. State) is to find a new audience for the works of a writer he feels has been unjustly ignored; but a reading of this rather pallid biography is not likely to send many to the library to seek out Phillips's works. The discussion of individual novels is not very stimulating, and weakest of all is the account of Phillips's vision as a novelist. We never learn fully why Phillips idealized the middle class and found the lower classes uninteresting. Filler does well, however, in discussing other writers and capturing the mood of the period.

A friend of Phillips was another muckraker fiction writer, but in *Alfred Henry Lewis* (WWS 32), Abe C. Ravitz tells us that Lewis's important achievement was in mythologizing the West in his Wolfville stories. Although Lewis described city life "with the sharp eye of an aggressive, perceptive journalist," writes Ravitz, it was in his Western books that he wrote with a conscious artist's dedication, preserving there the life of a typical, rowdy frontier town. Charles Alexander Eastman (Ohiyesa) was not strictly speaking a proletarian writer, but as a Sioux Indian he was concerned to interpret the life of his people for the white man. Marion W. Copeland discusses Eastman's work in WWS 33, focusing on the autobiographical writings. But neither Ravitz's essay on Lewis nor Copeland's study of Eastman introduces the authors very clearly or makes their works appear interesting to read.

Upton Sinclair is still the best remembered of the muckraking fiction writers but a recent article on *The Jungle* is only peripherally concerned with Sinclair as a reformer. In "Lithuanians in Upton Sinclair's *The Jungle*" (*Lituanus* 23[1977]:24–31) Alfonsas Šešplaukis says that although Sinclair "wrote with true compassion and insight into the stockyard worker's plight," he did not write very accurately about the Lithuanian national character, which is typically stoical, says Šešplaukis, in the face of misfortune. He sees this failure of Sinclair to understand "the Lithuanian soul" as symptomatic of a novel wherein the idea of social justice dominates over all else. An article on Robert Herrick is similarly less concerned with Herrick the reformer and more concerned with Herrick the artist. In "Robert Herrick's Post-War Literary Theories and *Waste*" (*ALR* 11:275–83) Phyllis Franklin shows how Herrick, after World War I, modified his fictional program so that autobiography and psychology became part of his writing as well as the use of allegory. Friedrich W. Horlacher

has compiled an annotated checklist of Robert Herrick's contributions to the *Chicago Tribune*. See *ALR* 10:191–210.

There were two recent articles on Traven, whose identity continues to fascinate and puzzle scholars. In his article "In Search of
Traven," *The Radical Reader* (Sydney: Wild and Wooley, 1977,
pp. 73–89) Jonah Raskin describes his relationship with Rosa Elene
Lujan, Traven's widow. Raskin tells us that he went to Mexico City
seeking her aid to write Traven's biography, but when he found that
she was glamorizing his memory, insisting that Traven was the son
of the Kaiser, he abandoned the idea of coauthorship. In a strictly
literary vein John M. Reilly in "The Voice of *The Death Ship*"
(*MinnR* 9[1977]:112–15) argues that Traven's narrator evokes none
of the romanticism of sea literature, but speaks as the voice of the
proletariat whose life is dictated by the machinery of the ship, not
by the sea or by nature.

xii. Women and Women Writers

In "Women Writers in the Mainstream" (*TSLL* 20:660–70) David
Stouck argues that women fiction writers have often been overlooked
because there has prevailed in America a definition of the novelist
as a ruggedly masculine figure, the type represented by London,
Hemingway, and Mailer. Stouck tries to show, however, that in the
fiction of Wharton, Stein, and Cather one can find the same archetypal themes and patterns that prevail in American literature as a
whole. Dorys Crow Grover in "The Pioneer Woman in Fact and
Fiction" (*HK* 10,ii[1977]:35–44) surveys the various fictional portrayals of women in Western fiction and compares them with some
of the historical portraits as found in the diaries and letters of
missionary women.

Research into forgotten 19th- and early 20th-century American
writings has recovered the fiction of Gertrude Atherton, once a very
popular California novelist. In a series of interesting essays, including *Gertrude Atherton* (WWS 23[1976]), Charlotte S. McClure has
been examining Atherton's fiction, particularly her treatment of the
willful, self-reliant woman. Her findings are presented in summary
fashion in "Gertrude Atherton's California Woman: From Love Story
to Psychological Drama" (*California Writers*, 1–19), where she locates Atherton's uniqueness in her theme of a woman's "attempting

to know herself and to develop common interests with a man before choosing to marry him." These heroines, says McClure, are not feminine in the traditional sense; rather they are vigorously healthy, are given to outdoor sports, identify with their fathers rather than with their mothers, and are devoted to developing their minds. Yet at the same time, says McClure, Atherton insists on their essential womanliness. Their problem, she observes, is to separate the romantic myth of love from the human reality. One of Gertrude Atherton's novels, *Perch of the Devil* (1914), is set in Butte, Montana, and in "Montana and the Lady Novelist" (*Montana: the Magazine of Western History* 27,i[1977]:40–51) Leslie A. Wheeler describes the novelist's visits to the mining town and her portrayal of the town and its people in fiction. Atherton, writes Wheeler, did not take Sinclair Lewis's approach to western towns, but in her fiction praised their combined sophistication and hardihood.

In "Ida M. Tarbell and the Ambiguities of Feminism" (*PMHB* 101[1977]:217–39) Robert Stinson discusses at length Tarbell's anti-feminist writings, published in book form in 1914 as *The Business of Being a Woman*, and shows how Tarbell's attitude was not a denial of her own career but rather the articulation of an old ambiguity wherein marriage and family still asserted a viable claim on her. Finally in *Ruth Suckow*, WWS 34, Abigail Ann Hamblen provides a useful introduction to the work of this writer, which she sees turning to the universal problems of loneliness, old age, and feminine frustrations. Suckow invariably presents women as victims, writes Hamblen, not however victims of men or society but of biology and the need for physical and emotional security. *The Folks*, says Hamblen, is Suckow's masterpiece, giving a perfectly realized picture of Iowa life, but her late works are also important, because they embody Suckow's wise conviction that only love, borne of sorrow and pain, can triumph over human adversities.

Simon Fraser University

14. Fiction: The 1930s to the 1950s

Jack Salzman

i. "Art for Humanity's Sake"—Proletarians and Others

Several book-length works were published in 1978 which, though not dealing with fiction of the Depression decade, are of importance in understanding and evaluating the literature that was produced in the 1930s. Bernard Bergonzi in *Reading the Thirties: Text and Contexts* (Pittsburgh) and Stephen Spender in *The Thirties and After: Poetry, Politics, People, 1930's–1970's* (Random) do deal with the literature of the thirties, but both are concerned primarily with the writers of Great Britain. Neither work adds very much to what already has been written about the period, but Spender's volume is of interest as a "kind of case history of a Thirties poet." More revelatory of the period is *Such as Us: Southern Voices of the Thirties* (N. Car.) edited by Tom E. Terrill and Jerrold Hirsch, which is offered as a sequel to the 1939 *These Are Our Lives*. Like the accounts in *These Are Our Lives*, those in *Such as Us* are life histories of people who live in a "rural, impoverished and segregated region" of the South—histories collected by fellow southerners employed by the Federal Writers' Project; and like its predecessor, *Such as Us* is moving and valuable.

Important to liberal thought in the thirties is the *New Masses*. David Peck has written a provocative essay, " 'The Tradition of American Revolutionary Literature': The Monthly *New Masses*, 1926–1933" (*Science and Society* 42:385–409), in which he argues that "the alteration in the basic character of American literature after 1930, in other words, the sudden emergence of an American proletarian literature in both creative and critical forms, was largely the achievement of the editorial policies of the *New Masses*." Although Peck's argument is not wholly convincing, it is an important attempt, at the very least, to acknowledge some of the very considerable achievements of the *New Masses*. One such achievement was the publication of the writings of one of its contributing editors, Herman Spector, whose writings and drawings have been collected in *Bastard in the Ragged Suit*, edited by Bud Johns and Judith Clancy (San Francisco: Synergistic Press, 1977). Spector's work has long been unavailable, and as a consequence he has become one of the truly neglected figures in American cultural history.

Not quite so neglected nor unknown is Max Eastman, the subject of William L. O'Neill's *The Last Romantic: A Life of Max Eastman* (Oxford). This is an uneven book, and if it is not very likely to change the situation which prompted the writing of the biography—O'Neill's "feeling that [Eastman's] best work has been neglected or undervalued"—chapters 7, 8, and 9 ("Politics and Literature 1924–1934"; "The Red Decade Begins 1930–1934"; "The Unmaking of a Socialist 1933–1940") are valuable for an understanding of Eastman's role in the literary class war which marked so much of the 1930s. Equally important for an understanding of this aspect of our literary history are several of the essays by Philip Rahv which were written in the thirties and are reprinted in Rahv's *Essays on Literature and Politics, 1932–1972*, edited by Arabel J. Porter and Andrew J. Dvosin (Houghton Mifflin), particularly his piece on "Proletarian Literature: A Political Autopsy." Some of the battles of the thirties also are considered by Malcolm Cowley in chapter 9 ("A Sense of Guilt") of his— *And I Worked at the Writer's Trade* (Viking). Cowley also offers a general assessment of the literature of the period in a chapter entitled "The 1930s: Faith and Works": "For the clearest expression of the age in its successive moods of anger, millennialism, and discouragement," Cowley contends, one must turn to *U.S.A., The Grapes of Wrath*, and *For Whom the Bell Tolls*. These accounts by Peck, Rahv, and Cowley share little in common and make clear what has been apparent for a while: a good cultural history of the 1930s is very much needed.

a. **James Agee.**   In the Agee part of *John Hersey and James Agee: A Reference Guide* (Hall), Nancy Lyman Huse offers a fairly comprehensive listing of the books, articles, and dissertations which have appeared on Agee from 1940 to 1977, and includes lengthy annota-

tions of the major studies "in order to present a strong picture of the
kind of explication Agee's work evokes and even requires." (One
of the items Huse annotates at length is Robert Coles's *Irony in the
Mind's Life: Essays on Novels by James Agee, Elizabeth Bowen, and
George Eliot*, which contains what is still one of the finest pieces on
Agee, "Childhood: James Agee's *A Death in the Family*." Coles's
study, which Huse erroneously lists under "Books for 1973" rather
than "1974," has been reissued by New Directions.) The bibliography
also lists a number of reviews but not all the reviews, "since the wealth
of other material required some selectivity." The entire volume,
however, runs to only 122 pages; surely there was enough room for
the inclusion of more reviews than the volume now lists.

Agee criticism is devoted almost exclusively to *Let Us Now Praise
Famous Men*. In "James Agee: Notes on the Man and the Work"
(*UDQ* 13,i:3–15), Jack Behard argues that Agee was an "encum-
bered man," a displaced or disappointed romantic whose concern
with ambiguities and ambivalences can be seen in the two kinds of
writing which are to be found in *Famous Men*: the "poetic and
meditative" and the "speculative and more nearly expository." Robert Zaller's "Let Us Now Praise James Agee" (*SLJ* 10:144–54) also
is concerned with *Famous Men* and notes that although the book
shames every other book written about poverty in America, "it is not
finally about three tenant families or social conditions in the deep
South but a ruthlessly unsparing autobiography and one of the most
sustained meditations on the relation between conscience and knowledge in our language." Wright Morris, on the other hand, is more
concerned with the language of *Famous Men* and contends in his
section on Agee (pp. 155–61) in *Earthly Delights* that words have
"seldom received such a charge of emotion to no other end than a
reverence for life." J. A. Ward, in what is perhaps the best of the
essays under consideration here, is concerned less with Agee's reverence for life than with his "persistent and obtrusive preoccupation
with silence," which grows out of his awareness of the limitations of
language. Despite Agee's wish to be as objective as a camera, Ward
writes in "James Agee's Aesthetic of Silence: *Let Us Now Praise
Famous Men*" (*TSE* 23:193–206), *Famous Men* "is a very personal
reaction—mainly aesthetic and religious—to a world in which he must
always be alien. The rhythms of silence and sound to which he is

ever alert gain their force and significance from the author's re-
sponding imagination."

b. **Jesse Stuart.** Stuart scholarship for the year once again owes
much to J. R. LeMaster, whose bibliography of Stuart criticism is
due next year. This year LeMaster is responsible for editing the
only work devoted to Stuart, *Jesse Stuart: Selected Criticism* (St.
Petersburg, Fla.: Valkyrie Press). As might be expected, the essays
vary not only in approach but in interest as well. Ruel Foster, in
"The Short Stories: Tales of Shan and Others" (pp. 145–68), fails
to make a very convincing case for his contention that "when the
definitive history of the American short story is written, Jesse Stuart's
name may well be near the top of the list of the best writers in this
genre," and Wade Hall in "Introduction and Background" (pp.
60–97) no doubt is right in arguing that Stuart relates directly to
two main schools of American humor—local color and the humor
of the Old Southwest—but his essay gives little reason to believe that
Stuart is one of our major humorists or that he has created "some of
the most memorable characters in American fiction." (Such adulation
merely detracts, I think, from Stuart's very real accomplishments.)
More convincing is Lee Pennington's "Symbolism and Vision in
Daughter of the Legend" (pp. 169–86), which argues that this is
Stuart's most unusual novel, one which most completely presents
his symbolism and vision. Everetta Blair no doubt overstates the
case somewhat when she writes in "The Poet as Teacher" (pp. 21–59)
that *The Thread that Runs So True* is "truly a great book," but she
does deal convincingly with the way in which "the poet has inspired
the schoolmaster, and the schoolmaster has brought to the poet
powerful material straight from life." Most convincing and best of
all, however, are Mary Washington Clarke's "Folk Life in a Primitive
Setting" (pp. 98–144), which contends that Stuart's writings present
"a regional museum containing variety and detail unsurpassed in
American literature," and LeMaster's "A Record of the Dream: The
Image in Practice" (pp. 187–209), which is concerned with Stuart's
early "experiments in imagery" and how the images changed once
he read Walt Whitman: "As Whitman had done before him, Stuart
hurled his ego into objects he found in nature and came to identify
it with the creative processes that he found there." Despite the exces-

sive adulation, then, this collection is an important addition to the growing body of Stuart criticism.

c. **John Steinbeck.** The major contribution to Steinbeck studies this year is Peter Lisca's *John Steinbeck: Nature and Myth* (Crowell), a volume in Crowell's Twentieth-Century American Writers series. Perhaps because of the series format, Lisca's book is briefer than it should be, but it nevertheless provides an excellent introduction to Steinbeck's work. The study begins with a biographical chapter, is followed by six chapters on the novels, and concludes with a chapter devoted to the short fiction and one to the nonfiction. Among the many virtues of the study is Lisca's refusal to either dwell upon or to ignore the failure of so much of Steinbeck's work after *The Grapes of Wrath*. Rather, Lisca concentrates upon showing how all the works are concerned with the themes of nature and myth. He does not hesitate to state that with few exceptions (notably *Sea of Cortez*), Steinbeck's nonfiction is not of the quality one would expect of a writer of his stature: his "real accomplishments are his eighteen volumes of fiction, and upon these his reputation rests secure." Certainly, as Lisca himself demonstrates, Steinbeck's "secure" reputation does not rest upon *all* eighteen novels, but one can hardly argue with Lisca's final assertion that it is "his ability to bring together in his novels and in his image of man both the scientifically described world and that of the intuition and imagination, nature and myth, without distorting either, that is Steinbeck's own unique genius."

In addition to Lisca's study, the most impressive contribution to Steinbeck scholarship once again has been provided by the Steinbeck Society. The Steinbeck Quarterly is celebrating its tenth year of publication, and in that time, as Warren French notes in a special message as president of the Society (*StQ* 11:69–72), the journal has consistently tried to serve three functions: "to provide a repository for information about Steinbeck and his work, to review in detail any books dealing in an important way with John Steinbeck, and to publish original articles about his work—especially the early efforts of young persons who will be the Steinbeck scholars of the future." That *StQ* has succeeded admirably in all three functions can be seen from even a cursory glance through the Cumulative Index to Volumes 1–10 (1968–77), which has been compiled by Donald Siefker (*StQ*

11:37–61). *StQ* is one of the best organs of its kind, and for that credit must go largely to the enthusiasm and dedication of the founder of the Steinbeck Society and editor-in-chief of the *StQ*, Tetsumaro Hayashi, who also is responsible (together with Yasuo Hashiguchi and Richard F. Peterson) for this year's volume (no. 8) in the Steinbeck Monograph Series, *John Steinbeck: East and West*, which is based on Proceedings of the First International Steinbeck Congress Held at Kyushu University, Fukuoka City, Japan, in August 1976.

Of the 11 essays included in the volume, those by Richard Astro and John Ditsky have previously been published. The other essays range from a consideration of the relationship between *The Great Gatsby* and *Cup of Gold* by Kiyohiko Tsuboi (pp. 40–47) to two studies of Steinbeck's women in *The Long Valley*—Fusae Matsumoto's "Steinbeck's Women in *The Long Valley*" (pp. 48–53) and Shigeharu Yano's "Psychological Interpretations of Steinbeck's Women in *The Long Valley*" (pp. 54–60)—to Noboru Shimura's "Mysticism in John Steinbeck" (pp. 83–90), which argues that Steinbeck's "acceptance of God does not change, but his idea of God shifts from a pagan to a Christian conception," from an "overwhelming animistic mysticism in *To a God Unknown* to a personal, Christian mysticism" in *The Winter of Our Discontent*.

The articles in *StQ*, as usual, touch on various matters with uneven results. Richard Peterson in "Homer Was Blind: John Steinbeck on the Character of William Faulkner" (*StQ* 11:15–20) offers some possible explanations for Steinbeck's intemperate remarks about Faulkner, and Ray Lewis White tells of a meeting in 1939 between Sherwood Anderson and Steinbeck (*StQ* 11:20–22), but neither piece adds up to much more than a footnote. In "Steinbeck, Jung, and *The Winter of Our Discontent* (*StQ* 11:87–96), Donal Stone offers some tentative observations about the Jungian sense of individuation which Steinbeck works out, consciously or unconsciously, in his novel, while Melanie Mortlock in "The Eden Myth as Paradox: An Allegorical Reading of *The Pastures of Heaven*" (*StQ* 11:6–15) concludes that although this work seems to be a collection of unrelated stories, Steinbeck has actually "ingeniously united form and content by utilizing the 'Munroe curse' as a unifying device" to carry the novel's thematic message—that man "must learn to accept the true meaning of the Eden myth and acknowledge the paradoxical nature of his attempts to create and sustain heaven on earth." The most interesting essay published this year in *StQ* is John Ditsky's brief but provocative "Ritual Murder in Steinbeck's Drama" (11:27–76), in which Ditsky addresses himself to Steinbeck's "apparent argument for murder." Ditsky can only speculate about Steinbeck's "troublesome affinity for murder," and finally suggests that this affinity is most "readily explainable as a response to the genre he had chosen, and to its accepted conventions and norms." It is an interesting proposition, but it is one which seems to leave Ditsky, as it does me, more than a little uneasy. Finally, for those who use *StQ* as a reference tool, there is a special section devoted to Steinbeck Research Libraries in the United States (11:96–105), in which the Steinbeck holdings of the libraries at San Jose State University, the University of Texas at Austin, Stanford University, and Ball State University are described.

Let me call attention to several essays on Steinbeck's fiction and film. In *The Modern American Novel* Russell Campbells criticizes the film adaptation of *The Grapes of Wrath* (in "Trampling Out the Vintage: Sour Grapes," pp. 107–18); and William Everson greatly admires the film version of *Of Mice and Men* (in "Thoughts on a Great Adaptation," pp. 63–69). A very similar view is held by Joseph Millichap (in "Realistic Style in Steinbeck and Milestone's *Of Mice and Men*," *LFQ* 6:241–52).

In "Steinbeck's *The Pearl* as a Nonteleological Parable of Hope" (*RS* 46:98–104) Charles R. Metzger is particularly concerned with those sections of *The Log from the Sea of Cortez* which offer "material deriving from a relevant part of Steinbeck's 'own life' that he called upon in fleshing out the original, true, but incredible parable." This material is "richly present" in chapters 10, 11, 12, 14, and 16 of *The Log*, and ultimately is concerned with survival, which also is the major theme of *The Pearl*. Despair, not survival, is the subject of Anthony F. R. Palmieri's "*In Dubious Battle*: A Portrait in Pessimism" (*ReAL* 3,i[1976]:61–71). The novel is a "portrait in pessimism," Palmieri writes; "No glimmer of hope, of optimism, of a better tomorrow illuminates, even faintly, the dark gloom of unutterable despair encountered in the pages of the book." *In Dubious Battle* is also the subject of Allen Shepherd's note in *NMAL* (2,iii:19). Shepherd takes exception to Peter Lisca's contention that Jim Nolan, the protagonist of *In Dubious Battle*, is an imitation of Christ, and argues instead that "Nolan is best understood as an inexact imitation of Milton's Satan." Shepherd is neither more nor less convincing than Lisca, which may eventually get us to the point that Nolan is at one and the same time Christ-like and Satanic. In another note in *NMAL* (3,i:1) Lewis Cobb points out that Guy de Maupassant's story "Idylle" and Steinbeck's *The Grapes of Wrath* "conclude with the same startling tableau: a woman feeds a starving man from her breast"; Steinbeck may have borrowed the scene from de Maupassant, Cobb notes, although he "uses the material of his French predecessor to achieve a culminating vision far beyond the intended scope of the original story."

Miles Donald, in a section devoted to Steinbeck in *The American Novel* (pp. 59–72) also is concerned with *The Grapes of Wrath*, but his intent is to defend the novel against some of the criticism which has been offered by such detractors as Henry Steele Commager, Harry T. Moore, and Edmund Wilson. Donald sees the book as "an *American* novel dealing with an American reality," and finds it hard "to accept the strictures which would keep it from its rightful place as an essentially *American* American novel, of great power." Karen J. Hopkins also takes on some of Steinbeck's critics in "Steinbeck's *East of Eden*: A Defense" (*California Writers*, pp. 63–78). Warren French and Charles Walcutt have dismissed what Hopkins refers to as Steinbeck's "most despised work," but Hopkins suggests that it was Steinbeck's intention in writing the novel to "annoy critics, because there are so few 'hidden' meanings and ingenuity in exploring the symbolism is unnecessary." No evidence is offered to support this rather extraordinary claim, and the rest of the essay never gets much beyond this level. If Steinbeck's work needs defenders, they will have to do a more tolerable job than either Donald or Hopkins has done. For the past few years just that kind of solid work has been done by John Ditsky, who in "The Friend at the Round Table: A Note on Steinbeck's *Acts*" (*AL* 49:633–35), not only identifies the reference to "Sir Tobinus Streat" in *The Acts of King Arthur and His Noble Knights* with Steinbeck's old friend Webster F. ("Toby") Street but also argues that *Acts* "provides the missing link, in terms of Steinbeck's developing fictional rhetoric on the subject of individual moral responsibility, between *East of Eden* and *The Winter of Our Discontent*," and adds that *Acts* contains "some of Steinbeck's finest writing—a reconstruction of Arthurian matter which is demonstrably better than Mark Twain's, for example." Not many critics seem to agree with his assessment of *Acts*, and it will be interesting to see if Ditsky chooses to write at length in defense of his position.

d. **Dahlberg, Farrell, Maltz, and Algren.** Three of the four writers considered here—all of whom were to varying degrees associated with the left wing in the 1930s—are the subject of full-length studies this year. Charles L. DeFanti's *The Wages of Expectation: A Biography of Edward Dahlberg* (NYU) is the first biography of Dahlberg, but it is a plodding, pedestrian, ill-written, over-footnoted work. One can gather as much about Dahlberg, perhaps more, from Frank MacShane's "Edward Dahlberg: 1900–1977" (*MR* 19:55–68). MacShane, who at one time had contracted to do a biography of Dahlberg, tells of his meeting, friendship, and eventual—almost inevitable—falling out with the man who rescued him "from the routine of literary scholarship that deadens so many professors of literature." Above all, Dahlberg was a moralist, and in his best work, *Because I Was Flesh*, he "was able to balance moral judgment with loving observation." But too often "morality got the upper hand" and became intolerable. As a consequence, McShane writes, Dahlberg may occupy a position in the literature of our time analogous to Thoreau's in the 19th century—"that of a man known mainly for one book [*Because I Was Flesh*] and for memorable sentences from his other writings."

Farrell, of course, is the author of more than 50 books, as well as being one of the most important figures in the literary battles of the thirties and forties, but much of this importance has been obscured by the fame of the *Lonigan* books, a matter Alan Wald tries to rectify in *James T. Farrell: The Revolutionary Socialist Years* (NYU). Wald offers a literary, political, and intellectual portrait of Farrell during his "revolutionary socialist years"—from the late 1920s until the late 1940s. He traces Farrell's movement from an interest in communism to an independent Marxist view, discusses at length Farrell's role in the work of the American Committee for the Defense of Leon Trotsky, and details some of Farrell's involvement in the literary battles of the period. At times the study strays too far from Farrell (when, for example, Wald writes about a prominent group of New York intellectuals), and at other times Wald's account is a little too sketchy. But, on the whole, the book is a good complement to Daniel Aaron's seminal study, *Writers on the Left*. The one real complaint to be made here is that the study still has too much of a dissertation sound to it. A different kind of problem is exemplified by William J. Lynch's "James T. Farrell and the Irish-American Urban Experience" (*PCLS* 9:243–54), in which Lynch simply goes over old ground as he writes about the corrosive effect the urban Irish milieu has on Studs Lonigan—a death symbol—and how Danny O'Neill—a symbol of hope—must reject Irish Catholicism to become a writer.

Unlike Dahlberg and Farrell, who are thought of primarily in terms of a particular work, Albert Maltz is identified almost solely with The Hollywood Ten. But as Jack Salzman argues in *Albert Maltz* (TUSAS 311), Maltz "was a far more significant figure in the history of American letters than is generally acknowledged." Salzman discusses Maltz's novels, plays, and short stories, as well as the various political and literary struggles in which Maltz has been engaged for much of his life, and concludes that "Maltz is one of the finest writers of social protest literature the United States has produced"—a writer who belongs in the company of such American writers of protest as Farrell, Steinbeck, and Richard Wright.

Although no book-length study was devoted to Nelson Algren this year, Robert Rosen's "Anatomy of a Junkie" (*The Modern American Novel*, pp. 189–98) does offer an interesting comparison of the novel and film version of *The Man with the Golden Arm*. Rosen points out that despite the fact that Algren's novel came out of the 1930s tradition of proletarian literature, it is "neither a novel of ideas nor one of social analysis." The novel's radicalism comes not from an analysis of capitalism, but through Algren's obvious sympathy for its more obvious victims. However, Otto Preminger's film version "transforms Algren's emotionally unsettling and subversive story into a voyeuristic slumming adventure with a glib 1950s resolution." Chicago is the subject of John Raymer's "A Changing Sense of Chicago in the Works of Saul Bellow and Nelson Algren" (*ON* 4:371–83), and as a consequence the piece offers little insight into Algren's work. Both Bellow and Algren have grown disenchanted with the city, Raymer points out, but Bellow has remained and Algren has left. Raymer glances at several works of Algren to show his changing sense of the city from his first novel completely about the city, *Never Come Morning,* to his most affectionate tribute, *Chicago: City on the Make,* to those works which show his disaffection in the late fifties and early sixties, perhaps best exemplified by the "sour observations" of *Who Lost an American?*

ii. Social Iconoclasts—West and Salinger

West was the subject of several articles this year, but for the most part none of the essays adds much to the continually growing body of West scholarship. Three of the pieces deal with cinematic versions of West's novels: Michael Klein concerns himself with *Miss Lonelyhearts* in "Miss L. Gets Married" (*The Modern American Novel,* pp. 19–28), while both Edward Jones in "That's Wormwood: *The Day of the Locust*" (*LFQ* 6:222–29) and Sidney Gottlieb in "The Maddening Crowd in the Movies" (*The Modern American Novel,* pp. 95–106) compare West's 1939 novel with John Schlesinger's film adaptation. More substantial than any of these essays is Maria Ujhazy's "The Satire of Nathanael West" (*ZAA* 26, iii:211–31), which contends that much of the proliferating criticism of West's work since the 1960s has offered "such an exegesis of his writings that they might serve the indirect apology of capitalist society." Critics have "purged West's novels of their vital element, their critical realism, and have allegorized and interpreted them into kinship with the critics' own outlook." What is most clear in West's work, Ujhazy notes, is that the target of his satire "is the manufacture and spread of religious and other illusions in the business and political interests of the ruling class, the delusion and self-delusions of the masses." The most specialized and the most interesting of the three essays is David Fine's "Landscape of Fantasy: Nathanael West and Los Angeles Architecture of the Thirties" (*California Writers,* pp. 49–62), in which Fine points out that the novel about Hollywood has had as its recurrent and major theme the distinction between illusion and reality; it is a nightmare world where the line between illusion and reality blurs. West, among all his contemporaries, "most pervasively and doggedly pursued the tangled relation between the fantasies manufactured on the studio lots and those constructed on the surrounding landscape."

The three essays on Salinger are second rate, it seems to me. In "Dostoyevsky's *Notes from Underground* and Salinger's *The Catcher in the Rye"* (*CRCL* 5:72–85) Lilian R. Furst argues the obvious: there are parallels between the two works. In "Salinger Revisited" (*CritQ* 20,i:61–88) Kerry McSweeney argues the dubious: the *Nine Stories* are little more than "professional pieces of work, textbook examples of the short-story form." In "Religious Symbols in Salinger's Short Fiction" (*SSF* 15,ii:121–32) James Finn Cotter's preoccupation with three symbols—the Fat Lady, the glass, and the ashtray—narrow the focus upon the stories and detract from their larger accomplishment.

iii. Expatriates and Émigrés

a. **Henry Miller.** Although 1978 saw the publication of volume 2 of "Book of Friends," *My Bike & Other Friends* (Santa Barbara, Calif.: Capra Press), the most important work to come out this year is not Miller's collection of essays (they really are rather flimsy), but Jay Martin's *Always Bright and Merry: The Life of Henry Miller* (Santa Barbara: Capra Press), part of which appeared as "The Last Book" in *Partisan Review* (45:611–26). For some reason the biography has failed to attract the attention it deserves. It is an unauthorized biography, to be sure, but it is much superior to most biographies of this kind and, indeed, it is considerably better than most biographies that are authorized. Martin says that Miller "never wavered in his belief that no one could write his biography." Yet he gave Martin access to read restricted material in libraries throughout the country, and the result is an exceptionally interesting book. As Martin notes in his "Programmatic Preface," *Always Bright and Merry* does not "propose to *be* Miller's life." But it is parallel to Miller's life; it does, as he hoped it would, exhibit "the process of Miller's life. It tells us about his life and work—and the inseparable nature of the two. It tells us more, too, of his relationship with women, more than we have ever known, especially about his relation with Anaïs Nin. And Martin tells it all in a prose that seldom falters. It is a fine work.

So, too, though necessarily to a lesser degree, are the essays about Miller's work which were published this year. In "Bergsonian Order in *Tropic of Capricorn*" (*ReAl* 4,ii:9–15), Mickey Riggs traces "the parallel opinions of a philosophical novelist [Miller] and an imagistic philosopher [Bergson] on the principle of order." Both Miller and Bergson ask similar questions: What is chaos? What is order? What is the response of the thinking being to the overpowering deluge of *forms* that the world forces on him? Miller asks one additional question: What is salvation? For him "it is the search for the vital order, the search for the autonomy rather than automatism." Mary Allen celebrates the one yea-sayer America has yet to meet head on in "Henry Miller: Yea-Sayer" (*TSL* 23:100–110). Miller writes convincingly of pain and anger, but he is one of the few writers who also records joyous feelings. His best work is *Tropic of Cancer*, Allen writes; it is "an incredible song of joy," whose real theme, as Miller says, is liberty. Donald Gutierrez also deals with *Tropic of Cancer* in "'Hypocrite lecteur': *Tropic of Cancer* as Sexual Comedy" (*Mosaic*, 11,ii:21–33). Although most critics have long been aware that Miller is, among other things, a comic writer, what remains to be explored "is the extent to which Miller's comedy is rooted in and exploits questions of sex and sexuality." Gutierrez undertakes such an exploration, and using *Cancer* as a case in point he concludes that although Miller's comedy is undeniably low, it is very much a work of art: "The artistic triumph of *Cancer* resides . . . in its characterization of males, in its vivid and variegated anecdotage of men stumbling through the mazes of their conceptions of women. Miller captures this activity with comic naturalism and psychological objectivity." Miles Donald's section on Miller in *The American Novel* (pp. 109–13) combines elements discussed by Allen and Gutierrez but concludes quite differently from either of them. Donald recognizes that Miller "the prophet of doom is also Miller the prophet of possibility and freedom," just as he acknowledges that "*Tropic of Cancer* contains some magnificant comic vignettes." But all of this just induces a feeling of regret—"regret that we do not have something more artistically complete than Miller's mauve memories, regret in a sense that the true momentum of the book, its desire for ecstatic revelation, does not have a broader or more concrete base."

b. **Anaïs Nin.**   This, the first year after Nin's death, has been marked by several important publications. To begin with, Harcourt has brought out *Linotte: The Early Diary of Anaïs Nin, 1914–1920*, translated by Jean L. Sherman. It is the first volume of Nin's *Diary* to be published essentially in the form in which it was written and covers the period from the time when Nin left Barcelona for New York in 1914 (when she began writing in French her "Childhood

Diary"), continues with her early years in New York, and concludes
with Nin in Richmond Hill, now writing in English. It is, it almost
goes without saying, an indispensable volume to anyone at all interested in Nin's life and work.

Of great value too is the special issue of *Mosaic* (11,ii), edited by
Evelyn J. Hinz, devoted to "The World of Anaïs Nin." Although the
essays deal with a wide range of topics—there are studies of the
fiction by Benjamin Franklin, V (pp. 95–106) and Keith Cushman
(pp. 109–19); "The Making of *Bell of Atlantis*" by Ian Hugo (pp.
77–80); of Nin's relationship with Lawrence Durrell by Ian Mac-
Niven (pp. 37–57) and of the importance of Otto Rank to her life
and work by Philip Jason (pp. 81–94), as well as a consideration by
Bernard Dick of the literary incompatibility of Nin and Gore Vidal
(pp. 153–62) and a particularly fine essay by Paul Kuntz on "Anaïs
Nin's 'Quest for Order' " (pp. 203–12)—the focus of most of the controversy in the collection, as Evelyn Hinz notes in her Introduction,
is "upon the question of how the *Diary* should be approached and
with the related questions of the kind of artistic excellence which
Nin's fiction evidences and the various traditions to which her work
may be allied." The essays by Duane Schneider, "Anaïs Nin in the
Diary: The Creation and Development of a Persona" (pp. 9–19),
and Lynn Z. Bloom and Orlee Holder, "Anaïs Nin's *Diary* in Context"
(pp. 191–202), are particularly fine. But, in fact, this first collection
of scholarly essays devoted to the work of Nin is one of the finest
collections of its kind that I have seen. Yet another important addition to the growing body of Nin scholarship, and one which will
prove to be of great value, is Rose Marie Cutting's *Anaïs Nin: A
Reference Guide* (Hall). This bibliography of secondary works on
Nin covers the period from 1937 to 1977 and includes all books and
articles in English and various foreign languages. Interviews with
Nin, biographical pieces, and articles in daily presses as well as some
college newspapers also have been included. The annotations are
evaluative rather than descriptive; there also is a sound and informative introduction, which is concerned largely with the critical response to Nin's work. Cutting's Reference Guide is one of the very
best to appear in the G. K. Hall Series.

This year's issues of *USP* were once again devoted to books about
Nin and her circle, as well as an interview with Sharon Spencer
(*USP* 9,ii:9–13), author of *College of Dreams: The Writings of Anaïs*

Nin, and reminiscences of Nin by Fraser Sutherland ("Anaïs Nin in Montreal," *USP* 9,iii:1–4) and Paula J. Peper ("International College's Tribute to Anaïs Nin," *USP* 9,iii:7–10). The pieces in *USP* tend to be somewhat informal, but the issues continue to be informative.

Anything but informal is Stephanie Demetrakopoulos' "Anaïs Nin and the Feminine Quest for Consciousness: The Quelling of the Devouring Mother and Ascension of the Sophia" (*BuR* 24,i:119–36). Demetrakopoulos, who contributed an essay on "Archetypal Constellations of Feminine Consciousness in Nin's First *Diary*" to the *Mosaic* issue devoted to Nin (pp. 121–37), here offers a "psychological analysis of the presence of the world mother and her personal mother in Anaïs Nin's psyche and literary works." It is a complex and difficult essay to follow but one which is worth the effort. Demetrakopoulos argues, among other things, that one of the most fascinating aspects of the *Diary* is its "detailed story of a woman artist fervently groping among alter egos to find herself. Each volume is a giant step toward the quest for self, a stripping away of artificial layers." Estelle C. Jelinek also appreciates Nin's "honesty and her struggle for a personal identity," but as she states in "Anaïs Nin: A Critical Evaluation" (*Feminist Criticism,* pp. 312–23) "she also was bored by her vanity and her endless descriptions of adoring and adored men." Jelinek sees the early diaries not so much as a quest for self but as "sourcebooks for her rather inept and inane novels." It is an angry and uncompromising essay which Jelinek offers, one which centers on her belief that Nin "holds views that are anathema to me and the women's liberation movement." Although Nin's admirers might prefer to dismiss Jelinek's essay, it is a provocative and challenging work that must be given serious attention.

c. Vladimir Nabokov. Contributions to Nabokov scholarship continue to be very uneven: some very substantial publications once again are mixed with slight, almost precious works which at times seem to be a parody of the Nabokovian style. The best study to appear this year is Marina Turkevich Naumann's *Blue Evenings in Berlin: Nabokov's Short Stories of the 1920s* (NYU), which focuses upon those early seldom-discussed stories written in Russian in the 1920s. Naumann starts with a chapter which centers on Nabokov's expatriate beginnings and emphasizes "the Berlin milieu in which his art developed and first received acclaim." Three chapters then are devoted to a detailed analysis of the 1920s stories, and a final chapter considers the degree to which these stories can be seen in the later novel, *Transparent Things*. *Blue Evenings in Berlin* is an important study of Nabokov's art which convincingly argues that these early stories "are more than youthful probings"; they "clearly bear the promise of Nabokov's eventual versatility and talent, which has been fulfilled in his last prose." Julian Moynahan is quite right in stating in his Foreword that this is "one of the very few works of Nabokov criticism . . . which every Nabokov admirer should read and own."

Less successful, though not without value, is Dabney Stuart's *Nabokov: The Dimensions of Parody* (LSU), much of which has appeared in different form in various journals during the past ten years. This is not an exhaustive study of Nabokov's work—*Lolita*, *Pale Fire*, and *Ada* are mostly ignored—but a "readings in" certain books by Nabokov. Nor does Stuart offer "an overriding theoretical coherence" to his essays. Rather, as he writes in his Preface, these readings in works by Nabokov are "specifications of parody"; the aim is to have the book "assumed by its subject, and the reader, a companion in these divagations, returned there, too." The insights and arguments are at times interesting enough, but the writing itself is almost always irritating and obtuse: a Nabokovian trying to outdo Nabokov. On the other hand, Stuart's prose is a model of clarity compared to Maurice Couturier's in "Nabokov's Performative Writing," one of the essays in *Les Américanistes* (pp. 156–81). Couturier offers an analysis of the performative nature of Nabokov's writings, "which happens to have a lot in common with that of the French New Novelists." He bases his study on the consideration of *Pale Fire*, *Ada*, and *Transparent Things*, in which he is primarily concerned with Nabokov's *récit*—"the narrative, the 'succession of events' related in the narrative, and the act of telling." Much of the essay seems to be a parody of literary criticism, but unfortunately seems not to have been written as parody.

Michael Rosenblum's position in "Finding What the Sailor Has Hidden: Narrative as Patternmaking in *Transparent Things*" (*ConL* 19:219–32) is clearly stated: "Reading Nabokov is an active process of making connections between different parts of the text: we become not mere readers, but finders of the narrative." Although *Trans-*

parent Things is not the most difficult of Nabokov's works, it is the most exemplary—what must be done in order to read the other novels must be done in exaggerated fashion in *Transparent Things*. To read *Transparent Things* means "being able to rearrange elements of the narrative into classes: book titles, authors, rooms, purchases, objects and persons which persist in time and space and those which do not." Pattern is also the concern of June Perry Levine, who in "Vladimir Nabokov's *Pale Fire*: 'The Method of Composition' as Hero" (*IFR* 5:103–08) suggests that the poem and commentary which comprise *Pale Fire* should not be seen as separate entities, as most critics see them. The heroes of *Pale Fire* are "methods of composition." The commentary and the poem create the tension of the whole and should be approached like a character. Nabokov differs from other writers who conceive of life as governed by accident to the extent that he does not "espouse despair, apathy, or anarchy. Like a modern physicist, he is a pattern hunter in a universe of chance."

In "On Human Freedom and Inhuman Art: Nabokov" (*SEEJ* 22:52–63), Ellen Pifer addresses the contention of such writers as Diana Trilling and Joyce Carol Oates that Nabokov is an aesthete who is indifferent to humanity and hostile to the ideals of democracy. Pifer argues that Nabokov has repeatedly "emphasized the distinction between the spheres of art and life. Only in the realm of art did he ever advocate dictatorship." To be sure, Nabokov's insistence on authorial dictatorship may be an unusual stance for a novelist, but "it is not meant to undermine the liberty of real people or of the essential humanity of literary characters."

Two out of three essays on *Lolita* treat it as film. In "*Lolita*: Novel and Screenplay" (*CollL* 5:195–204) Samuel Schumann finds the "translation into film a success because "it is itself a work of the imagination." Brandon French, however, shares none of this enthusiasm (in "The Celluloid Lolita, A Not-So Crazy Quilt," *The Modern American Novel*, pp. 224–35), believing that the various elements of the novel fail to coalesce in the film. William Vesterman deals with a more particular aspect of *Lolita* in "Why Humbert Shoots Quilty" (*ELWIU* 5:85–93). The reason, Vesterman suggests, is that Humbert must kill Quilty to be able to write his own version of his story, for it is through writing his story "that he makes his final and only successful attempt to possess Lolita." Only in that book will she be "my" Lolita; though they both are dead, in the book "Humbert will have finally imposed his imagination on the world, possessing Lolita by the metaphysical right of having created her."

Several shorter pieces should also be noted here. In "Vladimir Nabokov: The Emigré" (*Commonweal* 6 Jan.:18–20) Saul Maloff pays tribute to Nabokov's language and its constant astonishments: "It is a language evolved in the spirit of high play; the language of the consummate emigré, a courtly monarchical, archaic language, ceremonial, contemptuously graceful in a grand manner and in the grand manner not quite serious." Miles Donald also writes of Nabokov the emigré in *The American Novel* (pp. 133–40). Nabokov must be judged as an American writer, Donald contends, not merely because of his American citizenship but because in at least three of his novels—*Lolita, Pale Fire*, and *Ada*—"he commemorates and celebrates America with a beauty and understanding that is the greatest of personal tributes." Indeed, in *Lolita*, by deliberately portraying American society through the bizarre eyes of Humbert Humbert, Nabokov "gives us one of the most realistic portrayals of America ever."

John Mills suggests in "Homo Ludens: Vladimir Nabokov" (*WCR* 12,iii:41–42) that although it is too early to evaluate Nabokov's achievement, and despite the fact that most criticism has not been particularly helpful, we must recognize that his best work, *Lolita* and *Pale Fire*, are not only splendid achievements as works of 'Artifice,' they are also great comic novels. . . ." Laurie Clancy, too, is not very happy with some of Nabokov's critics, and in "Nabokov and His Critics" (*Meanjin* 37:150–56) she first gives a mixed response to Andrew Field's *Nabokov: His Life in Part* (see *ALS 1977*, pp. 285–86), then judges three of the novels: Lolita is "a highly moral and profoundly truthful book, qualities we are inclined to forget in the endless hunt after allusions"; *Pale Fire* is not only an empty book but finally, "in many ways, a boring one"; *Ada*, "unfortunately has attracted many of the kinds of critics it deserves."

iv. The Southerners

Southern writers did not fare quite as well this year as they did in 1977. There were no major studies published, though Robert Penn

Warren was the subject of a fine bibliography, Eudora Welty published a selection of her essays and reviews, and the Welty and Thomas Wolfe newsletters continued to keep their readers well informed.

a. **Robert Penn Warren and Allen Tate.** Neil Nakadate's *Robert Penn Warren: A Reference Guide* (Hall, 1977) will now replace Mary Nance Huff's 1968 *Robert Penn Warren: A Bibliography* as well as James A. Grimshaw, Jr.'s checklist of criticism on *All the King's Men* (see *ALS 1976*, p. 271). Nakadate covers the period from 1925 to 1977 and includes in his bibiography book-length studies, critical essays and articles, and reviews in quarterly journals and major newspapers. To the extent that Nakadate does not include many popular reviews and news releases, he is right in saying that his bibliography is not exhaustive, but it certainly will serve the needs of most students of Warren's work.

Unlike last year, when there were no new treatments of *All the King's Men*, there are four essays this year devoted to Warren's best-known work, three of which focus upon the character of Jack Burden. Luther Stearns Mansfield is concerned with "History and the Historical Process in *All the King's Men*" (*CentR* 22:214–30), and finds that although every character in the novel illustrates some aspect of these forces, the various ideas "were all brought together in Jack Burden, who was most notably a person of many selves." Mark Winchell's "O Happy Sin! Felix Culpa in 'All the King's Men'" (*MissQ* 31:570–85) posits the idea that Warren's vision in *All the King's Men* may reflect a secularization of the paradox of the Fortunate Fall. Rather than impose an artificially happy resolution upon the contradictions in the lives of his characters, Warren seems to accept such contradictions as inherent to the human condition. As such, "they can be resolved only if the effects of the Fall can be transcended. How this transcendence is achieved in the life of Jack Burden and fails fully to be achieved in the lives of Adam Stanton and Willie Stark is what *All the King's Men* is about." Richard Law's "'The Case of the Upright Judge': The Nature of Truth in *All the King's Men*" (*SAF* 6,i:1–19) is in many ways the most interesting of these three essays. Law finds that rather than a single center of interest, the novel has two counter-pointed plot lines: Willie Stark's political career and Jack Burden's struggle for understanding. With

the intrusion of Burden's consciousness into the action of the Stark
story, Law argues, "Warren turns the decline and fall of a great man
and public figure into a *Bildungsroman*. The fourth essay on the
novel is William Walling's "In Which Humpty Dumpty Becomes
King" (*The Modern American Novel*, pp. 168–77), a study of the
novel and Robert Rossen's film version of Warren's book. Walling
points out that in the novel the real drama "is meant to reside in
how, and what, Jack Burden learns from Willie Stark's career." In
Rossen's work Willie Stark is brought to the center of the viewer's
concern, and "both the tragedy and promise of the film version bring
us clearly into touch with an order of experience quite different
from Warren's, one in which we may even find the implication that
America is still capable of reordering its social and political destiny,
in a fashion wholly secular and humanistic."

This year there are only two pieces on Allen Tate that need be
mentioned and neither is of much consequence. Patrick Hundley
writes about "Harry Harrison Kroll's Unknown Vendetta Against
Allen Tate" (*SLJ* 10,ii:134–43) and informs the reader that although
Kroll was bitter that Tate had harshly reviewed his novel, *The Cabin
in Cotton* (1931), "when the final analysis is complete, one sees that
Kroll has the deepest respect for Tate and is at last overwhelmed that
Tate would choose even to respond to his work at all." William Mc-
Millen offers a note on "Memory in Allen Tate's *The Father*" (*NConL*
8,i:10), in which he states that what is facing us in Tate's only novel
"is parallel crises in the same character." Only after 50 years, and
in the face of his own death, "can the narrator understand what he
experienced as a boy. Now he can see that he was not only initiated
into life but that that initiation was brought about by the suffering
and death of others."

b. **Carson McCullers.**   Carson McCullers fared only a little better
than Tate this year. There is a nice but rather slight tribute by Wright
Morris in *Earthly Delights* (pp. 163–68) in which Morris writes
that "poetic truth lies in the image, not the demonstrations," and
McCullers, like Stephen Crane and Flannery O'Connor, creates
"images that are touched with a sense of the Orphic, of commonplace yet mysterious revelation." In "Androgyny and Musical Vision:
A Study of Two Novels by Carson McCullers" (*SoQ* 16,ii:117–24)
Patricia S. Box focuses upon *The Heart is a Lonely Hunter* and

Member of the Wedding as works which examine the problem of spiritual isolation. Both contain characters who struggle to become androgynous, and only androgyns, Box contends, are capable of experiencing the sexless love that can unite all human beings. Music is McCuller's metaphor for this type of love: it connotes harmony, and harmony between people is what a unified life is all about. A comparison of the plot structure, milieu, and revelation of theme in Carson McCullers's *The Heart Is a Lonely Hunter* and the 1968 film is offered by Robert Aldridge in "Two Plenary Systems" (*The Modern American Novel*, pp. 119–30). Although the film has been all but forgotten it deserves respect as "a quiet, principled complement to McCullers's vision." But at the same time it must be acknowledged that the novel "contains a far wider and more complex range of theme, plot, and characterization, as well as McCullers's undeniable genius," than the film, which is more modest in range.

c. Katherine Anne Porter. Like McCullers, Porter is the subject of one of Wright Morris's brief essays in *Earthly Delights* (pp. 105–11). Morris begins by observing that "To be fully conscious, to be one of those on whom nothing is lost, is to be aware of the ceaseless overlapping of the past and present. . . . In Katherine Anne Porter its haunting presence determines the subtlety and range of her style, and its civilized tone." He then goes on to consider elements in "Flowering Judas," *Old Mortality, Noon Wine,* and *Pale Horse, Pale Rider* and concludes that "although the downward path to wisdom is an insight that informs most of her fiction, its effect on the reader is one of life enchantment, rather than life negation."

Margaret Bolsterli also writes about Porter and McCullers—and Eudora Welty too—in "Bound Characters in Porter, Welty, McCullers: The Prerevolutionary Status of Women in American Fiction" (*BuR* 24,i:95–105). Bolsterli argues that characters developed by such writers as Porter, Welty, and McCullers illustrate a world view that imprisoned characters, readers, and writers alike in "a pattern which dictated that women could neither take their lives into their own hands nor achieve self-realization outside the roles society had chosen for them." And as diverse as they are, their stories can be fitted into a construct that defines the status of women in the first half of the 20th century: the Miranda stories present a dichotomy between women who strive to achieve a "feminine ideal" and those who seek independence; the Fairchild women in Welty's *Delta Wedding* exemplify those who devote themselves to the feminine ideal; McCullers's Miss Amelia Evans in *The Ballad of the Sad Cafe* is an example of the completely independent woman. Jane Flanders, in "The Other Side of Self-Reliance": The Dream-Visions of 'Pale Horse, Pale Rider'" (*RFI* 4,ii:8–13) also is concerned with patterns, but her concern is with the developing pattern of the dream vision of this work, which symbolically presents "the author/heroine relation to her family and her past, her response to a threatening, war-poisoned world, and a shattering revelation about the nature of her innermost self."

Two other pieces should be mentioned here, although they add little to our understanding of Porter's work. In "Myth and Epiphany in Porter's 'The Grave'" (*SSF* 15:269–75), Constance Rooke and Bruce Wallis note that criticism of the story has focused upon the few most obtrusive symbols—the dove and the grave, for example—but neglect the story's paradigm "of our most primal racial myth, that of the fall of man, which is itself the pattern of a primal experience in the life of each individual." And Joan Givner simply points out in "'The Plantation of this Isle': Katherine Anne Porter's Bermuda Base" (*SWR* 63:339–51) that in 1929 Porter spent five months in almost complete seclusion in Bermuda, living in a home which is similar to the family homes described in "Old Mortality" and "The Old Order."

d. **Eudora Welty.** The continually growing body of scholarship and criticism devoted to Welty shows no sign of abating. Nor does Welty's productivity show any indication of diminishing. In addition to the appearance in *SCR* (11,i:22–23) of the early short story, "Acrobats in the Park" (with a prefatory essay, "Remember How It Was with the Acrobats," by James Nordby Gretlund) this year saw the publication of *The Eye of the Story: Selected Essays and Reviews* (Random), works which date from 1942 to 1977. In addition to seven essays "On Writing," perhaps the most important section in the collection, there are sections "On Writers," "Reviews," and "Personal and Occasional Pieces." Almost without exception these pieces exemplify the accuracy of Johnathan Yardley's statement that "for Miss Welty, nothing is done or felt halfheartedly; she pours herself into the work she does, the books she reads, the opinions she holds, with total passion."

Not nearly as impressive a collection—if only because none of the contributors can write with anything like the brilliance of Welty—but an important collection nevertheless, is the volume edited by John Desmond devoted to Welty's work, *A Still Moment: Essays on the Art of Eudora Welty* (Scarecrow). Two of the essays, John Allen's and M. E. Bradford's, have been published previously; the remaining eight essays are published for the first time. None of them will greatly alter our way of seeing Welty's work, but almost all the essays are worth reading. More than half the pieces in the collection are concerned with specific books: Barbara Fialkowski deals with "Psychic Distance in *A Curtain of Green*: Artistic Successes and Personal Failures" (pp. 63–70), Charles E. Davis with "Eudora Welty's *The Robber Bridegroom* and Old Southwest Humor: A Doubleness of Vision" (pp. 71–81), Douglas Messerli with "Metronome and Music: The Encounter between History and Myth in *The Golden Apple*" (pp. 82–102), while William McMillen's essay discusses "Circling-In: The Concept of Home in Eudora Welty's *Losing Battles* and *The Optimist's Daughter*" (pp. 110–17) and John F. Desmond's "Pattern and Vision in *The Optimist's Daughter*" (pp. 118–38). The remaining essays treat such matters as "The Real Thing: Eudora Welty's Essential Vision" (Jerry Harris, pp. 1–11), "Time in the Fiction of Eudora Welty" (D. James Neault, pp. 35–50), and "The Poetics of Prose: Eudora Welty's Literary Theory" (Albert J. Griffith, pp. 51–62).

The most substantial single essay to appear about Welty this year is Lucinda H. MacKethan's "To See Things in Their Time: The Act of Focus in Welty's Fiction" (*AL* 50:258–75). MacKethan begins by quoting Welty's statement that "man can feel love for place; he is prone to regard time as something of an enemy," then notes that for Welty "the act of focusing" allows place to acquire the sense of identity "that men can use to measure themselves and to endure." Place yields to time, but still "exists as a mechanism of insight available to those who can 'stand still' to catch the fleeting moment when place reveals its mysteries." MacKethan goes on to discuss *Delta Wedding, The Golden Apples, Losing Battles*, and *The Optimist's Daughter* as works which "dramatize the demands made on characters whose main challenge is to perceive, understand,

and transmit the moments when place yields up its 'extraordinary' values." An interest in Welty's sense of place is also the concern of Bessie Chronaki, who finds in "Eudora Welty's Theory of Place and Human Relationships" (*SAB* 43,ii:36–44) that the major category of inspiration for Welty deriving from "place" is the family, and offers *Losing Battles* and *Delta Wedding* as examples to prove her contention.

Losing Battles is also discussed by Larry Reynolds in "Enlightening Darkness: Theme and Structure in Eudora Welty's *Losing Battles*" (*JNT* 8:133–44). Reynolds offers a strong case for believing that "the true strengths of *Losing Battles* lie beneath its entertaining surface where the story of an intense struggle for survival is subtly and carefully told." What the reader discovers, as Julia does before she dies, is that the Renfros and Beechams are a desperate people, "fighting a determined battle for survival." Ignorance is essential to that survival, for to recognize the truth of their existence would bring "unbearable loneliness and despair." Much less helpful is William Jay Smith's consideration of *The Optimist's Daughter* in "Precision and Reticence: Eudora Welty's Poetic Vision" (*OntarioR* 9:59–70). Smith admires the novel, but has little to tell the reader other than that Welty, "like the ancient lyric poet-storyteller has woven a multi-layered fabric of words, words concerned with the simplest but most important things we know," and in so doing "has enriched our language and given us in *The Optimist's Daughter* one of the true glories of modern literature."

Carol S. Manning is interested in "Male Initiation, Welty Style" (*RFI* 4,ii:53–60). In American literature, she notes, following the lead of Elaine Ginsberg, that the initiate is usually a male, and for a young male in the rural South the passage to a new identity is often the hunt. Manning discusses the originality, humor, and insight Welty brings to her portrayal of the initiation of Loch Morrison in "Moon Lake," and suggests that the originality of the portrayal derives from two perspectives which operate in the story: the author's combined perspective as realist, comedian, and female; and the female perspective of two young girls who observe the male initiate. Gary Carson argues in "Versions of the Artist in *A Curtain of Green*: The Unifying Imagination in Eudora Welty's Early Fiction" (*SSF* 15:421–28) that for Welty the artist is heroic "because it is in the imagination of the artist, if anywhere, that the tensions and contradictions in experience may be resolved in harmony and love and the perspectives of the primitive and the visionary may ultimately be reconciled." A case in point is the jazz musician Powerhouse in *A Curtain of Green*. Leroy Thomas, who also writes about Powerhouse in "Welty's Powerhouse" (*Expl* 36,iv:15–17), sees the story somewhat differently: not only does it mark a difference in Welty's technique, but it must be seen "as one of her most poignant treatments of the theme of alienation"; in fact, the various levels of Powerhouse's alienation "reveal him to be one of the most troubled of Miss Welty's characters." A troubled character is also the focus of Charles E. May's essay, "Why Sister Lives at the P.O." (*SHR* 12:243–49), which begins with the contention that the story "seems almost impervious to critical analysis," and then offers one of the most interesting readings of the story we have yet had. R. D. Laing rather than Freud seems to be the best guide here, according to May, for "in a very complex way the story illustrates the schizoid self-deception of the unembodied self. Moreover, it also dramatizes the results of a complex failure of communication when people not only refuse to listen to each other, but refuse to listen to themselves as well."

Several pieces deserve brief mention. Marilyn Arnold considers *The Robber Bridegroom* to be "Eudora Welty's Parody" (*NMW* 11,i:15–22) of the fairy tale. Patricia Chaffee examines psychological, emotional, and social functions of "Houses in the Short Fiction of Eudora Welty" (*SSF* 15:112–14). Concerning " 'Keela, the Outcast Indian Maiden': Studying It Out" (*SSF* 15:165–72), John Fischer says that the tale is "about deception, and itself deceptive, the tale illuminates through misdirection." Robert W. Cochran believes that Steve is as central a character as Lee Roy ("Lost and Found Identities in Welty's 'Keela, the Outcast Indian Maiden'," *NMAL* 2:item 14). Peggy W. Prenshaw has a note on "A Still Moment" (*NMAL* 2:item 17).

An essay of a totally different kind is provided by Joan Gruner, who describes "The Eudora Welty Collection, Jackson Mississippi" (*Descant* 23,i:38–48) in the Mississippi Department of Archives and History. The *Eudora Welty Newsletter* lists newspaper and magazine pieces about Welty which are to be found in the Department of Archives and History, and also lists recent additions to the Archives. *EuWN*, in fact, is the single best bibliographical source for writings by and about Welty. It may not be the most elegant of newsletters, but it certainly is one of the most valuable.

e. Thomas Wolfe. This was not a particularly good year for Wolfe scholarship. A. Scott Berg's *Max Perkins: Editor of Genius* (Dutton) does give us the most complete account to date of the relationship between Wolfe and his first editor, and Croissant & Co. (Ohio) has made available a reprint (with a Foreword by Aldo P. Magi) of Wolfe's 1938 *Vogue* piece, "Prologue to America," as well as Richard Walser's *Thomas Wolfe's Pennsylvania*, a pamphlet devoted to Wolfe's Pennsylvania heritage, with particular emphasis placed on the story of William Oliver Wolfe. Walser also is responsible for the publication of the facsimile edition of Wolfe's 1919 prize-winning essay, *The Crisis in Industry* (Hillsborough, N.C.: Ballinger's Book Service), for which he has written a *Prolegomena*. (The essay, without Walser's *Prolegomena*, also has been made available by Paleamon Press, Winston-Salem, N.C.)

But little else of importance has appeared this year. Elmo Howell finds in "Thomas Wolfe and the Sense of Place" (*SCR* 11,ii:96–106) that the reason critics continue to abuse Wolfe is not a problem in appreciation but a change in the critics' concept of what a novel should be. On the whole, contemporary criticism has shown little interest in place, "and Wolfe's Southerness is an essential element of his fiction, sometimes liked, sometimes hated, but always present to be dealt with in some way." Lawrence Maddock also is concerned with Wolfe's critical image, and in "Thomas Wolfe, a Stone, a Leaf, a Door" (*Ariz.Eng.Bull.*, 21,i:83–86) he suggests that we accept Wolfe as "a highly original writer of imaginative autobiography." Less conciliatory is Miles Donald's estimate in *The American Novel* (pp. 42–47), which acknowledges Wolfe's "remarkable development in bringing together twin nightmares—the repressiveness of the small town and the psychotic horrors of the family—but criticizes his "somewhat limited perceptions" and his inability to be selective.

Three other essays need be but briefly mentioned. In "Wolfe, O'Neill, and the Mask of Illusion" (*PLL* 14:87–90), Charmian Green tells us that in 1924, while Wolfe was at work on drafts of his play *Mannerhouse*, Eugene O'Neill was working on *Desire Under the*

Elms, which was "a probable catalyst for [Wolfe's] work in progress." Elizabeth Evans concerns herself in "Thomas Wolfe's Prelim-
inaries to *Of Time and the River*" (*MarkhamR* 8:5–7) with the six
preliminary pieces which precede the first page of book 1. John
Pleasant compares the fictional treatment of "Two Train Rides of
Thomas Wolfe" (*Innisfree* 4[1977]:3–14) to support his thesis that
"Wolfe's persona changed radically from the subjective, romantic,
egocentric Eugene Gant of *Look Homeward, Angel* and *Of Time
and the River* to the more objective, realistic, and humanitarian
George Webber of the posthumous novels." Of course, there are
several brief articles in *TWN,* but the most valuable sections of
TWN continue to be "Wolfe Trails: News and Notes," "The Wolfe
Pack: Bibliography," and "Wolfe Calls: Questions and Answers."
Now in its second year, *TWN* is an essential tool for anyone interested
in the work and life of Thomas Wolfe.

v. Humorists, Critics, and Others

Of the writers to be considered in this section, Dorothy Parker, for
a change, has been best served. In " 'I Am Outraged Womanhood':
Dorothy Parker as Feminist and Social Critic" (*RFI* 4,ii:25–34),
Suzanne L. Buner argues that Parker was not only a wit but a chronicler and harsh critic of 1920s' and 1930s' social roles. She uses her
"pitiable ridiculous women characters to criticize the society which
has created one-dimensional female roles and forced women to fit
into them." Buner suggests that a reexamination of Parker's poems
and short stories is in order. That reexamination is now to be found
in Arthur F. Kinney's *Dorothy Parker* (TUSAS 315), the best work
yet written about Parker. In four chapters Kinney provides first a
biographical sketch of Parker and an overview of the styles she
practiced; a study of her minor writing; a consideration of "Her
Accomplishment"—which "contains still some of the strongest examples of American periodical reviewing"; and a conclusion, which
briefly assesses her art as the "best epigramatic poet in our country,
in this century."

Another *New Yorker* author, James Thurber, has not been treated
nearly as well as Parker. Charles May offers an unconvincing reading of "Christian Parody in Thurber's 'You Could Look It Up'" (*SSF*

15:453–54); the story simply does not sustain the weight of May's
contention that Thurber's "ironic game . . . is not only to satirize the
'golden days of the national pastime,' but also to retell within a
modern American myth and idiom, the story of the golden days of
the Christian religion." As dubious and cloying as such a reading
may be, it is not nearly as distressing as the essays to be found in
*Grammars and Descriptions: Studies in Texts Theory and Text
Analysis* (Berlin: Walter de Gruyter, 1977). The volume, edited by
Teun A. van Dijk and Janos S. Petöfi, takes as its text Thurber's "The
Lover and His Lass" and subjects it to 13 types of linguistic dissec-
tion. I'm not sure what if anything is gained by such studies, but I do
know that the enjoyment of reading Thurber decidedly is not enhanced by a reading of these 400 pages.

A third *New Yorker* author, E. B. White, is the subject of no. 37
of the Scarecrow Author Bibliographies. A. J. Anderson's *E. B. White:
A Bibliography* (Scarecrow) attempts to cover everything White is
known to have published, from a short story in 1914 to his most
recent book, *Essays of E. B. White*, in 1977. Anderson includes a
listing of material of critical and biographical interest about White
and reviews of his books. This is an able job, but Scarecrow's production job, as usual, is dreadful.

One of our most influential students of language, Kenneth Burke,
is himself the subject of Frederic R. Jameson's "The Symbolic In-
ference; or Kenneth Burke and Ideological Analysis" (*CritI* 4:507–
23), in which Jameson first comments that the very greatest critics
of our time have construed the role of the critic to be the teaching of
history, and then regrets that "Burke finally did not want to teach us
history, even though he wanted to teach us how to grapple with it."
In a somewhat less technical framework, Dolores Rosenblum also
concerns herself with language as she discusses " 'Intimate Immensity': Mythic Space in the Works of Laura Ingalls Wilder" (*Where
the West Begins*, pp. 72–79). Rosenblum's inspiration is the French
critic Gaston Bachelard, whose definition of "intimate immensity" is
at the center of Rosenblum's consideration of Wilder's "Little House"
books—especially *The Little House on the Prairie*—in which Wilder
"defamiliarizes the known and familiarizes the unknown." The basic
"human plot of all of Wilder's narratives," Rosenblum points out in
her intriguing essay, "is 'to survive,' that is, to learn the rules—and

internalize them as self-regulation—so that you can enjoy life as a civilized human." Pam Doher examines "The Idioms and Figures of *Cheyenne Autumn*" (*Where the West Begins*, pp. 143–51) and finds that beneath the "easy flowing rhythms and simple vocabulary" of Mari Sandoz's novel lies an "intricate and complex pattern of language." There is a natural relationship of the language to the Indian people, as "the figurative language of *Cheyenne Autumn* aptly depicts the unity, the 'continuality' and the desperation of the Cheyenne and their land."

In "Joseph Wood Krutch: Persistent Champion of Man and Nature" (*WAL* 13:151–58), Paul N. Pavich considers the work of a writer who also was interested in the prairie, as he notes that after the pessimistic *The Modern Temper*, Krutch's critical works and philosophical essays reveal an intellectual evolution centered on a concern for the human being's role in nature. The Mormon writer, Virginia Sorensen, the author of eight books, most of which are about the American West, is the subject of L. L. Lee's and Sylvia Lee's *Virginia Sorensen* (WWS 31). The work is too brief and too simplistic to do much more than introduce the reader to Sorensen's work, but since few readers will be familiar with all of the novels and because so little has been written about them, this pamphlet is most welcome.

Finally, attention should be called to Hanna Wirth-Nesber's "The Modern Jewish Novel and the City: Franz Kafka, Henry Roth, and Amos Oz" (*MFS* 24:91–107), in which Wirth-Nesber notes that in *Call It Sleep, The Trial*, and *My Michael* "social and spatial experiences of the city have been translated into style," and that in Roth's book the Lower East Side "consists primarily of voices, and his style is garrulous, noisy, and colored by dialects overflowing into each other . . . the rapidity of his sentences, tripping over each other, conveys the city's density"; to James Gindin's "Storm Jameson and the Chronicle" (*CentR* 22:400–09), which tries to make a case for the Chronicle, "more shapeless than most," which Jameson wrote in the 1920s and 1930s centering on the family which begins with Mary Hervey; to William Baker's "Williams' 'The Use of Force'" (*Expl* 37,i:7–8), which argues the somewhat obvious point that there are two basic conflicts in the William Carlos Williams story: one within the girl and the other within the doctor; and, most important of all, to the republication by New Directions of Delmore Schwartz's 1938 collection of stories, *In Dreams Begin Responsibilities*, now issued with a brief introduction by James Atlas.

vi. Popular Fiction

a. Best-Sellers.   Unlike last year, when the popular literature of the 1930s to 1950s received relatively little critical attention, this has been a particularly good year for several writers of the period. Six short stories by Pearl Buck have been published under the title, *The Woman Who Was Changed and Other Stories* (Crowell). Matthew J. Bruccoli has edited *Just Representations: A James Gould Cozzens Reader* (So. Ill.), which includes the novel *Ask Me Tomorrow*, fifteen selections from six other novels, and three short stories and seven essays by Cozzens. Bruccoli also is responsible for three John O'Hara volumes. *Selected Letters of John O'Hara* (Random), as Bruccoli notes in his Introduction, documents aspects of O'Hara's career and character that a biographer can only summarize. Among the letters included are those O'Hara sent to several people at the *New Yorker*, to Bennett Cerf, his publisher at Random House, and to such writers as Fitzgerald, Hemingway, Steinbeck, and Cozzens. *"An Artist Is His Own Fault": John O'Hara on Writers and Writing* (So. Ill., 1977) has as its focal point three lectures O'Hara delivered at Rider College, two in 1959 and the third in 1961. To these Bruccoli has added several speeches, unpublished essays and forewords, several pieces on Fitzgerald, book reviews, interviews, and public statements. Both collections, of course, will be of considerable interest to O'Hara enthusiasts, but neither volume will do much to enhance O'Hara's reputation: he was neither a very interesting writer of letters nor a particularly discerning critic of writers and writing. Bruccoli's third contribution to the O'Hara concern this year is his *John O'Hara: A Descriptive Bibliography* (Pittsburgh). The bibliography builds upon his 1972 *John O'Hara: A Checklist*, and is both an excellent work of scholarship and an attractively produced volume.

Bruccoli was not responsible for the creation of the *John O'Hara Journal*—Vincent D. Balitas is the founder and editor of the new journal—but he is a contributor to the first number. The journal grew out of the John O'Hara Conference held in Pottsville, Pennsylvania, on 12 and 13 October 1978 and the first issue consists of papers delivered at the conference. Future issues, according to Balitas, "will publish articles, essays (both formal and informal), notes and queries, biographical information and reminiscences which deal both with O'Hara's life and work, and with the history of Schuykill County between 1890 and 1927."

Julie Gilbert's *Ferber: A Biography* (Doubleday) is the first biography of the author of *Show Boat*, but it really is not a very good book. Although Gilbert has made extensive use of Ferber's diaries and letters, the work is too admiring and anecdotal, and offers little insight into Ferber's work. The same is true to some degree of Lon Tinkle's *An American Original: The Life of J. Frank Dobie* (Little, Brown). This is the first major biography of Dobie, and it is a much more substantial work than Gilbert's *Ferber*. But, like Gilbert's biography, Tinkle's work does little to elucidate Dobie's writing. In his bibliographical note Tinkle mentions Larry McMurtry's negative assessment of Dobie's achievement, and says that as much as he values McMurtry's insights he thinks his judgment about Dobie to be wrong. But, he does not show *why* McMurtry's assessment is wrong; had he done so, the book might have been of considerably greater value. Much better by far is Willie Morris's *James Jones: A Friendship* (Doubleday), a moving and affectionate tribute which is neither a work of scholarship nor of literary criticism, but, as Morris writes, "it is an illumination of a friend, and perhaps of myself and others of us. . . ." A different kind of book, more traditional but less illuminating, is Robert Roulston's *James Norman Hall* (TUSAS 323)— the concluding chapter of which appeared in *Books at Iowa* (29:3–13). Roulston dutifully discusses the works Hall wrote in collaboration with Nordhoff, giving particular attention to the *Bounty* trilogy and *The High Barbaree*, and also considers the 16 volumes he wrote without Nordhoff, allotting the most space to the essays and sketches. Roulston offers little to suggest that Hall's writings, as he contends, deserve more critical attention than they have received.

Several other writers of popular literature of the period also received critical attention, though on a lesser scale than did the six above. Interviews with James Cain and Meyer Levin appeared this year, and both are of considerable interest. In the 69th interview published in the *Paris Review's* "The Art of Fiction" series (20:117–38), Cain speaks of his early years, his life as a writer, the origin of

The Postman Always Rings Twice and *Double Indemnity*, and "hard-boiled" writing. In "A Conversation with Meyer Levin" (*Mainstream* 24,i:39–43), Levin expressses his disquiet with writers like Roth, Bellow, and Malamud, whose audience "responded not only to their quality as writers but to a kind of hidden assimilationist quality in their work," and offers the opinion that of all his work *The Old Bunch* is the one most likely to endure.

Erskine Caldwell is the subject of a number of short essays this year. In " 'The Bogus Ones': A Lost Erskine Caldwell Novel" (*SLJ* 11,i:32–39), Guy Owen discusses one of Caldwell's early unpublished novels, which, though it has little merit, "is especially interesting to the Caldwell scholar for the additional light it adds to *Call It Experience* and, more significantly, for the way it anticipates the themes and techniques fully realized in Caldwell's major fiction of the 1930s." Owen also deals with unpublished material in "Erskine Cadwell's Unpublished Poems" (*SAB* 43,ii:53–57), and again concludes that although the poems are "not of a very high order," they are significant for revealing Caldwell's "early treatment of the important—even obsessive—themes of his major fiction of the 1930s." One of those major works, *Tobacco Road*, is the subject of Douglas Gomery's "Three Roads Taken: The Novel, The Play, The Film" (*The Modern American Novel*, pp. 9–18). Caldwell's novel is a throwback to 19th-century naturalism, according to Gomery, with sex, fear, and hunger as the primary human drives, and "there is a clear progression from the novel to the play to the film of excising the elements of determinism and substituting comedy." In *Media-Made Dixie: The South in the American Imagination* (LSU) Jack Kirby notes that another of Caldwell's major works, *God's Little Acre*, is the best selling southern book in history—exceeding sales of *Gone With the Wind* by more than a million copies—and contends that in the printed medium its author "must be ranked as the most influential communicator about the American South," a point which one wishes Kirby had considered at some length. An attempt to "facilitate a reexamination of Caldwell's short fiction" is the basic purpose behind Scott Mac-Donald's useful "An Evaluative Check-List of Erskine Caldwell's Short Fiction" (*SSF* 15:81–97), which describes the contents of every collection of Caldwell's stories published from 1929 to date and lists the first publication of each of his stories.

Gone With the Wind is the focus of three articles this year. Rob-

ert May's *"Gone With the Wind* as Southern History: A Reappraisal"
(*SoQ* 17,i:51–64) concludes that the novel's "positive aspects as
history have been hidden because of its uneven quality. It is one of
those rare instances when the sum of the parts is worth more than
the whole." Horst Breuer, in "Zur Ideologie eines Bestsellers: Bio-
ligismus und Sozialdarwinismus in Margaret Mitchells *Vom Winde
verweht*" (*AmS* 23,ii:260–69) contends that Mitchell's concern with
biologism and Social Darwinism in *Gone With the Wind* contributed
greatly to the novel's appeal during the post-Depression and post–
World-War-II eras, while Donald E. Sutherland, in "Southern Carpetbaggers in the North; or Ashley Wilkes, Where Are You Now?"
(*McNR* 24[1977–78]:9–17) writes about several southern carpetbaggers before turning to Ashley Wilkes, "potentially the perfect
carpetbagger," who like other, more successful carpetbaggers,
"feared being 'lost,' being buried in a post-war South threatened by
northern carpetbaggers, scalawags, freedmen, Scarlet O'Haras, and
all else that was unholy, unwholesome, and unpredictable."

Two of Ayn Rand's works are the subject of critical attention this
year. In "Ayn Rand and Feminism: An Unlikely Alliance" (*CE*
39:680–85), Mimi Gladstein acknowledges that *Atlas Shrugged* is
not generally considered to be philosophically feminist, but rather
unconvincingly contends that because Dagney Taggart is a heroine
"who not only survives but prevails," Rand has much to say that is
relevant to feminist issues. Just what it is that Rand has to say is
never clear. Less simplistic is Kevin McGann's "Ayn Rand in the
Stockyard of the Spirit" (*The Modern American Novel*, pp. 325–35),
which first discusses *The Fountainhead* and then the film version
of the novel and concludes that the torturous relationships in both
versions demonstrate that "respect and affection are difficult, trying, confusing concepts for their proudly selfish author."

Leonard F. Manheim's "An Author Wrecked by Success: Ross
Lockridge, Jr. (1914–1948)" (*HSL* 10:103–21) is concerned not so
much with *Raintree County* as it is with trying to explain why the
author of such a successful novel killed himself: he was ashamed,
Manheim suggests, of having stripped not only "his own inner
psyche but also the bodies and minds of those who were closest to
him." "Three Letters from Marjorie Rawlings to Emma Gray Trigg,"
which are printed in *EGN* (8:19–21), are concerned with Rawlings's
projected biography of Ellen Glasgow, but, like Manheim's essay

on Lockridge, they add up to very little. Much more substantial is Paul Ferlazzo's "The Midwest and the Expatriate in the Fiction of Glenway Wescott" (*ON* 4:25–35), which finds that "the relationship between the Midwestern expatriate and his home region is a complex mixture of pride and regret, of love and denial, of necessary dependence and inevitable rejection." Ferlazzo examines *The Grandmother* and *Good-Bye Wisconsin* to show that one of the significant thematic concerns of the two books is "the realization of the distance in more than mere miles between Kewaskum, Wisconsin, Wescott's birthplace, and Paris or Villefranche, where Wescott spent many years." W. D. Maxwell-Mahon looks at "The Novels of Thornton Wilder" (*UES* 16,i:35–44), not so much to offer an explication as to show that Wilder's attempt to use his craft to foster a sense of national identity in his readers resulted in the decline of his fiction into mediocrity.

b. **Detective Fiction.** Hugh Eames's *Sleuths, Inc.: Studies of Problem Solvers* (Lippincott) is a breezy and fairly entertaining look at the sleuths created by Arthur Conan Doyle, Georges Simenon, Dashiell Hammett, Eric Ambler, and Raymond Chandler; but there is nothing new here.

Chandler and Hammett fare better in some of the shorter pieces published during the year. Jonathan Holden's attempt to demonstrate in "The Case for Raymond Chandler's Fiction as Romance" (*KanQ* 10,iv:41–47) that a similarity exists between Chandler's fiction and medieval romance hardly seems worth the effort, but Winifred Fluck's "'Powerful but extremely depressing books': Raymond Chandler's Romane" in *American Studies* (23,iii:271–98) decidedly is worth the effort. Fluck argues that the realism of Chandler's social observations and the formal proprieties of the detective genre really mask his much more "overtly and obstinately moral concerns: the spectacle of an idealism, already infected by neurosis and obsessive behavior, in full retreat, though unrepentant and with nowhere to go." Richard Shatzkin offers an interesting comparison of the novel and film version of *The Big Sleep* (*The Modern American Novel*, pp. 80–94). Both works are confusing, Shatzkin contends, and in the filtering process from one medium to another become somewhat different works: "Chandler's story of his hero's failed individualistic and Romantic quest became on screen a dark romantic comedy that explores the feasibility of human and sexual commitment between a man and a woman." Perhaps most valuable to anyone interested in Chandler, however, is Natasha Spender's "Chandler's Own Long Goodbye: A Memoir" (*PR* 45:38–65), which among other things tells of Chandler's wary attitude toward psychoanalysis and his pride in being a "passionate moralist." Spender met Chandler in 1955, shortly after the death of his wife, and remained a friend until his own death. Her memoir offers one of the best portraits we have of Chandler.

The three essays devoted to Hammett are all worth reading. Best of all is H. H. Morris's "Dashiell Hammett in the Wasteland" (*MQ* 19:196–202), which sees the sum of Hammett's work as "a powerful jeremiad indicting virtually all of American society"—a wasteland "where evil and corrupt leaders will reach out to blight every level of society." In "Order and Disorder in *Maltese Falcon*" (*ArmD* 11:171), Donald Pattow discusses Hammett's use of pairing, which sets up the appearance of order but which ultimately is revealed to be illusory, "a facade masking a world in which no one can be trusted, a world in which emotion and greed rule, a world, in short of disorder," while in "Sam Spade–Lover" (*ArmD* 11:366–71), Peter Wolfe notes that most people have overlooked Sam Spade's tenderness and subtlety—he can "cope with dishonesty and even murder, but won't tolerate sexual betrayal."

Finally, in *ArmD* (11:257), John McAleer offers a self-interview about his relationship with Rex Stout and announces that Stout authorized him to start a *Rex Stout Newsletter*, and what better place to launch such a venture, he asks, than *ArmD*?

c. **Science Fiction.** Once again, work in the area of science fiction continues to be impressive. The projected volume on Robert A. Heinlein in the "Writers of the 21st Century" series which was mentioned in *ALS* 1977, page 300, has been published and continues the high standard set by the Asimov volume. Among the subjects treated in *Robert A. Heinlein*, edited by Joseph D. Olander and Martin Harry Greenberg (New York: Taplinger) are a reconsideration of Heinlein's "juvenile" novels, an analysis of his future history series and fantasies, an assessment of his preoccupation with the technique for survival, a consideration of the fiction based on the assumption that Heinlein's fiction is patterned upon Social Darwinism, the extent to which Heinlein treats the theme of sexuality in his fiction, a look at the major political and social elements in Heinlein's fiction, as well as an examination of *Stranger in the Land* and *Time Enough for Love*. A selected bibliography and biographical note complete this excellent volume.

Heinlein is also among the writers treated in *Critical Encounters: Writers and Themes in Science Fiction* (Ungar). Edited by Dick Riley, the volume includes studies of the work of Ray Bradbury, Isaac Asimov, Frank Herbert, Arthur Clarke, Samuel Delany, Ursula Le Guin, Robert Heinlein, and Theodore Sturgeon.

Finally a work on H. P. Lovecraft, Barton Levi St. Armand's monograph, *The Roots of Horror in the Fiction of H. P. Lovecraft* (Elizabethtown, N.Y.: Dragon Press, 1977). The volume runs to just more than 100 pages, but brief as it is, St. Armand has given us one of the best studies yet on Lovecraft as well as one of the most serious works we have on the horror tale. He sees Lovecraft as the Aristotle of the horror tale, but does not attempt to construct a *Poetics* of the horror tale from Lovecraft's work. Rather, he offers a close reading of Lovecraft's "The Rats in the Walls" as "a means of isolating fictional elements contributing to the creation of horror." It is an exciting, brilliantly constructed study, as St. Armand ranges from Poe and Radcliffe to Darwin, Jung, and Otto to show us the complex chain of Lovecraft's imagination. *The Roots of Horror* is an extraordinary achievement.

Hofstra University

15. Fiction: The 1950s to the Present

James H. Justus

Unlike an exasperated Hoover Shoats in *Wise Blood*—"That's the trouble with you innerleckchuls," he tells Haze Motes, "you don't never have nothing to show for what you're saying"—the reader of this chapter will no doubt feel that we have too much to show. The following survey of the year's work in contemporary fiction is longer than most previous ones, a fact which will confirm some enthusiasts in their belief that the state of both fiction and its critics is healthy. A careful scrutiny of this work is more sobering, however, since the rage for interviews, advocacy criticism, and generalized appreciation spreads unchecked, feminist criticism is growing so predictable that it has ceased raising either hackles or consciousness, essays on traditional authors like Bellow and O'Connor are voluminous and unvaried, and the once steady flow of work on Vonnegut, Kesey, and Heller is now a trickle. The bright spots seem even brighter against this gray picture: fresh, solid work on Mailer and Pynchon, innovative fictionists, and American Indian authors. Among the more than 50 reported dissertations on individual authors, those on Bellow (7) lead the list, followed closely by Oates (6), O'Connor, Mailer, and Pynchon (5 each). The topics of other dissertations include studies of "Holocaust-consciousness," naturalism, parody and satire in the Western, abstract characterization, "behavioral engineering," and the new journalism.

i. General Studies

a. **Overviews and Special Topics.** The most promising comprehensive study since Tony Tanner's *City of Words* (*ALS 1971*, pp. 245–46), Josephine Hendin's *Vulnerable People: A View of American*

Fiction Since 1945 (Oxford), is a disappointment, largely because it consists of generalizations that are as unexamined as they are provocative. Even the distinctions of the neat categories—"anarchic" and "holistic" fiction—grow progressively blurry from overlapping. The first is supposed to reflect a world as seen by suffering victim-heroes, the second as seen by parodists who fight the "abrasion and dispersal of the self" with self-conscious play; the "values" of the first are located in mechanisms that are regressive and disintegrative, those of the second are in those that promote clarity of perception. What is "seen" by both groups is the same: a world dominated by the random and the fragmentary. Hendin's relentlessly perky style does not encourage close analysis; this critic eschews notes and bibliography (but not pretentious epigraphs), and despite its modest elegance the book apparently dispensed with a good editor. Hendin favors the locution "different than," forgets the narrator's name in *One Flew Over The Cuckoo's Nest*, and chatters about "female heroines." The Guggenheim Foundation gave "generous support" for the writing of this facile book, portions of which appeared, predictably, in *Harper's*. The more substantial segments of *Vulnerable People* will be noted in appropriate places below.

More useful is a handsome reference work, Jeffrey Helterman and Richard Layman's *American Novelists Since World War II* (Gale), which contains biographical sketches of 80 writers: 18 are "master entries" (on such figures as Barth, Bellow, Pynchon, and Vonnegut) and the rest are "standard entries," which are devoted to novelists who are not yet "regarded as major forces in contemporary literature." The discursive accounts are both critical and factual and are followed by checklists of primary and secondary items. Some readers will doubtless note that certain innovative writers (Ronald Sukenick, Raymond Federman) do not earn even "standard" entries. Two more specialized books which should be noted here are Joseph F. Trimmer's *The National Book Awards for Fiction: An Index to the First Twenty-Five Years* (Hall) and Macel D. Ezell's *Unequivocal Americanism: Right-Wing Novels in the Cold War Era* (Scarecrow, 1977).

In a fine introduction to their anthology, *Writing Under Fire: Stories of the Vietnam War* (Delacorte), Jerome Klinkowitz and John Somer trace the fiction of the Indochina experience back to André Malraux, who saw it as early as 1930 as a metaphor for "man's anguished alienation from an absurd society within a meaningless universe." A generous sampling of work by Josiah Bunting, William Eastlake, James Simon Kunen, and others, *Writing Under Fire* also includes a "Chronology of Vietnam Conflict" (beginning in 207 B.C.) and a bibliography of American works issuing from that conflict. Philip D. Beidler glosses some of these same writers in a complementary piece, "The Vietnam Novel: An Overview, with a Brief Checklist of Vietnam War Narrative" (*SHR* 12:45–55), the very brevity of which says something about the feeble generative power of these experiences.

Also complementary are Gerald Peary's and Roger Shatzkin's *The Modern American Novels and the Movies* (Ungar) and James R. Messenger's "I Think I Liked the Book Better: Nineteen Novelists Look at the Film Version of Their Work" (*LFQ* 6:125–34). As Peary and Shatzkin note, Bellow, Barth, Ellison, Pynchon, and others constitute a generation of novelists whose "narrative structure, style, language, and self-reflexivity" are not easily "filmable," but even for the more filmable authors—James Leo Herlihy, James Jones, Herman Wouk, Bernard Malamud—Messenger finds unhappy but understandable responses to his questionnaire, but moralizes that for the "dedicated novelist, there could be worse things than a bad adaptation." The Peary-Shatzkin volume contains interesting but breezy essays on Edwin O'Connor, Truman Capote, John Updike, Thomas Berger, and James Dickey.

The feminist perspective on contemporary fiction is well served in three essays. Despite their banal title, "Second-Class Citizenship: The Status of Women in Contemporary American Fiction" (*What Manner of Woman*, pp. 297–315), Martha and Charles G. Masinton show persuasively how, amidst the hyperbolic extremes of contemporary art, the depiction of women derives still from myth and stereotype. Familiar observations about these types in Mailer, Updike, and Bellow are balanced by more original treatments of Alix Kates Shulman, whose technical problem has been to make interesting a character "whose life has been largely devoid of free choice and action," and the "somatic" novels of Joyce Carol Oates, Marge Piercy, and John Didion. Although she examines some of the liberated writers in "A Home of One's Own: Women's Bodies in Recent Women's Fiction" (*JPC* 11:772–88), Nancy Regan focuses on the "sexually conservative modern Gothics" to find that Victoria Holt and Phyllis A. Whitney transmute the concept of "what it's like to be inside a female body into what it's like to live in a mysterious house"—the dangers are libidinal and reproductive. Though female protagonists may not know what they want, Carolyn G. Heilbrun argues in "Marriage and Contemporary Fiction" (*CritI* 5:309–22) that they do know that the necessary change begins when they forsake marriage ties for a "flight into life." Rebecca Radner's "You're Being Paged Loudly in the Kitchen: Teen-Age Literature of the Forties and Fifties" (*JPC* 11:789–99) is an analysis which is as frothy as the subject.

Sarah Blacher Cohen has followed up her fine study of Bellow's humor (*ALS 1974*, pp. 295–96) with an edited volume of 16 essays, all but 2 of which are new and some of which will be discussed in appropriate segments below. Cohen's introduction to *Comic Relief: Humor in Contemporary American Literature* (Illinois), while summarizing subjects and methods of the individual essays, also manages to become a mini-history of the barbs, targets, and generating sources of 20th-century humor. The volume is rounded off with a 13-page checklist of criticism.

The longest, perhaps the best, and certainly the funniest essay in the collection is George Garrett's "Ladies in Boston *Have* Their Hats: Notes on WASP Humor" (*Comic Relief*, pp. 207–37), a wide-ranging piece that contrasts WASP humor with that of ethnics of various stripes and illustrates it generously from the work of Mark Twain ("its finest example"), Wright Morris, John Updike, and Tom Wolfe. Another of Blacher's authors, Earl Rovit, contributes "College Humor and the Modern Audience" (*Comic Relief*, pp. 238–48), which is serious but unsolemn in its exploration of the Max Shulman tradition and its elephantine subtlety and self-conscious shock effects. Rovit bravely numbers among the books that derive from this tradition William Gaddis's *The Recognitions*, Barth's *The Sot-Weed Factor*, and Pynchon's *Gravity's Rainbow*. Saad Elkhadem's "The Kitsch Novel" (*IFR* 5:150–52) is an important little definitional note which distinguishes the trivial and *Kitsch*.

Strother Purdy's *The Hole in the Fabric: Science, Contemporary Literature, and Henry James* (Pittsburgh, 1977) is a complex and provocative study that might better have been split into three books. Admitting that science, philosophy, and eroticism "are not assimilable," though they are all important to contemporary fiction through their links in James, Purdy speaks authoritatively on the "extension of man's mind into machines" and the momentous implications reflected in a broad range of fictionists.

The Fiction Collective is the subject of several assessments, two by one of its more prominent members, Larry McCaffery: "The Fiction Collective" (*ConL* 19:99–115), a straightforward historical sketch, and "The Fiction Collective, 1974–1978: An Innovative Alternative" (*ChiR* 30,ii:107–26), a plea for the establishment of even more organizations to insure the momentum of innovative fiction. Another member, Jonathan Baumbach, concentrates on the group's ability to counteract commercial alliances against experimental authors in "Who Do They Think They Are? A Personal History of the Fiction Collective" (*TriQ* 43:625–34); but Gene Lyons defends the bias of commercial publishers in "Report on the Fiction Collective" (*TriQ* 43:635–47), a confession by one who has not been able "to read any novel published by the Fiction Collective from beginning to end."

An aggrieved Fred Pfeil, in "Icons for Clowns: American Writers Now" (*CE* 39:525–40), excoriates alcoholism among writers; the Hemingway style, which he equates with a "sterile, impotent aesthetic"; macho programming for all American male writers; and the commercial corruption of talent epitomized by *Esquire*, whose 40th anniversary issue occasions the rage. In *American Visionary Fiction: Mad Metaphysics as Salvation Psychology* (Kennikat), Richard Finholt explores the tradition "that takes the inner self as subject because the deeply thinking mind is naturally drawn to its mysteries and the vision that arises from them." Finholt pretends to more originality than is real in his mining of subterranean depths in Mailer and Dickey, writers who, though they respect the "truth of the unconscious," simply illustrate clownishness in Pfeil's jeremiad.

John W. Tilton's *Cosmic Satire in the Contemporary Novel* (Bucknell, 1977) is a study whose premise is that no theory of traditional satire, based as it must be on past practice, can possibly embrace the contemporary versions of the mode: "Satire is and ought to be what the creative satirist makes it become." Much of this little treatise is a laying-out of appropriate critical approaches that can illuminate three novels: Anthony Burgess's *A Clockwork Orange*, Barth's *Giles Goat-Boy*, and Vonnegut's *Slaughterhouse-Five*. All three transcend topical targets to create a vision, "ultimately tragic in its implications, of man desperately refusing to face what he is and just as desperately—and unsuccessfully—trying to become what he thinks he ought to be."

b. **The New Fiction: Theories and Modes.** In a splendid and much-needed essay for delineating the points of contact between the old and the new, "Another Battle of the Books: American Fiction, 1950–1970" (*Prospects* 4:267–85), Chester E. Eisinger insists upon calling the practitioners of the new fiction "modernists" despite their protestations. Interested not in the predictable tensions between traditionalists and avant-gardists but in the major cultural phenomena which they both reflect, this critic is wide-ranging in his coverage of relevant artists and sensitive to the variety of the bases (epistemological, aesthetic, linguistic) by which we can discriminate the writing of the two groups.

Narrowing his focus to "American Fiction, 1974–1976: The People Who Fell to Earth" (*ConL* 19:497–530), Raymond M. Olderman finds that characters in these fictions are still adjusting to the "disruptive insights" of the 1960s: some embittered, hopeless, vengeful, others disoriented by drugs and sex, still others "scorched by what they have seen and think it is no longer possible to have God or moral order." Olderman is particularly perceptive in finding the new consciousness embodied in models (theoretical, as in Don De-Lillo and Ursula Le Guin; social and political, as in Marge Piercy and Ismael Reed). He appends a selective list of fictions from which he draws his generalizations.

Like Eisinger, Peter A. Brier is interested in continuities among the new fictionists; the purpose of his "Caliban Reigns: Romantic Theory and Some Contemporary Fantasists" (*UDQ* 13,i:38–51) is "to diffuse the aura of absolute originality that now surrounds writers like Pynchon, Barth, and Vonnegut" by finding the origins of their styles and mannerisms in the early romantic novel in Germany, with its ideas of imperfection in art and generic intermingling, and in the magazine humorists of the previous generation—Thurber, Perelman, and Benchley. Most of *Salmagundi* 42 is devoted to Gerald Graff's "The Politics of Anti-Realism" (pp. 4–30) and brief statements in response by Leslie Fiedler, Christopher Lasch, Patricia Spacks, Taylor Stoehr, and others. Graff's is a cogent and pungent critique of "cultural radicalism" as it derives from leftist romanticism, a frank declaration that some forms of realism and rationalism are needed to counteract the current avant-garde. Although "Fiction and Anti-Fiction" (*ASch* 47:398–406) pokes fun at the noisy "zietgeisters," especially their spot affairs with Barthelme, Barth, Beckett, and others before 1973, when they finally got their "Big Book" (*Gravity's Rainbow*), George P. Elliott's central point is that the antifictionists have developed a number of techniques which can be used by the traditional novelist for the advancement of realistic fiction, which has been "getting somewhat etiolated." Another target of innovative fictionists is the subject of an inconclusive but spirited symposium, "Character as a Lost Cause" (*Novel* 11:197–217), presided over by Mark Spilka and enlivened by Martin Price, Julian Moynahan, and Arnold Weinstein and with guest interruptions by John Gardner and Robert Scholes.

In "Prolegomena to the Study of Fictional *Dreck*" (*Comic Relief*, pp. 263–80), Philip Stevick detects at the very center of experimental fiction a shared set of assumptions toward and images of "the mass-cultural objects of our world." After World War I, Stevick argues, fiction began to respond "not merely to the growth of mass culture, but to the manipulated consciousness *of* mass culture that results from the new power of mass advertising." He discriminates among the users of *dreck*, from Updike and David Madden, to Vonnegut, Barthelme, and the most dazzling manipulator, Pynchon. This superb essay ends with a series of categorical generalizations toward "a grammar, as it were, of *dreck*."

Les Américanistes (Kennikat), edited by Ira D. and Christiane Johnson, is both a historical survey of French interest in (mostly) contemporary American fiction and a primer—valuable for those who need it—of French critical theories which have influenced the contemporary crop of critics of *Américanistes*. The various essays are liberally studded with "anastomosis," "enlisement," "diegetic," "metalepses," and other terms; but the chill felt by unreconstructed New Critics will come not from these contributors' respect for the text as artifact—indeed, the close readings border on the claustrophobic—but from the fact that the working theories derive from that old enemy, science. The anthropologists, linguists, and psychoanalysts may not much like what literary critics have done with their disciplines, but the appropriation goes grimly on. If most of these French observers of *Américanistes* lack humor, their prose style also lacks grace. The worst essays are not written so much as they are assembled; the notable exceptions, readable because they carry their theoretical baggage lightly, will be noted in appropriate spots below.

A fine general survey in the Johnsons' volume is "New Modes of Story-Telling in Recent American Writing: The Dismantling of Contemporary Fiction" (*Les Américanistes*, pp. 110–29) by André Le Vot, who argues vividly that James Purdy, William Burroughs, John Hawkes, Robert Coover, and Pynchon are "not the offsprings of spontaneous generation" but that their continuities are visibly evident. He traces two directions among innovationists: one derives from Djuna Barnes, the prophet of the "conjunctive mode"; the other from Nathanael West, the prophet of the "disjunctive mode." The first is characterized by "globality," abundance, hyperbole, polarization; the second emphasizes discontinuous narrative, flat characters, and the diction of a "walled-in consciousness."

A similar case for a continuing tradition can be seen in "Requiem for a Genre Very Much Alive or Il Fu Fiction Pascal" (*MFS* 24:509–19), in which Davy A. Carozza argues that though the traditional social novel has virtually disappeared, the innovative fictionists "are very much mimeticists," even as they break with the conventions of the realistic novel. Carozza sees fiction worldwide as healthy, thanks to the inventive modification of such types as the picaresque, the confession, movie-influenced fiction, new journalism, and black humor.

ii. Norman Mailer

The fact that the authors of two new books find it necessary to discriminate between Mailer the personality and Mailer the artist may signify a new (and certainly needed) phase in studies of this writer. Robert Merrill's *Norman Mailer* (TUSAS 322) is a sensitive examination of the books as aesthetic achievements, not as products of a contemporary legend or as documents of a performing self. And while he argues that Mailer is a writer who integrates his life and art, Philip Bufithis in his *Norman Mailer* (Ungar) believes that the huckstering hijinks of the public figure are crucial "to the *creation* of his work, not to its *promotion*." Both critics see Mailer's stylistic energy as a contribution to the coherence of his art rather than as an end in itself.

Merrill, for example, stresses the dramatic action of the narratives and comes up with particularly perceptive readings of *The Naked and the Dead* and *The Deer Park*. He is most original in his discussion of Mailer's efforts in the "fusion of novelistic traditions" and in the expert use of himself in his texts (as a failed Jeremiah, or his own hero, or as "interior" historian). Bufithis's depiction of Mailer's moral power, deriving from the clash of human will and imagination with "the forces of restraint," is impressive, but the strengths of his book lie in the separate readings of individual works. Bufithis claims (not entirely persuasively) that *Barbary Shore* is "a novel about the making of a novel"; he accurately names *An American Dream* as the first sign of Mailer's later mode of "mystic release and revelation." Others have seen Emerson and Hemingway lurking on the peripheries of the later work, but the most interesting chapter here, as in Merrill's book, incorporates a fresh treatment of *The Prisoner of Sex* and *Marilyn*. Merrill's book is valuable for those who appreciate Mailer as literary critic: despite the flaccid uncertainty in *Of a Fire on the Moon*, *Genius and Lust*, the tribute to Henry Miller, illustrates a "critical intelligence at its best." Those who favor a Mailer engaged in a large-scale intellectual tug-of-war will find Bufithis's book more satisfying.

Bufithis calls "The Time of Her Time" a satire on "the bromidic psychology of the 1950s," but in his excellent piece of critical scholarship, "Mailer's 'O'Shaugnessy Chronicle': A Speculative Autopsy" (*Crit* 19,iii:21–39), James Rother sees considerably more to what he calls a "Faustian epic." In this reconstruction of Mailer's grand scheme, which collapsed from its disproportion and which was abandoned in the early 1960s, Rother suggests that the Mailerian voices of both the later fiction and nonfiction are extensions of O'Shaugnessy.

Despite Mailer's priapic exploration of power as sexual energy, his novels, according to Josephine Hendin (*Vulnerable People*, pp. 117–44), are the products of ambition and frustration; like movie stars, his protagonists play one role forever, living "the myth of endless adolescence." Not so, says Richard Finholt (*American Visionary Fiction*, pp. 112–27), who asserts that the truths of the "old-time thinkers" of cosmology ("man acts as the agent of external, eternal, and omnipotent cosmic forces") are confirmed by the sometimes instinctual discoveries of Mailer; he cites *Why Are We in Vietnam?* as an example.

Finally, James E. Breslin's "Style in Norman Mailer's *The Armies of the Night*" (*YES* 8:157–70) is a thoughtful devaluation of the famous National Book Award winner. Despite its surface variety, the book describes actions which Breslin sees as repetitions of a single ritual test of manhood; its operatic style not only fails to distinguish any styles different from Mailer's own, but it also consistently empties events of their potential affecting power. Far from contesting "totalitarianese," *Armies* provides yet another instance of it.

iii. Flannery O'Connor

Eleven years after Melvin J. Friedman and Lewis A. Lawson's *The Added Dimension: The Art and Mind of Flannery O'Connor* (*ALS 1966*, p. 178), its editors have issued a second edition (Fordham, 1977), to which one important essay has been added: Friedman's " 'The Perplex Business': Flannery O'Connor and Her Critics Enter the 1970s," a survey of the books written on the author since 1966. Also useful as a critical overview is Friedman's "Flannery O'Connor in France: An Interim Report" (*RLV* 43[1977]:435–42), which sets the current French reputation of O'Connor (all of whose work is now available) in the context of the reception and translation of earlier American southerners in France.

One of those critics who has helped to make O'Connor's French reputation firm is André Bleikasten, who bluntly warns us that the author's public pronouncements on her art may not be the best guide to her fiction. In "The Heresy of Flannery O'Connor" (*Les Américanistes*, pp. 53–70), Bleikasten points out that though her intentions were doubtless orthodox, the "multivalence and reversibility" of her language suggest a bleak vision which differs little from "plain nihilism." In defining herself as a writer, O'Connor failed to acknowledge an insight admirably dramatized in her work: "that the self is not even master in its own house."

Marion Montgomery continues his investigation of O'Connor's conservative intellectual traditions. In "The Poet and the Disquieting

Shadow of Being: Flannery O'Connor's Voegelinian Dimension"
(*InR* 13[1977]:3–14), he explores the tangled interrelationships between aesthetic integrity and epistemology and finds that ideas of
Eric Voegelin are dramatized in such figures as Haze Motes and the
Misfit. In "Flannery O'Connor and the Jansenist Problem in Fiction"
(*SoR* 14:438–48), Montgomery distinguishes between authorial belief in free will and the aesthetic necessities of dramatic movement
which seems to establish deterministic fates for the characters; even
her agents, he says, can choose a final contingency: "Hell or Purgatory."

Michael Gresset once suggested that southern literature is to
American what Irish literature is to English. Now Patrick J. Ireland
argues that one of our most distinctive southern writers shows more
continuities with "the national literary mainstream" than divergences
from it. "The Place of Flannery O'Connor in Our Two Literatures"
(*FOB* 7:47–63) is pivotal: as both "insider and outsider" (as southerner and Catholic), O'Connor is useful for showing that both literatures offer some kind of "salvific loss of innocence to the romantic
dreamer." Others would agree with Ireland's thesis. In "The Artist
as 'a Very Doubtful Jacob': A Reflection on Hawthorne and O'Connor" (*SoQ* 16:95–103), Marion Montgomery observes that the southerner's poet-prophets are continuations of Hawthorne's attempts to
"rescue the poet to society," but O'Connor is able to build her argument upon the kind of authority which Hawthorne sought but could
never find—Aquinas. In "The Literary Theory of Flannery O'Connor
and Nathaniel Hawthorne" (*FOB* 7:101–13), however, Shannon
Burns warns us that O'Connor's "mysterious country," though linked
to Christianity, is not limited by it. As a romancer, her vision is virtually identical to that of Hawthorne, whose "neutral territory" is
the same as her "mystery." The aim of both is "not to limit, but to
expand, vision; not to answer, but to question."

Although Roberta Sharp declares that O'Connor's art "owes
something" to Poe's, in "Flannery O'Connor and Poe's 'Angel of the
Odd'" (*FOB* 7:116–28) she cites "odd imagery" as her meager evidence. More compelling links are advanced in "Varieties of Religious Experience in O'Connor and West" (*FOB* 7:26–46) by Laura
M. Zaidman, who argues that Haze Motes's "life-in-death quest"
follows the pattern in *Miss Lonelyhearts,* and both *Wise Blood* and
West's novel derive in part from William James.

According to George D. Murphy and Caroline L. Cherry's "Flannery O'Connor and the Integration of Personality" (*FOB* 7:85–100), a study of the short stories reveals "a kind of psycho-drama of the dynamics of personality: a chronically unresolved conflict between the conscious and unconscious elements of the mind." Though these critics refrain from citing O'Connor's personal situation as the source for this "war without armistice," Claire Kahane hesitates not at all. "The Artificial Niggers" (*MR* 19:183–98) contends that O'Connor's use of black characters are yet another version of her white dependent children, whose rage must be hidden behind conciliating social masks. Prominent among her examples are "Revelation," "The Enduring Chill," and "The Displaced Person." Despite her smug comfort with her own liberal premises, Kahane at last is saved by a Mrs. Turpin-like humility: her insight that O'Connor's South is "a metaphor for [all] our disturbed social relations."

Observing that all the central characters in *Wise Blood* are "wordsmiths, preachers who use words self-consciously," Melody Graulich in "'They Ain't Nothing But Words': Flannery O'Connor's *Wise Blood*" (*FOB* 7:64–83) concludes that these figures are forced to communicate truth through distortion, indirection, and ambiguity, since spiritual belief "is a mystery beyond words." John V. McDermott's "Dissociation of Words with the Word in *Wise Blood*" (*Renascence* 30:163–66) is an important footnote on the meaning of the title: man's free will is conjoined with God's when insight and grace coincide.

"From Fashionable Tolerance to Unfashionable Redemption: A Reading of Flannery O'Connor's First and Last Stories" (*FOB* 7: 10–25) is Ralph C. Wood's perceptive comparison of "Judgement Day," the author's final story, with "The Geranium," her first. The final story not only brings her career to a thematic culmination but also reveals striking new technical possibilities (such as convoluted flashbacks) which were cut short by death. Despite her extrapolation of O'Connor's single allusion to Job to the unprovable conclusion that the whole Book of Job "came to her mind while she was writing this story," Diane Tolomeo cites some persuasive parallels between Mrs. Turpin's experiences and the biblical sufferer's in "Flannery O'Connor's 'Revelation' and the Book of Job" (*Renascence* 30:78–90). It is more difficult to take seriously James Ellis's contention in "Watermelons and Coca-Cola in 'A Good Man Is Hard to Find':

Holy Communion in the South" (*NConL* 8,iii:7–8) that the grand-
mother's old suitor is "the gentlemanly counterpart to the crucified
Christ" and that his name (Teagarden) suggests the Garden of
Gethsemane. In "Julian's Mother" (*FOB* 7:114–15), Mary Frances
Hopkins is distressed that critics of "Everything That Rises Must
Converge" refer to the mother as "Mrs. Chestny"—she actually was
a Chestny "who married someone else."

iv. Saul Bellow, Bernard Malamud, Philip Roth

While his "Saul Bellow and Individualism" (*EdL* 1,i:3–28) offers
few new conclusions, James Schroeter's survey of a 30-year career
in which Bellow has defined and probed the meaning of consciousness and existence is admirably clear and fair, especially the observation of the novelist's ironic, uneasy relation to the other American
Nobel laureates.

"Saul Bellow's Chicago" (*MFS* 24:139–46) is more powerfully
evoked than any of his cities, says Sarah Blacher Cohen, although a
simultaneous attachment to and estrangement from the city account
for its different versions: whereas a stockyard past disallows errors
about the nature of man in *The Adventures of Augie March*, Chicago in *Humboldt's Gift* summons up local-color nostalgia to blot
out the fact of urban decay. Despite the characteristic urban setting,
however, Molly Stark Wieting points out in "The Symbolic Function
of the Pastoral in Saul Bellow's Novels" (*SoQ* 16:359–74) that the
corresponding pastoral element forms a consistent pattern in each
novel: though often illusory, the "flights to nature" signify affirmation and the possibility of spiritual renewal.

Citing such parallels as Henderson's age, themes of immortality
and death, and the gap between goal and method, and assorted instances of literary game-playing, Renée Sieburth says *Don Quixote*
is Bellow's "true model" for his African novel in "Henderson the
Rain King: A 20th-Century Don Quixote?" (*CRCL* 5:86–94). William J. Scheick's "Circle Sailing in Bellow's *Mr. Sammler's Planet*"
(*ELWIU* 5:95–101) is a succinct and detailed image study which
shows the novelist's use of the earth as a "macrocosmic analogue"
to human conflict, signaled not only by references to the bright and
dark sides of the moon and Sammler's good and blind eyes, but also
by Bellow's simultaneous attraction to and repulsion from his hero.

Modern Jewish Studies, the title given to a joint issue of *Yiddish* (3,iii) and *SAJL* (4,ii), features criticism on Bellow's later work. In "The Resonance of Twoness: The Urban Vision of Saul Bellow" (pp. 9–21), Daniel Walden suggests that a specific but chafing aesthetic-moral quest figures prominently in all the fiction; in "Meditations Interruptus: Saul Bellow's Ambivalent Novel of Ideas" (pp. 22–32), Sanford Pinsker argues that *Herzog, Mr. Sammler's Planet,* and *Humboldt's Gift* constitute a "loose trilogy" which concerns the impact of ideas on contemporary culture and "the comic interaction between both of these and an embattled spokesman; and in "Saul Bellow and Ghetto Cosmopolitanism" (pp. 33–44), Mark Shechner shows how the novelist exploits the "body-mind" problem for a "comedy of the cloaca," with an "inherited imaginative" technique of comic incongruity rooted in the ghetto experience. Two slight pieces, Leslie Field's "Saul Bellow: From Montreal to Jerusalem" (pp. 51–59) and Steven David Lavine's "In Defiance of Reason: Saul Bellow's *To Jerusalem and Back*" (pp. 72–83), round out the emphasis on the later work. One notable essay on the fiction in general is Keith Opdahl's "God's Braille: Concrete Detail in Saul Bellow's Fiction" (pp. 60–71), a convincing treatment of the "stereopticon effect" by which realistic scenes are rendered against a competing transcendental vision—an effect which results in Bellow's ambivalence toward the physical world.

Believing that a "basic ambiguity" underlies most of Bellow's writing, Jean-Pierre Vernier, in "Mr. Sammler's Lesson" (*Les Américanistes,* pp. 16–36), examines narrative techniques for hints of a system of values implicit in the novelist's most controversial works. He finds, among other things, that the point of view (third-person, blurred through "free indirect style") suggests, appropriately, the "flat perception" of a one-eyed man and concludes that although *Mr. Sammler's Planet* is clearly a didactic work, its ideological content is "far from clear." Michelle C. Loris, however, locates the source of that content in Sammler's uniqueness: he grounds his being in God, not, as in previous protagonists, in the "finite human self." "*Mr. Sammler's Planet*: The Terms of the Covenant" (*Renascence* 30:217–23) focuses on a loose apocalyptic movement "from judgment through the purification of flood and beatitude to the condition of promise," a movement which unifies the moral journey of the hero.

A Bellow number of *NMAL* (2,iv:Items 25–30) also features the later work. In "In 'Terror of the Sublime': Mr. Sammler and Odin," Blanche Gelfant relates the "orbital shape" of *Mr. Sammler's Planet* to its author's vision of "timelessness an as eternal return" in which his protagonist must reenact the sacrifices of ancient heroes. In "Epic Structure and Statement in *Mr. Sammler's Planet*," Suzanne F. Kistler appeals to C. M. Bowra and E. M. W. Tillyard to demonstrate that the novel is a spiritualized epic which moves from atheism to mysticism. Jo Brans ("The Balance Sheet of Love: Money and Its Meaning in Bellow's *Herzog*") focuses on Ramona, a sexual priestess who offers success and renewal to counteract Madeleine's "spiritual devastation." Sue S. Park's "The Keystone and the Arch: Another Look at Structure in *Herzog*" is a study of chapter divisions and what they reveal of time motifs. Alan Chavkin argues in "The Unsuccessful Search for 'Pure Love' in Saul Bellow's *Herzog*" that the protagonist is not masochistic, but that his failure with women stems from his naive belief in perfect love. In "The Politics of Message: Moshe the Masseur in *To Jerusalem and Back*," Robert F. Willson, Jr., believes that Bellow uses a minor character in his book on Israel to symbolize his own hopes for the Middle East.

Although "Artists and Opportunists in Saul Bellow's *Humboldt's Gift*" (*ConL* 19:143–64) is an account of the novel's two interlocking themes—the dangers of commercial success to the American artist and the "comic pathos of a vain intellectual's efforts to age with style and dignity"—Ben Siegel concentrates on the final scene in the cemetery, in which crocuses serve not as springtime renewal but as a play on words ("that all of *us croak*"). In this too-long piece, Siegel himself fails either to resolve the divergent notions about Bellow's meaning or to decide even if in this work Bellow "extends his familiar themes" or departs from them.

Everybody—academics, students, subject, author—smells of decayed roses in Mark Harris's "Saul Bellow at Purdue" (*GaR* 32:715–54), a mock-serious, quasi-confessional account of a 1970 visit which, even with generous samples from the visitor's remarks, becomes little more than an extended hate bouquet. Jerome Klinkowitz's "Words of Humor" (*WQ* 2:126–32) also takes as its point of departure a visit of the novelist to a midwestern campus, but this piece is both more genial and informative. Klinkowitz traces Bellow's response to scheduling difficulties and gaffes to a comedy of survival common to not only Jewish-American writers but also Updike, Heller, and others.

In *Saul Bellow: A Reference Guide* (Hall), Robert G. Noreen admirably annotates a checklist of writing about the novelist from 1944 through 1976 (foreign scholarship is "representative rather than exhaustive"). In his brief survey of critical trends, Noreen comments on the sparse substantive criticism of Bellow's short stories and plays. It is not his place, of course, to note that *substantive* criticism of Bellow generally is now thinning down to repetition and recapitulation.

Most of the work on Malamud this year appears in a special number of *SAJL* (4,i). Steven J. Rubin's contribution, "Malamud and the Theme of Love and Sex" (pp. 19–23), which continues and generalizes his observations in a note, "Malamud's Fidelman: Innocence and Optimism Abroad" (*NConL* 8,i:2–3), argues that Malamud's search for love is more hopeful than similar searches in Bellow and Roth and that his depiction of sex is less tinged with guilt and anxiety. In emphasizing the physicality of the fiction in "The Malamudian World: Method and Meaning" (pp. 2–12), Herbert Mann also discusses the recurring motifs relating to "connections." *Rembrandt's Hat* is the focus of "Insistent Assistance: The Stories of Bernard Malamud" (pp. 12–18) by Irving Saposnik, who sees the writer as a kind of verbal Chagall who transforms commonplace reality into significance; the form of the later stories, however, is a comment on the lack of human contact: "stories relate where humans cannot."

In "A Reinterpretation of Malamud's *The Natural*" (pp. 24–32), Marcia Gealy suggests that despite its being the novelist's only work without Jewish characters, *The Natural* as a Grail quest is a story of failure; but read in light of Hasidism, Roy Hobbs becomes a true schlemiel whose suffering earns him dignity. Marjorie Smelstor's argument in "The Schlemiel as Father: A Study of Yakov Bok and Eugene Henderson" (pp. 50–57) is that Malamud's and Bellow's protagonists are both schlemiels who, in conquering their fear of fathering and being fathered, learn that "paternity is a costly gift, the gift of self." While self-explanatory, Ita Sheres's "The Alienated Sufferer: Malamud's Novels from the Perspective of Old Testament and Jewish Mystical Thought" (pp. 68–78) suffers from a brevity disproportionate to its ambitious subject. In "Names and Stereotypes in Malamud's *The Tenants*" (pp. 57–68), David R. Mesher depicts Willie and Lesser as doubles and the author as the artist-landlord who is "unable to control his creation."

David Kerner, in "A Note on the Source of 'The Magic Barrel'" (pp. 32–35) offers a Yiddish folk story as "demonstrably" the source of Malamud's most famous story, but Laura Krugman Ray reads the story as an adaptation of *Great Expectations* in "Dickens and 'The Magic Barrel'" (pp. 35–40). Leslie Field discusses the periodical publications of *Dubin's Lives* in "Malamud-Dubin's Discontent" (pp. 77–78). Robert D. Habich's "Bernard Malamud: A Bibliographic Survey" (pp. 78–84) is a discursive piece which reminds us that in the midst of considerable critical interest in Malamud, he has yet to be the subject of scholarly work (no textual studes, no collected edition of letters or papers).

Fresh from his bibliographic work on Roth (*ALS 1974*, p. 300), Bernard F. Rodgers, Jr., has turned to critical analysis and evaluation in *Philip Roth* (TUSAS 318), the first substantive study to deemphasize Roth's Jewish-Americanism. Rodgers delineates three phases in the novelist's development: the first incorporating the fiction written before 1966, the second covering the period between *Portnoy's Complaint* and *The Great American Novel*, and the final one on the work since the baseball novel. Using "the interpenetration of reality and fantasy in the lives of representative Americans" as the unifying thread which supplies a "developmental logic" to the entire career, Rodgers explores Roth's literary continuities with Fitzgerald, James, Dreiser, the 19th-century American humorists, Chekhov, and Kafka. Individual readings are superb. *Letting Go*, though Dreiserian in its emphasis on environmental determinism and chance, betrays as well Jamesian psychological realism; *When She Was Good* ("his forgotten novel") uses women's magazine romance to challenge predispositions and to alter perceptions by focusing on ideas "imbedded deep within the American psyche." This volume is a solid achievement.

Rodgers's belief that Roth's work constitutes modulations on a fiction that is essentially realistic is confirmed by Alice R. Kaminsky, who in "Philip Roth's Professor Kepesh and the 'Reality Principle'" (*UDQ* 13,ii:41–54) discriminates between the techniques of "fantastic" (*The Breast*) and "icastic" imitation (*The Professor of Desire*), two divergent but complementary types of mimesis. It is possible, says Kaminsky, to view Kepesh "as a kind of *apologia pro sua* Portnoy." As befitting his title, "The Comic Anatomy of *Portnoy's Complaint*" (*Comic Relief*, pp. 152–71), Sheldon Grebstein explores Roth's most controversial novel with a keen eye for traditions and influences as well as its formal and linguistic properties. Though he finds in the novel traces of popular comedians no longer limited to Jewish audiences (Sid Caesar, Woody Allen), the most fascinating segment in this fine essay is Grebstein's account of a "line of succession" from Old Southwestern humorists and Mark Twain, which includes an unpromising but thoroughly persuasive comparison of Roth with the Sinclair Lewis of *The Man Who Knew Coolidge*.

v. Thomas Pynchon

"Criticism serves no useful purpose," says William M. Plater, "in burdening art with implications beyond its own pretensions," and Pynchon, though dazzling and esoteric, "never strays from fundamental conditions and ordinary themes." Thus with commendable common sense and discriminating clarity, *The Grim Phoenix: Reconstructing Thomas Pynchon* (Indiana) manages to demystify the Pynchonists without minimizing Pynchon. Four central chapters deal with the closed system, landscape, death and its transfiguring modes, and paranoia. If amid the conspiracies and plots of antilife, paranoia can be termed an aesthetic "form of life," the three novels which celebrate it are "local enclaves of organization taken from the chaos of infinite possibilities." In the single most spectacular segment Plater connects travel, travelers, and tours to the solipsistic journeys of Pynchon's protagonists. *The Grim Phoenix* is a useful, even necessary, book.

In a substantial introduction to his *Pynchon: A Collection of Critical Essays* (Prentice-Hall), Edward Mendelson also cuts through much of the cultist sludge while simultaneously affirming his high regard for this "greatest living writer in the English-speaking world." He brilliantly contrasts Pynchon with Joyce, isolating *Gravity's Rainbow* as a "national encyclopedic narrative" which, unlike *Ulysses,* leaves behind the ethical and linguistic bases of the Romantic aesthetic and its extension in Modernism. Mendelson's volume contains previously published criticism by Tony Tanner, Joseph W. Slade, Robert Sklar, Frank Kermode, and others and prints for the first time two essays, James Nohrnberg's "Pynchon's Paraclete" and Michael Seidel's "The Satiric Plots of *Gravity's Rainbow*." The first finds Marian analogues in the "calamitous annunciation" of Tristero to Oedipa in *The Crying of Lot 49*; the second touches on some of the formal inversions common to narrative satire in the third novel, especially the series of subverting strategies which "hatches plots against the book's own characters." If Nohrnberg finds the unresolved moment of *Lot 49* appropriate to the modal force of both testaments and apocrypha, Seidel believes the apparent end of "an entire paranoid civilization" in the third novel is modified in part by Pynchon's carefully timed love interludes and the Christmas vespers scene.

"Creative" is Mark Richard Siegel's operative word in *Pynchon: Creative Paranoia in "Gravity's Rainbow"* (Kennikat), an expansion of an earlier article (*ALS 1977*, p. 316); if Pynchon's third novel has often been read too ironically (thereby making it nihilistic), Siegel finds it a novel of "possibility" closer to the *engagé* existentialist novel than to absurdist fiction. Most readers will find the chapters on point of view and "socio-cultural metaphors" the most pertinent in the book. Of no pertinence whatever is "Thomas Pynchon and Western Man" (*Vulnerable People*, pp. 191–209) in which Josephine Hendin asks: "What happened to Pynchon between *V.*, the wildly sophisticated survival manual, and *Gravity's Rainbow*, the brilliant analysis of how you died?" If "Pynchon does not say," neither does Hendin, despite a two-paragraph attempt (unusual in this book) to talk critically about structure and pattern in the work of this "mournful genius." Mostly we get pithy observations useful only for cocktail parties: "Pynchon's most eloquent moral is himself" and "He plays Beethoven to Rilke's Schubert."

By locating the ideology of satire in pleasure rather than correction, Alfred Mac Adam makes Pynchon a latter-day disciple of Petronius, Apuleius, and Voltaire. In "Pynchon as Satirist: To Write, to Mean" (*YR* 67:555–66) Mac Adam suggests that the novelist's "*mise en scène* may be the only reason for calling his books novels," since his archeological precision in setting makes his readers comfortable; but his real interest is "the clash of personified ideas sur-

rounded by the things" of the 20th century. By making a mockery
of literary realism Pynchon directs our attention to the mind as
creator of unreal systems.

Mac Adam's point is reinforced by Richard C. Carpenter in
"State of Mind: The California Setting of *The Crying of Lot 49*"
(*California Writers*, pp. 105–13). The symbolic, generic, and archetypal quality of San Narciso, a setting marked by undifferentiation
and replicability, reflects the Menippean "arena of the mind" rather
than actual topography. In "Puritans, Literary Critics, and Thomas
Pynchon's *The Crying of Lot 49*" (*NConL* 8,ii:8–9), C. S. Pearson
warns that intellectual sleuthing will not reveal the truth that Oedipa
discovers; rational analysis must be accompanied by incarnational
insights.

Despite the title of his long and self-indulgent essay, "The Reader of Movies: Thomas Pynchon's *Gravity's Rainbow*" (*UDQ* 12,i
[1977]:1–46), Bertram Lippman stresses "verbal fetishism" in a
novel that is more "blueprinted" than plotted; and if science, sex,
myths, and fables are great resources for Pynchon, so is the *OED*.
In " 'Sacrificial Ape': King Kong and His Antitypes in *Gravity's Rainbow*" (*L&P* 28:112–18), David Cowart finds the old film's "racism
of the unconscious" relevant to Slothrop, whose fate beyond his
scapegoat role suggests the psychosexuality of racism. In "Cinematic
Auguries of the Third Reich in *Gravity's Rainbow*" (*LFQ* 6:364–
70), Cowart also perceives Pynchon's use of Fritz Lang's *Metropolis*
to reflect the cultural-psychological dispositions of Pökler. In "Beyond the Theater of War: *Gravity's Rainbow* as Film" (*LFQ* 6:347–
63), Scott Simmon argues that Pynchon's subject is the *theater* of
war because his book is studded with allusions to Hollywood genre
films of the 1930s and early 1940s and to German expressionist films
of the 1920s—all of which reflect patterns of technological control
by "directors and producers."

vi. John Updike and Joyce Carol Oates

Josephine Hendin (*Vulnerable People*, pp. 87–115) believes Updike's strength is directly related to his major "subject"—exposing
the myth of male freedom in a society structured by women; but in
the most substantial piece on Updike this year, "John Updike and
the Changing of the Gods" (*Mosaic* 12,i:157–75), Victor Strandberg

finds a more intricate pattern which unifies the disparate work: trauma occasioned by horror of death. The responses of the protagonists are varied: some resist through Christianity, some through eros, and others through art and metaphysical intuition.

In "Updike's Pilgrims in a World of Nothingness" (*Thought* 53: 384–400), George W. Hunt argues that religion in Updike's work goes beyond the moral level of debate (what is "right" or "wrong") to the ontological, a more radical level which can be seen in the "dialogic and dialectical" movement in the narrative. Both Christian and Jungian archetypes inform Hunt's reading in a better piece, "Updike's Omega-Shaped Shelter: Structure and Psyche in *A Month of Sundays*" (*Critique* 19,iii:47–60). Marshfield's omega-shaped motel reflects the circuitous movement of the diary, and while Hunt sees this 1975 novel incorporating earlier themes, he points out how Updike borrows some of the self-conscious techniques of Barth and Hawkes.

Contending that an "intextual shuttle" modifies the separate meanings of both *Rabbit, Run* and *Rabbit Redux*, Yves Le Pellec, in "Rabbit Underground" (*Les Américanistes*, pp. 94–109), shows how Updike varies the character of Angstrom through spatial metaphors, a device which especially illuminates Rabbit's "departures" in the first novel and the "trespassing" of his house in the second. In "Salvation by Death in *Rabbit, Run*" (*NConL* 8,ii:7–8), Wayne D. McGinnis argues that Rabbit's final beatitude is a kind of death, an Eastern grace whose direction is toward "the state of utterly free existence"; and in "Plato's 'Allegory of the Cave' in *Rabbit, Run*" (*NMAL* 2,ii:Item 15), James Ellis observes that Plato is as important as Kierkegaard in the design of this novel.

We now have by Joyce Carol Oates a body of fiction from a decade of war, assassination, riots, and malaise which not merely chronicles these events but sensitizes ordinary people to "the mystery and the sanctity of the human predicament." This crucial concept is the base of Mary Kathryn Grant's *The Tragic Vision of Joyce Carol Oates* (Duke), the strengths of which are not so much its critical insights, though they are both plausible and persuasive, but its accounting for Oates's literary links. Grant places her subject midway between the nonfictional literalists (Warhol and Capote) and the fabulators (Hawkes, Barth); she also finds connections with D. H. Lawrence, especially his fight against human debasement by an industrial society, and Flannery O'Connor, especially her treatment of violence as a means of transforming individual lives. Concentrating on three related themes—woman, the city, and the community—Grant advances what she sees as Oates's overarching theme: "human life is an inescapable tragedy which, unless and until it is so recognized, can never be transcended."

Joanne V. Creighton would agree with Grant that Oates is most successful when she is most conventional, as in her "scalpel-like control" in such stories as "In the Region of Ice" and "Where Are You Going, Where Have You Been?" "Joyce Carol Oates's Craftmanship in *The Wheel of Love*" (*SSF* 15:375–84) is the first of two pieces in which Creighton investigates the relationship of sexual love and the problem of selflessness in Oates's heroines. "Unliberated Women in Joyce Carol Oates's Fiction" (*WLWE* 17:165–75) studies the mothers and daughters who, in the midst of masculine violence, seek protection from emotion in passive withdrawal. Though few characters of either sex are ever liberated, Elena of *Do With Me What You Will* is "awakened to selfhood through love," which shows that even vacuous and immobile women can achieve "zestful independence."

Sanford Pinsker's "Joyce Carol Oates's *Wonderland*: A Hungering for Personality" (*Crit* 20,ii:59–70) is essentially a straightforward reading of a novel which the author herself has partly repudiated, perhaps because she as well as Pinsker now sees it merely as an "extended exercise in brooding." David Leon Higdon compares the differences in two versions of this novel in " 'Suitable Conclusions': The Two Endings of Oates's *Wonderland*" (*SNNTS* 10: 447–53). By focusing on the question of "inevitable" closure stemming from the tension between "fate" and "self," Higdon concludes that the revised ending tilts toward "self," and therefore suggests the possibility of change.

In "Existential Allegory: Joyce Carol Oates's 'Where Are You Going, Where Have You Been?'" (*SSF* 15:200–03), Marie Urbanski theorizes that Oates's most anthologized story is the biblical seduction myth updated by "existential initiation rites" to represent "*Everyman*'s transition from the illusion of free will to the realization of externally determined fate." Unpredictable forces, determinism, and entrapment are even more dominant in the fiction since *The Wheel of Love*, according to G. F. Waller in "Through Obsession to Transcendence: The Recent Work of Joyce Carol Oates"

(*WLWE* 17:176–80), and the apocalyptic strain in *The Assassins* and *Childwold* suggests that the novelist is moving close to the Eastern doctrine in which negation becomes the means of overcoming the self's egocentricity.

vii. John Barth, John Hawkes, Thomas Berger

Although the differences between the original (1956) and revised (1967) versions of *The Floating Opera* are widely known, Sherry Lutz Zivley has assembled all the relevant evidence—and more—in "A Collation of John Barth's *Floating Opera*" (*PBSA* 72:201–12), which should be read by every teacher of this novel. Zivley notes Barth's numerous revisions between the holograph and the first typescript and his revisions, beyond the changed ending, for the second edition, finding that they reflect not only efforts to appease the publishers but also opportunities which Barth took to mark his sense of his own novelistic development.

In "Fictions for Survival" (*Vulnerable People*, pp. 73–86), Josephine Hendin calls Barth "the grammarian of emotion" because of his virtuoso manipulation of voices proclaiming man as a fabricated thing, "a movable objet d'art"; but Linda A. Westervelt finds this "tangle of voices" the occasion for analysis rather than casual observation in "Teller, Tale, Told: Relationships in John Barth's Latest Fiction" (*JNT* 8:42–55). With his manipulation of first-person narrators in *Lost in the Funhouse* and *Chimera*, Barth creates personas who "rage about the inadequacies of their medium and prophesy the impending doom of story and civilization" while exploiting medium and conventions within their stories; thus the breakdown in love relationships is paralleled by the breakdown in language.

Strother Purdy (*The Hole in the Fabric*, pp. 182–97) finds Barth's "best book," *The End of the Road*, an "encapsulation of *nada*," illustrated by Jake's moral catatonia and repeated references to wordless lovemaking. Kenneth A. Thigpen offers little that has not been covered in previous studies in "Folkloristic Concerns in Barth's *The Sot-Weed Factor*" (*SFQ* 41:225–37), but he specifies some of the structural borrowings from folk narratives as they appear in various subplots.

The transcript of a 1976 conference, edited by Anthony C. Santore and Michael Pocalyko, is now available in an unattractive format as *A John Hawkes Symposium: Design and Debris* (New Directions, 1977). Albert J. Guerard shows up to engage in a dialogue with the novelist; John Graham discusses *The Cannibal* as a "revolutionary polemic"; a nicely wrought piece by Frederick Busch focuses on the connection between Hemingway and Hawkes and their mutual problem of self-influence. Other contributors include Marcus Klein, Enid Veron, Robert Steiner, Nancy Levine, and Donald J. Greiner, whose "Private Apocalypse: The Visions of *Travesty*" is one of the two new chapters appearing in the second edition of his *Comic Terror: The Novels of John Hawkes* (see *ALS 1974*, pp. 302–03). Greiner sees *Travesty* as the final volume in a trilogy. The guilt-free Papa, obsessed with "the harmony of paradox," is on a quest simultaneously for timelessness and cessation; though the narratives becomes progressively more lucid, the entire trilogy is a movement away from everyday reality toward death.

"*The Blood Oranges* as a Visionary Fiction" (*JNT* 8:97–111) is Steven Abrams's serious look at the narrative primarily through Hugh's death and the reader's too-easy moral judgment of the *menage à quatre*. An inadequate rendering of authorial stance is closely related to the "almost" omniscient Cyril, a technique which provides a correct view of the action while we are apparently "embroiled in the unsoundness of his own personality."

With a curious insistence upon the most general summary, Robert Scholes pays homage to "John Hawkes as Novelist: The Example of the Owl" (*HC* 14,iii[1977]:1–10). The surreal depiction of fascism in *The Owl* is morally and aesthetically justified because it destroys certain surface plausibilities in order to liberate realities that are "habitually concealed by habits of vision attuned only to the surface itself." In "Genesis and Functions of Hencher in 'The Lime Twig'" (*Les Américanistes*, pp. 138–55), Pierre Gault concludes that Michael and Margaret are "protagonists and eventually the victims of a very artificial plot, which is nothing but the projection of Hencher's dreams."

The freshest and most exciting segments of Stanley Trachtenberg's "Berger and Barth: The Comedy of Decomposition" (*Comic Relief*, pp. 45–69) deal with Thomas Berger's comic strategies involving a fragmented self. Trachtenberg argues that unlike traditional comedy, whose reassurance issues from "a vision of wholeness as a sanative norm," comedy in contemporary fiction dramatizes possibilities for "getting along with fragments." The characters in *Little Big Man* are reduced to "shadow projections" of myths and doubles, and the comedy of *Vital Parts* comes from the resilience of both the social self and its shadow.

In an equally rich essay, "Aspects of the American Picaresque in *Little Big Man*" (*Les Américanistes*, pp. 37–52), Daniel Royot traces in Berger's most famous novel its developing emblematic quality, from black humor to horror and solemnity, in light of the picaresque. The apocalyptic climax of Jack Crabb's "journey through myths" closes the "cycle of the Western Saga, floundering in grim absurdity." Along the way Royot pokes fun at French readers who cannot be satisfied that American social criticism is often transmuted into "either madcap fantasies or provocative exhibitionism."

viii. Kurt Vonnegut, Joseph Heller, John Gardner

Vonnegut is the hero of "the American male under siege" because he has transformed the pitiable ground-down man into "an unmistakable *model* of masculinity." To prove her slightly skewed thesis, Josephine Hendin (*Vulnerable People*, pp. 29–51) concentrates on *Slaughterhouse-Five*; most readers will find two other studies more useful.

John W. Tilton reminds us (*Cosmic Satire*, pp. 69–103) that Billy Pilgrim's vision is not authorially endorsed. By chronological dating, he shows that Vonnegut dramatizes the distance between his protagonist, whose escape to Tralfamadore in 1967 denies responsibilities to "wakeful humanity," and the author himself, whose flight to Dresden the same year becomes "an act of human responsibility." In a complementary essay, Robert Merrill and Peter A. Scholl respond to Lynn Buck's version of the cynicism and nihilism of this novel (see *ALS 1975*, p. 346) with "Vonnegut's *Slaughterhouse-Five*: The Requirements of Chais" (*SAF* 6:65–76). Although the Tralfamadorians' advice may please the not-very-bright Billy, Vonnegut himself projects a vision not of comic futility but of redeemable man.

It may be true that the novelist desires to create self-awareness on a new basis, but it is unlikely that a patronizing attitude toward his readers as quasi-children, "neophytes" in need of enlightenment, can restore "imaginative consciousness" in quite the way traced by John M. McInerney in "Children for Vonnegut" (*NMAL* 3,i:Item 4). Philip M. Rubens notes the double entendres and allusions in "Names in Vonnegut's *Cat Cradle*" (*NConL* 8,i:7), but a more useful note is "The Ambiguities of Bokononism" (*IEY* 26,vii[1977]:21–23, in which Wayne D. McGinnis argues that the mock religion of *Cat's Cradle*, founded on Johan Huizinga's sense of play, reflects the creative-destructive impulse of all human endeavor, including the new fictionists' emphasis on the value of artifice as artifice.

In "The Rhetorical Structure of *Catch-22*" (*NConL* 8,iii:9–10), Robert Merrill analyzes the Soldier in White episode and its successive variations as a satiric way of forcing the readers into a realization of their own responsibility for the horrors anterior to World War II. Susan Strehle Klemtner argues that unlike Yossarian of *Catch-22*, Bob Slocum maintains a deterministic belief in man as a helpless pawn in "'A Permanent Game of Excuses': Determinism in Heller's *Something Happened*" (*MFS* 24:550–56); but as Slocum tries to justify his failures and mediocrity, his creator destroys such a vision, thereby making his second novel a more subtle exploration of freedom and fate than *Catch-22*.

An obvious but needed essay for a generation ignorant of Old English, "John Gardner's *Grendel*: Sources and Analogues" (*ConL* 19:48–57) by Joseph Milosh, points out the liberties taken by the novelist in restructuring *Beowulf* and in more substantive shifts: humanizing the monster, injecting an antiwar theme, and downgrading the role of the *scop*. Picking up an ambiguous clue from Gardner, Craig J. Stromme in "The Twelve Chapters of *Grendel*" (*Crit* 20,i:83–92) examines the "philosophical center" of each chapter in a novel whose central concerns are "philosophical ways of living in the world." Since Grendel begins with solipsism and ends with empiricism, Stromme believes that the work can be read as "a complete history of man's progress."

In "*Nickel Mountain*: John Gardner's Testament of Redemption" (*Renascence* 30:59–68), Marilyn Arnold argues that, unlike O'Connor, whose doctrine demands that only Christ is redeemer, Gardner elevates human models of goodness to suggest their redemptive power. Unlike most examples of the genre, Marshall L. Harvey's "Where Philosophy and Fiction Meet: An Interview with John

Gardner" (*ChiR* 29,iv:73–87) has a focus: the novelist's comments on those philosophers he admires, the moral "effects" of good creative work, and the philosophical questions he deals with in his novels.

ix. William Styron, Walker Percy, and Other Southerners

Concentrating on structural design, language, and style, William J. Scheick gives a finely argued reading of Styron's first novel in "Discarded Watermelon Rinds: The Rainbow Aesthetic of Styron's *Lie Down in Darkness*" (*MFS* 24:247–54); he sees images of art, religion, and alcoholism interwoven to suggest a modern holocaust.

Despite its subtitle, old ground is being plowed again in "History as Self-Serving Myth: Another Look at Styron's *The Confessions of Nat Turner*" (*CLAJ* 22:134–46) by Harry D. Amis, who proposes that the direction and significance of this "meditation on history" stem from Styron's use of three basic (but unparallel) myths: the plantation tradition, southern femininity, and the black man as "impossible hero"; the acceptance of them led the novelist into assigning his own moral and ethical values to "another people's hero." Denise T. Askin, in "The Half-Loaf of Learning: A Theme in Styron's *The Confessions of Nat Turner*" (*NMAL* 3,i:Item 6), notes that Nat's being disturbed by the white man's pity and love rather than his abuse and hatred has its source in an incomplete education. In "*The Confessions of Nat Turner*: Styron's 'Meditation on History' as Rhetorical Act" (*QJS* 64:246–66), Mary S. Strine examines the sociopsychological circumstances of violence, their political implications for liberal humanism, and the novelist's use of "a public communicative genre" as a critique of "the intrapersonal consequences of violence as a strategy of social reform": a rather more extravagant accomplishment than most readers are willing to grant.

In the wake of last year's masterful bibliography by James L. W. West, III (*ALS 1977*, p. 330) come two complementary volumes of secondary checklists. *William Styron: A Reference Guide* (Hall) by Jackson Bryer with Mary Beth Hatem contains succinctly and judiciously annotated items from 1946 through 1978 in a chronological format. A brief introduction charts the curve of scholarship (and invective) occasioned by Styron's works. Unlike Bryer and Hatem,

Philip W. Leon, the compiler of *William Styron: An Annotated Bibliography of Criticism* (Greenwood), includes a checklist of Styron's works and omits annotation of reviews; divides his book into bibliographies, books and dissertations, chapters and "references" to Styron in books and critical essays; and invents a category ("Non-Literary References to Styron in *The New York Times*") to show that the author "does not shrink from controversy." The annotations are peremptory and promotional.

Walker Percy: An American Search (Little, Brown) is Robert Coles's graceful homage to the doctor-novelist who affected Coles's earlier training and the last two volumes of his *Children of Crisis*. Like most other critics, this one takes seriously the philosophical relationship between Percy's essays and the fiction; but, unlike most, his prose is clear, almost informally chatty. At once a biography and literary study, this book contains few new critical insights, but a single chapter, the epilogue, focuses more attention on how a particular writer works than most transcribed interviews.

Simone Vauthier applies the modified structuralist approach which worked so well with *All the King's Men* (see *ALS 1974*, p. 273) to Percy's most famous novel in "Narrative Triangle and Triple Alliance: A Look at *The Moviegoer*" (*Les Américanistes*, pp. 71–93): the dynamic relationship among "narrator, narratee, and narration." Especially perceptive in locating the blurred distinction of the inner dialogues between narrator and author, Vauthier argues that Percy's tensions deliberately keep the reader alternating between identification with and rejection of Binx Bolling. "Walker Percy's Language of Creation" (*SoQ* 16:105–16) concentrates on the "linguistic dysfunction" affecting so many of Percy's characters, which J. P. Telotte interprets as a metaphysical as well as a physiological problem. In "Walker Percy's *Lancelot*: Secular Raving and Religious Silence" (*SoR* 14:186–94), Robert D. Daniel says that the madness of Lancelot is double-edged: we sympathize with his attack on devalued language used to excuse sexual casualness though we are also suspicious of his clinical temperament. The book is a chronicle of "the failure of contemporary religion just as much as it is a satire on secularism."

Richard Finholt's segment on James Dickey (*American Visionary Fiction*, pp. 128–43) suggests that *Deliverance* borrows from the Homeric epic the indifference of the cosmos and the use of archery, that ancient sport which dramatizes the struggle "of mind to master matter and of will to master fear." For Linda Wagner, however, the novel is less an epic than "a *Pilgrim's Progress* of male egoism," whose resolution is far different from its characters' expectations. "*Deliverance*: Initiation and Possibility" (*SCR* 10,ii:49–55) is a serene account of what Gentry and Medlock learn through their "descent into hell," and Wagner's analysis of color imagery and the thematic recapitulations of Huck Finn is both perceptive and economical. Like Wagner, Linda Tarte Holley stresses the importance of the Before-and-After frame in "Design and Focus in James Dickey's *Deliverance*" (*SCR* 10,ii:90–98) and concludes that imagination, not methodical cunning, brings deliverance, which is an aloneness that "gives meaning and harmony to disparate matter." In "Learning the Hard Way in James Dickey's *Deliverance*" (*WAL* 12:289–301), Don Kunz studies the brief appearances of two female characters and the special imagery associated with both to show that Dickey deliberately sends his immature male characters to the wilderness "in order to liberate them from the captivating power of their conventional masculine fantasy."

An overview begins "A View of Peter Taylor's Stories" (*VQR* 54:213–30) by Jane Barnes Casey, who succinctly summarizes the thrust of his work as "the conflict between affectionate, civil society and chaos" before moving on to consider the ways in which Taylor's characteristic themes evolved into *In the Miro District*. In "Identity and the Wider Eros: A Reading of Peter Taylor's Stories" (*Shenandoah* 30,i:71–84), Alan Williamson also provides a wider range than we usually see in work on Taylor, but his concentration is on the stories which emphasize the problem of "identity and interidentity" and the "mystical oneness or transcendent love." Two notes on individual stories are Barbara B. Sims's "Symbol and Theme in Peter Taylor's 'A Wife of Nashville'" (*NMAL* 2,iii:Item 22) and Jan Pinkerton's "The Vagaries of Taste and Peter Taylor's 'A Spinster's Tale'" (*KanQ* 9,ii[1977]:81–85).

In "On Women and His Own Work: An Interview with Reynolds Price" (*SoR* 14:706–25), conducted by Constance Rooke, we get bright answers to intelligent questions. Price sees his books, among other things, as "an elaborate dialogue with the whole notion of free will and freedom, free will and compulsion," and feels his affinities with Racine and Tolstoy. A substantial segment is devoted to *The Surface of Earth*.

x. Wright Morris, N. Scott Momaday, and Other Westerners

Together with *Conversations with Wright Morris* (*ALS 1977*, p. 332), G. B. Crump's *The Novels of Wright Morris: A Critical Interpretation* (Nebraska) should help to correct the unjust neglect of a novelist who after 30 years and 25 volumes is still active. Crump astutely distinguishes two broad currents in Morris's art—its tentativeness (reflecting a belief in truth as a product of process) and its exploration of the tension between time and timelessness, not merely in the nostalgia of his midwestern novels but in all his fiction. Like most previous critics, Crump pays proper attention to the remarkable books of the 1950s (including *The Works of Love* and *The Field of Vision*), but he is most imaginative in his fine readings of *One Day* and *In Orbit*—the first which is Morris's thematic and structural tour de force, the latter which is a stylistic one. While he carefully cites literary influences (James, Lawrence, Mark Twain, Fitzgerald), Crump recognizes the novelist's originality. His book will be judicious and helpful even for that handful of seasoned Morris specialists.

The problem which Charles R. Larson sets for himself in *American Indian Fiction* (New Mex.) is to evaluate "the relationship between cultural background and aesthetic temperament" in 16 novels by such writers as N. Scott Momaday, D'Arcy McNichle, Dallas Chief Eagle, and Denton Bedford. After a knotty and not always convincing explanation of his methodology, Larson devotes two chapters to fiction prior to the mid-20th-century, characterized by an assimilationist impulse, and the rest to more recent fiction which, though diverse, depicts sympathetically the "changed attitude toward life on the reservation."

An "almost flawless novel" is Larson's estimate of James Welch's *Winter in the Blood*, one of the works discussed also in "Endings in Contemporary American Indian Fiction" (*WAL* 13:133–39) by David B. Espey, whose thesis is that the Indian concepts of time and death affect the structure of their fiction. Welch's novel is also the subject of two other pieces: William F. Smith's "*Winter in the*

Blood: The Indian Cowboy as Everyman" (*MichA* 10:299–306) and Don Kunz's "Lost in the Distance of Winter: James Welch's *Winter in the Blood*" (*Crit* 20,i:93–99). The latter's omission of any context damages its usefulness for those not already intimately familiar with the protagonist's problems. Smith argues that Welch merges white and Indian cultures, primarily by varying a search for personal salvation based loosely on the detective story.

In "The Art and Importance of N. Scott Momaday" (*SoR* 14: 30–45), Roger Dickinson-Brown finds *House Made of Dawn* "a memorable failure," citing its patches of awkward dialogue, affected description, false parallelisms, and evasive resolution; only its "intensely sensory and symbolic" landscapes are rendered successfully. He finds the associational structure of *The Way to Rainy Mountain* better controlled with more coherent symmetries. Baine Kerr, in "The Novel as Sacred Text: N. Scott Momaday's Myth-Making Ethic" (*SWR* 63:172–79), also itemizes the flaws of *House Made of Dawn*, but he senses that the seeming aesthetic lapses spring from within Indian experience, in which image is often more important than "story or sense"; however, by mythifying Kiowa consciousness in an Anglo form, Momaday succeeds in preserving rather than abusing it.

And if Kerr thinks that the novel is a form alien to the Indian consciousness, William Bloodworth sees the autobiographical impulse just as alien, even in *The Way to Rainy Mountain*. "Neihardt, Momaday, and the Art of Indian Autobiography" (*Where the West Begins*, pp. 152–60) nevertheless demonstrates that Momaday's writing is a personal articulation of tribal matter and manner derived from the verbal tradition of his ancestors. Mick McAllister concentrates on the importance of memory as a structural device in "The Topology of Remembrance in *The Way to Rainy Mountain*" (*UDQ* 12,iv:19–31), a fine essay which delineates three systems of organization derived partly from a study of the book's illustrations by Al Momaday. Pam Doher studies the cultural concepts of the Cheyennes as the source of Mari Sandoz's metaphors and similes in "The Idioms and Figures of *Cheyenne Autumn*" (*Where the West Begins*, pp. 143–51).

Glen A. Love's *Don Berry* (WWS 35) is the first substantial account of the diversely talented author of *Trask* and *A Majority of Scoundrels*. This latter work, an informal history of fur-trade in the

Mountain West which posits heroic individualism against well-knit social and business forces, complements the themes of Berry's fictional trilogy in which such qualities as ingenuity and will are internalized.

The work of Frederick Manfred is the subject of several pieces. Peter Oppewall's "Manfred and Calvin College" (*Where the West Begins*, pp. 86–98) shows in literal transcriptions the closely autobiographical nature of *The Primitive* and the other novels in Manfred's trilogy, *World's Wanderer*. Robert C. Wright argues that the priority of natural bonds over isolation, a common theme in the later novels, is also consistently visible in the early ones as well; "The Myth of the Isolated Self in Manfred's Siouxland Novels" (*Where the West Begins*, pp. 110–18) is unfortunately cluttered by a gratuitous historical sketch tracing the fortunes of the self in society. Anthony Arthur shows how the famous story of a Missouri River hunter in the 1820s became the stuff of epic in John G. Neihardt's *Song of Hugh Glass* and Manfred's *Lord Grizzly* in "Manfred, Neihardt, and Hugh Glass: Variations on an American Epic" (*Where the West Begins*, pp. 99–109).

Dorey Schmidt's gathering of mostly ill-assorted pieces for *Larry McMurtry: Unredeemed Dreams, A Collection of Bibliography, Essays, and Interview* (Edinburg, Tex.: Pan American Univ.) is clear indication that more reflection is needed before this novelist's work can be evaluated. Contributors are Andrew Macdonald, Dwight Huber, Donald E. Fritz, Gina Macdonald, Izora Skinner, and Violette Metz; but the most valuable item is the interview in which McMurtry speaks of his screen-writing experiences and his ideas about fictional regionalists.

In "Myth and Paramyth in John R. Milton's *Notes to a Bald Buffalo*" (*Where the West Begins*, pp. 80–85) Paul N. Pavich uses Eugene Jolas to illuminate the function of formal fragmentation, topographical description, Sioux myths, and the mingling of the literal and surreal in Milton's novel. Using Aristotle's concept of tragedy, Don Graham, in "Tragedy and Western American Literature: The Example of Michael Straight's *A Very Small Remnant*" (*UDQ* 12,iv:59–66) attacks the loose application of the term to Western subjects but concludes that Straight's novel is the real thing.

Fred Erisman picks up the later career of the most famous Western novelist of the 1950s in "Jack Schaefer: The Writer as Ecologist" (*WAL* 13:3–13) to show how *An American Bestiary* delineates the complex interrelationship of man and nature but reminds us that the direction is anticipated in such earlier books as *Shane* and *Monte Walsh*. Larry McCaffery argues that in the span of over 20 years, four novels, and several short stories, William Eastlake has created his own mythical county in New Mexico, using a basic Anglo-Indian opposition of traits as a structural framework. In "Absurdity and Oppositions in William Eastlake's Southwestern Novels" (*Crit* 19,ii [1977]:62–76), McCaffery links this novelist's black humor, two-dimensional characterization, and verbal excesses to the innovative fictionists which he knows so well. Finally, Donald C. Stewart contends in "The Functions of Bird and Sky Imagery in Guthrie's *The Big Sky*" (*Crit* 19,ii[1977]:53–61) that A. B. Guthrie's most famous novel is also his finest, partly because of its coherence, which derives from "interlocking skeins of bird and sky images."

xi. Jerzy Kosinski, Robert Coover, and Other Innovators

Krystyna Prendowska in "Jerzy Kosinski: A Literature of Contortion" (*JNT* 8:11–25) finds that this nonjudgmental, morally permissive fiction lies in an area between European "emotional lucidity" and the "hip coolness" of the American Beat and hipster traditions. The essay is finally nonjudgmental itself in refusing to answer its own question, Is cruelty Kosinski's "only beauty"? Gail L. Mortimer's psychological reading, " 'Fear Death By Water': The Boundaries of the Self in Jerzy Kosinski's *The Painted Bird*" (*PsyR* 63[1976–77]: 511–28), concentrates on the protagonist's experiences as attempts to create a viable self-definition. Schizoid clues are the language of the narrator, dreams of destruction and mutilation, and symbols of engulfment.

To the commentary on a tangled bibliographical matter of this novel (see *ALS 1974*, p. 308; *ALS 1975*, p. 355) should be added "The Three States of the Text of Kosinski's *The Painted Bird*" (*PBSA* 72:361–84) by Philip R. Rider, who discriminates among three states: the corrupt first edition (Houghton Mifflin), the "restored" edition (Pocket Books and Bantam), and the revised edition (Modern Library). Daniel J. Cahill's "An Interview with Jerzy Kosinski on *Blind Date*" (*ConL* 19:133–42) is important because the novelist pays tribute to Jacques Monod, the Nobel Prize winner in physiology and medicine whose work on cells showed the novelist that "there is no plan in nature, that destiny is written concurrently with each event in life, not prior to it, and that to guard against this powerful feeling of destiny should be the source of our new morality."

In exploring "The Exemplary Fictions of Robert Coover" (*Les Américanistes*, pp. 130–37), Régis Durand finds them "implosive" —an art which turns back upon itself through mock-beginnings, self-conscious use of the reader, shifting centers of vision, sliding narrative syntax, and "multiple exposures" of scenes and images. In a pertinent extrapolation, Durand also suggests that because structuralist modes of criticism have been incorporated within the fictional apparatus of postmodernist writers, the secondary bibliography is in danger of becoming a "tautology," a prospect which should please both these critics and subjects.

Although his "The Great American Game: Robert Coover's *Baseball*" (*ELWIU* 5:103–18) suffers from a blurred focus, Ronald Wallace is perceptive in his reading of *The Universal Baseball Association*, which he sees at once as a parody of baseball history, a satire of materialist American society, and a comic exposure of Waugh's own "artistry." Because baseball is linked with sex and religion, Coover's novel turns out to be a "comic allegory of the Christian myth." In "Coover's *Universal Baseball Association*: Play as Personalized Myth" (*MFS* 24:209–22), Neil Berman emphasizes the internalization of "myth, art, and religion" in Waugh's protean imagination; against a world actively hostile to the essential elements of play (human joy, freedom, and creativity), the attitude of play fosters rituals celebrating "significant" rather than "real" time.

"Obscuring the Muse: The Mock-Autobiographies of Ronald Sukenick" (*Crit* 20,i:27–39) is a solid and imaginative piece by Timothy Dow Adams, who discusses the form of Sukenick's three novels, Raymond Federman's *Double or Nothing*, Gore Vidal's *Two Sisters*, and Frederick Exley's *A Fan's Notes* as a hybrid of autobiography and the new journalism which ultimately derives from Gertrude Stein. In "Way Out West: The Exploratory Fiction of 'Ronald Sukenick'" (*California Writers*, pp. 115–21), Alan Cheuse associates the negation of conventional narrative in *Out* to the novelist's move from the East Coast to Laguna Beach (signaled by progressive linguistic sparseness as the narrator moves further west) and contends that the energy of Sukenick's third novel, *98.6*, derives from the "fusion of insouciance and seriousness" of its California setting.

The first in-depth study of another innovative fictionist, "Don DeLillo's Search for Walden Pond" (*Crit* 20,i:5–24), is by Michael Oriard, who finds that, like William Gass and Coover, DeLillo uses language as both subject and theme, even when the ostensible plots are the psychic journeys of media executives or rock musicians. In "Little Hans and the Pedersen Kid" (*NConL* 8,i:4–5), Bruce Bassoff finds that Gass's most successful story uses one of Freud's famous case studies as a counterpoint to the plot.

In "Matters of Life and Death: The Novels of Harry Crews" (*Crit* 20,i:53–62), Allen Shepherd finds an "anti-Disney savagery" in Crews's southern tales. Despite his self-indulgent grotesqueries (funerals, dwarfs, animate vehicles), Crews has a formidable if uneven talent. The finest example is *Car*, the thematic coherence of which Shepherd examines briefly in "Cars in Harry Crews' *Car*" (*NConL* 8,i:8–9). This novel, along with Kosinski's *Being There* and Robert M. Pirsig's *Zen and the Art of Motorcycle Maintenance*, is the central exhibit in Nancy Corson Carter's "1970 Images of the Machine and the Garden: Kosinski, Crews, and Pirsig" (*Soundings* 61:105–22): all three authors suggest that neither machine nor nature alone can save us, "that somehow we must effect a mythic *and* realistic reconciliation of the two."

xii. Others

a. **Jewish-American Fictionists.** "Jewish Messianism and Elie Wiesel" (*NDEJ* 11:33–46), a plodding piece by Byron L. Sherwin, is marred by antipathy to Jewish authors who write merely out of their experiences and not also out of Judaism (such as Roth) and those who write neither out of Jewish experiences nor out of Judaism (such as West). Because he is pivotal to the three central events in contemporary Jewry—"the Holocaust, Israel, and Soviet Jewry"—Wiesel stands above all others as spectator and witness. In "Choosing

Life: An Interpretation of Elie Wiesel's *The Oath*" (*Soundings* 61: 67–86), Ted L. Estess concentrates on the protagonists who commit themselves to action despite the inadequacy of rationalistic solutions, but especially those in his most recent work who "have inherited the burden but not the mystery" of the Holocaust.

Jakov Lind's 1962 novel and Edward Wallant's 1961 novel are the subjects of Stephen Karpowitz's "Conscience and Cannibals: An Essay on Two Exemplary Tales—*Soul of Wood* and *The Pawnbroker*" (*PsyR* 64[1977]:41–62), in which the emphasis is on blood rites, totem meals, and the cultural absorption of psychological forms of human sacrifice. Lawrence I. Berkove ranks Hugh Nissenson with Cynthia Ozick and Arthur Cohen as American-Jewish writers concerned with "a renewed commitment to Judaism," and in "American *Midrashim*: Hugh Nissenson's Stories" (*Crit* 20,i:75–82) demonstrates that the texts in *A Pile of Stones* are evidence of such a commitment.

In his imaginative study, "The Jew as Underground/Confidence Man: I. B. Singer's *Enemies, a Love Story*" (*SNNTS* 10:397–410), a profile of militant characters who feel they must confront the world with expediency and trickery, Ben Siegel argues that Singer is more existential than psychological, highlighting universal absurdities by combining individual insight and collective protest. Richard Burgin offers two interviews: "From Conversations with Isaac Bashevis Singer" (*HudR* 31:621–30) and "A Conversation with Isaac Bashevis Singer" (*MQR* 17:119–32). In the first the novelist asserts that after 25 years he still sees death as "the only redemption" and free choice as "the greatest gift of humanity"; the second reveals much about Singer's childhood and suggests some of his influences. In Grace Farrell Lee's "Stewed Prunes and Rice Pudding: College Students Eat and Talk with I. B. Singer" (*ConL* 19:446–58) we get trivial answers to trivial questions, but we now know this writer's favorite Howard Johnson's ice cream (strawberry).

Jacqueline A. Mintz discusses "The Myth of the Jewish Mother in Three Jewish, American, Female Writers" (*CentR* 22:346–55) in an attempt to discriminate among the versions of this much-maligned figure in Anzia Yezierska, Tillie Olsen, and Susan Fromberg Schaeffer. Sarah Blacher Cohen finds that the Jewish protagonists of Lois Gould, Alix Kate Shulman, Sue Kaufman, and Sandra Hochman are no different from their gentile counterparts when they play the sexual game; in "The Jewish Literary Comediennes" (*Comic Relief*, pp. 172–86), Cohen sees exceptions in the work of Gail Parent, Erica Jong, and Cynthia Ozick.

b. **Popular and Science Fictionists.** Because of the enormous outpouring of work on these writers what follows is rigorously selective. The two most important books are *Mark Harris* (TUSAS 304), in which Norman Lavers engagingly stresses the personal element in this popular author, and *James Jones: A Friendship* (Doubleday) by Willie Morris, who, while admitting that his work is neither scholarship nor literary criticism, nevertheless lays the groundwork which will prove useful for future work on this friend 15 years his senior. Lavers is particularly perceptive in his discussion of Harris's first Henry Wiggen novel, *The Southpaw*, but he thinks the finest achievement is *Something About a Soldier*, largely because in it Harris was able to get out of the trap of semiliterate language. William J. Schafer's "Mark Harris: Versions of (American) Pastoral" (*Crit* 19,i[1977]:28–48) comprehensively surveys the tensions between pluralist and conformist patterns in American life which each of Harris's books explores.

Bruce Jay Friedman, Woody Allen, Ken Kesey, and others constitute Sanford Pinsker's illustrations of "The Urban Tall Tale: Frontier Humor in a Contemporary Key" (*Comic Relief*, pp. 249–62), a fine essay which shows how the exaggerations of the tall tale are now being used to emphasize the protagonist's ineptness and inferiority "instead of his swaggering confidence." Tom Robbins's work has been dubbed "bubblegum fiction" by Jerome Klinkowitz, but the very title of Robert L. Nadeau's "Physics and Cosmology in the Fiction of Tom Robbins" (*Crit* 20,i:63–74) indicates that some readers are taking this pop innovator seriously.

David Ketterer, while admitting that humor is a commodity in short supply in science fiction, perceptively describes and distinguishes the varieties that he does find in "Take-Off to Cosmic Irony: Science-Fiction Humor and the Absurd" (*Comic Relief*, pp. 70–86); many of them stem from a comic tradition going back at least to Poe. Jacques Favier, in "Space and Settor in Short Science Fiction" (*Les Américanistes*, pp. 182–201), discovers that the tendency toward both animism and anthropomorphism in science fiction stories since 1950 links them more with the traditional folktale than with mainstream short fiction.

Brian M. Stableford contributes two pieces: "Science Fiction and the Image of the Future" (*Foundation* 14:26–34) and "The Science Fiction of James Blish" (*Foundation* 13:12–43). The first traces "futuristic alternativity" from the playful, cavalier fiction of the 1930s to its seriousness after 1945, when with the newer millennial thinking and variations of salvation myths it became less predictive and more analytical. The second is a survey of the career of a second-generation pulp writer who did much to eliminate sloppy writing from science fiction. Brian W. Aldiss has a breezier piece, "James Blish: The Mathematics of Behavior" (*Foundation* 13:43–51), which also traces Blish from his origins in *Astounding Stories*.

In "Delany's *Babel-17*: The Powers of Language" (*Extrapolation* 19:132–37), Jane Weedman praises a 1966 novel by Samuel R. Delany which helped the genre to grow up, primarily because of the use of linguistics to connect the plot with the realities of black culture in the 1960s. David N. Samuelson examines two 1977 works which were products of years of "speculation on and contemplation of the alien mystique" in "From Aliens to Alienation: Gregory Benford's Variations on a Theme" (*Foundation* 14:5–19). "Patterns of Science Fiction Readership Among Academics" (*Extrapolation* 19: 112–25) is Joe DeBolt's summary of a survey of 401 faculty members, which has passing sociological interest.

c. **Miscellaneous.** The most important essay in this group is "From *U.S.A.* to *Ragtime*" (*AL* 50:85–105), in which Barbara Foley superbly demonstrates that Dos Passos's masterwork is not merely a peripheral influence on Doctorow's novel but a "crucial model" for its blending of fact and fiction. Also important is "Tangled in the Language of the Past: Ken Kesey and Cultural Revolution" (*MQ* 19:398–412), in which James F. Knapp parallels McMurphy's games against symbolic control in *One Flew Over the Cuckoo's Nest* and Kesey's own games with his Merry Pranksters; he concludes that in fiction, as in life, Kesey offered "mixed signals": his flirtation with a warrior-Christ as myth fluctuated between aggressive individualism and self-destroying brotherhood.

Paul John Eakin's "Alfred Kazin's Bridge to America" (*SAQ* 77:

39–53) is the first substantial investigation of a critic who insists upon being generalized as "a *writer*." The theme of the autobiographies is alienation, which Eakin finds alleviated in *A Walker in the City* by Kazin's identification with Whitman, the Roeblings (the father and son who built Brooklyn Bridge), and Hart Crane; the dramatic structure of *Starting Out in the Thirties* is provided by a "conflict between the redemptive and the deterministic conceptions of history."

Josephine Hendin lumps together as "Angries: S-M as a Literary Style" (*Vulnerable People*, pp. 53–71) Donald Barthelme, Truman Capote, John Hawkes, William Burroughs, and Hubert Selby (reading the last, she says, is "like being mugged"). Burroughs's fans will find more help in Eric Mottram's *William Burroughs: The Algebra of Need* (London: Marion Boyars, 1977), which investigates both the increasing virtuosity of the composition and the social criticism which informs all of the work. The first half of Mottram's book is a revision of earlier published work, but the entire book is valuable because its depends heavily on interviews and fiction in hard-to-find little magazines.

In his preface to *Peter De Vries: A Bibliography, 1934–1977* (Texas), Edwin T. Bowden laments the tendency among those writing on De Vries to stress the darker undercurrent of his work, as if his tradition—Max Beerbohm and James Thurber—were somehow not a respectable one. This handsome volume is divided into three sections (books, contributions to books, contributions to periodicals) and includes paperback reprints. A comparison of William Gaddis's two novels is the central interest in " 'For a Very Small Audience': The Fiction of William Gaddis" (*Crit* 19,iii:61–73) by Susan Strehle Klemtner, who finds *JR* more entropic in its implications than *The Recognitions*. John Stark's "William Gaddis: Just Recognition" (*HC* 14,i[1977]:1–12) is a straightforward exercise, with general interpretation and only a dollop of critical specifics.

William Goyen's remark that language is "a quality of vision" is the insight governing " 'Marvelous Reciprocity': The Fiction of William Goyen" (*Crit* 19,ii[1977]:77–91) by Jay S. Paul, who bases his assessment on the *Collected Stories* of 1975. In " 'So Distinct a Shade': Shirley Ann Grau's *Evidence of Love*" (*SoR* 14:195–98), a brief analysis of the author's fifth novel, Mary Rohrberger finds traces of contemporary fictional experiments in the way meaning issues as much from gaps and silences as from fictive voices. "Conversation with Shirley Ann Grau and James K. Feibleman" (*CimR* 43:35–45) is Rohrberger's transcription of an interview with the writer and her philosopher husband.

Dorothy H. Lee's "Harriette Arnow's *The Doll Maker*: A Journey to Awareness" (*Crit* 20,ii:92–98) concentrates on the depiction of an archetypal journey from a pastoral to an urban setting, which becomes "a literal and metaphorical descent" from Eden to Hell. It is unlikely that Wendy Martin's "The Satire and Moral Vision of Mary McCarthy" (*Comic Relief*, pp. 187–206), with its political grievances and its failure to discriminate among the author's good and bad fictions, will do much to stimulate readers to return to McCarthy. In "'Isadora Icarus': The Mythic Unity of Erica Jong's *Fear of Flying*" (*RUS* 64,i:89–100), Jane Chance Nitzsche uses the flying theme as a clue to support her interpretation of the novel as a reworking of the Daedalus myth. Susan E. Lorsch's "Gail Godwin's *The Odd Woman*: Literature and the Retreat from Life" (*Crit* 20,ii:21–32) is just as dreary as the title promises—this is the story of a female academic whose "difficulty" is trying to choose an outer life over "the life of the imagination."

Donald J. Greiner pays tribute to two recent novels in "After Great Pain: The Fiction of Frederick Busch" (*Crit* 19,i[1977]:101–11) for their mastery of familial frustration in a painful, precise, and poetic prose. Dennis M. Welch argues in "Death and Fun in the Novels of Thomas McGuane" (*UWR* 14,i:14–20) that this novelist's protagonists become so conscious of mortality that they become antic, choosing not to negate absurdity but to "play around and have fun" with life. Larry McCaffery offers "Thomas McGuane: A Bibliography, 1969–1978" (*BB* 35:169–71).

Indiana University

16. Poetry: 1900 to the 1930s

Richard Crowder

Again this year Frost and Stevens outnumber the other poets of our period in brief items. For example, *Expl* published five comments on Frost and one each on Stevens, Hart Crane, and Ransom; *NConL*, one each on Frost and Stevens; and *NMAL*, two on Stevens and one each on Frost and Sandburg. The number of dissertations came to thirty-one, two more than last year. *DAI* 38:7–12 and 39:1–6 lists Robinson, Cummings, Aiken, H. D., and Ransom as subjects of one dissertation each, either alone or with other writers. Tate, Marianne Moore, and Millay figure in two each. Frost and Crane are treated in four each and Stevens in twelve, seven of which discuss him alone. Looking back at random, I find eleven dissertations on Stevens in 1975 and ten in 1977. Is he not perhaps being overworked at the expense of other interesting figures of our period? Granted he is interesting and offers many challenges, but such proliferation of graduate studies on a single writer cannot escape repetition and monotony. Possibly students could avoid useless duplication if they would begin by reading relevant abstracts in *DAI* for the ten years preceding their own undertaking. Their advising professors might profit by doing the same. A dissertation should be more than a mere exercise in research and report: it should record a fresh approach and original insights, proof that the young researcher is worthy of and ready for admission into the already crowded field of mature scholarship (which, let us admit, is weedy enough with mediocrity).

i. Women Poets

Mention of Amy Lowell and H. D. generally suggests Imagism, but articles about them this year remind us of their other interests. *NEQ* 51:489–508 presents "'Fireworks': Amy Lowell and the *Atlantic Monthly*," by Ellery Sedgwick, III, a narrative account based on letters exchanged between Lowell and the first Ellery Sedgwick, editor of the *Atlantic* from 1908 to 1937. Both correspondents were highly temperamental. Though Sedgwick had published several of Lowell's poems, he correctly declined to write an article on Lowell for the *Encyclopedia Britannica*, for the two were worlds apart in technical knowledge, literary goals, taste, and opinion, in spite of which fact the editor had described the poet at her death as "courageous, indefatigable, and gifted."

In "The Echoing Spell of H. D.'s *Trilogy*" (*ConL* 19:196–218), Susan Gubar explicates the poet's narrative, in which H. D. explores the meaning of World War II and analyzes her search for "female strength and survival." The verse often hides "private meanings behind public words." Gubar catalogues and explains various symbols, concluding that the echoing spell of the third poem of the *Trilogy* clears away any mystery about "enclosures" in the other two. Ever present is the circle, the center of which is mystery, but which one must always keep approaching. As female, H. D. becomes "the center of the universe," quite in contrast to the macho images she has inherited and must echo.

Elinor Wylie: A Life Apart, by Stanley Olson (Dial) is not what a scholar would hope for. It describes Wylie's three marriages, four unfortunate pregnancies, general poor health, and the fatal stroke at the last, as well as the suicides of three relatives. It pictures places (Washington, London, New York) and people (Carl Van Vechten, Sara Teasdale, Edmund Wilson, Frank Crowninshield, and others) that are familiar to most readers. It fails to give account of the large and vital literary world of the 1920s (except to refer to Wylie's embarrassing review of *The Waste Land*). On the whole, Olsen's image of writer and complex personality is weak. After all, Wylie was more than an elegant social figure, for she wrote some exquisite prose as well as some excellent poems. We must wait for a more adequate book to supplant this piece of shallow journalism.

On the other hand, in spite of many biases, Laurence Stapleton's *Marianne Moore: The Poet's Advance* (Princeton) is a valuable book for both old friends and new readers of Moore's poetry. Without stint, Stapleton writes sympathetically, disclosing new facts, describing the notebooks from which Moore wrote her poems, paraphrasing succinctly, solving problems of comprehension. Drawing chiefly from the poet's papers collected at the Rosenbach Foundation in Philadelphia, Singleton reveals her subject as a workaholic and strives constantly for meticulous clarity, as in, for example, her account of the translation of La Fontaine. Though the author never indicates that Moore, like Homer, sometimes nodded, was not always in top form, she provides rich allusion to the poet's relationships with her major contemporaries—Williams, Pound, Stevens, and Eliot (all born in the decade 1879–88). In sum, this is an important book.

In reviewing Stapleton's book in the *New Yorker* (16 Oct.:168–94), Helen Vendler, in imaginative phraseology, points to Moore's "princelesslike apprehension of every pea-size solecism," especially in the poems of 1921, her acidity being balanced by her tender feeling for people of moral strength and true beauty. Moore's severity shows itself in her picturing of "a whole gallery of self-recriminating fools." The later poems Stapleton sees as both rigorous and irrepressibly emotional (e.g., "Marriage"). She recommends rereading Jean Garrigue's 1965 Minnesota pamphlet on Moore for supplemental insights, and opines that most male commentators are uneasy with Moore's poetry, possibly because of the poet's sharp criticism of what she sees as male chauvinism.

Another in the guides to criticism published by G. K. Hall and Company (Boston) is Craig S. Abbott's *Marianne Moore: A Reference Guide*. (Also in the series is Nancy Joyner's *Robinson*; see below.) In addition to listing Moore's "principal works," Abbott includes chronologically all the substantial criticism with a summary statement of the contents of each item, beginning with H. D.'s review in *The Egoist*, August 1916. The seven items for 1976 (the last year of the survey) conclude with the entry of Patricia C. Willis and Clive E. Driver in *PBSA* for April–June, which criticizes as inadequate Abbott's own bibliographical treatment of the much-revised "Poetry." The compiler includes an account of the publication of Moore's books and of the trends in criticism. A detailed index provides such divisions as biography, dissertations, interviews, obituaries, and other useful references. Abbott's work, thorough and easily followed, should prove highly serviceable.

ii. The Harvard Connection

Hillyer, Fletcher, Cummings, Aiken, and Robinson were all students at Harvard at one time or another. So were Stevens and Frost, to be discussed later. "Does Anybody Here Remember Bobby Hillyer?" asks Phyllis Braunlich (*LGJ* 5,ii:9–10). Braunlich's article simply reminds us that Hillyer was conservative and patrician, was opposed to the avant garde, spoke out against Pound's receiving the Bollingen award in 1948, and maintained to the end his loyalty to the caesura and the spondee. He published many books, but was never a critical success. Braunlich shows, somewhat by way of paradox, that his friendship with John Dos Passos was lasting in spite of differences in poetic taste. She is not likely to cause a Hillyer revival.

John Gould Fletcher and Imagism, by Edmund S. de Chasca (Missouri), is in two parts, the first of which recreates the excitement, glamor, and excesses of the Imagist movement, especially between 1914 and 1917, and delineates Fletcher's role, in particular his relationship with Amy Lowell. The author has made use of the Fletcher papers at the University of Arkansas. In part 2 he clarifies the meaning of the word *imagism* and analyzes many of Fletcher's poems to see where they coincided with and differed from the received definition. He concludes that the Imagists were not hidebound doctrinaires but did share a life-vision.

Susan Gates's "E. E. Cummings' Spectatorial View" (*LGJ* 5,ii: 9,19) is chiefly about the poet's prison experience in World War I, which made a difference in his aesthetic and spiritual views: his creativity became more passionate and his spiritual vision more transcendental. Continuing his studies of Cummings as poet-artist (see *ALS 1975*, p. 372, and *ALS 1976*, p. 330), Rushworth M. Kidder, in " 'Twin Obsessions': The Poetry and Paintings of E. E. Cummings" (*GaR* 32:342–68) points out that Cummings turned ostensibly, in the late 1920s, from abstraction to representation, but always remained under the influence of abstraction. In his writing he tried consistently to use principles of other arts. With few exceptions he saw his poems as pictures, in proof of which the author explicates three poems to get at the poet's aesthetic—the identities of painting and poetry.

An absolute joy to read is *Selected Letters of Conrad Aiken*, edited by Joseph Killorin (Yale). The 245 letters (selected from 3,500, some located only after years of searching) focus on the theme of Aiken's life in literature—all of them unafraid, candid, outspoken, highly literate. They are widely varied in style, mood, and subject matter, often funny, often showing Aiken's amusement even at his own discomfitures. The editor has provided narrative setting in an introduction, headnotes, and quotations from *Ushant*. Recipients of the letters are amply identified in a "Cast of Correspondents." Two indices guide the reader to mention of Aiken's works and to the names of people referred to in the letters. Killorin's avowed aim is biographical: he generously lists other potential themes for future editors of other letters, including literary theory and technique, psychoanalysis as a force in the artist's life, and Aiken's narrative description of life at all levels, high and low. In the center of the book is a 19-page collection of interesting photographs. One could hope that this book —and Killorin's biography to come—would establish a productive curiosity about this sinfully neglected writer.

Underscoring what becomes evident in a reading of Killorin's book is Ted R. Spivey's "Aiken's Eliot: Toward a Revision" (*SoQ* 17:29–41). In a revival of interest in Aiken, emphasis would inevitably be placed on his lifelong friendship with Eliot and his assessment of Eliot's character and work. Even though he bowed to Eliot as the century's best poet, he nevertheless saw the two of them as being "on the same journey." In another article on the same subject, Spivey recounts the story of that friendship between the two poets from Harvard days to the death of Eliot in 1965. This narrative is titled "Conrad Aiken and T. S. Eliot: A Biographical Essay" (*EAS* 7:45–55).

After some years (see *ALS 1969*, pp. 263, 265, and *ALS 1970*, pp. 293–94), David H. Burton contributes another Robinson item, "Edwin Arlington Robinson and Morris Raphael Cohen" (*CLQ* 14:226–27). Burton contrasts the upbringing of philosopher Cohen with that of the poet. In telling of Cohen's introduction of Robinson's poems to Justice Oliver Wendell Holmes, he includes the jurist's deflating comment: "His music on the mystery of life does not quite enchant me." Donald E. Stanford takes a long look at a neglected poem in "Edwin Arlington Robinson's 'The Wandering Jew'" (*TSE* 23:95–107). Stanford considers such angles as the legendary, the symbolic, the psychological, the literary, and the personal. Agreeing with Winters that this is "one of the great poems . . . of our language," his study is thorough and broad-ranging. In 1977 Nathan C. Starr published "Edwin Arlington Robinson's Arthurian Heroines: Vivian, Guinevere, and the Two Isolts" (*PQ* 56:253–58). Starr's conclusion is that the power of these women lies in their strong mental ability,

their capacity for "the dialectic of frustrated desire." Though Isolt
of Brittany cannot contribute to "disputation," her "frustrated desire" is nevertheless "infinitely poignant." *Lancelot* is characterized
by "stormy love," *Tristram* by "fiery passion" and "terrible vicissi-
tudes." Vivian in *Merlin*, the most original of the four heroines,
"creates a wholly new pattern."

Nancy Carol Joyner's *Edwin Arlington Robinson: A Reference
Guide* (Hall) joins an important group of research aids including
Marianne Moore (see above). In her introduction Joyner describes
"The Shape of Robinson Criticism," material drawn from the more
than 1,400 entries in her book. She unselfishly indicates what remains
to be done in Robinson studies, including "a thorough, documented
biography," a careful analysis of the medium-length poems, and
more "stylistic analysis . . . and textual study." Also, she says, enough
material is available for a variorum edition. In discussing the "Scope
and Method of the Bibliography," Joyner cites Richard Cary, Charles
Beecher Hogan, and William White as principal sources, as well
as the listings in *PMLA* and *AL*.

The bibliography itself begins with selections from Richard
Cary's *Early Reception of Edwin Arlington Robinson* (see *ALS
1974*, p. 333), articles published 1894–1915. Then carefully year by
year Joyner itemizes with annotations (A) books and (B) shorter
writings about the poet arranged alphabetically by the critics' names.
The first entry is dated 15 July 1916; the last, Fall 1976. The index
directs the reader to authors and to titles of critical articles and
books. A serviceable lagniappe is a listing under "Robinson" of
themes and other specific material discussed by critics: e.g., "Classical influence," "Humor," "Naturalism," "Style," and "World view."
Joyner's bibliography is careful, thorough, and of enormous value.

iii. East, West, and South

Charles Reznikoff: A Critical Essay, by Milton Hindus (Black Sparrow [1977],) is an appreciative introduction to the work of a Jewish
poet of Objectivist persuasion who died in 1976 at the age of 82.
Among Reznikoff's books are *By the Waters of Manhattan* (1930,
1962) and *By the Well of Living and Seeing* (1974).

Four Decades of Poetry (*FDP*) is a new Canadian journal devoted to criticism of work published 1890–1930. In volume 2 are two

articles on Crane. Audrey T. Rodgers's "Hart Crane's 'Deathless Dance'" (pp. 1–24) is a long and elaborate study of dance as theme and image in *The Bridge*. The essay develops from a 13-line passage which the poet decided to omit from the final version:

> I'd have us hold one consonance
> Kinetic to its poised and deathless dance.

Rodgers draws evidence from both the poetry and the biographies. The other article (pp. 24–27) is by Roger Ramsey—"Crane's 'Twin Monoliths.'" Ramsey focuses on the first and last sections of *The Bridge*, saying that "Atlantis" was completed before any other parts of the book and that in many ways its imagery balances that of "Proem." Brooklyn Bridge itself, as Crane knew, was built from both banks—a "monolith" at each end (or beginning?).

HSL 10 takes as its theme "A New Anatomy of Melancholy: Patterns of Self Aggression among Authors: A Collection of Studies in Psychodynamic Interpretation." Of interest here, David Bleich shows in "Symbolmaking and Suicide: Hart Crane" (pp. 70–102) that Crane's constantly imminent psychotic self-destruction was the graphic demonstration of the truth and sanity in his firm belief that humanity could finally be saved through "words and language"—in the sublimation of ultimate frustration toward "ultimate satisfaction." To reach this conclusion Bleich draws on many of Crane's poems as well as life situations. In the struggle for such sublimation, Gregory R. Zeck sees the poet using deep symbolism that does double duty. "Identity and Form in Hart Crane" (*MichA* 11,i:19–24) develops the thesis that Crane's symbols express feeling that the poet cannot bring into the open in the world he has to face. At the same time they protect him from the shame of being "different."

Crane copiously defended *The Bridge* in a letter to Yvor Winters after a vicious review by Winters, who did not keep Crane's letter. Vivian H. Pemberton's article "Hart Crane and Yvor Winters, Rebuttal and Review: A New Crane Letter" (*AL* 50:276–81) is based on the carbon copy Crane sent to Allen Tate, who then returned it to Crane. Thomas Parkinson, on the other hand, has been able to use Crane's original letters in *Hart Crane and Yvor Winters: Their Literary Correspondence* (Calif.). Winters's letters to Crane have been lost or destroyed, but, by using Winters's letters to Tate (written at the same time), Parkinson has filled in the story of the Crane-

Winters connection. With urbanity and sound scholarship, the editor has interlaced a clarifying running commentary.

John G. Neihardt's autobiography continues with *Patterns and Coincidences: A Sequel to "All Is But a Beginning"* (Missouri). The poet's story begins here in 1901, just where the first volume ends. Neihardt carries his reminiscences through to 1908, at the start of his career as a mature writer. Completed shortly before his death in 1973, the book is full of anecdote and lively dialogue, including the account of his strange long-distance courtship and his marriage to Mona Martinsen.

In 1977 Lucile F. Aly contributed a fuller narrative, *John G. Neihardt: A Critical Biography* (Rodopi), no. 7 of *Melville Studies in American Culture*, edited by Robert Brainard Pearsall. Thoroughly documented and pleasantly readable, 11 chapters cover the life and work in uncomplicated chronological order from Neihardt's birth in 1881 to his death in 1973. Born in Illinois, Neihardt spent much of his adult life in Nebraska writing "epic" poems about Indians, white settlers, and the problems of life in the Great Plains. He also wrote fiction and criticism. Pearsall admits that critics have ignored Neihardt, a fact explained away by several causes: his predilection for "the great outdoors," his independence from literary fashions, and his unfamiliar brand of "dialectic, rhetoric, and poetic." A carefully prepared index would add greatly to the usefulness of the book, which, though not profound, deserves wide readership among devotees of Western literature.

Richard Messer's "Jeffers' Inhumanism: A Vision of the Self" (*California Writers*, 11–19) declares that the poet utters "a bitter protest against mankind's narcissim." Jeffers maintains that man should look outward "to Nature . . . to 'God,'" if you will. The "happiest and freest" of all men are scientists and artists, who investigate nature and admire it. Each individual ought to experience his primitive and violent dark side (Carl Gustav Jung's view) and practice "a sacramental relationship to nature" without interference from institutions and creeds. This is "inhumanism."

William H. Nolte has published two Jeffers items of interest. In an article, "Robinson Jeffers Redivivus" (*GaR* 32:429–34), Nolte traces the fall and subsequent resurgence of the poet's popularity, "a renaissance greater than that of any other modern poet." He details how critics and fellow poets felt and what caused their emotional reactions. In *Rock and Hawk: Robinson Jeffers and Romantic Agony* (Georgia) he defends the man and his opposition to the vogue of Nietzschean post-romanticism. Like Messer, Nolte pictures Jeffers as refusing to be egocentric and as denying the validity of "solutions" through such institutions as communism. For specialists the *Robinson Jeffers Newsletter* continues to publish bibliographical, biographical, and critical contributions of indispensable interest.

Winner of the Jules F. Landry Award for 1978, Louis D. Rubin's *The Wary Fugitives: Four Poets and the South* (LSU) goes far beyond the poetry of Ransom, Tate, Warren, and Donald Davidson, who were also essayists, writers of fiction, literary critics, and defenders of the Old South. Rubin considers them in the light of all these roles. He shows that Davidson is probably the only one of the four whose permanence rests on Agrarian regionalism. The author has set out for his readers in beguiling, even conversational style the story of these four men as they expressed the relation between what they wrote and the society they lived in. The result is fascinating.

Irv Broughton records "An Interview with Allen Tate" (*WHR* 32:317–36), in which Tate explains why he liked Minnesota, why Randall Jarrell turned against him, etc. He gives his opinion of Ransom, discusses aspects of the Civil War, delineates his problems with his fellow editors of *The Fugitive*, reminisces about Louise Bogan. He says he would like to have lived in the 18th century but to have written in the age of Elizabeth. He denies that there are any poets: "There are just some men who write poems." This interview covers considerable ground and sparkles with insight. In a somewhat ruminative mood, Tate recalls "the circumstances that prompted the writing of certain poems" in "Speculations" (*SoR* 14:226–32). For example, a "picnic at Cassis gave me three poems." Several pieces have classical backgrounds. He devotes considerable space to the provenance of "Seasons of the Soul" and concludes with a simple anecdote of his boyhood that he used 40 years later in "The Swimmers."

Three articles review Tate's *Collected Poems, 1919–1976*. J. A. Bryant, Jr., devotes the first part of "Allen Tate: The Man of Letters in the Modern World" (*SR* 86:274–85) to the revised edition of *The Fathers and Other Fiction*. When Bryant turns to the poetry (pp.

282–85), he shows how fear of death informs the early poems and how Tate's attitude gradually shifts to an ultimate love of God expressed in love of neighbor. Throughout the poems Bryant finds the presence of the female as complementing the persona of the speaker. At last, in Christianity the poet has found redemption through surrender and affirmation. Furthermore, as a man of letters Tate has made language "illuminate as well as shine." This article is rather biased and in fact says nothing particularly new.

Roy Fuller as a young poet was dazzled by "turns of phrase" in Tate's 1937 *Selected Poems*. He is still astounded and delighted by many of the "Early Poems"—"full of fancy, energy, cleverness, and cockiness," though, on the other hand, not enough of "frivolity" (to be derived from Eliot) to suit his taste. Fuller looks briefly at some problems in the scansion of these early verses. He thinks Tate was already "firmly fixed in his formative period," which is not saying he did not *grow*, but was never a poet of the 1940s or 1950s, say. Always he has provided "beauties and mysteries," has clung "to his highest aspirations," and has exercised "his talents so far as possible always at their best." Fuller's review is titled "Tate Full Length" (*SoR* 14:233–44).

The third review is by Donald Davie—"Theme and Action" (*Parnassus* 6,ii:64–73). Davie regards Tate's poems "with respect and even awe, but hardly with love," for the poet makes few concessions to the reader, who is distracted by echoes of past poets from classical times onward. Tate's principal fault, in Davie's eyes, has been to neglect the literal for the symbolical. (Tate's word is "anagogical.") Davie calls "Aeneas at Washington" one of the great American poems, though even it, like every Tate poem, is flawed: the poet is overcome, time and again, by forces he cannot master.

iv. Illinois

Marjorie A. Taylor traces Vachel Lindsay's use of Lincoln materials in his poetry of 1902–14 in her article "Vachel Lindsay and the Ghost of Abraham Lincoln" (*CentR* 22:110–17). In "Abraham Lincoln Walks at Midnight" she ingeniously finds concealed parallelism with the Gettysburg Address—the cadences of Lincoln's first two sentences being parodied in the first eight lines of the poem. The

author conjectures that Lindsay did not publicize this structural resemblance chiefly because he had made a virtual god of Lincoln
and did not want seeming "gimmicks" to intrude on the ideas of
the poem itself.

In *MidAmerica* 5:39–49 appears "'Awakened and Harmonized':
Edgar Lee Masters' Emersonian Midwest," by Ronald Primeau, who
stresses the Illinois poet's enthusiasm for the New Englander's style
and major themes. Through studying Emerson, Masters learned to
"celebrate the Midwest" and found support for his "own mix of
pride and self-reliance." Sixty-six sketches, mostly anecdotal and
arranged in roughly chronological order, make up Hardin Wallace
Masters's *Edgar Lee Masters: A Biographical Sketchbook about a
Famous American Author* (Fairleigh Dickinson), a son's eye view
of his well-known father. With two or three exceptions the pieces
are one or two pages long, written with affection but without sentimentality. The author welcomes future biographers "to my res-
ervoir of memories." In addition to a sympathetic introduction by
Charles Angoff, there are four appendices, listing the books owned
by Masters now in his son's library, the names of all persons who
had a major impact on the poet's daily life, the names of the American cities and towns to which Masters was most sensitive, and the
"feeding places" in Chicago and New York that he frequented most.
A bibliography and an index bring up the rear. This book would
appeal to all students of this period as well as to biography addicts
in general.

The centenary of Sandburg's birth brought forth a number of
celebrations, reviews, and tributes. Jay B. Hubbell, Sr., wrote on
"My Friend Carl Sandburg" (*Library Notes* [Duke Univ.] 48:5–17),
recollecting his contacts with the poet—at Southern Methodist and
Duke, in Flat Rock and Raleigh, and quoting from his own letters
as well as Sandburg's. His basic theme is that Sandburg was blessed
with the virtue of "magnanimity." Gwendolyn Brooks, who succeeded Sandburg as poet laureate of Illinois, pays tribute in "Carl
Sandburg, 1878–1967" (*Chicago Tribune*, Jan. 1: Sec. 7, p. 1). From
the beginning, Brooks says, Sandburg composed "a direct cool line"
born of passionate fire. She surveys the reception of the shocking
Chicago Poems (for readers were not ready for his "non-compromis-
ing reasonableness and realism"). He "crowned the 'common man'

with a rich-coarse stardust." He would probably face today's problems with the same "mighty faith," "strange courage," and "beautiful doggedness."

In the same issue of the *Chicago Tribune* (Jan. 1: Sec. 7, pp. 1–2) Karl Shapiro, reviewing the new book of poems (*"Breathing Tokens* by Carl Sandburg") ranks the poet with Poe, Whitman, Frost, and maybe Dickinson at the top of the list of truly American poets. Shapiro goes so far as to say that Sandburg is now probably "America's most official poet." He recalls that Sandburg was condemned by Edmund Wilson, Pound, and William Carlos Williams, but that Archibald MacLeish praised him for his faith in America and that Hemingway said, in accepting the Nobel Prize, that Sandburg deserved it more than he. Shapiro sees Sandburg as equal in influence on contemporary poetry to Pound or Williams. For example, there is, he thinks, not a great distance between Sandburg and Allen Ginsberg. Herbert Mitgang, editor of a volume of Sandburg letters (see *ALS 1969*, p. 273), recalls in "Carl Sandburg" (*NewRep* 14 Jan.:24–26) that in his occasional meetings with the poet, Sandburg "was a lot of fun to be with" and points up the poet's hatred of sham, his lasting political liberalism, his love of the commonplace, and his contempt for advertising jargon. Sandburg resisted the leadership of Ezra Pound, though he was independently influenced from time to time by the *haiku*. *Remembrance Rock* was a failure bcause it was too big and waved the flag too vigorously. In Mitgang's judgment *The People, Yes* is "Sandburg's finest verse work," a verdict liable to fierce contradiction from many competent quarters.

"'Moonlight Dries No Mittens': Carl Sandburg Reconsidered" is the title of Daniel Hoffman's lecture at the Library of Congress on Sandburg's 100th birthday, 6 January 1978. It was published in *GaR* 32:390–407. Hoffman quotes generously from *The People, Yes* to illustrate the poet's "ear for a good yarn, his sense of revealing detail, his empathy with folk wisdom, his unique ability to transform raw materials of common speech into a lyricism with a swing and rhythm recognizably his own." Sandburg can and does celebrate American life in all its "infinite variety," emphasizing as he does the phenomenon of living in contrast with Whitman's obsession with death. Hoffman finds Sandburg convinced that the people's lingo could be shaped into poetry and believes he increased "the possibilities of subject and language for other poets" of our time.

Another lecture, "The Influence of Carl Sandburg on Modern Poetry," was delivered by Richard H. Crowder in April at a Sandburg Symposium at Cornell College, Iowa, and published in *WIRS* 1,i:45–64. Crowder contrasts tone and technique in Eliot's *The Waste Land* (especially "The Fire Sermon") and Sandburg's "The Windy City" (especially the river bridge as central metaphor)—both poems from 1922. Sandburg's buoyancy contrasts with Eliot's *Weltschmerz*. Excerpts from younger poets (e.g., John Ashbery, Kenneth Koch, Galway Kinnell, and even Robert Penn Warren) show them to be nearer to Sandburg than they, perhaps, would be willing to confess. They are indeed indebted to Sandburg for his pioneering exploitation of new language and structure.

Helga Sandburg, the poet's youngest daughter, published *A Great and Glorious Romance: The Story of Carl Sandburg and Lilian Steichen* (Harcourt) on her father's centennial, 8 January. She traces the family roots back to Sweden and Luxembourg and finally gets around to telling of the eventual meeting of the two Social-Democratic Party workers (p. 104). Based as it is on some letters exchanged between the couple, the book ends oddly in mid-career (1926) with the publication of the first volumes of the life of Lincoln, *The Prairie Years*, without by any means accounting for the entire "story of Carl . . . and Lilian. . . ." It glosses over many of the intricacies of family life, including Carl's frequent and sometimes lengthy absences from home, and fails to mention middle daughter Janet's unfortunate accident. The author's stylistic eccentricities annoy the reader. Yet, of course, there are facts here that have not before been disclosed. The book, however, will be difficult for scholars to use because for one thing there is no index.

v. Wallace Stevens

Stevens scholars should examine the issues of *Wallace Stevens Journal* 2, which presents a wide range of pertinent items, including checklists of materials available at the University of Illinois and at the Huntington Library, explications of individual poems, and a linking of Stevens with the composer Charles Ives. In "Stevens' 'The

Emperor of Ice-Cream' and Emerson's 'The Poet'" (*FDP* 2:48–54),
Mario L. D'Avanzo sees Stevens as answering Emerson's visionary
idealism with a steady refusal to depart from this world. The poet
as emperor "presides over . . . earthly matters . . . rather than the
metaphysical. . . ." Stevens, at the same time, however, depends on
Emerson for his reasoning and much of his imagery

In a brief article aimed at identifying an allusion in the ongoing
process of enriching our feeling for Stevens's sensibility, Michael D.
Channing, in "'From the Packet of Anacharsis': A Tentative Identification" (*ELN* 16:51–54), suggests that in the poem under question, since Anacharsis and Puvis de Chavannes were actual people,
it is reasonable to assume that "Bloom" too is drawn from real life.
Channing proposes that he could be Hymen Bloom (born 1913), an
American painter of Latvian birth, and that Stevens could have
known Bloom's paintings, described in various sources as dazzling,
glittering, brilliant, visceral—not unlike much of the work of the
poet himself. One should be cautious of such speculations, of course,
though this one might bear up under further biographical research.
Philip Furia and Martin Roth discuss "Stevens' Fusky Alphabet" in
PMLA 93:66–77. Their central idea is that for Stevens the "fusky,"
"murderous" alphabet forms a fiction of the unreal, the unpleasur-
able, and the unchanging and is useful in imagining (i.e., creating)
heaven on earth. Not only do the authors discuss the function of
various letters (A, B, C, X, Y, Z) singly and in combination, but they
show how the poet's intricate and revealing code substantiates his
philosophic interests. This article is a solid contribution.

CritQ 20,ii:37–56 gives us Judith Weissman's "Stevens' War Poems: 'And Is Their Logic to Outweigh McDonagh's Bony Thumb?'"
Weissman examines chronologically the poems composed between
two world wars to discover how the poetry changed and proposes
that poets of the West have given up on "heroic poetry" in the interests of decency and civilization. She is, however, in the ironic
position of loving the *Iliad* in all its ferocity, but agreeing with
Stevens's ethics (faith in democracy, condemnation of war)—ethics
which, she concludes, must yield poems characterized by great limitations and undeniable coldness. From another angle, the earlier
"sensuality, heroism, tragedy, war, pain, loss all disappear from
Stevens's poetry, and . . . he never mourns their disappearance."
Cézanne's "concept of *réalisation* [was] much on Stevens's mind"

during his last two decades. This is the thesis Fred Miller Robinson pursues in "Poems That Took the Place of Mountains: Realization in Stevens and Cézanne" (*CentR* 22:281–98). Like the French painter, Stevens was perpetually concerned with the "rigorous and uncomfortable" task of trying as "subjective artist" to make "objective nature" real. Robinson explores at length a late poem, "As You Leave the Room," as an expression of the poet's need to "realize" and at the same time his doubt about succeeding in the process. As in the case of Cézanne, Stevens's ultimate subject could be only his subjective self.

Terrance King is writing a book on *Wallace Stevens' Poetry of Words*, from the preparation for which he has drawn two articles, both richly footnoted. "The Semiotic Poetry of Wallace Stevens" (*Semiotica* 23:77–98) considers Stevens' work as "a literal poetry of words" which can disclose a basic revelation concerning man in relation to his world. King sees Stevens as treating language as an external self, as an autonomy, and as a synopsis. He pronounces Stephens's "poetry of words" religious, epiphanic. The second article, though professedly borrowing from the first, is built on the theory that Stevens's language is not a product of thought, but is actual thought itself. "'Certain Phenomena of Sound': An Illustration of Wallace Stevens' Poetry of Words" (*TSLL* 20:600–14) uses the poem of the title as a firm example of visible language. King admits that part 3 of the poem is obscure because the poet is trying to use language to picture "the ambiguities inherent *in* language itself." He tries to analyze many of those ambiguities.

In *ALS 1974* (pp. 324–25) we reviewed Donald J. Greiner's *Robert Frost*. Now in the same series comes Abbie F. Willard's *Wallace Stevens: The Poet and His Critics* (ALA). As Greiner did in his book, Willard here selects and evaluates critical articles and books about Stevens as poet. The first chapter considers those critics who looked at the poems through biography, technique and theory, and emphases on early verse, later verse, and final poems. Some critics have seen no change at all over the years. (Willard is sharp when sharpness is called for.) Chapter 2, "Literary Heritage," presents those critics who emphasized the poet's debt or relation to American, French, and British literatures and to the "pre-modern" periods. A chapter entitled "Genre" discusses critics' interest in Stevens as philosopher, visual and musical poet, and psychologist.

"World View" analyzes critics' comments on such topics as Stevens on the theory of poetry, on imagination and reality, on actual practice (as opposed to theory) in metrics and language, on wit, on man in his various roles, and on death. The closing chapter considers critics' examination of *The Necessary Angel, Opus Posthumous*, the *Letters*, and *Souvenirs and Prophecies* by daughter Holly. Each of these chapters is followed by an elaborate list of "References." There are "Additional Study Guides" and a solid index. Both the *Frost* and the *Stevens* deserve the attention of every serious student of the poetry of our period.

vi. Robert Frost

A *Robert Frost Newsletter* is now published anually in November–December (College Station, Texas). Mainly of interest to Frost scholars, it contains notices of "publications, holdings, and events." *RFN* 2 features a section on "Frost Places" and an overzealous "Necrology" which cites the death of a very much alive Rabbi Victor E. Reichert, long-time friend of the poet.

Andrew J. Angyal has compiled "Robert Frost's Poetry before 1913: A Checklist" (*Proof* 5[1977]:67–125). Listing begins with two attributions dated 1899, goes through manuscripts in the Huntington Library, and ends with "The Subverted Flower," published in *A Witness Tree* (1942) but said to have been written in 1912 or earlier. One section is devoted to eleven "Doubtful Attributions and Datings." Seven appendices give various (and varying) lists of datings, including, for example, Frost's own list in Genevieve Taggard's copy of *Collected Poems*. The index directs readers not only to the "Writings" itemized in the checklist, but to the "Periodicals and Books" in which these early poems were first published and to the "Signatures" Frost used: e.g., Amnessel, Robert Lee Frost, R.L.F., etc. This study is a most important research tool in bringing Frost's juvenilia together for the attention of biographers and critics. It is a welcome addition to the bibliographical work of Frank and Melissa Christensen Lentricchia (see *ALS 1976*, pp. 319–20) and Linda W. Wagner (see *ALS 1977*, p. 356).

Philip K. Jason looks at "The First Writers in Residence: MacKaye and Frost" (*MQR* 17:377–91). Percy MacKaye, better known as playwright, perhaps, than poet, nevertheless published several volumes of verse and can be considered here. He was writer-in-residence at Miami of Ohio in the early 1920s. Frost was invited to establish residence at Michigan at about the same time. The two men thus began the now widely accepted practice of artist (of one kind or another)-in-residence. Jason tells, among other things, how Frost acknowledged that MacKaye's experience at Miami encouraged him in accepting the offer from Michigan. Details come from letters, family histories, interviews, third-party essays, and prefaces. Jason has written an interesting account of this period in the lives of two writers which has had a broad influence on the cultural growth of many campuses, large and small.

Frost is linked with Dylan Thomas, Eliot, and Pound in *Remembering Poets*. Donald Hall pictures Frost as mature, tough, self-preserving, able to face solitude, family tragedy, and inward "desert places." Quintessentially American, he had skill for survival, yet needed and soaked up admiration. Hall's impression is that Frost was kind and human really, in spite of views in Lawrance Thompson's biography. Hall is not so successful in making Frost's portrait exciting as he is with the other three subjects of his book.

Earlier writers who influenced Frost include Catullus, Tennyson, Dickinson, Thoreau, and Emerson as Helen Bacon demonstrated in the Elizabeth Drew Memorial Lecture at Bread Loaf in the summer of 1977. Her paper has been published in *MR* 19:319–34 under the title "Dialogue of Poets: *Mens Animi* and the Renewal of Words." The author's theme is that, though single poems of Frost are nearly always complete and intelligible in themselves, they become richer and more complex as one reads further into the whole of the poet's work—and over and over again. The process renews the words in any poem, whether by Frost or by Catullus of old Rome, whose dictum was that *mens animi* is thus made more sensitive and broad. Rereading poems, renewing the past (Bacon is aware of Frost's knowledge of classical writers), is "to escape from the confinement and provincialism of our time and place. . . ." As usual, the author draws on her own rich inheritance of classical writers to make her profound point.

Robert Fleissner, in "Frost and Tennyson: New Points" (*AN&Q* 16:72–73) proves to his own satisfaction that Tennyson was Frost's favorite Victorian poet (rather than Arnold, Browning, or Hardy). Among other reasons for his choice are the similar "melancholy or darkness" in the imagery of the two poets, their status as poets of popular appeal, their mutual admiration of Keats, their roles as "nature poets," their interest in the interlocking of science and culture, and so on. The wary reader of this catalogue wishes for a full development of the suggestions made here.

In two articles George Monteiro presents the case for Emily Dickinson's influence on Frost, especially in the early poems (1894–1901). "Robert Frost's Dickinson Books" (*EDB* 33:3–7) is a descriptive listing of the Dickinson volumes in Frost's library, a useful tool in the study of influences. "Emily Dickinson and Robert Frost" (*PrS* 51:369–86) proposes that much can still be done concerning the poet's early debt to Dickinson. "My Butterfly," e.g., has antecedents in two Dickinson poems, and butterfly poems elsewhere in Frost have her tone and even thematic similarities. Other images and themes from Dickinson found their way into Frost's early work (e.g., children playing hide-and-seek). In fact, the poems with her influence were the first works Frost was able to find publishers for. Dickinson was always to be "an example, a resource, a warning, a challenge, and, above all, a threat."

One of the early poems, "The Quest of the Orchis" (1901), later called "The Quest of the Purple Fringed," is related to a passage in Thoreau's journal, especially in its sexuality, according to Michael West. His "Versifying Thoreau: Frost's 'The Quest of the Purple Fringed' and 'Fire and Ice'" (*ELN* 16:40–47) maintains that "Fire and Ice" is related to Thoreau much more than to "the bardic stance" of "Uriel" (Emerson). It echoes "Thoreau's steady matter-of-factness, tough, observant, ultimately perhaps a trifle whimsical."

In two sound articles, Darrel Abel clarifies Frost's self-reliance. "Emerson's 'Apparition of God' and Frost's 'Apparition of the Mind'" (*UTQ* 48:41–52), through the examination of several poems, demonstrates that Frost thinks of one's perception of reality as changing—as resulting not only from object but also from atmosphere, which does not yield all "of God's truth." Thus, clarity of observation is not equivalent to clarity of understanding. When objects and experiences are "diminished" by changing atmosphere (and the passing of time), one must exercise "the fullest imaginative power . . . to sustain the experienced fact." The empiricist relies on his own imagination, not on an Emersonian Oversoul. "Robert Frost's 'True Make-Believe'" (*TSLL* 20:552–78) is a thoroughly documented study of Frost's belief in the efficacy of "creative faith." Abel divides his analysis into four parts: "Believing Things In," "Self-Belief" (Abel uses the neglected "Maple" to illustrate the "pragmatic postulate" of believing oneself "into existence"), "The National Belief," and "God Belief." This article makes substantial an often superficially accepted side of Frost's poetry and character.

Also on the subject of "True Make-Believe in Robert Frost" (*MSE* 5,iii:1–5), Lewis H. Miller, Jr., analyzes particularly "A Boundless Moment" to show how serious Frost is about his playfulness. Quoting from the frequently cited "Directive," Miller concludes that the poet finds salvation centered in "the very temple of make-believe." The author supports his thesis by reference to Joseph Campbell, Reuben Brower (albeit on Wallace Stevens), and a Frost letter to R. P. T. Coffin. He decides that Frost's chief characteristic at his most playful is "the dialectics of assertion and denial of readily identified fictions."

Justin Replogle, in "Vernacular Poetry: Frost to Frank O'Hara" (*TCL* 24:137–53), pronounces Frost our best theorist of the voiced vernacular as well as its best maker (along with Marianne Moore). His skill is easily shown in the earlier works: e.g., "The Housekeeper," "Wild Grapes," and "New Hampshire." Syntax and diction of a "literary" sort, however, are mixed in with the idiom of the familiar. Moore is, perhaps, more parsimonious and precise; but it is vernacular intonation that makes clear her "elegant, complex syntactical constructions." Neither Frost nor Moore is totally "speechlike," however, as the younger Frank O'Hara is. Frost, nevertheless, thought no game more important than that of vernacular poetry.

A double issue of the periodical *Pebble* (nos. 14–15) is dated 1976 but, with customary casualness, just recently published. Frost is here the subject of 14 essays by such well-known critics and poets as Philip Booth, William Meredith, Richard Wilbur, Louis O. Coxe, and John F. Lynen. For the most part the articles explore single poems, generally popular ones such as "After Apple-Picking" and "Mending Wall." Alan T. Gaylord ("The Imaginary State of 'New Hampshire,'" pp. 1–52) goes through his chosen poem thoroughly for 40 pages and adds 93 footnotes. Maxine Kumin (pp. 63–64), on the other hand, uses less than two pages to demonstrate how the style of "Provide, Provide" saves it from simple pietistic didacticism. These essays are varied, wise, and useful as we continue to delineate the always evasive picture of the mind and art of Robert Frost.

Frost: Centennial Essays III, edited by Jac Tharpe (Miss.), continues the series begun in 1974 (see *ALS 1974*, pp. 328–29, and *ALS 1976*, p. 321). Included are recollections about Frost at Bread Loaf, especially Peter J. Stanlis's "Acceptable in Heaven's Sight: Frost at Bread Loaf, 1939–1941" (pp. 179–311), a remarkably detailed account of Frost's seasons at the famous summer school. Dorothy Tyler's essay, "Robert Frost in Michigan" (pp. 7–69), narrates and reflects on many of the incidents and personal relationships the poet experienced at the first university where he served as poet-in-residence. (See Philip K. Jason's article, reviewed above.) Tyler supports her statements with 97 conscientious footnotes. Several essayists (including Lesley Frost, briefly) tackle Frost's religious beliefs. In "'The Death of the Hired Man': Modernism and Transcendence" (pp. 382–401) Warren French looks at several poems against a broad-ranging discussion of what he sees as the temper of Frost's time, invoking Jacques Barzun, Kierkegaard, Stephen Crane, F. Scott Fitzgerald, and others. In all, there are 13 essays, some by critics who have contributed to the two earlier volumes. A number of pictures add another perspective to this book, which, however, lacks the verve and vitality of the 1974 volume.

Purdue University

17. Poetry: The 1930s to the Present

James E. Breslin

Critical writing about contemporary poetry increases almost as rapidly as the poetry itself. For 1978 this chapter includes discussion of 19 books and about 60 essays; at least another 30 essays were read but omitted as trivial. Yet the quality of even the selected portion of this immense critical effort is often dreary. Much of the criticism repeats what has already been said—a surprising phenomenon in a field that is relatively open and uncluttered; but then there is safety in restating established truths. Other essays remain cautiously myopic: they adopt a narrow focus—a single poem or book of poems— then steadfastly refuse to mention other works or authors, much less to introduce broad theoretical or historical perspectives. Sometimes this limited vision results from a partisanship which leads the critic to be swallowed up by his or her poet. Still other writers have been swallowed up by current developments in literary theory, which they then use to devour their helpless authors. Nevertheless, some genuinely distinguished work was done in 1978 by critics who have been stimulated by their poets and by contemporary theory yet who maintain a critical distance from both: Marjorie Perloff on Williams and on Ashbery and O'Hara; Charles Altieri on Williams and on Ashbery; Robert von Hallberg and Sherman Paul on Olson.

i. General Studies

Ambitious projects with large scope and bold, broad formulations were sparse in 1978. Only one book attempted anything like an overview—Louis Simpson's *A Revolution in Taste* (Macmillan). Simpson promises an exploration of the radical shift of poetic values that took place in the late 1950s, and he proceeds by concentrating on four key figures: Dylan Thomas, Allen Ginsberg, Sylvia Plath, and Robert Lowell. Yet the rich theoretical and historical possibilities of this subject are never realized as the author reduces complex issues to simple, schematic generalities. In the fifties "Auden ruled with wit and a knowledge of verse forms," but the quality missing from the fashionable poetry of the time was, Simpson declares, "passion." Thus, the impact in America of Thomas, who was "demonic" while Auden was "rational." The chapters on particular poets combine anecdotal biography with superficial critical analysis; they lean heavily on published criticism and offer little that is new. Too often Simpson's own contributions are sagacious pronouncements from the literary armchair: "It is not wrong to interpret the meaning of a poem—it is only wrong to interpret too much." No one will accuse Simpson of overinterpretation.

In "Contemporary Poetry and the Metaphors for the Poem" (*GaR* 32:319–31) Charles Molesworth similarly deals with the transformation of American poetry in the late 1950s. The shift, he argues, was from a "dominant sense of a poem as an autotelic, self-explaining" object, to "at least three other metaphoric images for the poem: 1) the poem as a force-field; 2) the poem as a 'leaping' or associatively linked cluster of nondiscursive images; and 3) the poem as commentary on some unspoken myth—what Galway Kinnell has called a 'palimpsest.'" But the essay does not fully deliver on this promising beginning; its sections on each of these three metaphors for the poem are too brief to be substantive.

Surrealism has emerged as perhaps the prevailing fashion of the late seventies and Paul Breslin in "How to Read the New Contemporary Poem" (*ASch* 47:357–70) offers a penetrating and sardonic critique of this mode. Breslin views surrealism not as a technique but as "a shared set of implicit assumptions about poetry and reality" —as a literary ideology—and he attacks its solipsistic dismissal of "the quotidian world," its taking refuge in a sentimental, Jungian idea of the unconscious as "the wellspring of religious revelation." But his main objection is specifically literary: he shows how many stock images of the new surrealism (jewels, stones, silence, darkness, etc.) come into the poem "already charged with significance" rather than developing their meaning in a specific poetic context.

Confessionalism, the dominant trend of the sixties, was the subject of two essays last year. The most interesting of these, "Impersonal Personalism: The Making of a Confessional Poetic" (*ELH* 45: 687–709) by Steven K. Hoffman, asserts that confessionalism constitutes "a definable poetic," one that has strong continuities with both romantic and modern poetry. Hoffman stresses the "dramatic element" in confessional poetry, its transformation of private psyche to public concern and its characteristic structural progression "from necessity and entrapment to qualified liberation." Harry Stessel in "Confessional Poetry: A Guide to Marriage in America" (*MSpr* 72: 337–55) repeats the familiar account of confessional verse as a reaction against modernist impersonality, but does add the interesting argument that this literary mode was also a reaction against the fifties' cult of domesticity.

"The Treatment of American Indian Materials in Contemporary American Poetry" (*JAmS* 12:81–98) is studied by Peter Easy, who discusses the use of Indian myths as subjects in poems by Gary Snyder and Barry Gifford, the problems of translating Native American poetry, the history of such translations and Jerome Rothenberg's attempts at "total translation" of these texts.

An issue of *TriQuarterly* (43) contains three reminiscences by founding editors of little magazines: Cid Corman on *Origin*, Reed Whittemore on *Furioso*, and Jack Conroy on *Anvil*.

ii. William Carlos Williams

No critical book on Williams was published in 1978, but the essays by Perloff, Altieri, and Bruns—among the most provocative and substantial dealt with in this chapter—testify to Williams's continuing importance and to the energy of his critics. Two book-length works did contribute to the project of defining Williams's relation to the visual arts. *William Carlos Williams and the American Scene, 1920–1940* (Calif.) by Dickran Tashjian is the catalog from last winter's Whitney show. The catalog itself, with 16 color plates and 127 black and white reproductions, has been beautifully produced. In his text Tashjian does not claim any influence between Williams and the artists but views Williams as typifying the American artist's struggle during the twenties and thirties to reconcile European avant-garde procedures with native materials. No startling contributions to our knowledge of Williams emerge, but Tashjian does synthesize an abundance of detail and insight about Dada, Marsden Hartley, Charles Demuth, Charles Sheeler, Alfred Stieglitz, and the issues raised by the use of ethnic, proletarian, and regional subjects during the period.

In *A Recognizable Image: William Carlos Williams on Art and Artists* (New Directions) Bram Dijkstra has collected Williams's extensive prose writings on art and artists, most of the essays previously unpublished or uncollected. In his "Introduction" Dijkstra asserts that Williams was "trying to do in words what the painters were doing with paint on canvas" and that the artists who most affected Williams were the French moderns, along with Hartley, Marin, Demuth, Stella, and Stieglitz. Dijkstra's lengthy Introduction also attempts a Marxist demystification of Williams. Williams viewed art, according to Dijkstra, as "the privileged realm of transcendent experience" and refused to acknowledge his unconscious assimilation of his culture's "dominant ideology"—evident in his anti-Semitism, racism, and sexism. To some extent Dijkstra berates Williams for simplifications of his views attributed to him by Dijkstra, but his critique of Williams raises legitimate questions about many of the leading clichés of Williams criticism.

Both Tashjian and Dijkstra stress the "visual" quality of Williams's imagination, but Marjorie Perloff in her superb " 'Lines Converging and Crossing': The 'French' Phase of William Carlos Williams" (*MoR* 2,i:89–123) argues that what Williams derived from the French painters was "a rejection of *mimesis*, of representational art." At the same time Perloff shows in careful readings of passages from *Kora* and of poem no. 12 in *Spring and All* that Williams is also an "anti-Symbolist" whose metonymic art creates verbal constructs in which particulars "refuse to cohere" into visual images. Williams's true predecessor, she argues, is Rimbaud. In "The Design of Experience: William Carlos Williams and Juan Gris," Rob Fure contends that in "The Rose"—based on Gris's "Roses"—Williams "offers striking visual images" of his subject, yet his poem "advances its argument securely within the medium of poetry" (*WCWN* 4,ii:10–19).

The question of the referentiality of his language has now emerged as the central issue in Williams criticism, as it is in contemporary theory. In "Presence and Reference in a Literary Text: The Example of Williams' 'This Is Just to Say'" (*CritI* 5:489–510) Charles Altieri uses Williams's poetics as the basis for an attack on Derridean skepticism about the referentiality of language. Williams's poetry does not strive to present objects, but neither does it, as Joseph Riddel has argued, create a self-referential realm of fictive structures. Rather, according to Altieri, Williams "constructs poetic spaces which reveal the qualities of human actions, of minds creating meanings in a middle space between origins and ironic self-conscious fictive reflections on the emptiness of our figures." This "middle space"—which can account for the fact that we are able to understand and appreciate complex utterances—becomes the ground on which Altieri bases his alternative to "deconstruction."

Gerald L. Bruns examines a kind of utterance that must be situated right at the border of that middle space—the improvisation ("De Improvisatione," *IowaR* 9,iii:66–78). Since an improvisation "is ungeneric almost by definition," Bruns's subtle meditation circles around this "unplanned discourse," exploring its "elusiveness of form," its divergent speech as "a mode of violence" that seeks "refreshment" and "originality." The improvisations of *Kora in Hell* do, however, have a kind of "law"—the principle of contradiction.

In the American Grain was the subject of a single article ("Against the American Grain: William Carlos Williams between Whitman and Poe," *TSE* 23:123–42), which begins by questioning why Williams devoted "a whole chapter to Edgar Allan Poe and only one sentence to Walt Whitman." E. P. Bollier concludes that Williams sought in Poe an "*American* rationale for a poetic method" that was "remarkably similar" to that of "The Waste Land" or the *Cantos.* The essay, however, does not get very specific about this "poetic method"; nor does it have much new to say about *In the American Grain.*

In "The Politics of Description: W. C. Williams in the 'Thirties" (*ELH* 45:131–51) Robert von Hallberg studies a neglected period of Williams's career, a time when he was struggling "to reconcile the political demands of a disruptive decade with the kinds of descriptive and often delicate poetry he was then accustomed to writing." Von Hallberg emphasizes *An Early Martyr*, "its concern with the problematic relationship between two poles of discourse, explanation and description."

Paterson continued to elicit considerable and varied attention. Paul Mariani in "*Paterson* 5: The Whore/Virgin and the Wounded One-Horned Beast" (*UDQ* 13,ii:102–30) traces the genesis of *Paterson* 5 in an essay that is richly detailed, carefully researched and evocatively written. According to Paul Bové in "The World and Earth of William Carlos Williams: *Paterson* as a 'Long Poem'" (*Genre* 11:575–96), all previous critics of Williams have been covertly "metaphysical"; they have reified Williams's poems into artifacts which achieve a "timeless stasis" and possess the power both to present and to be objects. Yet Bové's own notion of *Paterson* as a dynamic process of gathering and dispersal sounds new only because of the Heideggarian language and his simplifications of previous criticism.

In "Williams's *Paterson*: Doctor and Democrat" (*YES* 8:77–94) Stephen J. Tapscott stresses the poem's "dual perspective"; "to know the world, Paterson needs to be objective, a doctor, who can glimpse the 'thing' itself. To know the mind, Paterson needs to be an individuated, democratic citizen, with his own prerogatives of internality." In "'A little touch of / Einstein in the night': Williams' Early Exposure to the Theories of Relativity" (*WCWN* 4,i:10–13) Carol C. Donley establishes that by 1921 Williams "was interested in the new physics but that he had not created any formal poetic analogs to it." This he did in *Paterson*, as Donley shows in "Relativity and Radioactivity in William Carlos Williams' *Paterson*" (*WCWN* 5,i:6–11).

James Swafford's "Temples on the Rock: Religion and the Rhythms of *Paterson*" (*ELWIU* 5:75–84) stresses Williams's structural use of ascent/descent patterns and his use of religious motifs to "celebrate the union of spirituality with sexual fertility," but, brief and schematic, the essay offers little that is fresh. Williams "got" his idea of imagination as dream from Freud, according to David Hurry in "William Carlos Williams' *Paterson* and Freud's *Interpretation of Dreams*" (*L&P* 28:170–77), but the profound differences between Williams and Freud are never even acknowledged in this essay.

Steven Ross Loevy has edited and written a useful introduction (pp. 1–11) to "Rome" (*IowaR* 9,iii:12–65), a prose improvisation written while Williams was there in the spring of 1924.

iii. Robert Lowell, W. D. Snodgrass, John Berryman, Theodore Roethke, Elizabeth Bishop, Robert Penn Warren

The year's main contribution to Lowell studies was Steven Axelrod's *Robert Lowell: Life and Art* (Princeton). Axelrod's Lowell is a poet who repudiated Modernism, its valuing of "impersonal, self-reflexive art structures," to return to the American tradition of experiential verse; his poems are "structures of experience." Few of Lowell's readers will find this characterization startling. In his account of Lowell's development Axelrod stresses *Lord Weary's Castle, Life Studies,* "For the Union Dead," "Near the Ocean," and *The Dolphin,* and his readings of these works are detailed and perceptive. What is most valuable in this book, however, derives from Axelrod's use of Lowell's manuscripts and unpublished correspondence; he gives a much fuller account of Lowell's life than we've had before and his astute analysis of the relation between Lowell and Williams shows how archival work can generate important critical insights.

Donald Hall's "Robert Lowell and the Literature Industry" (*GaR* 32:7–12) fulminates against the sloppy writing he sees in *Day by Day*—a book that receives a more patient and penetrating reading in Helen Vendler's "Lowell's Last Poems" (*Parnassus* 6,ii:75–100). *Day by Day,* she argues, offers a "redefinition of lyric." Suggestively tracing the evolution of a new poetic that first appeared in a few poems in *For the Union Dead,* Vendler powerfully demonstrates that Lowell ended his career as a poet of "disarming openness" whose sacrifice of "plot and rhyme" was motivated by a "double aesthetic —the obligation to notice and to be subject to the present moment in its present configuration."

"Looking for Robert Lowell in Boston" (*LitR* 21:285–303), Richard Fein recollects a literary pilgrimage that produced valuable information about public persons and places in Lowell's poems, especially "For the Union Dead." Christopher Butler's "Robert Lowell: From *Notebook* to *The Dolphin*" (*YES* 8:141–56) declares the failure of *Notebook, History,* and *For Lizzie and Harriet* to achieve what Butler will accept as form, but argues that *The Dolphin,* willing to compromise with literary conventions, does work. That Lowell's changing attitudes generated his changing forms is the not-too-surprising thesis of "The Morality of Form in the Poetry of Robert Lowell" by William Bedford in *ArielE* (9,i:3–17).

Except for a 1975 essay by J. D. McClatchy, the poetry of W. D. Snodgrass has not received the attention it merits. Unfortunately, Paul Gaston's effort to remedy this situation in *W. D. Snodgrass* (TUSAS 316) achieves only mixed results. Abjuring "a controlling critical thesis," Gaston offers close readings of major works as an introduction to Snodgrass's work. Individual chapters deal with *Heart's Needle*, the pseudonymously published *Remains*, *After Experience*, five poems on paintings, *The Führer Bunker*, Snodgrass's translations and criticism. The book is weak when it deals with anything like a theoretical issue—e.g., the nature of confessional poetry. Its readings are thorough but—perhaps because they lack the edge a controlling thesis would provide—more competent than exciting.

John Berryman was similarly ill served by a single, undistinguished book. Gary Arpin's *The Poetry of John Berryman* (Kennikat) places Berryman in the Symbolist tradition to show how he departs from its "rarefied" language to adopt a tougher idiom capable of dealing with "the absurdity and pain" of our lives. Berryman's solution to pain and loss, Arpin argues, becomes "a realization of the importance of love and work." But in the brief chapters dealing with Berryman's major works neither the stylistic nor the thematic thesis is pushed hard enough to turn up much that is new.

The relations between Lowell, Berryman, Roethke, and younger contemporary poets offer a rich set of possibilities for studies of poetic influence—a subject that is opened in a book missed last year: Harry Williams's *"The Edge Is What I Have": Theodore Roethke and After* (Bucknell, 1977). Chapters on "The Lost Son," "Meditations of an Old Woman," "North American Sequence" argue that these three long poems mark stages in Roethke's psychic journey toward reconciliation with his parents, but Williams's interpretations do little to extend what recent Roethke critics, notably Richard Blessing and Rosemary Sullivan, have said. On his reading of these three poems Williams bases his characterization of "The Roethkean Mode"—an unmasked speaker, present tense, free verse, intuitive imagery—a formulation he then uses to identify Roethke's "legacy" to such poets as Wright, Bly, Dickey, Plath, and Hughes. This chapter accomplishes a solid beginning in a study of Roethke's influence,

although the connections that Williams finds are often too generalized (e.g., animism) to be convincing.

Elizabeth Bishop was the subject of three essays, none of them
opening any significantly new perspectives on her work. The best
of the three, Willard Spiegelman's "Elizabeth Bishop's 'Natural Heroism'" (*CentR* 22:28–44) persuasively argues her revision of heroism: Bishop's poetry ironically scrutinizes conventional ideas of the
heroic in order to locate it in a Wordsworthian natural piety. In
"Elizabeth Bishop's Originality" (*APR* 7,ii:18–22) Lorrie Golden-
sohn sees Bishop "amplifying awareness of the incongruities and unexpected congruences of all object categories, but at a cool remove"
in her early work, then "magnifying the child at the distant center
of oneself" in *Geography III*. Jerome Mazzaro focuses on "Crusoe
in England" in "The Recent Poems of Elizabeth Bishop" (*SCR* 10,i:
99–115) and argues that the poem's full meaning lies in "the various
contexts the work calls up"—in travel literature, children's literature,
natural history, Defoe, Bishop's earlier work. Not all these contexts,
however, are convincingly related to the poem itself.

Since the publication of his *Selected Poems, 1923–1975*, more and
more critics have assigned Robert Penn Warren to major status in
contemporary poetry. In last year's only overview of Warren's career
A. L. Clements in "Sacramental Vision: The Poetry of Robert Penn
Warren" (*SAB* 43,iv:47–65) traces the poet's evolution of a "sacramental vision," increasingly expressed in long poetic sequences. The
remaining contributions to the study of Warren were solid, mainly
thematic accounts of individual volumes of poetry. According to
Richard G. Law in "*Brother to Dragons*: The Fact of Violence vs.
the Possibility of Love" (*AL* 49:560–79), Warren's historical poem
marks "a wholly new dimension" in his work: impersonal remove is
shed for the risks of "self-involvement" and "stoical acceptance" is
replaced by "joyous affirmation." Two essays by Guy Rotella focus
on Warren's later poetry. In "'One Flesh': Robert Penn Warren's
Incarnations" (*Renascence* 31:25–42) Rotella declares that book
part of the poet's "attempt to counter the threat of solipsism, now
with emphasis on the oneness of all flesh," while Rotella's "Evil,
Goodness, and Grace in Warren's *Audubon*: A Vision" (*NDEJ* 11:
15–32) sees Warren proposing the naturalist as "a mythic model
for all men" in his "discovery of the wondrous, irreducible mixture
of filth and hope which is reality." In "A Meditation on Folk-History:

The Dramatic Structure of Robert Penn Warren's *The Ballad of Billie Potts*" (*AL* 49:635–45), William Bedford Clark justifies the reflective passages that many critics have found intrusive in Warren's folk ballad.

iv. Charles Olson, Louis Zukofsky, Robert Creeley, Ed Dorn

From the beginning of his career Olson has been the most controversial figure in contemporary poetry, the polemics between his worshipping admirers and his merciless detractors allowing for little sense of a middle ground. This year saw publication of three book-length critical studies of Olson, plus a *Guide* to his major work, *The Maximus Poems*. All four are written by Olson admirers, and they illustrate some of the ways in which partisanship can become a force for well or ill in literary criticism. In his *A Guide to The Maximus Poems of Charles Olson* (Calif.), George Butterick manifests his commitment to Olson by the painstaking care with which he has assembled over 4,000 annotations, drawn from Olson's wide reading, his unpublished papers, his conversation. Butterick's entries, moreover, are fuller and much more informative than those, say, in the *Annotated Index to the Cantos of Ezra Pound*. The *Guide* establishes Olson as the village polymath of Gloucester—a zealous, eccentric, extensive reader; and Butterick's work provides the ground on which all subsequent critical estimates of the poem must be built.

Paul Christensen, on the other hand, is an Olson enthusiast whose dutiful attention to his ideas too often turns Olson's work into the flat abstractions he abhorred (*Charles Olson: Call Him Ishmael* [Texas]). Looking for the "underlying unity" beneath the eccentric surface of Olson's work, Christensen locates it in the poet's concern "to restore to human beings their own primal energies"—a thesis that fails to distinguish Olson from many another poet since Blake. Beginning by defining Olson's "New Reality" as revealed in his prose writing, Christensen nicely connects the opposition between Ahab's will to power and Ishmael's "open consciousness" in *Call Me Ishmael* with the antithesis between closed and open forms in "Projective Verse." But the readings of the short poems are too brief and schematic and while Christensen has a provocative thesis about the overall form of *The Maximus Poem* as "a modern mystery play," the chapter on Olson's epic is too brief to substantiate this notion fully.

In his *Charles Olson: The Scholar's Art* (Harvard) Robert von Hallberg adopts a more independent perspective, from which he generates a specific and fruitful thesis. Von Hallberg does not approach Olson by way of the poet's own literary polemics; Olson, von Hallberg contends, conceives of the poet as a teacher rather than as a maker and his "expository poetics," entailing a referential language and a logical organization, distinguishes Olson from his Modernist predecessors. At times the book seems straining to effect a truce between Yvor Winters and Charles Olson, and von Hallberg does not fully confront the discrepancy between his pedagogical Olson and Olson's claims to have repudiated discursive thinking. But *Charles Olson: The Scholar's Art* is a subtle, solid, and valuable achievement. Von Hallberg assesses Olson's debt to and difference from Pound, Williams, Whitehead with a just complexity. More interested in poetics than poems, von Hallberg still says many perceptive things about Olson's rhythms, diction, tone, syntax. While arguing that Olson's "willfully prosaic" language derives not from ineptitude but from his didactic concerns, von Hallberg also concedes Olson's limits, his extravagances, and his real failures.

In *Olson's Push* (LSU) Sherman Paul approaches Olson by way of the poet's own theories; but rather than being swallowed up by his subject, Paul generates a sympathetic and penetrating opening of Olson's poetic premises—at the same time that Paul's wide reading in modern poetry and transcendentalist literature allows him to place Olson fully in the American literary tradition. In a tight, evocative prose Paul uncovers Olson's push "to recover beginnings"; he suggestively describes Olson's struggles to emerge as a poet in the oppressive postwar social and literary climate—an account that culminates in a powerful reading of "The Kingfishers." Olson's strivings against the fathers provide a motif that Paul productively follows throughout Olson's career, and Paul's long chapter on *The Maximus Poems*, his tracing of the "twistings and turnings" of their "circular and multidimensional" form, provides the best *literary* account we have so far of Olson's major work.

A special issue of *Paideuma* (7,iii) collects poems, brief tributes, letters, memoirs, and critical essays about Louis Zukofsky. Statements by Robert Duncan and Charles Tomlinson testify to Zukofsky's role as an "enduring resource" for younger poets. Among the critical contributors Hugh Kenner contrasts Zukofsky's translation

of Calvalcanti's "Donna mi prega" with earlier versions by Pound;
Barry Ahearn amply documents "The Adams Connections," especially in "A"-8; John Taggart justifies the sestina form in "Mantis";
Peter Quartermain analyzes the 12th poem of *Anew*; and Burton
Hatlen defends Zukofsky's translation of Catullus from academic
accusations of ignorance. These essays all deal with fairly narrow
subjects, as if the character and standing of Zukofsky's poetic achievement could be taken for granted. Don Byrd's "The Shape of Zukofsky's Canon" attempts an overview and offers some provocative
statements about "A," *Bottom*, and *Catullus* as "intersubjective lyr-
ics." What Zukofsky criticism needs now is not close readings of
individual poems, not another meeting of the Zukofsky fan club
(the poet chumily referred to as "Zuk"), but the proposal of broad
avenues of approach to his work. Viewing "A" as a collage, Barry
Ahearn's "Origins of 'A': Zukofsky's Materials for Collage" (*ELH*
45:152–76) promises such a perspective—and the essay does provide useful annotations and show Zukofsky's early struggle to re-
nounce idealism, but it wanders, makes some dubious claims about
Zukofsky's sources and influences, and fails to show how collage
works as a formal principle in "A."

"The way a poem speaks," "not the matter, proves its effects,"
Robert Creeley insists. His poetry requires a criticism that is carefully attentive to the working of his language and yet is willing to
take on the theoretical issues raised by his experiments with language. The first two books to be written about Creeley appeared
in 1978; both are written with clarity and enthusiasm and both are
primarily contributions to the practical criticism of Creeley. Cynthia
Dubin Edelberg's *Robert Creeley's Poetry: A Critical Introduction*
(New Mex.) studies the poet's development through his preoccupation with the activity of thinking, love, and poetry itself. *For Love*
manifests a tension between the "dispassionate intelligence" and the
frustrating realities of love and language; *Words* questions "analytic
thinking" and modifies Creeley's ideals of love and language, while
Pieces accomplishes a "fusion of analytic and intuitive" modes.
Edelberg also shows Creeley's gradual evolution toward poetic
forms that are looser yet more complex—a progress that culminates
in the autobiographical immediacy of *A Day Book*; her perceptive
accounts of Creeley's language, its shifts of tone and pace constitute

the strongest part of the book. In his *Robert Creeley* (TUSAS 310) Arthur L. Ford establishes biographical and critical contexts for Creeley's work, then discusses *Pieces, Words, For Love*, and the fiction. Ford approaches *For Love* through the themes of love and loneliness; *Words* struggles to capture the physical object; *Pieces* views the word itself as object. Like Edelberg, he values *Pieces* as Creeley's major work, but whereas Edelberg argues a romance quest myth structuring *Pieces*, Ford sees the book as less linear—as a journal with the search for "perception of self" and "perception of form" as recurring motifs. Ford's enthusiasm for the poems as poems generates what is best in his book: a devoted and precise attention to the linguistic movements of the poems in *Pieces* and *Words*.

A double issue of *Boundary 2* (6,iii;7,i), containing an interview, memoirs, poems, and essays, provides what amounts to another book-length study of Creeley. In addition to statements by fellow poets such as Duncan, Ginsberg, Dorn, Levertov, and Clark, the collection includes critical essays that range in approach from Paul Mariani's use of archival research to establish a detailed narrative of the Creeley-Williams relationship, to Sherman Paul's journal of his rereading of Creeley, to the speculative, philosophical approach of Charles Altieri. Among the more significant contributions, Robert Kern, characterizing Creeley as a "humble witness rather than the organizing manipulator of the poem's occasion," unfolds the complexities of Creeley's relations to both Modernism and post-Modernism; Robert von Hallberg contends that Creeley is a "discursive" poet who, rather than constructing systems to understand history, "*discovers* systematic behavior in the people he observes or imagines"; John Vernon shows that for Creeley the body becomes the "field" proposed by Olson, but the body "is also closed, and often deflects the intended gesture of the poem"; Paul Diehl demonstrates how Creeley makes emotion literal in the poem by junctures of breath; Nathaniel Mackey and Marjorie Perloff show "projectivist" principles at work in the fiction; concentrating on the prose published after *Pieces*; Michael Davidson argues that whereas before "the poem maintained a tension between transcendence and objectivity," "the new writing collapses these alternating poles into a single gesture of recognition"; and in a compact, richly suggestive discussion of the later poetry, Charles Altieri identifies Creeley's "poetics

of conjecture" "whose aim is not so much to interpret experience as
to extend it by making a situation simply the focus for overlapping
reflexive structures."

Ed Dorn's concern with the dynamic relation between self and
place is the subject of William Lockwood's "Ed Dorn's Mystique of
the Real: His Poems for North America" (*ConL* 19:58–79).

v. Sylvia Plath, Anne Sexton, Adrienne Rich, May Swenson

Is there a women's poetry that is generically different from the poetry written by men? Two excellent articles—Alicia Ostriker's "The
Nerves of a Midwife: Contemporary American Women's Poetry"
(*Parnassus* 6,i[1977]:69–87) and Dianne F. Sadoff's "Mythopoeia,
The Moon, and Contemporary Women's Poetry" (*MR* 19:93–110)
—propose that there is. Ostriker cites "four elements" in the contemporary flowering of women's poetry that make it distinct: "the quest
for autonomous self-definition; the intimate treatment of the body;
the release of anger" and "the contact imperative." Her rich essay
probes these themes in numerous contemporary women poets. "I
would not be surprised to find that certain traditional images and
symbols reveal new facets for women artists," Ostriker remarks.
Sadoff studies the different ways in which Denise Levertov, Nancy
Willard, and Diane Wakowski transform legends of the moon. If
traditional myths project the moon as virgin and whore, "the source
of inspiration and madness, the life-giver and -destroyer," contemporary women imagine the moon as embodying "female self-doubt
and fear of sexual involvement" as well as "the transforming power
of female sexual desire." Sadoff could have extended her argument
to a wide range of women poets from Sylvia Plath to Louise Gluck,
but the readings of the three poets she does deal with are subtle
and compact.

Study of Plath took some fresh and important turns in 1978.
Sandra M. Gilbert's "'A Fine, White Flying Myth': Confessions of
a Plath Addict" (*MR* 19:585–603) combines autobiography with incisive literary analysis to argue that "being enclosed" "and then
being liberated from an enclosure by a maddened or suicidal or
'hairy and ugly' avatar of the self" is the core of the Plath myth and
of much women's writing of the last two centuries.

Caroline King Bernard's *Sylvia Plath* (TUSAS 309) is relatively slight. The book, which begins with a chapter on *The Bell Jar* and then offers a developmental study of the poetry, defends Plath against the old accusations that her poems are merely private and formless. But Barnard's claim that the poems have a public vision merely gives a new name ("apocalyptic") to the same pattern (confinement generating a wish for purifying release in death) that critics have always seen there, and her insistence on the "formalizing process" in Plath's verse is not bulwarked by *specific* analysis of technique in the poems.

M. L. Rosenthal and Sally M. Gall in "'Pure? What Does It Mean?'—Notes on Sylvia Plath's Poetic Art" (*APR* 7,iii:37–40) stress poetic structure to argue that while the poems "use the intensities and explosiveness of hysterical or hallucinated states," "they are constructs rather than symptoms." More psychological in approach, Jeannine Dobbs's "'Viciousness in the Kitchen': Sylvia Plath's Domestic Poetry" (*MLS* 7,ii:11–25) explores the poet's "ambivalence toward men, marriage, and motherhood," the ensuing guilt and self-punishing gestures. "Sylvia Plath's Bee Poems" are "an attempt to renew and purify the male principle, and to incorporate it, so that the power of death would be the power of life," according to Janet McCann (*S&W* 14,iv:28–36), while Plath's views of therapy and her ambivalent attempts to make writing into therapeutic exorcism provide the focus of Jeffrey Berman's "Sylvia Plath and The Art of Dying" in *HSL* 10:137–55. In his "A Stylistic Analysis of Sylvia Plath's Semantics" in "Fever 103" Thanh-Binh Nguyen draws on a very technical linguistic terminology to yield fairly minimal results (*Lang&S* 11:69–81).

Beverly Tanenhaus explores the "Politics of Suicide and Survival: The Poetry of Anne Sexton and Adrienne Rich" (*BuR* 24,i:106–18) only to find that the pain of a traditional woman's life prompted both poets to transformation, but whereas Sexton remained a powerless victim dependent on external figures, Rich evolved an historical and political consciousness that made change possible. J. D. McClatchy's *Anne Sexton: The Artist and Her Critics* (Indiana) gathers three interviews, the poet's worksheets for "Elizabeth Gone," reminiscences by such figures as Robert Lowell, Denise Levertov, Maxine Kumin, important reviews of Sexton's books, and four critical overviews of her career. These four essays vary in both scope and quality. Jane McCabe worries the conflict between her commitments to feminism and aesthetic values, then drops the issue to discuss Sexton's search for identity. Robert Boyers declares Sexton's *Live or Die* "the crowning achievement of the confessional mode," but then tries to prove its literary merit by examining its psychological themes. Richard Howard provocatively argues that Sexton gradually came to substitute melodrama for "care" "for the poem's *making*." But the most valuable contribution is McClatchy's detailed and incisive developmental account of Sexton; his essay also speculates very interestingly on the "confessional aesthetic" by way of Theodor Reik's *The Compulsion to Confess*.

In "May Swenson and The Shapes of Speculation" (*APR* 7,ii:35–38) Alicia Ostriker concentrates on the shaped poems of *Iconographs* in order to show how, "apart from producing some beautiful things to look at, the method extends an observer's eyebeam to a new dimension" of speculation that is "balanced between the patterned and the random."

vi. Allen Ginsberg, Kenneth Patchen

Paul Portugés, in his *The Visionary Poetics of Allen Ginsberg* (Santa Barbara, Calif.: Ross-Erikson), has mapped out an important and even dramatic subject in contemporary poetry, and he's asked the right questions about it. Portugés narrates Ginsberg's visionary experiences of 1948, follows Ginsberg's struggle to embody those visions in his verse during the next eight years, and shows their ultimate effect on the poet's theory of spontaneous composition, his ideas of prosody, and his conception of the poet as prophet. The book concludes with excerpts from interviews with Ginsberg. Portugés writes about Ginsberg's mysticism with a sympathetic enthusiasm, but his interpretations of Ginsberg's life and writing are persistently superficial; he adds little to what Ginsberg himself has already told us. Had Portugés made greater use of the papers in the Allen Ginsberg Archives at Columbia he could have created a more thickly textured narrative of Ginsberg's early development, one that would have questioned the myths that Ginsberg has promoted about his career.

At the start of his *Kenneth Patchen* (TUSAS 292) Larry R. Smith announces that his subject requires a "radically new criticism." Patchen aspired to be "the poet-prophet for his age" and so what must be stressed about his work is its "message." Hence the criticism that Patchen needs—and here gets—is some old-fashioned thematic analysis. The book explores Patchen's social vision, his belief in an engaged art, his themes of madness and romantic wonder, then turns to the *Journal of Albion Moonlight*, his "poetry-prose" experiments, his anticipation of concrete poetry, his involvement in the poetry and jazz fad of the late fifties, his "irrational tales and verse," his multimedia experiments in "painting and writing forms." Smith is an ardent advocate but the case for Patchen has yet to be made.

vii. James Wright, Robert Bly, James Dickey

Two essays comment favorably on Wright's recent poetry, which has not been as well received as his work of the midsixties. Stephen Yenser's "Open Secrets" (*Parnassus* 6,ii:125–42) characterizes the tension between extravagant adventuresomeness and a plain straight-forwardness that informs all of Wright's work. In *Moments of the Italian Summer* and *To a Blossoming Pear Tree*, Yenser believes, Wright "means to have it both ways"; at his best, his "extravagance is directness." With *Two Citizens* Wright became "our most scrupulously honest, our least pretentious poet," according to William S. Saunders in "Indignation Born of Love: James Wright's Ohio Poems" (*ON* 4:353–69). Sentimentality, always the danger in Wright, is now checked by a self-consciousness which allows him to season "his love with a new realism."

Charles Molesworth's "Domesticating the Sublime: Bly's Latest Poems" (*OhR* 19,iii:56–66) provocatively offers an historical perspective on Bly. Concentrating on *This Body is Made of Camphor and Gopherwood*, Molesworth views Bly as repudiating the late modernist "traps of autotelism and excessive self-consciousness" by affirming a beyond, "a realm where value is generated and confirmed." At the same time Bly seeks to share his ecstatic visions by deifying "the data of consciousness not understood as thought, but as bodily sensation."

George S. Lensing locates James Dickey in a different historical context in "The Neo-Romanticism of James Dickey" (*SCR* 10,ii:20–32). In Lensing's version of Dickey's career, the poet begins by rejecting Eliotic impersonality, is stimulated by Roethke's concept of metaphor as a means toward "fusion of inner and outer states"; but just where Lensing should become most precise and specific—in characterizing "the audacious metaphor" in Dickey—he is too brief and too vague. "James Dickey's *The Eye Beaters*: 'An Agonizing New Life'" by Ronald Baughman (*SCR* 10,ii:81–88) reveals Dickey's inward turn. In *The Eye Beaters* Dickey presents a self threatened by "age, disease, uncertainty, terror," but a self that persists in struggling toward "momentary truth." In "Shamanism Toward Confessionalism: James Dickey, Poet" (*GaR* 32:409–19) Linda Mizejewski argues that the failure of Dickey's *Zodiac* derives from his failure to distance himself sufficiently from the hero.

viii. John Ashbery, Frank O'Hara, A. R. Ammons, W. S. Merwin, Howard Nemerov, Richard Hugo, Mark Strand

In "Motives In Metaphor: John Ashbery and the Modernist Long Poem" (*Genre* 11:653–87) Charles Altieri makes a major advance in the study of Ashbery. Although Ashbery now ranks as a leading figure in contemporary poetry, we lack any real practical criticism of his problematic texts, except for David Kalstone's chapter in *Five Temperaments*. Altieri's brilliant essay provides rich readings of "No Way of Knowing" and "Self-Portrait in a Convex Mirror." More than that, he expounds Ashbery's poetic, comparing him with Olson and Creeley, and he shows how "Self-Portrait" departs from the premises of the modernist long poem: Ashbery is willing "to continue the ambitious cultural questioning of his modernist predecessors while adapting imaginative strategies that both deflate and reinterpret their versions of the imagination as counterpressure to oppressive cultural realities and reductive models of the psyche." At the other end of the spectrum of Ashbery criticism, Richard Jackson responds to the difficulties of the poetry by locating some all-too-predictable Derridean themes—decentering, the "prison-house of language," an infinitely deferred meaning—in *Houseboat Days* ("Writing as Transgression: Ashbery's Archeology of the Moment," *SHR* 13:279–84).

Ashbery and O'Hara are often discussed as if their poetic projects were identical; carefully unfolding their early developments, Marjorie Perloff's " 'Transparent Selves': The Poetry of John Ashbery and Frank O'Hara" (*YES* 8:171–96) identifies the link between the two as "an aesthetic of *presence*" which "replaces one of transcendence." But Perloff then goes on to discriminate their poetic sensibilities: O'Hara's "daily journeys through the streets of Manhattan" juxtapose "real and surreal, serious and comic," while Ashbery's quests, "at once quite literal" yet possessing "the obsessive persistence of dreams," are more "elusive, shadowy, archetypal." Justin Replogle's "Vernacular Poetry: Frost to Frank O'Hara" (*TCL* 24:137–53) shows how O'Hara makes use of ellipsis and syntax to become "that *completely* vernacular poet the tradition hadn't produced before."

In "'Tangled Versions of the Truth': Ammons and Ashbery at Fifty" (*APR* 7,v:5–11) Marjorie Perloff points out the tired self-imitativeness of *The Snow Poems* while the author of *Houseboat Days* is writing "at the top of his form." Her essay also unfolds the fundamental difference between these two poets: "If Ammons is supremely the poet of the outdoors, of the actual American land-scape as seen by the descendants of Emerson and Whitman, Ashbery is, to my mind, an indoor poet, one who *invents* his own dream landscapes or, as he calls them in a poem from *Self-Portrait in a Convex Mirror*, his 'Märchenbilder.'" John E. Sitter's brief but very suggestive "About Ammons' *Sphere*" (*MR* 19:201–12) declares Ammons's long work a "poetic theodicy"; in *Sphere* Ammons manages to write "a poem of the middle in a largely middle style, tries to balance more than unbalance" and thus refuses the irony many modern poets have adopted to avoid the "bathos" potential in this genre.

Evan Watkins's theoretical *The Critical Act* (Yale) closes with an excellent section on W. S. Merwin's *The Lice, The Carrier of Ladders*, and *Writings to an Unfinished Accompaniment*. Watkins subtly contends that "Merwin's poetry is directed less toward escaping the limitations of the subject, the self and its idiosyncrasies, than toward a renunciation of the peculiar psychic greed which could constitute the nuclear identity of a personality." Starting out by defining their obsession "with the meaning of America" as their (rather vague) common point, L. Edwin Folsom concludes in "Approaches and Removals: W. S. Merwin's Encounter with Whitman's America" (*Shenandoah* 29,iii:57–73) that the laconic poet of the void and the expansive bard of transcendent Spirit are fundamentally different.

The publication of his *Collected Poems* in 1977 has prompted a reassessment of Howard Nemerov. Mary Kinzie's lengthy "The Signatures of Things" (*Parnassus* 6,i:1–57) lacks the concentration and direction a strong thesis would provide but the essay does deal perceptively with Nemerov's use of particulars, his figurative language, and his relation to such predecessors as Frost and Stevens.

Richard Hugo, now editor of the Yale Series of Younger Poets, has achieved sufficient reputation for Alan Helms to question it in "Writing Hurt: The Poetry of Richard Hugo" (*MPS* 9:106–18). Citing instances of "forced diction," "convoluted syntax," "private associations" and "unsure rhythms," Helms relates all these stylistic defects to the absence of any "coherent center" in Hugo's work.

"Beginnings and Endings: Mark Strand's 'The Untelling' " (*LitR* 21:357–73) by Robert Miklitsch concentrates on this poem from *The Story of Our Lives* to show how Strand's simple "use of syntax and metaphor" work to create a complex "emotional and linguistic interplay."

ix. Theodore Weiss, John Logan, Younger Poets

Weiss and Logan are two poets at mid-career who have yet to achieve reputation, much less serious critical study. Surveying Weiss's seven books, Reginald Gibbons in "The Cure: Theodore Weiss's Poetry" (*MPS* 9:18–33) makes the case for his poet by expounding his method: rather than "isolated brilliancies," Weiss's meditations give the reader "the time-bound unfolding of an emotional progress." Four essays about John Logan appeared in *MPS* (9,iii). None of the articles offers an overview of Logan's work, but Elinor Cubbage (pp. 168–78) and Robert Phillips (pp. 178–86), focusing (respectively) on *The Zigzag Walk* and *The Anonymous Lover*, emphasize the gradual secularization of Logan's verse. Alfred Barson (pp. 191–96) examines walking as metaphor for the creative process in the "Dublin Suite" and "Elegy for Dylan Thomas," while Phyllis Hoge Thompson (pp. 197–210) sees a "journey from doubt" "through loss of faith" "to a new and broader belief" in *The Anonymous Lover*.

In his long, provocative, and brilliant "Chapter and Verse" (*APR* 7,i:21–32 and 7,iii:21–32) Stanley Plumly, surveying about 20 recent books of poetry, attempts to characterize the state of the art in the late seventies. Plumly finds two major trends: a free verse "that is preoccupied with its own voice and rhetoric, the voice of the emotion, a voice tested by its ability to create and control tone" and a more "formal" verse, "a voice that has idolatrized as well as idealized the image." The essay, rich with both broad formulations about Symbolism, Surrealism, Imagism and with subtle, precise readings of poems, provides a model of the kind of literary criticism younger poets most need.

University of California, Berkeley

18. Drama

Winifred Frazer

i. From the Beginning

Historical studies of the American theatre provide each year new data on subjects as varied as minor figures and major trends, all interpreted in the light of new scholarship. *The Revels History of Drama in English*, Volume 8—*American Drama* (Methuen)—includes in three sections extensive essays by well-known American critics. In "The American Drama: Its Range of Contexts," Travis Bogard covers the history of the American theatre as an art, as a political force, and as a reflector of American values; Richard Moody treats "American Actors, Managers, Producers, and Directors"; and Walter J. Meserve, who is writing a multivolume work on the subject, describes the history of American playwriting in "The Dramatists and Their Plays." A helpful reference volume as well, *The Revels History* includes a 40-page chronological chart of theatrical events, first performances of notable plays, and biographical data about important dramatists.

In a treatment of the earliest history, "The Development of Theatre on the American Frontier, 1750–1890" (*ThS* 19:63–78), Douglas Mc-Dermott describes in detail the players, the theatres, the audiences, and the repertoires of numerous frontier troupes which existed on every frontier as the country moved westward. The process consisted of first, a few strolling amateurs playing in barns and warehouses; second, a troupe of semiprofessionals utilizing whatever town theatres existed and performing perhaps two dozen standard and new plays; and third, touring or resident companies of professionals putting on the best European and American drama available. James S. Moy in "Entertainments at John B. Ricketts's Circus, 1793–1800" (*ETJ* 30: 187–202) adds details about an extremely popular form of theatre, which competed successfully in every major east coast city of the period with the legitimate theatre companies. Erecting circus buildings in Philadelphia and other cities, Ricketts mixed serious horse-back riding with comic pantomimes, involving many riders and a musical band accompaniment—in performances which George Washington himself quite often attended. During the same decade popular in the legitimate theatre was William Dunlap's *André: A Tragedy in Five Acts*, which Miriam J. Shillingsburg describes in "The West Point Treason in American Drama, 1798–1891" *ETJ* 30:73–89) as the first of a number of versions of Benedict Arnold's treason and the hanging of Major John André as a spy. In later dramas the portrayal of Washington changed from classic man of reason to superhero, and in the centennial versions of Ingersoll Lockwood, P. Leo Haid, and Martin F. Tupper he much overshadowed the characters of the traitor and the spy. William Johnson's end-of-the-century version illustrates a new psychological interest in Arnold's near-fateful treason. The last decades of the 18th century also saw the beginning of the minstrel show, which, according to Gary D. Engle in *This Grotesque Essence: Plays from the American Minstrel Stage* (LSU), was, between the 1840s and the 1870s, the dominant form of American popular art. Engle's book consists of some 20 short afterpieces—farces, Shakespearean burlesques, and lampoons of contemporary fads—essential components of "that grotesque concoction of song, dance and theatrical comedy" featuring the black-face clown. So popular was the form that by 1860 New York alone had ten resident companies, a vigorous democratic art, making fun of pretension and deflating the highbrow.

Still another popular type of 19th century theatre—the musical spectacle—as experienced by one of its important stars, is the subject of Barbara M. Barker's "The Case of Augusta Sohlke vs. John DePol" (*ETJ* 30:233–39). A ballet star brought to New York to be featured in *The Devil's Auction*, Sohlke was not allowed by a one-sided contract to dance elsewhere when the production failed in 1867, until a legal battle revealing the exploitation of actors by managers made it possible for her to star in *The Black Crook*.

Shakespearean plays, also well-received, are the subject of Peter James Ventimiglia's "Shakespeare's Comedies on the Nineteenth-Century New York Stage: A Promptbook Analysis" (*PBSA* 71:415–41) and his "The William Winter Correspondence and the Augustin Daly Shakespearean Productions of 1885–1898" (*ETJ* 30:220–28). In the first, an analysis of eight promptbooks from the second half of the century reveals adaptations similar to those of British productions of the era, in attempts to produce the bard accurately while removing subplots and minor characters to emphasize the main action and excising indecorous phrases, classical allusions, and descriptive passages. In the second, the drama critic for the New York *Tribune* from 1865 to 1909 is shown to have been the secret adaptor of many of Daly's Shakespearean productions—a fact which neither critic nor producer wished to publicize. In a third article, "Shakespearean Prototypes and the Failure of Boker's *Francesca da Rimini*" (*ETJ* 30:211–19), Oliver H. Evans relates the baleful influence of Shakespeare on George Henry Boker, whose characters of Paolo and Francesca are well realized, but whose Lanciotto merely echoes elements from *Richard III, Macbeth, Lear,* and *Hamlet.*

ii. 20th Century

Turn-of-the-century historical accounts seldom avoid mention of the syndicates, so powerful an influence on the theatre of the time. Such is the case with Larry T. Menefee's "A New Hypothesis for Dating the Decline of the 'Road'" (*ETJ* 30:343–56) and Weldon B. Durham's "The Tightening Rein: Relations Between the Federal Government and the American Theatre Industry During World War One" (*ETJ* 30:378–97). To counteract the easy explanation that the Road, which had flourished since the 1880s, was by 1920 done in by the movies, Menefee shows through graphs and statistics that Syndicate Road shows out of New York began to decline in Little Rock (a typical road-circuit town) about 1903. He leaves it to others to build on his evidence the causes of the disappearance of the Road, which at the turn of the century meant that "Broadway" stretched from coast to coast and was immensely more profitable than the theatre district in New York from which it sprang. Durham documents theatre history in a year of crisis. The Commission on Training Camp Activities, which built or acquired 44 camp theatres in 1918, expected the syndicated theatrical profession to provide free or low-cost entertainment, resulting in much friction between government and actors, writers, and managers, whose monetary expectations differed from those of the bureaucrats.

Moving into the post-World-War-I era, Cynthia Sutherland in "American Women Playwrights as Mediators of the 'Woman Problem'" (*MD* 21:319–36) describes the work of four middle-class playwrights, born in the 1870s and 1880s—Zona Gale, Zoë Akins, Susan Glaspell, and Rachel Crothers—who exposed the situation of American women in a patriarchal society as forcefully as they could in an era when most women opted for home and motherhood. Although the endings of their plays often depended on some concession to public taste, they raised important questions about women's roles in American culture. At the end of the proletarian thirties Franklin Roosevelt (perhaps at the behest of Eleanor, who had seen the production at least six times in New York) invited the cast of the International Ladies' Garment Workers Union to perform their popular left-wing revue at the White House. Harry Morton Goldman in "*Pins and Needles*: A White House Command Performance" (*ETJ* 30:90–101) assesses his interviews with some 60 survivors of this great event in their lives. A splendid view of the entire Federal Theatre Project—pictures and commentary—is now available in *Free, Adult, Uncensored: The Living History of the Federal Theatre Project* (Washington, D.C.: New Republic Books), edited by John O'Connor and Lorraine Brown. It makes that remarkable experiment come alive.

Philip K. Jason in "The First Writers in Residence: MacKaye and Frost" (*MQR* 17:377–91) documents the beginnings of a widespread practice today. Percy MacKaye was the first writer in residence at Miami University in Oxford, Ohio, in 1920, where he worked productively on American dramas based on the folklore of the Kentucky mountains. MacKaye's publicizing and extolling his appointment resulted in a similar position for Robert Frost at the University of Michigan and an increasing number of such appointments for writers in the decades since.

iii. Ruth Draper, Sidney Howard, Lillian Hellman, Robert Anderson

Three playwrights and Ruth Draper, creator of her own monologues, are the subjects of useful biographical volumes. In the foreword to *The Letters of Ruth Draper, 1920–1956: A Self-Portrait of a Great Actress*, edited by Neilla Warren (Scribner's), John Gielgud calls Draper (along with Martha Graham) "the greatest individual performer that America has ever given us." Thirty-six of her best-known monologues, in which she evoked some 310 characters on the stage, are described in an appendix, whereas her letters to family and friends balance the lonely rigors of touring against her great successes on the stages of the world.

Considering his fame in the twenties and thirties and the lasting character of some of his work, the Twayne biography—*Sidney Howard* by Sidney Howard White (TUSAS 288[1977])—is overdue. From *They Knew What They Wanted* (1924) through *The Silver Cord, The Late Christopher Bean, Alien Corn,* to *Yellow Jack* (1934), Howard provided original plays for Broadway and was equally important to Hollywood, adapting a number of his own plays, and writing screenplays, including *Gone With the Wind,* before an accident cut short his life. In *Robert Anderson* (TUSAS 300) Thomas P. Adler has most competently analyzed the life and work of the playwright whose "theme is loneliness." From *Tea and Sympathy* in 1953 through later plays like *Double Solitaire* and *I Never Sang for my Father,* Anderson has written well-crafted dramas, exploring the "pervasive isolation" of the contemporary human condition. An excellent critic of modern American playwrights, Doris V. Falk, has written a biography, *Lillian Hellman,* in the Modern Literature Monographs series (Ungar), pointing out that Hellman has been in the news for five decades as playwright, political liberal, or autobiographical best-seller. Falk describes a consistently serious character, not always happy, not always popular, but always in search of enlightenment about the times and about herself.

iv. Eugene O'Neill

Some reputations come and go, but O'Neill's remains high from year to year. Interest continues in his plays, dramatic theories, and biography. At the 1978 MLA Convention in New York an O'Neill Society was formed, whose secretary, Jordan Miller, University of Rhode Island, Kingston, may be contacted for further information. Highlights for the third year and third volume of the *Eugene O'Neill Newsletter,* edited by Frederick Wilkins, are in the January issue, plus a series of four short articles on *The Hairy Ape* by Michael Hinden, Virginia Floyd, Ann D. Hughes, and Horst Frenz. In the May issue James Robinson writes on Christianity in *All God's Chillun* and Kristin Morrison on the sea plays of O'Neill and Conrad. In the September issue *Hughie* is the subject of short pieces by Edward I. Shaugh-

nessy and by Frederick I. Carpenter, who has also this year revised
and updated *Eugene O'Neill* (TUSAS 66). In each issue are production notes for performances of O'Neill plays by various American and
foreign groups as well as accounts of the historic restoration of
O'Neill's childhood home, Monte Cristo Cottage, in New London,
Connecticut, and of Tao House, near San Francisco, where he wrote
his last great plays.

The most important of all living memorials to O'Neill is the
O'Neill Theatre Center overlooking the Thames River in Waterford,
Connecticut, near New London. The National Playwright's Conference held there annually under the direction of Lloyd Richards affords
the opportunity for some 16 to 20 playwrights to participate in staged
readings and criticism of their plays. The Rufus and Margo Rose
Theatre Barn on the grounds provides four large working areas for
the various conferences which meet there, which include the National Theatre of the Deaf and the Creative Arts in Education Program for elementary-school teachers. The Theatre Collection and
Library continually expands its holdings from the original Harriet
Whitmore Enders collection of dramatic literature and the Dale
Wasserman collection of theatre books and periodicals. As an international clearinghouse for research materials on O'Neill, it is fittingly
located on the grounds and will later be housed in Monte Cristo
Cottage. Testimony to interest in the project abroad is an article in
England's *ThQ* 8,xxxi:61–65, "Playwrights Front and Centre: the
O'Neill Conference at Work," by Arthur Ballet, who claims that the
conference serves playwrights, and hence all theatre, better than any
other operation in America.

In a study of an O'Neill character, *A Role: O'Neill's Cornelius
Melody* (Humanities Press) Lennart Josephson, besides describing
the role from an actor's point of view, also analyzes the characters
around Melody, the social class from which he came, and the sources
from life and literature which may have inspired O'Neill to create
the role. As volume 19 in the Stockholm Studies in History of Literature series, this book is one more proof of Sweden's continued interest
in O'Neill. Eliciting nothing very new, it does make clear how O'Neill's
knowledge of Adler's psychology informs the character of the anti-
hero of *A Touch of the Poet*. Taking a very different approach, Elinor
Fuchs in "O'Neill's Poet: Touched by Ibsen" (*ETJ* 30:513–16) claims
that this play shows Ibsen's influence, not most importantly in theme

or details of action from *Hedda Gabler* and *The Wild Duck*, but as "a pivotal work" toward the new ironic, compressed method of O'Neill's late plays in the Ibsenist mode.

Iceman is the subject of two essays. Dennis M. Welch plows some old ground in "Hickey as Satanic Force in *The Iceman Cometh*" (*ArQ* 34:219–29) and perhaps makes the case for Hickey as an image of Milton's Lucifer no stronger than O'Neill himself explicitly has in portraying the devilish nature of the rebel against man's God—illusion. In a most original treatment, "The Theater in *The Iceman Cometh*: Some Modernist Implications" (*ArQ* 34:230–38), James G. Watson, however, makes a case for *Iceman* as being not about illusions but about theatre. In the same self-contained modernist mode of *Ulysses* or "Gerontion," each character plays a part for the audience on stage, a theatre which "Theodore" Hickman almost kills. Assuming the role of madman, however, Hickey restores the theatre, proving O'Neill's modernist tenet that objective truth is insanity, that art is the sole hope for man in a world gone mad. Up to now perhaps all too little has been done to pull O'Neill into the intellectual mainstream of his lost-generation times. Watson makes a formidable beginning. Another article, William Wasserstrom's "Notes on Electricity: Henry Adams and Eugene O'Neill" (*PsychocultR* 1:161–78) also stresses O'Neill's modernism, but from a different view. O'Neill's early play, *Dynamo*, which was professionally produced in 1976 by Arthur Storch at Syracuse Stage, reveals the playwright's concern with the optimism of Walter Lippmann and Charles Beard in contrast to the pessimism of Henry Adams and D. H. Lawrence concerning the effect of modern mechanization on the human psyche. The play is thus not only a revelation of O'Neill's antagonism toward his mother as dynamo, but also a modernist dramatization illustrating the destructive power of technological progress.

O'Neill's influence on Thomas Wolfe is the subject of Charmian Green's "Wolfe, O'Neill, and the Mask of Illusion" (*PLL* 14:87–90). In Wolfe's play, *Mannerhouse*, as in O'Neill's expressionistic plays of the twenties, characters are alienated by masked faces, and in *Look Homeward, Angel*, Eugene Gant's encounter with the ghosts of his emerging identity may pay tribute to O'Neill, whom Wolfe greatly admired. In contrast to those pieces relating O'Neill to his times is Paul Voelker's "Eugene O'Neill's Aesthetic of the Drama" (*MD* 21:87–99) in which he, like others, has tried to formulate from

O'Neill's brief comments his theory of the dramatic art. Voelker shows the playwright's consistent view that in his own creations theme precedes plot, which precedes character, which precedes dialogue. O'Neill thus worked from idea to plot to scenario to dialogue draft, and he wished his plays to be judged by how successfully the audience responds to Life in terms of the lives he portrays.

Whether serious modern drama meets the criteria of classic tragedy is often debated. Apparently assuming that it should, Mara Lemanis in "*Desire Under the Elms* and Tragic Form: A Study of Misalliance" (*SDR* 16,iii:46–55) avers that O'Neill has written a "miscegenated tragedy," for Abbie is unconscious of a moral dilemma in the murder of her baby and Ephraim, who has tragic stature, experiences no rebirth. As to biography, Dorothy Commins in *What Is an Editor? Saxe Commins at Work* (Chicago) adds details to those already known about the friendship of O'Neill for his editor, Commins. She describes their relationship through the years and their grieved parting as O'Neill struggled at the end of his life to reconcile his differences with Carlotta.

Each year a number of doctoral dissertations are concerned with O'Neill, the man and artist. His theory and practical use of masks, his view of cyclic and lineal time in his proposed cycle and in his biographical plays, the eternal mother-son relationship as it emerges in many of his dramas are typical subjects of investigation. A useful bibliographic study appears to be Clarence Sturm's "Scholarly Criticism of Eugene O'Neill in Periodicals, 1960–1975, with a Bibliographical Overview of the American and German Studies" (*DAI* 38A:5469). The study includes abstracts of the articles during the recent period, a bibliography of German studies (which are extensive) since 1920, and a bibliography of significant works in English since 1915.

v. Arthur Miller, Tennessee Williams, Edward Albee

A number of the 23 pieces in *The Theater Essays of Arthur Miller*, edited by Robert Martin (Viking), have been anthologized and reproduced often in the past three decades, "Tragedy and the Common Man" having been the rallying cry of the critics opposed to Krutch's "The Tragic Fallacy." Although in an introduction Miller wishes that he "had never said a word on the subject of tragedy," he did not, after 1949, stop writing pragmatic commentaries on such matters as a repertory theatre at Lincoln Center, the difficulty of getting good plays on Broadway, and the nature of the American social life which the drama reflects. Disavowing a theoretical or scholarly stance, Miller's best known essays, mainly from the fifties, elucidate his own work and that of his contemporaries.

Avoiding the old question of whether Willy Loman is a tragic figure, Alfred R. Ferguson in "The Tragedy of the American Dream in *Death of a Salesman*" (*Thought* 53:83–98) posits that Willy as the personification of the American dream—the word made flesh—provides a tragic vision of the death of the myth, heightening our awareness of what it means to be human, as all great tragedy does. Compiled by George H. Jensen, *Arthur Miller: A Bibliographical Checklist* (Columbia, S.C.: J. Faust, 1976) is a scholarly volume recording the various publications of Miller's books, articles, speeches, and interviews. Since it is often easier for students of American drama to come by information on details and dates of productions of various plays than it is to discover publication data relating to American playwrights, Jensen's work will be appreciated and will serve as a model for such works on other important playwrights.

None of our three great playwrights—O'Neill, Miller, or Williams—can be commended as dramatic theorists. In *Where I Live: Selected Essays* (New Directions), editors Christine R. Day and Bob Woods include 30 of Tennessee Williams's very short pieces written between 1944 and 1978, published in various papers, journals, and books, and consisting of introductions to new plays, commentaries about the theatre and about his work—in one Williams interviews himself—none of which reveal a serious consideration of drama as an art. Many do, however, reveal Williams's sense of humor: Liz Taylor was miscast in *Suddenly Last Summer*, for she "would have dragged Sebastian home by his ears and so saved them both from considerable embarrassment that summer." Too casual to be called essays, the selections abound in original descriptions of Williams and other personalities on the American scene since he hit the big time with *The Glass Menagerie*.

Susan Snowden Palmer's "An Interview with Tennessee in Georgia" (*NOR* 6:28–30) might well have been included in *Where I Live*, being the playwright's commentary on play revision, specifically the creation of *Tiger Tale* from *Baby Doll*, as well as Williams's happy satisfaction with his life at this time. His personal life is also of in-

terest abroad, as illustrated by Dotson Rader's "The Private Letters
of Tennessee Williams" (*London Mag.* 18:18–28). Landing hard on
Donald Windham for publishing the letters which Williams wrote
him between 1940 and 1965 without permission, and on Gore Vidal
and Robert Brustein for their carping at the playwright's life and
work, Rader makes a rousing defense of Williams, for his weathering
of the death of Frankie Merlo in 1963, and a plea for his need of
understanding in the face of a betrayal like Windham's.

Williams, as might be expected, comes in for lengthy treatment
by Georges-Michel Sarotte in *Like a Brother, Like a Lover: Male
Homosexuality in the American Novel and Theatre from Herman
Melville to James Baldwin* (Anchor). Using the stage for concealed
psychotherapy, Williams, while identifying with his female characters, keeps his homosexual males offstage (often deceased before the
curtain rises) and makes his virile machos of foreign descent. Much
as the subject has been covered, Sarotte adds some new details. The
book originally was published in French in 1976.

In an extremely useful start on a comprehensive bibliography of
Williams's work, Drewey Wayne Gunn in "The Various Texts of
Tennessee Williams's Plays" (*ETJ* 30:368–75) lists 70 published or
produced plays and screenplays with annotations on various versions
of some. Numerous other plays in manuscript form are among the
Williams papers at the University of Texas Humanities Research
Center. Signi Falk has revised and updated her volume on *Tennessee
Williams* (TUSAS 10) this year, and a semi-annual, *Tennessee Wil-
liams Newsletter*, under the editorship of Stephen S. Stanton, University of Michigan, Ann Arbor, appeared in April 1979.

Edward Albee is the only American playwright treated by John
M. Clum in "Religion and Five Contemporary Plays: The Quest for
God in a Godless World" (*SAQ* 77:418–32). His *Tiny Alice*, however,
illustrates, as do plays by Stoppard, Shaffer, and Ionesco, the thesis
that man lives in a meaningless void—boxes within boxes—for nothing
but death at the end. If Lucina P. Gabbard is right, a later Albee play
has a more optimistic message. In "Albee's *Seascape*: An Adult Fairy
Tale" (*MD* 21:307–17), Gabbard sees Albee illustrating that an aging
human couple can attain a sense of rebirth to a higher plane through
encounter with two primeval creatures on their way up the evolutionary ladder—all in a manner typical of the rites of passage of many
a fairy tale.

Even if Sarotte (see above) notes the possibility of playing *Who's Afraid of Virginia Woolf?* with four male characters (perhaps two in drag), he might become convinced of the heterosexuality of the couples considered by Terry Otten, who, in "'Played to the Finish': Coward and Albee" (*StHum* 6,i:31–36), sees *Hay Fever* as one source of the play. Playing of staged games by a family of four to the chagrin of four guests in Coward's play is closely paralleled by half the number of characters in Albee's, the older couple of which subject the two guests to humiliation and exposure through four harrowing games. Although Coward's light tone is not paralleled by Albee, the technique of the plays, as Otten points out, is in innumerable instances remarkably similar.

An essay explaining Albee's social philosophy in terms of his dramaturgy is "In the Bosom of the Family: Contradiction and Resolution in Edward Albee" (*MinnR* 8:133–45) by Rachel Blau Duplessis. Claiming that evasion is Albee's method of avoiding the resolution of social problems, Duplessis suggests that Albee's plays conclude traditionally with husband in charge of family (George comforting submissive Martha) in a "privatized" solution which disregards the implications of George's failure as a professor or the peril of mechanized man in Nick's biology. Likewise in *A Delicate Balance* the solution to threat from outside is found in normalizing relationships at home. Duplessis may think Albee's endings sanctimonious and his dramas overpraised, but the number of articles on his various plays each year testify to the scholar's continuing interest in his work.

vi. Contemporary

Speculative books on comedy and tragedy are Robert B. Heilman's *The Ways of the World: Comedy and Society* (Wash.) and Alfred Schwarz's *From Buchner to Beckett: Dramatic Theory and the Modes of Tragic Drama* (Ohio), both of which emphasize foreign rather than American drama. Longtime drama professor Heilman, acceding to the modern assumption that whether or not tragedy is dead, comedy is alive, tries to get at the nature of comedy on the stage and considers plays of Americans O'Neill, Williams, and Robert Sherwood in the process. In his book on the tragic, Schwarz treats Arthur Miller at great length in a chapter, "After the Fall," citing the change in Miller's view of man as the victim of social ills to the tragic view that "the fate of society is mirrored in the nature of man." O'Neill's characters "fight their private battles of passion and conscience" as do those of Tennessee Williams, but no American playwright illustrates Beckett's tragic pessimism that man's misfortune is that he exists at all.

In *Family, Drama, and American Dreams* (Greenwood) Tom Scanlan makes the case that American drama concerns the family with its dream of the security of a home in conflict with the need for individual freedom and social communication. O'Neill looked deeply into the question in plays like *Desire, Mourning, Journey,* and *Wilderness.* Miller saw the question as how to make of the outside world a home. Williams's characters are driven from or escape from the warring family, always to be haunted by its memory. Neither can Lillian Hellman's Hubbards, Clifford Odets's Bergers, nor Edward Albee's George and Martha solve the dilemma, posed originally by Joseph Jefferson's *Rip Van Winkle,* of how, as a family member, one can have both individual and social freedom. In a closely related article, "On the Moral Character of the American Regime: *A Thousand Clowns* Revisited" (*SAQ* 77:225–41), Thomas J. Scorza proposes that the popularity of Herb Gardner's play on stage and screen illustrates America's devotion to the bourgeois family, with Murray succumbing to marriage and commonplace decor to provide Nick a home, a situation which neglects the civic responsibility which Tocqueville saw as a higher virtue.

The diversity of the contemporary theatrical scene in America is testified to by many serious short pieces and books. *The Performing Arts and American Society,* edited by W. McNeil Lowry (Prentice-Hall), consists of articles analyzing various kinds of performances in the last two decades in America—"a period of the most rapid expansion in the performing arts in the history of this or any other nation." There is emphasis upon the move from Broadway to off- and off-off-Broadway and the growth of resident companies throughout the land. Gerald Weales in "American Theater Watch, 1977–1978" (*GaR* 32:515–27), reinforces the thesis, noting that New York has become "little more than a receiving station for pre-tested goods" and that the American critic today needs eyes all over the country in order to keep a watch on the many active regional theatres where the best American plays now originate. Craig Werner in "Primal Screams and Nonsense Rhymes: David Rabe's Revolt" (*ETJ* 30:517–29) writes on one of America's promising playwrights, who, confronting the disunities of the American experience during the Vietnam war, attempts in his trilogy to create a language to overcome the alienation caused by evasion of reality.

Very specialized kinds of theatre which gained popularity in the 1970s are the subject of analysis by theatre and social critics. In "Feminist Theatre: A Rhetorical Phenomenon" (*QJS* 64:284–94) Patti P. Gillespie suggests that at least 40 identifiable theatrical groups to promote the interests of women elicit the support of activists as well as women to whom the theatre has no implications of violence. The rhetorical paradox of proclaiming equality while asking society to grant it is thus solved by feminist theatre. A regional theatre promoted by Texas A. and I. University to bring drama to underprivileged Mexican-Americans in their native language and in English is the subject of Joe Rosenberg's "La Compañia de Teatro Bilingüe" (*ETJ* 30:240–52). Now a year-round professional company brings border towns and school children bilingual theatre and through music and dance encourages South Texas audiences to test the work of Latin-American playwrights.

An informative book on a third kind of theatre ever increasing in popularity is George Latshaw's *Puppetry: The Ultimate Disguise* (New York: Richards Rosen) in the Theatre Student series. Interest in semiprofessional and professional groups which perform religious and classical dramas with a variety of puppets and marionettes is increased by the popularity of this form of theatre on educational television and more recently on commercial TV by the prize-winning Muppets.

Avant garde theatre in America and abroad is covered each year by the *Drama Review* (*TDR*). The issue on the "Occult and Bizarre" includes Carol Rosen's "The Bird and the Dirt" (22:97–106), explaining the origin of this play in Old Philadelphia—a combination of mysticism, religion, superstition, song, dance, and chant brought from Brazil by Jonas dos Santos. Also an historical article on the mystic Gurdjieff, whose performances had considerable influence on America in the 1920s, is of interest to students of that period. In an "Analysis" issue (vol. 22, no. 3) various kinds of criticism are applied to the description of certain avant garde theatre performances. An article on the play, *Andy Warhol's Last Love* by Adele Edling Shank and Theodore Shank describes its production for the West 23rd

Street Squat Theatre. There follow an "Anthropological Analysis" by
Richard Schechner and an "Organic Analysis" by Noël Carroll, who,
disavowing Marxism, psychoanalysis, feminism, structuralism, or
phenomenology, searches for coherence between different elements
of the play. In the same issue Ingrid Nyeboe describes Mabou Mines's
The Shaggy Dog Animation in production, which is followed by a
Jungian and also a Trans-Semiotic analysis, whereas the play *Cops*
by Richard Schechner is followed by a Gay analysis. In the 'Workshop" issue (vol. 22, no. 4) besides discussion of such techniques as
that of Jacques Copeau in Paris during World War I, the Suzuki
Method in Tokyo, Bertolt Brecht's experiments in discourse making,
and the American Abstract Spaces Workshop, there is general discussion of three types of workshop—special skills, production-oriented,
and self-exploration—at least one of which is frequently associated
with each avant garde theatre company.

Noteworthy news items for the year are that the *Educational
Theatre Journal*, longtime publisher of scholarly articles on theatre,
became in 1979 *Theatre Journal*, indicating a national blurring of
the lines between educational, community, and professional theatre,
and that history repeats itself in reverse as Robert Brustein leaves
as dean of the Yale School of Drama to assume the directorship of the
Loeb Drama Center at Harvard, whereas George Pierce Baker left
Harvard in 1925 to found the Yale School of Drama.

vii. Reference Works

A useful work of primary source material is *Scenes from the Nineteenth-Century Stage in Advertising Woodcuts* (Dover, 1977), which
contains some 300 advertising cuts from one old pictorial catalogue,
supplemented by numerous miscellaneous notes by editor Stanley
Appelbaum. This year's reprint in 21 volumes of *America's Lost Plays*,
edited by Barrett H. Clark (Indiana), will be welcomed by many
libraries which are otherwise unable to obtain many of the plays
included.

Helpful to those studying America's present interest in Shakespeare is *The Shakespeare Complex: A Guide to Summer Festivals and
Year-Round Repertory*, edited by Glenn Loney and Patricia MacKay
(New York: Drama Book Specialists). Besides many photographs,
the volume includes the history of some 25 theatre groups and the

details of numerous Shakespearean productions. In this period of
proliferation of theatres throughout the country, Stephen Langley's
Theatre Management in America (New York: Drama Book Specialists) provides essential graphic detailed information of great help
to commercial, stock, educational, or community theatres which work
under economic as well as aesthetic strictures.

Helpful information guides this year include Don B. Wilmeth's
American Stage to World War I: A Guide to Information Sources
(Gale), which contains items written during the past 200 years on
all aspects of the American stage (excluding drama as literature);
a four-volume biographical dictionary of theatrical figures, *Who Was
Who in the Theatre, 1912–1976*, originally compiled by John Parker
(Gale); *Contemporary American Theatre Critics: A Dictionary and
Anthology of Their Works*, edited by M. F. Comtois and Lynn F.
Miller (Scarecrow, 1977); and the second volume of the series *New
York Theatre Annual, 1977–1978*, edited by Catharine R. Hughes
(Gale) and covering plot summaries, review excerpts, cast lists, and
production photographs for all shows opening or continuing on Broad-
way and off-Broadway.

Of even more interest to the specializing scholar are the many
theatre collections becoming available throughout the country. Ted
Perry's third volume of *Performing Arts Resources* (New York:
Drama Book Specialists, 1977), copublished with the Theatre Library
Association, describes a number of these. William C. Young in "Thea-
tre Collection Notes" (*ETJ* 30:294–95) lists others, among them the
Schubert Archives, now being catalogued in New York, the Kennedy
Center Library of the Performing Arts, the Curtis Collection at the
University of Pittsburgh, and the American Avant-Garde and Radical
Theatre Collection at the University of California in Davis. The
wealth of emerging primary source material bodes well for productive work in various fields of American drama, just as growth in the
number and quality of theatrical groups and playwrights foretells a
healthy resurgence of participation in American theatre throughout
the country.

University of Florida

19. Black Literature

Darwin T. Turner

It is more difficult to teach courses in Afro-American literature today than a few years ago because significant anthologies, novels, dramas, and volumes of poetry no longer are in print. Nevertheless, journals and a few publishing houses continue to be interested in scholarship about black literature—especially in the necessary bibliographical information. If the number of essays and books about black literature was slightly less in 1978 than in preceding years, it is nonetheless impressive.

I wish to explain briefly one arrangement in the following essay. Several Afro-Americans have created distinguished work in more than one literary genre. To avoid separating the criticism about such authors according to the genre to which it applies, I have placed all of the criticism within the genre to which I have assigned the author: Alice Dunbar-Nelson, Arna Bontemps, James Baldwin, Ishmael Reed, and Al Young in "Fiction"; Amiri Baraka (LeRoi Jones), Langston Hughes, and Gwendolyn Brooks in "Poetry"; Joseph S. Cotter in "Drama." For the most part, however, I have listed interviews and bibliographies separately from the criticism section. Furthermore, I have not included criticism of motion pictures except for one discussion of Richard Wright's efforts to convert *Native Son* into a film.

i. Bibliography

Esther Spring Arata's *More Black American Playwrights* (Scarecrow) expands *Black American Playwrights, 1800 to the Present* (1976). The book has three sections: (1) an alphabetized listing of black playwrights (and whites who collaborated) and their works, together with criticism, reviews, and a record of awards; (2) a general bibliography; (3) an index of play titles. Almost 500 playwrights

are included. The bibliography has weaknesses: dates of birth are
included for some authors but not for most; items are missing from
the general bibliography; authors' names are sometimes misspelled
(for example, Zora Neale Hurston is identified once as Nora Zeal
Hurston). The most serious deficiency, however, is insufficient publishing information about the plays. To cite only one of many examples, Langston Hughes's *Little Ham, The Emperor of Haiti, Simply
Heavenly,* and *Tambourines to Glory* have been published; but the
bibliography does not record that information. Despite limitations,
the bibliography should be very useful.

Black American Writers: Bibliographical Essays (St. Martin's)
is a two-volume work edited by M. Thomas Inge, Maurice Duke,
and Jackson R. Bryer. Volume 1 includes five essays: "Early Writers:
Jupiter Hammon, Phillis Wheatley, and Benjamin Banneker" by
Jerome Klinkowitz; "Slave Narratives" by Ruth Miller and Peter
Katopes; "The Polemicists: David Walker, Frederick Douglass,
Booker T. Washington, and W. E. B. DuBois" by W. Burghardt
Turner; "Modern Beginnings: William Wells Brown, Charles Wad-
dell Chesnutt, Martin R. Delany, Paul Laurence Dunbar, Sutton E.
Griggs, Frances Ellen Watkins Harper, and Frank J. Webb" by Ruth
Miller and Peter Katopes: "The Harlem Renaissance: Arna W. Bon-
temps, Countee Cullen, James Weldon Johnson, Claude McKay,
and Jean Toomer," also by Miller and Katopes; and "Langston
Hughes" by Blyden Jackson. A more conservatively structured second volume is limited to "Richard Wright" by John M. Reilly, "Ralph
Ellison" by Joanne Giza, "James Baldwin" by Daryl Dance, and
"Amiri Baraka" by Letitia Dace. Each essay includes an introduction, an annotated bibliography, a discussion of editions of the
author's work, a record of holdings of manuscripts and letters, an
evaluation of any biographies or biographical articles, and an evaluation of the criticism of the authors. The bibliographical facts
(titles, sources, etc.) will be valuable to students and beginning
scholars, but some more advanced scholars will question the evaluations and the omissions. The design of volume 1 probably was
too large for a book of slightly more than 200 pages. The result is a
work highly uneven. In a judicious essay of 20 pages Klinkowitz
discusses three writers, including Banneker, who would not be
taught in most courses in Afro-American literature. W. B. Turner
justifiably requires 86 pages to discuss Walker, Douglass, Washing-

ton, and DuBois. But Miller and Katopes use only 90 pages to dispose of slave narratives and all significant black creative writers—except Langston Hughes—from 1850 to 1930. Moreover, the Miller-Katopes sections are weakened by a tendency towards exuberant evaluations of works as "definitive," "excellent," "outstanding," and "absolutely essential." (The "absolutely essential" crown is awarded to Addison Gayle's *The Way of the New World* for its perception about the Harlem Renaissance, as if the Renaissance had not been understood before the appearance of Gayle's book.) Since the volume suggests inclusiveness, one wonders why such writers as Wallace Thurman, Zora Neale Hurston, Nella Larsen, Jessie Fauset, and perhaps W. S. Braithwaite were omitted from the Renaissance. Such omissions distort the history of Afro-American literature. That is, conventionally the Harlem Renaissance is taught as a period during which, for the first time in the history of the United States, numbers of Afro-American writers were courted and printed by American publishers; but volume 1 of *Black American Writers* fails to reflect this increase. DuBois, Washington, Chesnutt, Dunbar, and Griggs represent the 1890s, and only five writers represent the Renaissance. (The separate chapter on Hughes even implies that he is not to be considered part of the Renaissance.) Because of its limited focus on four writers, the second volume seems more rational. Although one might desire biographical essays about authors other than Wright, Ellison, Baldwin, and Baraka, one must admit that they are the most frequently discussed. In addition to his bibliographic chapter on Wright, Reilly has published *Richard Wright: The Critical Reaction*, discussed later in this essay.

Donald Gibson and Geneviève Fabre published significant bibliographical essays on Afro-American fiction and drama in the annual bibliography issue of *American Quarterly*. In "Afro-American Fiction: Contemporary Research and Criticism, 1965–1978" (*AQ* 30: 395–409), Gibson intelligently discusses criticism about the Black Aesthetic, recent monographs on fiction, biographies (calling attention to the need for more), anthologies, and bibliographies. Because of space limitations, Gibson excludes black folklore and critical essays; but, in the very short essay, he provides a comprehensive survey of the major works and some of the lesser known. His evaluations of monographs and anthologies should be of special value to students and general readers seeking a limited number of books through which to gain an introduction to Afro-American literature. Generally conservative in his appraisals, he becomes harsh only when he warns readers against critics he considers contemptuous of or condescending toward Afro-American writers. In particular he warns against Robert Bone, who "oversimplies and . . . distorts" and "inclines toward easy and overly imaginative readings"; David Littlejohn, who "evinces little respect for the authors of whom he writes"; and C. W. E. Bigsby, who "cannot conceal the sense of superiority he feels toward the work of black writers and critics." Interestingly, Bigsby apparently has now decided to pretend that black writers do not exist. In a review of American dramatic criticism 1945–1978, published in the same issue of *American Quarterly*, Bigsby mentions Amiri Baraka in a list of playwrights who received critical attention in *Modern Drama*, names Charles Gordone without identifying him as black, and disposes of the rest of black drama of the past four decades with only this statement: "Blacks, Mexican Americans, and Puerto-Ricans dramatized their plight. . . ." One would never suspect that Bigsby himself has written about Lorraine Hansberry, LeRoi Jones, and James Baldwin or that he included more than 100 pages of criticism about black dramatists in his two-volume anthology of criticism of Afro-American literature.

A more honest attempt to place blacks in American theatre is "American Drama, 1918–1940: A Survey of Research and Criticism" (*AQ* 30:298–330) by Jackson R. Bryer and Ruth M. Alvarez. The essay calls attention to bibliographies by James Hatch and Abdullak and by Arata and Nicholas Rotoli. It describes anthologies by Hatch and Theodore Shine, Alain Locke and Montgomery Gregory, and William Brasmer and Don Consolo. It describes books of criticism, and it includes Langston Hughes among the playwrights surveyed. In the same issue, a more extensive bibliographical essay, "Afro-American Theatre: A Bibliographic Survey" (*AQ* 30:358–73) by Geneviève Fabre, discusses checklists and bibliographies, anthologies, critical books and articles on books, magazine articles, and black periodicals devoted to drama, documentary and historical studies, and the Black Aesthetic. Trying to cover a wide range of materials within a relatively short essay, Fabre has been selective. There are some omissions and some misinterpretations of criticism, and the author seems weakest when reviewing the history of black theatre briefly; nevertheless, the essay is perceptive and useful. *Bibliographic Guide to Black Studies, 1978* (Hall) lists publications (by subject) catalogued during the previous year by the New York Public Library and the Library of Congress. The *Guide* is useful but incomplete.

Black American Fiction: A Bibliography by Carol Fairbanks and Eugene Engeldinger (Scarecrow) provides an alphabetized list of Afro-American authors, a list of works by those writers, and a list of reviews of the works. There is also a general bibliography.

A useful annotated bibliography of Afro-American literature is regularly prepared by Ernest Kaiser in the quarterly issues of *Freedomways*. Kaiser's ranks among the most intelligent criticism of black literature. *Obsidian: Black Literature in Review* regularly reviews black literature—as do *Black American Literature Forum, First World,* and *Black Books Bulletin.*

Several checklists or bibliographies of individual authors were published during the year. Joe Weixlmann and John O'Banion published "A Checklist of Ellison Criticism" (*BALF* 12:51–55), an updating of Jacqueline Covo's *The Blinking Eye*, criticism through 1972. Leonard J. Deutsch prepared "A Corrected Bibliography for Rudolph Fisher" (*BB* 35:30–33). Ishmael Reed collaborated with Joe Weixlmann and Robert Fikes, Jr., in "Mapping Out the Gumbo Works" (*BALF* 12:24–29), which includes published and soon-to-be published works by Reed as well as biography and criticism. Elizabeth and Thomas Settle compiled *Ishmael Reed: An Annotated Checklist* (Carson: Calif. State College/Dominguez Hills, 1977). In *James Weldon Johnson and Arna Wendell Bontemps: A Reference Guide* (Hall), Robert E. Fleming has prepared an annotated checklist which offers a year-by-year listing of materials about the authors.

Thomas Inge's "Contemporary Southern Black Writers: A Checklist" (*MissQ* 31:185–90) seems to have been researched carefully but includes individuals not known for poetry, fiction, or drama. Andrea Rushing has published part of a bibliography that, when completed, will describe African and new world images of women. This very brief bibliography, "An Annotated Bibliography of Images of Black Women in Black Literature" (*CLAJ* 21:435–42), does not distinguish original publishing dates from reprint dates.

ii. Criticism of Fiction Writers

a. **Brown, Webb, Delany, Griggs, Dunbar-Nelson, Chesnutt.** This
year's scholarship verifies Renate Simpson's complaint that Afro-
American fiction of the 19th century is a neglected field. In fact, the
quality of some of the essays suggests that it is an abused field. In
"The 1850's—The Maturation of the Black American Novel" (*RAIC*
1,i:1–11), Simpson compares William Wells Brown's *Clotel,* Frank
Webb's *The Garies and Their Friends,* and Martin Delany's *Blake*
in their emphasis on black survival through independent spirit and
reliance on black identity. Seeking to encourage teachers to include
these works in the curricula, Simpson enthusiastically commends
the timely themes and well-developed characters of the novels.

If Simpson may be excessively generous in her praise, Roger
Whitlow is excessively harsh when he ridicules two novelists in
"The Black Revolutionary Novels of Martin R. Delany and Sutton
Griggs" (*Melus* 5,iii:26–36). The essay deserves mention only as
an example of that kind of criticism which denies the black novelist
the traditional latitude of imagination in fiction (if indeed political
or personal antagonism is not at work). Whitlow is not willing to
permit Delany in *Blake* the right of an imaginative writer to fashion
events about a revolution to free slaves. Similarly, in regard to
Griggs's *Imperium in Imperio,* he feels it beyond belief that there
could be a massive conspiracy to establish a black empire—in a work
of fiction.

Writing about Alice Dunbar-Nelson, who does not offend his sensibilities, he is more generous. Describing the themes he perceives
in *Violets and Other Tales* and *The Goodness of St. Rocques and
Other Stories,* Whitlow identifies her, in "Alice Dunbar-Nelson: New
Orleans Writer" (*RFI* 4,i:51–61), as a regional writer who should
be better known.

If Whitlow's essay about Delany and Griggs stimulates some
scholars to protest against the demand that black writers validate
their material, so Gloria Oden's "Chesnutt's Conjure as African Survival" (*Melus* 5,i:38–47) at least provokes questions. After praising
Chesnutt as the first writer after the Civil War to explore the spiritual
uses of folk belief, Oden seeks to authenticate the African origins
of Chesnutt's tales by analyzing them in relation to N. N. Puckett's
Folk Beliefs of the Southern Negro and Newman White's discussion

of improvisation in black folksong. One wonders, however, why she believes that Puckett and White should be considered the touchstone of truth against which a black writer should be measured. Surely, one might suspect that Chesnutt, a black reared in the South, was as competent as Puckett to learn what southern blacks believe. Perhaps Puckett's statements should be measured against Chesnutt's. Another work on Chesnutt is Frances Keller's biography, discussed later in the biography-interview section of this essay.

b. **Fauset, Hurston, Schuyler.** The Harlem Renaissance fiction writers received surprisingly scant attention in 1978. In "Literary Midwife: Jessie Redmond Fauset and the Harlem Renaissance" (*Phylon* 39:143–53), Abby Johnson reviews briefly the favorable criticism of Fauset's novels by W. E. B. DuBois, Alain Locke, Montgomery Gregory, and George Schuyler and the later, unfavorable criticism of her content by Robert Bone. Johnson insists, however, that Fauset's major significance is her work as the literary editor of *The Crisis*. There she sometimes reflected conflicting attitudes: as a critic, she wanted to emphasize objective literary standards, but as a Negro writer she felt a need to evaluate books according to their relationship to black culture. Discussing Fauset's essays, poems, fiction, biographical sketches of prominent blacks, and fervent support of Pan-Africanism published while she was literary editor, Johnson echoes Langston Hughes's conviction that Fauset was important to the Harlem Renaissance.

By a plot summary interspersed with commentary, Erlene Stetson proposes an interesting reading of Zora Neale Hurston's best-known novel. In *"Their Eyes Were Watching God:* A Woman's Story" (*RFI* 4,i:30–36), Stetson describes Janie Starks, the protagonist, as an antiromatic image of the mulatto, who, unlike mulattoes in earlier novels, harbors no guilt about her color. Janie Starks is a black woman, Stetson concludes, who has a bank account but does not insist on maintaining a class privilege and who defines sexuality in terms other than the physical ability to bear children. (In reading I must have observed casually that Janie Starks does not become pregnant, but I had never really considered the fact in analyzing the novel. Thus does a female critic surpass a male.)

George Schuyler, a black novelist of the Harlem Renaissance, is rarely discussed anymore. As caustic as H. L. Mencken in his journalism, Schuyler once had a wide audience among black readers, but his conservative-reactionary statements of recent years have alienated many blacks, who choose to remember him only as a once-black writer and the father of a musical prodigy. In "George Schuyler: Paradox among 'Assimilationist' Writers" (*BALF* 12:102–06), Ann Rayson, after a brief review of Schuyler's imaginative literature, describes his career of socialism, followed by the anticommunism that led to his support of Barry Goldwater for President, his attacks on the Civil Rights Movement, and his membership in the John Birch Society. Indicating that his autobiography is an argumentative tract rather than a personal confession, Rayson cites the contradictions between Schuyler's actions and writings emphasizing his interest in blacks, and the autobiography that denies it.

c. Petry, Wright, Baldwin, Ellison.   Vernon Lattin insists that Ann Petry has received too little analysis because of the tendency of some scholars to want to fit black writers into the category of assimilationist or nationalist. In "Ann Petry and the American Dream" (*BALF* 12:69–72) Lattin supports Addison Gayle's assessment that Petry is an iconoclast and a rebel against assimilationism and romanticism. He examines her three novels to show how they reveal her rebellion against the American Dream, falsification of life, and everything that would distort reality. *The Street* demands that the American Dream be seen as false and that the American way be destroyed as it has destroyed Lutie Johnson, the black protagonist who tries to realize the Dream. In *Country Place*, a white protagonist returns from a war he has fought to safeguard the American Dream, which he expects to realize partially through the ironically named Glory, his unfaithful wife. The white characters are living in illusions eventually destroyed by a hurricane, a force of nature. In *The Narrows* a black man and a white woman succumb to the forces of racism and materialism that have ended the American Dream.

The Richard Wright Reader (Harper), edited by Ellen Wright and Michel Fabre, with notes by Fabre, has the usual virtues and vices of an attempt to compress a major author into a volume of less than 900 pages. It includes essays not readily available—"Joe Louis Uncovers Dynamite" (a news account of black reaction to Louis's winning the heavyweight championship), "Blueprint for

Negro Writing," and "There's Always Another Cafe." It also includes less well-known poems, such as "The Fb Eye Blues," a few letters, a review of a book by Gertrude Stein, two stories from *Uncle Tom's Children*, and two from *Eight Men*. Most of the volume consists of excerpts from all of Wright's nonfiction books and all of his novels. Fabre has also provided a carefully written introduction, a chronology of the writer's life, and a bibliography of his published poetry, nonfiction, fiction in book form, and his most important, uncollected short, nonfiction pieces. In "Richard Wright and the French Existentialists" (*Melus* 5,ii:39–51), Michel Fabre attempts to refute the concept of Wright's indebtedness to the French existentialists by discussing his relationship with Camus, Sartre, and Simone de Beauvoir. Insisting that existentialism was not a fad for Wright, Fabre states that it was an important part of his thought even before he was introduced to the word by Dorothy Norman, a columnist for the *New York Post*. Although Wright met Sartre in 1946, there seems to have been little literary influence between the two. Sartre probably took his perspective on the Negro problem from Wright, whom he saw as a representative man rather than as an artist; Wright's similarities to Sartre's prose existed before he met Sartre. Fabre admits that Camus's *The Plague* may have influenced *The Outsider* but argues that the seeds of the book are in "Down by the Riverside," written long before Wright met Camus in France. Camus's *The Stranger*, however, may have influenced Wright's plan to rewrite *The Outsider* in the first person. Although he notes the close relationship between Wright and Simone de Beauvoir, Fabre finds little evidence of literary influences. Wright's existentialism, he concludes, came from his own philosophy and from his reading of Heidegger, Nietzsche, Dostoevsky, and Kierkegarde.

John M. Reilly's *Richard Wright: The Critical Reception* (New York: Burt Franklin) is a useful companion to *The Richard Wright Reader*. In the introduction Reilly summarizes trends and patterns in the criticism of Wright. The work itself is organized chronologically according to the publication of Wright's books. Each chapter includes significant and representative reviews that appeared soon after the American publication of the book. Each chapter concludes with a checklist of additional current reviews. Reilly's book will provide scholars with primary evidence of reactions of critics who were Wright's contemporaries. It also provides interesting observations for the reader who is merely scanning it: a hostile review of *Uncle Tom's Children* by Zora Neale Hurston, whom Wright had previously castigated for "minstrel-show" characters in *Their Eyes Were Watching God*; the absence of any reviews of *Strange Holiday*; Reilly's amused summary of the reactions of scholars who, not knowing that most of *American Hunger* had been published previously in the 1930s and 1940s, hailed its discovery and speculated about reasons for its previous "suppression."

In critical essays on Wright, Charles De Arman and Nina Cobb differed in their attitudes about Wright's concept of individualism. In "Bigger Thomas: The Symbolic Negro and the Discrete Human Entity" (*BALF* 12:61–64), De Arman writes that, until the last two pages of *Native Son*, Bigger confuses the individual self—what he must create—with his social, representative, symbolic self. In the last two pages, however, he begins to define his individual self to a perplexed Max, who continues to see him only as a symbol. In "Richard Wright: Individualism Reconsidered" (*CLAJ* 21:335–54), Cobb, however, argues that Wright's ambivalence towards individualism caused his decline as a writer. Although she admits that free will best explains Bigger's transformation, she argues that, because alienation was both the cause and effect of his freedom, Wright could neither reject nor endorse individualism. Too much of the essay is wasted on material that scholars already know: a summary of *Black Boy* and Wright's life, a pedantic (and unnecessary) observation that "no one can work on Richard Wright today without consulting Michel Fabre's meticulous study."

For several years I have worried that I would see in print the pseudo-Freudian analysis of *Native Son* that argues that, when Bigger suffocates Mary, he is not reacting against the whiteness in the situation but is gaining vengeance on his black mother, who nearly suffocated him when she breast-fed him. Diane Hoeveler comes close in "Oedipus Agonistes: Mothers and Sons in Richard Wright's Fiction" (*BALF* 12:65–68). Insisting that violence towards women in Wright's fiction results from the "unreconcilable oedipal dilemmas that afflict his heroes," Hoeveler writes that "women do not appear in Wright's fiction except as mothers or surrogate-mothers" and cites *Savage Holiday* as an excellent example of his substituting women for his mother. She does not discuss the young prostitute that Fish loves or the prostitute whom Damon deserts.

Some criticism from abroad is even worse. R. Orlova, in "Richard Wright: Writer and Prophet" (*Twentieth Century American Literature: A Soviet View*, Moscow, Progress [1976]:384–410) describes how Bigger "full of rage and lust, drags her [Mary] to bed," and reads *Black Boy* as a personification of "the deadening horror that marks the existence of all men, black and white . . . who become the step children of contemporary urban civilization." Orlova also argues that Wright was the first black writer to let uneducated southern black emigrants speak for themselves and the first to use the genuine language of black America.

In "Two Rights, One Wrong" (*The Modern American Novel*, 131–42), Peter Brunette provides an interesting discussion of Wright's problems with the filming of *Native Son*. After Wright refused one man who proposed to make Bigger an oppressed white and after the French stopped production for fear of arousing antagonism in America, *Native Son* was filmed in Argentina with the part of the sister played by a Brazilian learning to speak English, Bessie transformed into a graduate of a southern school for women, and Bigger played by the 50-year-old Wright. The production was sanitized: Bigger's hatred of whites is discarded along with the dialect; Jan is the leader of a labor union; and Bigger submits to religion.

The kind of criticism against which Michel Fabre would protect Wright is evidenced by Charles De Arman's "Bigger Thomas: The Symbolic Negro and the Discrete Human Entity" (*BALF* 12:61–65), in which the author's analysis of Bigger Thomas is based more on Jean-Paul Sartre's existentialist philosophy than on Wright's racial concerns. More cautious is J. F. Gounard's opinion, in "Richard Wright's *The Man Who Lived Underground*, a Literary Analysis" (*JBlackS* 8:381–86) that Wright developed an existentialist philosophy through which his characters may be considered symbolic of all oppressed people.

As usual, Ralph Ellison's only published novel received considerable critical attention. In "The Ambiguities of Dreaming in Ellison's *Invisible Man*" (*AL* 49:592–603), Robert Abrams examines the dreams, nightmares, and hallucinations, which he considers to be contradictory to the waking epistemological assumptions.

M. Celeste Oliver, "*Invisible Man* and the Numbers Game" (*CLAJ* 22:123–33), argues analogues between the novels and a numbers game. Like a numbers runner, the protagonist is given slips of paper that keep him running; the numbers 3–69 on the tank in the paint factory symbolize failure in the world of the numbers player; the Brotherhood operates like a numbers racket; and Rinehart actually is a numbers runner. Another explanation of the grandfather's riddle is propounded by Joseph Trimmer in "The Grandfather's Riddle in Ralph Ellison's *Invisible Man*" (*BALF* 12:46–50). Arguing that the riddle is a key to all episodes in the novel, analyzing it in terms of solutions proposed by the narrator in the epilogue Trimmer sees three possible meanings: (1) that we are to affirm the principles of democracy rather than the people who practice it; (2) that we are to affirm the reality of the victimization as well as the ideal of democracy in black people, who become more human and humane because of their victimization; (3) that we affirm the principle that blacks are linked to others in a universal humanity. The solution, Trimmer concludes, is to affirm the self and the complex heritage of the self. Examining the rhetoric of the novel in "Ellison's *Invisible Man*: The Old Rhetoric and the New" (*BALF* 12:43–45), Robert Bataille argues that the importance of the rhetoric cannot always be defined as the conflict between the old rhetoric (manipulative and deliberate) and the new (spontaneous and candid). Although the abuse of rhetoric is an important theme, one must analyze the thought and conduct of the protagonist—who practices a rhetoric of self-discovery, exhortation, and community—as a mixture of the old and the new. In "Ralph Ellison and the Example of Richard Wright" (*SSF* 15:145–53), Joseph Skerrett, Jr., reexamines the influence of Wright on Ellison. Postulating that T. S. Eliot and André Malraux had influenced Ellison before he met Wright, Skerrett suggests that Ellison turned to Ernest Hemingway and especially to Wright as an expression of modern sensibility. "The Birthmark" (*New Masses*, July 1940) displays the influence of Hemingway and Wright even though Ellison is more cynical than either. Ellison's projected novel of the late 1930s, *Slick Gonna Learn*, echoes Wright's *Lawd Today* in its emphasis on troubles related to women and pregnancy in urban, lower-class life. "Afternoon," "Mister Toussan," and "That I Had the Wings," all centered on two black male children, Buster and Riley, reveal Ellison's development in craft.

Whereas Ellison's first stories show the influence of Wright's earliest writings, the later stories show not only the influence of Mark Twain, Hemingway, and James Joyce but also Ellison's reliance on his private world.

In "The Little Man at Chehaw Station: The American Artist and His Audience" (*ASch* 47[1977–78]:25–48) Ellison admonishes artists never to underestimate or be contemptuous of the artistic comprehension of an audience even though it may seem to be as insignificant as an anonymous man in a tiny town. To illustrate the reason for his beliefs, he recounts a time when, approaching an apartment in Harlem, he overheard a sophisticated discussion of operatic technique. Amazed to hear such evaluation from the apparently crude and unlettered group in the apartment, he learned that their long experience as laborers at the Metropolitan Opera House had stimulated their interest in opera and had provided knowledge and judgment far beyond that of the average person attending an opera.

It seems that, as scholars once measured new black writers against Richard Wright, they now compare black writers with Ellison. In a thoughtful essay, "The Heirs of Ralph Ellison: Patterns of Individualism in the Contemporary Afro-American Novel" (*CLAJ* 22: 101–22), Elizabeth Schultz discusses six novels published between 1970 and 1975 to show how contemporary Afro-American novelists endorse Ellison's belief in the possibility and the need to shape art, individual identity, and cultural identity from the multiple elements in American society. The novels of character growth Schultz examines are Charles Johnson's *Faith and the Good Thing*, Leon Forrest's *There Is a Tree More Ancient than Eden*, John Wideman's *Hurry Home*, Albert Murray's *Trainwhistle Guitar*, Al Young's *Who Is Angelina?*, and John McCluskey's *Look What They Done to My Song*. Each of these, she writes, reveals the author's agreement with Ellison that individuals can shape their own destiny and that the attempt is not only cyclical and mythical but also governed by accident, death, and racism. There is, however, a significant difference between Ellison and his heirs: whereas Ellison's protagonist developed a personal, aesthetic plan suitable for an individual isolated from a group, the newer writers suggest that the contemplative individual must be an active social being, part of a community.

Another to use Ellison as a touchstone is Kimberly Bentson, who in "Ellison, Baraka, and the Faces of Tradition" (*Boundary* 6:333–

54) describes the similarities between the two authors. Both Ellison and Baraka have emphasized the importance of black music—especially the blues—the effect of slavery on black life, history as a philosophical and mythological construct, and the relationship between the individual and the contingent culture. Both believe that the black past is not a static ideal but a protean idea to be rethought by individual consciousness in order to preserve and improve the best aspects of the black self. Bentson admits differences between the two writers—especially in their aesthetic: Ellison espouses an eclecticism that, drawing from all traditions, stresses beauty and durability, whereas Baraka endorses a nationalistic creed that Afro-American writers must develop new, post-Western forms of expression that supplant both Euro-American and Afro-American traditions. Nonetheless, Bentson concludes, the two authors are surprisingly similar as critics and creators of tradition who seek to improve the black Self.

Despite the restriction suggested by her title, "The Eye as Weapon in *If Beale Street Could Talk*" (*Melus* 5,iii:54–66), Trudier Harris examines several aspects of Baldwin's novel. In addition to noting how eyes can be used as weapons, especially by the white policeman Bell, Harris emphasizes that James Baldwin's characters also communicate love through their looks. The female narrator provides a new dimension for Baldwin's fiction, and the innocence and perception of the narrator encourage empathy. In the novel, Harris believes, Baldwin finally achieves the family relationship he has been struggling to portray in earlier novels; the characters love each other, are committed to love, and even find religion in each other.

d. **Marshall, Williams, Reed, Gaines.** Paule Marshall's volume of short stories receives some needed critical attention from L. Lee Talbert in "The Poetics of Prophecy in Paule Marshall's *Soul Clap Hands and Sing*" (*Melus* 5,i:49–56). Despite his title and his conclusion that Paule Marshall is a prophet of the new world consciousness, Talbert seems more concerned with an analysis of Marshall's fictive techniques and her themes: reliance on Western literary traditions, man's capacities to destroy and to survive, concern with the cyclical character of life. He concludes by analyzing each of the four stories to show how the male protagonist attempts to assert himself parasitically through a female.

Examining the novels of John A. Williams, C. Lynn Munro argues that, experimenting continuously and studying survival and social change from a variety of vantage points, Williams leads readers from time-honored myths to an understanding of the historically bound present. In "Culture and Quest in the Fiction of John A. Williams" (*CLAJ* 22:71–100), Munro contends that Williams moves from cautious optimism (*The Angry Ones, Nightsong,* and *Sissie*), to a "grasping and tortured" tone (*The Man Who Cried I Am, Captain Blackman,* and *Sons of Darkness, Sons of Light*), to mellowness (*Mothersill and the Foxes, The Junior Bachelor Society*). In the essay Munro seems to define "time-honored myths" as synonymous with "popular beliefs."

The question of Ishmael Reed's aesthetics constitutes the core of two essays. In "Ishmael Reed and the Black Aesthetic" (*CLAJ* 21: 355–66) Nathaniel Mackey argues that Reed has opposed the Black Aesthetic formulated by Addison Gayle, Larry Neal, and Hoyt Fuller because Reed considers the Neo-HooDoo Aesthetic to be "Blacker." With frequent allusions to *Mumbo-Jumbo, The Last Days of Louisiana Red,* and *Flight to Canada,* Mackey identifies similarities between the Neo-HooDoo Aesthetic and the Black Aesthetic: (1) a renunciation of Western civilization and a proposal for a new philosophy to be used as an alternative to the collapsing West; (2) the belief that black writers have been "victimized by the chauvinistic uninformed assumptions of white critics," who almost always employ criteria that are alien to the guiding principles and central concerns of black artists; (3) an insistence on the existence and dignity of an African-based culture to which black Americans have ties; (4) use of the oral tradition and celebration of a black folk culture. Reed's major departures from the Black Aesthetic, Mackey concludes, are his insistence that artists be permitted to practice their individual beliefs and his rejection of Marxism. The thoughtful article is weakened by a confusion that clouds many discussions of "The Black Aesthetic": "The Black Aesthetic Movement" is sometimes used interchangeably with "Black Nationalism." In "Backgrounds of the Black Arts Movement," a lecture presented at the University of Iowa in 1978, Larry Neal has explained a fact essential to a discussion of the Black Aesthetic, a fact which I believe could be inferred from a careful study of the literature: The early Black Arts writers who conceived an idea later identified as the

"Black Aesthetic" were politically aware but did not insist that the "Black Aesthetic" must espouse a particular ideology; influenced by the political activities of the 1960s, they sought to create a literature that would draw upon Afro-American traditions of the church, street oratory, music (especially the black music exemplified by Art Ayler, Sun Ra, Charlie Parker, James Brown, and John Coltrane), and oral presentation to create a literature that would heighten the consciousness of Afro-American people. Although such literature can be identified as a segment of the Black Nationalist movement, such literature is not identical with it. Specific political ideologies were later additions, sometimes by individuals who were not the writers. The social, political, economic separatism and the armed revolutions, rejected by some black and most white scholars, were not part of the original concept of a Black Aesthetic. Moreover, Marxism must be considered incidental since Amiri Baraka, symbol of the movement, opposed Marxism until he moved away from the Black Cultural Nationalism that supports the concept of the Black Aesthetic. It is also ironic that in 1979, speaking at the University of Iowa, Ishmael Reed stated that he used Neo-Hoodoo as an experimental method rather than as a permanent philosophy. I have expanded this discussion, not to criticize Mackey, who writes more intelligently than many who discuss the Black Aesthetic, but to caution scholars to consider carefully the complexities of any discussion of the Black Aesthetic. In this particular situation it might have been more accurate for the scholar to say that the iconoclastic Ishmael Reed emphasizes the importance of black culture and traditions but defends the black writer against any black or white theoretician who prescribes a path for that writer.

Studying such poems as "Railroad Bill, a Conjure Man" and "I Am a Cowboy in the Boat of Ra," Chester Fontenot in "Ishmael Reed and the Politics of Aesthetics, or Shake Hands and Come Out Conjuring" (BALF 12:20–23) argues that "Reed wants to merge the ethereal artistic world of platonic universals with reality by employing voodoo tales in the structure of the narrative.

Ernest Gaines was the subject of a special issue of Callaloo (vol. 1, no. 3; May). In two entries, "Miss Jane and I" (pp. 23–38) and an interview by Charles H. Rowell, " 'This Louisiana Thing That Drives Me': An Interview with Ernest J. Gaines" (pp. 39–51), Gaines describes his writing and the influences on it. In "Miss Jane and I"

Gaines reviews his life and his intellectual development, especially his discovery of 19th-century Russian writers, who "wrote truly about peasantry or . . . truer than any other group of writers in any other country." He concludes with an analysis of the evolution of the *Autobiography of Miss Jane Pittman* from an idea sketched in "Just Like a Tree" to the one-voice narrative by a black woman, who is not "a capsule history of black people in the rural South during the last hundred years" but who is simply Miss Jane telling the truth as she remembers it. In Rowell's interview, Gaines discusses his family background in Louisiana, his belief that at present he can write only about life in that state, his preference for the first-person point of view, his experiments with multiple narrators and the omniscient point of view, his earlier novels, and his belief that he derived a sense of style from reading Faulkner and an interest in the theme of "grace under pressure" from reading Hemingway. Gaines believes that the black author "should write about the black condition." But he also insists that writers must have the freedom to write whatever they want as long as they write truthfully about the human condition and their experiences, whether direct or vicarious.

Five essays in the May *Callaloo* analyze various aspects of Gaines's work. Michel Fabre's "Bayonne or the Yoknapatawpha of Ernest Gaines" (pp. 110–23) insists that every black novelist who writes about the South will inevitably be compared with Faulkner because "his racial myths are the most indestructible." Like Faulkner, Gaines has created a distinctive fictive universe, which is essentially stable; his characters are thinkers. Fabre suggests that the tragic metaphor of Gaines's Louisiana is the disappearance of Creoles, thinned out by the Cajuns with the complicity of the planters. But their story is not told by narrators favorable to lost causes: Their decline is described by blacks who have identified their aspirations with Creole success but who are now claiming what is owed by mulattoes and whites. Gaines's blacks exhibit the endurance, dignity, compassion that Faulkner described. Faulkner, however, inscribed the blacks within the hierarchy of white domination to be tools to serve whites or instruments for their redemption. But Gaines's black and Creole protagonists heroically refuse to obey this definition of their role. Raoul Carmier, Fabre suggests, more closely resembles a Faulknerian planter whose dynasty is dying than the traditional mulatto. The major difference between Faulkner and

Gaines, Fabre concludes, is that, despite his compassion, Faulkner never could have exulted as Gaines does in the successive, sometimes triumphant black assaults on the monolithic South. Alvin Aubert, "Ernest J. Gaines's Truly Tragic Mulatto" (pp. 68–75), agrees with Fabre that the Creole is a metaphor, but a metaphor of the plight of Afro-Americans in general. Raoul Carmier, Aubert tries to demonstrate, is a tragic hero in the Aristotelian sense. In *"Of Love and Dust*: A Reconsideration" (pp. 76–84) novelist John Wideman analyzes the persona of the narrative, Gaines's use of repetition, and his language. In "Jane Pittman and the Oral Tradition" (pp. 102–09) novelist Barry Beckham also praises Gaines's language and art. Gaines draws upon three aspects of the oral tradition —black southern pronunciation and grammar, pleasant orality, and verbal wit—and he employs narrative techniques of the story within a story, episodic tension, and incidental directness (asides to the listener). In a carefully reasoned essay, "Scene and Life Cycle in Ernest Gaines' *Bloodline*" (pp. 85–101), Todd Duncan analyzes the structure as a series of stories, each told from a more advanced perspective of age, portraying childhood or youth in relation to literal or symbolic parenthood, and demonstrating the importance of the relationship between the generations, the importance of family, and the concept of the human life cycle as a developing and culminating experience.

e. **Walker, Young.** Chester Fontenot contends, in "Alice Walker: The Diary of an African Nun and DuBois' Double Consciousness" (*JAAI* 5[1977]:192–96), that the story is the supreme statement of the universality of the dilemma for blacks. Analyzing the six sections of the story, Fontenot shows how the African nun, who is uneasy because she has rejected traditional African values and religion, questions her image as projected by her white oppressors, some of whom question whether such a beautiful woman can be dedicated to the church. Viewing herself as part of the Christian world but aware of the contrast between the realistic sensuality of traditional African religion and the aloofness of Christians, the nun regrets Christian asexuality and repression of passion. Finally, judging Christianity to be spiritually decadent but a material salvation, the nun resolves to adopt the "enlightened" stance of the Europeans even though this choice will remove her from reality and the culture and goals of her world. Relating the nun's choice to the behavior of such black writers as Alice Walker, Fontenot concludes that Afro-American writers may resolve their own double-consciousness (black and American) if they presume that they are merely adopting "American" values that can be removed as easily as clothes.

In addition to being considered as a literary heir of Ralph Ellison, Al Young has been evaluated as a novelist who has used thematic and structural forms of the blues to explore the lives of black Americans. In "Al Young's *Snakes*: The Blues as a Literary Form" (*Obsidian* 4,ii:28–36) R. G. Billingsley identifies the humor, sexuality, folklore, folk motifs, and folk speech that he finds in both *Snakes* and the blues.

f. General Criticism of Fiction. Michael Popkin's *Modern Black Writers: A Library of Literary Criticism* (Ungar) is a collection of reviews about various authors. Among the authors not included are Alice Childress, Charles Gordone, Owen Dodson, and Ann Petry.

Amritjit Singh's sympathetic study of Hughes's *Not Without Laughter*, Baldwin's *Go Tell It on the Mountain*, and Killens's *The Cotillion* is weakened by false perceptions. In "Self-Definition as a Moral Concern in the Twentieth Century Afro-American Novel" (*IJAS* 8,ii:23–38), Singh writes erroneously that, before *Native Son*, Afro-American novels were concerned only with middle-class octoroons; the 20th-century Afro-American novel "has been written predominantly by writers who are alienated from the bourgeois values of their backgrounds and who have variously expressed their sense of solidarity with the black masses through suggestive portrayals of the problems facing their individual characters; and that *Go Tell It on the Mountain* reveals *Baptist* (italics are mine) conversion. Despite these and comparable fallacies about black history and culture, Singh's analyses of the novels are perceptive.

Arthur Davis, a distinguished scholar of Afro-American literature, has examined some recent Black novelists in "Novels of the New Black Renaissance: A Thematic Survey" (*CLAJ* 21:457–90). Omitting such writers as Barry Beckham, Donald Goines, Jason Grant, and Samuel Delaney, Davis considers James Baldwin, John Killens, Paule Marshall, John Williams, Amiri Baraka, William Kelley, Ronald Fair, Ishmael Reed, Kristin Hunter, Sam Greenlee, Louise Meriwether, Ernest Gaines, Sarah Wright, Cecil Brown, Toni

Morrison, George Cain, Alice Walker, Al Young, Leon Forrest, John McCluskey, [John] Edgar Wideman, Charles Johnson, Clarence Major, and Gayl Jones. Davis offers the following conclusions: (1) most black novels of the past two decades focus on the urban northern ghetto with emphasis on its drabness; (2) the novels focus primarily on such themes as animosity against the white man, black-man–white-woman sexual patterns, black jazz musicians as heroes and jazz as an antidote to life, brutal treatment of black women by black men, and civil rights activities as motivation and inspiration; (3) many novels are blues-type narratives by female narrators; (4) there is considerable experimentation, with Clarence Major and Ishmael Reed leading the way; (5) novelists are using "Black English"; (6) the most memorable characters are Ernest Gaines's Miss Jane Pittman, Alice Walker's Granges Copeland, Ishmael Reed's Loop Garoo, William Kelley's Tucker Caliban, and Toni Morrison's Sula. The black novelist, Davis concludes, is penetrating more deeply into the mainstream of American life and letters.

Believing that the study of Afro-American short fiction has been ignored by critics or badly treated in Robert Bone's *Down Home* (which is criticized for vague categories, simplistic views, and lack of a precise critical framework), Peter Bruck, from the distance of Holland, encouraged a number of teachers and students to write studies of selected short stories, 1889–1965. The resulting collection was published as *The Black American Short Story in the 20th Century* (Amsterdam: Grüner, 1977)—a very uneven group of essays. In addition to Bruck's introduction and essay on the influence of D. H. Lawrence on Hughes's "The Blues I'm Playing" (pp. 71–83), there are two other pieces worthy of special notice: David Galloway's discussion of the protagonist's experience in William Melvin Kelley's "The Poker Party" (pp. 129–40); and Peter Freese's views of James Baldwin's effective detachment from his materials in "Going to Meet the Man" (pp. 171–85).

In "The Promise of America and the Black American Novel" (*JAAI* 5[1977]:135–42) Clifford Harper analyzes Chesnutt's *The House Behind the Cedars*, Hughes's *Not Without Laughter*, and William Attaway's *Blood on the Forge* to show that the essential substance of novels by black Americans is the dichotomy between black Americans' belief in the promise of America and the oppressive realities of black experience. This essay, Harper writes, is an introduction to a larger study of the black American novel.

iii. Criticism of Poets: Brooks, Baraka, Wheatley, Spencer, Hughes

Scholars gave relatively little attention to Afro-American poetry in 1978. In "Define . . . the Whirlwind: *In the Mecca*—Urban Setting, Shifting Narrator and Redemptive Vision" (*Obsidian* 4,i:19–31) R. Baxter Miller argues that *In the Mecca* culminates Gwendolyn Brooks's efforts to write an Afro-American epic. In *Annie Allen*, "The Anniad," Miller contends, sank to the level of mock epic because the style was too lofty for the theme. After practicing the techniques of focus on one character and use of an undramatized narrator in *Maud Martha*, Miller concludes, Brooks created a successful epic in *In the Mecca*, where verse and ballad succeeded as rime royal and the sonnet had not. In part 2, "After Mecca," Miller suggests, Brooks elevates such figures as Medgar Evers and Malcolm X to the level of myth.

The poet who received the most attention was Amiri Baraka (LeRoi Jones), the subject of *Boundary 6*. In "Anonymous in America" (*Boundary* 6:435–42), Sherley Anne Williams, praising Baraka's mastery of technique in poetry, suggests that, by combining theory with political action, Baraka emulated DuBois and Malcolm X. Praiseworthy for liberating language, Williams states, he might have had no impact on literature if he had not been politically active. After this introductory statement Williams reviews Kimberly W. Bentson's *Baraka: The Renegade and the Mask* and Theodore Hudson's *From LeRoi Jones to Amiri Baraka*. Neither Bentson nor Hudson, Williams argues, places Baraka within a black tradition. Hudson, she writes, primarily describes major themes; and Bentson draws upon Hudson for biographical support. Favoring Bentson above Hudson because of superior analysis, Williams concludes that Bentson's major weakness is the failure to integrate Baraka the writer with Baraka the activist and to see both within a black culture.

In his 338-page study of Baraka—*Amiri Baraka/LeRoi Jones: The Quest for a "Populist Modernism"* (Columbia), Werner Sollors continues to examine Baraka. In "Does Axel's Castle Have a Street Address, or, What's New? Tendencies in the Poetry of Amiri Baraka (LeRoi Jones)" (*Boundary* 6:387–413) the imaginative Sollars traces Baraka's evolution from his affinity with Beatnik poetry to his Marxism in the late 1970s. Contending that Baraka wanted to move be-bop into literature, Sollars examines the William Carlos Williams–T. S. Eliot influences on Baraka's poetry and proposes that Baraka's characteristic trait is an antithetical structure. Baraka is also concerned with the problem of identity under masks, frequently explored through a middle-class young black alienated from his bourgeois surroundings. Crucial to his later poetry is the concept of a new poet emerging from an old shell to cut through lies and turn people into potential revolutionaries. To do so, he experiments with ways to destroy and rebuild poetic language, develop a black voice, and create a Black Aesthetic. Obviously distressed by Baraka's movement towards black nationalism and a Black Aesthetic, Sollars complains about the anti-Semitism and the love of violence that he finds in the Black Arts poetry of Baraka, which he considers inferior to the earlier, European-oriented work.

Also tracing Baraka's evolution from Greenwich Village poet to Marxist, Nathaniel Mackey, "The Changing Same: Black Music in the Poetry of Amiri Baraka" (*Boundary* 6:355–86), proposes that music, an impulse (life-style) and theme in Baraka's work, can be used as a focal point for a study of his thought. Black music, Mackey suggests, is the meeting ground for two contending forces in Baraka's thought: (1) acknowledgment that life and art are affected by social contingencies, and (2) respect for aspirations to other-worldliness. Mackey further suggests that, as Baraka moved toward a nationalist position, his poetry moved toward direct statement; but that, in *Hard Facts*, in which he renounces nationalism to favor Marxism, Baraka returns to his earlier practice of blending the explicit with the oblique.

Working on a more restricted scale than most 1978 critics of Baraka's poetry, Jay Wright tries to prove, in "Love's Emblem Lost: LeRoi Jones's 'Hymn for Lanie Poo' " (*Boundary* 6:415–34), that the poem from *Preface to a Twenty-Volume Suicide Note* reveals Baraka's early effort to create an emblem of love. A reading of the poem, Wright suggests, will disclose that Baraka was influenced by Dante and Rimbaud; but, Wright concludes, the poem fails because Baraka did not fully appropriate the best of what is valuable in Dante and tradition. Interestingly, it is this kind of criticism that caused Baraka/ Jones and many other young black poets of the 1960s to endorse a Black Aesthetic to dissuade critics from the inevitable comparison with European or Euro-American writers.

Analyzing *It's Nation Time*, Phillip B. Middleton, "The Rage for Order in Baraka's Political Philosophy" (*JAAI* 5[1977]:161–65), discovers four themes: security, progress, stimulation, and identity. For Baraka, Middleton suggests, poetry has a two-fold purpose—to express disgust and to manifest hope. Sometimes his rage for order, Middleton concludes, is unsettling (to white readers?).

Owen Brady considered Baraka's dramas. In "LeRoi Jones's *The Slave*: A Ritual of Purgation" (*Obsidian* 4,i:5–18), Brady compares *Dutchman* with *The Slave*. *The Slave*, he accurately proposes, calls for the revolution that Clay implies in *Dutchman*. Brady vitiates his argument, however, by contending that Walker Vessels, accepting guilt for all America, redeems life for all America. This is a more accurate assessment of James Baldwin's thought than of Jones/ Baraka, who—even while admitting his attraction to Euro-American/Western culture—has never proposed that blacks sacrifice themselves to redeem whites.

An early LeRoi Jones reappears in a 1960 interview by David Ossman, "Le Roi Jones: an Interview on *Yugen*" (*TriQ* 43:317–23). Jones discusses his literary influences: Lorca, Creeley, Charles Olson, T. S. Eliot, William Carlos Williams, Ezra Pound, the Imagists. At this time Jones believed that his being Negro influenced his writing, but he did not want to be identified as a Negro writer: "It's always been a separate section of writing that wasn't quite up to the level of other writing."

An interesting note confirming the fact that some poets recognize the realities of life is found in Mukhtar Ali Isani's "Phillis Wheatley in London: An Unpublished Letter to David Wooster" (*AL* 51:255–60). Recounting her tour of London, Wheatley evidences her interest in the money she might derive from sales of her volume of poetry because, as a free woman, she needed money.

Frequently identified by Renaissance writers and scholars as one of the more talented poets of the era, Anne Spencer deserves greater recognition. But Erlene Stetson's "Anne Spencer" (*CLAJ* 21:400–09) distracts readers from the poet. Arguing that the Harlem

Renaissance restricted the Anne Spencers by the male belief that women should be "refined versifiers" (with no apparent confirmation from Spencer that this attitude governed her writing), Stetson writes too little about Spencer's poetry.

Another Renaissance figure, Langston Hughes, receives more literary treatment from Dellita Martin, "Langston Hughes's Use of the Blues" (*CLAJ* 22:151–59), who analyzes three poems from *Fine Clothes to the Jew* to show an interrelationship between form and content. After discussing the blues form, Martin examines "Suicide," in which the blues functions as a safety valve in social relationships; "Lament over Love," in which a blues singer affirms love; and "Young Girl's Blues," in which the persona's fear of loneliness in old age underscores the blues mood.

iv. Criticism of Dramatists: Grimké, Cotter, Branch, Carter

Examination of Afro-American playwrights continues to be sparse. Jeanne-Marie Miller, however, has provided a useful introduction to a black woman playwright. In "Angelina Weld Grimké: Playwright and Poet" (*CLAJ* 21:513–25), after summarizing Grimké's education and her career as a teacher, Miller identifies her with the "Black Genteel School" (Georgia D. Johnson, Anne Spencer, Jessie Fauset, Countée Cullen, W. S. Braithwaite) that ignored the seamier side of black life, described positive and progressive aspects, often treated universal themes, and desired to write in the manner of other American authors. Grimké's drama *Rachel* (produced in 1916), Miller states, is significant as an early black protest work (against lynching) whereas the unproduced *Mara* calls attention to the helplessness of southern black women against lustful white men. Miller also discusses Grimké's introspective poetry, her occasional poems, and her raceless poems.

In "Wearing the Mask: Joseph S. Cotter, Sr.'s *Caleb the Degenerate*" (*Melus* 5,iii:37–53), Betty Cain contends that the drama by Grimké's contemporary is subject to two levels of interpretation. Literally, it seems to support Booker T. Washington by endorsing industrial education and ridiculing the idea of black emigration to Africa; however, interpreted symbolically with emphasis on Olivia, a young black teacher, as the focal point, it calls for a great black leader more militant than Washington.

Reviewing Branch's drama about Frederick Douglass, "Now and Then: William Branch's *In Splendid Error*" (*BALF* 12:110–12), Melvin G. Williams argues that, although the play succeeds as propaganda by using a 19th-century setting that does not threaten 20th-century whites, by depicting white assistance in the blacks' struggle for freedom, and by picturing heroic, active blacks, it fails artistically because it oversimplifies good and evil.

A younger dramatist, Steve Carter, receives attention in Ian Watts's review of the British production of *Eden,* "Echoes of Romeo and Juliet" (*AfricaI* 80:111–12). Winner of the Andelco Award for the best production of 1976, *Eden* depicts cultural interracial clashes between blacks from the American South and blacks from the West Indies in the Harlem of the 1920s. The author of *One Last Look, The Courage and the Grace,* and *Nevis Mountain Dew,* Carter has won an Outer Critics Circle Award.

v. Autobiography as Genre, Slave Narratives

Although only a few essays about autobiography and slave narratives have appeared within the past two years, oral reports attest that those two genres continue to be important in many courses focused on black literature. In "After *Black Boy* and *Dusk of Dawn*: Patterns in Recent Black Autobiography" (*Phylon* 39:18–34), Albert E. Stone suggests the importance of design: "The discovered design is the truth of all autobiography." In black autobiographies Stone sees two dominant patterns: one, the flight from oppression; the other, confrontation of the problems of minority existence. In "The Place of Frederick Douglass's *Narrative of the Life of an American Slave* in the Development of a Native American Prose Style" (*JAAI* 5[1977]: 183–91), Henry Dan Piper tries to demonstrate that the 1845 *Narrative* is stylistically the best of Douglass's autobiographies because it is the least verbose. Piper attributes the increased verbosity in later autobiographies to Douglass's attempt to emulate the "Latinate, polysyllabic, inflated rhetoric" of such eminent Victorian contemporaries as James Russell Lowell and William Lloyd Garrison, who averaged 28 to 33 words in each sentence. In contrast, the average in the 1845 *Narrative* is only 18, a figure that Piper says approximates the average of a sentence by Abraham Lincoln, Benjamin Franklin, Mark Twain (in *Huckleberry Finn*), or the young Ernest Heming-

way (in *In Our Time*). Whereas Hemingway contended that an
indigenous American prose style began with *Huckleberry Finn*,
Piper suggests that it originated with Franklin, Douglass, and Lincoln. In "Wit and Humor in Slave Narratives" (*JAAI* 5[1977]:125–
34), Daryl Dance demonstrates the way in which humor is developed from varied ideas and situations: the ludicrous contrast between slavery and the idealistic political documents of America; the
hypocrisy of masters and ministers who espouse both Christianity
and slavery; satirical accounts of the adultery, vulgarity, ignorance,
and duplicity of masters; contrasts between the idealized southern
woman and descriptions of actual mistresses; stories of the slaves'
success in outwitting the masters, gaining revenge, or pretending
to lament the master's illness or death.

vi. Criticism and Literary History

Continuing a complaint that has been voiced frequently since World
War I, Sheila Hill and Haki R. Madhubuti (formerly Don L. Lee)
call for the development of an educated black audience. Suggesting
that lack of knowledge may cause blacks to be uninterested in black
theatre, Hill, in "Black Theatre and Audience Development" (*Freedomways* 18:39–42), asks black artists to try to turn spectators into
participants. In "Black Writers and Critics: Developing a Critical
Process without Readers" (*BlackS* 10:35–42), Madhubuti warns that
education, the Black Consciousness Movement, and Black Studies
programs have failed to create a "serious literate black public." Black
writers and critics, he states, still are outsiders in the minds of
whites who control publication in this country. Regardless of their
appeal to white readers, even the best black writers (Reed, Morrison, Brooks, John A. Williams), are merely "talented tokens" in the
minds of publishers; the best black critics (George Kent, Hoyt Fuller, Eugenia Collier, Darwin T. Turner, Stephen Henderson, Carolyn
F. Gerald, Sherley Anne Williams) receive no requests to review
black literature for major periodicals (*New York Times Book Review*, *Saturday Review*, *Commentary*, etc.). Defining the role of
black critics, Madhubuti urges them to locate the wisdom and inconsistencies in the writers' work; to assist in defining racial, political,
social, and artistic consciousness; to promote black literature; and
to aid the writer in finding the ear of black people.

In "Introductory Remarks about the Black Literary Tradition in the United States of America" (*BALF* 12:140-47) Darwin T. Turner insists that it should be possible to define a literary tradition of black American writers. Turner identifies certain elements through which black American literature can be distinguished as unique. One is purpose (educating blacks and educating whites); a second is theme, such as liberation, pride in an African past; a third is what Stephen Henderson identifies as "saturation," a complex cluster that can include psychological forces, traditions, legends, language, rhetoric, and such; and a fourth, influence of the church and the sermon. Turner calls for scholars to look at black literature afresh, to find the qualities which produce a black American literary tradition—as yet poorly understood.

Equally concerned with the approaches by critics, Gloria Hull, Barbara Smith, and Erlene Stetson offer varying proposals. In "Rewriting Afro-American Literature: A Case for Black Women Writers" (*RadT* 6[1977]:10-13), Smith argues that black women writers must be studied separately because they have been excluded from most surveys. Listing writers who should be included in literature surveys, she includes several who are important as black leaders but who would not be considered creative writers: Sojourner Truth, Harriet Tubman, Mary McCleod Bethune, Ida B. Wells are among these. Among the recent writers who deserve additional study are Alice Walker, Gayl Jones, Toni Cade Bambara, Sonia Sanchez, Mari Evans, Sarah Wright, and Audre Lorde. From a different perspective, in "Notes on a Marxist Interpretation of Black American Literature" (*BALF* 12:148-53), Hull insists that critics need to focus on five tasks while examining Afro-American literature from a Marxist perspective: (1) compiling an annotated bibliography; (2) analyzing from a Marxist perspective writers whom she identifies as Marxist (Hughes, McKay, Wright, Frank Marshall Davis, DuBois, and Baraka; (3) analyzing Marxist elements in such non-Marxist works as *Invisible Man* or Melvin Tolson's "Dark Symphony"; (4) discussing literature according to Marxist categories (realism, modernism, socialist realism); and (5) comparing Marxist tenets with other literary theories. Hull considers black literature especially rich for Marxist analysis because generally it is functional and cause-oriented, does not emphasize consciousness of technique, respects the communicative aspect, and emphasizes oral-folk culture. She also proposes that Marxist perspectives be used to analyze black critics. In "Toward a Black Feminist Criticism" (*RadT* 7:20–27) Barbara Smith insists that there must be the development of black feminist criticism and a discussion of black lesbian writing. It is not sufficient, Smith writes, to assume that black women writers can be studied by white feminists, for they either ignore black and Third World women writers or reveal incompetent readings of them. Such novels as *The Bluest Eye* and *Sula*, she writes, can be analyzed effectively from a lesbian perspective. Black feminist criticism is needed to create a climate for such Black lesbian writers as Audre Lorde and Pat Parker. Black feminist critics whom Smith mentions for praise are Gloria Hull, Lorraine Bethel, and Elaine Scott. In "The Black Writer, The Black Aesthetic, and Western Art" (*JAAI* 5[1977]: 173–82), Erlene Stetson insists that the Black Aesthetic must cull from black literature the ironic inversions through which black writers have turned metaphors of the majority culture upside down. She discusses the mulattoes in Chesnutt's *The Wife of His Youth* and Johnson's *Autobiography of an Ex-Coloured Man* to illustrate this concept.

Also concerned with an aesthetic analysis of black literature is James Spady, who, in "Indigene=Folkski Equations in the Black Arts" (*BlackS* 10:24–33), suggests new ways of looking at black literature through improvisation, humor, African religions, fatalism, and music. To evidence his argument that readers must "become more adept at detecting cultural dynamisms in several art forms" when analyzing black literature, Spady insists that the free narrative style, form, and content of Toomer's *Cane* should be studied in relation to Will Marion Cook's compositional techniques in jazz.

Some persons writing on black writers cannot agree on just what are "writers" (including, for example, politicians and educators) and some do not clearly define "southern" (including, for example, persons born in Maryland and Washington, D.C.). Such weaknesses are found in Julian Mason's "Black Writers of the South" (*MissQ* 31:169–83).

In *The "Hindered Hand": Cultural Implications of Early African-American Fiction* (Greenwood), Arlene A. Elder proposed to examine the writers' explorations of social and psychological clashes between the individual and society and to show that their artistic choices and difficulties reveal them as examples of the problems they wrote about. Perhaps the major value of the work, however, is the discussion of rarely mentioned novelists, such as Victoria Earle and J. McHenry Jones. Writing for a dual audience, Elder argues, black novelists of the 19th century were influenced by popular literature of the white culture. Even when writing for black audiences, they endorsed white models: middle-class virtues and Caucasian-featured protagonists. Less frequently they drew upon the black traditions of realistic and satiric oratory, autobiography, and oral narrative. They concentrated on four themes: (1) the rise to prominence of a lowly slave, (2) the dangers inherent in slavery and caste, (3) the sudden reversal of fortune of mulattoes, and (4) an examination of miscegenation and its consequences. Too frequently, they endorsed the American dream and created counter-stereotypes of black protagonists gifted with the talents requisite for success in business. The most important influence from a black tradition was the portrayal of realistic folk characters, usually as minor figures. With interesting comments, Elder analyzes the work of Sutton Griggs, Paul Laurence Dunbar, and Charles W. Chesnutt.

For reasons of economy, let me briefly mention three essays worth attention. Two focus upon character types. Della Burt examines "The Legacy of the Bad Nigger" (*JAAI* 5,ii:111–24) and John Tedesco, "The White Character in Black Drama, 1955–1970: Description and Rhetorical Function" (*ComM* 45:64–74). In "The Black in Anti-Utopia" (*BALF* 12:107–10) John Reilly argues that George Schuyler's *Black No More* is an anti-utopian satire revealing that assimilation is an impossible ideal, whereas William Kelley's *A Different Drummer* is anti-utopian in its stress on the disintegration of a social order.

vii. Biography, Interviews

The only book-length biography of a black writer during the year was Frances Keller's *An American Crusader: The Life of Charles Waddell Chesnutt* (Brigham Young), which emphasizes Chesnutt's role as a race historian by discussing his essays, articles, speeches, and correspondence, more than his fiction.

Interviews with writers continue to multiply. Probably the most frequently interviewed author was Alex Haley, whose *Roots* was considered more often as a successful media event (on television) than as a novel. Typical of the Haley interviews are "Alex Haley talks to Jeffrey Elliot (*Negro Hist. Bull.* 41:782–85) and Godwin Matatu's "Well, Which Way Did the Ship Go?" (*AfricaI* 69:94–95). After recalling that the novel *Roots* won the Pulitzer Prize and that the television version was nominated for a record 39 Emmys, Elliot leads Haley through a discussion of the novel (the Africa section is too long, but Haley hated to have Kunta captured), the author's loss of privacy, the impact of *Roots* (Haley did not envision its popularity), and the author's family and his future plans. In the interview with *Africa* magazine, Haley compares *The Autobiography of Malcolm X* with *Roots* (one is the symbol of individuals; the other is the symbol of a people) and suggests his concern for blacks throughout the diaspora ("The only real difference between Blacks in the USA and in the Caribbean is simply which way did the ship go").

In "Work: Beginning to Write at Fifty" (*AR* 36:422–36) Cyrus Colter, in interview form, reviews his career, the writers who influenced him—especially the Russians—his criticism of the manner in which the New York establishment discourages new and unknown writers, and his concept of the artist's need to perfect the craft.

In Jane Bakerman's "The Seams Can't Show: An Interview with Toni Morrison" (*BALF* 12:56–60), Morrison discusses the emotions attendant upon her writing. First, she wrote to ease loneliness; now she writes from compulsion but ends in depression. Discussing her process of construction, her enjoyment of revision, her symbols and characterization, Morrison says that she wants to write for herself.

A different approach to an interview is found in Charles Lynch's "Wesley Brown Speaks of *Tragic Magic*" (*First World* 2,ii:47–49). Needing to identify the novelist, Lynch summarizes Brown's educational background and publishing record before leading Brown into a discussion of the novel: the theme of a black man's struggle for identity, the difficulty of writing prison scenes, Brown's interest in the black idiom as a "way of dealing with chaos through the instrument of languages, and the influence of jazz."

Also feeling a need to introduce his subject, Nathaniel Mackey, "Interview with Al Young" (*Melus* 5,iv:32–51), summarizes Young's professional activities as writer and editor. Then he skilfully leads Young to discuss his influences (music and life more than literature), his attempts to reproduce southern speech and the style of southern story-telling, his opposition to the Black Aesthetic, and his belief in a West Coast ethic (neither he nor Mackey finds an ironic conflict in Young's discovery of a regional ethic but rejection of a racial aesthetic).

University of Iowa

20. Themes, Topics, Criticism

Michael J. Hoffman

The year 1978 was busy in literary criticism and theory. Before choosing the titles reviewed in the following pages, I read between 90 and 100 books. American literature saw the publication of a few works of a general nature that will almost surely become classics. The field of literary theory witnessed the continuing translation of works by major figures such as Roland Barthes and Jacques Derrida. In relation to theoretical books composed in English, there is now evident an increasing acceptance of works influenced by the "new criticism" of European origin, particularly by houses such as the Johns Hopkins and Indiana University presses. Overall, 1978 was a good year for books with relevance for this chapter. Good, but not spectacular.

i. American Literature

a. **Historical Approaches.** I shall deal with the books in this section in roughly chronological order. *Poetry in America: Expression and Its Values in the Times of Bryant, Whitman, and Pound* (Duke), by Bernard Duffey, attempts a major overview of American poetry, of the scope of Roy Harvey Pearce's *Continuity of American Poetry* or of similar books by Hyatt Waggoner or Albert Gelpi. Duffey's historical thesis is that American poetry can be divided into three periods. The first preceded the Civil War and constitutes what Duffey calls the "fiction of coherence." This phrase suggests "the degree to which poetry was felt to be most itself, most truly poetical, as it found images of reconciliation and harmony of feeling." The second stage began in the 1860s when "American poetry came more to depend on one form or another of the opposite quality, on contradiction between feeling and fact, on singularity, on a breadth of prospect that exceeded simple and unified feeling, or, finally, on a sense of the world as fragmented, or at war with itself or with individual aspiration."

The third phase was created by poets born "not later than 1920," for whom "the sense of poetry was to depend less upon such larger hopes or doubts and more on seeking a particular being of its own." The general nature of the thesis does not lend itself well to close readings of individual poems. What Duffey does, in fact, is present an overview of each poet he treats—including all American poets of any consequence—in accordance with the way he or she fits Duffey's thesis. What emerges is more a history of ideas in American poetry and less one of American poetry as a literary form. Duffey is an erudite author who knows his subject well and writes comfortably about it. Nonetheless, because he depends too much on a thesis worked out only in a general sense and because he moves from text to ideas without enough analysis, the book is ultimately unsatisfying. Its ideas are insufficiently novel to remain fresh and one's interest in them tends to flag after a while.

A more impressive work is Sacvan Bercovitch's *The American Jeremiad* (Wis.), an altogether admirable sequel to his *Puritan Origins of the American Self* (see ALS 1975). Bercovitch views the jeremiad as a positive shaping force for the United States' view of itself as a middle-class society with a political mission stated in overtones of religiosity. He traces the form from Puritan times through those of Henry Adams, showing how the rhetoric of Puritan ideas and language pervades political thought from the time of John Winthrop on, in such images as the City on the Hill and the Errand into the Wilderness, and such practices as the Fast Day and the Election Sermon. With regard to the latter, Bercovitch shows how it was transformed by an increasingly secular America into such holidays as the Fourth of July, with Independence Day addresses becoming jeremiads in the mouths of such lay priests as Daniel Webster.

I consider this book to be a major statement about American culture. Bercovitch makes a strong case for the belief that the jeremiad and the rhetoric it embodied was a central force leading to the development of what he calls the American consensus. All sides, he points out, in the argument over the nature of the American polity— whether from the right or the left—tend to see the United States in religious terms as a country with a special mission, in an ideological line springing throughout the generations from its origins in the Puritan jeremiad. An important book.

Edwin M. Eigner's *The Metaphysical Novel in England and*

America: Dickens, Bulwer, Hawthorne, Melville (Calif.) is probably the most sophisticated attempt yet to define the romance (roughly equivalent to what the author calls the philosophical novel) as a genre common to both British and American fiction. Early in the book Eigner makes the following distinctions: "Realism is profoundly psychological precisely in the sense that it is interested in the effects of experience on individuals. Metaphysical romance is more seriously concerned with the nature of experience itself . . . [it] may justly be called metaphysical, for it is primarily concerned with explaining the *why* rather than the *how* of reality, its philosophical or metaphysical meanings rather than its psychological effects." Eigner talks about the divided nature of the metaphysical novel, noting that "its characters are sometimes presented on one page as ideal types and on another as realistic portraits" and that "in the matter of setting, the metaphysical novelists did not use either the never-land of their Gothic predecessors or the everyday, Dutch-genre-painting world of the realists."

Eigner defines the various characteristics of the metaphysical novel according to conventional, widely used categories. He talks about writer and audience, about the depiction of character, about certain distinctive character types common to many romances, about the ways in which writers in this genre manage to give a "romantic" aura to familiar things, and he concludes with a convincing discussion of various kinds of structures used in metaphysical novels. The basic scholarship of this book is excellent. Eigner is throughly familiar with his subject, writes well, and convincingly conveys the metaphysical and visionary dimension of the genre.

Myth and Literature in the American Renaissance (Indiana), by Robert D. Richardson, Jr., is a study of the use of myth by writers in the American Renaissance. It is not, however, a "myth" study in the sense of trying to prove a thesis concerning a contemporary theory of myth. It is a historical study based in the notions of myth that would have been current in the intellectual milieu of Emerson, Thoreau, Hawthorne, Melville, and Whitman. Richardson outlines the basic theories of and approaches to myth developed from the late 17th century to the time of Theodore Parker, Bronson Alcott, and Emerson as a context for studying the use of myth by the major authors of the period.

An excellent piece of basic scholarship, this is not really a work of criticism but rather one in the history of ideas. There are long chapters on the sources of myth in the works of all the writers mentioned above, with an especially impressive chapter on Melville. The annotated bibliography is first-rate. This will be a useful sourcebook for scholars of the period.

Henry Nash Smith has made another contribution to the study of 19th-century American literature in *Democracy and the Novel: Popular Resistance to Classic American Writers* (Oxford). More a collection of essays than a unified book, *Democracy and the Novel* centers on the theme of how the major 19th-century American writers responded to what Smith variously suggests was the popular mind, culture, assumptions. The kinds of responses can be charted in the following paradigmatic authors: those who resisted (Herman Melville); those who gave in (William Dean Howells); those who transmuted (Henry James).

While in terms of specific new insights there is not much new here, as an overall document the book presents some fresh perspectives. There is a fascinating chapter on Henry Ward Beecher's now little-known or -read novel, *Norwood*, as a book that embodies all the assumptions of the "genteel tradition." There is also an excellent chapter on Mark Twain, an author Smith knows extremely well, and a good one on the popular reception of Henry James. While not up to the standards of Smith's major works on Mark Twain and the American West, *Democracy and the Novel* is a solid contribution to the scholarship on the period.

Two works published in England deserve short notice: Ann Massa and Scott Donaldson, *American Literature: Nineteenth and Early Twentieth Centuries*, and Miles Donald, *The American Novel in the Twentieth Century* (both Newton Abbot, Eng.: David & Charles). These are low-level chapbook approaches to their subjects. It is difficult to say which students could benefit from reading either volume. Scholarship is minimal, the insights conventional. High-school students could possibly benefit if they were not to fall prey to the faulty scholarship. The best advice would be to leave these books on the shelves where they belong.

H. Wayne Morgan's *New Muses: Art in American Culture, 1865–1920* (Oklahoma) is a short survey of the cultural context out of which American painting developed during the period. "The book is deliberately designed to sample themes common to the era's entire cultural development." The chapter titles indicate the author's concerns: "A New Art World," "Ideals and Conflicts," "Studying Art at Home and Abroad," "Impressionism," "Modernism and a New Century." The latter two chapters, in particular, present good overviews of the period. This well-written book provides a well-documented survey of the period that will be useful to literary scholars. It contains a number of good black-and-white photographs and reproductions.

The final book in this section is *Les Américanistes: New French Criticism on Modern American Fiction* (Kennikat), edited by Ira D. and Christiane Johnson. In this collection of essays the subjects are all recent American writers of fiction, and the authors are without exception *Américanistes* at French universities. Most of the essays reflect various emphases of contemporary French criticism, including structuralism, phenomenology, semiotics, and Marxist approaches, and the quality is high. The American writers covered range from Saul Bellow and John Updike to Robert Coover, John Hawkes, Thomas Berger, and Vladimir Nabokov, with most of the essays in the mode of the *explication de texte*. I recommend in particular the essays by Jean-Pierre Vernier, Yves Le Pellec, and André le Vot. Overall, the book is a good introduction to French academic criticism.

b. **Thematic Approaches and Cultural Criticism.** In this section the books are organized less on historical bases and more by their focus on thematic, topical, or cultural issues. One of the most interesting books of the year, and one that defies easy categorizing, is Leslie Fiedler's *Freaks: Myths & Images of the Secret Self* (Simon & Schuster). This fascinating book is best described as a cultural/psychological study rather than a literary one. Its subject is "teratology," the study of "freaks." The materials with which Fiedler deals are such physical aberrations as dwarfs, giants, hermaphrodites, and Siamese twins. Fiedler explores the place they played as display pieces in American and British culture, as well as the ways in which so-called normal people have responded deeply to them out of the anxiety of knowing that these freaks are strange extensions of our own humanity.

In the first half of the book Fiedler develops each major category of freaks both historically and definitionally. In the second half he uses the categories metaphorically, asking such questions as, Why do we need freaks? and How do we use them in our lives? The final chapters—"Freaks and the Literary Imagination," "Freaking Out," "The Myth of the Mutant and the Image of the Freak"—are of most use to literary scholars. There are a number of touching descriptions of the more famous 19th- and 20th-century freaks and a number of wonderful photographs. Fiedler ranges throughout literature, the circus, and the movies (including a fine analysis of Todd Browning's classic film, *Freaks*) with his usual penchant for sweeping generalizations. A disturbing book, not to be put aside easily.

A very different kind of study is Martha Banta's *Failure & Success in America: A Literary Debate* (Princeton), a captivating work about the long literary debate over what constitutes success in this country. Banta describes the book's general structure as follows: "The three main foci are the thoughts, the feelings, and the language of Americans caught in the press between winning and losing. Certain philosophers, psychologists, and historians furnish supplementary material, using the expository prose forms native to their professions. The major arguments are provided, however, by the poets of the imagination, who are apt to approach meaning through metaphors."

In her exploration of the problems of winning and losing in America, Banta ranges widely through all forms of prose and poetry. The book is organized thematically, although it is thoroughly grounded in history. Banta seems equally at home in all periods and with all forms. She writes well, often at times poetically, and she has no real axe to grind. Although there are no footnotes, there is a very wide range of reference and an extensive bibliography. Unquestionably the definitive work on its subject, the book is a pleasure to read.

Judith R. Berzon's *Neither White Nor Black: The Mulatto Character in American Fiction* (NYU) claims to be the first study of the mulatto character in American fiction. Berzon introduces her theme from historical, sociological, and psychological points of view. She touches on the history of the mulatto in such novels as *Puddn'head Wilson, Melanctha,* and *Band of Angels,* exploring her subject through a series of topics. A rewritten doctoral thesis, the book is solidly researched and well written. It is worth reading, although it could have been more concise.

In *American Visionary Fiction: Mad Metaphysics as Salvation Psychology* (Kennikat) Richard Finholt takes Herman Melville as the beginning "of an *intellectual* tradition in American fiction, a tradition that takes the inner self as subject because the deeply thinking writer is naturally drawn to its mysteries and the vision that arises from them and not because of some Byronic fascination with morbid emotions." In the opening half of this short book Finholt writes a series of essays on *Moby-Dick* to analyze various metaphors for the visionary madness suggested by his title. Having established his categories, he then uses them to analyze works by Edgar Allan Poe, Ralph Ellison, Norman Mailer, and James Dickey. The book contains a number of interesting essays, but it does not cohere as a totality. Finholt is in many ways extending the thesis Harry Levin developed in *The Power of Blackness,* and although he has the intervening years of American literature to draw upon, his book is more valuable for individual insights than theoretical freshness.

H. Bruce Franklin's provocative study, *The Victim as Criminal and Artist: Literature from the American Prison* (Oxford), attempts to establish for literary study a tradition of American literary works written by prisoners. Some of Franklin's metaphors of the prison are slavery and the treatment of sailors on ships in the 18th and 19th centuries. He examines both slave narratives and such early Melville novels as *Redburn* and *White Jacket.* His analyses of Malcolm X's *Autobiography* and the works of Malcolm Braly and Chester Himes are excellent and so is his early chapter on Melville. This well-written book, with a Marxist perspective, occasionally forces a point to prove its thesis, but it is successful in forcing us to rethink many basic assumptions about our American heritage.

Sol Gittleman's *From Shtetl to Suburbia: The Family in Jewish Literary Imagination* (Beacon) straddles with reasonable success the line between the scholarly and popular study. Gittleman's subject is the development of Jewish writing from its beginnings in Yiddish to its present high status in contemporary American writing. The book contains an excellent brief summary of the development of Yiddish from a language that lacked the prestige of Hebrew into an increasingly respectable serious language of study and literature by a number of authors throughout the 19th and early 20th centuries. Gittleman is quite good on such early Yiddish writers as Sholem Aleichem, but he is less good on Jewish-American authors such as Bernard Malamud and Philip Roth. The book's unifying concept is the idea of the Jewish family as it developed in fiction from purely Yiddish writers to contemporary Americans writing in English. The book is entertaining and thoughtful, but it should be supplemented by Irving Howe's masterpiece, *The World of Our Fathers* (see *ALS 1976*).

American Indian Fiction (New Mex.), by Charles R. Larson, surveys the fiction written by and about American Indians. A good overview of the field, it traces the tradition from John Smith to such little-known works as *Cogewea* by Hum-Ishu-Ma, and Jon Mockingbird's *The Wokosani Road*. Although it is not a "major" work, in our growing consciousness of the multi-ethnic character of American culture this is a welcome book.

c. **Major Figures.** I begin this section with brief mention of a fascinating book by Dorothy Commins, *What Is an Editor? Saxe Commins at Work* (Chicago), which is basically a collection of letters from and to Saxe Commins by such major figures as Eugene O'Neill, William Faulkner, Sinclair Lewis, W. H. Auden, Etienne Gilson, and others whose works Commins edited during his long tenure at Random House. The letters are strung together skillfully by narrative provided by Commins's widow. The total package conveys a rich sense of Saxe Commins's devotion to his editorial tasks, as well as good insights into many 20th-century writers and literary groups. My favorite sections are the ones on Faulkner and O'Neill, the latter of which provides a harrowing insight into that playwright's tortured life.

Malcolm Cowley's—*And I Worked at the Writer's Trade: Chapters of Literary History, 1918–1978* (Viking) is a mixture of memoirs and literary essays, some of the latter on specific authors and some on more general topics. All were written during the last 20 years, although their subjects often range back for 50 or more. There is much variety here, with authors as diverse as William Faulkner, Conrad Aiken, Jules Laforgue, Robert Coates, and S. Foster Damon. Although Cowley is most at home with his familiar subjects, prominent writers of the twenties and thirties, he also tackles new writers; particularly absorbing is his chapter on Damon. The book is best in those sections in which the author takes a perceptive though restrained look at his own experience.

A more important work is Alfred Kazin's *New York Jew* (Knopf), the third memoir in a series following *A Walker in the City* and *Start-*

ing Out in the Thirties. While it is not quite as good as either of its predecessors, *New York Jew* is full of excellent writing, interesting situations, and perceptive analyses. The best parts are the continuously interesting character studies and vignettes of such writers as Sylvia Plath, Edmund Wilson, Delmore Schwartz, Saul Bellow, the staff at the *New Republic*, F. O. Matthiessen, Lionel Trilling, and Hannah Arendt. These are all solid intellectual portraits but the brooding presence that recurs often is Edmund Wilson, clearly Kazin's intellectual hero. The author's grasp of the forties and fifties is convincing, but with the sixties Kazin seems unsure and at times rushed. He also attempts to write about his sexual life with the kind of openness Edmund Wilson attempted in his journals, particularly in his book on the twenties, but he is restrained. The result is a mixture of honesty and coyness. Still, this is a book not to be missed. Although not all it might have been, *New York Jew* is an important writer's assessment of his times.

An unusual but fascinating work is *Rat & the Devil: Journal Letters of F. O. Matthiessen and Russell Cheney* (Archon), edited by Louis Hyde. It contains a large selection from among 3,000 letters exchanged by Matthiessen and Cheney during the more than quarter century they were friends and lovers. Because they were a homosexual couple during a time when this fact was very difficult to acknowledge openly, only a few friends shared a relationship with them as a couple. "Rat" is Cheney, a good minor painter with poor health and a weakness for alcohol; Matthiessen is the "Devil." The letters are organized chronologically but in sections, each of which is introduced by the editor, who was a lifelong friend of both men. The letters and the attendant introductions provide excellent insights into each man, the nature of their relationship, and their various friends. This book is clearly a labor of love as well as a useful chronicle of intellectual life in the United States between 1924 and 1945, the year of Cheney's death.

John Wain has edited *Edmund Wilson: The Man and His Work* (NYU), with essays by Alfred Kazin, Angus Wilson, Larzer Ziff, John Wain, John Updike, and others. The essays treat three sides of Wilson—the man, the critic, and the artist. Some of the best pieces deal with Wilson's involvement in national cultures through his treatment of American, French, and Russian writers. Most of the essays seem

to have been written for the occasion and mix reminiscence with
critical responses to some of Wilson's own works. The quality is
high, with excellent pieces by Ziff, Kazin, Helen Muchnic, and Wain.

d. **Women in Literature and Feminist Concerns.** Lillian S. Robinson's collection of essays, *Sex, Class, and Culture* (Indiana) combines Marxist and feminist approaches to cultural studies. The
biographical introduction relates how Robinson embraced both ideologies in the late 1960s. The book is divided into two parts, the first concerned with theory, the second with more practical kinds of criticism.
The first section contains such titles as "Dwelling in Decencies: Radical Criticism and the Feminist Perspective," "Modernism and History," and "Criticism: Who Needs It?"; the second, "On Reading
Trash," "What's My Line? Telefiction and the Working Woman," and
my favorite piece, "Who's Afraid of A Room of One's Own?," the first
of Robinson's essays in her "radical" mode. This is an interesting collection with a perspective that provides fresh insights into familiar
subjects.

Communities of Women: An Idea in Fiction (Harvard), by Nina
Auerbach, is a study of the idea of a community centered on women
as it was developed in a series of classic 19th-century British and
American novels. There is also discussion of one 20th-century novel,
The Prime of Miss Jean Brodie. The 19th-century works are *Pride
and Prejudice, Little Women, Cranford* (by Elizabeth Gaskell),
Villette, The Bostonians, and *The Odd Women* (by George Gissing).
In all these novels Auerbach analyzes the concept of sisterhood. In
the introduction she establishes a theory of community which discusses stereotypes of women, power relationships, matriarchies, and
the religious, familial, and cultural expectations placed on women.
All the analyses of individual works use concepts developed in the
introduction and are themselves perceptive and persuasive. Another
well-written, solidly researched book is Barbara J. Berg's *The Remembered Gate, Origins of American Feminism: The Woman and
the City, 1800–1860* (Oxford), in which the author demonstrates how
American feminism emerged from the urban experiences of women
in the 19th century. The book, part of the Urban Life in America
series, is a historical rather than a literary study, full of insights
useful to literary scholars. Berg begins by discussing the situation of
"American Women in the Eighteenth Century" and continues by

treating such topics as "The Fading Order: Cities in Collision" and "The Woman-Belle Ideal." In the second half of the book, entitled "Towards Feminism," Berg traces the 19th-century movement toward that century's version of women's liberation. This book, if supplemented by Ann Douglas's *The Feminization of American Culture* (see *ALS 1977*), provides a good overview of the situation of American women in the years up to the Civil War.

Nina Baym's *Women's Fiction: A Guide to Novels by and About Women in America, 1820–1870* (Cornell) studies the most popular women novelists of that period. Most of the writers—such as Catharine Sedgwick, Maria McIntosh, Ann Stephens, and Caroline Chesebro'—are largely unknown to contemporary readers, but their works were "best-sellers" of the previous century. Although not a strongly feminist work itself, this book attempts to establish the "ideology" within which most of the last century's women's fiction was written. Baym sets the context well, particularly in her opening two chapters, "Introduction and Conclusions" and "The Form and Ideology of Woman's Fiction," both of which ought to be read by all students of American fiction. The chapters on individual authors are surprisingly interesting, particularly in light of the fact that their works are almost totally unknown. Baym has a rare ability to make minor writers interesting without letting their literary mediocrity trivialize her book.

The major thesis of Judith Fetterley's *The Resisting Reader: A Feminist Approach to American Fiction* (Indiana) is stated early: "American literature is male. To read the canon of what is currently considered classic American literature is perforce to identify as male. . . . Our literature neither leaves women alone nor allows them to participate. It insists on its universality at the same time that it defines that universality in specifically male terms. . . . the female reader is co-opted into participation in an experience from which she is explicitly excluded; she is asked to identify with a selfhood that defines itself in opposition to her; she is required to identify against herself." Women are thus the resisting readers because of the fact that American literature is male and they (women) are asked to identify in fact against themselves. Some of the works which Fetterley analyzes in light of her belief that literature is a primary political act are "Rip Van Winkle," "A Rose for Emily," "The Birthmark," *A Farewell to Arms, The Bostonians, The Great Gatsby,* and *An Ameri-*

can Dream. She develops a number of examples and arguments to demonstrate the various ways male writers create resistance in female readers. Conversely, she shows the paradox in *The Bostonians* that has the opposite effect. Because that novel is written from a point of view somewhat sympathetic to a feminist position, it arouses resistance among male readers. Male and female readers alike can learn from Fetterley. Her book is ideological and mildly polemical, but it is well written, thoughtful, and convincing.

e. Humor. One of the important comprehensive works of 1978 is *America's Humor: From Poor Richard to Doonesbury* (Oxford), by Walter Blair and Hamlin Hill. This is the definitive work on the subject, the result of a lifetime of specialized scholarship by both authors. *America's Humor* is informed by the latest theories of humor, even though it is not itself a theoretical work. A historical survey of its subject, the book is in fact an excellent history of American culture as seen through the medium of humor. The opening section establishes basic principles of organization and theories of humor, both of which are followed carefully in the chapters that follow and cover the subject from the Puritans to the 1970s. By no means exclusively literary, the subjects cover such diverse sources of humor as television, standup comics, and comic strips. Especially good, and not surprisingly, is a long chapter on Mark Twain. Students of American literature will want to keep this book on their night tables.

A more limited study of a similar subject is *American Humor in France: Two Centuries of French Criticism of the Comic Spirit in American Literature* (Iowa State), by James C. Austin, with a concluding chapter by Daniel Royot. The work studies the responses of a cultural elite: those French writers with sufficient interest and proficiency in American literature and the English language to write about the subject. Austin's study rests on solid scholarship, although his own writing is not sufficiently humorous and witty. What is most interesting is the way the book illuminates the response of one culture to another. Humor is the cultural attribute most difficult to translate, as Americans in France have often noted when listening to French intellectuals extolling the comic genius of Jerry Lewis. Specialists in American humor will want to read this book. Generalists will probably want to pass it by.

Comic Relief: Humor in Contemporary American Literature (Illinois), edited by Sarah Blacher Cohen, is the outgrowth of an MLA seminar on the subject. The essays are original contributions by a distinguished group of American literary scholars and cover a variety of authors and topics. Among the best essays are the following: Richard Pearce, "Nabokov's Black (Hole) Humor: *Lolita* and *Pale Fire*"; Stanley Trachtenberg, "Berger and Barth: The Comedy of Decomposition"; Allen Guttmann, "Saul Bellow's Humane Comedy"; Wendy Martin, "The Satire and Moral Vision of Mary McCarthy"; Ruby Cohn, "Camp, Cruelty, Colloquialism"; and John Vernon, "Fresh Air: Humor in Contemporary American Poetry." The book has a useful checklist, and it is well worth the time of any student of contemporary American letters.

f. The West.   Two books comprise this section. The first, by Frederick Merk, *History of the Westward Movement* (Knopf), is a monumental work that traces the movement westward over the American continent. Its survey begins with the first settlements of the English in Virginia and moves all the way to the mid-1970s. The successor at Harvard to Frederick Jackson Turner in the course on the West, Merk instills in this book a lifetime of scholarship and lecturing. This beautifully written work of history is now the definitive treatment of the subject. While clearly influenced by Turner, Merk has his own voice. This is narrative history at its best and all students of American literature will want to read it. C. L. Sonnichsen's *From Hopalong to Hud: Thoughts on Western Fiction* (Texas A&M) is a more modest book. A collection of essays by a lifelong scholar of the West, it discusses how western fiction can be used as an index to the development of American culture. The book treats both "popular" and "serious" fiction through a variety of topics such as "The West That Wasn't," "The Ambivalent Apache," "The Sharecropper in Western Fiction," and "Sex on the Lone Prairie." This is a pleasantly written, relatively lightweight series of essays.

g. The Film and Other Media.   There were fewer distinguished books on film this year than in the recent past, but four deserve brief mention. Jack Temple Kirby's *Media-Made Dixie: The South in the American Imagination* (LSU) discusses the ways the image of the South has been created in the public mind largely by its use as a setting in popular media forms such as fiction, films, and television.

Kirby, a southern historian, is well versed in his subject, and although
the tone of the book is light and often amusing, it is based on good
scholarship.

Politics and Cinema (Columbia), by Andrew Sarris, is a collection of essays and reviews, most of which appeared in *The Village
Voice*. The introduction outlines Sarris's basically political approach
to films. What follows are his reviews of films that have orientations
which lend themselves to Sarris's political interpretation. Examples
are *The Candidate, the Front, The Godfather,* and *The Sorrow and
the Pity*. There are also interesting essays on Norman Mailer's *Marilyn*
and on "Semiotics and the Cinema." While Sarris is clearly one of
the intelligent critical voices dealing with motion pictures, he prides
himself on a wise-guy, insider's tone, which keeps him at a contrived
distance from the reader. Because of this, I find it difficult to warm
to his work even when I agree with him.

A different kind of tone controls the essays on film of Charles
Samuels, who died by his own hand in 1974 after four years as film
reviewer for *The American Scholar*. Samuels brought to his film criticism the tools of the literary critic which had manifested itself in
books on John Updike and Henry James. *Mastering the Film and
Other Essays* (Tenn, 1977), edited by Lawrence Graver, is a collection of Samuels's essays on film, along with an incomplete book,
Mastering the Film. Samuels was not a theorist but rather a solid
practical critic of sensitivity, sensibility, and a strong moral bent.
He had little patience with such matters as semiotic theories, and his
essays largely treat individual films and directors. *Mastering the
Film,* as much as we have of it, consists of essays on Carol Reed, Jean
Renoir, Alfred Hitchcock, and Federico Fellini. Some of the individual films discussed are *Bonnie and Clyde, Zabriskie Point,* and *A
Clockwork Orange*. The essays we have are literate, intelligent, and
unpretentiously provocative.

Charles Eidsvik's *Cineliteracy: Film Among the Arts* (Random)
attempts to give an "overview of the languages of film" and "an aesthetic of the cinema from the perspective of the film-viewing experience." It is a well-written introductory text for readers who wish
to understand some of the languages and approaches current in film
criticism. The book is organized topically and its author is well
versed in cinematic and aesthetic theories. There are long analyses

of a number of major films as well as a number of stills chosen to illustrate the author's points.

ii. General Literary Works

a. Major Figures. *Reflections: Essays, Aphorisms, Autobiographical Writings* (Harcourt), edited and introduced by Peter Demetz, is the second volume of Walter Benjamin's essays and occasional writings to appear in English, the first being the celebrated *Illuminations*. The earlier volume concentrated primarily on literary essays, but this one attempts to show the range of Benjamin's mind by also including essays of philosophical and sociological character as well as a number of autobiographical fragments. In many ways Benjamin was the finest of all Marxist critics, although to categorize him lightly is a mistake. Coming from a cosmopolitan tradition of German scholarship and letters, Benjamin was truly catholic in his interests. The work here ranges from a number of fascinating essays on various of Benjamin's favorite cities—Moscow, Berlin, Marseilles, and Paris—to marvelous pieces on surrealism, Karl Kraus, and Bertholt Brecht. There is scarcely a page in this book that does not contain an insight worth remembering. For those who wish simply to dip into the book, may I recommend "Parts, Capital of the Nineteenth Century," "The Author as Producer," and "On Language as Such and on the Language of Man."

A very different type of critic is represented by the next two books. The first, *Northrop Frye on Culture and Literature: A Collection of Review Essays* (Chicago), edited and introduced by Robert D. Denham, is a book-length set of 21 review essays by Northrop Frye, 14 of which first appeared in the *Hudson Review*. They were all composed between 1946 and 1960, a period that spans the composition of Frye's book on William Blake and his most famous work, *Anatomy of Criticism*. The collection is organized in two parts, the first covering reviews of books whose primary subject is cultural, the second reviewing works primarily literary. Some of the major authors about whom Frye writes are C. G. Jung, Ernst Cassirer, Arnold Toynbee, Susan K. Langer, and Mircea Eliade. Frye's range and erudition have always been enormous, but what is most fascinating about this book is the chance to watch his central ideas emerge and develop.

Robert Denham's excellent introduction analyzes Frye's basic ideas and their evolution.

The second book is a full-length exposition, also by Robert Denham, entitled *Northrop Frye and Critical Method* (Penn. State). This volume complements the above collection of essays and treats in greater depth much of the material covered in the introduction to the other volume. It is an excellent, systematic treatment of Frye's critical program and deals with Frye's critics as well as with Frye's work. The book is organized topically, with chapters on such matters as theories of modes, symbols, myths, and genres. Anyone interested in Northrop Frye's work and in contemporary criticism in English will want to read this book.

A new collection of essays by William H. Gass, *The World Within the Word* (Knopf), is one of the more interesting works in this section. A novelist, philosopher, and critic of distinction, Gass is one of the most literate essayists now active. The work in this collection ranges from the literary to the philosophical. Most of it was written for the *New York Review of Books*, but the essays do not read like occasional pieces. There are fine discussions here of Malcolm Lowry, William Faulkner, Gertrude Stein, Jean-Paul Sartre, and Sigmund Freud ("The Anatomy of Mind"). Everything is marked by Gass's characteristic wit and philosophical depth, and the book is marred only occasionally by the author's tendency toward glibness.

The late Philip Rahv's *Essays on Literature and Politics, 1932–1976* (Houghton Mifflin) have been edited by Arabel J. Porter and Andrew J. Dvosin and are preceded by a delightful, much-too-short memoir by Mary McCarthy. Rahv's best-known pieces are all here: "Paleface and Redskin," "The Cult of Experience in American Writing," "The Dark Lady of Salem." In rereading them and in reading many others for the first time, I find that Rahv's work holds up well. A wide-ranging critic, he wrote on many literatures and many non-literary topics with erudition and firmness. Clearly a Marxist in all his writing, Rahv was nonetheless not bound by ideology, and his Marxist perspective makes his political essays seem particularly acute. It is only in his tastes that Rahv seems dated. He does not express much admiration for recent literature—with the exception of Saul Bellow. More at home with the classic 19th-century novelists, Rahv sometimes allows his impatience with the new to make him seem crotchety. Still, students of literature should take the time to read these essays. They are products of a mind with which it is well worth arguing.

George Steiner's latest collection is entitled *On Difficulty and Other Essays* (Oxford). These essays have primarily to do with the relationship to literature of language and communication systems and are in many ways both followup and supplementary to Steiner's profound study of language, *After Babel* (see *ALS 1975*). The discourse is always rich in reference and sinewy in argument. One of the most erudite of all contemporary critics, Steiner is the best writer I know at bringing together problems common to linguistics and literary interpretation. All the essays in this book are interesting, but I especially recommend "Eros and Idiom," "The Distribution of Discourse," and the title essay.

b. **Marxist and Sociological Criticism.** George Bisztray's *Marxist Models of Literary Realism* (Columbia) is an analytical-historical study of Marxist literary criticism organized around the concept of "realism." Bisztray focuses further on the subconcepts of "critical realism" and "socialist realism" and on the problems caused by both terms. His distinctions are clear and well thought out. Tracing the concept of realism from pre-Hegelian times, he then uses Hegel to trace the concept throughout the 19th and well into the 20th century. A Marxist himself, Bisztray's discussions of such figures as Karl Marx, Friedrich Engels, V. I. Lenin, and Georg Lukacs are well written and not doctrinaire. A useful book.

Audrey Borenstein, in *Redeeming the Sin: Social Science and Literature* (Columbia), attempts to show how literature and social science cover the same territory and deal in similar ways with the same materials. The author, who is both a sociologist and a writer of fiction and poetry, is versant in the classics of both literature and social science. In organizing her book thematically, Borenstein tries to draw evidence from both fields to show that the operatives in each are after the same kinds of understanding of human activity. There is a certain romanticism in her approach that is convincing in spite of occasional lapses of intellectual rigor. Borenstein is at all times well informed and informative, but her book does not leave a lasting imprint.

In *Literary Sociology and Practical Criticism: An Inquiry* (Indiana) Jeffrey L. Sammons has written a study of current trends in the

European sociological theory of literature. The book is Marxist in orientation, and for the most part it stresses the contributions of German socioliterary theory. The categories through which Sammons has organized his work include "Analogy, Homology, Equivocation," "Truth and Time," "Value," "Endurance," "Elitism," and "Extrinsicality." The book develops a number of interesting ideas about the application of literary sociology to the interpretation (practical criticism) of works of literature, but it is limited by a plodding style that often reads like a translation from another language. I quote the book's concluding passage to indicate both the basic thesis and the weaknesses in style that make this a difficult, though often rewarding book: ". . . 'literary sociology' has become a name, perhaps a not wholly fortunate one, for a complex and contentious effort to integrate the fact and the experience of literature into the whole diachronic and synchronic fabric of human reality, proceeding from the elementary principle that consciousness is a derivative of social relations, so that the dialectical distance and deviance of consciousness that we call the faculty of imagination, or, alternatively, of creative freedom, is the object of a rational, practical criticism."

c. Fiction. Seymour Chatman's *Story and Discourse: Narrative Structure in Fiction and Film* (Cornell) applies to the study of narrative those principles of European semiotics which maintain that literature is best treated as a system and that poetics is the study of the nature of literature rather than of works of literature in and of themselves. Chatman's introduction establishes his basic principles. The next four sections are divided equally between "story" and "discourse," which are distinguished by having narration be part of the discussion of discourse rather than of story. Story is divided into "events" and "existents"; discourse into "nonnarrated stories" and "covert versus overt narrators." Within these larger categories Chatman writes discrete examinations of smaller topics having to do with a variety of aspects of his larger topics. This erudite work is informed by a number of different disciplines and makes available to the study of fiction well-explained terminology imported from semiotics and linguistics and from such theorists as the folktale theorist, Vladimir Propp.

Dorrit Cohn's *Transparent Minds: Narrative Modes for Presenting Consciousness in Fiction* (Princeton) is a study of the various ways narrative consciousness is made manifest in prose fiction. The book's first section treats third-person narrative; the second, narrative in the first-person. Cohn's topical treatment of her subject leads her into a number of individual discussions of various problems and characteristics of narrative technique, all of which are notable for their thoroughness and range. Unlike Chatman, however, Cohn does not try to import modish critical terms and techniques. Rather, she is earnest, straightforward, and empirical in her examination of various books and passages in relation to her thesis. This is a well-written, though not exciting work. But it is a solid contribution to the theory of fiction and it is certainly one of the most thorough and understandable treatments of the problems of narrative I have ever read.

John Gardner is a novelist and Chaucer scholar of some note, as well as a literary critic of very definite beliefs. His new work, *On Moral Fiction* (Basic), seems almost to have been written as a corrective to the excesses of contemporary literature and criticism. Gardner adopts a deliberately old-fashioned, impassioned moral attitude that is strikingly antimodernist and sometimes almost hysterical in tone. His models are the great 19th-century masters of narrative, his enemies almost anyone in contemporary letters who is obscurantist by his definition or who does not meet his moral criteria for worthwhile works of literature. The book is fun to read, although some of it goes on too long to remain interesting.

Lawrence L. Langer's *The Age of Atrocity: Death in Modern Literature* (Beacon) is a sensitive, well-written book by the author of *The Holocaust and the Literary Imagination* (see *ALS 1975*). Langer claims that the character of death has been changed in this century by the history and image of mass slaughter, particularly but not exclusively by the fact of the Holocaust that overtook European Jewry during the Second World War. "This book," Langer says, "explores some of the implications of an age that has imposed on the traditional idea of death the prospect of atrocity; it records and hopes to illuminate a shift from the habit of satisfying spiritual appetites to the more urgent predicament of avoiding psychological starvation." The book opens with two splendid chapters, "The Examined Death" and "Dying Voices," that establish the thesis, and continues with attention paid to Thomas Mann, Albert Camus, Aleksandr Solzhenitsyn, and a lesser-known writer, Charlotte Delbo. *The Age of Atrocity* is a compelling book, not only because of its subject but also because of the committed integrity and concern of its erudite author. It is a meaningful supplement to *The Mortal No*, Frederick J. Hoffman's classic study of death in modern literature.

In *Expositional Modes and Temporal Ordering in Fiction* (Hopkins) Meir Sternberg has attacked one of the thornier problems of narrative technique, the matter of the temporal ordering of fiction. His innovative approach to the problem shows how the author's choice of certain expositional modes forces the development of a particular type of chronological unfolding. Sternberg explores a number of types of novelistic chronology, drawing his examples from novels in a number of languages and literatures. The definition of exposition in the first chapter alone makes the book worth the time of anyone interested in the theory of narrative, but the book contains many other riches. My only serious complaint is that the style is often turgid and cluttered with jargon. A good, strong-minded editor could have made these ideas more accessible.

A study of time in fiction is contained in Patricia Drechsel Tobin, *Time and the Novel: The Genealogical Imperative* (Princeton). Tobin's approach is heavily anthropological, her thesis being that the genealogical structuring of society provides the basic temporal structure for the classic novel. "In order," she says, "to bring Time out of hiding and give it the sharpest focus, I offer the metaphor of the 'genealogical imperative.' It equates the temporal form of the classical novel—the conceptualized frame within which its acts and images find their placement— with the dynastic line that unites the diverse generations of the genealogical family." We get our sense of time, Tobin claims, from the passage of generations, and the classic novel follows this pattern. She discusses novels which fit her thesis: Thomas Mann's *Buddenbrooks*, D. H. Lawrence's *The Rainbow*, William Faulkner's *Absalom, Absalom!*, Vladimir Nabokov's *Ada*, and Gabriel Garcia Marquez's *One Hundred Years of Solitude*. Her concluding chapter, "Whither the Novel: The Wager on the Surface," is an interesting piece of speculation. A well-written but modest contribution to the theory of fiction.

d. **Theories of Literature.** In *The Act of Interpretation: A Critique of Literary Reason* (Chicago) Walter A. Davis has attempted to construct a viable theory of pluralistic criticism. Using Faulkner's *The Bear* (the longer version) as the fictional basis for trying out various theories, Davis develops paradigms of three different types of criticism which he in turn applies to Faulkner's novella. The three paradigms are the theory of emotional form (R. S. Crane); rhetorical theory (Kenneth Burke); and dialectical theory (Northrop Frye, Martin Heidegger, Claude Lévi-Strauss), or literature as a special way of knowing. Davis applies each critical approach to *The Bear* with great persuasiveness. He then asks which of the theories we can take most seriously and which we have to exclude. Davis follows by examining each theorem to discover its philosophical basis, his technique here being much influenced by Richard McKeon. In another chapter he examines each interpretation of *The Bear* for its particular weaknesses. As the analyses emerge it becomes clear that Davis has sympathies that lean mostly toward Burke with some strong residual attraction for the work of Crane. The book prescribes a commonsense approach that is much influenced by the Chicago school of criticism. One does not finish this book, however, with much of an instrumental theory to use.

Eugene Goodheart is represented by a new volume, *The Failure of Criticism* (Harvard). This polemical book argues that modernism—through its destruction of any genuine semblance of certainty—has destroyed the possibility of a moral or humanistic basis for criticism. The focus of criticism has become the act of interpretation itself rather than an act performed on behalf of any encompassing social or moral values. Criticism has been captured by the forces of culture, technology, and the modern "creative" spirit. The extremes of this tendency are represented for Goodheart by such critics as Marshall McLuhan and Susan Sontag. The essays that make up this book have among their subjects T. S. Eliot, F. R. Leavis, Philip Rieff, Stendahl, Flaubert, and Joyce. Goodheart's tone is Laurentian, and his moral attitudes seem to stem from Lionel Trilling. This basically conservative book is both erudite and compelling, although its author seems to fancy himself a prophet crying in the wilderness.

The essays in *What Is Literature?* (Indiana), edited and introduced by Paul Hernadi, were commissioned especially for this volume to explore the question asked in the book's title. Many distinguished theorists are represented here, including René Wellek, E. D. Hirsch, Monroe Beardsley, Murray Krieger, Morse Peckham, and Robert Scholes, and they represent many points of view. The book is divided into four sections, "Definitions," "Theory and History," "Canon-

Formation: Forces and Procedures," "Literature: Acts, Effects, Artifacts," each of which contains a number of first-rate essays. While the book is continuously stimulating, what emerges is not so much a coherent theory of literature as a fascinating potpourri.

The Critical Circle: Literature and History in Contemporary Hermeneutics (Calif.), by David Couzens Hoy, is a stimulating philosophical discussion of the major issues in hermeneutics. Hoy begins by taking on E. D. Hirsch's theory of intentionality. He examines a number of other figures famous in hermeneutics and announces himself as a follower of Hans-Georg Gadamer. Hoy dissects a number of theories of history, following this by discussions of such literary critics as Harold Bloom, Michael Riffaterre, and Stanley Fish. Much of this book is highly technical, and while it contains an effective analysis of a number of problems important to literary theory, it is best read by someone a bit schooled in hermeneutic theory.

Louise M. Rosenblatt's *The Reader, the Text, the Poem: The Transactional Theory of the Literary Work* (So. Ill.) is an effective presentation of the transactional theory of literary experience. Rosenblatt makes a basic distinction between the text and the poem. The reader responds to the text, and the interaction of the two evokes the poem. The third chapter suggests an interesting though questionable distinction between two types of reading: the "efferent" (nonaesthetic), which is reading just for the sake of remembering, and the "aesthetic," whereby one reads for the experience of reading. This sensible but unexciting book is based heavily on the author's experience in the classroom.

The latest volume of the Yearbook of Comparative Criticism (volume 7), edited by Joseph P. Strelka, is *Theories of Literary Genre* (Penn. State). This collection is divided into three sections: "Basic Theoretical Problems," "Special Aspects of Genre Theory," and "Contemporary Genre Criticism." The authors include Albert William Levi, Robert Champigny, and Paul Hernadi. A lot of the essays are fairly technical, although by the end of the book the reader will have a good understanding of the current state of genre theory, within certain limitations. These limitations are, however, crucial. There is almost no representation here of structuralist critics, a school of criticism much of whose major work has been in the area of genre theory. In his Preface Strelka is critical of the theories of Tzvetan Todorov, a bias that obviously was a limiting factor in his choice of authors for this volume. That choice gives this book a certain one-sidedness of which readers ought to be aware.

Evan Watkins, *The Critical Act: Criticism and Community* (Yale), presents a theory of dialectical criticism that examines the interaction between the reader and the poem as well as that between poem, author, and society. The first part of the book discusses contemporary criticism and poetry, including sections on critics who are structuralists, hermeneuticists, and phenomenologists. The second section discusses Marxist theory and has a chapter on *Absalom, Absalom!*. Watkins's final chapter, "Criticism and Community: On Literary Value," is an interesting statement about the interrelationship between the concept of community developed in works of literature and the literary value of the works themselves. This well-written book makes a lot of sense, but I find myself unsatisfied by its ultimate lack of coherence as a basic statement. It does not fully rise above its being a collection of essays tied together loosely by a common theme.

e. **On the Cutting Edge.** The following are works which, in my opinion, lie on the cutting edge of contemporary criticism and point some of the future directions that criticism will take. First of all, a good introduction to current thinking in the field of semiotics is a collection edited by Richard W. Bailey, Ladislav Matejka, and Peter Steiner, *The Sign: Semiotics Around the World* (Ann Arbor: Michigan Slavic Publications). This collection contains essays by some of the best and most well-known people currently active in the field. The book demonstrates well the range of semiotics as a method and the situation of semiotics in a number of national cultures. I especially recommend essays by Tzvetan Todorov, "The Birth of Occidental Semiotics"; Elmar Holenstein, "Semiotic Philosophy?"; Ladislav Matejka, "The Roots of Russian Semiotics of Art"; James A. Fanto, "Speech Act Theory and Its Applications to the Study of Literature"; and Walter Mignolo, "What Is Wrong with the Theory of Literature?"

Two more of Roland Barthes's books have been translated into English. *Image–Music–Text* (Hill & Wang, 1977) is a set of essays not previously collected in English. None of these appeared in *Critical Essays*, a volume that was published in 1972 by the Northwestern University Press. The subject matter covered in *Image–Music–Text* includes imagery, photography, Eisenstein's films, mythology, music,

and a host of other topics, some of them literary, some not. Barthes's
mind is amazingly fertile and his methodology is adaptable to the
analysis of almost anything in the world that has structure. This is
an excellent introduction for readers who do not know Barthes's
work. *A Lover's Discourse: Fragments* (Hill & Wang) was first published in France in 1977. It is similar in format to *The Pleasure of
the Text* (see *ALS 1975*) by being composed primarily of discontinuous fragments organized alphabetically by the French names of
the terms Barthes ostensibly defines. The assumption behind this
book is that the highly conventional language of lovers is controlled,
by and large, by literary models. The basic texts to which Barthes
constantly refers come from two great literary models of amorous
behavior, *The Sorrows of Young Werther* and *Remembrance of
Things Past*. There are 80 terms such as "jealousy," "magic," "night,"
"affirmation," "absence," "objects," "obscene," and "clouds," around
which Barthes organizes his quotations and analyses. He presents a
great many literary quotations and performs impressionistic analyses
of his key terms, but beyond this statement it is difficult to summarize
the book. Barthes's mind is one with which it is always stimulating to
be in contact. He constantly has insights that surprise. While *A
Lover's Discourse* is not exactly a work of literary theory or analysis,
it is full of profound literary as well as philosophical and psychological insights.

Another important work of European semiotic theory has been
translated into English, Maria Corti's *An Introduction to Literary
Semiotics* (Indiana). One of the better introductions to the subject,
the book describes literature as part of a total information system, by
examining the various communicative values of literary signs, actors,
and situations. The five broad areas into which the book is organized
indicate the general thematic tendencies: "Literature and Communication," "Sender and Addresses," "The Linguistic Space," "Hypersign," "Literary Genres and Codifications." In common with other
works in this discipline the book tends to look at literature as a particular communication system with definite rules governing its discourse. In order to read such a book profitably it is important to
accept the language (jargon?) that is conventional to the discipline.
As an example, I shall quote from the definition of the work of literature as a "hypersign": "The term 'hypersign,' used here for the work
of art considered in its semiological perspective, attests to the fact

that the work can produce a high yield of information precisely because the work-as-a-whole strengthens the complex of its constituent
signs." Aside from the difficulties of adjusting to the diction, the
book makes insufficient reference to specific works of literature.
Still, this is one of the most accessible introductions to semiotics,
easier for the uninitiated than either Barthes's *Elements of Semiology*
or Umberto Eco's *A Theory of Semiotics* (see *ALS 1976*).

One of the most important texts of recent French criticism has at
last been published in English: Jacques Derrida's *Writing and Difference* (Chicago), translated and edited by Alan Bass. This collection of essays was first published in France in 1967, the same amazing
year that saw the original appearance of Derrida's *Speech and
Phenomena* and *Of Grammatology*. The first six essays of *Writing
and Difference* establish the basic principles which Derrida systematically applies in the final five. The difficult concept of "difference" vs.
"differance" is discussed and elaborated here. To translate Derrida is
extremely difficult not only because his work treads the line between
criticism and philosophy but also because Derrida, like a number of
other French critics, is extremely playful in his use of language, pun-
ning constantly and making other kinds of linguistic jokes. Much of
this word play can only be approximated in English, and Derrida's
Hegelian dialectic is often quite abstract. Nonetheless, certain of
these essays have become classics in critical literature and are good
entrées into Derrida's work. I especially recommend "Force and
Signification," "Genesis and Structure and Phenomenology," "Freud
and the Scene of Writing," and "Structure, Sign, and Play in the Discourse of the Human Sciences."

The final book in this review has had a controversial reception,
but I am one of those who thinks it a brilliant attempt at a kind of
analysis with which I am fundamentally out of sympathy: ideological
criticism. Edward Said's *Orientalism* (New York: Pantheon Books)
is one of the first attempts in English to apply a full-scale analysis
in the manner of Michel Foucault to a large ideological topic. Said's
claim is that "Orientalism" is basically a political-ideological topic
and that all statements and claims concerning the Orient as a subject
of study are fraught with assumptions that are little understood by
those making them. The most basic assumption of Western scholars
and Westerners in general is that the Orient is an area that must
naturally be dominated by the Occident. Therefore all scholarship—

no matter how it may pretend to "objectivity"—is imperialialist in its orientation and is full of assumptions about the inferiority of the subject colonial peoples. The following lengthy quotation gives a succinct idea of the theoretical methodology underlying Said's analysis: "A text purporting to contain knowledge about something actual, and arising out of circumstances similar to the ones I have just described [circumstances whereby texts reinforce ideologies] is not easily dismissed. Expertise is attributed to it. The authority of academics, institutions, and governments can accrue to it, surrounding it with still greater prestige than its practical success warrant. Most important, such texts can *create* not only knowledge but also the very reality they appear to describe. In time such knowledge and reality produce a tradition, or what Michel Foucault calls a discourse, whose material presence or weight, not the originality of a given author, is really responsible for the texts produced out of it."

Said's study focuses on the Islamic Near Orient. He examines the history of Orientalism as a field of study and the ways the ideology connected with this study managed to develop. He also attempts to show how Orientalist assumptions continue today in the average Westerner's feelings and attitudes toward "Arabs," attitudes that are extremely damaging to intercultural understanding. Said does not offer an alternative. He intends his book to demonstrate how there is a nearly inescapable ideology connected with any topic such as this that involves complex historical and political interrelationships like those between Orient and Occident. Said himself is a Palestinian and he feels his ideas passionately. Orientalists will almost surely take offense (and already have done so, in print), and I do not take any position on the factual accuracy of what Said has to say. It is his methodology that has much to offer to English readers. This book is much more clearly written than *Beginnings* (ALS 1975) and is more accessible than any of Foucault's works. Aside from the timeliness of the topic, the book has a great deal to teach in the way of understanding a certain type of ideological analysis, and I recommend it highly.

University of California, Davis

21. Foreign Scholarship

i. French Contributions

Maurice Couturier

More and more doctoral dissertations in American literature are being written in France every year, but it seems that fewer and fewer are being published because of rising publishing costs. This is partly compensated by the increasing number of articles published in periodicals.

Two interesting books came out this year, both dealing with contemporary literature. *Les Américanistes: New French Criticism on Modern American Fiction* (Kennikat) is a collective work. In their opening essay the joint editors, the late Ira D. Johnson and his wife, Christiane Johnson, have provided a brief summary of the avatars of American literature with the French audience, from de Tocqueville to Sartre, and a very clear sketch of the contemporary critical background that can be assumed for all the contributors, from Russian Formalism to Barthes, Kristeva, and psychoanalysis. Each article deals with a specific author or a specific work. In "Mr. Sammler's Lesson" (pp. 16–36) J. P. Vernier investigates Bellow's fictional discourse and suggests that on a number of points Sammler may be "the mouthpiece for Bellow's views" (p. 32). "Aspects of the American Picaresque in *Little Big Man*" (pp. 37–52) by Daniel Royot examines the case of Jack Crabb, the actor-narrator in Thomas Berger's novel, as central intelligence, social archetype, and American folk hero. André Bleikasten's "The Heresy of Flannery O'Connor" (pp. 53–70) contrasts the novelist's "professed ideological stance and the textual evidence of her fiction" (p. 54), and declares her to be of the Devil's party. "Narrative Triangle and Triple Alliance: A Look at *The Moviegoer*" (pp. 71–3) by Simone Vauthier gives a neorhetorical reading of Percy's novel, concluding that "read-

Professor F. Lyra's report on East European contributions was not received in time for inclusion this year. It will be included in next year's essay.—*J.A.R.*

er and writer have become co-celebrants in the rites of symbolic communication" (p. 93). In his essay about Updike, "Rabbit Underground" (pp. 94–109), Yves Le Pellec concentrates on Rabbit's apprehension of "the poetry of space . . . and on the metaphors which express it" (p. 95), and declares that Updike has probably completed the Rabbit cycle. With "New Modes of Story-Telling: Dismantling Contemporary Fiction" (pp. 110–29) André Le Vot offers an enunciative and psychoanalytic theory of postmodern fiction; he distinguishes between two narrative modes, the disjunctive (Coover, Brautigan, Hawkes, Barthelme) and the conjunctive (Pynchon, Barth . . .). "The Exemplary Fictions of Robert Coover" (pp. 130–37) by Régis Durand and "Genesis and Functions of Hencher in *The Lime Twig*" (pp. 138–55) by Pierre Gault deal with the "disjunctive mode"; Durand tries to define the kind of critical discourse which suits this kind of fiction best, whereas Gault makes a structuralist analysis of one of Hawkes's novels. Maurice Couturier's "Nabokov's Performative Writing" (pp. 156–81) provides an enunciative study of three novels, *Pale Fire, Ada,* and *Transparent Things,* emphasizing the distortions which pervert the discursive status of the writing. In "Space and Settor in Short Science Fiction" (pp. 182–201), Jacques Favier singles out two structural elements of the science fiction setting and emphasizes the animist and anthropomorphic bias of the genre. The essay which concludes the collection, Robert Silhol's "Portrait of an Ideal Critic" (pp. 202–15), does not specifically deal with American literature but with some of the theoretical dilemmas the contemporary critic must face. *Les Américanistes,* despite the variety of subjects it touches, is not an arbitrary collage but a whole; this is largely due to the fact that the contributors have the same theoretical background.

The second book, *Le théâtre américain d'aujourd'hui* (Paris: Presses universitaires de France) by M. C. Pasquier, is a very well documented study of the American stage in the sixties and seventies. The first part of the book, which is by far the more important of the two, concerns the explosion that took place in the sixties; it focuses upon specific phenomena: the Open Theatre, the Bread and Puppet Theatre, the Teatro Compesino, and the Black Theatre. It lays particular emphasis upon the social and political environment in which this new theatre developed. In the second part Pasquier tries to make a quick portrait of the seventies where, as far as she is concerned, four names stand out: Andrei Serban, Meredith Monk, Robert Wilson, and Richard Foreman. Considering the magnitude of the subject, this is a very good and useful book: Pasquier has not only provided a comprehensive introduction (with a thorough chronology and bibliography) but also a very intelligent analysis.

The most important contribution made by the French scholars this year may well be the double issue of *Delta*, about Melville's "Bartleby the Scrivener." These two volumes (6 and 7) offer an unprecedented variety of readings of Melville's tale. Mathieu Lindon in "Descriptions d'un combat" (6:5–27) and Hélène Rosenberg in "Huis-clos dans 'Bartleby'" (6:29–35) study Bartleby's special rapport with writing as both a record-making and an artistic practice. In "A propos de 'Bartleby': Compilation" (6:37–42) Jean Roudaut suggests that the tale can be taken as either the story of a ritual murder or the portrait of an exemplary sage. The next two articles, Cathy N. Davidson's "Courting God and Mammon: The Biographer's Impasse in 'Bartleby'" (6:41–59) and Renaud Zuppinger's "'Bartleby': *Prometheus Revisited*: Pour une problématique de la confiance, ou, la sortie du souterrain" (6:61–77), develop an enunciative reading of the story: they underline the shortcomings of the unreliable narrator and the phatic dimension of the narrative. In "The 'Incurable Disorder' in 'Bartleby'" (6:79–93) Thomas P. Joswick interprets Bartleby's "I would prefer not to" as a refusal to take writing as a remedy against universal disorder. The next article, Régis Durand's "Le cadre de la fiction" (6:95–107), also deals with the problem of writing, or rather with the relationship between writing and knowledge viewed from a metaphysical angle. This first volume ends with an interesting interview of Maurice Ronet, the French actor turned film director, who has recently made a film out of the tale.

The first two articles in the second volume, Francine S. Puk's "'Bartleby the Scrivener': A Study in Self-Reliance" (7:7–20) and Joseph Moldenhauer's "'Bartleby' and 'The Custom House'" (7:21–62), make a careful comparison between the tale and the texts of Emerson and Hawthorne. One of the most ambitious articles in this series is Claude Fleurdorge's "'Bartleby': A Story of Broadway" (7:65–109): it tries, first of all, to decide what the real object of the tale is and who the actual subject is who assumes it; then it draws a parallel between the "easiest way" of the narrator and the "broad way" mentioned in the Gospel according to St. John. In "Le pharmakos au gingembre" (7:111–26), an article strongly influenced by Derrida, Gilbert Laurens tries to show the relationship between the tale and Plato's *Phaedo*. Claude Coulon's "Pour une dramaturgie de Melville dans 'Bartleby' " (7:131–41) is an attempt to single out the dramatic elements in the tale and to view the text as a protracted soliloquy. In the following articles, "Bartleby l'idée fixe" (7:143–53) and "Mourning and Melancholia in 'Bartleby' " (7:155–68), François Laroque and Nancy Blake give a psychoanalytic reading of the story, suggesting that Bartleby's neurosis springs from his failure to come to terms with the "Other," his unconscious. Pierre Vitoux and Annette Lanoix in the last two articles, " 'Bartleby': Etude du récit" (7:173–89) and "Les différents types de discours, ou les problèmes de l'énonciation dans 'Bartleby' " (7:191–202), analyze two complementary aspects of the "récit," the "récit as a story" (Vitoux) and the "récit as a discourse" (Lanoix), to borrow Todorov's terms. Taken as a whole, these two volumes no doubt constitute the most elaborate examination of the story to date; it is a landmark in Melville scholarship.

The April issue of the *Revue Française d'Etudes Américaines* is mostly devoted to 19th-century literature. In "The Age of Reform: A Reappraisal" (5:7–18) Ronald Creagh questions many of the clichés concerning the "eccentric" period between 1820 and 1870, taking a more positive view of the so-called utopian communities and of the various brands of idealism which developed during that period. Yves Carlet, in " 'Respectables iniquités': le Transcendantalisme et l'ordre social" (5:18–31), argues, along the same lines, that the American scholar of the Transcendentalist era had a keener sense of his social mission than he has usually received credit for. The next two articles reappraise two literary works of the period: in "Analyses structurales de 'Rip Van Winkle' " (5:33–45) Jean Béranger takes Irving's story as a series of dreams which he analyzes both structurally and psychoanalytically; Michel Granger's "Le bras du cannibale: aspects de la régression primitiviste dans *Moby Dick*" (5:47–61) is less ambiguously psychoanalytic: it suggests that Melville has used the exotic setting to distract the reader from the obsessive presence of cannibalism. Next, Jean-Marie Bonnet, in "Aristarques et poètes: notes préliminaires à une analyse du discours critique sur la poésie dans les revues américaines de 1783 à 1837"

(5:63–72), sums up the critical opinions developed in the American periodicals of the early 19th century concerning poetry and explains that they were tainted with political conservatism. In "The Profane and the Sacred: An Initiation to the American Romance" (5:73–82) Viola Sachs combines Richard Chase's well-known theory of the romance with Mircea Eliade's views concerning myths in order to define a new approach to that typically American genre, as well as to American imagination in general. The last two articles bridge the gap between the Transcendentalist and the contemporary era. Maurice Couturier's "Zona Gale, transcendantaliste de Main Street" (5: 83–92) analyzes the peculiar transcendentalism of the author of the "Friendship Village" stories and of *Miss Lulu Bett*, who was largely influenced by Swedenborg and Gurdjieff. Finally, in "Whitman, Williams, Ginsberg: histoire d'une filiation" (5:93–108), Jacqueline Saunier-Ollier traces the links between these three poets who often relied upon the same poetic devices.

The third issue of *Annales du CRAA* contains four excellent articles about American Naturalism. "Dorothy Parker, héritière du naturalisme ou humoriste féministe" (3:121–37) by Rolande Diot, inquires upon the illocutionary value of Dorothy Parker's work: is it an impassive statement concerning social evils, or the militant discourse of a feminist? Françoise Brousse in "Le 'Machismo' de Norman Mailer" (3:139–50) stigmatizes the male chauvinism of Mailer, whereas Jean Demanuelli in "Politique et femmes fatales: Portraits d'intrigantes dans le roman du 'Gilded Age'" (3:151–76) proposes a feminist reading of the novels of the Gilded Age, and shows that the many scheming shrews who turn up in these works are the offsprings of Victorian puritanism. In the last article, "La contribution du journalisme au 'réalisme' de Stephen Crane" (3: 187–202), Jean Cazemajou explains how Crane's journalistic experience may have helped him to evolve his special kind of realism in his fiction.

After the publication of the first volume of Faulkner's *Oeuvres romanesques*, edited by Michel Gresset and reviewed in *ALS 1977*, *La Quinzaine Littéraire* (270 [Jan. 1–15]) published a series of articles to celebrate the event. Philippe Jaworski's "William Faulkner: Le désir et l'exigence d'écriture" (p. 4) is a eulogistic review of the book. It is followed by the translation of an unpublished preface to *The Sound and the Fury*, written by Faulkner in

1933, and of a letter Faulkner wrote to his agent, Ben Wasson, in 1929, telling him how much he resented the corrections he had made in *The Sound and the Fury.* "Encore le temps Faulknérien" (pp. 6–7), by Pierre Pachet, is a new reading of the articles Sartre wrote in 1939 about Faulkner, and a phenomenological study of *The Sound and the Fury.* In "Un écrivain du mal absolu," an interview (p. 8), Philippe Sollers analyzes Faulkner's personal stake in his writing. The last article in the series, "L'impossible répétition" (p 8), by Roger Laporte, briefly examines another preface to *The Sound and the Fury* in which Faulkner insisted upon the genesis of his novel. This interesting dossier also includes a bibliography of the Faulkner scholarship in France.

Michel and Geneviève Fabre, who are specialists in black literature, have published four very well documented articles. In "Richard Wright's Image of France" (*Prospects* 3[1977]:315–29) Michel Fabre explains that Wright did not know France too well but did his utmost to publicize black American culture in France, and in "The Richard Wright Archive: The Catalogue of an Exhibition" (*YULG* 53:57–78) he lists the items that were exhibited in the Beinecke Rare Book and Manuscript Library in November 1977. Both of Geneviève Fabre's articles deal with the black theatre: "The New Black Theatre: Achievements and Problems" (*Caliban* 14:122–29) describes the past achievements and the present decline (due to financial difficulties) of the black theatre; "Afro-American Theatre: A Bibliographic Survey" (*AQ* 30:358–73) provides useful guidelines for the study of the Afro-American theatre.

Two more articles deserve to be mentioned. Geneviève Hily-Mane's "Les versions successives de *The Sun Also Rises,*" published in *Actes du Congrès de Saint Etienne* (Paris: Didier, pp. 267–86), describes the five stages which led to the final version of the novel and shows that Hemingway's corrections always helped make the text more suggestive and less redundant. In "L'espace imaginaire de Melville dans les *Encantadas* et les significations des trois symboles thériomorphes" (*RLV* 44:15–27), Monique Pruvot studies the main theriomorphic symbols (bird, fish, tortoise) present in *The Encantadas.*

As a conclusion, one can say that the French scholars are becoming more and more interested in the writers of the transcendentalist and post-transcendentalist period, Melville especially, and in the contemporary novel. This does not exclude other fields of research, but it seems, for instance, that the "Great American Novel" of the twenties and thirties, which was so popular in France during the existentialist era, is attracting less and less attention. I suggest that this new tendency may spring from the widespread materialistic (some will call it antihumanist) stance of many French scholars at the moment. This ideological presupposition has encouraged the development of a formalist approach which is more easily applicable to the romance, on the one hand, and to postmodern fiction, on the other. Perhaps there is more in common between these two corpora than meets the eye!

Université de Nice

ii. German Contributions

Hans Galinsky

Continuity and change once again determine the general picture of German contributions in 1978. Last year's number of items, around 120, was reached once more, with book-length publications, volumes of essays from several hands, and annotated editions of literary texts accounting for one fourth. The essay volumes still prefer the survey type, embracing more than one literary period. They usually focus on one genre only, and, aside from a historical introduction, concentrate on the 20th century. The pattern persists with the late Edgar Lohner and Rudolf Haas, editors of *Theater und Drama in Amerika: Aspekte und Interpretationen* (Berlin: Schmidt), a German-British-American enterprise. Another well-organized specimen by Jens Peter Becker and Paul G. Buchloh, editors of *Der Detektivroman: Studien zu Geschichte und Form der englischen und amerikanischen Detektivliteratur* (Darmstadt: Wissenschaftliche Buchgesellschaft) is binational. It enjoyed a revised and enlarged second edition. More and more often operating on an even larger, multinational scale, many surveys including American literature come under "Comparative Studies" (section *b*). As this section also comprises "Literary Criticism and Theory," another binational sur-

The author wishes to apologize for an error in last year's account (*ALS* 1977:479, 531). Claus Rüdiger should read Rüdiger G. Schlicht.–*H.G.*

vey, *Englische und amerikanische Literaturtheorie: Studien zu ihrer historischen Entwicklung*, edited by Rüdiger Ahrens and Erwin Wolff, vol. 1: *Renaissance, Klassik und Romantik*, AF 126 (Heidelberg:Winter), will be conveniently reserved for section *b*. In the field of didactics, too, the essay-volume type continues its hospitality to American themes as is evidenced by the interdisciplinary volume *Landeskunde und Fremdsprachenunterricht*, edited by Horst Arndt and Franz-Rudolf Weber for the monograph series *Schule und Forschung* (Frankfurt: Diesterweg). The preponderance of articles over single authors' book-length studies is yet another persistent characteristic.

Change enters via a new interest in (1) editing American texts, (2) applying a comparative view to American literature not only in European, but also in Puerto-Rican, Canadian, and East Asian contexts, (3) increasingly attempting to understand and evaluate literature, both "belles-lettres" and "popular," with the help of political and/or economic science, psychoanalysis, linguistics, and semiotics, reception esthetics, and 'reader manipulation strategies.' Myth criticism, perhaps because of its anthropological and theological presuppositions, is much less applied.

a. **Literary History—General.** *Theater und Drama in Amerika* opens with a comprehensive introduction (pp. 9–41) by Haas. It incorporates material left by Lohner at the time of his premature death. The joint view of drama and theater, the perceptive and balanced judgment on the Americanness of American drama, and the firm grasp of its complex history render this essay a major achievement. In a book of smaller historical scope, ranging from Poe to the "hard-boiled" detective story since 1945, Rainer Burckhardt interprets the development of the genre along two lines usually kept apart, psychoanalysis and Marxism. The title of this monograph, *Die "hartgesottene" amerikanische Detektivgeschichte und ihre gesellschaftliche Funktion*, EurH, ser. 14, Angelsächsische Sprache und Literatur 59 (Frankfurt: Lang) omits the fact that chapter 2 (pp. 35–96) includes the "classic" detective story and chapter 3 tries to understand it in psychological and sociological terms. Naturally, the social function of the genre is defined as providing "escape" varying in accordance with the intellects of middle-class readers.

a–1. **Colonial, Revolutionary, and 19th Century.** Focusing predominantly on one period each and often on one literary genre only is the continuing mark of scholarly activity. An exception to the rule, in spite of its chief title, is Karl Heinz Göller's "Amerikanische Unterhaltungsliteratur im 19.Jahrhundert" (*DVLG* 52:1–25). As is clarified by the subtitle "Von der Captivity Narrative zur Dime Novel," the colonial origin of the form type is not neglected. It is looked upon as a transatlantic offshoot of the English "chapbook." Restricting itself to the early colonial period, Gustav H. Blanke's "Early Images of North America and Shakespeare's *The Tempest*" (*Landeskunde und Fremdsprachenunterricht*, pp. 72–83), competently distinguishes primitivist from antiprimitivist views, their representatives ranging from Parmenius to Wigglesworth. *The Tempest* is held up as the "one English literary work which bridges the gap between primitivistic and antiprimitivistic imagery." This essay is most profitably read in conjunction with Stephen J. Greenblatt's "Learning to Curse: Aspects of Linguistic Colonialism in the Sixteenth Century," a contribution to vol. 2 of *First Images of America* (Berkeley, Calif., 1976, pp. 561–80). As for the Revolutionary era, an international response to the Bicentennial, at length rendered audible by *Other Voices, Other Views*, edited by Robin W. Winks (Greenwood), includes a German voice. Along with the others, it does not sound a revolutionary theme. The period is considered, but in comparative contexts only (see section *b*).

Late 18th-century and early 19th-century writing has become the target of useful editorial enterprise. Hans Borchers has edited and introduced *Charles Brockden Brown, Memoirs of Stephen Calvert*, Studien und Texte zur Amerikanistik, Texte 2 (Frankfurt: Lang). The fruitful cooperation of Hans-Joachim Lang and Benjamin Lease continues in their joint venture, *The Genius of John Neal: Selections from His Writings*, Studien und Texte zur Amerikanistik, Texte 1. This sampler offers four tales, extracts from five novels, eight specimens of "Essays and Criticism," and three examples of Neal's advocacy of women's rights. In their introduction (pp. vii–xxiv) the editors neatly balance Neal's contemporaneous significance and modern appeal in his role as critic, writer, and social reformer. Their claim that Neal's *Brother Jonathan* "stands alone in its exuberant vitality and epic sweep as a direct forerunner of *Moby-*

Dick" will surely turn critical attention to this "novel of the American Revolution." Third of the editorial enterprises, Sybille Haage's *Edgar Allan Poe, Tales of the Folio Club and Three Other Stories,* Studien und Texte zur Amerikanistik, Texte 3 (Frankfurt: Lang) is supplemented with the editor's attempt at reconstruction. This companion volume, *Edgar Allan Poe's "Tales of the Folio Club": Versuch der Rekonstruktion einer zyklischen Rahmenerzählung,* Studien und Texte zur Amerikanistik, Studienband 7 (Frankfurt: Lang) and the edition of the text are two thoughtful contributions to international Poe scholarship in the neglected field of short story 'macrostructure.' Normally bypassed, too, early 19th-century drama is inspected by Astrid von Mühlenfels in "James Nelson Barker: *The Tragedy of Superstition"* (*Drama und Theater in Amerika,* pp. 194–218). In previous German survey-type collections of essays the American stage of the time was excluded. Thus a play of Barker's makes its first appearance in von Mühlenfels's stimulating analysis. It blends sound knowledge of American research with firsthand expertise, achieving a pilot study in waters usually avoided by German explorers. A near-contemporary of Barker's and U.S. citizen of Austrian descent, who served as a literary purveyor of his political conception of America to German-speaking Europe and, in a much lower degree, to his adopted country, turns up in Alexander Ritter's "Charles Sealsfield: Literaturgeschichtliche Standortbestimmung und philologischer Auftrag," *Deutsche Dichter des 19.Jahrhunderts,* edited by Benno von Wiese, second revised and enlarged edition (Berlin: Schmidt), pp. 98–117. Josephinism, the Austrian Catholic variant of the late Enlightenment, especially with Bernard Bolzano for its spokesman in Bohemia, and Republicanism concretized in Jacksonian brand of southern Agrarianism, a harmonious order the return to which is looked upon as a "historical necessity," are found to be the basic ingredients of Sealsfield's image of America. New England's rising industrialism is negated but subconsciously feared. Ritter's rejection of Sealsfield's assignment to "the narrative tradition of escapist exotism" is cogent. His view of him as "an author of the Austro-American late Enlightenment" might be contested.

All of the major representatives of the generations of the 1800s and 1810s, from Emerson through Melville, Whitman excepted, come up for discussion. Emerson the poet forms the subject of a penetrating investigation by Franz H. Link ("Idee und Wirklichkeit in den Gedichten Emersons," *Literaturwissenschaftliches Jahrbuch der Görres-Gesellschaft*, New Series, 19:317–57). Aware of the paucity of studies in Emerson's poetry over against the host of publications on his essays, Link inquires into possible reasons for this disparity. Of the two questions posed—(1) Can the vision expressed in the poetry be called a success? (2) Is the deficient mastery of a style traceable to a deficient congruity of vision?—the first receives a negative, the second an affirmative answer. Hawthorne research can register a rewarding sign of international recognition. The soundness of Hans-Joachim Lang's 1969 essay, "*The Blithedale Romance*: A History of Ideas Approach," is deservedly acknowledged by its inclusion in the Norton Critical Edition of *Nathaniel Hawthorne: The Blithedale Romance. An Authoritative Text, Backgrounds and Sources, Criticism*, pp. 324–37. Hawthorne's probable service as a source for a play by Wilder will be chronicled in the context of German Wilder scholarship (section a–2). Poe, already mentioned as the subject of reediting and reconstruction, returns in Peter Krumme's *Augenblicke —Erzählungen Edgar Allan Poes*, SAVL 12 (Stuttgart: Metzler) and in an essay by Marianne Kesting, which for its comparatist slant will be discussed in section *b*. Melville this year benefits from the steady increase, noticeable since the 1960s, of German reception studies accompanied by several theories of "reception esthetics." This general trend is reflected in Arno Heller's "Herman Melvilles 'Bartleby the Scrivener'": Eine kritische Rezeptionsanalyse" (*Sprachkunst* 9:316–27). Heller rejects such older approaches as the biographical, psychoanalytical, and philosophy- or religion-oriented ones for their subjective "projection, selection and construction" in the process of interpretation. Instead, he approves of the analysis of the multilayered and indirect form of (narrative) communication, which on the author's part obviously stems from a "tendency to disguise." According to Heller, Melville's reader is stimulated less to identify himself with than to critically reflect on "the text as the product of subjective narration." "Bartleby the Scrivener" is suggested to present "the analysis of an epistemological process, i.e., the attitude of man when confronted with an indifferent reality that cannot be seen through by reason." Discoveries of literary thematizations of epistemological processes have multiplied in German-speaking countries ever since Hans Robert Jauss's reception esthetics. Wolfgang Wittkowski's "Unbehagen eines Praktikers an der Theorie: Zur Rezeptionsästhetik von Hans Robert Jauss" (*Colloquia Germanica* 12[1979]:1–27) was not yet available to Heller at the time. It makes instructive collateral reading in view of Heller's innovative essay.

Interest in the later 19th-century figures dropped to a mere trickle of one article—and that not on a major writer. Horst Kruse's "Der Aufstiegsmythos in der amerikanischen Trivial-literatur des 19. Jahrhunderts im literarhistorischen Kontext" (*Amst* 23:213–29) evidences the same interest in popular literature that permeated Göller's comprehensive essay (see section *a–1*) and occasionally surfaced in Ritter's article on Sealsfield. By concentrating on Timothy Shay Arthur, William Makepeace Thayer, and the inescapable Horatio Alger, Kruse succeeds in demonstrating the influence of not only Franklin's *Autobiography* but also a work dear to it, Bunyan's *The Pilgrim's Progress*.

a–2. **20th-Century Poetry, Drama, and Fiction to 1945.** As usual, the lion's share of publications goes to the 20th century. Unusual, however, is a slight change of predominant interest from post-1945 to pre-1945 literature. A more intense rediscovery of the "near-past," as it were, grandparents' and parents' past, a trend asserting itself in political and art history, but also in fashion and interior decoration, seems to have reached the middle and the young generation of German Americanists. More remarkable still, there is a "change within the change." Pre-1945 poetry and drama have grown more attractive than pre-1945 fiction. The publication of *Theater und Drama in Amerika*, refocusing attention on those three pre-1945 "golden decades" of the American theater, has reenforced the trend and channeled it into a network of survey-type and individual work-centered interpretations.

As for poetry, a rare guest at the table of German scholars, John Gould Fletcher, is the subject of Gisela Hergt's *Das lyrische Werk John Gould Fletchers, MSzA* 10 (Frankfurt: Lang). An "estheticist" phase of Romantic, neo-Romantic, and French-symbolist models and imagist experiments is distinguished from a religion-oriented middle span of a syncretism trying to fuse elements of Eastern and Western religions and philosophies whereas a last phase is seen as dominated by an expatriate's return to southern regionalism. Detailed analyses of representative poems support the underlying thesis of a three-phase process. The climax of achievement is asserted to have been reached early, i.e., in the years 1915–21. Two of Fletcher's contemporaries, Pound and Eliot, prove again their hold on scholars. Link continues his contributions to Pound explication in "Two Notes on the Early Poetry" (*Paideuma* 7:185–86). "A Note on 'Passing' in 'Gentildonna'" explains "passing" with reference to Exodus 33.18–20, and "the beauty of the lady" as "associated with Christ" by Pound's paraphrasing John 1.14. "A Note on the Honey-Comb in 'Ballad of the Goodly Fere'" detects a direct allusion to Luke 24.42. Simon Zelotes's view of Christ is convincingly suggested as a view of a Christ "reincarnated in Dionysus." It is primarily not the work but its author that is the object of explanation or rather of anthropological meditation in Eva Hesse's "Von der Spaltbarkeit des Menschen—Zum Fall Ezra Pound" (*Akzente* 25:559–83). Even after this thoughtful and stirring statement by Pound's most constant translator and critic in German-speaking Europe, the debate on the wished-for matching of ideological rectitude and literary creativity will probably not cease in our time as it has not done after the publication of William M. Chace's *The Political Identities of Ezra Pound and T. S. Eliot* (see *ALS 1973*: 304–05, 311–12).

A friend of Pound's since Philadelphia student days, Hilda Doolittle has found in Link, Pound's explicator, an outstanding interpreter: "Bild und Mythos in der Dichtung Hilda Doolittles," *LJGG* n.s. 18 [1977]:271–303. Considered together with Link's article on Emerson, the essay on H. D. is even more penetrating. Both rank as the best of the year's German contributions to the interpretation of 19th- and 20th-century American poetry. Intimate knowledge of primary and secondary sources underpins interpretations especially of the postimagist trilogy composed of the cycle, "The Walls Do Not Fall" (1944), "Tribute to the Angels" (1945) and "The Flowering of the Rod" (1946). The interpretation extending to the last poetry, concentrates on "Helen in Egypt." Myth, Christian Revelation, and poetry are pointed up as "equally valid forms by which spiritual realities communicate themselves." Twentieth century drama links up with poetry in Peter Drexler's *'Escape from Personality': Eine Studie zum Problem der Identität bei T. S. Eliot* (Braunschweig, privately printed). One of the most-treated problems, of contemporary life, if understood as "personal identity," is traced back to the earlier decades of our century and exemplified in the work of its most influential literary critic and poet. Drexler applies a social-science-oriented concept of identity to Eliot's work instead of deriving one or more concepts of identity from the work itself. He consistently tests its usefulness in (1) clearing up the interrelations between Eliot's, the artist's, self-perception, and his cultural and social criticism, and (2) unraveling the thematic development of the identity problem in the poems and plays. Drexler frankly states, and modestly overstates, the small contribution his problem-centered study can make to the literary evaluation of Eliot's achievement.

Pre-1945 drama studies make up almost one-half of the largest, 20th-century, part of *Theater und Drama in Amerika.* Of the contributors, who are German residents in the United States or Americans living in Europe, predominantly Germanists, one knowledgeably informs the reader about basic "movements" (Anton Kaes, "Zwischen Avantgarde und Massenkultur: Die Anfänge der amerikanischen Theaterbewegung," pp. 44–66). Comparisons with the contemporaneous situation in German theater life are useful. Kaes is also the author of "Dokumentarismus—Fiktionalität—Politik: Anmerkungen zum deutschen und amerikanischen Dokumentationstheater der 20er und 30er Jahre" (pp. 91–107). Here the comparative, German-American, viewpoint is even more pronounced. Two other contributors, Charlotte Körner in "William Vaughn Moody: The Great Divide" (pp. 219–34), and Peter Juhl in "Eugene O'Neill's *The Hairy Ape*" (pp. 235–53), present analyses of a less well-known and a very well-known play. Among the cisatlantic German interpreters Susan Vietta in her essay "Darstellungsformen des proletarischen Dramas in den USA" (pp. 108–26) takes up a subject of the 1930s. Vietta illustrates it by means of Marc Blitzstein's *The Cradle Will Rock,* Clifford Odets's *Waiting for Lefty,* Irving Shaw's *Bury the Dead,* and Paul Green's *Hymn to the Rising Sun.* The plays chosen, with the exception of Odets's, are largely unknown to German critics and theatergoers but their relevance to the German theater has increased ever since the 1960s. Of less immediate but more intrinsic significance is 20th-century historical drama as investigated in Kurt Tetzeli von Rosador's "Formen des amerikanischen Geschichtsdramas im 20. Jahrhundert" (pp. 67–90). With a sharp eye for the existence but also the limitations of the "Americanness" of America's historical drama, von Rosador selects the pageant, the living newspaper, "the poetic historical drama of Maxwell Anderson" and "forms running counter to the traditional historical drama," e.g., Arthur Kopit's *Indians* and Paul Foster's *Tom Paine.* "Formal variety, and the shaping of American value concepts, ideologies, and problems" are thought to constitute the Americanness of the genre. The inclusion of Kopit and Foster proves that post-1945 developments are not overlooked. Of pre-1945 prominent dramatists Robert Sherwood goes unnoticed. While this essay enlarges the survey aspect of *Theater und Drama in Amerika,* Siegfried Melchinger's "Die Yankee-Elektra" (pp. 254–62) extends the perspective on O'Neill as already applied in Juhl's interpretation of *The Hairy Ape.* Melchinger's approach is that of the comparatist. Aeschylus' *Oresteia,* occasionally Sophocles' and Euripides' versions, are drawn upon but only crucial analogues and differences are pinpointed. Contrasts such as (1) the state vs. society, i.e., the Greek *polis* vs. the New England class structure, (2) the public vs. the seemingly private, yet profoundly human, define the differences. The American, Puritan, elements count for less than "the concatenation of hate and love in the human soul." Apparently not availing himself of abundantly existing research, Melchinger relies on the intuitive grasp of essentials. In the pre-1945 segment of *Theater und Drama in Amerika,* Berthold Schik contributes a study of Wilder: "Thornton Wilder und das 'total Theater': The Skin of Our Teeth" (pp. 263–77).

As we would expect, no pre-1945 major dramatists other than O'Neill and Wilder figure in research outside the *Theater und Drama in Amerika* collection. O'Neill furnishes the subject of the only book-length study devoted to an American playwright in 1978, and of two periodical articles as well. Günther Ahrends's *Traumwelt und Wirklichkeit im Spätwerk Eugene O'Neills* (Heidelberg: Winter) ties together the great many threads of international research on *The Iceman Cometh, Hughie, A Moon for the Misbegotten, Long Day's Journey Into Night, A Touch of the Poet,* and *More Stately Mansions.* Although the "dream-reality" polarity is not new to O'Neill scholarship, both American and foreign, it has never been tested as systematically and methodically as in this detailed piece of work. By no means does it restrict itself to, but it only concentrates on, the "last" plays. In "O'Neills 'Open Boat'" (*LWU* 11:222–29) Jürgen Wolter does confine himself to such early plays as *Thirst* and *Fog.* Almost exclusively resting his case on internal evidence, Wolter

Foreign Scholarship

points out parallels between them and Crane's short story. The radical test of actual and particularly of functional differences of recurrent features might have been applied to determine the extent and the significance of similarities. Not a literary but a psychological source, the analytical psychology of C. G. Jung, is more comprehensively treated than ever before in a new study by Loring Sittler. "*The Emperor Jones*—ein Individuationsprozess im Sinne C. G. Jungs?" (*Amst* 23:118–30) interprets the play with the aid of dream criticism ("oneirocriticism"). Sittler answers his question in the affirmative. In a respect only touched upon by Ahrends (op. cit., pp. 107, 223) he deepens our understanding of the dream element in O'Neill's dramatic world. Not psychoanalysis or depth psychology but "critical realism" is claimed to characterize O'Neill's *Desire Under the Elms*. Anna Maria Stuby's "Tragödie und Privateigentum: Zu *Desire Under the Elms* von Eugene O'Neill" (*Gulliver* [Berlin: Argument Verlag] 3:78–96) presents the dramatist as an innovator of the tradition of "the American folk drama" and the "rural environment exposure plays." The motif of private property undoubtedly forms part of the texture of the play but the obsession with private property seems to be overemphasized by the interpreter, and this at the expense of a mid-19th-century New England pride in painfully yet successfully obeying Jehovah's command of "subjecting the earth." Not by chance does the California motif of the Golden West serve as countermotif of easily acquired, gold-rush wealth. However, Stuby gives cause to reconsider O'Neill's literary uses of his knowledge of Max Stirner's *Der Einzige und sein Eigentum*. Once again a source study, Rainer Sell's "Hawthorne and Wilder: From Main Street to *Our Town*" (*LWU* 11:141–60) leans on internal proof as did the before-mentioned article on O'Neill and Crane published in the same periodical. Sell sets up six classes of parallels between Hawthorne's sketch "Main Street" (*The Snow Image and Uncollected Tales*, Centenary Edition, 11, Ohio State Univ. Press, 1974) and Wilder's play: (1) Main Street as dominant spatial concept in both works, (2) journey as movement in space and time, (3) Hawthorne's showman and Wilder's Stage Manager, (4) audience and imagination, (5) atmospheric detail, (6) allegory. Constituting a topos, item 2 furnishes the least "remarkable affinity." The borrowings seem plausible.

When assessed in terms of book-length publications, the attractiveness of pre-1945 literature is still highest in the very generic field in which articles are scantier than in the field of poetry and drama. Narrative genre has three monographs, one each on Robert Herrick, Upton Sinclair, and Sherwood Anderson. To these author-centered studies has to be added a "movement"-oriented monograph on the Muckrakers. A basic problem of realism in literature, the relationship between the empire and the fictional world, is at the center of Friedrich W. Horlacher's inquiry *Die Romane Robert Herricks: Empirie und Fiktion, Studien und Texte zur Amerikanistik,* Studienband 5 (Frankfurt: Lang). The book is intelligently designed and studded with perceptive insights. A poetological and a formal topic are treated in Alfons Klein's *Figurenkonzeption und Erzählform in den Kurzgeschichten Sherwood Andersons,* Palaestra 201 (Göttingen: Vandenhoeck & Ruprecht). A primarily ideological interest prevails in Dieter Herms's *Upton Sinclair, amerikanischer Radikaler: Eine Einführung in Leben und Werk* (Frankfurt: März Verlag). Klein concludes that "the attempt to confront the individual figures and the reader [of Anderson's short stories] with [the] existential situation of 'accepting the half-tragic experience of one's own insignificance in "the scheme of existence" intends "to free them from the ambitious self-interest of the illusory promises of the American dream." This "belief in the healing force of the imagination" is also claimed to explain the narrative form of Anderson's stories. Not only the Sinclair centennial but also the rising interest in the literary representation of American radicalism may account for Herm's Sinclair monograph. In view of Sinclair's popularity with German readers and his impact on Brecht, a monograph on this social critic and reformer was overdue. Symptomatically, two passages taken from Sinclair's *The Jungle* are among the 41 "one- to two-page excerpts from macrotexts" that constitute the material on which Alfred Hornung's *Narrative Struktur und Textsortendifferenzierung: Die Texte des Muckraking Movement (1902–1912),* Amerikastudien Schriftenreihe 52 (Stuttgart: Metzler), is based. As to its method, the significance of this inquiry as a pilot study deserves special praise. It combines literary with linguistic procedures. The latter are those of transformational grammar. The application of two of Michel Foucault's studies to the understanding of early 20th-century prose texts, expository and imaginative, indicates a most welcome French-German cross-fertilization. Of similar theme

but a different, more conventional, method is Klaus Walter Vowe's
*Gesellschaftliche Funktionen fiktiver und faktographischer Prosa:
Roman und Reportage im amerikanischen Muckraking Movement*
(Frankfurt: Lang).
Articles, occasionally in the shape of afterwords to translated
novels, choose either the same subjects as the monographs did or
advance toward others, e.g., an amusingly disparate trio consisting
of Lovecraft, Margaret Mitchell, and Hemingway. Herms follows
his interest in Sinclair by contributing " 'Reds I Have Known': Upton Sinclair's Verhältnis zum Kommunismus" (*Gulliver* 4:118–40)
and "An American Socialist: Upton Sinclair" (*Upton Sinclair Centenary Journal*, Los Angeles, pp. 42–54). Herms has also written
"afterwords" to German editions of *The Jungle* (*Der Dschungel*)
and *Boston* (Frankfurt: März), pp. 459–64; 937–40. Dietrich Wachler's "Die Präexistenz und das Böse: Technik und Magie im Werk
von Howard Phillips Lovecraft" *STZ* 6:230–40) as well as Horst
Breuer's "Zur Ideologie eines Bestsellers: Biologismus und Sozialdarwinismus in Margaret Mitchells *Vom Winde Verweht*" (*Amst*
23:260–70) exemplify the before-mentioned continuing trend toward popular and best-seller literature in German scholarship.
Wachler is uncertain whether Lovecraft "designed perspectives of
anxiety and horror with inadequate devices" but stresses the political and social importance of this Rhode Island author's presentation of evil and his difficulty in finding names for "things unnamed
yet." Breuer chooses for his Mitchell study a history-of-ideas approach. The congruence between a conservatism of narrative technique and a conservative world view is just as acutely observed as is
the ambivalent tension between an anti-aristocratic Social Darwinism and a 'rather aristocratic ideology of heredity' in the novel. Klaus
P. Hansen in "Ernest Hemingway: Dialektik der Idylle" (*Amst* 23:
98–117) "attempts a reinterpretation of Hemingway's works with
the intention of clarifying his social and historical relevance by approaching them from the notion of the pastoral." The traditional
meaning of the genre is extended so as to cover "a structure designed as an extra-ordinary domain and as a contrast to a certain
societal conception of ordinary reality." Hansen detects a paradox
between a pastoral offered by Hemingway as an escape "from society," and the upholding of "fundamental mechanisms" of this very
society, i.e., "the achievement principle and group conformity." To

what extent a detailed textual analysis of literary form as conveyor of meaning will support this interpretation remains to be seen.

a–3. **Fiction since 1945.** Two novelists who started out toward the end of World War II and continued or still continue writing, Raymond Chandler and Saul Bellow, receive concise and penetrating treatment. Winfried Fluck's " 'Powerful, but extremely depressing books': Raymond Chandlers Romane" (*Amst* 23:271–98), taking W. H. Auden's verdict for title and point of departure, is the most perceptive and adequate essay on Chandler's works that so far has been written by a German Americanist. Historically sound and thoroughly familiar with the German reception of Chandler, it advances the claim that "by projecting the insistence on a self-reliant moral integrity onto a cynical detective, Chandler attempts another renegotiation of a moral ideal and a set of (masculine) values that has been in crisis for longer than this century." Fluck has set the stage for further study ready to test his central thesis by a more detailed ideational and formal analysis of individual novels. Brigitte Scheer-Schätzler's "Epistemology as Narrative Device in the Works of Saul Bellow" is an important contribution originally made to a Brussels symposium. E. Schraepen has edited the papers as *Saul Bellow and His Work* (Brussels: Vrije Universiteit, available from the editor). Scheer-Schätzler's printed essay, with exemplary clarity and cogency, advances two theses: (1) "in Bellow's novels the striving for knowledge represents a key concept; the desire for it is partly aroused and partly gratified by a perception of beauty; its attainment precedes the highest manifestation of virtue," (2) "Bellow, in trying to discover the universal in the particular, echoes the Transcendentalist epistemological quest and reenforces important concerns of the American imagination. "The second claim opens up a profitable history-of-ideas line of hoped-for research. A second, book-length study, Walter Hasenclever's *Saul Bellow: Eine Monographie* (Koln: Kiepenheuer & Witsch), benefits from an outstanding professional translator's sensitivity and a nonacademic critic's fresh perceptiveness.

Concerning novelists who came to the fore in the 1950s, one short-lived, Jack Kerouac, and another still going strong, Bernard Malamud, have stimulated scholarly activity. Kerouac serves as a focal point for a monograph that, due to oversight, went unnoticed in the 1977 report. Gertrude Betz's *Die Beatgeneration als literarische und soziale Bewegung, untersucht am Beispiel von Jack Kerouac, "The Subterraneans," "The Dharma Bums," und "Desolation Angels," KASL 2 (Frankfurt: Lang)*, reflects in its methods of interpretation modern trends toward combining literary sociology with previously mentioned reception esthetics. The rise and the effect of the Beat Generation is seen as being typified by the literary career and the impact of a prototypal literary author. As for Malamud, *The Assistant* is examined in Tobias Hergt's "Vom Gehilfen zum Helfer: Das Thema der Mitmensohlichkeit in Bernard Malamuds *The Assistant*" (*NsM* 31:74–81). Permeating the structure and the language of the novel, the theme of human fellowship is unraveled in all its ramifications. Its didactic potentialities (for German high-school teaching) are competently assessed. Limited to only one novel out of the many which comprise Kurt Vonnegut's work to date, Hansjörg Gehring's article "Die Anti-Struktur des Anti-Kriegsromans *Slaughterhouse-Five* von Kurt Vonnegut" (*LWU* 11:93–96) resumes earlier interpreters' notions of the theme-form congruence in this novel. Gehring extends them to the effect that the anti-novel structure of Vonnegut's antiwar novel includes its 'inner' structure and its 'microstructure.' The rapid spread of the anti-structure principle in novel writing is rightly asserted to limit its effect on the critical reader.

Regarding scholarship aware of post-1945 developments of narrative subgenres, Horst Schroeder's *Science Fiction Literatur in den USA: Vorstudien für eine materialistische Paraliteraturwissenschaft* (Giessen:Forum Verlag) embraces the years 1945 through 1972. A volume of 519 pages, it prepares itself for a thorough exploration of the field by examining relations between ideology and literature, it investigates the commercial aspect of science fiction, and it dissects its ideologies. Comparisons, mainly with British science fiction, statistics of authors and their educational background, and several indexes testify to the exceptional industry of the researcher. He might have given more consideration to atypical works which have turned science fiction into an art, thus transcending 'paraliterature.' Credit for a solidly informed and critical survey of black autobiography since 1960 goes to Klaus Ensslen for his "Schwarze Autobiographie in den USA seit 1960" (*Gulliver* 3:96–116). It is the only ethnicity-centered article of the period to appear in a periodical.

a–4. **Drama and Poetry since 1945.** In the framework of such a
survey as *Theater und Drama in Amerika* post-1945 black literature
fares considerably better. Werner Sollors, now a German resident in
America, brings his customary expertise in the whole field to a review of its drama section. His "The New Black Theatre" (pp. 136–
53) is well-informed and blends sensitivity with shrewd evaluation.
Of black plays selected for close analysis, at least James Baldwin's
Blues for Mister Charlie" (pp. 328–52) and Lorraine Hansberry's
The Sign in Sidney Brustein's Window (pp. 364–73) come up for
discussion by Peter Freese and Werner Habicht respectively. Iris
Bünsch joins them with "Tennessee Williams: *Orpheus Descending*"
(pp. 278–94), Hannes Razum follows with a moral-problem topic,
"Schuld und Verantwortung im Werk Arthur Millers" (pp. 310–20).
Not an original play but the stage adaptation of a well-known novel
has been selected by Marianne Kesting for her contribution, "Truman Capote: *Die Grasharfe*" (pp. 321–27). Razum's other contrib-
utive essay, "Edward Albee und die Metaphysik" (pp. 353–65),
sketches the life and career of the author, emphasizing his musical
interests. The selective survey leads up to *Tiny Alice*, which is central to Razum's essay. It is understood to be a religious problem
play, posing the question of the perception of the imperceptible.
Its contrapuntal design is clearly recognized. In "Mythos and Rol-
lenkonflikt in Arthur Kopits *Indians*" (pp. 375–87) Uta Denecke
places Kopit's play in the neighborhood of the 'theater of the absurd' and its formal experiments. The "myth of the 'western hero'
as the target of satire" and the psychological complexity of Buffalo
Bill as an individual are felt to be dramatically concretized in a conflict of roles. Off-off Broadway comes to life in Jürgen Brinkmann's
survey essay, "Off-Off Broadway: Das neue amerikanische Theater"
(pp. 154–67).

　　Beyond the confines of *Theater und Drama in Amerika* one of the
West Coast theater groups, the San Francisco Mime Troupe, gets
a hearing in Arno Paul's "Engagement, Commitment and Fresh Air':
Die politische Ästhetik der San Francisco Mime Troupe—dargestellt
an den Stücken 'Los Frijoles' und 'False Promises'" (*Gulliver* 3:
123–43). Paul G. Buchloh is unique in attempting a survey of contemporary drama in the shape of a periodical article. Intentionally
generalizing, "Das zeitgenössische amerikanische Drama" (*LWU*
11:178–89) propounds seven theses ranging from the significance

of trans-European theater traditions like the showboat, and the individual impact of O'Neill to a reawareness of a "cult-determined" religious or philosophical theater. Although broadly based on East Coast commercial theater phenomena as this thought-provoking generalization is, and not explicitly dealing with developments in Houston, Los Angeles, and San Francisco, it does expect new impulses from "the regional stages and the drama departments of the major universities." Ethnic contributions to the post-1945 theater might have received greater attention.

On the whole much less satisfactory is scholarly involvement with the poetry of the last three decades. Undoubtedly the best contribution comes from an, as it were, migrant scholar, now teaching at a Canadian university. Ekbert Faas's *Towards a New American Poetics: Essays & Interviews* (Black Sparrow) is a unique combination of interpretation and dialogue between poets and their interviewer-interpreter. Poets presented comprise Charles Olson, Robert Duncan, Gary Snyder, Robert Creeley, Robert Bly, and Allen Ginsberg. While the late Olson could have only an essay dedicated to him and Duncan is represented only in an interview, both forms are available to the reader in the other parts of this fascinating volume. Such a union of forces as that of John Martin, a devoted West Coast private press owner and publisher, with a brilliant younger German scholar is a rare and most gratifying event. Wolfgang Binder's "Puertoricanische Lyrik aus New York" (*Puertoricaner in New York —Volk zwischen zwei Kulturen*, Erlangen: Städtische Galerie) merits special mention as what appears to be the first German venture into the ethnic pluralism of American poetry. It complements Sollors's study "The New Black Theatre."

b. **Literary Criticism and Theory, Comparative Studies.** Whereas German and foreign, and with it American, political and socioeconomic criticism has often been found to influence choice of theme and/or criteria of literary judgment, exploration of American literary criticism and theory has been scanty. Contrary to expectations aroused by its title, the first volume of *Englische und amerikanische Literaturtheorie: Studien zu ihrer historischen Entwicklung* (AF 126), edited by Rudiger Ahrens and Erwin Wolff, finds a niche only for the "literary theory and practice" of New England Puritanism. It is treated in Klaus Lubbers's instructive essay, "Literaturtheorie und literarische Praxis der neuenglandischen Puritaner" (pp. 175–98).

Restricted to the American domain are but two publications, one again a contribution to a collective enterprise, another a monograph. Winfried Fluck's "Aesthetic Premises of American Studies," contributed to previously mentioned *Other Voices, Other Views* (see *a-1*) (pp. 21–30) offers new perspectives on an often discussed, admittedly basic, problem. Romeo Giger in *The Creative Void: Hemingway's Iceberg Theory* (Bern: Francke), a book overlooked last year, elucidates and evaluates a subject frequently commented on, yet widely unexplored. In two other studies works of American literary criticism serve as illustrative material within international comparative contexts or specimens of American literature furnish examples to inquiries into general literary theory. Symptomatically, these publications always concern the art of narration. In "Der Roman und das Geschichtenerzählen" (*DVLG* 52:296–345) Edward Reichel discusses Robert Scholes and Robert Kelly, *The Nature of Narration*, Ronald S. Crane, "The Concept of Plot and the Plot of *Tom Jones*" (*Perspectives on Fiction*), *The Theory of the Novel*, edited by Philip Stevick, and Wayne C. Booth, *The Rhetoric of Fiction*. The insight yielded into the slow academic critical reception of relative oldtimers is instructive. *Zeitgestaltung in der Erzählkunst*, edited by Alexander Ritter, Wege der Forschung 447 (Darmstadt: Wissenschaftliche Buchgesellschaft) includes works by Melville, Sinclair, and Faulkner as examples of both narrative treatment of time and academic analyses of such treatments.

A complementation of these time studies by a space study and a unique combination of poetology with literary history are provided by Gerhard Hoffmann's *Raum, Situation, erzählte Wirklichkeit: Poetologische und historische Studien zum englischen und amerikanischen Roman* (Stuttgart: Metzler). Based on a formidable mass of British, Anglo-Irish, and American material, this mighty tome of almost 900 pages links literary theory to comparative literature studies. The American corpus examined comprises close to 100 works, many of them classics. Their authors range from Cooper to Barthelme. America's literary handling of space, a research topic of increasing popularity since the early 1960s, is seen by Hoffmann particularly from the angles of "space as designed," "spatial structures and models of meaning," "the referential character of space as

symbol, allegory, and stimulus of associations," and "spatial macrostructure in the novel." Aside from this systematic arrangement, Hoffman, by a network of subdivisions, provides for a historical view of
literary handlings of space. Sound in detailed analysis and system-
atization, the book's value to American literary scholarship lies especially in the meaningful comparison of American and non-Ameri-
can trends in the literary mastery of space. The careful integration
of previous international research with this new magisterial work
can be tested by means of what is the most comprehensive bibliography to date on the topic of "space in literature," especially in its
narrative genre. Both English and American material, once again
of narrative provenience, are also made use of in Paul Goetsch's
Literarische und soziale Bedingungen erzählerischer Kurzformen
(Tübingen: Deutsches Institut für Fernstudien).

Not any longer accompanied as it was by literary theory, especially poetology, in Hoffmann's magnum opus, the comparative
view of American literature is more popular and more varied than
ever. Its old form, source or model detection in foreign works, is
still alive in Gerd Schmidt's *"Far-Sourced Canticles": Kompara-
tistische Studien zu T. S. Eliot und Ezra Pound*, SUF 1. The handy
volume gathers together the author's revised and updated source
studies originally published between 1967 and 1975. The originality
of Poe's detective Dupin is subjected to an industrious attempt at
reducing it by Marianne Kesting in a sprightly essay "Auguste
Dupin, der Wahrheitsfinder und seine Leser: Inwiefern Edgar Allan
Poe nicht der Initiator der Detektivgeschichte war" (*Poetica* 10:
53–65).

Inquiries into the foreign reception of American authors show
a welcome increase. By juxtaposing German and American criticism
of Wallace Stevens, Ulrike Rix-Lorenz's essay "Tendenzen der
neueren Stevens-Forschung" (*LWU* 11:42–54) enables the reader
to compare aims and methods within the same binational reception
process. Helmut Bonheim reports on "William Carlos Williams in
Germany" (*WCWN* 4:14–18), and Manfred Markus comments on
"Bellows Vermächtnis: Zur Rezeption eines Nobelpreisträgers in
der Bundesrepublik Deutschland" (*ZK* 28:101–09). Happily, earlier
authors of American literature have not been neglected either. Probably due to the effect of the Bicentennial, two essays deal with
Franklin's German reception. In " 'Eripuit coelo fulmen sceptrumque

tyrannis': Benjamin Franklin als dis Personifizierung der amerikanischen Revolution" (*Amst* 23:19–29) Horst Dippel investigates
Franklin's German reputation on "the basis" of "several hundred
private, mostly unpublished, letters written by Germans to Franklin in the 1770s and 1780s." This intimate picture is complemented
by a public, literary one in Reiner Wild's "Prometheus–Franklin:
Die Gestalt Benjamin Franklins in der deutschen Literatur des 18.
Jahrhunderts" (*Amst* 23:30–39). The interplay of myth and reality
operating in this identification is seen against the background of the
revived 'Querelle des Anciens et des Modernes.' Likewise an echo
of the Bicentennial but sketching in the pre-1776 period as well,
Hans Galinsky's "Zwei Jahrhunderte amerikanisch-deutscher Liter-
aturbeziehungen (1776–1976)" (*Nassauische Annalen* [Wiesbaden:
Steiner] 89:49–77) deals with American-German literary interrelations on the levels of reception, influence, and imagology (literary
images of the 'other' country). Interrelations established by stimulus
and effect are treated more fully than those resting only on comparison. Also focusing on the recipient and the creative transformer
of what was received, but limiting herself to one author only, Sigrid
Mayer contributes "Die Amerikakomponente im Werk" to vol. 1 of
Max Frisch: Aspekte des Prosawerks, Studien zum Werk Max
Frischs, ed. Gerhard P. Knapp (Frankfurt: Lang). These binational,
German-American, effect-based (inter-)relationships for the first
time expand from American-European to intra-American ones. The
gradual growth of Canadian studies in Germany is mirrored in Bern-
hard Beutler's pioneering study *Der Einfluss des Imagismus auf die
moderne kanadische Lyrik englischer Sprache* (Bern: Lang).

Binational (inter-)relations viewed as part of multinational ones
abound. Tri-national, though still moving in the English-language
orbit, as Hoffmann's blend of literary theory and comparatistics already did, is Buchloh's "Umsetzung und Dramenanalyse" (*LWU* 11:
supp. 54–62). It is rooted in the field of translation, the border region
between reception and creative impact, and competently explores
translation problems, e.g., cultural differences, connotations lacking
in the translator's language, regional and social dialects. The German translator confronted with English (and Anglo-Irish) as well
as American plays stands at the center of observation. Trinational
and unigeneric, dramatic, again is the material scrutinized by Hennig Thiess's *Namen im Kontext von Dramen* (*RAAA* 13). It pursues

nature and function of an onomastic phenomenon, names of persons. Two different genres, the epic and the dramatic, their interpenetration in 20th-century drama, are investigated in Dietrich Jäger's "Über Episches und Dramatisches im neueren Drama" (*LWU* 11:75–95). Wilder's *Our Town*, Williams's *The Glass Menagerie*, Miller's *A View from the Bridge* and *After the Fall* as well as O'Neill's *Long Day's Journey Into Night* are analyzed in comparison to Shakespeare, Fry, Osborne, Pinter on the English, Brecht on the German side. Problems arising from the sources or models of whole genres are taken up by three other researchers. Two of them examine the detective story, a subject already discussed along uninational, American lines in a new, comparative light. One researcher chooses for comparative treatment the picaresque narrative, a topic so far new to German Americanists from a comparative angle. Peter J. Brenner's "Die Geburt des Detektivromans aus dem Geiste des Unheimlichen" (*LWU* 11:1–13) points up German "Schauerroman" and the English Gothic novel as cultivators of the uncanny and the sinister, with the classical, American type of the detective story as their heir "domesticating" the uncanny in a rationalistic world. Not the international genesis of its classical type, but the international transformations, English, American, Belgian, French, Swedish, and Italian, are of primary interest to Ulrich Broich's "Formen des modernen Detektivromans" (*NsM* 31:65–73). This is one of the best and most well-written essays of the whole year. As for the picaresque, Klaus Poenicke's "Das Rad der Fortuna und die Revolution: Zur Geschichtsideologie pikarischen Erzählens" (*Amst* 23:90–97) selects modern Anglo-Irish, 16th-century Spanish, 18th-century Scottish, and 19th-century American examples, i.e., Beckett's *Waiting for Godot*, *Lazarillo de Tormes*, Smollett's *Roderick Random*, and Melville's *Moby-Dick*. Poenicke asserts that *Moby-Dick* "in a certain sense" "ends where once the exposure of the 'classical' picaro to an episodic, unstable form of existence began: in a loss of original confidence, a grave disturbance of a child-relationship transferred from the biological father to a long series of personal and institutional father substitutes." The reason for the recurrence of "picaresque motifs" is seen to be "the breakdown of romantic self-reliance." The thesis will surely stimulate debate.

While all of these studies treat of general problems of the literary work or of literary genres in contexts multinational but including, with varying degrees of intensity, American literature, Peter Boerner's article "Amerikabilder der europäischen Literatur: Wunschprojektion und Kritik" (*Amst* 23:40–50) chooses America for the unifying center to be shown refracted in the prism of European writing. Even more than Mayer's and Galinsky's essays did, does his concentrate on imagology. Image-makers are recruited from early 19th-century French, English, German, and what is particularly instructive, Russian authors. Not only do the variegated facets of the image of America stand out clearly but also a usually neglected factor emerges: "America itself, through events such as its separation from Britain, acted as a catalyst to form new images."

Comparatist views of American literature mostly remain within the literary field of reference. Crossing the border from the verbal art to art in another medium is practiced only once. Friedmar Apel's "Der Baumeister der Träume: Wirklichkeit und Gedankenspiel bei Charles Simonds" (*STZ* 67:149–65) inquires to what extent the physical and the verbal architect, the latter speaking in *Three People* and *Floating Cities*, illuminate one another.

A rate of publication as high as in 1977 tries to keep pace with an ever-growing variety of topics, perspectives, and judgments. Subjects omitted or of declining attraction are particularly telling, even in this far from complete survey.

Johannes Gutenberg Universität, Mainz

iii. Italian Contributions

Rolando Anzilotti

The work of Italian Americanists is evidenced this year by a large number of full-length works as well as by a good many articles and essays. Quality and range of subjects vary; all periods and genres are represented, but prose and fiction, especially modern, draw most scholarly attention. The art of translation has again provided occasions for introducing on a scholarly basis lesser known or difficult works to students and general readers of American literature.

In this interesting field of literary production, we must record that the most arduous task for a translator was undoubtedly that undertaken by Sergio Perosa, who in his *Canti onirici e altre poesie*

(Torino: Einaudi) has turned John Berryman's poetry into Italian. Perosa had already translated *Homage to Mistress Bradstreet* most competently in 1969; this time he has made a wide and intelligent selection from *Dream Songs* and other collections of Berryman, rendering with great skill and admirable faithfulness the poet's complex, highly experimental language. The accurately annotated volume opens with a thoughtful introductory essay in which Perosa points out that the poet's self is a reflective power field that becomes "a kind of trans-biological, overpersonal I or you," like "a mirror or sounding board of the living mind's panorama and of the spectacle of the world's dissociation." Berryman's poetry, Perosa finds, is not "confessional," but deals with "here and now, with the disconnected language and the expressive hallucination"; in its mature achievement "it is a perfect example of post-modern poetry." Laura Coltelli's translation and presentation of John Woolman's *Journal* (*Giornale*, Pisa: Nistri-Lischi) inaugurates a new series of works of American literature which have never before appeared in Italian. One is struck by the way Coltelli's style does wonderful justice to the humble Quaker's plain writing in the carefully edited, soberly elegant volume, ably introduced and annotated by the translator herself. *Molti amori: Un sogno d'amore* (Torino: Einaudi) is the Italian title of Vincenzo Mantovani's translation of W. C. Williams's *Many Loves* and *A Dream of Love*. In the ingenuous but somewhat overworked introduction Barbara Lanati maintains that "desire" instead of "possession" of love is the object of the poet's analysis: his theatrical pieces take the form of content, that is, content *is* form in them, and, because of their self-reflecting, self-analyzing character, they rightly belong to the "historical avant-garde." Tommaso Pisanti's *Poesia americana del Novecento* (Napoli: Guida), though not exciting, is an honest effort at giving a panorama of 20th-century American poetry in translation. It includes 118 poems by 59 authors, from E. A. Robinson to Aram Saroyan and Louise Slück; the line-by-line translations are rather flat, but reliable, apart from a few slips; the introduction is concise and in line with accepted patterns of interpretations.

Sound scholarship, clear reasoning, and accurate writing are qualities to be found in a symposium of four essays (the first of a forthcoming series) on the oriental influence on American literature edited by Elémire Zolla, *L'esotismo nella letteratura anglo-ameri-*

cana (Firenze: La Nuova Italia). The book is a fresh, original discussion of a particular aspect of American literature. In the introduction Zolla sketches a brief history of the East-West philosophical confrontation to show that America is the place where oriental philosophy finally finds acceptance, if not adoption. Fedora Giordano conducts an examination of the works of the American travelers who came in contact with the Islamic world before the advent of Transcendentalism. Her conclusion is that beyond the romance of travel nothing can be found in them of the inner conflict and the stirring ideas and intuitions that characterized the major writers at midcentury. The well-researched essay by Andrea Mariani accurately describes the Japanese influence on the American painter and writer John La Farge. Caterina Ricciardi deals with the influence of oriental art and thought on Wallace Stevens, and persuasively proves how certain poems such as "Significant Landscapes" and "Thirteen Ways of Looking at a Blackbird" must be read not in a Cubist key, but as patterned on Chinese and Japanese prints. Marina Camboni delineates Allen Ginsberg's poetics and cogently demonstrates the impact of Zen and Hinduistic thought on this idea and practice of poetry writing.

   E. A. Poe, Dal gotico alla fantascienza, edited by Ruggero Bianchi, is also a symposium, but centered on a single writer who acts as the point of encounter of 21 essays by various specialists. This thick volume is rich in adventurous and, at times, stimulating suggestions, but it is uneven and not so satisfactory from the point of view of scholarship when, in some cases, texts by Poe are analyzed in their Italian translation. As Bianchi states in the introduction, the collection grew out of an interdisciplinary seminar held at the Facoltà di Magistero of Turin University with the professed aim of bringing together and comparing different methodologies and critical schools which were to be applied to the work and the personality of a single writer. The essays, written by specialists in various fields (comparative literature, history, psychoanalysis, the visual arts) are all there; what one misses is a specific unifying theme that would make each individual essay interact more significantly with the others. The best critical piece, in my opinion, is Barbara Lanati's "Poe e la scrittura del corpo." Starting from a minor Poe story ("A Predicament") and making use of the ideas of Barthes's and Foucault's, this extends into a very penetrating analysis of the most important tales. Piero Bairati is also very good on Poe and American society. Placing the writer's work in its social and historical context, Bairati finds that Poe, who always avoided all political and social identifications, is a stranger in his own country; his belief in the literary ideal of a united national culture was an unrealistic hope in a nation that grew up by fission rather than aggregation.

Three works stand out as original or noteworthy individual contributions. Guido Fink's *I testimoni dell'immaginario* (Roma: Edizioni di Storia e Letteratura) deals with four major 19th-century writers—Irving, Hawthorne, Poe, Melville—and incorporates a chapter already noticed as an essay in *ALS 1975*. Although the subtitle seems to promise a comprehensive treatment of narrative techniques, Fink wisely limits himself to the exploration of one crucial device: the role of the narrator—the narrator as the *mask* of the author—throughout the prose work of the four writers. The main line of his reasoning can be described as follows: as the narrator shifts his observation post from more elevated points to lower ones, the degree of his involvement with the observed reality increases accordingly, while the certitude of his judgments, even the possibility of making them, decreases towards a sort of vanishing point. Fink's command of the whole canon of the writers examined is impressive; less so his lavish display of various literary and cultural references, insofar as this burdens the argument, and, in generating distraction and confusion, may point to a certain inconclusiveness. However, though weak if I may say so, in architectonics, the author is strong on decoration; he has perceptive ingenuity and writes well. His book recommends itself for providing a unifying perspective on pre-Jamesian fiction—a perspective concerned with *form*, and not, as is more often the case, with the *themes* of fiction.

Marilla Battilana's *Il tranello diabolico* (Venezia: Neri Pozza) is a thoroughly researched and documented study on the visual arts in American literature. It traces the development of art appreciation, from the Puritans' ethical mistrust of the arts (beauty as "the devil's trap" to which the title alludes) to Henry James's view of art as ethical justification. The crucial factor in this development appears to have been the quality of the landscape: whether the manifestation of God's splendor, or the source of untold dangers, or the promise of fulfillment, its vastness induced a feeling for form and for functional beauty. Less concerned with Franklin's strictly practical views, Battilana concentrates on Edwards's sense of spiritual "fitness," its functionalist evolution in Emerson, the organicism of Thoreau and Whitman on the one hand, and the deviations into Art as spirituality (Hawthorne) and Art as manifestation of the unconscious (early Melville and Poe) on the other, to end up with Henry James's synthesis of the two elements. Artistic sensitivity, sharp intuitions, and sound reasoning, all applied to extensive reading of so many authors of the early and middle periods of American literature, make this compact book a meaningful contribution.

In her *Studi su poeti e narratori americani* (Cagliari: EDES) Margherita Guidacci has collected essays, articles, and reviews written over the years on Poe, Twain, Henry James, Jewett, Pound, Stevens, Cummings, and Elizabeth Bishop. To these she has added two hitherto unpublished pieces: a keen, soberly stated recapitulation of that all-inclusive aspect of Dickinson's poetry—its religious dimension, and a lovingly perceptive analysis of *Geography III*, where the continuity between this book and Elizabeth Bishop's earlier work, as well as the pivotal role played by space in the poet's inspiration and poetic method, are stressed. Guidacci has no axes to grind, no predetermined theses to prove. She strives instead to adhere to her texts and to highlight what is distinctive in them. Such is the clarity of her style that at times the justness, the depth even, of her insights are not immediately visible. A poet herself, she is proof of Pound's pronouncement (Pound is the most fully represented author in her book) that only writers can be good critics.

Two standing series of short monographs on contemporary authors have brought out three new items that deserve mention. Carlo Pagetti's *Theodore Dreiser* (Firenze: La Nuova Italia) is the first book to appear on the novelist in Italy. The author follows the stages of creation of each work, describing and analyzing all of them with critical acumen and sound information. As an introduction to Dreiser, this is a worthy booklet scattered through with an abundance of original remarks. Giordano de Biasio's *Erskine Caldwell* (Firenze: La Nuova Italia) is the first Italian attempt to assess Caldwell's value. De Biasio is wholeheartedly committed to his subject and fully conversant with the scholarship that goes with it, but the awkwardness he displays in discussing narrative techniques, and his uncritical acceptance of broad generalizations from the sociology of literature as well as from Leslie Fiedler's *Love and Death*, fail to impress or convince the reader. That Caldwell's best fiction should be read not as belonging to the naturalistic tradition but to the tradition of romance, is an interesting insight which is unfortunately not elaborated upon. *Invito alla lettura di Pound* (Milano: Mursia) by Laura Cantelmo Garufi is an honest description of the poet's work, clear, informed, essential but not superficial, that serves its purpose of introducing and rendering Pound accessible to student and layman.

Interpretazioni di Twain (Roma: Savelli) is a thematic anthology of some 50 chosen essays in a series that is meant to offer a vast spectrum of interpretations of major authors. In his lengthy introduction, editor Alessandro Portelli gives his own sociological, Marxian interpretation of Mark Twain, whom he sees as a "bourgeois moralist, honest and consistent," an intellectual "marked in every aspect by contradictions," a writer "committed" within the limits of his political thought. Particularly interesting, even if sketchy, are the considerations and observations on Twain's fortune in Italy, especially as an author of children's literature, and also on his influence on the cinema, the theater, and some modern novelists. Sergio Duichin and Alessandro Gebbia are two devotees of Jack Kerouac who feel that the human and artistic dimensions of the man and the writer need to be vindicated in Italy. They have collected and translated some reminiscences and appreciations (three of them apparently never published before) by American friends of the late writer, and have also contributed an unconventional introduction and a personal essay each to *Kerouac Graffiti* (Roma: Arcana Editrice). The book stands as a fond tribute to the Beat hero, certainly not as an assessment of his work; and yet one may find it interesting, especially Duichin's essay on the complex and conflicting reactions to the Kerouac myth in Italy.

One book belongs to literary theory. Francesco Binni's *Modernismo letterario anglo-americano* (Roma: Bulzoni) is a thick volume that includes chapters on English and American authors (such as Snodgrass, Robert Bly, James Wright), but is mainly concerned with a discussion of the theory of "Modernism." It is impossible for me to give a fair account of it in a few sentences, but I shall try to draw one of the conclusive lines of its argument. Starting from the ideas of Wright Mills, John Fekete, and Gerald Graff, Binni argues that postmodern fiction (superfiction, surfiction, metafiction) feeds

on an amorphous consumer society whose morality is sluggishness—
a society that is unable to maintain any links with historical reality.
This fiction is made up of narratives which are neutral recordings
of experiential situations. Even the most ambitious works of American fiction, like Barth's *Giles Goat-Boy* and Pynchon's *Gravity's
Rainbow*, fail to perceive that "besides disaster history can offer
possibilities of achievement and fulfillment." Literary works, Binni
concludes, should not be seen as literary values in themselves, and
their authors should not be regarded as detached historical figures.
He asks for a new social history of the intellectuals that will see
them as more involved in and concerned with the real problems of
contemporary society. Based on a great amount of reading, written
in a style that is difficult and elliptic, it is an uneven book, inconclusive at times. It can be considered an earnest attempt to examine
and understand the "permanence" and the "unreal situation" of the
literary and artistic movement that characterizes the time we live in.

Most of the articles and essays that appeared this year are contained in the volume of *Studi americani* 21–22 (1975–76), whose
publication was long delayed. Including two historical essays, there
are 17 pieces in all, of uneven value and varied interest: they go
chronologically from "Ponteach: una tragedia indiana" by Gianna
Gatti to Javier Coy's "A thematic and character approach to Henry
James," Loretta Valtz Mannucci's "I saggi di Frank Norris," Paola
Ludovici's "Oliver La Farge e i nuovi indiani," Daniela Montanari's
"Il personaggio nero nei romanzi di William Faulkner," Mario
Strano's "La visione entropica di Norman Mailer," Donatella Abbate
Badin's "Roethke and Rimbaud: a case of identity," Annalisa Gol-
doni's "Robert Duncan o la poesia come religione," Giovanna Sil-
vani's "L'isola di Robert Creeley," Maria Antonietta Saracino's
"*Bread and Puppet Theatre* fra utopia e impegno," Marilla Battilana
Shankovski's "Sull'umorismo americano." Since doing justice to each
literary contribution would take more space than it is convenient to
use for this article, I shall limit myself to giving an account of those
which I have found particularly original and valuable.

Paola Cabibbo's "L'invenzione di Pocahontas" (*SA* 21–22[1975–
76]:7–29) is a finely written, subtly argued piece of research.
Analyzing Book III of John Smith's *General History of Virginia*,
and comparing it with the 1612 version, and also with *A True Relation*, Cabibbo finds in the creation of Pocahontas a shrewd literary

manipulation of the text with the intention of making the Indian
princess a reassuring symbol of native acceptance and support of
the white colonization fostered by the author. "*The Enormous Room*
e la visione del pellegrino" (*SA* 21–22:153–99) by Renzo S. Crivelli
is a brightly readable, penetrating, mostly psychoanalytic reading
of Cummings's "novel," which is seen as a lay equivalent of Bunyan's *Pilgrim's Progress*. Taking the "excremental vision" as a metaphor, Crivelli shows how Le Nouveau's experience is a pilgrimage
of 20th-century man towards salvation "to find how much has remained intact, in man himself, after the devastation carried out by
organized civilization, religious hypocrisy and science." Le Nouveau
escapes the neurotic, hypocritical, aseptic 20th-century Western civilization by his very immersion in the excremental filth of prison
life: a soul-saving immersion, a sanctifying communion of each of
the prisoners with his own body (and, therefore, soul) and with
the body (the soul) of his fellow-sufferers. Maria Vittoria D'Amico's
thesis in her ample study "Cinque versioni del trickster" (*SA* 21–22:
221–74) is that most traits of the trickster figure, as it appears in
many American Indian oral traditions, recur in the characters of
swindlers and con-men one frequently meets in contemporary fiction. After shrewdly underlining that the former is an archetype
(and thus to be considered not so much as a literary source but as a
mythological matrix for the latter), the author concentrates on Rinehart of Ellison's *Invisible Man*, Dr. Tamkin of Bellow's *Seize the
Day*, the Doctor of Barth's *The End of the Road*, Matthew O'Connor of Djuna Barnes's *Nightwood*, and, through perceptive distinctions and appropriate qualifications, points out differences and anal-
ogies among the four characters as well as between each of them
and Wakdjunkaga, the trickster of the Winnebago tales. Geoffrey
Moore's "American Poetry, 1900–1950: Notes toward a Re-assess-
ment" (*SA* 21–22:383–422) is an essay admirable for its concise
thoroughness and lively style. Moore succeeds in his attempt to
provide us with "a brief summary of those characteristics . . . which
mark American poetry" in the first half of this century "off from the
English." According to him, the American poet is usually "a preacher
or experimenter or both," while his poetry has not the "memorability
of diction" of his English counterpart, who much more often than
not is conventional in form "and in morality (at least as publicly

expressed)," but whose "professionalism is superb," and for whom "music is all."

The whole issue of *Calibano*, a new biannual review of English and American studies, is devoted to literary forms of mass communication. Using Marx as a key, the authors try to penetrate all the hidden meanings of commercialized culture. Barbara Lanati's "Una Ligeia, cento Ligeie: ovvero del 'perturbante' ostentato e rimosso" (*Calibano* 2:45–76) is an essay on Poe that can be seen as complementary to her other one mentioned above in Bianchi's book. Both essays explore with great subtlety the division of the self and the death desire in Poe's tales by scrutinizing in depth the connection between the act of writing and the description of sick or maimed bodies. But whereas the first essay deals mainly with Poe as a writer of literary fiction, this one looks at Poe's rapport with his readers and his techniques in the writing of commercial fiction. In Lanati's view, the characters' progressive loss of *sanity* is the main and most controversial feature in Poe's short fiction. It represents an obvious metaphor of man's weakness and impotence, while at the same time (together with the exotic, improbable setting) serves to remove the average reader's fears: in fact, all the horrors in the stories seem to belong to alien worlds, either to the world of pure madness or to the decadent world of Europe. This ambiguity, Lanati concludes, is reflected in Poe himself, in his being a dangling "literary histrio," a writer continually torn between the rigors of real art and the commercial rules of magazines for which he produced his work. Guido Carboni's "Un matrimonio ben riuscito? Note sul giallo d'azione negli USA" (*Calibano* 2:109–37) is both an attempt to evaluate the influence of economic and sociological factors on the development of the hard-boiled detective story and a study of its structural paradoxes: the coexistence in it of utopia and violence, realism and romance, emotional involvement and ironic detachment. Well-informed, accurate, competently combining a sociological approach with a structural one, it is a brilliantly argued piece. Isaac Asimov's short stories and novels, seen as outstanding science fiction and strictly representative of its conventions and rules, are examined by Alessandro Portelli in his intriguing essay "Asimov: il presente come utopia" (*Calibano* 2:138–84). Portelli suggests that Asimov's "neutral," familiar style as a writer, and his characters' adoption of a

colloquial, everyday language, and of a set of values that closely
reflects the ethics, the ideals, the fears and the obsessions of the
American middle class, contribute to make of his future worlds and
societies an obvious though undeclared metaphor of the present.
But this "present," as a synthesis of the American Dream and the
liberal and capitalistic state, is utopian, because "when it is claimed
that it exists in every time and place, its *historical* existence is denied, particularly here and today."

Four more essays deserve to be noticed this year. Mario Materassi conducts a short and able structural analysis in his "Le due
fabulae di 'A Rose for Emily' di Faulkner" (*SpM* 9:76–82). In
Faulkner's story Materassi identifies two *fabulae* (the story of Emily
and the narrator's reconstruction of the story) which act within the
concentrical circles (temporal, environmental, and personal) that
constitute the mechanism of the text. Guido Carboni's "Donald
Barthelme: tre modi di costruire il reale" (*Sigma*, 11,i:79–105) is a
stimulating essay whose readability would, however, have profited
a great deal from more careful proofreading. After pointing out and
intelligently discussing the constructive principles at work in three
different stories ("Critique de la vie quotidienne," "The Glass
Mountain," and "Will You Tell Me?"), the critic concludes that
Barthelme's acceptance of everyday *dreck*-laden language and manipulation of literary conventions show that the writer's aim is to
direct the reader's attention to the shaping process more than to the
meanings of his fictions, to the *how* more than to the *what*, and that
this method is an act of political significance, one fostering changes
in reality. Fedora Giordano's "Jack London" (*CeS* 63–64:119–30)
furnishes an interesting Jungian approach to London's fiction. Focusing on one of the recurring situations, the confrontation with
the wilderness, Giordano discusses its mythical, ritual, and psychological implications, showing good use of scholarship and offering some interesting critical comments. Franco Meli provides a
careful reading of Thoreau's *The Maine Woods* in his "Thoreau: un
Anteo americano" (*Paragone* 342:29–63), which throws some light
on a frequently slighted aspect of Thoreau's complex personality:
his attitude towards the wilderness and its living symbol, the American Indian. In the presence of the mountains and forests of Maine,
Thoreau's self-reliance becomes irrational awe, his faith in the
benevolence of Nature is shattered, his contradictions explode, and

the result is an ambiguous attempt at exorcizing both his white man's conscience (as in the case of his relationship with Joe Polis, the Indian guide) and his primeval terrors of an inhuman world.

University of Pisa

iv. Japanese Contributions

Keiko Beppu

For the past consecutive years this review has begun with a list of Japanese translations of works by American novelists and poets. The list has grown each year, and continues to grow both in quantity and quality, and it still is maintained that a good translation is an interpretation—even the most natural way of introducing works by foreign authors. Let it suffice this time, however, to say that the scholars whose books are here surveyed are also prolific translators: for Hawthorne, Whitman, and writers of the American Renaissance, Masayuki Sakamoto, or Shunsuke Kamei; for Faulkner, Kenzaburo Ohashi or Kichinosuke Ohashi; for contemporary writers (Bellow, Barth, Barthelme, Roth, Updike), Iwao Iwamoto, Yokichi Miyamoto, or Masao Shimura. Which is to name only a few of active translators of American writers.

As ever, Japanese scholarship on American literature for 1978 is impressive in the field of fiction. The 1978 issue of *Studies in American Literature* (Kyoto: American Literature Society of Japan) has a checklist covering the past 15 years. The journal is our major publication in the field and is an indicator of our scholars' critical interests. Faulkner leads the list with 13 articles; next comes Hawthorne with 8; Whitman, 6; James, 5; Melville, 4; and Bellow, 3.

The year 1978 saw two monumental general studies of American literature: Kenzaburo Ohashi's *Shosetsu No Tameni: America-teki Sozoryoku To Konnichi No Bungaku* [*For the Novel: The American Imagination and Contemporary Literature*] (Tokyo: Kenkyusha) and Masayuki Sakamoto's *America Bungaku O Do Yomitoruka: Bungakushi No Kochiku O Mezashite* [*Interpretations of American Literature: Toward the Construction of Literary History*] (Tokyo: Chukyoshuppan).

Ohashi's book, *For the Novel*, borrows its title from Robbe-

Grillet's *Pour un Nouveau Roman,* which constitutes, together with
James's "The Art of Fiction," a point of departure and the basis for
Ohashi's exploration on the theme. *For the Novel* is a collection of
the author's articles and essays which appeared in various journals
and magazines during the past ten years or so. In book form these
articles become one long monologue of our eminent scholar about
the fate and possibility of the novel. Ohashi's theory of the novel
form is a natural growth out of his close reading of Faulkner's works
and other American authors inclusive of 19th-century writers and
very "new writers"—Updike, Bellow, Kozinski, and Nin. The question of "the point of view" and the narrator leads Ohashi to the art
of biography, discussing Anaïs Nin's *Journals* and showing a positive
reading of Joseph Blotner's biography of William Faulkner. *For the
Novel* is also a recapitulation of his lectures and discussions in class;
in such sections Ohashi's tone becomes confessional (and sometimes
reminiscent) and he *talks* about the teaching of literature to college
students and about the profession of literary criticism. And on the
art of translation Ohashi offers some valuable guidelines for future
translators of American authors, pointing out the two major linguistic differences between English and Japanese that our language
lacks—"tense" sequence and the sense of "otherness" (pp. 230–32).
Ohashi's passion for the cause of the novel is one constant in the
resourceful book. He is attached to the novel form and sees the continuity of the tradition through Hawthorne, Melville, Faulkner, to
Updike. *For the Novel* can be thus read as a literary history not in
chronology, but in the sense that the literary history is an organic
structure, *the* thesis in Sakamoto's book, *Interpretations of American
Literature: Toward the Construction of Literary History.*

Sakamoto has been established here and abroad (through *ALS*)
as an expert on the writers of the American Renaissance, and as the
author of *Hawthorne* in the Tohjusha's British and American Writers' Series (1977). Like Ohashi's book, Sakamoto's work is a collection of articles written for various periodicals for the past ten years.
Interpretations of American Literature has a tighter organization;
the argument in the book is clear-cut and direct. In the first chapter,
entitled "Search for Methodology," Sakamoto poses the question,
What are comparative studies? It has been suggested that, in view
of the increasing penchant for this critical approach employed by
our scholars, a methodology be established (see *ALS 1977,* p. 504).

The opening chapter is a timely answer to the need. Sakamoto contends that comparative studies of literature are futile without some solid research into the structure of subject materials compared and contrasted. He expounds the theory, using a concrete example: "Romanticism in America and Japan" is an exploration of Emerson juxtaposed against Kitamura Tohkoku. The two intervening chapters are thoughtful discussions of the American Renaissance writers: Emerson, Whitman, Poe, Melville. Sakamoto reserves an entire chapter, naturally, for Hawthorne. The concluding chapter, which is on Thomas Wolfe, may strike the reader as an anomaly, but it proves to be a continuation of the first and the second chapter, an attempt to find coalescence between Whitman and Thomas Wolfe. The chapter illustrates an application of his theory of comparative studies proposed in the first chapter. The section entitled "Thomas Wolfe and the City" is a readable essay in itself; and the chapter is a reassessment of the novelist. *Interpretations of American Literature* becomes a good demonstration of Sakamoto's thesis that literature is an organic entity. Both Ohashi and Sakamoto have some scruples about the fact that their books are anthologies of previously published articles, but both works are not mere collections of their essays. And as Sakamoto's subtitle indicates, these studies provide a framework for various researches conducted by our scholars with different backgrounds and diverse interests in American literature.

As is evident from the foregoing summary, the resources for Ohashi and Sakamoto have been such 19th-century authors as Poe, Melville, Hawthorne, and James. The year 1978 saw significant studies on these individual writers.

Toshio Yagi's *Poe: Grotesque To Arabesque* [*Edgar Allan Poe: The Grotesque and the Arabesque*] (Tokyo: Tohjusha) is a new addition to the Tohjusha's British and American Writers' Series. The book is Yagi's second publication on the poet-critic-writer. Yagi devotes nearly half of the book to Poe's poetry; his main objective, however, is to present a unified image of Poe as "romantic ironist." In the chapter, "The Grotesque and the Arabesque," Yagi questions the facile classification of Poe's fiction into either the grotesque or the arabesque. In this Yagi's attempt is not new, preceded by G. R. Thompson's *Poe's Fiction: Romantic Irony in the Gothic Tale* (1973). Rather Yagi pursues the question, using Poe's story, "Metzengerstein," and succeeds in explaining the diversity of Poe's achievement in mixed genres. His contention is that Poe's own classification of his stories into grotesque and arabesque is arbitrary and that the grotesque includes the arabesque—which establishes Poe as "romantic ironist."

Melville has received careful and constant critical attention in this country, and the completion of a bibliography of Melville studies will solidify such a position. Concentrated research and labor have gone into *A Bibliography of Herman Melville Studies in Japan* (The Faculty of Literature, Shimane University), edited by Masao Tsunematsu and Sanford E. Marovitz. The bibliography is indispensable to Melville scholars here and abroad, since it shows the extent and depth of Melville reception in this country. It is hoped that similar attempts will be made on major American writers in future. With compilations of such investigation in view, it may be proposed that our studies in American literature have come of age, as it were. Hawthorne scholarship for 1978 is represented by Sakamoto's chapter, "Hawthorne Notes," in *Interpretations of American Literature*. Here an article on the novelist deserves mentioning: it is Katsumi Okamoto's "Dimmesdale and the Problem of Self-Realization" (*SELit* 55:227–40).

Another popular novelist among our scholars is Henry James; his reception is reflected in the number of translations of his novels and short stories, and in the publication of anthologies of stories and textbooks. Yet no good independent study has been produced in recent years. The fact may strengthen Hisayoshi Watanabe's contention that there is nothing in James except the language in his *Henry James No Gengo* [*Henry James and the Language*] (Tokyo: Hokuseido). The book is an excellent analysis of James's prose, which shows Watanabe's critical insight, solid scholarship, and sensitivity to the language, and the "composition." Watanabe's discussion of Henry James as the artist of words is a valid assessment of the novelist, and it provides in turn a model for stylistics and linguistic examination of literary works. But to declare that nothing counts in James except the language is to risk the sin of commission —the mutilation of the "precious moral of everything else" in *The Ambassadors*. All the same, Watanabe does full justice to James as the artist of words—the sole objective in *Henry James and the Language*. Furthermore, in consideration of the scarcity of research of this kind in this country, his achievement deserves much credit.

Compared with the 19th-century American writers here surveyed, Mark Twain seems to have been neglected by our academicians. Yorimasa Nasu's *Mark Twain Ronko: Taigu No Henreki* [*A Study of Mark Twain: The Pilgrimage of "A Great and Sublime Fool"*] (Tokyo: Shinozakishorin) is the fourth book-length study of Twain and is worth special review here. Nasu's treatment of the subject is unique, appealing to our visual sense. The book begins with the colored picture of the Gateway Arch in St. Louis, beside the Mississippi. Nasu reads in this "artificial rainbow" the telling symbol of Twain's dream—an atonement with "the Great Plains," "the Great River," and "the Grand Empty Space." Similarly, the author illustrates the *ambiance* of Twain's works by drawing the "horseshoe curve," which shows graphically the movements of Twain's characters and the stories. Nasu argues that if Twain's hero is on the move, he is nevertheless equipped with a round-trip (not one-way) ticket. Nasu's *Mark Twain* is delightful reading despite the fact that it is a serious study of the humorist, and its author is in earnest, in love with Mark Twain. Twain receives another reference in Shunsuke Kamei's essay about the culture of the Gilded Age (to be surveyed later).

Studies of 20th-century and contemporary literature for 1978 are as overwhelming as in the previous year; this is reflected in the number of translations and in the output of numerous papers and research done on the subject.

Toshio Takada's *Faulkner No Sekai* [*The Fictional World of William Faulkner*] (Tokyo: Hyoronsha) is a handy student-guide and introduction to Faulkner's major novels and stories. It should be remembered here that Faulkner is the frequent subject in Kanzaburo Ohashi's aforementioned book, *For the Novel*. There are an essay and notes on the novelist which deserve at least mentioning: Keiichiro Takaya's "William Faulkner's 'Past'—in the Case of *The Sound and the Fury*" (*SALit* 15:16–34) and Masa Yamamoto's notes, "The Use of Smell in Faulkner" (*SALit* 15:35–49).

Our scholars' concern with southern writers and with feminist literature is noted in Shizuo Suyama's *Kami No Nokoshita Kuroi Ana: Gendai Nambu Bungaku* [*The Black Hole Left by God; Contemporary Southern Novels*] (Tokyo: Kayohsha) and in Hideo Inazawa's *America Joryusakka Ron* [*Three American Women Writers: Willa Cather, Pearl Buck, and Carson McCullers*] (Tokyo:

Shimbisha). Inazawa chooses these three women writers for their popularity among Japanese readers, and for their different attitude toward life and art. He assumes a feminist point of view in his reading of these writers, and shows a well-balanced judgment of each. His discussions of Cather's novels, O Pioneers! and My Ántonia in particular, are of special interest. He contends that Lena (My Ántonia) and Marie (O Pioneers!) are precursors of an independent woman, and that Cather could not fully develop the type, not because of her inhibition or moral scruples, but because of her artistic credo of selection and simplification. And in McCullers, Inazawa finds a significant change in the treatment of women characters, because in McCullers's works the feminist perspective is replaced by the novelist's preoccupation with man's existential condition per se.

Among contemporary writers Jewish authors enjoy quite a favorable reception, since they have been made accessible to general readers through translations of their works. They also receive serious critical attention among our scholars for their sheer productivity. There was a symposium on Jewish writers at the 50th Convention of the English Literary Society of Japan; the discussion is reported by Shigeo Hamano (EigoS 124:132–34). Naturally, the Tohjusha Series on British and American Authors includes one on Saul Bellow: Yuzaburo Shibuya's Bellow: Kaishin No Kiseki [Saul Bellow: The Conversion of "the Sick Soul"] (Tokyo: Tohjusha). Shibuya takes a biographical approach to the novelist, as he sees a close connection between Bellow's personal heritage and his art. The book is divided into two equal parts: a detailed examination of his background and as detailed discussions of Bellow's major novels from Dangling Man through Humboldt's Gift. He illustrates the process of what William James called "the conversion of the sick soul," or what Shibuya explains as transformation from a rationalist to a "Blakean" visionary. Shibuya's Bellow is a valid assessment of the novelist, even though in the concluding chapter the critic changes into an enthusiast.

Shigeo Hamano discusses various reactions to the contemporary milieu as registered in representative contemporary American writers, Jewish and non-Jewish, in Konnichi No America Sakka Gun [Contemporary American Writers] (Tokyo: Kenkyusha). The writers represented are Updike, Malamud, Cheever, Bellow, Purdy, Vonnegut, Kozinski, Barthelme, and Brautigan. Hamano's book presents a rough sketch of these writers as a group; the conclusion is no more than a summary of the foregoing arguments or a redundancy. On the other hand, Iwao Iwamoto's article, "A Perspective on the American Novel" (*EigoS* 124:438–39), is a sensible assessment of recent trends in contemporary fiction from the fifties through the seventies, and a speculation on the American Novel in the eighties that the coming decade may see a new realism in fiction. Iwamoto's critical appraisal of Mary Gordon as illustrative of new realism, it seems, is well-founded. One more essay on the theme needs a quick glance: Masao Shimura takes up the issue of virtuosity and the "new writers" in his article, "Painting and the Novel" (*EigoS* 124:429–31). Shimura's discussion of the impact of modern painting on the practice of contemporary novelists brings this review for 1978 back to Ohashi's concern with the fate of the novel form.

In the sphere of American poetry Japanese scholarship for the year is very limited. Yet Hisashi Noda's "Whitman and Dickinson" (*EigoS* 124:4–7) is a readable essay, which contrasts these two poets and clarifies the differences between Whitman and Dickinson. Hiroko Uno's notes on "The Two Emily Dickinsons" (*EigoS* 124:418–19) is an evidence of our modest yet continued interest in "the belle of Amherst." Uno's query may establish a linkage between Dickinson and William Carlos Williams. This last-mentioned poet is the subject of Minoru Hirooka's "An American Cubist Poem: William Carlos Williams's *Paterson*" (*SALit* 15:1–15). Hirooka's article written in English is a solid study of the poem. Hirooka demonstrates how cubist innovations in modern painting influenced the making of Williams's *Paterson*. The only book-length study on poetry is Masuo Funaki's book, *T. S. Eliot No Bungaku: Annji To Kaishaku* [*A Study of T. S. Eliot: Suggestion and Interpretation*] (Tokyo: Hokuseido), a good introduction to the poet and as such deserving due attention.

The survey of Japanese scholarship on American literature for 1978 should include some significant publications in the field of American Studies. Michiko Inugai's *American America* (Tokyo: Bungeishunju) is a collection of the author's essays which appeared in one of the major magazines; it is quite a readable book about American culture and history, a good companion to readers of American literature. Some of Inugai's observations are outdated, based on her experience of the country back in the forties, yet on the whole her commentary on various aspects of life in America is judicious and insightful, supported by her avid reading and thorough investigation in relevant historical documents. If *American America* is enjoyable nonfiction, *Matenro wa Kohya ni Sobie* [*The Appearance of Skyscrapers in the Wilderness*] (Tokyo: Nipponkeizaishimbunsha) by Shunsuke Kamei is expertise par excellence on American culture, the most recent work by an authority on the subject. Two articles by the same critic are supplements to his book: "The Gentleman in America" in three installments (*EigoS* 124:377–79, 466–68,518–20) and "The Days of Circus: The Culture of the Gilded Age" (*EigoS* 123:438–41). The first-mentioned essay is a clear-cut thesis that Cooper's Natty Bumppo is the specimen of the "American Gentleman," who played an important role in the making of the American people and the nation. The other article, to which reference has been made earlier, is an exploration of Kamei's idea that the roots and identity of America's cultural vitality are traced to the Gilded Age and its culture.

Quite an interesting analysis (though new-fangled) of contemporary culture in the States is made in Yoshiaki Sato's essay, "For a New Culture to Wear: An essay on Contemporary Counter-Cultural Literature" (*SELit* 55:291–302). Sato's article has won the Shinjinsho for 1978—the Prize has been founded by the English Literary Society of Japan in commemoration of the Society's 50th Anniversary and will be awarded every year to promising new scholars of English and American literature. Sato examines different modes of resistance to the "packaged culture" and ways of creating the "counter-culture" manifested in the writings of Kesey, Castaneda, and Pynchon. It is noteworthy that our young scholar's essay has won recognition, an indication of the diversified studies done by Japanese scholars on American literature.

Kobe College

v. Scandinavian Contributions

Rolf Lundén

The main interest of Scandinavian scholars in 1978 was directed towards 20th-century literature, with a special emphasis on contemporary fiction and poetry. However, two weighty books on 19th-century writers also appeared, both written by Danish critics. As usual scholars devoted their efforts primarily to analyzing American fiction, though poetry received somewhat greater attention than in the last few years. American drama is often neglected in Scandinavia, and this year was no exception: not a single article on drama was published.

The colonial period was represented by only one article. Karl Keller's "Edward Taylor and the Mathers" (*MSpr* 72:119–35) investigates Taylor's indebtedness and services to Increase and Cotton Mather. As Keller admits, many of the interrelations between these colonial writers have already been noted by Norman S. Grabo. What Keller adds are mostly speculations. He suggests for instance that Taylor's *Metrical History of Christianity*, as well as several of his shorter naturalistic poems, may have been written in response to a request from Increase Mather, but Keller presents no proof. The main contributions of the article are that the complete text of the elegy Taylor wrote on Increase Mather's death in 1723 is printed for the first time, and that Keller makes clear that Mather, in his *Illustrious Providences*, used a report from Taylor on a hailstorm in Springfield in 1682.

One of the Danish books mentioned above is Erik A. Nielsen's *Fortolkningens Veje* [The Ways of Interpretation] (Copenhagen: Gyldendal) with the subtitle "A Didactic Essay on Edgar Allan Poe." Nielson admits initially a disbelief in too strict a method and advocates rather what might be called an intuitive method. This introduction sets the tone for the rest of the book, which is concerned with Poe's interpretation of reality. Poe's central motif, Nielsen seems to say, is the quest for clarity, for truth. The creative moment, or the moment of artistic completion, is a common denominator in most of his stories. "The Gold Bug" is then about the glorious moment when the interpreter's speculative calculations are confirmed by experience. It is about intuition in a rationalistic world, about the need to pursue what seems foolish in order to find a meaningful order. Nielsen further argues—and argues well—that Poe's detective stories are not incompatible with the rest of his work. Like the narrators of "The Tell-Tale Heart" and "The Black Cat," detective Dupin is trying to sort out what really happened. He becomes a

poet seeking the moment of clarity. Although Nielsen's study does
not examine all of Poe's stories, it still constitutes a perceptive contribution to an understanding of Poe's art.

The other Danish critic writing on the 19th century is Ole Storm,
who has published a very attractive two-volume set, consisting of
an anthology of stories and articles by Mark Twain and a biography
called *Mark Twain og Mr Samuel L. Clemens* (Copenhagen: Lade-
mann). As the title of the latter suggests, Storm continues the long
discussion of Twain's split personality initiated by Van Wyck
Brooks. But he does not agree with Brooks's conclusions. Twain's
mother and wife did not play the destructive roles assigned to them
by Brooks. Storm's emphasis is rather on Twain's ambivalent attitude towards sex, morals, religion, money, his family, and his art.
For instance, while Twain often shows an inclination towards sensuality and even pornography, he appears at other times to be as
puritanical as his wife. Storm also pays attention to Twain's manic-
depressive nature, which may explain much of the writer's ambivalence. He has avoided the danger of making the study too thesis-
ridden, and the result is a well-balanced presentation for the general
reader of a complex personality.

Four contributions were devoted to 20th-century poetry. The
most significant of these was Marianne Thormählen's *The Waste
Land, A Fragmentary Wholeness* (Lund: Gleerup), which sets
out to "bring the 433 lines of *The Waste Land* back into focus."
Thormählen tries to get close to Eliot's text by analyzing various
components such as language, meter, myths, voices, and time. Her
main emphasis, however, is on symbolic imagery. In the last chapter
she widens her view to encompass such aspects as unity, content,
and continuity. Thormählen is impatient with earlier critics who
have neglected to acknowledge their sources, and this impatience
becomes the basis of her method. Throughout the study she scrutinizes the readings of earlier scholars and points out obvious misreadings and plausible interpretations. The book sometimes reads
like a history of *Waste Land* criticism, and from that point of view
it is excellent. Thormählen's discussion is usually convincing; she is
a level-headed scholar who often manages to bring clarity to the
fog of Eliot scholarship. The danger of her method is that sometimes she focuses not on Eliot's text, as she says, but on earlier
readings of the text. Another weakness is that the study becomes

somewhat imprecise: it seldom becomes clear what exactly Thormählen's own contribution consists of.

To the constantly growing scholarship on Pound's sources for the cantos John Driscoll has added an article titled "Canto LX and Ezra Pound's Use of *Histoire Générale de la Chine*" (*SN* 50:215–32). Driscoll's aim is to discover principles behind source selection and to examine Pound's method of using de Mailla's chronicle history to "construct" poetry. By following the texts very carefully Driscoll succeeds in pointing out Pound's omissions, misunderstandings, and additions. We get a penetrating glance into Pound's workshop. What makes his selections and transformations into poetry, if it is poetry, remains to be answered, but this does not fall within Driscoll's present field of investigation.

Two articles were written on contemporary American poetry, both of a more or less introductory character. In "The New Romantics" (*AmerSS* 10:51–64) Ulf Lie is concerned with Black Mountain poetics and how the postmodernists have reacted against the modernist view of human creativity being superior to nature. These new romantics rather see themselves as "representative men penetrating the veil of cultural layers, uncovering the archetypal, the universal values." Lie also points to similar attitudes toward art in painters such as Pollock, Rosenberg, and Kline. Harry Stessel devotes his interest to "Confessional Poetry: A Guide to Marriage in America" (*MSpr* 72:337–55). Having given a general background to the confessional writings of poets such as Lowell, Berryman, Sexton, and Plath, Stessel narrows his discussion down to their treatment of marriage. The confessional poets, Stessel argues, reacted against the Cult of Domesticity of the fifties, and the popularity of these poets today is a reflection of the general discontent with an earlier marriage ideal.

With one short exception, all contributions on 20th-century fiction were devoted to the post-World-War-II period. Grete Ek traces in "A 'Speaking Picture' in John Steinbeck's *The Grapes of Wrath*" (*AmerSS* 10:111–15) what might be a parallel between the last chapter of Steinbeck's novel and Caravaggio's *Seven Arts of Mercy*. Knut Ahnlund managed a literary scoop of the first order when he published his book, *Isaac Bashevis Singer* (Uppsala: Brombergs), shortly before Singer received the Nobel Prize. Ahnlund's well-written study introduces the Yiddish-American author to the Swedish reader. It is divided into three sections dealing with Singer's life, his work, and his language. The introductory nature of the book means much re-telling of plots, but Ahnlund is an intelligent critic who also presents readings full of insight. He has further realized the need to depict the historical and autobiographical backgrounds to Singer's tales.

Another Jewish writer who received attention from Scandinavian scholars was Saul Bellow. In "Saul Bellow and Wilhelm Reich" (*AmerSS* 10:81–91) Helge Normann Nilsen discusses *Seize the Day* and *Henderson the Rain King*. He comes to the conclusion that Bellow is sympathetic towards Reich as a psychological and social revolutionary but skeptical of his belief in vegetotherapy as a means of regenerating the individual psyche. Nilsen is more convincing in his analysis of *Henderson the Rain King* than of *Seize the Day*. Astrid Holm investigates another influence on Bellow in "Existentialism and Saul Bellow's *Henderson the Rain King*" (*AmerSS* 10: 93–109). According to Holm, none of Bellow's protagonists are able to accept reality because of their intense fear of facing death as the only certainty in an absurd world. Lapsing into what Sartre called "bad faith," they identify themselves with "things" in order to escape death. Henderson realizes eventually that he must acknowledge his own mortality and accept his freedom to choose his own life.

David Minugh also focuses on a protagonist's quest for meaning in "John Gardner Constructs *Grendel's* Universe," in *Studies in English Philology: Linguistics and Literature Presented to Alarik Rynell*, SSE 46, edited by Mats Rydén and Lennart A. Björk, pp. 125–41 (Stockholm: Almqvist & Wiksell International). Minugh shows how Gardner has used the zodiac signs, one for each chapter, to structure *Grendel*, and how Ariel, Taurus, Gemini, etc., color the development of Grendel's education towards "an understanding of the self in the universe, particularly the role of man as Shaper."

The postmodernist novelists were subjected to observation in two articles. Rolf Lundén gives an introduction to the "fabulators" in "American Fiction Today" (*AmerSS* 10:65–72). He discusses their rejection of reality and their deliberate attempts to break down the traditional way of telling a story. The only reality these writers seem to recognize, Lundén says, is the actual writing of their fiction, the creative process. They see themselves as creators of their own world, which explains their common use of the intrusive voice. In "Ford Madox Ford, John Hawkes: Their Variations on a Theme" from *Occasional Papers, 1976–1977*, edited by Graham D. Caie, Michael Chestnutt, Lis Christensen, and Claus Faerch (Copenhagen: Akademisk Forlag), Anne R. Clauss compares Ford's *The Good Soldier* with Hawkes's *The Blood Oranges*. Both novels, she states, appeal to the psyche rather than the intellect; they are "testimonies to the powers of conceptual, rather than chronological, logic." As key scenes Clauss selects similar visits in the two books, one to Luther's castle and the other to a ruined fortress, where the protagonists experience symbolic returns to the past.

University of Uppsala

Bibliographical Addendum

J. Albert Robbins

The most energetic publishers of bibliographies and other reference books are G. K. Hall and Company, Boston, and Gale Research Company, Detroit. Their various new bibliographical guides to individual authors should be noted in the appropriate author and genre chapters, above. The more general, multivolume sets I call attention to below, along with some titles overlooked in the preceding chapters and a few which fit only this addendum.

Of those works which fall to me for notice, the most exciting is a book which is seven-eighths literary history and one-eighth bibliography—a study of the "little mag." Frederick J. Hoffman's *The Little Magazine in America: A Modern Documentary History* (1946) was the first formal work on this genre of publishing in this country. Now, 30 or so years later—and thousands of little mags later—there is a sequel: *The Little Magazine in America: A Modern Documentary History*, edited by Elliott Anderson and Mary Kinzie. It comes in two packages: as *Tri-quarterly* 43, without an index; and as a book by Pushcart Press (Yonkers, N.Y.), with index—a fat book of 770 pages enlivened with many photographs. There are 9 general articles, 27 essays treating 30 magazines; 3 essays on Corinth Books, the Pushcart Press, and the Fiction Collective; and an extremely useful "Annotated Bibliography of Selected Little Magazines" by Peter Martin (pp. 666–750) giving essential and hard-to-come-by facts on 84 magazines. The essays, memoirs, and interviews are generally by founders or close associates and serve to preserve intimate details of purpose, policy, funding, contributorship, and readership which in due time would be largely unrecorded and largely lost. This is literary history by the participants and, as a result, alive and vibrant: Robert Creeley on *Black Mountain Review*, William Phillips on *Partisan Review*, Gilbert Sorrentino on *Neon* and *Kulchur*,

LeRoi Jones on *Yugen*, Clayton Eshleman on *Caterpillar*, George Plimpton on *Paris Review*, and so on.

The lavish, large, hefty, and expensive set—*First Printings of American Authors: Contributions Toward Descriptive Checklists*, edited by Matthew Bruccoli, C. E. Frazer Clark, Jr., Richard Layman, and Benjamin Franklin, V (4 vols.; Gale, 1977–79)—reached its second and third volumes in 1978 and its fourth in 1979. Professor Woodress noticed it in *ALS 1977* (p. 512) and I shall try not to duplicate what he has said there. With the final volume also before me as I write this, I would like to cite some exact statistics about the set. The publisher avers that it includes 361 authors. I count 350, of which 66 are starred (signifying extended treatment: that is, including English first printings also and indicating whether these are reprinted or reset). There are 4 authors of the 17th century, 12 of the 18th, 28 of the 19th, and 306 of the 20th. With such preponderant attention to our century, I would have liked to see them segregated: four volumes, *FPAA, 20th Century*; and a fifth, possibly sixth, *FPAA, 19th Century*. The 17th and 18th centuries might have come along later in a concluding volume. Obviously the orientation is toward the 20th century, yet the user of the set must not expect to find all major writers included. Three Nobel winners are missing: Eliot (considered British?), Bellow, and Singer (considered Polish?). Other sample absentees are Ezra Pound, James Baldwin, Anne Sexton, E. E. Cummings, Edgar Rice Burroughs, Tillie Olsen. The inclusions at times are whimsical—authors both literarily insignificant and, so far as I know, of no interest to book collectors: such writers as Charles Portis, Frederick Exley, Edith Summers Kelley, Larry Woiwode, C. D. B. Bryan, and Humphrey Cobb (*one* book).

We have, of course, the essentials—title; publisher, place, and date; size of edition. While they were at it, it would have taken the contributors little extra effort to record the size of the volume in pages and the genre (novel, stories, play, essays, memoir). These facts would have enlarged its usefulness to the general user. In last year's *ALS* Professor Woodress quoted the price for the set as $140. The figure now is $180.

For all this, *FPAA* is a bibliographically informed and useful brief description of American authors' first printings. The selected references at the ends of author entries are very useful. Let us hope that the editors will now give more than token attention to the 19th century, and to the 18th and 17th.

Back in 1963 Gale gave us (of course, at a stiff price) *CA* (*Contemporary Authors*), then in 1973 *CLC* (*Contemporary Literary Criticism*), and now in 1978 a new one, *TCLC* (*Twentieth-Century Literary Criticism*). These are all massive, large-format, weighty, multivolume enterprises of international scope, but they have useful information and are usefully indexed (if you master the serialized index system). *CA* gives essential biographical facts, and *CLC* and *TCLC* excerpt criticism at some length. *CLC* treats about 175 authors per 600-page volume; *TCLC*, about 50 authors per 600-page volume. Obviously the new *TCLC* gives greater depth. For example the entry for F. S. Fitzgerald in *TCLC*, volume 1, occupies 42 double-columned pages with excerpts from 64 articles and books from 1922 to 1976. Both novices and specialists, I think, will find it useful. (How many of us do not have authors we have not really "kept up" with in recent years?).

This is not all. In the same large format Gale has in 1978 commenced another series of another sort: *DLB—Dictionary of Literary Biography*. These are intended to supply a need for detailed, up-to-date biographical essays on groups of American writers. Volume 1, edited by Joel Myerson, covers *The American Renaissance in New England*—a relatively slender volume of 224 pages giving detailed essays of eleven major writers and shorter sketches of 87 lesser figures. Volume 2, edited by Jeffrey Helterman and Richard Layman, treats *American Novelists Since World War II*—a weighty volume of 557 pages giving detailed essays of 18 major writers and shorter pieces on 62 others. Both volumes are the work of a large staff of scholar-contributors and both are lavishly illustrated. There is a list of "Books for Further Reading," but no index. Author entries provide biographical facts; commentary on major works; a listing of major and some minor publications; and selected references. With reliable and relatively complete information on living novelists hard to come by in a single volume, *American Novelists Since World War II* is especially welcome. During the past few months I found myself reaching for and consulting it frequently, with profit. But they are not cheap at $42 per volume.

A useful English series, published by St. James Press, London, is now complete. The earlier volumes include *Contemporary Poets* (2nd ed., 1975), *Contemporary Novelists* (2nd ed., 1976), *Contemporary Dramatists* (2nd ed., 1977); and the new addition is *Contemporary Literary Critics* (1977). All volumes include British and American writers; and to basic facts about biography and career are added commentary about work and ideas, and a bibliography about the biographers.

A new serial index appeared in 1978, volume I of *Index to Reviews of Bibliographical Publications, 1976*, edited by L. Terry Oggel and Rosalie Hewitt (Hall). This work of modest proportions (150 pp.) indexes relevant reviews in 323 journals, primarily by bibliography author and secondarily by 27 subject headings. You are sure to find material if you know the bibliography author; less sure if you must use the general subject index (for example, enumerative bibliography; indices and concordances); helpless if you seek reviews of a checklist of single-author criticism (for example, item 172, "A Bibliography of Dickensian Criticism, 1836–1975"; there is no "Dickens" in the index). It does well what it purports to do and, though admittedly specialized, gives us yet another tool in library reference collections.

Two works open up new areas bibliographically. In one, a new bibliography on current "native" literature, a sizable body of 2,024 numbered items is placed on record in Angeline Jacobson's *Contemporary Native American Literature: A Selected and Partially Annotated Bibliography* (Scarecrow, 1977). The collection itemizes the work by American Indians, Eskimos, and Canadian and Mexican tribal writers. The other records a large (253-page) body of black dramatic works: *Black Playwrights, 1823–1977: An Annotated Bibliography of Plays* (Bowker, 1977), edited by James V. Hatch and OMANii Abdullah. The list is alphabetical by playwright, but unfortunately lacks birth and death dates. There is information about first performance and publication. The back matter consists of useful lists: bibliographies of published studies, anthologies, dissertations, taped interviews, awards, and current addresses of playwrights and agents.

Another work on drama is Don B. Wilmeth's *The American Stage to World War I: A Guide to Information Sources* (Gale), organized into 13 categories—for example, state and local histories;

actors and acting; stagecraft, theatre collections; "paratheatre" (panoramas, minstrels, variety theatre, wild west shows, burlesque, showboats, and such). Useful and thorough.

The most esoteric of the Gale works which I shall notice is Eugene L. Huddleston and Douglas A. Noverr's *The Relationship of Painting and Literature* (vol. 4 in the American Studies Information Guide Series). As we would expect, all but a few pages (those on fiction) cite painting and poetry: poems reacting to paintings; poems treating subjects of paintings; poems close to paintings in subject, imagery tone. Both paintings and poems are located and dated. The three indexes enable one to locate items from several approaches: by authors; by painters; by paintings, books, poems, and first lines of poems.

Barbara Haber has edited a broad work on recent books on women: *Women in America: A Guide to Books, 1963–1975* (Hall). It is arranged by 18 topics from "Abortion" to "Work" and includes annotations. There is a section on "Literature, the Fine Arts and Popular Culture."

Because it is a standard guide to the genre, I will simply call attention to the updated, 3rd edition of Warren S. Walker's *Twentieth Century Short Story Explication: Interpretations, 1900–1975, of Short Fiction Since 1800* (Shoe String, 1977). It has, of course, grown fat over the years—880 pages.

Because they are mentioned nowhere else, I call attention to two thoughtful studies of fiction published by David and Charles (Newton Abbot, Eng.) in a series inaptly called "Comparative Literature." (I find nothing comparative in either volume.) One is *American Literature, Nineteenth and Early Twentieth Centuries*, by Scott Donaldson and Ann Massa. (That title is misleading, for it is almost wholly on *fiction*: major novelists from Cooper to Twain, Howells, James, and Stephen Crane.) The study considers thematic opposites: city and country, dreams and nightmares, individual and society, and so forth. The other is *The American Novel in the Twentieth Century*, by Miles Donald, focusing upon Fitzgerald, Hemingway, Thomas Wolfe, Dos Passos, Steinbeck, Faulkner, Updike; and, segregated in the later chapters, such writers as Henry Miller, William Burroughs, Kerouac, Nabokov, blacks, Jews, and the writers of SciFi and detective fiction.

Author Index

Subject Index

DATE DUE